RECASTING
BOURGEOIS
EUROPE

RECASTING BOURGEOIS EUROPE

•

STABILIZATION IN FRANCE,

GERMANY, AND ITALY

IN THE DECADE AFTER

WORLD WAR I

•

CHARLES S. MAIER

PRINCETON

UNIVERSITY

PRESS

Library of Congress Cataloging in Publication Data will
be found on the last printed page of this book

Publication of this book has been aided by a grant
from The Andrew W. Mellon Foundation

This book has been composed in Linotype Caledonia

Printed in the United States of America
by Princeton University Press
Princeton, New Jersey

To my parents

CONTENTS

CONTENTS

PREFACE

This book originated in an ambition to extend my study of European history beyond the national frontiers that usually structure teaching, research, and writing. This is not to diminish the value of sensitive and well-researched national history; but there are many students who have had the chance for immersion in individual European cultures to a much greater degree than I have. As an American scholar I believed that I might take advantage of my distance to examine the interconnectedness of Europe's societies and their politics. I have not sought to homogenize the diverse national (and regional) experiences into one entity known as "Europe." Instead I have attempted to construct an analytic framework that will relate parallel conflicts and compromises even as it illuminates what developments remain unique from country to country.

One major impulse behind this enterprise has been the awareness of middle-class commonality: specifically a sense of the rhythms of bourgeois life as they have pulsed through business activity in Milan or Düsseldorf, family walks in the Villa Borghese or Champs de Mars, anxieties about keeping up a decent style of life in the midst of civil disorder in Bologna or inflation in Berlin and Paris. From the North Sea to the Mediterranean intense political effort went into defending communities built on precarious mixtures of respectability, Sunday kinship rituals, work involving supervision of others, and general exclusiveness from the encroaching "masses." I have not sought to recreate that social universe, but I have tried to analyze its underpinnings in the world of power. It is the political and economic girders and buttresses that have claimed my attention during the making of this book.

A further inquiry has motivated this investigation. In a small way it addresses a continuing question concerning Western society. How has it remained so stable despite the widely differential rewards it provides? I continue to find its persisting inequality a source of wonder and a challenge to explanation. This book represents no celebration of stability. Perhaps it does testify to the willingness of most men and women to live with their subordinate roles in the hierarchies that exist rather than wager the limited rewards and values that sustain them. More directly, it is a study of those who had important stakes in continuity. I have examined the powerful, less for their own sake than to understand their success. This entails understanding the transformations they resisted and those they finally sanctioned so as to avert more drastic changes of fortune.

The underlying structure of the arrangements between classes, parties, and interests was more durable than suggested by the fragile stability attained in the 1920's. The nationalism aggravated by war, especially the persistence of German power and ambition, and the continuing imbalances of the Atlantic economy quickly shattered the settlement of the twenties. Still, the elements of stability in that era adumbrate the political and economic foundations of our own. Despite the intervening depression, fascist successes, and war, the social truces of the 1920's prefigure the more durable internal armistices on which, so far at least, Western capitalism has rested since 1945.

The labor on this book has been long and preoccupying enough to strain the confidence of professional associates and the patience of my friends and family. Along the way I have incurred many debts, especially because of the assistance needed in grasping three national experiences.

The Foreign Area Fellowship Foundation funded two years of thesis support when they began their West European Program. Among those who facilitated research were Costanzo Casucci and the staff of the Archivio Centrale dello Stato; Dr. Thomas Trumpp and the staff of the Bundesarchiv in Koblenz; M. Laloy at the Archives of the French Foreign Ministry; Agnes Petersen who permitted filming of selections from the Louis Loucheur papers at the Hoover Institution at Stanford; Giambattista Gifuni at the Biblioteca Comunale "Ruggero Bonghi" in Lucera; the staff of the Deutsches Zentralarchiv in Potsdam; Mme. Guillemin and the staffs at the Archives Nationales and the French Ministry of Finance; plus many others who helped at the United States National Archives; the Bergbau-Archiv in Bochum; the Volksverein für das katholische Deutschland, held at the Mönchen Gladbach municipal library; the manuscript division of the Bibliothèque Nationale; the Bibliothèque de Documentation Internationale Contemporaine, the Emeroteca of the Biblioteca Nazionale in Rome, the Baker Library at the Harvard University School of Business Administration, and most continually: Harvard's Widener Library in Cambridge, above all Michael Cotter and the staff of the Document Division.

I am grateful to the guardians of private collections: Friedrich Freiherr Hiller von Gaertringen who allowed consultation of the Westarp papers; Erich Warburg, who permitted the use of the Max Warburg papers; Bodo Herzog who facilitated research at the Firmenarchiv of the Gutehoffnungshütte in Oberhausen; the President and directors of the Compagnie de Saint-Gobain-Pont-à-Mousson, who departed from traditional French reluctance to open their archives in an especially gracious and enlightened manner; likewise to Graf von Zedwitz Arnim of Friedrich Krupp, A.G. for equivalent privileges. Jacques Millerand permitted use of his father's political memoir and contributed reminiscences as well as friendship. André François Poncet and Mme. Louis Marin vouchsafed their memories of the 1920's.

Personal debts are least equally compelling. Gerald Feldman first pointed out to me the value of the German industrial archives and has unselfishly shared his expertise and counsel from the inception of this project through its final drafting. Stephen Schuker, whose own research promises a major synthesis of the financial and diplomatic resolution of the international predicaments left from the First World War, generously shared his knowledge of sources, archives, and financial issues of the era. Harold Hanham took my manuscript in hand for a detailed reading and editorial revision at a time when I badly needed encouragement and guidance. I am grateful to my original thesis director Franklin L. Ford for letting me embark upon the dark waters of comparative history and expressing his confidence that a useful contribution would result. H. Stuart Hughes, who shared the burden of supervising the thesis which this project first yielded, contributed a penetrating critique that forced a better focusing of questions. John Clive, Patrice Higonnet, Ernest May, and Hans Mommsen have all offered acute and sympathetic commentary, and David Landes has provided continuing encouragement and sound advice. Arno J. Mayer has given the tribute of taking the work of his former student seriously and has remained teacher and friend.

Other assistance that requires acknowledgment includes that of Henry A. Turner, Guido Di Meo, Denise Artaud, Malcolm Anderson, David Goldey, Michael Rust, and Peter Stern who all helped me find my footing in various archives. Charles Sabel read the manuscript carefully and helped sharpen its sociological argumentation. Peter Christian Witt scrutinized Chapter 6, part one. Alan Kovan of Berkeley and Rudolf Tschirbs of Bochum arranged some filmings; Anne Sa'adah, Jeremiah Riemer and Max Rudman aided with the apparatus. Jacqueline Jordan, Laura Margolis, Marcia Fernald, Susan Carlson, and Patricia Brennecke assisted with manuscript preparation. As editor, Lewis Bateman proved an encouraging disciplinarian. Elizabeth C. Moore took it upon herself to aid me in proofreading.

Scholarly work is nurtured in intellectual milieux even if it rests finally on individual labor. Stanley Hoffmann has made the Center for European Studies a foyer for interdisciplinary research; my association with Leverett House at Harvard has provided fellowship for all the time this book was in process; as neighbor and friend Barrington Moore has come to represent for me a model of how analytic scholarship can be fused with sympathy for many human conditions. Finally my wife Pauline has contributed intellectual fellowship as well as family: she gave the manuscript a helpful reading and has never offered spurious praise. For Andrea and Nicholas this book has represented a life-long claim upon their father. Jessica, who arrived with galleys, has incurred only brief deprivation. Ultimately, it is their common assertion of continuity that must redeem and justify the concern lavished on the past. Whether this particular work can be justified must be left to its readers. The book is offered to my parents, Muriel and Louis Maier, whose faith in the author has gone beyond the limits of prudence and reason alone.

Cambridge, Massachusetts, December, 1974

ABBREVIATIONS

Archives (For full references see the Bibliography)

ACS, Rome: Archivio Centrale dello Stato. The major collections used fall under the heading: Min. Int., Dir. Gen. P.S., Div. Aff. gen. e ris.: Ministero dell'Interno, Direzione Generale della Pubblica Sicurezza. Divisione: Affari generali e riservati.

AN, Paris: Archives Nationales, Paris.

BA, Koblenz: Bundesarchiv.

DZA, Potsdam: Deutsches Zentralarchiv.

FO: British Foreign Office microfilms (FO 371: Political Correspondence, and FO 408: Confidential Prints, Germany).

GFM: German Foreign Ministry Microfilms from the National Archives, Washington (Series T 120). Films will be cited by the serial number, roll number and frame numbers as identified in George O. Kent, *A Catalogue of Files and Microfilms of the German Foreign Ministry Archives*, 4 vols. (Stanford, 1962–1964), vols. I and II. For citations from the Stresemann Papers, the original volume numbers will be included with the serial number that corresponds to each. Generally the letter prefix or suffix on the frame numbers has been dropped if not needed for identification.

GFM:ARK: German Foreign Ministry, Alte Reichskanzlei. (Films of Chancellery with documents and cabinet protocols.)

GHH: Archives of the Gutehoffnungshütte, Oberhausen.

Min. Aff. Etr.: Archives of the French Foreign Ministry, Quai d'Orsay.

Min. Commerce: Archives of the French Ministry of Commerce (F^{12}).

Min. Finance: Archives of the French Ministry of Finances (F^{30}).

PAM: Archives of former Compagnie de Pont-à-Mousson (now: Cie de Saint-Gobain-Pont-à-Mousson) at La Châtre (Indre).

PRO:CAB: Public Records Office: Cabinet Office Papers.

Seg. Part.: Segreteria Particolare del Duce. This is available directly at ACS, Rome, but generally the National Archives microfilm copy (Serial T 586) will be used for citation with reel and frame numbers.

In archival citations, folder, volume, or carton numbers will generally be separated from the collection designation by a slash-line. Non-numbered items will be designated with B. (Busta); f. (fascicolo, fascicule, folder); or sf. (sottofascicolo, subfolder, etc.), as appropriate.

Public Documents

AP: Camera: *Atti Parlamentari, Discussioni della Camera dei Deputati*.

AP: Senato: *Atti Parlamentari, Discussioni del Senato*.

JOC: *Journal Officiel*, Chambre des Deputés.

JOS: *Journal Officiel*, Sénat.

VNV:SB: Verhandlungen der verfassungsgebenden deutschen Nationalversammlung: *Stenographische Berichte*.

VDR:SB: Verhandlungen des deutschen Reichstags, *Stenographische Berichte*.

ABBREVIATIONS

Newspapers and Periodicals

NP(K)Z: Neue Preussische (Kreuz-) Zeitung, Berlin.
BT: Berliner Tageblatt.
CdS: Corriere della Sera, Milan.
GdI: Giornale d'Italia, Rome.
JI: Journée Industrielle, Paris.
RDM: Revue des Deux Mondes, Paris.
RPP: Revue Politique et Parlementaire.
   Le Temps, La Stampa, and other organs will be cited without abbreviation.
RFP:APS: British War Office, *Review of the Foreign Press: Allied Press Supplement.*
RFP:EPS: British War Office, *Review of the Foreign Press: Economic Press Supplement.*

Political and Economic Groups

DNVP: Deutschnationale Volkspartei (German National People's Party; sometimes shortened to Nationalists).
DVP: Deutsche Volkspartei (German People's Party).
DDP: Deutsche Demokratische Partei (German Democratic Party; shortened to Democrats).
ZAG: Zentralarbeitsgemeinschaft (Association of labor leaders and industrialists, formed in November 1918).
VdESI: Verein deutscher Eisen- und Stahlindustrieller (Union of German Iron and Steel Industrialists).
RWR: Reichswirtschaftsrat (Reich Economic Council).
SPD: Sozialdemokratische Partei Deutschlands (German Social Democratic Party; shortened to Socialists).
USPD: Unabhängige Sozialdemokratische Partei Deutschlands (Independent Social Democratic Party; shortened to Independents).

In addition, Reichsverband will be used for Reichsverband der deutschen Industrie (Reich Federation of German Industry); Zentrum or Center will be used for Deutsche Zentrumspartei (the Catholic Center Party).

SFIO: Section Française de l'Internationale Ouvrière (French Socialist Party).
CGT: Conféderation Générale des Travailleurs (General Confederation of Labor).
PLI: Partito Liberale Italiano.
PPI: Partito Popolare Italiano (shortened to Popolari, the Italian Catholic or early Christian Democratic Party).
PSI: Partito Socialista Italiano.
PCI: Partito Comunista Italiano (Communists).
PNF: Partito Nazionale Fascista (Fascist Party; formed from the fascist movement in late 1921).
CGL: Confederazione generale del Lavoro (General Confederation of Labor).

In addition, Confindustria will be used for the Confederazione generale della Federazione della Industria; Federterra will be used for the Federazione dei Lavoratori della Terra (the Federation of Agricultural Workers).

RECASTING
BOURGEOIS
EUROPE

INTRODUCTION:
FROM BOURGEOIS TO
CORPORATIST EUROPE

In an era of upheaval, it is continuity and stability that need explanation. The premise of this study is that European social hierarchies in the twentieth century have proved strikingly tenacious when men often expected otherwise. Violence is not always a midwife of history: despite world wars and domestic conflict much of Europe's institutional and class structure has showed itself tough and durable; the forces of continuity and conservatism have held their own. Real changes have certainly taken place—growing enrichment, loosening family structures, broader educational opportunities. But these have occurred more as a product of the last quarter century's stability than of prior social turmoil, and they have not dispossessed the privileged groups. The Fiats and Renaults of the workers may now push to the campgrounds of the Riviera, but the Mercedes and Jaguars still convey their masters to Cap d'Antibes or Santa Margherita. Industrialists, now as after World War I, can still lament the intrusion of labor unions upon their prerogatives; the respectable press can still denounce public service strikes; Ruhr managers command awe in Germany; the nation-state persists. This is not to claim that the relative social stability of the last quarter century may not finally disintegrate under new pressures. But it is to call attention to the persistence of social hegemonies that a half century ago seemed precarious if not doomed.

This study examines a critical period in the disciplining of change, in the survival and adaptation of political and economic elites, and in the twentieth-century capitalist order they dominated. The years after World War I are especially instructive, because security was apparently wrested from profound disorder and turbulence. If in the turmoil of 1918–1919 a new European world seemed to be in birth by the late 1920's much of the prewar order appeared to have been substantially restored. Both perspectives were skewed: the transformations of 1918 had been in good part superficial, and so was the stability of the 1920's. Nonetheless, despite the limits of the restoration, the decade rewarded conservative efforts with striking success.

The process by which this occurred is the subject of this study. In retrospect, it is easy to note that the forces actively pressing for major social or political changes constituted a minority, and a badly divided one at that. But this response is not very revealing; it discourages investigation of how so great a degree of hierarchical social ordering was preserved when mass parties, "total war," and economic dislocation made some social leveling inevitable. And if the weakness and divisions of the attackers are well known, the strategies of social and political defense remain unexplored. Political and economic institutions served as the outworks of a fortress—so Tocqueville had described them while waiting for the assault on private property he feared as the revolution of 1848 approached.[1] How in the decade after 1917 were the fortifications challenged? How were they defended? The strategy and the ultimate stakes were not always apparent. Partisans of order and partisans of change, besieged and besiegers, too often served as Tolstoyan commanders, mapping delusory tactics for misconceived battles. Noisy clashes were not always significant ones. The spectacular conflicts of the era were not always the important ones in shaking or reestablishing the structures of power. For every March on Rome, Kapp Putsch, or general strike, there were equally determinative disputes over factory council prerogatives, taxes, coal prices, and iron tariffs. These were quieter but still decisive struggles.

In the wake of World War I, these confrontations formed part of an overarching development. That long and grueling combat imposed parallel social and political strains upon the states of Europe, and for years after dictated a common rhythm of radicalism and reaction. All Western nations experienced new restiveness on the left after the Russian Revolutions of 1917 and continuing radical turmoil from the 1918 Armistice through the spring of 1919. The "forces of order" had to make their peace either with political overturn, as in Germany, or, at the least, new attacks on capitalism. Yet, by 1920–1921, they had recovered the upper hand and pushed the "forces of movement" onto the defensive. By 1922–1923 a new wave of nationalist, sometimes authoritarian, remedies replaced the earlier surge of leftist efforts. Right-wing schemes, however, could not durably settle the economic and social dislocations the war had left. By the mid-1920's each country had to find a new and precarious equilibrium, based less on the revival of traditional ideological prescriptions than upon new interest-group compromises or new forms of coercion. Despite their many differences, France, Germany, and Italy all participated in this postwar political cycle.

This common tidal flow of politics virtually calls for comparative examination. In a more general work, post-World War I developments could be set in an even wider context of conservative reaction

[1] *The Recollections of Alexis de Tocqueville*, Alexander Teixera de Mattos, trans. J. P. Mayer, ed. (Cleveland and New York, 1959), p. 10.

or liberal crisis. Other countries, Austria and Spain, and from some perspectives Great Britain and the United States, might also have been included. This book sacrifices a broader range through space and time for intensive examination of three countries during one critical decade.

The three countries, moreover, do form a coherent unit for political and social analysis, despite the fact that Italy ended up under fascism, the German Republic as of the mid-1920's remained vulnerable to authoritarian pressures, while France maintained parliamentary institutions until its military defeat in 1940. Despite major differences, the three nations all had traditions of sharp ideological dispute and fragmentation, concepts of liberalism and labels for class distinction that set them apart from Britain or the United States. France, Italy, and Germany certainly do not provide the only matrix for comparison, but they do offer a logical one.

In the last analysis, there can be no *a priori* validity or lack of validity in historical comparison. The researcher can group together any range of phenomena under some common rubric. The issue is whether the exercise suggests relationships that would otherwise remain unilluminated. Some comparative approaches are more fruitful than others. Comparative history remains superficial if it merely plucks out elites in different societies—or working-class organizations, or party systems, or revolutionary disturbances. Flower arranging is not botany. A bouquet of historic parallels provides little knowledge about society unless we dissect and analyze the component parts. What is important to learn is what functions were served by supposedly comparable historical phenomena in establishing and contesting power and values. Organized parties, for instance, were critical in Germany but less so in Italy and France, so to follow parties alone would distort historical perspective. Issues deemed vital at one moment often lose the symbolic importance with which they were originally charged. Nationalization of the French railroads was bitterly contested in 1920, yet it meant little when it was finally accomplished in 1937. Issues and associations, therefore, must be scrutinized not according to their external form, but according to the changing roles they played in revealing the stress lines of European society. For this reason, comparative analysis starts here, from the disputes wherein the basic distributions of power were contested or at least exposed.

The analytical description needed here is complicated because what the contestants themselves described as the stakes of conflict was often misleading. The defenders envisioned their struggle in terms of the clashes they knew from before the war. They entered the interwar years with an inherited imagery of social and political conflict. Borrowing their terminology, this study uses the term *bourgeois* to denote

5

the arrangements which conservatives felt they were defending. In many instances the imagery of bourgeois defense was inadequate for understanding the new institutional realities that were emerging. To describe these new realities we cannot borrow from the terminology of the era, but must impose our own unifying concept. I have chosen the notion of corporatism. Each of these terms oversimplifies—distorting, on the one hand, conservative aspirations, and, on the other, the emerging institutional reality. Taken together, however, they force us to keep in mind the tension between aspiration and achievement.

What conservatives naturally aimed at was a stability and status associated with prewar Europe. "Bourgeois" was the most general term of orientation they invoked; they employed it as a shorthand for all they felt threatened by war, mass politics, and economic difficulty— in short, as the common denominator of social anxiety and political defense. For an observer suddenly transplanted from Restoration France or Germany before 1848, the conservative connotations of "bourgeois Europe" might have been startling. In those earlier eras the bourgeoisie had spearheaded the liberalization of economy and politics against the prescriptive claims of dynasties and agrarian traditionalists. But during the course of the nineteenth century, bourgeois spokesmen achieved the civil rights and, at least partially, the access to power they desired. Increasingly, in Western Europe they formed long-term associations with the old elite. Universities, government bureaucracies, boards of directors, and marriage beds could not produce a complete fusion of classes, but they did offer new chances to combine the assets of land, capital, public service, and education.

Bourgeois reformers, moreover, had always had potential enemies to the left: democrats, artisans, spokesmen for working-class grievances. Except in periods of crisis, cooperation with these volatile forces was short-lived, even during the era of bourgeois reform. From the advent of mass suffrage in the 1860's and after, the left became even more threatening, especially as it advocated major changes in property relationships. Under this pressure, too, members of the old elites perceived the same dangers as did bourgeois leaders. Tory radicalism, or the effort to outflank bourgeois elites with working-class alliances, yielded meager results and was never popular for very long among conservative constituencies. By the twentieth century most of the old elites had formed a conservative cartel with bourgeois political representatives. They identified the same enemies and defended the same prerogatives. As the most preoccupying enemy, social democrats set the terms of attack for the defenders of the social order as well as for themselves. More consistently than any other group, the socialists challenged existing property and power relationships as the foundation of a bourgeois society that rested upon economic exploitation, sacrificed democracy to elitism, and created suicidal international conflicts to preserve its internal structure. Under the pressure of growing social-democratic strength, both sides focused upon bourgeois society as the ultimate stake of political and economic conflict.

Yet in what sense was "bourgeois" a meaningful class category by 1918; or had it already been bled of all sociological precision? In the mid-1920's, Croce, for one, complained of the careless usage that "bourgeois" was receiving as a historical term.[2] He argued that it had really come to mean little more than modern and secular. Similar reservations could be made of its widespread use by social commentators. But its broad use also suggests that "bourgeois" really did evoke the basic social divisions of a market economy and industrial social order. Frequent recourse to the term revealed a nagging preoccupation with inequality and class antagonism. Conservatives liked to claim that class conflict as Marxists portrayed it was merely conjured up by agitators and demagogues. And yet they devoted major efforts to shoring up the very institutions that anchored class domination in the eyes of the left: they extolled the nation-state, fretted about nationalization of coal mines or railroads, praised property and entrepreneurship. As men of the 1920's employed the term, bourgeois invoked fundamental questions of social hierarchy and power. It remained the code word for a matrix of relationships defined in opposition to what socialists suggested as alternatives.[3] For the elites of the 1920's, bourgeois Europe was both elegiac and compelling: the image of an *ancien régime* that was still salvageable and whose rescue became the broadest common purpose of postwar politics.

This is not to claim that bourgeois defense was the stake of all political conflict in the 1920's. Disputes between Catholics and anti-clerical liberals remained deep enough to influence party organization in each country and to cut across the issues of social defense. Italian fascists or German right-radicals would also have rejected any claim

[2] Benedetto Croce, "Di un equivoco concetto storico: la 'Borghesia,'" *Atti della Academia di Scienze Morali e Politiche della Società Reale di Napoli*, LI (1927); reprinted in *Etica e politica* (Bari, 1967), p. 275. Although valid as a cross-national designation, the term "bourgeois" still suggested different qualities from country to country: "civic" in Germany, a ruling elite in Italy, and refined, perhaps smug upper-middle-class leisure in France.

[3] For the generation of class division: cf. Stanislaw Ossowski, *Class Structure in the Social Consciousness*, Sheila Patterson, trans. (London, 1963), pp. 72–73, 133; Ralf Dahrendorf, *Class and Class Conflict in Industrial Society* (Stanford, Calif., 1959), pp. 162–179, 201–205; useful surveys of the literature are in T. B. Bottomore, *Elites in Society* (Baltimore, 1966), and *Classes in Modern Society* (New York, 1968). Cf. also the essays in André Béteille, ed., *Social Inequality* (Baltimore, 1969).

that they sought to strengthen bourgeois Europe, for they fundamentally despised its parliamentary institutions. Even before the war a "new" European right had moved beyond the conservatism of agrarian, business, and bureaucratic elites to embrace a strident chauvinism, anti-Semitism, and antiparliamentarism. This new right comprised distressed farmers, retired officers, intellectuals and university youth, clerical employees and hard-pressed small businessmen and shopkeepers. Yet ironically, this rag-tag right-radical constituency could also contribute to the defense of bourgeois Europe. By the 1920's both the old and new right were attacking Marxist socialism (and communism) as an evil incubated by liberal democracy. The gains of socialism testified to a bourgeois failure of nerve; they made counteraction urgent and sanctioned a violent assault on liberalism itself. Thus, even as the radical right rhetorically lashed out against the parasites of finance or corrupt party politics, it moved with violence against the major organized opposition to bourgeois institutions. Disillusioned liberals, traditionalist conservatives, nationalists, and new right-radicals converged in their hostility to socialism and the democracy that permitted it to thrive.[4]

Nonetheless, this book focuses neither on the old nor the new right *per se*, but upon the process of stabilizing institutions under attack. It must, in fact, explore positions that were never considered to be on the right at all, in the militant sense usually given to that word. The right incorporated only one of two possible approaches to protecting the social order. While the right accepted a clear clash of ideologies and aimed at repressing change, moderate and democratic leaders dreaded Armageddon and hoped to disarm the attackers by reformist initiatives. Both strategies come under study here insofar as both envisaged a social order according to bourgeois criteria. To reconsolidate that social order was the overriding aim of conservative thought and action after 1918. It was the essential effort for the old right, often catalytic for the emergence of the radical new right, and a preoccupation as well for many progressives not on the right at all. To anticipate our conclusions, it was an effort that was largely successful, even if the victory required significant institutional transformation.

[4] For an introduction to concepts of the right: Hans Rogger and Eugen Weber, eds., *The European Right* (Berkeley and Los Angeles, 1965); René Rémond, *The Right Wing in France from 1815 to de Gaulle,* James M. Laux, trans. (Philadelphia, 1966); Ernst Nolte, *Three Faces of Fascism,* Leila Vennewitz, trans. (New York, 1966), pp. 29 ff., 429 ff.; Armin Mohler, *Die konservative Revolution in Deutschland, 1918–1932* (Stuttgart, 1950); Karl Mannheim, "Das konservative Denken. Soziologische Beiträge zum Werden des politisch-historischen Denkens in Deutschland," *Archiv für Sozialwissenschaft und Sozialpolitik,* 57, 1 and 2 (1927), pp. 68–142, 470–495.

For there was no simple restoration. While Europeans sought stability in the image of a prewar bourgeois society, they were creating new institutional arrangements and distributions of power. What began to evolve was a political economy that I have chosen to call corporatist.[5] This involved the displacement of power from elected representatives or a career bureaucracy to the major organized forces of European society and economy, sometimes bargaining directly among themselves, sometimes exerting influence through a weakened parliament, and occasionally seeking advantages through new executive authority. In each case corporatism meant the growth of private power and the twilight of sovereignty.

Most conspicuously, this evolution toward corporatism involved a decay of parliamentary influence. Already effaced during World War I, parliaments proved incapable of recovering a decisive position of power. Even in Germany, where the Reichstag had always been subordinate, the Weimar Republic's parliament proved a reflection and not a source of effective power. In part, parliamentary incapacity was a consequence of the harsher political tasks imposed by the 1920's. Not the fruits of growth but the costs of war had to be distributed: parliaments faced dilemmas of economic reallocation and relative deprivation that strained older party alignments and precluded coherent majorities. Ultimately, the weakening of parliament also meant the undermining of older notions of a common good and a traditionally conceived citizenry of free individuals.[6]

In the liberal polity, decisions demanded periodic ratification by a supposedly atomized electorate. The new corporatism, however,

[5] Like an emergency paper currency, the concept of a "corporatist" Europe is assigned a given value for internal use within the argumentation of this book. I make no claim that the term has a universal value. In fact, it is chosen hesitantly since it generally suggests "estatist" or a society of legally defined "orders." Political scientists might prefer "pluralist," but this notion usually suggests a free competition among social forces. And while I have resorted to the term "corporative pluralism" elsewhere it is inappropriate to deal with fascist Italy as pluralist. The Germans have tried "organized capitalism," but I wish to emphasize the political more than economic transition; hence "corporatist" as a provisional description of social bargaining under fascism and democratic conditions alike. On the general theme see my own and others' essays in Heinrich August Winkler, ed., *Organisierter Kapitalismus, Voraussetzungen und Anfänge* (Göttingen, 1974). For discussions of analogous developments within the United States, cf. Grant McConnell, *Private Power and American Democracy* (New York, 1966); Theodore J. Lowi, *The End of Liberalism: Ideology, Policy, and the Crisis of Public Authority* (New York, 1969). Samuel Beer, *British Politics in the Collectivist Age* (New York, 1967), also introduces comparable concepts.

[6] On this problem: Brian M. Barry, *Political Argument* (London, 1965), pp. 187–291; "The Public Interest," *Proceedings of the Aristotelian Society*, suppl. vol. 38 (1964), pp. 1–18. Cf. Jürgen Habermas, *Strukturwandel der Öffentlichkeit* (Neuwied, 1965), for the loss of the idea of the public in liberal society.

sought consensus less through the occasional approval of a mass public than through continued bargaining among organized interests. Consequently, policy depended less upon the aggregation of individual preferences than upon averting or overcoming the vetoes that interest groups could impose at the center. Consensus became hostage to the cooperation of each major interest. If industry, agriculture, labor, or in some cases the military, resisted government policy, they could make its costs unacceptable.

The leverage that each major interest could exert had further institutional consequences. It tended to dissolve the old line between parliament and the marketplace—between state and society—that continental liberals had claimed to defend. The political veto power of an interest group came to depend upon its strength in the economic arena. Conversely, viability in the marketplace required a voice in determining the political ground rules for economic competition, such as tariffs and taxes or the rights of collective bargaining.[7]

Consequently, too, the locus of policy making changed. Parliamentary assemblies grew too unwieldy for the continuing brokerage of interests. Bargaining moved outside the chamber to unofficial party or coalition caucuses, and to government ministries that tended to identify with major economic groupings, such as the Weimar Republic's Ministry of Labor.

Even the modalities of exerting influence altered. The liberal polity had always sanctioned discreet compacts between powerful individuals and ministers or parliamentary delegates. Influence was also transmitted less directly but just as pervasively in the clubs, lodges, schools, and regiments that formed the social milieu of the governing elites. But in the emerging corporatist system, new social elements had to be consulted, above all labor leaders who had earlier been outside the system. Domestic policy no longer emerged intact from the foyers of the ruling class, no longer represented just the shared premises of the era's "best and the brightest." Policy formation required formal confrontation in offices and ministries between old social antagonists. Political stability demanded a more bureaucratic and centralized bargaining. If Marx, in short, dictated the preoccupations of bourgeois society, Weber discerned its emerging structures of power.

[7] Cf. Rudolf Hilferding's analysis of "organized capitalism" as it developed between 1915 and 1927, esp. "Probleme der Zeit," *Die Gesellschaft*, 1 (1924), pp. 1–13; "Die Aufgaben der Sozialdemokratie in der Republik," Sozialdemokratischer Parteitag 1927 in Kiel, *Protokoll* (Berlin, 1927), pp. 166–170; also Wilfried Gottschalch, *Strukturveränderungen der Gesellschaft und politisches Handeln in der Lehre von Rudolf Hilferding* (Berlin, 1962), pp. 190–193, 207; and Heinrich August Winkler, "Einleitende Bermerkungen zu Hilferdings Theorie des Organisierten Kapitalismus," Winkler, ed., *Organisierter Kapitalismus*, pp. 9–18.

10

It would be wrong to exaggerate the suddenness of this transformation, which began before World War I and is really still underway. Labor and tariff disputes spurred the organization of modern pressure groups in the late nineteenth century. Cartelization further signaled the consolidation of economic power. Observers of the same era noted the growing affiliation of political parties with economic interest groups; and they discussed how party competition was changing from a clubby and whiggish rivalry into a professional mobilization of opinion through electoral machines. These developments quietly altered the nature of representative government.[8]

But they did not create a corporatist polity. Two further significant developments emerged only with the massive economic mobilization of World War I. The first was the integration of organized labor into a bargaining system supervised by the state. This accreditation of labor also had been underway, but the urgency of war production accelerated the process. Adding labor to the interest groups bargaining around the table suggested that a new division between those producer groups which could organize effectively and the fragmented components of the middle classes might become more politically significant than the older class cleavage between bourgeois and worker.

A second decisive impulse was the wartime erosion of the distinction between private and public sectors. As the state claimed important new powers to control prices, the movement of labor, and the allocation of raw materials, it turned over this new regulatory authority to delegates of business, labor, or agriculture, not merely through informal consultation but also through official supervisory boards and committees. A new commonwealth that dissolved the old distinction between state and economy seemed at hand; and some of its beneficiaries looked forward to extending wartime organization as the basis, in Rathenau's phrase, of a "new economy."

[8] Michael Ostrogorsky, *La démocratie et l'organisation des partis politiques*, 2 vols. (Paris, 1903); Max Weber, "Politics as a Vocation," and "Class, Status, Party," in Hans Gerth and C. Wright Mills, eds., *From Max Weber* (New York, 1958), pp. 99–112, 194–195; Robert Michels, *Political Parties, A Social Study of the Oligarchical Tendencies of Modern Democracy*, Eden and Cedar Paul, trans. (New York, 1915); Vilfredo Pareto, *Les systèmes socialistes* [1902] (Geneva, 1965). On interest-group development: Hans-Jürgen Puhle, "Parlament, Parteien und Interessenverbände 1890–1914," in Michael Stürmer, ed., *Das kaiserliche Deutschland* (Düsseldorf, 1970), pp. 340–377; Thomas Nipperdey, "Interessenverbände und Parteien in Deutschland vor dem Ersten Weltkrieg," now in Hans-Ulrich Wehler, ed., *Moderne deutsche Sozialgeschichte* (Cologne-Berlin, 1970), pp. 369–378; Heinrich A. Winkler, *Pluralismus oder Protektionismus. Verfassungspolitische Probleme des Verbandswesens im deutschen Kaiserreich* (Wiesbaden, 1972); Étienne Villey, *L'organisation professionnelle des employeurs dans l'industrie française* (Paris, 1923); Mario Abrate, *La lotta sindacale nella industrializzazione in Italia 1906–1926* (Turin, 1967), pp. 31–61.

Advocates for this parceling out of sovereignty spoke out from different points along the political spectrum. Men of the left, right, and center noted the new tendencies at the turn of the century: the growing web of interest groups and cartels, the obsolescence of the market economy, the interpenetration of government and industry. But they hoped to rationalize and order what they saw taking place as an unplanned evolution before 1914 and as an emergency response during the war. Rather than just a new centralization of interest-group bargaining, they wanted to leave brokerage behind entirely and create a planned and harmonious productive system based upon technological or moral imperatives. On the moderate left, guild socialists, Marxist revisionists, and some democratic liberals envisioned a gradual dissolution of central state authority and the growth of works councils and industrial self-government. Their premise was that if normally antagonistic groups, such as the workers and entrepreneurs of a given industry, could be seated at the same table to hammer out common policy, the result must be impartial enough to guarantee the public interest as a whole. Their concept of decentralization sometimes borrowed from French and Italian syndicalism, but the syndicalists envisaged a more radical elimination of the entrepreneurs.

There were also spokesmen for an older corporatism on the right, represented by writers from La Tour du Pin in the 1870's to Othmar Spann a half-century later. These theorists felt that they could undo the social ravages of an atomistic liberalism by creating an estatist representation. This vision differed in an important respect from the new corporatism that was actually emerging, because it envisioned not merely a *de facto* representation of economic forces, but a society of legal orders. As on the left, the corporatism invoked by conservatives was designed to secure a social harmony that transcended mere pressure-group bargaining. The new corporatism, however, did not eliminate class transactions but merely centralized them.

Finally, a technocratic vision of a new industrial order emerged from the ranks of professional engineers and progressive businessmen. American enthusiasts joined Europeans in blueprinting the future industrial commonwealth. Herbert Hoover's crusade for an orderly community of abundance and Walther Rathenau's more mystical revery of a postcompetitive industrial order both drew on the promises of technology and organization. Both men envisaged moving beyond an often wasteful *laissez-faire* economy, subject to cycles of boom and bust and to overproduction in some sectors and shortages in others. Horizontal association among producers would eliminate wasteful competition. Vertical association between industry and labor would ultimately rest upon technological determination of how to share the rewards of productivity.[9]

Each of these groups rejected the Manchesterite, bourgeois state, but their final visions remained different. Socialist and syndicalist theorists, who eschewed the term "corporative" because of its reactionary overtones, hoped to move beyond state authority to a less coercive and more egalitarian economy. Corporatists of the right, however, sought to re-create earlier hierarchies. The old ladders of subordination and domination, deference and largesse, reflected an ethical universal ordering that liberalism and the commercial spirit had shattered. Technocratic spokesmen denied class objectives in favor of a new efficiency, enhanced productivity, and a society of abundance.

History was to play tricks on each group; for the new corporatism encouraged restriction of output as much as abundance, and it led neither to radical liberation nor to recovery of an estatist social order. Instead it brought enhanced control for the very elites that had come to prominence under parliamentary auspices. Nor could any far-seeing statesman oversee the transformation: there was no Bismarck for the bourgeoisie as there had been for the Junkers. Rather, corporatist stability arose out of new pressures and false starts: as noted, wartime demands upon industry and labor for massive industrial production with a minimum of conflict; the accompanying wartime inflation, which permitted big business and the unions to reward themselves jointly—or at least to lose less than the other, less organized sectors of the economy; thereafter, the failure of liberal parliamentary leaders to solve postwar economic and social problems by traditional coalition compromises; finally, the terms of American economic intervention and of stabilization in the mid-1920's. It was this sequence of events that helped to consolidate the new relationships between private and public power, the development of which is presented below.

It is not claimed here that the trend was uniform throughout Europe. By the mid-1920's the thrust toward corporatism was clear in Germany, emerging under authoritarian auspices in Italy, but only embryonic in France. Corporatist trends in the Weimar Republic could build upon estatist patterns of authority and economic organization that had

---

[9] For corporatism on the right: Ralph Bowen, *German Theories of the Corporative State: With Special Reference to the Period 1870–1919* (New York, 1947); Matthew Elbow, *French Corporative Theory, 1789–1948* (New York, 1953); Herman Lebovics, *Social Conservatism and the Middle Classes in Germany, 1914–1933* (Princeton, N.J., 1969), pp. 109–138; on the left, cf. M. Beer, *A History of British Socialism* [1919] 2 vols. (London, 1953), II, pp. 363–372; G. D. H. Cole, *Self-Government in Industry* (London, 1917); also the writings cited below for chapter three, part one.

survived the nineteenth century in Germany. In Italy the traditional elites were more isolated and less protected by guild-like economic organization or by vigorous local self-government. A corporatist defense could not emerge from the fragmented pattern of business groupings and antiquated bourgeois parties. It had to be imposed by political coercion. In France, corporatist developments were even more retarded. Estatist patterns had been pulverized by prerevolutionary and postrevolutionary regimes, while a gentler pace of industrialization than Germany's lessened the scope and impact of powerful pressure groups. Less buffeted by radicalism, too, the French could preserve a bourgeois society through the parliamentary institutions of the Third Republic. Yet even in France the incapacities of the parliamentary regime pointed the way toward corporatist development.

The notion of corporatism is applied to all three countries, in any case, not as a simple description but rather as an ideal type. As such, it helps us to make sense of French tendencies as well as German ones and to forecast the structure of stability throughout Europe. The decade after World War I was a decisive era in this regrouping of conservative forces. The legacy of war precluded any simple return to the model of the liberal polity; and the role of the United States— a society marked by a new cooperation of government and business in the wake of wartime mobilization—helped advance the transformation in Europe.[10] The Depression, World War II, and subsequent American aid in reconstruction would thrust the evolution of corporatism even further along. After 1945, it would no longer be necessary or even comforting for conservatives to imagine the restoration of a bourgeois society as the endpoint of their efforts. The corporatist structure that was emerging in the 1920's as the instrument of social reconsolidation became a goal in its own right by the end of World War II. To reestablish the given hierarchies in Western Europe by the late 1940's, it was sufficient to assure the independence of private industry and interest groups. Conservative goals were less utopian than they were after 1918, less fraught with nostalgia for a deferential and stable bourgeois order. After 1945 bourgeois Europe neither existed nor ceased to exist: an ideological construct, it faded from concern.

[10] For diverse perspectives on trends in the United States: Gabriel Kolko, *Railroads and Regulation, 1877–1916* (Princeton, N.J., 1965) and *The Triumph of Conservatism: A Reinterpretation of American History, 1900–1916* (New York, 1963); Robert Wiebe, *Businessmen and Reform, A Study of the Progressive Movement* (Cambridge, Mass., 1962); Wiebe, *The Search for Order, 1877–1920* (New York, 1967); Paul A. C. Koistinen, "The 'Industrial-Military Complex' in Historical Perspective: World War I," *Business History Review*, XLI, 4 (1967), pp. 378–403; Ellis W. Hawley, *The New Deal and the Problem of Monopoly* (Princeton, N.J., 1966), pp. 8–13, 36–42; and Hawley's essay in *Herbert Hoover and the Crisis of American Capitalism* (Cambridge, Mass., 1973).

Stratification, inequality, and corporatist power remained, but few had sought to abolish them.

Bourgeois society, considered in retrospect, amounted to a conservative utopia.[11] It incorporated a collection of images, ideas, and memories about desirable ranking in a tensely divided industrial Europe. As a utopia it spurred conservative, and ultimately corporatist strategies, once simple restoration proved beyond reach. These corporatist arrangements not only helped reentrench prewar elites, but also rewarded labor leadership and injured the less organized middle classes. The history of stabilization after World War I thus involved, not a political freeze or simple reaction, but a decade of capitalist restructuring and renovation. The tension between bourgeois utopia and corporatist outcome—part of history's constant dialectic between men's intentions and their collective realization—provides the interpretive structure for what was a key era of conservative transformation.

[11] Cf. Karl Mannheim, *Ideology and Utopia* (London, 1960), pp. 206–211.

PART I
THE CONTAINMENT OF
THE LEFT

· 1 ·

THE DIMENSIONS OF SOCIAL
CONFLICT AT THE END
OF WORLD WAR I

The defense of bourgeois Europe must be mapped in three dimensions—in terms of class, elite, and interest groups. Class is the most troublesome variable—troublesome first to define, then to apply in concrete historical situations. What distinguished class, insofar as the historian encounters it, was not directly a group's relationship to the means of production or its relative wealth, but a sense of an overriding collective struggle for independence or hegemony. "Classes are valuable as myths, forces that constantly renew themselves and contend for power," wrote the young Italian antifascist, Piero Gobetti, in 1924. "In the messianic struggle of two ideal principles—the one alive as dream, the other as economic and political reality—history does not admit of solutions of continuity, but employs myths, faith, and illusion to renew its eternity."[1] Influenced by the Marxism of his Turin contemporary, Antonio Gramsci, Gobetti did not blink at the fact that society was profoundly divided. Indeed, he insisted that social progress had to start from a frank recognition of real inequalities—a view that appalled many Italian liberals. On the other hand, Gobetti never accepted the Marxist view that the proletariat's perspective on society was more objective and correct than the bourgeois: the collective self-appraisals upon which class was based, he suggested instead, were necessarily limited in insight on both sides.

The view of class that follows is akin to Gobetti's. The nomenclature of class is used here to convey what Europeans perceived as the fundamental social antagonisms arising from the unequal distribution of power and authority.[2] Class divisions doubtless derive in large measure from structural economic situations, from the positions that men occupy in the world of work or consumption. But stratification, whether based on economic power or on wealth, produces class division only insofar as there is awareness of collective competition for power and

[1] Piero Gobetti, *La rivoluzione liberale. Saggio sulla lotta politica in Italia* [1924] (Turin, 1964), p. 150. For the metaphor of three dimensions, see: W. C. Runciman, *Relative Deprivation and Social Justice* (London, 1966), pp. 36 ff.

[2] Cf. Ralf Dahrendorf, *Class and Class Conflict in Industrial Society* (Stanford, Calif., 1959), pp. 201–205; also Dahrendorf, "On the Origin of Inequality among Men," *Essays in the Theory of Society* (Stanford, Calif., 1968), pp. 151–178.

19

the right to distribute rewards. Class affiliation, whether expressed as "bourgeois" or in other coded terms, thus represented an allegiance and a collective commitment.

Overlapping the idea of class but not identical to it was the notion of elite. Turn-of-the-century sociologists were newly preoccupied with the concept. Mosca in part, then Pareto maintained that the elites in different fields of endeavor generated a selection of the forceful and intelligent who came to wield influence and power in society as a whole.[3] While a class could not really be discussed without at least implicit reference to an opposing class, the elite could be defined independently as a privileged stratum enjoying power, wealth, honor, or combinations of all three.

What makes the historian's task difficult is that elites were usually designated by a term suggesting class: the Italians referred to the ruling or "directing" class—though sometimes with more precision to the ruling stratum (ceta dirigente). Along with the French, they employed the term "bourgeoisie" much as Anglo-American usage today employs "upper class," more to suggest an elite than a class strictly speaking. In his last and fragmentary reflections on the problem, Max Weber sought to clear away this sort of ambiguity. Elites were groups enjoying elevated status; classes represented divisions of the economic world. But two principles of class structure existed side by side: "occupational classes," ranking those with differing professional and marketplace advantages, and "property classes," arrayed according to wealth and styles of consumption. Weber's occupational classes verged upon being interest groups, while privileged property classes, he admitted, formed the nuclei for social elites defined according to prestige and honor.[4] Weber's distinction helps the historian to illuminate some revealing national differences in class perception. French commentators tended to define class in terms of consumption and style of life;

[3] Gaetano Mosca, Elementi di scienza politica [1896, 1923], trans. Hannah D. Kahn, and ed. Arthur Livingstone as The Ruling Class (New York, 1939), esp. pp. 394–464; Vilfredo Pareto, Trattato di sociologia generale [1916], Andrew Bongiono, trans., Arthur Livingstone, ed., as The Mind and Society, 4 vols. (New York, 1935), IV, pp. 1421–1432 (§§2026–2059). Cf. also Franz Borkenau, Pareto (New York, 1936), pp. 106–164; James H. Meisel, The Myth of the Ruling Class: Gaetano Mosca and the "Elite" (Ann Arbor, Mich., 1958), pp. 57–61 ff.; H. Stuart Hughes, Consciousness and Society. The Reorientation of European Social Thought, 1890–1930 (New York, 1961), pp. 249–274.

[4] Max Weber, The Theory of Social and Economic Organization, Talcott Parsons, ed. and trans. (New York, 1964), pp. 424–429. (I have used different English equivalents for Erwerbsklassen and Besitzklassen.) Cf. Robert Michels, "Beitrag zur Lehre von der Klassenbildung," Archiv für Sozialwissenschaft und Sozialpolitik, 49, 3 (1922), pp. 561–593. Michels uses Weber's distinction, but also adds "social classes" to convey an overriding stratification.

Germans, too, never forgot these distinctions but increasingly emphasized class rivalry in the world of production. The difference makes sense in light of the fact that by the late nineteenth century the French bourgeoisie had achieved status as a social elite, while German bourgeois groups were still battling for uncertain power and prestige.

Still, despite the analytic clarity of Weber's categories, it is easier to discuss conflicts here in terms of class, elite, and interest groups. Weber's rigorous terminology was aimed more at classifying the social-structural determinants of class than at probing the ordinary language of group competition. Participants and observers did not readily separate the rewards of power, social rank, and economic success, since each ultimately depended upon the others. Even the distinction between class as a perceived "conflict group" and elite as a privileged stratum must be imposed *ex post facto*. In the turmoil of social conflict, concepts of class defense and elite defense remained snarled and intertwined. It is easier to keep the concept of interest group separate from that of class and elite. Interest groups claimed less of their members' identity than classes or elites, and they sought more tangible and professional objectives. From the late nineteenth century on, they emerged ever more centrally as points of orientation for political and economic rivalry. The treatment here, then, can usefully follow the order suggested by these three dimensions of social division: first the preoccupations embodied in the language of class (and sometimes of elite), then the actual precariousness of elite positions, and finally the strategy of interest groups.

Naturally there remain analytic problems. Men were members of classes or elites and of interest groups simultaneously: the entrepreneur was both steel industrialist and bourgeois. As he was to learn, it was easier to defend his specific prerogatives as industrialist than his privileges as bourgeois, for the goals were more concrete and the tactics clearer. Nevertheless, in different countries the defense of class or elite status was initially more compelling and not always easily separable from interest-group affiliation. In Germany the defense of corporate interest came to override that of class, so that businessmen came to feel that to defend the power of the entrepreneur was to defend the essential attribute of their social position. In Italy, on the other hand, the corporatist defense of industry and agriculture was only slowly disengaged from the more general political reaction on the part of the "directing class." Yet in each country, through the 1920's, it became clearer that successful conservative action required corporate organization and identity. Preoccupations about class or elite status might catalyze political defense, but new interest-group and corporatist strategies became increasingly important to its success.

The Language of Class Anxiety
(1900-1925)

If the proletarian supposedly had no fatherland, the bourgeois certainly did. His class awareness (and, of course, that of the worker as well) was molded within a national history and culture. Conservatives throughout Europe were preoccupied with class divisions and the vulnerability of their own favored stations in life, but their sense of vulnerability emerged in different language and day-to-day disputes. French social defensiveness was revealed directly by continuing justification and discussion of the bourgeoisie, while in Germany the fixation with the Social Democratic Party and in Italy the defense of "liberalism" disclosed underlying class malaise.

These differences emerged within a pervasive anxiety about social polarization. Admittedly, this concern had changed everywhere from the raw fear of urban *jacquerie*, which had marked the middle third of the nineteenth century with its June days and Paris Commune. Violent uprising was the product not of industrialized society but of the transition to that society—the explosion of workers and humble businessmen who were urbanized but not necessarily in factories or unions and who took to the streets for lack of more institutionalized alternatives. By about 1900 in France and Germany, perhaps a decade later in Italy, the major threat from the working class appeared less one of primitive upheaval than of long-term rivalry through political machines and industrial unions. Vocabulary and rhetorical images of social division had evolved correspondingly, from the premodern notions of rank and station to the language of class, from mob to proletariat, from concern for "the social question" to social democracy.[5]

This change did not mean, however, that bourgeois spokesmen could be less concerned. On the eve of the new century, Vilfredo Pareto warned that "slowly but surely the socialist tide is rising in almost every country of Europe. State socialism is opening the way

[5] For this evolution: Asa Briggs, "The Language of 'Class' in Early Nineteenth-Century England," in Asa Briggs and John Saville, eds., *Essays in Labour History* (New York, 1967), pp. 69–73; Wolfram Fischer, "Social Changes at Early Stages of Industrialization," *Comparative Studies in Society and History*, xi (1966), p. 71; Werner Conze, "Vom 'Pöbel' zum 'Proletariat.' Sozialgeschichtliche Voraussetzungen für den Sozialismus in Deutschland," in Hans-Ulrich Wehler, ed., *Moderne deutsche Sozialgeschichte* (Cologne-Berlin, 1968), pp. 111–136. For some earlier reactions to insurrectionary danger, see the Tocqueville *Recollections*, cited, Introduction, n. 1; Werner Pöls, *Sozialistenfrage und Revolutionsfurcht in ihrem Zusammenhang mit den angeblichen Staatsstreichplänen Bismarcks* (Lübeck and Hamburg, 1960); Heinrich von Treitschke in the *Preussische Jahrbücher*, June 10, 1878, included in *Zehn Jahre deutscher Kämpfe* (Berlin, 1897). Cf. Theodor Schieder, "The Problem of Revolution in the Nineteenth Century," *The State and Society in Our Times*, C.A.M. Sym, trans. (London, 1964), pp. 25–27.

to revolutionary socialism."[6] Pareto was less worried about the potential for violence of the working-class movement than its political challenge to a bourgeoisie that had come to doubt its own moral authority. The socialists were only the latest contender in a ceaseless struggle between aspiring and established elites, a struggle in which the bourgeoisie had grown soft because of misplaced humanitarianism, "its tearful apparatus of sentimentality and asceticism."[7] The political maverick, Georges Sorel, also arrived at a diagnosis of bourgeois flabbiness: "In the course of the nineteenth century," he reflected during the last weeks of peace in July 1914, "the bourgeoisie was so troubled by the fear of revolution that it accepted out of resignation the claims of a democracy whose inevitable triumph had been predicted by so many ideologies."[8] The task of Sorel's famous myth, with its incitement to class tension and creative violence, was to reinvigorate the elites as well as the proletarian challengers.[9] Both Sorel and Pareto shared a new and still unusual bourgeois hostility to liberalism. Yet it was significant that in decrying a crisis of European culture, they summoned up the rhetoric of class confrontation. Social conflict had become preoccupying enough to call into question the entire legacy of Enlightenment rationality and humanism.

While Pareto and Sorel saw the humanistic teachings of liberalism as the major symptom of class default, for most European spokesmen liberalism really suggested a doctrine of class defense. Because it had once attacked estatist society in the cause of equal opportunity, liberalism justified the hierarchies formed subsequently as meritocratic. By 1900, liberalism in all the Continental countries was narrowing into a nostalgic defense of an uncontested bourgeois leadership. The danger now was that what liberals held valuable would be swamped by de-

[6] Vilfredo Pareto, "La marée socialiste" [1899], now in Pareto, *Mythes et idéologies*, Giovanni Busino, ed. (Geneva, 1966), p. 162.

[7] Letter of April 1, 1905, in Vilfredo Pareto, *Lettere a Maffeo Pantaleoni, 1890–1923*, Gabriele De Rosa, ed., 3 vols. (Rome, 1962), II, p. 442. Cf. letter of July 15, 1908, III, p. 107, for the hope that syndicalist pressure would spark bourgeois combativeness. On the long-term struggles among elites: Pareto, *Les systèmes socialistes* [1902] (Geneva, 1965), p. 455; also, "Deux socialismes" [1903], *Mythes et idéologies*, p. 215. For the role of elite theory, see Hans P. Dreitzel, *Elitebegriff und Sozialstruktur* (Stuttgart, 1962), p. 39; T. B. Bottomore, *Elites in Society* (Baltimore, 1966), pp. 17–20.

[8] Georges Sorel, *Matériaux d'une théorie du proletariat* (Paris, 1917), p. 17; and for despair with liberalism, Sorel, *Les illusions du progrès* [1906–1908] (Paris, 1947). Cf. Michel Freund, *Georges Sorel, Der revolutionäre Konservatismus* (Frankfurt, 1932); Irving L. Horowitz, *Radicalism and the Revolt against Reason, the Social Theories of Georges Sorel* (Carbondale, Ill., 1967).

[9] Georges Sorel, *Réflexions sur la violence* [1908] (Paris, 1950), pp. 117–120, 193–195.

mocratization: "The failure of liberalism might very well be the characteristic trait of the nineteenth century," the French literary critic, Émile Faguet, typically lamented. "Everything, it seems to me, is pushing toward the triumph of an integral equality. . . . Europe is thus heading toward despotism by tending toward collectivism. In this regard there cannot be the slightest illusion."[10]

Nowhere was the stress upon liberalism as a class concept so intense as in Italy, where the *Risorgimento* had legitimized the historical role of the liberals in unifying the country. But from describing a vanguard of patriots engaged in nation building and modernization, the designation of liberalism had become a mantle for class politics. The Liberal Party, confessed one of its most conservative leaders, Antonio Salandra, in 1912,

> is not a class party. . . . Still, it cannot be denied that it finds its strength above all in the middle class, in what with an expression that is vague and poorly defined but not devoid of content, is usually called the bourgeoisie. The Italian bourgeoisie can boast of a dual title to glory: first it was the principal architect of the *Risorgimento* and the founder of the new united state. Since then, it has been the agent of the wonderful economic development of so many sections of the country. . . . It is still by far superior to other classes and other possible groupings of our society, who remain quite far from the day when they will dispose of as many of the elements of vigor and virtuous discipline needed to govern a state.[11]

Salandra's Liberal Party represented no more than a network of local political associations. But it claimed a moral and ideological preeminence and had encountered few challenges for a generation. The liberals of the nineteenth century composed virtually the whole body politic of the Italian nation before the rise of socialism in the 1890's. They comprised the business classes and civil servants throughout the peninsula, the progressive gentry of Piedmont or Tuscany, the lawyers and the so-called humanistic petty bourgeoisie of the Southern urban centers—Masons and spiritual heirs of the *Carbonari*. Traditionalist conservatism, often tied to the great landlords or the "black aristocracy," largely defaulted in the political arena; for it had been closely connected with Catholic resistance to the conquest of Rome, and until

[10] Émile Faguet, *Problèmes politiques du temps présent* (Paris, 1901), p. xi. Cf. also his preference for a republic with "aristocratic institutions," in "Une Étude sur Le Play," *RDM*, December 15, 1912, p. 897. For general discussion of this attitude: Theodor Schieder, "The Crisis of Bourgeois Liberalism," *The State and Society in Our Times*, pp. 39–64; also Dreitzel, *Elitebegriff*, p. 40.

[11] Antonio Salandra, *La politica nazionale e il partito liberale* (Milan, 1912), pp. xxi, xxii.

1904 the Vatican did not permit its faithful to participate in the politics of the despoiling state. Within the broad liberal camp, moreover, the divisions that did arise between right and left, the more conservative and the more democratic, usually yielded to the blandishments of *trasformismo*. Epitomized by the 1882 reconciliation of the Left with its former opponents of the "Old Right," *trasformismo* was the practice of joining with the opposition to erase ideological distinctions and construct a broad liberal coalition based on patronage and the enjoyment of power. Thus, with the exception of republicans, radicals, and occasional socialists on the left and the handful of clericals on the right, to belong to the political class or to sit in parliament meant to commit oneself as a liberal.[12]

Despite the original ruling party consensus, the spurts of industrialization and the growth of a militant labor movement sharpened political alternatives. The issues of how far to democratize the governing system—based until 1912 on a restricted suffrage that disenfranchised the Southern peasantry on grounds of illiteracy—how far to concede the right to strike, and how to deal with the new socialists in parliament, produced significant political differences by the first decade of the twentieth century. Seeking to keep political leadership in the hands of a reinvigorated but narrow political elite, Sidney Sonnino (Premier: 1906 and 1909–1910) envisaged a modernized restoration of the Old Right's conservative and administrative approach to governance. Financial and social reform accompanied a search for enhanced executive authority in an effort to hold back the encroachments of the new mass movements. Sonnino's attitude differed in emphasis but not in fundamental conception from that of the man who dominated the cabinets of 1901 to 1914, Giovanni Giolitti (Interior Minister, then Premier, 1901–1903, 1903–1905, 1906–1909, 1911–1914). For Giolitti, the best way to manage Italy's dynamic industrialization without social upheaval was gradually to assimilate the working class into Italian politics. Rejecting the repression attempted during the late 1890's, Giolitti tolerated strikes and sought to treat labor's claims as interest-group grievances, not class attack. Rejecting, too, Sonnino's search for clear-cut political alignments, Giolitti became a master at manipulating broad and disparate coalitions of interests and shunned

---

[12] For these developments, consult Mario Vinciguerra, *I partiti italiani dal 1848 al 1955* (Rome, 1956); Carlo Morandi, *I partiti politici nella storia d'Italia* (Florence, 1965), pp. 25 ff.; Federico Chabod, *Storia della politica estera italiana dal 1870 al 1896*, 2 vols. (Bari, 1965), i, pp. 375 ff.; Giampiero Carocci, *Agostino Depretis e la politica interna italiana dal 1876 al 1887* (Turin, 1956); G. Spadolini, *L'opposizione cattolica da Porta Pia al 1898* (Florence, 1955); Gabriele De Rosa, *Storia del movimento cattolico in Italia*, 2 vols. (Bari, 1966), i, pp. 265 ff., 283 ff., 437–462.

polarized, ideological blocs. His efforts to domesticate socialism, to win the reformist labor leaders to his program, and to deal with their aspirations as legitimate bargaining demands offended both right and left who desired ideological consistency. Nonsocialist radicals condemned Giolitti's iron hold over Southern political fiefs; the right distrusted his dissolution of the liberal governing elite. In this political context, therefore, to reassert the role of the Liberal "Party," as did Sonnino and his lieutenant Salandra, signified a disenchantment with the Giolittian program, a desire for bloc confrontation, and an unwillingness to surrender bourgeois power and influence.[13]

With the new century, the liberals' worry about the role of the bourgeoisie was reinforced by the strident claims of a new nationalist right. As early as 1882, Pasquale Turiello had condemned the disintegration of Italian society under the liberals, above all the harsh cost of liberal policies for the South. As a remedy Turiello envisaged a new war with Austria, which might help the state to become a martial and conservative rallying point.[14] By 1900, nationalist propagandists had introduced the idea of Italy as a "proletarian nation," arguing that the working class was less exploited than the country as a whole was abused by the richer and more developed powers to the north. The implication was that Italy's proletariat should cease pressing its own class demands and support the governing elite in an imperialist drive that would enrich the country as a whole. For Giovanni Papini and Giuseppe Prezzolini, nationalism and colonial expansion could assist in the task of "reawakening the bourgeois class by means of aristocracy to lead it against socialist or semi-socialist democracy."[15] For Enrico Corradini and Alfredo Rocco, domestic class division was to be submerged in a militant national commitment and a union of the productive elements of society—workers of hand and of mind together. Stressing the "march of the producers" led the nationalist ideologues beyond liberalism, to a defense of the bourgeoisie as a vanguard of industrial innovation and technological leadership. Interest reinforced ideology: the Italian Nationalist Association (and thereafter Party), which Corradini, Luigi Federzoni, and Rocco established in the years before

[13] Giampiero Carocci, *Giolitti e l'età giolittiana* (Turin, 1961); A. William Salamone, *Italian Democracy in the Making, 1900–1914* (Philadelphia, 1945); Nino Valeri, *Giolitti* (Turin, 1971), pp. 165 ff.; Gaetano Natale, *Giolitti e gli italiani* (Milan, 1949); G. Ansaldo, *Il ministero della buona vita* (Milan 1950); recent summary of the literature in Franco De Felice, "L'età giolittiana," *Studi Storici*, x, 1 (1969), pp. 114–190.

[14] Pasquale Turiello, *Governo e governati in Italia*, 2 vols. (Bologna, 1882), esp II, pp. 306, 311–312, 337, and chapter vii, *passim*.

[15] Giovanni Papini e Giuseppe Prezzolini, *Vecchio e nuovo nazionalismo* (Milan, 1914), p. 23.

World War I, quickly forged important links with Italy's large iron and steel producers.[16]

The emergence of the new authoritarian Nationalist Party was just one of many developments in the turbulent period from 1911 to 1915 that brought an end to the conditions under which either Salandran or Giolittian varieties of liberalism might have functioned successfully. Giolittian compromises, particularly, depended upon moderation on the part of the working-class opposition, upon economic prosperity so that both labor and capital could share in the benefits of growth, and finally upon insulation from international disturbances. But these conditions all vanished. With the advent of universal suffrage (1911/12), which Giolitti conceded to the left, and the Libyan conquest he granted to the right, with a slowdown in economic growth, the radicalization of the Italian Socialist Party in 1912, and the tormenting controversy over intervention in World War I after August 1914, the fragile bases of the liberal national achievement became painfully overstrained. Giolitti had to resort to bargaining for organized Catholic support for his parliamentary candidates in 1913, but he thereby alienated the anticlerical left wing of his own majority, and he thought it best to step down from power in the spring of 1914. The ministerial succession this time fell logically enough to Salandra, who seemed ready to work in the spirit of Giolitti's democratic initiatives but was really far more conservative. Salandra remained profoundly elitist and parochial, a small-town Apulian lawyer and *notable* who reaffirmed the most traditional formulas of the liberal right. Salandra's new administration, moreover, was shaken at its outset by the riots of Red Week (June 1914), which helped trigger a conservative reaction in key urban elections.[17]

Intervention in the European war, the outbreak of which had left Italy poised between rival alliances, seemed to offer a chance to reconsolidate "liberalism" as Salandra understood it. For the premier and

[16] For the movement and its spokesmen: Franco Gaeta, *Nazionalismo italiano* (Naples, 1965); Paola Maria Arcari, *L'elaborazione della dottrina politica nazionale tra l'unità e l'intervento (1870–1914)*, 3 vols. (Florence, 1934–1939); Enzo Santarelli, *Origini del fascismo (1911–1919): Studi storici* (Urbino, 1964), esp. part II: "Il socialismo nazionalista"; Paolo Ungari, *Alfredo Rocco e l'ideologia giuridica del fascismo* (Brescia, 1963), pp. 13 ff.; Enrico Corradini, *La marcia dei produttori* (Rome, 1916); and Corradini, *Discorsi politici (1902–1923)* (Florence, 1923).

[17] Richard Webster, "From Insurrection to Intervention: The Italian Crisis of 1914," *Italian Quarterly*, v, 20 and vi, 21 (1961 and 1962), pp. 27–50; Brunello Vigezzi, "Il suffragio universale e la 'crisi' del liberalismo in Italia (dicembre 1913–aprile 1914)," *Nuova Rivista Storica*, 48, 5–6 (1964), pp. 529–570; Carocci, *Giolitti*, pp. 138 ff.

for Sonnino, whom he chose as Foreign Minister in September 1914, the war offered territorial acquisitions and, equally important, the opportunity to strengthen executive authority and subdue the parliamentary majority originally loyal to Giolitti. The ex-premier himself favored staying neutral and extracting concessions from the Central Powers in return. This stance accorded by and large with the neutralist sentiments of the socialists and the organized Catholic political forces. For both leftist and conservative opponents of Giolitti, however, intervention in the war promised a way out of his "system" of ideological fuzziness and clientele politics. More generally, intervention promised to offer a new function and vitality to the bourgeois political class.[18]

In the political clashes between 1911 and 1922, when the fascists came to power, an ever more intense rhetorical invocation of "bourgeoisie" and "liberalism" disclosed the uneasiness and isolation of the traditional ruling groups.[19] The ideological output was often self-contradictory: seeking to deny the importance of class division, the liberals insisted on the historical contribution of their own elite. While constantly reiterating the merits of the bourgeoisie, the *Giornale d'Italia*, for example, still claimed that "society does not break down into classes but presents instead the spectacle of strata having the most diverse interests," strata in turn that were "extremely mobile in the sense that they are unceasingly changing their social molecules, that is, the individuals who compose them."[20] There were no classes, but the bourgeoisie had to be preserved! By the early 1920's, many liberals agreed that only Mussolini could force Italians to accept this social paradox, that only political violence could impose class rule while simultaneously denying class conflict.

Admittedly, on the liberal left there were challengers to this elitism. The democratic interventionist Ivanoe Bonomi argued that the liberals identified their own political elite with a national good transcending other class interests. Since modern history generated progress through class and party rivalry, "A regime . . . that opposes the abstract idea of the Nation to the concrete reality of social life can resist only with coercion."[21] Like Bonomi, Gobetti, too, demanded that the liberals

[18] Internal significance of the intervention in: Edgar Rosen, "Italiens Kriegseintritt im Jahre 1915 als innenpolitisches Problem der Giolitti-Ära," *Historische Zeitschrift*, 187, 2 (1959), pp. 289–363; Brunello Vigezzi, *L'Italia di fronte alla prima guerra mondiale*, vol. 1, *L'Italia neutrale* (Milan, 1966); interpretive exchanges in *Atti del XLI Congresso di Storia del Risorgimento italiano* (*Trento, 9–13 Ottobre 1963*) (Rome, 1965).

[19] Brunello Vigezzi, *1919–1925. Dopoguerra e fascismo. Politica e stampa in Italia* (Bari, 1965), p. xvii.

[20] "Fuori del maleficio della lotta di classe," *GdI*, December 21, 1923.

[21] Ivanoe Bonomi, *Dal socialismo al fascismo* (Rome, 1924), pp. 156–157.

champion the class struggle and not a fictive and self-serving national interest. He condemned the conventional liberal's praise of the bourgeoisie's role in the *Risorgimento* as reflecting "the moment of inertia and renunciation in which all elites redescend as they approach their twilight." But even Gobetti was not prepared to abandon the mission of the bourgeoisie. Accepting the challenge of class struggle was not to do away with elites but to renew them: "The class struggle has been the experimentum crucis of liberal practice; only through the class struggle can liberalism demonstrate its riches."[22] Italy's present elites, Gobetti realized, had become trapped in a conservative desire to retain the old, unchallenged hegemony that an industrialized Italy no longer sanctioned. Still, for Gobetti as for Giolitti and Pareto, there had to be some elite. And if the problem of good governance remained that of finding a worthy elite, then perpetual class division was presupposed. The debate over the nature of liberalism thus involved a defense of hierarchy in its very posing of alternatives. It revealed an underlying consensus on the continuing importance of the ruling elite as well as new anxiety about the challenges to it.

This agonized discussion over liberalism would have seemed irrelevant in France. As a historical tradition, liberalism played less of a role in a country whose national achievements were largely Jacobin or imperial. "Orleanism," the tradition of parliamentary liberalism and middle-class fitness to rule, did indeed represent a strong current in French political life, but it never monopolized the loyalties of the dominant political contenders as did the equivalent in Italy. Furthermore, the notion of "bourgeois" was less politically restrictive in France. It suggested a broader-based national transformation; for the break with the *ancien régime* had involved wider popular participation than the *Risorgimento*.[23] More immediately, as of 1900 French bourgeois political values still faced a bitter right-wing assault, a continuing attack upon the secular democratic republic. This meant in turn that divisions between bourgeoisie and working class could not so monopolize the French political scene, at least before 1905. Then, with the close of the harshest phase of the Church–state battle, with the advent of a unified French Socialist Party, and with the ever more ominous German rivalry, social and national issues emerged as more

[22] Gobetti, *La rivoluzione liberale*, pp. 146–147; cf. pp. 48–59. For an evaluation: G. Arfé, "La rivoluzione liberale di Piero Gobetti," *Rivista Storica Italiana*, 74, 2 (1962), pp. 313–323.

[23] Cf. Antonio Gramsci, *Il Risorgimento* (Turin, 1966), esp. pp. 69 ff., 87 ff.; Rosario Romeo, *Risorgimento e capitalismo* (Bari, 1963), pp. 17–51; A. William Salamone, "The Risorgimento between Ideology and History: The Political Myth of *rivoluzione mancata*," *American Historical Review*, LXVIII, 1 (1962), pp. 38–56.

important than those of religion and regime. These new developments finally made the socialist–bourgeois split more critical than the old enmity with the reactionary right.

Paradoxically, the more modern French social structure permitted indulgence in a more reactionary rightist ideology than in Italy. The moderate political results of the *Risorgimento* were accepted with less active dissent in Italy than were the implications of the democratic revolution within France. The effort of Italian conservatives went into agonizing about the vulnerability of their social leadership. The relative security of the French elites—their social and economic insulation from mass movements—allowed a mandarin's intellectual fixation upon older political issues and more "purer" counterrevolutionary ideas. But when bourgeois security was shaken after 1905 and more significantly after 1918, the old-fashioned ideologies of the counterrevolutionary right, such as the Action Française, appeared antique and beside the point.[24]

A less flamboyant but more enduring conservative tendency of the period between 1890 and 1920 is better described in terms of the politics of "concentration"—the migration of bourgeois republicans to the right over economic and social issues. The governments of the 1890's drew majorities from moderate republicans and nondoctrinaire conservatives, notably to pass tariff protection. Antisocialism and a harsh reaction to labor-union organization also characterized the last decade of the century. By reopening the older questions of religion and regime, the Dreyfus Affair, however, reimposed a traditional left–right confrontation. As a result of the political passions aroused, the Radical Socialist Party emerged as the dominant Chamber grouping—a democratic and fiercely secular electoral machine based on the middle-class and lower-middle-class elements of small-town France. Yet by 1910, after the eruption of syndicalist agitation, even the moderate Radicals ran on socially conservative platforms. Finally, growing tension with Germany played a major role in creating a coalition of centrists and conservatives around issues of national defense. The formation of Raymond Poincaré's 1912 government, his election to the French presidency a year later, and the restoration of three-year military service

[24] For the far right, there is a large literature. Among recent studies: René Rémond, *The Right-Wing in France from 1815 to de Gaulle*, James M. Laux, trans. (Philadelphia, 1966), pp. 208 ff.; Ernst Nolte, *Three Faces of Fascism*, Leila Vennewitz, trans. (New York, 1966), part II; Eugen Weber, *Action Française* (Stanford, Calif., 1962); Robert Soucy, *Fascism in France: The Case of Maurice Barrès* (Berkeley, Calif., 1972); Claude Digeon, *La crise allemande de la pensée française (1870–1914)* (Paris, 1959), pp. 434 ff.; and the reminiscences in Henri Massis, *Maurras et notre temps*, 2 vols. (Geneva, 1951).

all signified the renewal of a "concentration" majority preoccupied with labor unrest and the state's growing economic role at home and with German assertiveness abroad.[25]

In the elections of 1914, advocates of a strong defense posture, relaxation of anticlerical measures, and postponement of a progressive income tax ran together against an alliance of the French Socialists (SFIO) and Radical Socialists. While the left bloc prevailed in its popular demand for reinstatement of two-year conscription, it was the electoral alignments and not the election results that were most revealing.[26] French elections were becoming a contest for the conscience and interests of the moderate Radical Socialists. If, from motives of economic conservatism, the Radicals could be separated from the Socialists as in 1910, then ultimately a coalition built around social and nationalist issues might achieve a center-conservative majority. The prewar elections thus forecast the potential of the 1919 Bloc National.

Such a coalition could not be constructed around the liberal label. This term had little popular resonance; moreover, it had been claimed at the turn of the century by Catholics who rallied to the regime but demanded an end to anticlericalism. Counterrevolutionary slogans were also anathema to all but the extreme right. All other French political forces claimed the designation of "republican" as their own. While political coalitions were built increasingly around economic questions, little specific language of class was pressed into service for the prewar elections.

But class awareness was still rife, even if the prewar elections did not fundamentally test class divisions. Instead, preoccupations about the bourgeois role as social elite testified to anxiety, "The bourgeoisie has the pretension to be an *elite* and to be recognized as one," one commentator noted.[27] By elite he meant to suggest an aristocracy of merit, not merely privilege. All parties in fact shared a belief in the significance of elites. Throughout the nineteenth century a notion of professional elites had been central to Orleanist liberalism and to Saint-Simonian ideas. Spokesmen for the left might condemn the two hun-

[25] For these developments: Pierre Sorlin, *Waldeck-Rousseau* (Paris, 1966), pp. 356–364; Michel Augé-Laribé, *La politique agricole de la France de 1870 à 1940* (Paris, 1950), pp. 72–80, 219–220, 237–240; Eugene O. Golob, *The Méline Tariff: French Agriculture and Nationalist Economic Policy* (New York, 1944); the new coalitions behind nationalism in Eugen Weber, *The National Revival in France, 1905–1914* (Berkeley, Calif., 1959); cf. Pierre Miquel, *Poincaré* (Paris, 1961), pp. 208 ff.

[26] Georges Lachapelle, *Élections législatives des 26 avril et 10 mai 1914: Résultats officiels* (Paris, 1914); François Goguel, *La politique des partis sous la IIIᵉ République* (Paris, 1958), pp. 129–150.

[27] Edmond Goblot, *La barrière et le niveau* [1925] (Paris, 1967), p. 9.

31

dred families, but they shared a commitment to intellectual meritoc-racy.[28] Middle-of-the-roaders described democracy as little more than a system for recruiting new elites. Just as Italian political thinking could not pose the problem of governance without reference to a political class, French concepts of social order required positing a directing elite. But to be part of an elite meant less fortune than toil and sacrifice: "The bourgeoisie is essentially an effort," wrote one apologist, "individual effort (culture, moral tenor), family effort (profit, patrimony), social effort (propriety, personal merit), political effort (authority, competence)—above all in France."[29] What is more, the elite was accessible to all of ability: the French bourgeoisie was "not a privileged corporation, but a very open, very fluid category furnishing the country with its general staff, and constantly renewed by the elites of the urban and rural proletariat."[30] One inequality, at least, was implicit in this description: bourgeois elites gloried in being bourgeois; proletarian elites were elites precisely because their mem-bers could escape the proletariat. Yet it was clear that despite the impediments of recruitment, the narrowness of higher education, and the inheritance of wealth, enough of middle-class France accepted the inevitability of an elite—and shared enough of its *laissez-faire* preju-dices—to provide broad social consensus.

Two particular trends emerged in the current of bourgeois self-celebration: first an aesthetic snobbism, which during the postwar era influenced the efforts of Léon Bérard, Poincaré's Minister of Ed-ucation from 1922 to 1924, to tighten up classical language training for the *baccalauréat*. Bérard claimed that he was merely trying to re-inforce national values, but "under the simple pedagogical question," wrote the sensitive commentator Edmond Goblot, "there is the ques-tion of social class. . . . The bourgeois needs a culture that differen-tiates an elite, a culture that is not purely utilitarian, a culture de luxe."[31]

[28] Michalina Clifford-Vaughn, "Some French Concepts of Elites," *The British Journal of Sociology*, xi, 4 (1960), p. 329; on Orleanist elites: Rémond, *The Right-Wing in France*, pp. 99–124.

[29] René Johannet, *Éloge du bourgeois français* (Paris, 1924), p. 95.

[30] André Lichtenberger, "Le bourgeois," *RDM*, November 15, 1921, pp. 339–340. For discussions of French bourgeois attributes over the course of a century: Adeline Daumard, *La bourgeoisie parisienne de 1815 à 1848* (Paris, 1963); Jean Lhomme, *La grande bourgeoisie au pouvoir (1830–1880)* (Paris, 1960); A. Bar-doux, *La bourgeoisie française* (Paris, 1893); the impressionistic snapshot in Jacques Chastenet, *La France de M. Faillères* (Paris, 1949), esp. p. 148; J. Aynard, *La bourgeoisie française, Essai de Psychologie* (Paris, 1934); Emmanuel Berl, *Frère bourgeois, mourez-vous? Ding! Ding! Dong!* (Paris, 1938).

[31] Goblot, *La barrière et le niveau*, pp. 81, 85–86; see also Theodore Zeldin, "Higher Education in France, 1848–1940," *Journal of Contemporary History*, ii, 3 (1967), reprinted in Walter Laqueur and George L. Mosse, eds., *Education and*

In addition to this cultural elitism, bourgeois spokesmen turned to a technocratic self-justification that stressed entrepreneurial and scientific leadership. Saint-Simonian ideas reinforced this trend, while conservatives could also justify a paternalism of expertise from the writings of Le Play. After the war, new economic difficulties and the emphasis on industrial reorganization and production would encourage a bourgeois managerial elitism: "The bourgeois is not, as he is accused," wrote the young François Poncet, "a privileged being. For where are, what are his privileges? But he is a favored being. By chance or by birth he has had the intelligence, or by the circumstances surrounding the first years of his life, the faculty of deferring the moment when he would have had to earn his living, and of acquiring education and culture that have placed him on the superior echelons of society. It is doubtless vain and absurd to imagine that this fundamental inequality could be suppressed. It is in the air. It is in nature. Even were you 'dictators of the proletariat' you could not dictate the laws of nature."[32] A few years later Ernest Mercier, a product of the École polytechnique and an organizer of the modern electrical industry, called upon men of education and character to act together as a directing cadre. "The mass of workers" might not second this allegedly nonpartisan effort, but it was perilous to entrust the masses with real control before they enjoyed "sufficient education" and a "technical and moral formation."[33] Mercier's appeal in the late 1920's was the logical endpoint of French bourgeois adaptation to issues of social stratification. The search for a technocratic elite really implied the preservation of a given social hierarchy universally described as bourgeois. The filtering of the educational system and the adoption of a functional view of class justified social hierarchy in a society of supposed egalitarian commitment.

Bildung und Besitz (culture and property) as a pillar of a privileged social order had long been a commonplace notion across the Rhine. Nonetheless, German conditions produced a far harsher sense of social threat and class response. The adjective "bourgeois" invoked far less of a contribution to national unification than in Italy. It remained

---

Social Structure in the Twentieth Century (New York, 1967), pp. 74–78. Cf. Léon Bérard, "Ce que j'ai voulu faire," *RDM*, October 1, 1924, pp. 513–526; and Bérard, *Au service de la pensée française* (Paris, 1925).

[32] André François Poncet, *Réflexions d'un républicain moderne* (Paris, 1925), p. 127.

[33] Ernest Mercier, "Réflexions sur l'élite," *RDM*, February 15, 1928, pp. 383, 389–390; cf. Richard F. Kuisel, *Ernest Mercier, French Technocrat* (Berkeley, Calif., 1957), esp. pp. 45 ff.

less suggestive of social preeminence or managerial leadership than in France. As Max Weber and other writers pointed out, middle-class elements remained under the spell of "feudal" and aristocratic values and aspirations.[34] The constitutional system of the Reich and the three-class Prussian suffrage, as well as the continuing dominance of the army and bureaucracy, preserved the power of the Junkers until 1918 and even beyond.[35]

Just as critical in shaping the language of class defense, the centrifugal social forces of the new Reich could really be held together only by brandishing some grave domestic or foreign peril. Confronted with the massive growth of the industrial working class, urban and Southern liberals and agrarian conservatives might come to see their own conflicts over army bills, canals, and tariffs as secondary. Bismarck's early policy of rapprochement between industrial and agricultural leaders —the so-called coalition of rye and iron—broke down in the early 1890's when the agrarians became antagonized over Chancellor Caprivi's reduction of tariffs. Adopting what initially seemed a rewarding tactic of anti-Semitic agitation, organizing themselves in a powerful Agrarian League, the East Elbians sought to limit the incursions of liberalism and industrialism. Given the need to placate the reactionary majority of the Prussian Landtag, the political leaders of the later 1890's and early 1900's, Johannes Miquel and then Bernhard von Bülow, found it easier to yield in part to the agrarians. In 1897 Miquel announced that new concessions would be granted to both industrial and agricultural interests to consolidate the "forces loyal to the state."[36]

[34] For German notions of the bourgeoisie, Hansjoachim Henning, Das westdeutsche Bürgertum in der Epoche der Hochindustralisierung 1860–1914 (Wiesbaden, 1972), pp. 5–38; Werner Sombart, Der Bourgeois (Munich and Leipzig, 1913); Weber's critique in Wolfgang Mommsen, Max Weber und die deutsche Politik (1890–1920) (Tübingen, 1959), pp. 61–62, 103–109.

[35] On the constitutional system: J.C.G. Röhl, Germany without Bismarck, The Crisis of Government in the Second Reich, 1890–1900 (Berkeley and Los Angeles, 1967); Arthur Rosenberg, Imperial Germany: The Birth of the German Republic, 1871–1918, Ian F. D. Morrow, trans. (Boston, 1964), pp. 32 ff. For the social role of the army, Gerhard Ritter, Staatskunst und Kriegshandwerk: Das Problem des "Militarismus" in Deutschland, II, Die Hauptmächte Europas und das wilhelminische Reich (1890–1914) (Munich, 1965), pp. 117–132; Martin Kitchen, The German Officer Corps, 1890–1914 (London, 1968). For bureaucratic conservatism: Eckart Kehr, "Das soziale System der Reaktion in Preussen unter dem Ministerium Puttkamer" [1929], now in the essays collected by Hans-Ulrich Wehler, ed., Der Primat der Innenpolitik, Gesammelte Aufsätze zur preussisch-deutschen Sozialgeschichte (Berlin, 1965).

[36] Hans–Jürgen Puhle, Agrarische Interessenpolitik und preussischer Konservatismus im wilhelminischen Reich (1893–1914) (Hanover, 1967), pp. 226 ff.; Alexander Gerschenkron, Bread and Democracy in Germany (Berkeley, Calif., 1943), pp. 51–64; Kenneth Barkin, The Controversy over Industrialization in Germany (Chicago, 1970), pp. 211 ff.; Johannes von Miquel, Reden, Walther Schultz and Friedrich Thimme, eds., 4 vols. (Halle, 1914), IV, pp. 278–281, 283–287 (July 15 and 24, 1897).

The agrarians won a new and higher tariff; the industrial National Liberal community could participate in the mission of *Weltpolitik* and the naval arms construction it supposedly required. And since, by 1900, piecing together a Reichstag majority required Center Party support if the Socialists were to be excluded, Catholics also won new benefits, as anticlerical legislation was dismantled. This grand log-rolling operation, in fact, revealed that interpenetration of state and business interests which would characterize the German political economy during and after World War I. As it would again in the 1920's, the government summoned representatives of business and the Chambers of Commerce to participate in the tariff advisory council set up to work out the new duties. But unlike the later experience of *Interessenpolitik*, there was no effort to woo labor. Overarching the tangible payoffs to each party remained the fear of Social Democratic advance. While in Italy Giolitti sought to woo the Socialist moderates into the liberal system, the Bismarckian constitution led Miquel and Bülow to govern the unwieldy Reich precisely by rallying its major elites against the SPD.[37]

This task was not easy: the agrarian conservatives resisted even the small degree of political liberalization in Prussia that the middle-of-the-road National Liberals desired, as the crisis over suffrage in 1910 revealed. Indeed, the National Liberals became a decisive bellwether party since they were internally divided between left and right wings —as would be their successors during the Weimar Republic. Frustrated by the rigid Junker defense of the Prussian suffrage, the left of the National Liberals sought a cautious approach to the Social Democratic reformists. The Party's right wing, based on Rhenish heavy industry, persisted in viewing the Marxists as the ultimate enemy. Despite limited electoral collaboration with left-liberals and Social Democrats in 1912, rightist tendencies generally prevailed. The Social Democratic electoral success of 1912 (110 of 390 Reichstag seats), the rising nationalism of the post-Agadir period, and the important bills for enlarging the army worked to prevent a major breakdown between conservative and liberal elites as war approached.[38]

[37] Eckart Kehr, *Schlachtflottenbau und Parteipolitik 1894–1901* (Berlin, 1930), esp. pp. 189–207; Dirk Stegmann, *Die Erben Bismarcks. Parteien und Verbände in der Spätphase des wilhelminischen Deutschlands* (Cologne, 1970), pp. 97 ff., 128–130; Hartmut Kaelble, *Industrielle Interessenpolitik in der wilhelminischen Gesellschaft. Centralverband deutscher Industrieller (1895–1914)* (Berlin, 1967), pp. 51–61, 123–147.

[38] Hartwig Thieme, *Nationaler Liberalismus in der Krise. Die national–liberale Fraktion des preussischen Abgeordnetenhauses 1914–18* (Boppard am Rhein, 1963), esp. pp. 46–49; Carl Schorske, *German Social Democracy, 1905–1917* (Cambridge, Mass., 1955), pp. 224 ff. For the tensions of the Bülow Bloc: Theodor Eschenburg, *Das Kaiserreich am Scheideweg* (Berlin, 1929); and for continuing

35

Despite some efforts among left-liberals and progressive National Liberals, the German "bourgeois" parties thus remained preoccupied with the proletarian challenge. The SPD's rejection of the monarchical form of government made the ideological demarcation all the more glaring. The Socialists' creation of their own cultural and political enclave within the wider society by means of an all-embracing party organization reinforced political exclusiveness on both sides. Even more than elsewhere, the Social Democrats were depicted as a party set against the nation:

> While the socialist parties in other countries, especially in the Latin lands, joined their national political life, and, above all, followed the practical goals of day-to-day politics, German social democracy adopted the distant and clearly utopian goals of Marxist concepts as their program, proclaimed a new order of state, society, and nations, and thus too a stance beyond any other in existing German national political life.[39]

German bourgeois consciousness thus developed into little more than rampant anti-Marxism. Once Germany moved beyond a confederation of cities and states, what other substantive qualities could be attributed to the *Bürgertum?* German bourgeois liberals maintained pride in their role during unification, but with more ambivalence than their Italian counterparts. Piedmont, after all, had created a nation; the Paulskirche had not. The German middle class continued to reproach itself for its alleged ideological rigidity and cosmopolitanism. The fact, too, that in Germany parties increasingly corresponded to well-defined social and religious divisions accentuated this development. East Elbian landlords, urban patricians, middle classes, workers, and Catholics all had their parliamentary representation, hence political and sociological description overlapped more than elsewhere. "Bourgeois" became an attribute easily applied to political divisions as well as social ones, hence a characteristic eventually to be shared by

---

suffrage disputes, Reinhard Patemann, *Der Kampf um die preussische Wahlreform im ersten Weltkrieg* (Düsseldorf, 1964). Valuable insight into strains on the ruling coalition from Peter-Christian Witt, *Die Finanzpolitik des deutschen Reiches von 1903 bis 1913* (Lübeck and Hamburg, 1970), esp. pp. 58–80, 304–311, 356–376; and the cautions against seeing too monolithic a bloc of elites in Hans-Jürgen Puhle, *Von der Agrarkrise zum Präfaschismus* (Wiesbaden, 1972), pp. 50–59; also Wolfgang Mommsen, "Domestic Factors in German Foreign Policy before 1914," *Central European History,* VI, 1 (1973), pp. 3–43.

[39] Bernhard von Bülow, *Deutsche Politik* (Berlin, 1916), pp. 236–237, 239; cf. Karl Erich Born, *Staat und Sozialpolitik seit Bismarcks Stürz* (Wiesbaden, 1957), pp. 176–177. J. P. Nettl, "The German Social-Democratic Party, 1890–1914, as a Political Model," *Past and Present,* 30 (1955), pp. 65–95, and Guenther Roth, *The Social Democrats in Imperial Germany* (Totowa, N.J., 1963), pp. 117 ff. both discuss the SPD "subculture."

agrarian or ennobled foes of socialism as well as by middle-class opponents. The adjective "bourgeois" thus vaulted from reference to medieval citizenship rights to antisocialism. The older sense of "civic" was never really shed; but the intervening phase of reference to a generalized nation-state citizenship—such as the French Revolution had bestowed upon *citoyen*—never became prevalent. "Bürger" had been a title of pride in old Lübeck, but was little more than an antisocialist referent in the new Empire.[40]

Given this political terminology, social democracy defined class conflict and anxiety during the Wilhelmian era. "The task of the government," noted Hans Delbrück in 1895, even as he condemned government muzzling of the press and assembly, "is not at all to educate social democracy to decent behavior, but to suppress it, or if that is impossible at least to hinder its further growth."[41] In 1913, even the Centrist politician Matthias Erzberger, who was to cooperate with the SPD after the war, wrote that the Reich's greatest domestic challenge was "the shattering of the mighty power of social democracy; compared with this central question of political life all others take second place."[42] Likewise the German Conservative Party saw the SPD as the overriding evil of national life and supposedly the major spur to its own mission of diehard reaction during the last decade of the Empire. If elsewhere the problem of class conflict appeared in the growth of labor agitation, or international allegiances, in Germany it was epitomized by the role of the Social Democratic Party.[43]

Left-liberal intellectuals, or the National Socialists around Friedrich Naumann, might have wished to bridge the gap, but their own ideas of German nationhood precluded success. Friedrich Meinecke, for example, condemned the conservatives' "latent civil war against the Social Democrats conducted with police-state weapons" and believed that liberals should meet the prodigal brothers "on the common ground of the national state." But until August 1914, the socialists refused to accept the nation-state as a common ground, precisely because it was so central to bourgeois values.[44]

[40] On the connotation of "citizen," Georg Lukács, *Essays on Thomas Mann*, Stanley Mitchell, trans. (New York, 1964), pp. 42–43; Ralf Dahrendorf, *Society and Democracy in Germany* (Garden City, N.Y., 1967), pp. 67 ff.

[41] *Preussische Jahrbücher*, LXXXII (1895), p. 559.

[42] Kuno Graf von Westarp, *Konservative Politik im letzten Jahrzehnt des Kaiserreiches*, 2 vols. (Berlin, 1935), I, p. 338.

[43] *Ibid.*, II, p. 641.

[44] Friedrich Meinecke, "Sammlungspolitik und Liberalismus" [1910], *Politische Schriften und Reden* (Darmstadt, 1968), p. 41; "Die Nationalliberale Partei," *ibid.*, p. 59. On left-liberal efforts at dialogue with the SPD: Roth, *The Social Democrats*, pp. 136–158; Theodor Heuss, *Friedrich Naumann. Der Mann, das Werk, die Zeit* (Munich and Hamburg, 1968), pp. 151–158.

On the other hand, most German liberals could not accept even a simple democratic commitment. They felt that democracy must mean social democracy, mass leveling, and despotism. Even remote eras of antiquity taught this lesson to the historian of the social question in the ancient world, who concluded that the classical era proved democracy degenerated into socialism and mob rule.[45] Opposing this notion in the early years of the Weimar Republic, Meinecke, for one, sought to make democracy acceptable to liberals by stressing the Kantian concept of self-imposed legislation that was common to both liberalism and democracy. But even the historian felt that he was fighting an uphill battle. "One became frightened before the specter of democratic levelling and mass rule," he conceded. "Bourgeois advocates of democracy," he warned during the war, "are struggling in truth not against, but for the bourgeoisie."[46] Naturally, this is what working-class spokesmen recognized as well: even among left-liberals, democracy was urged in the name of the nation-state and bourgeoisie. Hence the salient ideas and images that defined class divisions for both sides persisted even as some liberals sought to transcend them.

Each country, then, worked out different parameters of hierarchy and the threats to hierarchy. In view of the varying emphases upon what was crucial to the bourgeois order, different issues were likely to trigger future crises. In Italy, the political vulnerability of the *classe dirigente* prompted constant, ritualistic reaffirmations of liberalism. This meant in turn that any erosion of the parliamentary majority that liberals enjoyed before 1919 really entailed a profound and total social challenge. Taking the measure of their overall cultural and social hegemony by the ability to manipulate Chamber majorities, the liberals would see their whole regime shaken by the success of mass parties after World War I. The French conception of bourgeois, on the other hand, suggested other dangers as being critical. "Bourgeois" evoked less a political cadre and more a privileged but deserving social stratum. Preservation of the congenial environment that nurtured

[45] Robert von Pöhlmann, *Geschichte der sozialen Frage und des Sozialismus in der antiken Welt*, 2 vols. (Munich, 1912), i, p. vii, 157; cf. 367–368.

[46] Meinecke, "Das deutsche Bürgertum im Krieg" [1918], *Politische Schriften und Reden*, p. 250. For the relationship of liberalism and democracy, see the debate between Meinecke, "Zur Geschichte des älteren deutschen Parteiwesens," and Erich Brandenburg, "Eine Erwiderung," in *Historische Zeitschrift*, 118, 1 (1917), pp. 46–62, and 119, 1 (1918), pp. 63–84. Evaluations of Meinecke's stance in Richard Sterling, *Ethics in a World of Power: The Political Ideas of Friedrich Meinecke* (Princeton, N.J., 1958); Sergio Pistone, *Federico Meinecke e la crisi dello stato nazionale tedesco* (Turin, 1969), pp. 313 ff.; Robert A. Pois, *Friedrich Meinecke and German Politics in the Twentieth Century* (Berkeley, 1972), pp. 23–25.

the elite became the utmost priority. The major threat to that environment and the bourgeois milieu was likely to be indirect, such as the peril of inflation in a culture that emphasized family saving. Finally, in Germany, the public role of the Social Democratic Party threatened to be far more explosive than any of its actual policies might warrant. Just the presence of the SPD in a cabinet could provoke bitter reaction, regardless of the nature of SPD policy.

Out of each national perception of class structure, therefore, there arose characteristic dangers: nightmares emerging from common class anxieties but appearing in diverse images. Thus, too, each society created its own grammar and logic of conflict—a logic that shaped future issues and disputes. But it was a logic created by history, by the distribution and arrangements of power over time. In turn, these had been set by the path to nationhood, by the middle-class contribution to economic development and the thoroughness of industrialization, by the claims of a manorial countryside, and by the strains of international competition and war.

ELITES—RESILIENT AND VULNERABLE

The world war, lamented a conservative commentator in November 1918, "has so profoundly overturned the conditions of life for the French bourgeoisie that it is undergoing a crisis whose gravity just cannot be exaggerated."[47] Throughout the 1920's, diagnoses of middle- and upper-class anguish provided a ready theme for sociologists and cultural critics. Certainly they testified to a great sense of transition, doubt, and political insecurity. Distress and dislocation were natural for bourgeois elements whose values rested so much upon a commitment to prewar continuity, to "the need for security" itself.[48] But what relationship the gloomy assessments bore to the real conditions of life for the well-off or middle strata is harder to ascertain. The fate of those with a stake in the social order was far from uniform. It depended upon circumstances that were often unfamiliar and little understood: whether one held wealth in traditionally prestigious bonds or new industrial equity, in rural land or urban buildings with frozen rents; whether power and status were keyed to old posts of public eminence or to the new corporations, to industrial associations or political party bureaucracies. Not only the political thrust of the left, but the seismic pressures exerted by the rise of new occupational groups, concentration of industry, and the stately or precipitous fall

[47] André Lichtenberger, "Le bourgeois," *RDM*, November 15, 1921, p. 338.
[48] Joseph Aynard, *La bourgeoisie française. Essai de psychologie* (Paris, 1934), p. 13.

in the value of currencies brought new hazards and distributed new rewards.

Who was on top; who was vulnerable? Germany has benefited from the most exhaustive analysis. Despite great stratification and hierarchy, the Reich still possessed neither a unified *Bürgertum*, nor a cohesive political class as of 1918. The so-called *Mittelstand*—roughly, a lower middle class of artisans, clerks, and shopkeepers—underwent its own peculiar agony in the inflation and later depression.[49] Economically fragmented, it was to mobilize successfully only behind the Nazis a decade and more after the war. At a higher level, business leaders had married into the aristocracies of the German states, and their kin comprised an important component of the civil service, which had developed into a "noble-bourgeois aristocracy of office."[50] As a self-assertive group, entrepreneurs enhanced their influence and public role under the benevolent eye of Chancellor Bülow (1900–1909), who always felt that gathering together Germany's men of quality was the only way to govern the unwieldy state. But the upper class was hardly more than what Ralf Dahrendorf has called a "cartel of anxiety" cemented together in opposition to the society below.[51] Business leaders, managers as well as owners, were to become crucial components of the Weimar leadership. Imbued with as intense a corporate sense as the civil service or university teachers, they maneuvered single-mindedly on behalf of their interests, which they graciously attributed to the public at large. Just as other professional cadres tended to become self-recruiting from generation to generation, by 1930 only 10 percent of business leaders had come from working-class or petit-bourgeois backgrounds and 29 percent from the middle levels of society; 23 percent were scions of the old aristocracy or officialdom;

[49] For aspects of this social group, cf.: Theodor Geiger, *Die Soziale Schichtung des deutschen Volkes* (Stuttgart, 1932), pp. 84–89, 97–138; Emil Lederer and Jakob Marschak, "Der neue Mittelstand," *Grundriss der Sozialökonomik*, IX/I (Tübingen, 1926), pp. 120–141; Josef Schumpeter, "Das soziale Antlitz des deutschen Reiches" [1929], *Gesammelte Aufsätze zur Soziologie* (Tübingen, 1953), pp. 214–226; Heinrich A. Winkler, *Mittelstand, Demokratie und National-sozialismus. Die politische Entwicklung von Handwerk und Kleinhandel in der Weimarer Republik* (Cologne, 1972).

[50] The description is Otto Hintze's, *Der Beamtenstand* (Leipzig, 1911), p. 45; cited in John R. Gillis, "Aristocracy and Bureaucracy in Nineteenth-Century Prussia," *Past and Present*, 41 (December 1968), p. 108. Cf. J.C.G. Röhl, "Higher Civil Servants in Germany, 1890–1900," *Journal of Contemporary History*, II, 3 (1967), republished as *Education and Social Structure in the Twentieth Century* (New York, 1967), pp. 101–122.

[51] Ralf Dahrendorf, *Society and Democracy in Germany* (Garden City, N.Y., 1967), pp. 269–275. On elites: Wolfgang Zapf, *Wandlungen der deutschen Elite. Ein Zirkulationsmodell deutscher Führungsgruppen 1919–1961* (Munich, 1965); Gillis, "Aristocracy and Bureaucracy"; Nikolas von Preradovich, *Die Führungs-schichten in Österreich und Preussen (1804–1918)* (Wiesbaden, 1955).

and 38 percent were the offspring of fathers already engaged in big business.[52]

German society, therefore, contained encapsulated competitive spheres of attainment, with the members of each often edgy and defensive under their strident claims to eminence. Contrast this situation with England, where the social structure was virtually as elitist or pyramidal, but the elites had learned to function together as a result of various factors, such as the undercutting of agricultural interests, the commercial spirit of the landed classes, and more recently the work of the public schools. A self-confident "establishment" dealt with challenges from the left within a liberal institutional framework, although it would be misleading to deny the potential fraying of this liberalism that was produced by the crises of 1910 to 1924.[53]

In France, too, there were significant differences. If the war and the advent of Weimar brought to Germany a bitter competition among diverse leadership groups for state power, in France a virtual gentlemen's agreement prevailed. Once the passion of the Dreyfus struggle quieted, the old social elites tacitly acquiesced in the rise to power of a political cartel that represented the middle and lower-middle classes. Consequently, a political cadre developed—less a "class," strictly speaking, than a network of men who derived their living from politics, who attended the ritual banquets at elections, who sat on the departmental *conseils-généraux* or in their own city halls, who ascended to the Chamber, then the Senate, wielding *bonhomie* and assurances of economic development for their "homefolks," making Paris a fount of patronage while subscribing to the generous platitudes of republicanism. These men, even if they represented the grandsons of the druggist Homais or the local tavern keeper, might share domination of the Assembly so long as they did not seriously attempt to curtail economic privilege. The old elites conceded political power to purchase social immunity. In Germany, however, such a compromise was impossible. The German socialists were unwilling to accept such a trade in 1918, while in France they were not strong enough to challenge it until 1936. Nor were the traditional German elites, who had renounced power only in the embarrassment of military bankruptcy,

[52] Wilhelm Treue, "Der deutsche Unternehmer in der Weltwirtschaftskrise 1928 bis 1933," in *Die Staats- und Wirtsschaftskrise des deutschen Reiches 1929/33*, Werner Conze and Hans Raupach, eds. (Stuttgart, 1967), p. 91.

[53] For an approach to the British elite, see: W. L. Guttsman, *The British Political Elite* (London, 1963); and Guttsman, ed., *The English Ruling Class* (London, 1969), pp. 1–20; on the strains before World War I: George Dangerfield, *The Strange Death of Liberal England 1910–1914* (New York, 1961); Standish Meacham, " 'The Sense of an Impending Clash': English Working-Class Unrest before the First World War," *American Historical Review*, LXXVII, 5 (1972), pp. 1343–1364.

likely to accept that surrender of public control by which the French upper classes sought to preserve their own private domains.[54]

The Italian situation is harder to summarize because of the extreme differentiation of development throughout the peninsula. Nowhere was there more self-consciousness on the part of a supposedly coherent *ceta dirigente*. But the components of the "ruling class" varied from place to place: in Milan, the established powers of finance and textiles owned the *Corriere della Sera* and supported the club-like liberal party associations; in Genoa, newer parvenu industrialists, the Perrone brothers of the giant Ansaldo works, sought to buy their way to influence; the Agnelli dynasty of Fiat in Turin maintained a rewarding connection with the prevailing Giolittian adherents, who made Piedmontese liberalism more open and democratic than Milan's variety. In Bologna, the old aristocracy played an important role, and the urban elite still kept up important agricultural domains in the Emilian countryside. In Naples, business interests looked to Francesco Nitti—not because of his self-designated "radicalism" but for his technocratic espousal of local development. In the rural South, elitist politics often rested upon traditional sources of authority: the law courts, estates, and local government. The upper crust of the former Neapolitan realms still enjoyed a patriarchal eminence that they hired out to Northern politicians in return for continuing patronage. The tissue of loyalties, and thus of power, was determined, therefore, less by ideological alignment or even clear economic division, than by clientele politics and local interests.[55]

In general, the elites of the North rested their claims upon a modern economy, those of the South upon the traditionalist claims of the land, the law, and not least important, the patronage of a provincial cultural life. For both groups, the self-consciousness of belonging to a unified

[54] Cf. Stanley Hoffmann, "Paradoxes of the French Political Community," Hoffmann et al., *In Search of France* (New York, 1965), pp. 15 ff. For descriptions of the mores of the Third Republic: Jacques Fourcade, *La république de la province* (Paris, 1936); Daniel Halévy, *La république des comités: Essai d'histoire contemporaine (1895–1934)* (Paris, 1934); Robert de Jouvenel, *La république des camarades* (Paris, 1914).

[55] For local history and social description see Valerio Castronovo, *Economia e società in Piemonte dall'unità al 1914* (Milan, 1965), esp. pp. 325–352; G. Prato, *Il Piemonte e gli effetti della guerra sulla sua vita economica e sociale* (Bari and New Haven, 1925); Raffaele Colapietra, *Napoli tra dopoguerra e fascismo* (Milan, 1962); Dominique Schnapper, "Storia e sociologia: Uno studio su Bologna," *Studi Storici*, vii, 3 (1967), pp. 550–578. On the upsurge of the iron and steel interests, Luigi Einaudi, *La condotta economica e gli effetti sociali della guerra italiana* (Bari and New Haven, 1933), pp. 264–269; Rosario Romeo, *Breve storia della grande industria in Italia* (Bologna, 1963), p. 120; Alberto Caracciolo, "La crescita e la trasformazione della grande industria durante la prima guerra mondiale," in Giorgio Fuà, ed., *Lo sviluppo economico in Italia*, 3 vols. (Milan, 1969), iii, pp. 212–239.

elite was strengthened by the concentration on law and administrative science in the universities—a discipline that filtered businessmen as well as bureaucrats and professors through a cultural accreditation closed to the lower strata of society.[56] The sense of serving a true *classe dirigente* made the Italian elite more cohesive than the broader and less clear-cut French bourgeoisie. But with the exception of old local aristocracies, the maintenance of preeminence in any sphere, whether social or cultural, was felt to depend upon control of the political apparatus in Italy for a generation longer than it did in France. This meant that the Italian upper class shared the anxieties of the German, although its internal clashes of interest were regulated more easily than in Germany by different tariff rates and tax bases. If the German ruling groups remained a socially fractured "cartel of anxiety,"[57] the Italians might well be described as a regionally differentiated fraternity—equally besieged but more cohesive.

Challenging the upper classes after the war was not only the immediate thrust of the left, but what they well might have termed the silent revolution, the transformation of economic and social status threatened by the growth of state intervention or inflation. Total war meant social transformation, the centralization of power, equalization of income, the concession of new rights to the working classes. Measurement of the changes is rough at best, but some indices are available. From the perspective of the upper classes they reveal a somber, but far from catastrophic picture. How could one wage a four-year war without the destruction of wealth and savings, whether from the spectacular losses on Russian bonds in French hands, or the indirect toll of capital levies imposed by inflation? In France, for instance, the inheritances that were passed on in 1925 had only twice the nominal value of those in 1913, despite the franc's three- to fivefold loss of value between those years. Alfred Sauvy estimates that 1913 fortunes were cut by more than one-half their value by 1929. It is not surprising that with such devaluations, new tax demands, and the erosion of income, sad stories about the evils of inflation multiplied.[58]

[56] Robert Michels, *Umschichtungen in den herrschenden Klassen nach dem Kriege* (Stuttgart and Berlin, 1934), pp. 72–74.

[57] For discussions of the Italian elites and middle classes: A. Fossati, *Le classi medie in Italia* (Turin, 1938); Giuliano Pischel, *Il problema dei ceti medi* (Milan, 1946), which distinguishes *ceti medi* from *borghesia*, giving the former a rough equivalence to the German *Mittelstand*; also Nello Quilici, *La borghesia italiana* (Milan, 1942); Giacomo Perticone, *La formazione della classe politica nell'Italia contemporanea* (Florence, 1954); Renato Treves, "Le classi sociali in Italia," *Nord e Sud*, XII, Nuova seria 65 (=126) (May 1965), pp. 67–88.

[58] For an impressionistic survey of the changes wrought by inflation throughout Europe: Richard Lewinsohn, *Die Umschichtung des europäischen Vermögens*

It was logical that accumulated wealth should be vulnerable, but there were income effects as well. Not only did the public sector requisition previously amassed claims on national resources, it helped shift the distribution of current claims. The shares of national income to the bourgeois elements of society, in short, dropped; the resulting distribution may not have appeared radically different, but the changes were substantial in proportion to the customary stability of income streams. Throughout Europe the strata of the population deriving income from capital assets—land or building rents, fixed-interest securities, or stocks—watched their income decline as a portion of their respective national products. Given the state of the estimates, it is hard to say which nation's bourgeoisie fared most harshly, but a significant change is evident.[59] Great Britain experienced the sharpest decline in the share of national income earned by capital assets, as a result of the war, but then Britain had previously bestowed a far higher proportion of its income on capital assets than had been the case elsewhere. Even after a major change in the distribution of income, Britain still remained a country of vast inequalities. Everywhere, however, not only did the factor share of capital assets fall, but the per-capita share of entrepreneurial income dropped in proportion to the per-worker share of wages and salaries. So, too, did the income going to the upper strata of society.[60] Besides these financial attainders,

---

(Berlin, 1925). Statistique générale de la France, *Annuaire statistique*, XLVI (1930), p. 128, provides inheritance tables. Cf. savings accounts, 1914–1928, *ibid.*, pp. 156–157. For Sauvy's estimate: *Histoire économique de la France entre les deux guerres*, I, *De l'armistice à la dévaluation de la livre, 1918–1931* (Paris, 1965), p. 294. See also the pathos-filled works of André Bouton, *La fin des rentiers* (Paris, 1932), p. 177; and Germain Martin, *Les finances publiques de la France et la fortune privée (1914–1925)* (Paris, 1925). Cf. discussion below, Chapter Seven, section three, pp. 466–470.

[59] Simon Kuznets, "Quantitative Aspects of the Economic Growth of Nations, IV: Distribution of National Income by Factor Shares," printed as *Economic Development and Cultural Change*, VII, 3, part II (1959), pp. 45, 86 ff. Cf. Kuznets, *Modern Economic Growth: Rate, Structure, and Spread* (New Haven and London, 1966), pp. 168–170, table 4.2. According to Kuznets, the French share of income to assets remained much steadier than that of the other European countries after World War I; but for the difficulty with the obsolete French statistics that Kuznets uses, see Tihomir J. Markovitch, "L'industrie française de 1789 à 1964: Sources et méthodes," in Institut de Science Économique Appliqué, *Cahiers, série D, Le revenu national*, Nr. 7: *La croissance du revenu national depuis 1870*, Série AF 4, 163 (July 1965). Cf. also Sauvy's estimates in *Histoire économique*, I, pp. 275–276.

[60] For per-worker shares in wages and salaries *vis-à-vis* entrepreneurial income: Kuznets, "Quantitative Aspects, IV," pp. 44–51, 89; for distribution of income to the top 5 or 20 percent of the population in England, Germany, and the United States: "Quantitative Aspects . . ." VIII: "Distribution of Income by Size," *Economic Development and Cultural Change*, XI, 2, part II (1963), pp. 58–61; or *Modern Economic Growth*, pp. 208–209. For the limits on redistribution of wealth

the war years and the economic vicissitude of the 1920's—deflationary squeezes as well as inflationary ones—tended to consolidate business under larger organizations. Even if a man's income survived, his sense of independent status must often have succumbed in such takeovers.

Despite these changes, it would be misleading to join those who sounded the knell for the bourgeoisie. Those groups who presumably drew most of their income from capital assets were still a narrow elite with a massive share of national income. Railroad bonds might fall in France, and government obligations come to mean little more than disguised capital levies; nevertheless, many investors were switching to more active portfolios. Railroad stock and bonds represented 42 percent of all French tradings in 1900, but only 3.2 percent in 1932 as other industrial ventures boomed.[61] If in both France and Germany a bank account that had not been touched since 1913 was worth about 15 to 20 percent of its original value by 1929,[62] most individuals had probably not merely hoarded paper. The sacrificial burden of holding on to given fixed-interest securities was often spread over several different investors between 1914 and the mid-1920's—each confident in turn that the franc or the mark had sunk as far as it could. Their optimism cost them dearly, but it spread the burden of devastation.

Moreover, other buttresses of the social order were not equally hit. As Robert Michels observed about the social effects of the German inflation, status was a function of the stable occupational positions a man held; it did not vary with passing economic circumstances. Daughters contemplated careers, but somehow bourgeois dignity might survive even a position as saleslady or secretary.[63] *Dérogation* from the bourgeoisie took at least a generation. The number of domestic servants—the reserve army of the concealed unemployed—shrank drastically in the war, but not in the 1918–1931 era.[64] Most important,

in interwar England, see the argument of G. W. Daniels and H. Campion, *The Distribution of National Capital* (Manchester, 1936).

[61] Jules Denuc, "Dividendes, valeur boursière et taux de capitalisation des valeurs mobilières françaises de 1857 à 1932," *Bulletin de la Statistique Générale de la France*, xxiii, 4 (1934), pp. 691–767; cf. Sauvy, *Histoire économique*, i, pp. 391–408.

[62] It must be remembered that although German paper money was reduced to negligible value during the height of inflation, 1922–1923, bank accounts and privately issued obligations (mortgages, industrial bonds held since 1920) were restored by law up to 25 percent of preinflationary values. For the political ramifications of the disputes involving revaluation, see below, Chapter Eight, section one.

[63] Michels, *Umschichtungen in den herrschenden Klassen*, pp. 104–105; also Ferdinand Dauriac, "Le travail des femmes en France devant la Statistique," *Revue d'économie politique*, xlvii (1933), p. 99.

[64] Sauvy, *Histoire économique*, i, p. 219. In England servants increased in numbers during the 1920's, as industrial employment lagged. See Guy Routh,

perhaps, the educational system did not shed its class character. Completion of a *baccalauréat* or *Abitur*, not to say university training, remained a bourgeois attainment. Lycée, Gymnasium, or university classroom doors might begin to open to the lower middle classes, but hardly ever to working-class children.[65] Mobility, if one measured it as the advance of laborers' sons into clerical or white-collar work, had traditionally been substantial, according to some estimates.[66] But mobility in terms of lower-class sons who came to occupy important ministries, executive positions, or the judicial bench—least of all the embassies!—remained infinitesimal. The important political transformations of the interwar period brought the party delegates of working-class backgrounds into parliament and ministries, but did not really change the composition of private or public bureaucracies.

Finally, it must be recalled that mobility is compatible with hierarchies: a theoretically perfectly mobile society, with every career open to talents, is still a society that ranks functions in terms of prestige and material rewards. Specifically, the principles of hierarchization after the war remained those of before the war. World War I did not drastically rupture the class categories of bourgeois Europe. Despite the hazard of old fortunes, elite categories remained the same. Their individual members could well feel defensive, might in fact succumb to the new perils, or might prosper; but the cadres of ranking, the principles demanded, the values reinforced, remained steady. That continuity bracketed all the intervening turbulence.

One elite in particular deserves special scrutiny: the Italian. Nowhere else did the traditional "establishment" conceive of itself both as so rightfully influential and as so threatened. Its sense of crisis led

---

Occupation and Pay in Great Britain, 1906–1960 (Cambridge, 1965), p. 33. See the frequent laments about the difficulty of the servant problem even before the war: Georges d'Avenel, "Le train de maison depuis sept siècles—les domestiques," *RDM*, April 1, 1912, pp. 632–655; also Lichtenberger, "Le bourgeois," p. 342: "His daily life is cruelly transformed by the scarceness or virtual disappearance of domestic servants." For a general survey of related issues: Marguerite Perrot, *La mode de vie des familles bourgeoises 1873–1953* (Paris, 1961).

[65] Michels, *Umschichtungen in den herrschenden Klassen*, pp. 62–66, 72; for numbers and discussions of French higher education: Jean Zay and Henri Belliot, *La réforme de l'enseignement* (Paris, 1938); P. Bourdieu and Jean-Claude Passeron, *Les héritiers* (Paris, 1964). For Germany cf. Fritz K. Ringer, "Higher Education in Germany in the Nineteenth Century," *Education and Social Structure in the Twentieth Century*, pp. 123–138; and *The Decline of the German Mandarins* (Cambridge, Mass., 1968).

[66] Seymour M. Lipset and Reinhard Bendix, *Social Mobility in Industrial Society* (Berkeley, Calif., 1967), for the emphasis on intergenerational mobility in Europe, but note the reservations on elite positions, pp. 278–279; and the implicit contrast with Zapf's approach in *Wandlungen der deutschen Elite*.

to the destruction of the liberal state precisely because its members could not regain security through mastery of parliament as in France, or manipulation of the economic arena as in Germany. In Italy, furthermore, the difficulties of the agrarian and industrial leadership, or of local *notables*, most quickly evolved into the crisis of a general political system, for the same restricted circle felt vulnerable in many areas. The stronghold of the liberal bourgeois state might be stormed by mass parties and new voters, undermined by the erosion of deference politics, starved out by new labor demands.

Agitation in the countryside provoked anxiety more intense than elsewhere. France faced no political problems from agrarian labor; her widespread and relatively well-off peasant proprietors ensured stability, not reaction. German agrarians, it is true, suffered political eclipse between 1918 and 1923, leaving bourgeois defense to business and industry. But in Italy the agrarian danger was more central: there was greater interdependence between urban and rural elites and a better organized radical opposition. Eastern Germany had numerous agricultural laborers, but except for a brief vote for social democracy in January 1919, and agricultural strikes in the summer of that year, they remained under the Junker thumb. Not so in Italy: the organization of agricultural labor there exceeded that of any other country. Before the war the socialist-affiliated "red leagues" of the National Federation of Agrarian Workers—Federterra, for short—had unionized about a quarter of a million farm laborers, landless salaried workers known as *braccianti*. The *braccianti* sustained the agricultural economy in the Po Valley, especially in Emilia and Romagna where, hired job by job in the local village squares, they sowed and harvested the estates won by land reclamation.[67]

The war brought more massive organization and greater bitterness. An alienated and mistrustful peasantry resented even subscribers to Red Cross drives and war bonds as men who had supposedly brought them into war.[68] The interventionists in the countryside comprised the so-called rural bourgeoisie who owned or leased the land, and the Socialists were quick to argue that the rich had wanted the war. Peasant conscripts, moreover, served most conspicuously in the in-

[67] Renato Zangheri, *Lotte agrarie in Italia: la Federazione dei Lavoratori della Terra 1901–1926* (Milan, 1960), pp. xxxviii ff.; Luigi Preti, *Le lotte agrarie nella Valle Padana* (Turin, 1955), pp. 46 ff., 211 ff.; Luigi Arbizzani, "Lotte agrarie in provincia di Bologna nel primo dopoguerra," in Renato Zangheri, ed., *Le campagne emiliane nell' epoca moderna* (Milan, 1957), pp. 283–299; Franco Cavazza, *Le agitazione agrarie in provincia di Bologna dal 1910 al 1920* (Bologna, 1940), pp. 40–67, 133–160.
[68] Luigi Peano, *Ricordi della guerra dei trent'anni, 1915–1945* (Florence and Bari, 1948), pp. 46–47; also Prato, *Il Piemonte e gli effetti della guerra*, p. 224, for similar observations on Giolitti's province of Cuneo.

fantry, where casualties were heavy: some indication of the suffering that the harsh and often mismanaged mobilization of Italy's resources imposed upon an unlettered and subjugated class was revealed by the massive rate of desertions and courts-martial.[69] On the other hand, those peasants who remained at home and retained some control over their own crops—whether by the common terms of payment in kind or by a system of share-cropping (*mezzadria*)—could benefit from the inflation. For proprietors, real income might well drop as rents were eroded by inflation. The proprietor saw himself relatively worse off than his more prosperous tenants; the peasant felt that his landlord had dispatched his son to the trenches for the honor of the rich. Mutual antagonism between *braccianti* and proprietor also deepened. Although the gains in peasant wealth did not filter down to the *braccianti*, who retained no crops to market, the laborers, at least, won the prolongation of all agrarian contracts for a year after the end of hostilities, thus assuring themselves of secure work and wage increases determined by arbitration. This fixing of contracts, however, antagonized the proprietors, who faced a squeeze between the escalating prices they paid in the city and the returns for their own crops as regulated by the government for the duration.[70]

By the fall of 1919, the Federterra had more than doubled its wartime complement to reach 457,000 militant members and redoubled it again to almost 900,000 a year later. Although less disciplined and combative, the Catholic "white leagues" reported almost 1.2 million adherents by 1920. Their constituency lay among the share-croppers, small proprietors, and tenants, whom the socialist Federterra distrusted and felt were doomed to extinction as a rural proletariat. The white leagues spurned collectivism and held instead a Christian-social ideal of diffused small holdings; however, this vision had its own radical implications by the end of the war. Repeated promises of "land to the peasants"—an apocalyptic dream of redistribution spread by the left as well as by the nationalist propagandists who sought to boost morale during the war—spurred agrarian unrest. The promise of land reform especially enticed the Southern peasants who eked out livings as tiny landholders and as peasants on the large, capital-poor *latifondi*. In hilly Piedmont there was a "yeoman" peasantry, but (except for Apulia) the South had no buffer between dwarf holdings and backward estates. There were perhaps 5 million proprietors in Italy, but nine-tenths of them owned less than half a hectare (1.23 acres) each.

[69] Cf. Alberto Monticone and Enzo Forcella, eds., *Plotone di esecuzione* (Bari, 1968). For the percentages of peasant contingents in Bologna: Arbizzani, "Lotte agrarie," p. 293.

[70] Arrigo Serpieri, *La guerra e le classi rurali italiane* (Bari and New Haven, 1930), pp. 34–35, 41–43, 146–155.

Unfortunately, "land to the peasants" was at best a pious hope and at worst a hoax. The democratic groups in the chamber might agree in calling for the creation of national reserves to be taken from uncultivated *latifondi* and state lands to assign to peasants. But the Opera Nazionale per i Combattenti, founded in 1917 to distribute state lands to veterans' cooperatives, had too little new land and worked too bureaucratically to ease the pressure of a resentful and radicalized peasantry.[71]

Industrial workers, too, shared revolutionary aspirations. During 1919 the membership of the CGL rose from about 350,000 to 800,000 adherents in industry, while the Socialist Party to which the CGL was affiliated itself lurched to the left. In the autumn of 1918, "maximalist" leaders imposed a platform on the PSI that called for an early dictatorship of the proletariat and immediate mass strike action.[72] Such radical rhetoric was made potentially explosive because of the severe Italian inflation, which doubled 1914's retail prices in Rome and more than tripled them in Milan. Wages kept up only in certain war-affiliated industries. In general their real level fell to less than two-thirds that of 1913.[73]

Agitation against rising prices also encouraged nonsocialist radicalism. The interventionists of the left—syndicalists, Mussolini's adherents, and also the Republicans—offered no collectivist model, but demanded a transformation of bourgeois values. As a self-proclaimed

[71] On the Leagues: Zangheri, *Lotte agrarie in Italia*, pp. lxxxiii–xcii; Preti, *Le lotte agrarie*, pp. 349–350, 354–358, 372–375; Serpieri, *La guerra e le classi rurali*, pp. 83–86; Amos Zanibelli, *Le leghe "bianche" nel Cremonese (dal 1900 al "Lodo Bianchi")* (Rome, 1961), pp. 38–59; Luigi Einaudi, *La condotta economica e gli effetti sociali della guerra italiana* (Bari and New Haven, 1933), pp. 290–291. For the emergence of the land issue during the war see Antonio Papa, "Guerra e Terra 1915–1918," *Studi Storici*, x, 1 (1969), pp. 3–45. On land distribution, Einaudi, p. 5; Friedrich Vöchting, *Die italienische Sudfrage* (Berlin, 1951), pp. 281–285, 290–292, 307–309, 341 ff.

[72] Figures in Einaudi, *La condotta economica*, p. 312 (I have subtracted the Federterra component of the CGL); maximalism and 1918 congress in: Angelo Tasca, *Nascita e avvento del fascismo*, 2 vols. (Bari, 1965), I, pp. 20–21; Gaetano Arfé, *Storia del socialismo italiano (1892–1926)* (Turin, 1965), pp. 261–269; Roberto Vivarelli, *Il dopoguerra in Italia e l'avvento del fascismo (1918–1922)*, I, *Dalla fine della guerra all'impresa di Fiume* (Naples, 1967), pp. 68 ff.

[73] For prices and wages, Prato, *Piemonte e gli effetti della guerra*, pp. 184–185; C. Gino, "Sul livello dei salari reali nel dopoguerra in Italia in confronto al loro livello prebellico," *Rivista di Politica Economica*, XIII (1923), pp. 357–384; Antonio Fossati, *Lavoro e produzione in Italia. Dalla metà del secolo XVIII alla seconda guerra mondiale* (Turin, 1951), pp. 634–635; Cesare Vanutelli, "Lavoro e salari in Italia," in *L'economia italiana dal 1861 al 1961* (Milan, 1961), p. 570; Paolo Spriano, *Torino operaia nella grande guerra (1914–1918)* (Turin, 1960), pp. 187 ff. The end of Anglo-American wartime pegging of the lira hurt badly; by the end of 1919 it had depreciated to two-fifths of par. See Einaudi, *La condotta economica*, pp. 353–355, also his "L'abolizione dei controlli sui cambi," *CdS*, April 9, 1919.

revolutionary, Agostino Lanzillo, a future fascist syndicalist leader, announced that the war had proved the bankruptcy of socialism but also the inadequacy of Italian bourgeois reformism. By shattering capitalist and pacifist values it cleared the ground for a new revolutionary syndicalism. In common with the veterans' groups, Mussolini invoked a "productive" collaboration of industry and labor that would likewise reject bureaucratic social democracy and carry the activist spirit brought home from the trenches into economic activity. These and similar attitudes were briefly channeled into the vague concept of a new Constituent Assembly that would renovate and recast Italian institutions. The constituent idea aroused radicals, republicans, and syndicalists, but the Socialist Party opposed it as a diversion from the true Marxist path to revolution. It was too impregnated with the interventionist celebration of the war to reunite the left. As the young Pietro Nenni wrote, it created "feverish months . . . in which opposed sentiments flowed together in an almost mystical exaltation of the rights of the veterans."[74]

Interventionist radicalism could trouble conservatives; on the other hand, it was a current that tough-minded industrial or political leaders might try to harness against Giolittians or socialists. Many university youths had been interventionist spokesmen, then veterans; some had become *arditi*, the shock troops chosen for difficult assaults, and by 1918 were addicted to danger and discipline. They were courted by Mussolini as an avant-garde whose political radicalism he hoped to exploit for his own leadership. According to the Prefect of Milan, the local aristocracy, the Banca Commerciale, and Senator Crespi of the textile dynasty and shareholder of the *Corriere* were also helping to subsidize the *arditi*'s newspaper and expenses.[75] Veterans' groups elsewhere also attracted the right. In Florence the *Giornale dei Combattenti* attacked the old corrupt class of profiteers and politicians while advocating an extreme nationalism that sought "to educate the colonial consciousness of Italy." In Tuscany, as elsewhere, the veterans' attack on "plutocracy" and war profiteers easily became a diversionary theme that the right itself could safely emphasize, especially when it was coupled with the demand for an end to wartime economic controls and an appeal for "a directing audacious minority, strong and capable

---

[74] Pietro Nenni, *Il diciannovismo* (*1919–1922*) (Milan, 1962), p. 19; for revolutionary syndicalism: Agostino Lanzillo, *La disfatta del socialismo* (Florence, 1918), esp. pp. 109 ff., 165, 271 ff. For "productivism" see Renzo De Felice, *Mussolini il rivoluzionario 1883–1920* (Turin, 1965), pp. 465 ff.; and more critical Vivarelli, *Il dopoguerra in Italia*, pp. 234–238, 257–258.

[75] ACS, Rome: Min. Int., Dir. gen. P.S., Div. Aff. gen. e ris. (1903–1949), B. 585, f. "Stampa cessata," sf. "Milano." Valuable for the atmosphere of the veterans' return to civilian life: Emilio Lussu, *Marcia su Roma e dintorni* (Rome, 1945), pp. 15 ff.

of using force in the supreme interest of the country."[76] As of 1918–1919 this rhetoric was immensely plastic. In many areas the *combattenti* merged into the radical and republican left, and Gaetano Salvemini was to run as one of their candidates in November 1919. Elsewhere their fierce antisocialism, hostility to the so-called *rinunciatari*, who shunned extensive annexations, and resolute praise of *laissez-faire* suggested that traditional elites might do well to coopt their vigor, if they had cynical sense enough to discount the formulas of revolution.

For most bourgeois, however, the radical enthusiasm was to be deplored or endured with distaste. By December 1918, Maffeo Pantaleoni, once a free-trade liberal, now a rightist, fretted,

> There is no doubt that we are in full chaos. Projects for renewal of the social world overwhelm us. Every Italian is being transformed into a *sandwich man*. He has a placard in front and another in back. Each placard tells how Italy must be transformed and says it differently from every other one.

For Pantaleoni, all the proposals were variants of bolshevism—whether the eight-hour day, land to the peasants, or annulment of the interest on the public debt. "Today every citizen is presenting a bill to the state for one of so many innumerable effects produced by the war"; socialists and Giolittians were sabotaging the Chamber; "bolshevik and corrupt deputies" were running the country.[77]

But panic was not the only response, as some of the liberal right called for cautious reform. The Liberal Association of Milan suggested further social insurance, aid to the South with state intervention to deal with the problem of uncultivated land, and recognition that war burdens had to be assumed by the wealthy classes. Faced with the radicalism of the veterans, the Congress of Liberal Associations agreed in April that the pace of reform had to be accelerated. Before socialist and labor pressure, the eight-hour day was conceded with hardly a murmur during the spring of 1919.[78]

It was not merely fear, however, that prompted reform, but also

---

[76] Carla Ronchi Bettarini, "Note sui rapporti tra fascismo 'cittadino' e fascismo 'agrario' in Toscana," in *La Toscana in Italia Unita* (Florence, 1962), pp. 346–348.

[77] Maffeo Pantaleoni, "Caos e programmi del dopo–guerra," in *La fine provisoria di un' epopea* (Bari, 1919), pp. 85–86.

[78] Report from Prefect of Milan to the Ministry of the Interior, ACS, Rome: Min. Int., Dir. gen. P.S., Div. Aff. gen. e ris. (1914–1926), B. 45, f. "Milano," for the Liberal Association; also Tasca, *Nascita e avvento del fascismo*, i, p. 22; CdS, April 1, 1919. On the eight-hour concession: Einaudi, *La condotta economica*, p. 311; Riccardo Bacchi, *L'Italia economica nel 1919* (Città del Castello, 1920), pp. 399–402.

the vague hope that somehow the old liberal elites could justify their leadership in a period of renovation and renewal. "The war," said Orlando, on November 20, 1918, "is at the same time the greatest political and social revolution history records, exceeding even the French Revolution." Even Salandra conceded, "Today it is authoritatively said that the war is a revolution. . . . No one believes that with this tempest over, a peaceful return to the past is possible."[79] Reform represented more than a mere attempt to forestall revolution; it could prove psychologically necessary to the self-conceived function of the political elite. In the postwar era, liberals understood that it was not solely revolution that might undermine their role, but also political obsolescence. Throughout the liberal polemic and embedded in the advocacy of cautious reform there lay a certain stranded moralism, a claim to allegedly distinterested leadership buffeted by the crasser demands of the masses. Liberal leaders offered reform precisely to prove their disinterestedness, to demonstrate that the old classes were still worthy of hegemony and neither superannuated nor selfish. The wager on reform was necessary, because ultimately the status of the liberal bourgeoisie was tied up with the patrician heritage of administering the Italian political community.

Underneath both the efforts at cautious reform and the out-of-hand rejection of leftist demands lay indeed a common conception of the state—shared by men from Pantaleoni on the right to the editor Luigi Albertini and even to the more democratic Giovanni Amendola. In apparent paradox, the same liberal Italians who opposed government interference in the economic sphere all called for a strong state. Pantaleoni lamented the "presenting of accounts" to the state by various interest groups, while Einaudi and Albertini felt that the state must transcend competing economic interests. Rooted in Italian liberal thought—at least the strand that derived from the secular traditions of the Piedmontese right—was the conviction that when the state became enmeshed in the regulation of economic affairs it was soiling itself in the very interest-group clashes that it was supposed to transcend. When Giolitti sought to reconcile the working class, the more conservative liberals felt, he was not seeking to represent a broad spectrum of social currents but was demeaning the state by paying blackmail to subversives.[80]

[79] Tasca, *Nascita e avvento del fascismo*, I, p. 18.

[80] For this view: Guido Ruggiero, *The History of European Liberalism* [1927], R. G. Collingwood, trans., (Boston, 1959), pp. 275–343, 370–387; cf. also F. Burzio, *Politica demiurgica* (Bari, 1923), pp. 42–43, cited in Vivarelli, *Il dopoguerra in Italia*, p. 94, n. 221. For the displacement of the liberal elite in a suddenly polarized urban situation: Claudo Silvestri, *Dalla redenzione al fascismo. Trieste 1918–1922* (Milan, 1959), pp. 6–7 ff.

Given these strandards, liberals might feel increasingly isolated and out of touch with interest-group politics and mass parties. In 1915, Albertini had written revealingly to his associate, Andrea Torre:

> I too may feel passions, cede to weaknesses; but I assure you that it is my boast and my title of pride to see that my personal sentiments do not influence my public action, in which I desire to have as guide only equity and the interest of Italy. These are not rhetorical phrases, but a method which constitutes our honor and force. Perhaps because of this we are not feared and respected as would be our due, because it is known that our conduct shall never be determined in respect to men and problems by sympathies or antipathies, love or rancor.[81]

Albertini remained convinced that Italian participation in the war would reinfuse the liberal elite with the disinterested patriotism he sought to exemplify. As often before, public spokesmen relied on rhetoric to disguise the massive social costs of the national cause. Their success was limited and brief, for the wartime experience radicalized workers, rewarded a new industrial class, and mobilized masses of men politically as it moved them from their villages to the trenches. Entered into to cement liberal leadership,[82] the war threatened to destroy it. The liberals might resent interest-group politics, but they would soon face the issue of whether they could maintain their political and social leadership by clinging to outmoded class concepts and elitist strategies.

BUSINESS ACCOMMODATION IN GERMANY AND FRANCE

The successful defense of privileged positions in the turbulence of 1918–1919 required new organization, not aristocratic nostalgia. German heavy industry developed the most coherent response as a threatened interest; French as well as Italian industrialists remained more fragmented and less purposeful. While German capitalism faced the gravest political threat on the morrow of defeat and revolution, the peculiar pattern of the German upheaval created opportunities as well as perils. With the eclipse of the former dynastic and bureaucratic leadership, industrialists inherited a new prominence; with the economic burdens of defeat they could claim needed expertise.

[81] Letter of September 15, 1915, ACS, Rome: Carte Andrea Torre, f. 4, sf. 14; cf. *CdS*, January 15, 1919: "For our part we shall continue on our own path, unperturbed, disdaining a false and momentary popularity . . . ," cited in Piero Melograni, ed., *Corriere della Sera (1919–1943)* (Bologna, 1965), p. 9.

[82] Cf. Antonio Salandra, *La neutralità italiana (1914). Ricordi e pensieri* (Milan, 1928), pp. 203, 371–372.

The key to capitalist continuity in Germany rested on the parallel behavior of industry and labor. Politically, German business and labor confronted each other across the traditional divide between the bourgeois parties and social democracy. But in their very moment of political adversity, major industrialists found it advantageous to secure economic immunities by astute alliances with the trade-union leaders. A double effort thus distinguished the "bourgeois" reaction to the German revolution: a fore-ordained class competition with the socialists, but simultaneously a coalition on the part of key industrialists with organized labor to carve out a corporatist autonomy profitable for both partners.

The revolution itself threatened major economic change only briefly, because a large terrain of implicit agreement existed between the socialists who inherited power and the more conservative forces. While the Social Democrats foreswore any abandonment of parliamentary pluralism, the right, in effect, renounced contesting the form of the new regime. The question of SPD power and objectives was crucial, no longer that of the crown. As even the head of the Junker-dominated Agrarian League wrote to his chief collaborator, the essential was to create a new force to guarantee "the bourgeois social order. Whether we wish to adopt republican or monarchical forms is not an issue for today."[83]

In the month after November 9, the central concern of all moderates and conservatives was whether the constituent assembly announced by the socialists would actually convene to establish a parliamentary system, or whether what they feared as a Soviet-model republic of councils (*Räte*) would prevail. Until that issue was settled, all the forces of the old order, even those who had traditionally despised the Reichstag, could become ardently parliamentary.[84] Meanwhile three

[83] Conrad von Wangenheim to Gustav Rösicke, November 13, 1918, in DZA, Potsdam: Wangenheim Nachlass/13. There was a lively debate on abdication and the fate of the monarchy, but only during the armistice negotiations with Wilson and before the proclamation of the Republic. See Erich Matthias and Rudolf Morsey, *Die Regierung des Prinzen Max von Baden. Quellen zur Geschichte des Parlamentarismus und der politischen Parteien,* I. Reihe, Bd. II (Düsseldorf, 1962), pp. 442, 501, 582–598; Stresemann Nachlass, esp. statements in GFM:6889= 180/3068/133574–575, 6896=187/3069/13450–502, 6891=182/3068/133896–897; Conservative prescriptions in the crisis, in Kuno Graf von Westarp, *Die Regierung des Prinzen Max von Baden und die konservative Partei 1918* (Berlin, 1928), pp. 64 ff.

[84] For the nonsocialists' campaign for parliamentary representation and the controversy sparked when Konstantin Fehrenbach, Reichstag President and Centrist leader, sought to reconvene the Reichstag, see Fehrenbach's recollections printed in Erich Matthias and Suzanne Miller, eds., *Die Regierung der Volksbeauftragten. Quellen zur Geschichte des Parlamentarismus und der politischen Parteien* (Düsseldorf, 1966), I. Reihe, VI/1, pp. 381–392. Cf. Richard Müller, *Vom Kaiserreich zur Republik,* 2 vols. (Berlin, 1924–25), II, pp. 178–179; and Wil-

Social Democrats and three Independent Socialists shared provisional executive power as "People's Commissioners" (*Volksbeauftragten*) under the chairmanship of Friedrich Ebert. The divisions among the socialist representatives, and the greater cohesion of the SPD, along with Ebert's decision to summon an elected constituent assembly, which was endorsed by the delegates of the Worker and Soldier Councils in mid-December, ensured that the new republic would be a parliamentary one. This meant eventual representation of conservative and antidemocratic currents alongside those of the left.[85] As a conservative analyst later wrote, the decision was "the salvation of bourgeois Germany."[86]

Applauding Ebert as a force for order while the parliamentary issue was still in doubt, the far right kept the liberty to turn against him once it was confirmed. "Preservation of order," the Conservatives' *Kreuzzeitung* had written in November, "is the reason for which all of bourgeois society presently stands beside this government." But the day after the Berlin Spartacist uprising was stopped and the last major challenge to a parliamentary regime apparently was crushed, the issue became that of "fighting the idea of socialism and the socialist republic" to the hilt. "A socialist regime will shatter the whole structure of bourgeois existence. Whether this amputation happens

---

helm Gröner, who encouraged Fehrenbach and then backed down, in Gröner's *Lebenserinnerungen*, Friedrich Freiherr Hiller von Gaertringen, ed. (Göttingen, 1957), p. 472; BA, Koblenz: Erich Koch-Weser Nachlass 13, p. 555. For the Conservatives' demand for parliamentary government, Werner Liebe, *Die deutschnationale Volkspartei 1918–1924* (Düsseldorf, 1956), p. 11; similar People's Party views in Wolfgang Hartenstein, *Die Anfänge der deutschen Volkspartei 1918–1920* (Düsseldorf, 1962), p. 59. For the same campaign on the part of the agrarians, see Rösicke's prompting of the *Deutsche Tageszeitung*'s editor, Paul Bäcker, in BA, Koblenz: Rösicke Nachlass/2, p. 10; also Rösicke's suggestion that the Agrarian League promise support for any government protecting order and convening a National Assembly, in his letter to Wangenheim, December 3, 1918, DZA, Potsdam: Wangenheim Nachlass/13.

[85] Eberhard Kolb, *Die Arbeiterräte in der deutschen Innenpolitik 1918–1919* (Düsseldorf, 1962), pp. 24–55, 114–182; Müller, *Vom Kaiserreich zur Republik*, II, pp. 214–216, also 105–113 on economic compromises; Matthias and Miller, eds., *Die Regierung der Volksbeauftragten*, pp. lxxx–lxxxi, cvii–cviii; Allgemeiner Kongress der Arbeiter- und Soldatenräte Deutschlands vom 16. bis 21. Dezember 1918 im Abgeordnetenhause zu Berlin: *Stenographische Berichte* (Berlin, 1919), pp. 105–112, 115, 123, 127–128, 137–142. Peter von Oertzen, *Betriebsräte in der Novemberrevolution* (Düsseldorf, 1963), pp. 51–67, 84–93. For the bureaucracy's contribution to limiting the revolution: Wolfgang Elben, *Das Problem der Kontinuität in der deutschen Revolution. Die Politik der Staatssekretäre und der militärischen Führung vom November 1918 bis Februar 1919* (Düsseldorf, 1965).

[86] Johann Victor Bredt, *Der Deutsche Reichstag im Weltkrieg*. Das Werk des Untersuchungsausschusses der Verfassungsgebenden Deutschen Nationalversammlung und des Deutschen Reichstages. 4. Reihe: Die Ursachen des deutschen Zusammenbruches im Jahre 1918, Bd. 8 (Berlin, 1926), p. 371.

radically *à la* Spartacus or gradually *à la* Ebert-Scheidemann is, in the last analysis, only a question of time."[87] The Moor had done his work, the Moor could go!

This ambiguous response—the distrust of Social Democratic hegemony on the one hand, the fear of weakening Ebert before the more radical Independent Socialists and Spartacists on the other—prompted a general regrouping of bourgeois parties. In the disarray among German liberals as the monarchy lost its vestiges of authority, the amateurs of the bourgeois left, such as the sociologist Alfred Weber and the editor of the *Berliner Tageblatt*, Theodor Wolff, organized a new German Democratic Party (DDP) intended to restrain liberals from becoming cowed into voting for the Social Democrats even while it cooperated with them. After exclusion from the new Democratic Party because of his wartime annexationism, Gustav Stresemann and his adherents reworked the remaining National Liberal organizations into a German People's Party (DVP).[88] The continuing division among the liberals had been lamented often but probably meant little. Democrats and People's Party often worked as one group in parliament after 1920, and they failed as one group in the early 1930's when their combined following largely deserted to splinter parties and to National Socialism. At the time of their birth, moreover, they disagreed over more than personality. The Democratic Party initially sought to overcome the old bourgeois-socialist antagonism by a fresh emphasis on democracy and republicanism. The recruits to the People's Party protested instead with the characteristic question of nineteenth-century liberalism: "Can one be a democrat at all without becoming a social democrat?"[89] In the election of January 1919, the DVP fared badly, primarily because the formation of the rival Democratic Party had shattered many of the former National Liberal local organizations required to support candidates. The Democrats seemed to have cre-

[87] "Die innere Politik der Woche," *NP(K)Z*, November 18, 1918, January 13, 1919.

[88] See the letters and accounts in the Stresemann Nachlass, GFM: 6896=187/3069/134519–620, and 6895=186/3069/130436–467; also BA, Koblenz: R 45 II (DVP)/1; Hartenstein, *Anfänge der deutschen Volkspartei*, pp. 7–33; Henry A. Turner, Jr., *Stresemann and the Politics of the Weimar Republic* (Princeton, N.J., 1963), pp. 14 ff.; Otto Nuschke, "Was die Deutsche Demokratische Partei wurde, was sie leistete, und was sie ist," in Anton Erkelenz, ed., *Zehn Jahre Deutsche Republik* (Berlin, 1928), pp. 24–30; Theodor Wolff, *Through Two Decades*, E. W. Dickes, trans. (London, 1936), pp. 138–142.

[89] Cited by Stresemann from a Würzburg party leader, December 10, 1918, and reproduced in Gustav Stresemann, *Von der Revolution bis zum Frieden von Versailles* (Berlin, 1919), pp. 58–59. Cf. Stresemann's campaign speech in Osnabruck, December 19, 1918: "We confess ourselves openly as a bourgeois party and as fundamental enemies of Social Democracy," *ibid.*, p. 87.

ated a powerful liberal-democratic nucleus, but half their voters would desert in a year and a half. Meanwhile, on the far right, the new German National People's Party (DNVP)—designed to broaden and modernize the old agrarian German Conservatives—suffered from association with a bankrupt military annexationism. Yet even its limited support disclosed a strength in the cities and outside East Elbia that its predecessor had never attained.[90]

The real victory for conservative forces, however, did not lie in the small number of seats they rescued in the 1919 voting. It consisted of the failure of the two socialist parties to secure a majority between them and, even more fundamentally, the fact that an elected Assembly was actually to convene and decide the future constitutional order. Less than two months after the revolution, therefore, bourgeois and even antiliberal forces had won the pluralist institutional framework and created the new parties that would allow their political revival.

This political continuity could not have been achieved without parallel continuity in the economic arena. As Franz Neumann recognized, the real framework of the Weimar Republic comprised a set of treaties among the powerful social and political forces of Germany. The cooperation between Social Democrats and the Supreme Command to prevent "bolshevism" formed one; a further compact between the leaders of heavy industry and of organized labor constituted a second.[91] Industry and labor unions achieved new influence as a consequence of the demands of "total war." The government turned to businessmen to organize the war economy, summoning Walther Rathenau to the key Raw Materials Section of the Prussian War Ministry and turning over procurement, rationing, and planning to committees of officers, businessmen, and civil servants. Heavy industry especially won new dominance and privileges: its trade associations claimed hefty price increases for its patriotic collaboration, and it captured the directorships of the "war companies"—joint private-public corporations that had important responsibilities for purchasing and distributing scarce raw materials. Union leaders won a new influence, too, as bureaucrats and the army commanders who took over regional

[90] Official results in the *Vierteljahrshefte zur Statistik des deutschen Reiches*, 28. Jg. 1919, *1. Ergänzungsheft* (Berlin, 1919), "Die Wahlen zur verfassungsgebenden Deutschen Nationalversammlung am 19. Januar 1919." Cf. Hartenstein, *Anfänge der deutschen Volkspartei*, pp. 67–71, 224–230; Bernhard Vogel, Dieter Nohlen, and Rainer-Olaf Schultze, *Wahlen in Deutschland* (Berlin, 1971), pp. 139–141.

[91] Franz Neumann, "Der Funktionswandel des Gesetztes im Recht der bürgerlichen Gesellschaft," *Zeitschrift für Sozialforschung*, VI, 3 (1937), pp. 571 ff.; also Neumann, *Behemoth: The Structure and Practice of National Socialism* (New York, 1966), pp. 11–13.

governing responsibilities—including guidance on wage and price disputes—sought labor cooperation for the duration.[92]

As labor and industry, moreover, each gained new power, the state's resort to inflationary finance created a community of interest between them. The government avoided rigorous taxation and relied increasingly on unsecured banknotes issued through the Reichsbank. While real income declined for those on fixed revenues, working class families employed in war-related industry may have eked out higher real, as well as money, incomes. Employers reaped even steeper price increases, until finally even the friendly Supreme Command denounced the gains by early 1918.[93]

The implicit logrolling also extended to political and social prerogatives. As compensation for the Auxiliary Service Law, which the Supreme Command won at the end of 1916 to enhance their control over the economy, the unions extracted "Worker and Employee Chambers," established to mediate factory conflicts. Where once lock-out and yellow union had prevailed, the new committees meant an important encroachment upon the prewar *Herr im Hause* prerogatives, according to which "the worker becomes the subject of the employer; he must subordinate himself to him; the employer thus becomes his master."[94] Perspicacious managers understood, however, that compromise with labor leaders was preferable to facing left-wing socialists or the enthusiasts for a government-controlled planned economy who had won key footholds in the Berlin ministries. Following occasional discussions concerning Germany's economic future, business leaders and

[92] Albrecht Mendelssohn-Bartholdy, *The World War and German Society. The Testimony of a Liberal* (New Haven, 1936), pp. 195–220; Gerald Feldman, *Army, Industry, and Labor in Germany 1914–1918* (Princeton, N.J., 1966), pp. 31–38 on war administration, 45–52, 149 ff. on businessmen; Werner Richter, *Gewerkschaften, Monopolkapital und Staat im 1. Weltkrieg und in der Novemberrevolution* (Berlin, DDR, 1958), pp. 96–103 on war companies. Cf. W. F. Bruck, "Die Kriegsunternehmung. Versuch einer Systematik," *Archiv für Sozialwissenschaft und Sozialpolitik,* 48, 3 (1921), pp. 547–595.

[93] On inflation, profits, and wages: Feldman, *Army, Industry, and Labor,* pp. 63, 385 ff., 464–472, 480 ff.; Waldemar Zimmermann, "Die Veränderungen der Einkommens- und Lebensverhältnisse der deutschen Arbeiter durch den Krieg," in Zimmermann, A. Günther, and R. Meerwarth, *Die Einwirkung des Krieges auf Bevölkerungsbewegung, Einkommen, und Lebenshaltung in Deutschland* (Stuttgart and New Haven, 1932), pp. 469–471; Leo Graebler, "The Cost of the War to Germany," in Graebler and W. Winkler, *The Cost of the World War to Germany and Austria-Hungary* (New Haven, 1940), pp. 59–66. Jürgen Kocka, *Klassengesellschaft im Krieg 1914–1918* (Göttingen, 1973), pp. 12–27, 71–75.

[94] Citation from the employers' federation of 1906 is in Otto Neuloh, *Die deutsche Betriebsverfassung* (Tübingen, 1956), p. 89; cf. pp. 36–40. For the evolution of labor conditions, Feldman, *Army, Industry, and Labor,* pp. 168 ff., 203–217, 247–249, 473–477. Cf. also Hans Josef Varain, *Freie Gewerkschaften, Sozialdemokratie und Staat. Die Politik der Generalkommission unter der Führung Carl Legiens (1890–1920)* (Düsseldorf, 1956), pp. 88–90.

union officials conferred in October 1917 about labor support for industry's annexationist projects as well as about limiting the potentially revolutionary effects of sudden demobilization. Nonetheless, industrialists resisted full recognition of the unions, and the parleys remained inconclusive.[95]

Contacts were renewed more urgently during October 1918, as it became clear that virtual surrender was near and industrialists feared that the reform government of Prince Max von Baden would also collapse. As Jakob Reichert, executive director of the Union of German Iron and Steel Industrialists (VdESI), explained, the traditional middle class and the discredited Junkers were undependable bulwarks against the expected political upheaval: "Allies for industry could be found only among the workers; these were the unions."[96] In Berlin, Hans von Raumer, a representative of the relatively progressive electro-technical industry, began negotiations with labor leaders in the hope that Berlin industry might have to yield fewer concessions than the coal and iron concerns. The Ruhr leaders were realistic but not prepared to panic. Supported even by Alfred Hugenberg, Hugo Stinnes began talks with the mineworkers' chief, Otto Hue, and prepared the way for general conferences in Essen from October 18. From the outset the Ruhr mine owners conceded *de facto* recognition of the unions as official bargaining agents. But they postponed renouncing their own company unions and tenaciously sought to limit the scope of the prerogatives they yielded, so as to avoid union control over the pits.[97] Meanwhile Stinnes took effective leadership over the Berlin talks, too. The revolution finally compelled the employers to accept a general eight-hour day and renounce company unions in the final agreement, which was worked out between Stinnes and Carl Legien, head of the SPD-affiliated Free Trade unions, between November 12 and 15. But industry still managed to channel union grievances. The Stinnes-Legien pact established a pyramid of labor-management arbitration committees. The new structure was designated the Arbeitsgemeinschaft—a term suggesting a cooperative association of labor and management—and its major organ, the Central Arbeitsgemeinschaft (ZAG), was officially recognized by the early decree

[95] Richter, *Gewerkschaften, Monopolkapital und Staat*, pp. 156–162; Gerald Feldman, "German Business between War and Revolution: The Origins of the Stinnes-Legien Agreement," in Gerhard A. Ritter, ed., *Entstehung und Wandel der modernen Gesellschaft (Festschrift für Hans Rosenberg)* (Berlin, 1970), pp. 323–325.

[96] J. Reichert, *Entstehung, Bedeutung und Ziel der Arbeitsgemeinschaft* (Berlin, 1919), p. 6.

[97] Hans Mommsen, "Die Bergarbeiterbewegung an der Ruhr 1918–1933," in Jürgen Reulecke, ed., *Arbeiterbewegung an Rhein und Ruhr* (Hanover, 1973), pp. 282–286.

legislation of the revolutionary regime. Industry's sacrifices really remained minimal: the German eight-hour day was made conditional on its international adoption; moreover, employers found the new "parity" committees, which gave labor and management an equal voice in the formation of social policy, preferable to workers' councils or factory councils which included no industrialists.[98]

The employers viewed the concessions as inoculation against further radicalism. Dissident business leaders worried more about the bypassing and obsolescence of the traditional economic associations and the new preeminence of heavy industry. At the November 14 Executive Committee meeting of the Union of German Iron and Steel Industrialists, no real criticism emerged. Even the chairman, Ewald Hilger, proprietor of Silesian coal interests and a bitter opponent of labor claims, thought the compact more favorable than he had believed possible. Identifying himself as a former zealous adversary of the unions, Hilger now confessed:

> I stand before you as a Saul become Paul. Unless we negotiate with the unions we can go no further. Yes, gentlemen, we should be happy that the unions are still prepared to negotiate as they have; for only by negotiation, above all, with the unions, only through agreement with the unions, can we avoid anarchy, bolshevism, Spartacist rule and chaos—call it what you will.[99]

Not all industrialists, however, remained so acquiescent once the pressures of the revolutionary months ebbed. By March 1, 1919, the erstwhile Saul become Paul, Hilger himself, was complaining that

> the workers are not unemployed but unwilling to work. Above all else they want to avoid difficult labor because they now have much better unemployment insurance. . . . No work gets done in the pits, but many speeches are given and the most difficult problems are being resolved. When a blast goes off they sit down and converse about political matters which are very interesting, such as the Polish question etc.[100]

As a Silesian mine director, Hilger represented an industry that was organized differently from the one whose leaders had personally

---

[98] Accounts in Feldman, "German Business between War and Revolution," pp. 325–336; Richter, *Gewerkschaften, Monopolkapital und Staat*, pp. 203–210, 237–243; Hans von Raumer, "Unternehmer und Gewerkschaften in der Weimarer Zeit," *Deutsche Rundschau*, 80, 5 (1954), pp. 428–432; cf. Heinrich Kaun, "Die Geschichte der Zentralarbeitsgemeinschaft der industriellen und gewerblichen Arbeitgeber und Arbeitnehmer Deutschlands," Diss. (Jena, 1938).

[99] BA, Koblenz: R 13 I (VdESI)/155, p. 15. Cf. the optimistic Stinnes evaluations in the same meeting.

[100] BA, Koblenz: R 13 I (VdESI)/156, p. 12.

negotiated the Arbeitsgemeinschaft. The managerial class of the Ruhr and the surrounding Rhenish-Westphalian region often had a less proprietary stake in their corporations and could afford more costly experiments with conciliation. In Silesia, however, the mines often remained family patrimony, and managers confronted a partly Polish labor force, "with greater Polish as well as Bolshevik aspirations."[101]

Light industry—the smaller machinists, the optical, food, and clothing producers who were politically stronger in South Germany and Saxony—also worried about the new commitments entailed by the Arbeitsgemeinschaft. This stance involved a turnabout, for generally prewar labor relations in light industry had been more progressive than in the giant coal and steel firms.[102] Now, however, its representatives feared that heavy industry would make a separate peace with organized labor at a price in wages and hours that light industry could ill afford.

In fact, the cooperative attitude of Ruhr heavy industry was a transient one and remained dependent upon pervasive inflationary conditions and a vigorous export demand. Still, in the months immediately after the revolution, the Westphalian entrepreneurs often seemed to be dangerous gamblers. Ernst Borsig, heir to the massive locomotive, turbine, and machine works in Berlin and chairman of the ZAG, was complaining to General Schleicher as early as December 1918 about the working classes' lack of understanding for Germany's difficult economic situation. In 1920, when the spirit of concession was fast dissipating, he attacked Rhenish-Westphalian leaders for allowing German industry to be "politicized" and found that the ZAG he had once defended had become far too radical.[103] Basically, entrepreneurs such as Hilger and even Borsig felt that workers were not to be coddled but commanded. But Stinnes and Albert Vögler, General Director of the Stinnes-affiliated German-Luxemburg mining

[101] For Silesian attitudes, see BA, Koblenz: R 13 I (VdESI)/158, pp. 95–96, a retrospective glimpse from late 1920; also the discussion of Upper Silesian conditions in the ZAG Vorstand, January 27, 1919: DZA, Potsdam: 70 Ze 1 (ZAG)/28; for management trends, Ingolf Liesebach, "Der Wandel der Führungsschicht der deutschen Industrie von 1918 bis 1945," Diss. (Hanover, 1957), pp. 22 ff. On the new collegial administrative style in Ruhr industries which helped prepare for Arbeitsgemeinschaft ideas: Neuloh, *Die Betriebsverfassung*, pp. 146–147.

[102] Ruhr labor relations in Neuloh, *Betriebsverfassung*, pp. 121–135, 147; for light industry Helga Nussbaum, *Unternehmer gegen Monopole. Über Struktur und Aktionen antimonopolistischer bürgerlichen Gruppen zu Beginn des 20. Jahrhunderts* (Berlin, 1966); cf. Hans Jäger, *Unternehmer in der deutschen Politik 1890–1918* (Bonn, 1967).

[103] Borsig to Schleicher, BA, Koblenz: Schleicher Nachlass/12; his 1920 judgment on BA, Koblenz: R 13 I (VdESI)/158, pp. 30–31, and in the controversy after the Kapp Putsch, *ibid.*, 157, pp. 30–32, 38.

concern, were corporate organizers, not field commanders; their success was a function of management skills and financial legerdemain. Both men created huge industrial combinations: Stinnes' conglomerate enterprises embraced coal mines, iron and steel plants, related electrical power sources, wharves and shipping lines, forests, newsprint, and even a politically active newspaper. When the structure collapsed after Stinnes' death in 1924, Vögler reconstructed a giant steel trust on its ruins, the Vereinigte Stahlwerke. The Rhinelanders were driven by an entrepreneurial expansionism and were willing to work face to face with labor leaders—if these leaders would endorse their business acquisitions and defer to their expertise. Family-firm owners, however, continued to be guided by the patriarchal urge to preserve harsh and traditional hierarchies.[104]

In the postrevolutionary months, the Central Arbeitsgemeinschaft served both sorts of businessmen well. Leaders of industry and labor used the association to enhance their own power and deflect threats to their own leadership. Confronting the government jointly, they could claim that their direction of the demobilization economy was in the public interest. Through their joint pressure they extracted a new, independent Demobilization Office armed with decree power. With the end of the war imminent, industry wished to eliminate the authority of the Reich Economic Office (RWA), an agency of the Economics Ministry that was resented for its bureaucratic regulation and what was felt to be its effort at backdoor nationalization. They found their spokesman in Rathenau's successor in the Raw Materials Division of the Prussian War Ministry, Colonel Joseph Koeth, who attacked the unpopular rival agency and demanded an independent authority for the problems of deconversion. The Max von Baden government resisted ceding so much power; so too did the Independent Socialist People's Commissioner, Emil Barth, after November 9. And so too did textile manufacturers, who feared that heavy industry would win further leverage. Nevertheless, faced by the confusion of the postarmistice economy and confronted with the insistence of trade-union leader Legien as well as industrialists, the Ebert government placed Koeth at the head of an Office for Economic Demobilization, which was to fix the legal relationships between industry and labor for the next five years. As technocratic dictator, Koeth called upon the Arbeitsgemeinschaft partners to establish further parity committees to manage the difficult economic dilemmas of the postwar blockade winter. "Self-regulation" of industry was thus carried into

[104] Cf. Gert von Klass, *Alfred Vögler, einer der grossen des Ruhrreviers* (Tübingen, 1957) and his *Hugo Stinnes* (Tübingen, 1958) both hagiographic; also Hugo Brinckmayer, *Hugo Stinnes* (Munich, 1921).

the postwar period, but divested of radical implications and the earlier threats of government control. Economic survival, not restructuring, preoccupied all parties, and Koeth specifically renounced any rash socialization measures: "Only after demobilization can political projects come to practical fulfillment."[105]

The new partnership clearly benefited industry during the troubled months when a "revolutionary" government had the power to decree extensive nationalization and might have done so to appease the radicals. Trade-union leaders, too, had a stake in the success of the ZAG and its related parity committees; they also wished to control the channels of labor grievances. This meant containing the potentially explosive factory-council movement, which threatened to displace the well-entrenched, nation-wide union hierarchies in favor of direct workers' representation in the plant. Labor leaders, in fact, preferred to share their influence with management representatives on parity committees rather than gamble on the left wing in the *Räte* movement.

Spokesmen for the traditional and the new forms of labor representation had different political allies in the government. While the Independent Socialists were responsive to the factory councils and the radical "shop steward" movements centered in Berlin's metal manufacturing plants, the Majority Social Democrats reflected the suspicions of their affiliated unions. The two socialist delegations reached a compromise by November 23 on the powers to be granted the workers' committees, but the unions refused to ratify it. Pressure, moreover, continued from below: labor turmoil in the Ruhr and the appointment by the Essen Workers' and Soldiers' Councils of a Commission of Nine to socialize the Ruhr mines slowly pushed the Berlin government to further concessions. By Socialism, the active mineworkers' delegates meant less nationalization than local labor takeovers. But this outran the determination of the SPD and the Mine Workers' Union to keep control over the turbulent Ruhr movement. Berlin sent its own socialization commissioners (the inclusion of Vögler indicated the scope of socialism intended!), and after much temporizing agreed to new and more powerful Labor Chambers, which were now to represent workers not only in the plant but on a regional basis. This was still insufficient to appease the factory-council advocates. In the wake of another gen-

---

[105] Cited in Elben, *Das Problem der Kontinuität*, p. 80, who discusses Koeth's and Eugen Schiffer's conservative roles, pp. 72–96; Richter, *Gewerkschaften, Monopolkapital und Staat*, pp. 228–234, 282–296; Feldman, "German Business between War and Revolution," pp. 327–330, 333–335. For the preeminent role of Koeth's office, see BA, Koblenz: Nachlass Moellendorff/160, "Niederschrift der Besprechung . . . am 21.XI.18," where it was recognized that the Demobilamt enjoyed executive power and could not be interfered with.

eral strike in Berlin during March, the SPD finally agreed to "anchor" the factory-council system in the new constitution, along with a provision for a pyramid of worker-management councils from the local to the national level. A further cycle of strikes, quasi-insurrections, and military suppression convulsed the Ruhr during April, but the government's emissary, Carl Severing, finally managed a grudging pacification of the area. The settlement confirmed the establishment of local factory councils; on the other hand, disputes with management were to be mediated by parity committees, and if need be, decided by appeal to the Mayor of Essen, Hans Luther.[106]

Both industrial and labor delegates to the ZAG objected to the government concessions of these turbulent months. Until the SPD finally felt it necessary to guarantee factory councils in the constitution, businessmen and labor leaders fought together for extension of the parity principle of joint representation. In the ZAG Executive on January 27, employers complained about institution of new labor chambers—that is, the regional working-class delegations—for the Ruhr and Upper Silesian coal districts, while Legien and his lieutenant, Theodor Leipart, also claimed that an extension of the Arbeitsgemeinschaft mechanisms to the regional level would be preferable.[107] On January 30, Legien and steel-industry spokesman Reichert called jointly upon the workers not to abuse their temporary power and to behave responsibly; and the next day union and industry spokesmen petitioned together to postpone legal implementation of the labor chambers, "since the Arbeitsgemeinschaft is working excellently in heavy industry."[108] As the cabinet made further concessions under the pressure of mass strikes, Reichert warned that "the second phase of the revolution has begun," and suggested appealing to industry's Social Democratic friends in the government, Gustav Bauer and Rudolf

[106] Oertzen, *Betriebsräte*, pp. 80–82, 109–132; see also Oertzen, "Die grossen Streiks der Ruhrbergarbeiterschaft im Frühjahr 1919," *Vierteljahreshefte für Zeitgeschichte*, 6, 2 (1958), pp. 240 ff.; Mommsen, "Die Bergarbeiterbewegung," pp. 292–295. From the viewpoint of the Majority Socialists, Carl Severing, *1919/1920: Im Wetter und Watterwinckel* (Bielefeld, 1927), pp. 9–55; cf. Hans Luther, *Politiker ohne Partei. Erinnerungen* (Stuttgart, 1960), pp. 72–75; and for a prounion view: Varain, *Freie Gewerkschaften, Sozialdemokratie und Staat*, pp. 142–147. The army's account of Ruhr disorders: Kriegsgeschichtliches Forschungsamt des Heeres, *Die Wirren in der Reichshauptstadt und im nordlichen Deutschland 1918–1920* (Berlin, 1940); and industry's perspective in Hans Spethmann, *Zwölf Jahre Ruhrbergbau*, 4 vols. (Berlin, 1928), I, pp. 251–331.

[107] DZA, Potsdam: 70 Ze 1 (ZAG)/28, Zentralvorstand session, January 27, 1919.

[108] BA, Koblenz: R 13 I (VdESI)/190, "Aufzeichnung über die am 31. Januar abgehaltene Besprechung über Einrichtung von Arbeitskammern." Cf. Richter, *Gewerkschaften, Monopolkapital und Staat*, pp. 320, 323; also Oertzen, *Betriebsräte*, pp. 187–193, for union views toward the ZAG.

Wissell, to postpone inauguration of the Labor Chambers. On March 4, the ZAG again resolved to seek a delay.[109]

SPD cabinet officials faltered between the claims to economic sovereignty on the part of union leaders as well as industrialists and the impatient demands for socialization and power-to-the-*Räte* emanating from the workers in mine fields and factories. At its party congress on March 22 and 23, the SPD leadership, as noted above, finally reaffirmed its commitment to the councils with the promise to include them in the constitution. Two weeks later, following massive strikes in the Ruhr, Ebert announced introduction of appropriate legislation. Although the employers remained hostile, the unions began to soften their own hostility in light of rank-and-file militancy and the SPD commitment. Unsuccessful in preventing the establishment of labor chambers and factory councils, they began to compromise with the government to win important modifications in the proposed legislation.[110]

Given the change in the labor leaders' position, employers could no longer muster a united opposition in the Arbeitsgemeinschaft. Further antagonism between industry and unions, moreover, would emerge by summer over issues of economic planning and nationalization. Nonetheless, the Stinnes-Legien collaboration and the Arbeitsgemeinschaft had served as a critical moderating force throughout the revolutionary months. Jealous of their newly won privileges, legitimately concerned about production and employment, the trade-union principals in the ZAG worked to forestall those social experiments that exceeded their own mild prescription as actively as did the industrial leaders.

While union executives distrusted new forms of working-class representation, business leaders feared further efforts at government control of industry. Under the impetus of Wichard von Moellendorff, formerly Rathenau's assistant in organizing war production and, in 1918–1919, State Secretary under Rudolf Wissell, the Economics Ministry was generating new and complex planning schemes. As a continuation of wartime regulatory agencies and expression of his commitment to a non-Marxist "conservative socialism," Moellendorff envisioned dual pyramids of planning boards based on region and

[109] Reichert in BA, Koblenz: R 13 I (VdESI)/155, pp. 47–51; March 4 Vorstand decision in DZA, Potsdam: 70 Ze 1 (ZAG)/28; cf. Richter, *Gewerkschaften, Monopolkapital und Staat*, pp. 335, 339.
[110] Varain, *Freie Gewerkschaften, Sozialdemokratie und Staat*, pp. 147–149; Oertzen, *Betriebsräte*, pp. 109 ff., 153–164. For employers' defeat, see Fritz Tanzler, *Die deutschen Arbeitgeberverbände 1904–1929* (Berlin, 1929), pp. 150–157.

type of industry. The final draft proposal did not appear until late spring 1919, but initial projects for uniting producers, labor delegates, and consumer representatives of each major industry were sufficient to antagonize businessmen. Ruhr industry wanted their clients in manufacturing to have no voice over prices or the allocation of goods for domestic consumption and for export.[111]

The delegates of industry in the Arbeitsgemeinschaft convinced labor representatives to second their plea that the Arbeitsgemeinschaft must first be allowed to get organized. Wissell, however, pointed out impatiently that strong resistance had arisen to the Arbeitsgemeinschaft. Some industries resented its claims, while the government itself wanted quicker organization of economic sectors outside the purview of heavy industry, such as in "trade" and "agriculture." Borsig claimed that the conflicts of interest between heavy industry and "commerce" lay too deep for cooperation.[112] This was true. Bankers, manufacturers, and shipping interests all had stakes in spurring exports and preserving low prices at home for primary coal and iron products. Iron and steel producers, on the other hand, sought an advantageous dual market, with the opportunity for unrestricted exports to hard-currency countries and a rationing by high prices of the quota left for domestic manufacturers. Stinnes' advocacy of collaboration with labor, for example, fit into a vaster vision of continuing inflation and low real wages, hence vigorous export demand and new opportunities for corporate expansion through borrowing of an ever-depreciating currency. His projection of a labor shortage despite demobilization was welcome to business and government; but the critical question was who was to benefit at the cost of whom.[113]

All industrialists in Germany shared a commitment to strong demand, high employment, and a minimum of central regulation. But Ruhr producers of basic steel products often had different tariff and

[111] For the Moellendorff plans see below, Chapter Three, part one; cf. also *Der Aufbau der Gemeinwirtschaft; Denkschrift des Reichswirtschaftsministeriums vom 7. Mai 1919* (Jena, 1919), which embodied his and Wissell's planning ideas. See also BA, Koblenz: Moellendorff Nachlass/153, "Uber die kritische Zeit im Reichswirtschaftsamt. Briefwechsel mit Paul Wissell"; and Moellendorff, *Konservativer Sozialismus* (Hamburg, 1932), esp. pp. 118–124. Wissell's memoirs in BA, Koblenz: Rudolf Wissell Nachlass/7–8, are skimpy.

[112] Vorstand meetings of March 18/19, 1919, in DZA, Potsdam: 70 Ze 1 (ZAG)/ 28; cf. Richter, *Gewerkschaften, Monopolkapital und Staat*, pp. 335–339; also BA, Koblenz: R 13 I (VdESI)/190, Rundschreiben Nr. 1114 (March 18, 1919), for account of industrialists' meeting with Bauer, Wissell, and Moellendorff. Cf. the employers' attitudes expressed in "Gewerkschaften und Arbeiterräte," *Deutsche Arbeitgeber-Zeitung*, April 6, 1919.

[113] Stinnes' optimism in BA, Koblenz: R 13 I (VdESI)/155, pp. 43–44 (Hauptvorstand of November 14, 1918); cf. Feldman, "German Business between War and Revolution."

export preferences from the manufacturers of machines, not to say textiles, paper, leather, or chemicals. Before the war, the Central Association of German Industry (Centralverband deutscher Industrieller) had represented the interests of coal and steel producers, while the Industrialists' League (Bund der Industriellen) arose in competition to provide a voice for the finishing and export sectors and smaller firms in general. The Centralverband had fought for high tariffs and against unionization and social democracy; the Industrialists' League defended more moderate duties and some degree of collective bargaining. Members of the Centralverband affiliated themselves with the German Conservative Party and the National Liberals, where they reinforced the latter party's right wing. (After 1924, many of the same pool of industrialists, who had originally enlisted with the People's Party in 1918–1919, regrouped in the Nationalists.) Manufacturers in the light industries, on the other hand, did not feel at home among the prewar Conservatives. They gravitated toward the progressive wing of the National Liberals and sponsored reformist business associations such as the Hansa-Bund. Stresemann himself, who had begun his career in the beer trade and then became an official of the Association of Saxon Industry and of the Industrialists' League, spoke for his organizations when he tried to lead the prewar National Liberals toward accepting cautious social and political reform. Significantly, Stresemann had misgivings about the post–1918 prominence of heavy industry. The merger of the two industrial associations into the new Reichsverband der deutschen Industrie might be necessary as a counterweight to the Social Democrats' new hegemony. But there were disadvantages. Heavy industry was likely to be more vulnerable to socialization and costly labor demands, according to Stresemann. More generally, he feared that small manufacturers would lose influence to the right-wing Alfred Hugenberg, late of the Krupp firm and founder of a mass communications empire, or to Borsig, Stinnes, Felix Deutsch of AEG, or Carl Duisberg of the chemical industry.[114]

Stresemann was correct about the growing power of the industrial giants, but less accurate, as it turned out, in his view of their vulnerability. Heavy industry, in effect, was a government ally because of the very difficulties that the German economy was facing. The new Demobilization Office under Koeth, the old National Liberal State Secretary at the Treasury, Eugen Schiffer, who stayed on as a "nonpolitical" expert after November 9, and finally the SPD executive itself, all subordinated plans for collectivization to economic survival. The continuing Allied blockade, the approaching winter, and the sur-

---

[114] Stresemann to Bund der Industriellen, January 30, 1919, and March 31, 1919, in Stresemann Nachlass, GFM: 6818=114/3051/122925–926, and 122937.

render of railroad cars and other goods required by the Armistice terms inhibited drastic experimentation. The major preoccupation of the government became the recovery of exports to support the mark, pay for food, and absorb veterans into the labor market. In part intentionally, in part because of bureaucratic delay and the desire for thorough preliminary study, the new regime avoided quick nationalization. Faced with labor unrest and declining output, the government and union leadership exhorted workers to remain at their jobs with slogans such as "socialism means work." The cabinet approved an aid fund for Krupp and other industrialists who faced deconversion difficulties, removed the wartime price controls on metals, and lifted export restrictions.[115]

These actions favored the dual-market strategy of heavy industry, since they facilitated sales abroad and the maintenance of high prices at home. Over the objections of the manufacturing industries, Reichert, Stinnes, and Vögler explained that higher prices were needed to ration domestic sales and thus allow for exports. Exports for what end, however? On November 8, Reichert and others told the Economics Ministry that exports would strengthen the mark, but the Ruhr industrialists did not really share this objective.[116] Stinnes' interests diverged from government goals precisely in his need for continuing inflation. Depreciation of the mark facilitated exports, as the government wanted, but it meant shrinking tax revenues. Industry, meanwhile, could indulge in aggressive corporate expansion on borrowed money. Its leaders recognized their own stake in inflation: by 1920 its spokesmen boasted of having disgorged only 5 percent of their foreign-currency proceeds to the government, which had orginally stipulated that 40 percent of export returns be exchanged for marks. And as Reichert revealed to members of the Iron and Steel Industrialists later in 1920, the mark's temporary recovery was distressing exporters. Bourse insiders, the Reichsbank, and Reichert himself, however, predicted a reversal of the recent stabilization and further depreciation, making it foolish, therefore, to cease purchase of foreign currencies. Beginning in 1918, German industry was gambling on inflation and exports, while Berlin officials wanted exports precisely to strengthen the currency.[117]

[115] Matthias and Miller eds., *Die Regierung der Volksbeauftragten*, I, pp. 319–343 (cabinet session of December 12); Richter, *Gewerkschaften, Monopolkapital und Staat*, pp. 228–234, 282–296; Elben, *Das Problem der Kontinuität*, pp. 70–100; Hans Schieck, "Der Kampf um die deutsche Wirtschaftspolitik nach dem Novemberumsturz 1918" (Diss., Heidelberg, 1958), pp. 81 ff.

[116] See BA, Koblenz: R 13 I (VdESI)/189, pp. 3–5, "Aufzeichnung der . . . Verhandlungen über Aufhebung der Ausfuhrverbote," November 8, 1918.

[117] Reichert's statement on the 5 percent currency surrender in BA, Koblenz: R 13 I (VdESI)/158, pp. 64–65; and his advice against the mark, *ibid.*, R 13 I/194, memo of March 13, 1920. On mark dumping see the testimony from Paris of Raymond Philippe, *Le drame financier de 1924–1928* (Paris, 1931), p. 28, n. 1.

For those interested in economic policy, the question remains whether the government could really have stabilized the mark and maintained high employment. Was Stinnes' enrichment the price of high demand? A definite answer is precluded; any alternative policy, though, would have demanded more rigorous exchange control so that Berlin effectively tapped the foreign-currency proceeds exporters accumulated. The real point is that the Social Democratic government did not yet see the potential divergence of interests between heavy industry and national economic recovery. Preoccupied by the dilemmas of production, they overlooked those of equity and income distribution. This perspective derived in turn from the war experience, when the interests of their own working-class constituency and the interests of industry had often coincided, largely because of the effects of inflation. Only as inflation accelerated after 1920 did organized labor come to understand its contribution to the political power of heavy industry.

The cooperation that industrialists received from the new government in the fall of 1918 did not make their overall economic position a cheerful one. During the war, industry had enjoyed exceptional rewards. Firms had accumulated large reserves, even in real terms; prices paid by the Reich had been set to allow for rapid amortization of new investment; the halving of the mark's domestic value reduced debt burdens. But there were deconversion difficulties; markets had been lost abroad; industry faced what the pro-business *Kölnische Zeitung* called "the insane wage demands and extortions of the working classes."[118] Productivity did fall sharply in revolutionary Germany; between October 1918 and February 1919 coal output per worker dropped an average of 25 to 30 percent, as strikes and clashes with troops disorganized the coal fields. This followed an earlier 30 percent decline during the war, stemming in large part from the inability to renew equipment, the departure of experienced workers, and poor health and nutrition. Rather than hire extra workers to compensate for shorter working days and new shifts, industries curtailed production and banked their furnaces. Coal shortages and railroad difficulties further hurt the steel, textile, and chemical industries. For many entrepreneurs the first eight months after the war were frightening and costly.[119]

[118] *Kölnische Zeitung*, January 18, 1919, cited in *RFP:EPS*, 6, pp. 240–241. On the overall situation of industry, cf. Graebler, *The Cost of the War*, pp. 62–66, 70–71.

[119] Graebler, *The Cost of the War*, pp. 33–34, 70, 88. On productivity see also the mid-decade inquiry into economic conditions, the so-called Enquête-Ausschuss: Ausschuss zur Untersuchung der Erzeugungs- und Absatzbedingungen der deutschen Wirtschaft, IV. Unterausschuss, Bd. 2, *Die Arbeitsverhältnisse im Steinkohlenbergbau in den Jahren 1912 bis 1926* (Berlin, 1928), which concludes that no

By the summer of 1919, however, foreign demand soared, and the second half of the year saw both political stabilization and an orgy of exports.[120] Government commissions were still weighing some sort of socialization plans as of mid-1919, and eventual legalization of factory councils was now a written commitment. Nonetheless, major changes in ownership or management henceforth required legislative compromise among a Reichstag majority that comprised bourgeois as well as socialist representatives. Brought together reluctantly with the unions during wartime, heavy industry had learned that the collaboration legitimized a new thrust for interest-group power. No German businessmen would have chosen the revolution, but their collective influence gained from it. Too late to serve as a bourgeois revolution, too weak to become a socialist one, the reorientation of German politics in 1918 served as a corporatist revolution instead.

French commentators rarely failed to point out that the German penchant for organization was alien to their own traditions. The cliché was well founded, even though "total war" imposed economic and administrative centralization on both sides of the Rhine. Like their German counterparts, the big French metal producers did seek to organize and exert collective power. The Clemenceau government of 1917–1919 also sponsored industry-wide associations. But these efforts met indifference or resistance; moreover, French business as a whole was less willing to work with organized labor than German industry.

Both the aloofness toward the unions and the difficulty of organizing powerful industrial associations derived from an underlying discomfort with voluntary collective action. The French could not have arrived at a Stinnes-Legien agreement without the state's intervention. Throughout the postwar years, government agencies often sought more cohesiveness and aggressive interest-group policies for the sake of national economic performance against foreign competitors. Yet when industrialists organized, it was to ask authorities to wrest international advantages or to limit foreign and domestic competition.

---

single cause can be blamed for the fall in production. Cf. Bureau International du Travail, *Enquête sur la Production*, 4 vols. (Geneva, 1921–1922), with similar conclusions, esp. for France.

[120] See *Schmollers Jahrbuch für Gesetzgebung, Verwaltung und Volkswirtschaft im Deutschen Reiche*, 43 (Jena, 1919–1920), pp. 933 ff. No official export statistics were published until 1924. The French complained, and authoritative Germans conceded, that in view of reparation demands, German exports were consistently and deliberately underreported. In December 1919, Reichert estimated, however, that German monthly exports had reached 4 billion paper marks, imports only 1.5 billion. Cited in Richter, *Gewerkschaften, Monopolkapital und Staat*, p. 358.

Joint action was largely defensive, aimed at consolidating and harmoniously dividing existing markets rather than conquering new ones. The roster of associations was as impressive in France as in Germany, but their solidity and inner dynamic were less imposing.

Before 1914 the steel industry had organized *comptoirs* or joint marketing associations which set prices and assigned market quotas. Since 1864, the Comité des Forges, which grouped major steel industrialists, had also intervened to influence government tariff and social policies. The war gave its leaders new power and responsibility, as state agencies in charge of raw material and production sought out unified industrial authorities with which to deal, giving the Comité des Forges authority, for instance, to supervise sales of steel abroad and the purchase of coal in London.[121]

Meanwhile, the Comité des Forges formulated its own demands for the coming peace settlement through study groups under Humbert de Wendel, who with his brother François represented the major steel dynasty of Lorraine. Even these demands reflected the traditional defensive mentality of French industry. The Comité des Forges, it is true, asked for cession of the Saar and reannexation of Alsace-Lorraine and the transfer of Luxembourg from the German Customs Union to a new Union with Belgium. But these were more moderate objectives than the plans of German industrialists for further annexations in Briey and long-term domination of Belgium. Only a few individual iron magnates, such as Camille Cavallier of Pont-à-Mousson, wanted the Left Bank of the Rhine. The Comité's aims for long-term elimination of competition were more significant. Preoccupied about an "unprecedented crisis of overproduction" after hostilities ended, the Comité des Forges sought to prevent any postwar German incursion into French steel markets while securing free access of Lorraine goods back to traditional German purchasers. In fact, the minority reports of the war-aims study committee, written by Jean Schneider of the Schneider-Creusot firm in central France, called for a tax on each ton of raw iron or of "semiproducts" sent to Germany for processing.[122] Schneider's

---

[121] Henri Flu, *Les comptoirs métallurgiques d'après-guerre (1919–1922)* (Lyon, 1924), pp. 16–17, 38. On the background of French steel organization, see Rolf Bühler, *Die Roheisenkartelle in Frankreich. Ihre Entstehung, Entwicklung und Bedeutung von 1876 bis 1934* (Zurich, 1934), pp. 11–25, 67–100; Comité des Forges de France, *La sidérurgie française, 1864–1914* (Paris, 1921); Jacques Lapergue, *Les syndicats des producteurs en France* (Paris, 1925), pp. 130–139, 147–162, 197–204, 216–227.

[122] The Comité des Forges set up a special Peace Treaty Commission under Humbert de Wendel, August 19, 1915. (See Camille Cavallier's notes on the meeting of the Comité de Direction in PAM/6673.) For its report on the "future peace" see PAM/12119, which also contains the "Note de M. Schneider et C¹ᵉ pour la Commission de Direction du Comité des Forges," June 24, 1916. Wendel's

policy was evidently designed to offset the advantages of the Lorraine steel producers, who would otherwise benefit from nearby German customers; it would also place an implicit tariff on many of the German products competitive with Schneider engineering in France. The reasoning and mechanisms were typically defensive. Schneider did not win an export tax on raw iron. Given the strength of the Wendel interests, Schneider's suggestions were never adopted by the Comité des Forges. Industry did gain five years of duty-free entry for Lorraine and Saar products into Germany, and it won the right to incorporate the Saar economy into its own customs frontier for fifteen years, until a plebiscite would determine the political future of the autonomous territory. The French state acquired the German-Lorraine iron and steel concerns at bargain prices and transferred them to new French condominiums. Likewise French steel firms exploited Paris's economic hold to pool resources and to acquire seven of the nine major Saar steel firms. But they could never reconcile the implicit conflict of interests between their precarious Saar holdings and their permanent Lorraine acquisitions, and by mid-decade were willing to write off their Saar assets despite the foreign-policy reasons for keeping control.[123]

Secrecy enhanced the reputation of the Comité des Forges for great influence and power. Behind the walls of its headquarters at 7, rue de Madrid, however, there was often more division than coherence. The government was often to disregard its wishes, but likewise found

---

study commission emphasized the need to guarantee access for French metal exports to Germany, presumably by keeping a defeated Germany's tariffs down; it likewise expressed the urgency of Britain retaining her low-tariff policy. Schneider stressed the need to develop a French engineering industry and to keep iron and steel products out of the hands of the powerful German firms in competition. Wendel announced at the July 20 meeting that he had amended the original report to "mix" both solutions; in fact the Schneider proposal received only perfunctory attention (PAM/12122). For disagreements between steel men on the Rhine frontier, see the exchange of letters between Cavallier and Léopold Pralon of the Steelworks of Denain et d'Anzin, June 23 and 27, 1916, in PAM/12120. The Wendel commission's report on the "future peace" cited only recovery of Alsace-Lorraine and the Saar. It allowed vaguely that further extension of frontiers would simplify the economic problems raised by incorporating Alsace-Lorraine and the Saar, but did not seriously urge such annexations.

[123] See Chapter Three, n. 160; also: Bühler, *Die Roheisenkartelle*, pp. 130–138; Paul Berkenkopf, *Die Entwicklung und die Lage der lothringisch-luxemburgischen Grosseisenindustrie seit dem Weltkriege* (Jena, 1925), pp. 25–27, 57–65; Henry Laufenberger, *L'industrie sidérurgique de la Lorraine désannexée et la France* (Strasbourg, 1924), pp. 124–133, 136–143. The new condominiums were formed by large French iron and steel producers who pooled capital but held their acquisitions firm by firm. One group alone was formed by auto firms, smaller steel manufacturers and other iron consumers; on the other hand, the largest German-Lorraine property had been controlled by Wendel before the war and remained in its hands.

it a weak agent for carrying out the policies it would have liked to delegate. Probably the wartime situation of scarcity brought its influence to its height. By 1918 the Comité des Forges was administering a system of industry-wide levies and subsidies (*péréquation*) designed to equalize metal prices despite the differential costs for various producers. The organization continued briefly after the Armistice. To handle deconversion and reconstruction, steel producers wanted to rely on further self-regulation through their *comptoirs* and to avoid state control. Étienne Clémentel, Clemenceau's Minister of Commerce, and Louis Loucheur, his more remarkable Minister of Armaments and later of Reconstruction, also promoted schemes of industrial centralization. In touch with Loucheur, the Comité des Forges suggested new and more effective postwar *comptoirs*. The Minister of Armaments—himself a corporate financier who had organized electrical industries in the North—feared a postwar glut in the steel market, especially in view of the doubling of capacity that reannexed Lorraine would bring. Loucheur wanted a disciplined industry ready to compete in the export market, and was ready to use the Comité des Forges as his instrument in reorganization. But he did not offer the secure shelter for a traditionalist management at which the prewar associations had aimed. He decreed sharp price cuts for steel products; on the other hand, he promised equivalent decreases in the prices of government-supplied coal and coke, dangled subsidies for companies in need, and promised to absorb 80 percent of the losses on steel stocks manufactured before his retroactive price cuts. As a condition for the compensatory benefits, steel firms had to join the new marketing organizations he was helping to establish. For arbitration of intra-industry disputes, Loucheur planned a five-member commission with two representatives of the new *comptoirs* or the Comité des Forges. He encouraged a new hematite pig-iron *comptoir* and provided it with scarce coke for distribution among its own members. Similarly, he promised to provide the new Comptoir Sidérurgique, formed between December 1918 and January 1919, with a monopoly over all steel products sequestered in Lorraine. The Comité des Forges would have the authority to mediate among the divergent interests of different steel producers and consumers.[124]

[124] Flu, *Les comptoirs métallurgiques*, pp. 36–46, 50–56, 98 ff. Cf. also François de Wendel, President of the Comité des Forges, to Loucheur, December 21, 1918, confirming that to win lower iron prices, the government must reduce coke prices; give "allocations" through the newly formed Comptoir Sidérurgique to firms who could not, for reasons beyond their control, get prices down to desired levels; absorb 80 percent of the losses on inventory produced before November 11, 1918; restrict competitive imports from Alsace-Lorraine; and requisition metal products from German firms west of the Rhine. Loucheur's response of January

Loucheur thus sought to continue the collaboration of the steel industry with the state by deliberate reinforcement of the industry's large firms and strong associations—a monopoly strategy to preserve an international competitive position. Other industries and smaller producers naturally reacted suspiciously. Within a few months of Loucheur's initiatives, a major attack upon the Comité des Forges and the new *comptoirs* appeared in the press. In the Chamber of Deputies, the Socialist Barthe charged that the French Air Force had deliberately refrained from bombarding the Wendel ironworks in German-occupied Briey in order to protect the family's investment. A special committee of investigation decided that the indictment was groundless and declared that insufficient air power had spared the furnaces. Nonetheless, the charges increased public antagonism and stung the Secretary-General of the Comité des Forges, Robert Pinot, into a book-length defense of the group's wartime role. Not only the left, but small-scale industry resented the growing control of the large iron and steel firms. Loucheur retreated and withdrew his plan for permitting the new *comptoirs* to distribute the steel products taken in Lorraine. His new pig-iron *comptoir* had to dissolve provisionally in March 1919, and while it emerged again by the summer, it no longer possessed its original monopolistic powers.[125]

Without the lure of tangible privileges, the movement toward industrial reorganization lagged. In contrast to its cooperation with Loucheur, the Comité des Forges, for instance, remained lukewarm toward the initiatives of the other advocate of industrial federation, Étienne Clémentel. Clémentel was inspired by wartime cooperation to promote a nation-wide scheme of industrial self-regulation similar to the ideas of the planned economy current in Germany. Without the metaphysical underpinnings of Rathenau's "New Economy," Clémentel designed pyramids of interlocking associations based both upon regional bodies and industry-wide boards. The regional associations were to emanate from the local Chambers of Commerce, which enjoyed official public status in France. In Lille, for instance, a constituent meeting on March 1, 1919, organized the economic grouping of the North. Clémentel's representative explained that the regional bodies would serve first to arbitrate conflicting local interests and then

---

1, 1919, confirmed the last point and summoned a committee to work out particular allocations. For the general situation of the industry after the war: M. Brelet, *La crise de la métallurgie. La politique économique et sociale du Comité des Forges* (Paris, 1922).

[125] Cf. Flu, *Les comptoirs métallurgiques*, pp. 55–60; for the Barthe interpellation, see JOC, 1919, pp. 204 ff. (January 24), 350 ff. (January 31); for Pinot's defense, *Le Comité des Forges de France au service de la Nation* (Paris, 1919).

to counsel the government on local economic needs. In March Clémentel summoned representatives to constitute boards for the mining industry, light-metal manufacturing, chemicals, art and luxury trades. A group for heavy metallurgy was formed under François de Wendel and Robert Pinot. Both men disliked Clémentel's scheme but were determined not to let any new organization escape their control. By mid-April Clémentel convened the thirty-one "syndicates" thus formed to constitute a Fédération Nationale des Syndicats, which was to serve as a government advisory organ. Alongside the employer groups he planned to establish employee confederations by industry. Delegates of these associations would converge with the regionally based councils to form a Conseil National Economique—the French equivalent of the National Labor Chamber envisaged by planning enthusiasts across the Rhine. In the meantime, Clémentel grouped the business representatives into a Confédération Générale de la Production Française (CGPF).[126]

In reality, this represented an effort at corporatism without either carrot or stick, imposed on a business community deeply distrustful of collaboration. The National Economic Council remained a Radical Socialist project. But it was not instituted until the left came to power and even then remained feeble. The CGPF was inaugurated in 1919 but remained a loose and relatively unimportant grouping. Still, the move toward industrial concentration and away from individual competition, Clémentel felt, was taking place in all countries. His "syndical" federation represented a natural outgrowth of modern industrial concentration. His plans, he insisted, envisaged no administrative mechanism directed from above. Unfortunately, however, distrust of *étatisme* still pervaded the business community. "Too many remain indifferent," Clémentel noted ruefully, "to the advantages of collective effort."[127]

Indifference, if not indeed hostility, impeded Clémentel's organizational efforts. Smaller producers, first of all, clung to old attitudes even though their own trade and employers' associations had become significant during the years of labor unrest in the early years of the century. But enter the state and most businessmen reacted defensively; they wished to evade regulation and not systematize it, and they shared the opinion of *Le Temps* after the Armistice that wartime controls must be lifted, consortiums and monopolies had to be liqui-

---

[126] *JI*, March 8–9, 1919, for early organization; April 16, 1919, for the Fédération Nationale des Syndicats. The report of the March 1 meeting at Lille is in the annex to the minutes of March 17, *Archives de la Chambre de Commerce de Lille*, 54 (1919), pp. 94–101.
[127] Articles by Clémentel, in *JI*, April 25–28, 1919.

dated.[128] Second, the iron and steel firms that found tangible market benefits in Loucheur's corporatist schemes saw no equivalent rewards in Clémentel's bureaucratic structures. As in Germany, heavy industry did not want its own special relationship with government undercut by inclusion of consumers or light industries on joint planning boards. Heavy industry may have objected with the traditional arguments of *laissez-faire*; however, it was the terms of Clémentel's associational efforts, not the links with government *per se*, which dismayed them. Although the Union des Industries Métallurgiques et Minières (UIMM)—in effect, the arm of the Comité des Forges that dealt with social questions—participated in Clémentel's CGPF, rivalry continued between the two groups. Clémentel's schemes foundered on the mutual distrust of the forces he had hoped to group together.[129]

But even from the viewpoint of the state or public interest, his concept was flawed. The belief that one could hand over public economic regulation to industrial groups originally designed to protect only their own market quotas and security was a peculiar vision of 1919. It was possible only in the wake of a war that had temporarily made business devote full efforts to maximization of production and had facilitated cooperation by means of inflationary price and wage increases that could be passed along to the public. Neither the commitment to cooperation nor that to abundance was well rooted, however, in French entrepreneurial habits.[130]

The differences between French and German businessmen emerged even more strikingly on the labor question. Navigating in revolutionary currents, German industry found it opportune to work with the unions. There was less political need for such collaboration in France and more residual hostility to the workers' organizations. Nonetheless, there had to be some changes. As Robert Pinot wrote to the chairman of the UIMM in August 1917, the war was imbuing workers with a greater sense of their collective power. Mobilization, the relocation

[128] "Pour la libération totale," *Le Temps*, November 18, 1919.

[129] On the weakness of the CGPF and the reluctance of the UIMM to cooperate: Etienne Villey, *L'organisation professionnelle des employeurs en France* (Paris, 1923), esp. pp. 30, 42–46, 57–60; Brelet, *La crise de la métallurgie*, pp. 99–103, 155–164, 169 ff., 175 ff.; André François Poncet, *La vie et l'oeuvre de Robert Pinot* (Paris, 1927), pp. 260–262.

[130] Cf. David Landes, "French Business and the Businessman in Social and Cultural Analysis," in Edward M. Earle, ed., *Modern France* (Princeton, N.J., 1951), and Landes, "French Entrepreneurship and Industrial Growth in the Nineteenth Century," *Journal of Economic History*, 9, 1 (1949), pp. 45–61; Charles P. Kindleberger, *Economic Growth in France and Britain: 1851–1950* (New York, 1969), pp. 113–123; instructive on the limits of French organization is Gerd Hardach, "Französische Rüstungspolitik 1914–1918," Heinrich August Winkler, ed., *Organisierter Kapitalismus. Voraussetzungen und Anfänge* (Göttingen, 1974), pp. 111–113.

of factories, the draft-sheltered status of armaments workers, the favorable treatment conceded by the Minister of Armaments, and wage increases would all contribute to postwar collective strength. The lesson for Pinot was that French industry must organize its own forces more effectively to win its own concessions from the government. Pinot understood and accepted the terms of an impending interest-group competition; but few French businessmen looked forward to the idea of corporatist collaboration.[131]

The French debate over the eight-hour day in early 1919 revealed some of the differences between the situations in France and Germany. Labor had already secured this long-standing objective in various government enterprises before the war, and coal miners had won eight-hour contracts in 1913. Clemenceau personally supported the reform and felt that delaying it would only radicalize the working class, especially when German labor achieved it in November 1918, and Italian workers in February 1919.[132]

As was the case in Germany, the eight-hour day came to France as the result more of wartime collaboration than of conflict. By the time the Confederation of Labor (CGT) threatened militant action in 1919, it had already won other important rights. Government agencies now required collective bargaining procedures of their suppliers—a practice legally sanctioned (though not required) for all industry by legislation of March 1919. Those industries labeled as essential to national defense during the war had had to introduce compulsory arbitration along with parity committees of employers and management to work out disputes. SFIO members of the National Assembly had even joined in wartime cabinets. The political and economic trends naturally aroused conservative uneasiness—demonstrated, for instance, when the allegedly "defeatist" Minister of the Interior, Louis Malvy, was reproached in his wartime trial for having favored workers over employers in industrial disputes. Government guidelines to establish grievance committees and workers' delegates within factories met fragmentary resistance in Rouen, Rennes, Le Mans, Tours, and else-

[131] Robert Pinot to the President of the UIMM, Humbert de Wendel, August 23, 1917, in PAM/7385, f. "UIMM."

[132] General J. Mordacq, Le Ministère Clemenceau, journal d'un témoin, 4 vols. (Paris, 1931), III, pp. 252–253. On the pressure for the law, see André François Poncet and Emile Mireaux, La France et les huit heures (Paris, 1922), pp. 7–30; Gabriel Guyot, La loi des huit heures en France et ses conséquences économiques (Paris, 1922), pp. 11–16; also William Oualid and Charles Picquenard, Salaires et tariffes, conventions collectives et grèves: la politique du Ministère de l'Armement (Paris and New Haven, 1928), pp. 277–319, 413ff.; Roger Picard, Le mouvement syndical durant la guerre (Paris and New Haven, 1927), pp. 102–104, 118–138; Pierre Laroque, Les rapports entre patrons et ouvriers (Paris, 1938), pp. 282–295.

where. But opposition was unavailing, and labor had gained potentially important rights.[133]

Winning the eight-hour day would climax labor's gains and reward its wartime cooperation; it would also help the union leadership to reunite radicals and reformists within their movement. The staunch *Union Sacrée* socialists, Renaudel and Thomas, introduced eight-hour legislation in late January 1919; and the government sent the bill, not to the customary Chamber commission, but to a committee of workers and employers' delegates already established to discuss the international agreements on labor that might be written into the Paris peace settlement. In fact, there was no serious resistance; the parallel steps taken abroad and the anxiety about blunting "bolshevik" propaganda made ratification inevitable. What remained, as the influential *Journée Industrielle* conceded in mid-February, was the "question, albeit an important one, of the mode and delay in application."[134]

Public argument centered upon the costs in terms of productivity, especially in view of the losses France had suffered in the war. The Paris Chamber of Commerce and the Comité Central des Houillères de France—the major coal owners' association—predicted ruinous falls in output and higher prices.[135] The industrial representatives on the commission agreed: they foresaw a fall in productivity of 30 percent and warned that shortages of coal and the predominantly small workshop organization of French industry precluded any significant compensation by mechanization. The businessmen threatened agricultural ruin as well, since farm areas would be depopulated to meet new urban employment demand. Industrial representatives hesitated, however, to oppose an international trend. They thus acquiesced in the commission's report and expressed hope that labor would allow the necessary exceptions in application. The two legislative chambers approved the bill by mid-April after minimal discussion.[136]

Heavy industry was more ready to deal with the unions. On the

---

[133] Picard, *Le mouvement syndical*, pp. 117, 129; Oualid and Picquenard, *Salaires et tariffes*, pp. 423, 435 ff. For an insight into the government's delicate treatment of labor, see Louis Loucheur's record of a conversation with Briand in Loucheur, *Carnets secrets, 1908–1932*, Jacques de Launey, ed. (Brussels and Paris, 1962), pp. 21–22.

[134] Jean Hardy, "Notre enquête sur les lois de huit heures," *JI*, February 19, 1919. Cf. François Poncet and Mireaux, *France et les huit heures*, pp. 10 ff.

[135] François Poncet and Mireaux, *France et les huit heures*, p. 19; *JI*, March 6, 1919.

[136] On the industrialists' attitude, see Picquenard's statement in Bureau International du Travail, *Enquête sur la production*, iv/2, pp. 767–769; for the protracted and inconclusive argument on productivity in the wake of eight-hour legislation, *Enquête*, ii/2 and iv/2, passim. On passage of the legislation, François Poncet and Mireaux, *France et les huit heures*, pp. 23–54; JOC, 1919, pp. 2018–2020 (April 16), 2029–2042, 2048–2060 (April 17).

eve of formal enactment the steel industry's UIMM signed its own collective eight-hour agreement with the metalworkers. Pinot, the Secretary of the UIMM as well as of the Comité des Forges, did not like the formal recognition of the union that a contract implied, nor was he happy about the eight-hour stipulation, but he wished above all to avoid governmental intervention in the bargaining process.[137]

As in Germany, real controversy over the eight-hour day would arise later, in 1921 and 1922, following economic recession and a political balance more favorable to the employers' viewpoint. The discontent of 1919, however, still testified to French business attitudes. Before legislative passage, and then again in late summer 1919, the *Journée Industrielle* pointedly surveyed the predictably hostile opinion on the opportuneness and practicality of the law. Occasional respondents blasted "socialist agitators and politicians," and the Lille Chamber of Commerce felt that the law revealed a new and unhealthy degree of CGT power in general. Most complained, however, only that the hour was badly chosen or the reform too sweeping and ultimately counterproductive.[138] Beneath the economic arguments lay a residue of bourgeois paternalism. Workers, it was claimed, would suffer most from the inflationary rise in prices resulting from the legislation. The two hours liberated daily could easily go to unworthy pursuits or, as Alexandre Ribot, Chairman of the Senate Commission to review the bill, suggested, to an "idleness contrary to health and life." The hostile columnist of the *Journée Industrielle* regretted that the worker merely created new and frivolous needs with his higher income: instead of improving his lodgings or food he bought a bicycle or went to the theatre. If the worker devoted his extra time to the cabaret, François Poncet asked when the question was revived later, would he have been rendered a service? With a few hours off from work, apparently, the French proletariat was subject to all the vices of the bourgeoisie.[139]

What the eight-hour controversy finally revealed was the strength,

[137] "Une date," *JI*, April 19, 1919; François Poncet, *Robert Pinot*, pp. 279–283; also *Le Temps*, April 21, 1919.

[138] For political complaints see the condemnation by the Rennes Chamber of Commerce and the statement of M. Bienaimé, President of the Syndicat des Industriels Français, in *JI*, February 25 and March 8, 1919; for complaints of inopportune timing: *Archives de la Chambre de Commerce de Lille*, 54 (1919), pp. 127–130; also those of St. Étienne's industrialists in *JI*, April 9, 1919. *JI*, August 30–31, 1919, felt compelled to deny that its press campaign was hostile to the reform.

[139] Ribot's concerns in Bureau International du Travail, *Enquête sur la production*, iv/2, p. 667. (Alcoholism, incidentally, dropped after 1919, *Enquête*, p. 675); the theatre and bicycle deplored by Pierre Moire in *JI*, June 25, 1919; the cabaret, by François Poncet and Mireaux, *France et les huit heures*, p. 2.

not the weakness of the French *patronat*. Neither in Italy nor Germany in 1919, did businessmen enjoy the freedom from other worries for so sustained a discussion about working time. In Italy the issue aroused little apparent concern in view of general strikes, agrarian unrest, and political violence. In Germany businessmen protested, but in general leading industrialists accepted the eight hours as a dike upon which the radical tide could break. By 1922, the issue would arouse German entrepreneurs more than the French; but for the moment the Germans were anxious more about factory councils and nationalization. In France these seemed remote perils. Although the government had authorized factory delegates in 1917, the system soon fell into desuetude, and even during the war the cabinet sharply curtailed any claims by the delegates to speak collegially for their plant as a whole. They were to serve only as individual shop stewards for their own workshops.[140]

The prevailing security of French business groups showed up, too, in the diversity of their economic complaints. These revealed a host of small and often local resentments but few overriding issues: raw materials were too expensive; railroad service was insufficient, especially in the North where barge transport had been cut back by wartime destruction. Northern business, too, had special concerns about reparation for damages. They disliked the projected system of evaluating compensation due for confiscated inventories. Lille asked for special exemptions in application of the eight-hour law; Roubaix woolen manufacturers complained that clothing manufacturers were buying finished wool abroad, whereas by importing half the amount of raw wool, France's own wool finishers could produce the same amount and get needed orders. Industrialists in the North condemned Lyon's desire to export silk; Lyon's Chamber of Commerce wanted early restoration of trade with Germany and blamed the *vie chère* on import duties. Marseilles merchants demanded suppression of the luxury tax; Northern ones wanted it preserved. When Loucheur visited the Nord in August 1919 he was to hear a whole requisitory of complaints against the government: railroad inadequacies, "a wave of inertia on the part of the working class," abuses of the dole, high coal prices, and a worsening transport crisis.[141]

---

[140] Oualid and Picquenard, *Salaires et tariffes*, pp. 431–435, 440, 502–509; Laroque, *Les rapports entre patrons et ouvriers* (Paris, 1938), pp. 300 ff.

[141] For these complaints, see the *Archives de la Chambre de Commerce de Lille*, 54 (1919), as follows: meeting of January 17, 1919, on evaluation of damages, pp. 25–27 (this issue dragged on and on); March 21, on the eight-hour day, pp. 127–130; June 20 on taxes, pp. 290–292; August 6, coal question and Loucheur visit, pp. 411 ff.; complaints on linen exports, pp. 487–488, 510–511, 620–621, 634–636. Coal complaints again in January 1920 in *Archives de la*

What the economic laments revealed was a chafing discontent with the shortages and restrictions of the wartime economy and wartime losses. Actually, the general situation for 1919 was relatively satisfactory by contrast with the shortages and strains of the war; gradual demobilization, departure of foreign workers, organization of reconstruction, all eased the threat of unemployment, which by the end of 1919 was no worse than at the outbreak of war.[142] But collective discipline, naturally, was strained. The sociologist Lévy-Bruhl pointed to a general European reaction toward self-interest after the exertions of war had ceased. Speculation by the wealthy, "laziness" on the part of the workers, he felt, indicated a general traumatic response; and he compared the phenomenon with the aftermath of the plagues or the Thirty Years War.[143] But in Germany self-interest suggested the formation of new pressure groups and collective accommodation with other social forces, whereas in France the absence of an overriding revolutionary danger allowed more traditional responses and a concern with scattered economic complaints. Unless the government held out concrete incentives, businessmen pursued their own private causes.

The differences between the French and German response was further disclosed in fiscal questions and tax complaints. No business group anywhere was happy with the steeper taxes introduced in wartime, and especially not in France, where the progressive income tax with a tax declaration under oath had been finally introduced.[144] Writing as "Custos" in the conservative *Echo de Paris*, François-Marsal of the Banque de l'Union Parisienne, later Finance Minister under Millerand, praised the old taxes based on "external signs" of wealth as a fiscal system in line "with the necessities of the situation, the habit—we will even say prejudices—of Frenchmen, which necessitates as little contact as possible between citizen and treasury," and condemned the progressive income tax: "Any measure which has the effect of ranging citizens in classes, of establishing differential treat-

Chambre de Commerce de Lille, 55 (1920), pp. 40–41, etc. Also, cf. "Le cri d'alarme du Nord," *JI*, March 25, 1919, for discouragement in the North. Lyon's desire for reopening of trade is in *Compte rendu des travaux de la Chambre de Commerce de Lyon* (1919), pp. 242–245, 521.

[142] Arthur Fontaine, *French Industry during the War* (New Haven, 1926), p. 90.

[143] See his letter to the Bureau International du Travail in *Enquête sur la production*, IV/2, pp. 44–46.

[144] For tax developments during the war and their limits: Robert M. Haig, *The Public Finances of Post-war France* (New York, 1929), pp. 5–41, 315 ff.; Martin Wolfe, *The French Franc between the Wars, 1919–1939* (New York, 1951); for a general treatment of the income surtax: Edgard Allix and Marcel Lecercle, *L'impôt sur le revenu*, 2 vols. (Paris, 1926); Germain Martin, *Les finances publiques de la France et la fortune privée (1914–1925)* (Paris, 1925), pp. 56–82.

ment based on money or birth . . . is a law in reaction against liberty and contrary to the fundamental principles on which French society rests."[145] But the French notoriously resorted to individual evasion, while the Germans opted for concealed tax forgiveness through inflation. The two responses reflect the differing social and economic structures into which business fitted in the respective societies. In Germany debt liquidation took place with the implicit connivance of heavy industry, which accepted inflation as a means of financing corporate expansion, creating an export premium, and avoiding real tax burdens. The fate of a wider middle-class constituency, which lived on fixed incomes and held its savings in government bonds, became unimportant in these calculations. In France, however, industrialists were bourgeois first and businessmen second; they saw themselves as savers and bondholders. Even the large entrepreneurs of France generally shared a conservatism about investment and expansion that marked middle-class attitudes in general. The structure and values of French industry were part of a greater bourgeois homogeneity than existed in Germany, and one based upon the expectation that the value of money would stay constant.[146]

Entrepreneurial styles in the two countries were a product both of the common behavior imposed by the logic of modern corporate enterprise and of deep cultural divergences. In France as well as Germany the notion of management—of the organization and leadership of an enterprise apart from its ownership—was encouraging new *patronal* attitudes. The self-consciousness of proprietorship, the desire to "remain master *chez soi*," central in the nineteenth century, yielded to a more functional view of enterprise. The nature of appropriate management might well be contested: some business leaders, in line with the new vogue of scientific management, stressed the mastery of organization; others inherited military or civil-service models and emphasized strong-willed decision making, a new *mystique des chefs*. Moreover, much of the old paternalism pervaded the new science of administration. Pinot and François Poncet, not industrialists but spokesmen for them, felt that industrial leaders must form a self-conscious elite, but they still looked to older theorists of paternalist re-

[145] Custos, "L'effort financier," *L'Echo de Paris*, April 25, 1919; "Le code fiscal," *L'Echo de Paris*, June 14, 1919; also François-Marsal, "Impôts réels ou impôts personnels," *RPP*, cii (January 1920), pp. 13–16; cf. Carl Shoup, *The Sales Tax in France* (New York, 1930), p. 13.

[146] Cf. Joseph Aynard, *La bourgeoisie française*, pp. 424 ff., 467 ff.; for day-to-day opinion on current monetary questions, see Marguerite Perrot, *La monnaie et l'opinion publique en France et Angleterre de 1924 à 1940* (Paris, 1955). Cf. Raphaël Georges-Lévy, *Finances de Paix*, i, *RDM* (January 15, 1919), pp. 421–422, for orthodox views.

sponsibility. Their elitism allowed for no conception of equality. None-theless, in the new elite, rationality and expertise, not ownership *per se*, were to be paramount values. When the workers refused to give in, when they supported "demagogic" agitators, the French saw the offense as one against an imperious rationality: *lèse majesté* became *lèse logique.*[147]

The new managerial class reacted similarly in Germany. Although old-fashioned authoritarian attitudes were to revive from 1924 to 1945, the logic of the corporation was evolving a more flexible leadership in both societies. Still, there were important differences. The Germans brought a model of civil service leadership into the factory: the state hierarchy legitimized the rankings of private enterprises. While French relationships did not allow for mingling between employers and work-ers or any other groups that stood on the different divides of the command structure, the German patterns allowed subordination and dependence to be noninvidious, visible, and even honorific. Employers could mingle more directly with their workers and take pride in their common sharing of productive efforts and imposed hardships. German industrialists could deal directly with union leaders and exclude the state; French attitudes remained and continue to remain far more rigid and hostile.[148]

Ultimately these contrasting approaches rested on different national attitudes toward authority and organization in general. French rivals would rather call in the impersonal and distant state than surrender authority to equals; the consequence was weak voluntary associations unless coercion or rewards were compelling. Associations that mediated between the individual and the sovereign traditionally appeared

[147] Discussions of management in Jean-Paul Palewski, *Le rôle du chef d'entre-prise* (Paris, 1924), p. 508; cf. Georges Rives, *La conception du chef d'entreprise d'après la méthode administrative* (Paris, 1924); and Robert Pinot, "Le chef dans la grande industrie," *Revue de France*, 1, 1 (1921), p. 116. For the persistence of older paternalist styles, see Camille Cavallier, *Notes économiques d'un métal-lurgiste* (Paris, 1921), pp. 44–45, on the *patron* as *père* and pp. 50–51, on factory solidarity. These attitudes remained mixed with newer ones: see Robert Pinot on Le Play, in "Les institutions sociales dans la grande industrie," *RPP*, cxviii (February 1924), pp. 235–237; and for the continuing influence of Le Play, Edouard Dolléans and Gerard Dehove, *Histoire du travail en France*, 2 vols. (Paris, 1955), ii, p. 19; also Laroque, *Les rapports entre patrons et ouvriers*, p. 321. For a study of entrepreneurial styles in the nineteenth century and how they might vary between newer and older industries, in this case linen and cotton, see: Jean Lambert-Dansette, *Quelques familles du patronat textile de Lille-Armentières* (Lille, 1954), esp. pp. 91–93, 740 ff.
[148] For styles of management in Germany, see Jürgen Kocka, "Industrielles Management: Konzeptionen und Modelle in Deutschland vor 1914," *Vierteljahr-esschrift für Sozial- und Wirtschaftsgeschichte*, 56, 3 (1969), pp. 332–372; and Kocka, *Unternehmensverwaltung und Angestelltenschaft am Beispiel Siemens 1847–1914* (Stuttgart, 1969).

factious or subversive. Only a minority strand of liberalism—running from Montesquieu to Tocqueville and then to the *progressiste* Waldeck-Rousseau—insisted on the value of intermediate bodies. Political and economic organizations, even in the celebrated law of associations of 1901, existed on the sufferance of the state. This discomfort with voluntary initiatives, the difficulty of sustaining effective associations, and the fear of conspiracy in any that did exist, inhibited business organization along with other group efforts.[149]

In Germany after 1890 the right of an organization to come together was less contested than its arrogation of quasipublic powers. While French law conceded groups the very right of existence, German public-law liberalism parceled out sovereign power, which remained indivisible in corresponding French concepts. In Germany, intermediate bodies from municipalities to student fraternities to the Officer Corps provided all-inclusive and publicly sanctioned solidarity. The organization and hierarchy imposed by the corporation was thus more acceptable; there still existed in fact a legacy of a former corporatism to be revived. Each group, moreover, sought its own profitable relationship with the state. In France that state was to be summoned as an arbiter only because men could not organize collectively unless they invoked higher authority; in Germany the state was the accepted supporter for any group—so long as one's competitors did not gain domination. Both systems produced characteristic bureaucratic dysfunctions or deformations. French organization was fragile and ephemeral: delegation of authority to agents or superiors was conditional at best. Within organizations there was vertical and horizontal fragmentation and rivalry. In Germany organizations were more cohesive; but there was a strong tendency for what was rational from the viewpoint of the association to take precedence over the ends rational from the perspective of the public interest. In short, French and German associational efforts offered a choice between stratification or satrapies.[150]

[149] For the considerations on organization, see Michel Crozier, *The Bureaucratic Phenomenon* (Chicago, 1964), esp. part 4; Jesse Pitts, "Continuity and Change in Bourgeois France," in Stanley Hoffmann et al., *In Search of France* (New York, 1965), esp. pp. 254 ff.; also François Bourricaud, "France," in Arnold M. Rose, ed., *The Institutions of Advanced Societies* (Minneapolis, 1958). For the liberal strain: Sorlin, *Waldeck-Rousseau*, pp. 208–214, 236–264; Rémond, *The Right-Wing in France*, pp. 99–124.

[150] For public-law liberalism see Heinrich Heffter, *Die deutsche Selbstverwaltung im 19. Jahrhundert. Geschichte der Ideen und Institutionen* (Stuttgart, 1950), esp. pp. 372–403 on Gneist; also Ruggiero, *The History of European Liberalism*, pp. 257–262. For the clash of private and public ends see Karl Mannheim on "functional" versus "substantial" rationality: *Man and Society in an Age of Reconstruction* (New York, 1954), pp. 53 ff., as applied in Feldman, *Army, Industry, and Labor in Germany*, p. 519.

These were traits of long duration; they can be illustrated by organizational responses throughout the two countries' modern history. Certainly, the behavior of business leaders in 1918–1919 confirmed their tenacity. French entrepreneurs sought to entrench themselves against labor and state regulations; the Germans sought to construct a new corporatism that eventually set the terms of Weimar politics. The initiative for creating an organized social "partner" originated with industry itself and produced the Arbeitsgemeinschaft. French industrialists accepted Loucheur's corporatist effort only when offered new monopolies, and they generally resisted the less rewarding schemes of Clémentel as well as any new overtures to the unions. (When really pressed by labor, as in 1936, entrepreneurs deferred action until the state could mediate the dispute and dictate the Matignon accords.)

Thus, while the French industrialists faced a lesser challenge than the Germans in the spring of 1919, they never seized so large an influence over public policy. They remained less articulated as a distinct interest group and less set apart from bourgeois France as a whole. The Third Republic did not have to confront so self-assertive a business interest as did Weimar. Its policy shifts remained more responsive to the moods of the fragmented electorate, and its parliament acted freer of interest-group determination (although it remained more heedful of local constituency pleas). Business and industry in France remained an interest of certain citizens, albeit powerful ones; business and industry in Germany became a dominating force within the regime.

The behavior of Italian industry does not require the same extended discussion here. Loosely organized in various associations from before the war, it played a growing collective role after the formation of the General Confederation of Italian Industry (the "Confindustria") in February 1919. Like the Reichsverband der deutschen Industrie, Confindustria grouped diverse industries and worked to augment the influence of the more powerful ones. But unlike Germany, there were no coherent party groupings that represented industrial interests in parliament. Industry gained institutional leverage in the political system only with the fascist reconstructing of the state (see Chapter Eight, part three). Also in contrast to Germany and France, there was no cohesive organization by type of industry: no Association of Iron or Steel Industrialists of consequence, nor a Comité des Forges. Instead firms were clustered together because of their credit dependencies upon particular large banks. Rivalry between the industrial nexus around the German-founded Banca Commerciale and that around the Banca di Sconto was intensive and involved jockeying for patronage and favors from successive ministries. But this search for subsidies represented an older type of lobbying, not the new corporatism.[151]

As in France and Germany, however, there was a divergence between the interests of heavy and light industry. Giolittian tariff policy and then the war fostered the hothouse growth of industrial giants: the steel companies Ansalso and Ilva, the chemical firms of Montecatini and Snia Viscosa, Pirelli rubber, and hydroelectric interests. Large industry knew how to exploit wartime and postwar inflation; the electrical industry, for instance, raised its corporate indebtedness from 58 percent of its equity in 1914 to 66 percent by the end of 1918 and 113 percent by the close of 1922.[152] The major high-cost steel firms, whose profit had depended upon tariffs and government orders, were in no hurry to remove wartime government controls, while smaller firms, commercial interests, and the export-oriented textile manufacturers echoed French pleas in their call for a return to *laissez-faire*. Luigi Einaudi, the *liberista* economic columnist for the *Corriere della Sera*, repeatedly attached restrictions and controls;[153] and at convocations in late November 1918 and January 1919, industrialists demanded the release of restricted war materials and an end to prohibitions on exports. In these attitudes they reflected the impatience with wartime intervention that characterized light industry throughout Europe.[154]

Ultimately, the political role of Italian industry remained limited

[151] Cf. Roland Sarti, *Fascism and the Industrial Leadership in Italy, 1919–1940* (Berkeley, Calif., 1971), pp. 7 ff. Mario Abrate, *La lotta sindacale nella industrializzazione in Italia 1906–1926* (Turin, 1967), pp. 31–61, and Valerio Castronovo, *Economia e società in Piemonte dall'unità al 1914* (Milan, 1969), pp. 325–352, both discuss Turin's organization. For the bank affiliations and their major role: Rosario Romeo, *Breve storia della grande industria in Italia* (Rocca San Casciano, 1963), pp. 67–71, 75–82; Franco Bonelli, *La crisi del 1907. Una tappa dello sviluppo industriale in Italia* (Turin, 1971), pp. 13 ff., 164–169, which stresses how central the state was for economic development.

[152] Alberto Caracciolo, "La crescita e la trasformazione della grande industria," pp. 219–236; Luigi Einaudi, *La condotta economica e gli effetti sociali della guerra italiana*, pp. 99–178; Eugenio Scalfari, *Storia segreta dell'industria elettrica* (Bari, 1963), pp. 40 ff., a leftist exposé in tone and approach but with helpful data.

[153] "I problemi urgenti del dopoguerra," *CdS*, November 16, 1918; also the pieces reproduced in Luigi Einaudi, *Chronache politiche e economiche di un trentennio*, v (Turin, 1961), pp. 360–367, 476–489. For a discussion of Einaudi's *liberismo*, see Ciampiero Carocci, *Giolitti e l'età giolittiana* (Turin, 1961), pp. 128–130; for the 1918–1919 clash with protectionist demands: Franco Catalano, *Potere economico e fascismo. La crisi del dopoguerra 1919–1921* (Milan, 1964), pp. 39–57.

[154] Report in *CdS*, November 27, 1918, and on the Bergamo meeting of January: Einaudi, "Licenziare i padreterni," *CdS*, February 1, 1919, now in Einaudi, *Chronache politiche e economiche*, v, pp. 47–49.

in the early postwar period because it had not yet learned to work coherently for unified goals. Smaller firms sought only an end to intervention, and the giants pursued their own private interests. Just as important, the great political contest underway in Italy did not seem to involve industrialists in their professional capacity, but rather in their role as members of the ruling class. Just as the French businessman was first a bourgeois, so most Italian economic leaders—with the exception of enthusiastic entrepreneurs and organizers, such as Ettore Conti of the electrical industry or Antonio Benni and Gino Olivetti of the Confindustria—reacted first as members of an elite that measured its security and status according to the yardsticks of traditional liberalism.[155] For the moment the sense of peril as a "ruling class" or as an elite was what remained the catalyst of social and political defense.

But could the Italian bourgeois prevail as a traditional elite? Everywhere the world war had undermined the distinctions that defined Europe's class society. At the same time, the war had enormously increased the opportunities for pressure-group strategy. Cartelization, the formation of interest groups, the partial integration of unions into a bargaining system had all started to emerge before 1914. But the war accelerated the trend and placed it under government sponsorship: the imperatives of assuring the flow of material to battle theaters, hence to command output and transport, to allocate scarce fuels and ores and credit, to impose regularity upon volatile markets, enormously favored the advance of corporatist political economics. Just as World War I helped complete the nineteenth-century politics of nationalities, so it was a key chapter in the rationalization of nineteenth-century capitalism. In August 1914, poets saw the gods of heroism and sacrifice unchained, but at their side were those of bureaucracy and interest groups. The challenge to elites, to the forces of order, or even of orderly change, was thus to utilize the opportunity to reassert their older social hegemony in the context of corporate capitalism, to use pluralist competition to regain political preeminence—in short, to work for old dominance under new conditions.

---

[155] For these leaders, see Abrate, *La lotta sindacale*, pp. 100–102, 456–460; Felice Guarneri, *Battaglie economiche tra le due grandi guerre*, 2 vols. (Milan, 1953), I, pp. 67–70; and Ettore Conti, *Dal taccuino di un borghese* (Milan, 1946), for the self-satisfied diary of the electrical magnate.

· 2 ·

POLITICS AMONG THE VICTORS:
ISSUES AND ELECTIONS
IN NOVEMBER 1919

For more than a generation, left and right, socialist and bourgeois bitterly condemned each other's international policies. Before 1914 the Second International met and debated general-strike strategies that would make it impossible to unleash war, while middle-class and conservative spokesmen discovered the elemental claims of the national community, the dangerous ambitions of their neighboring states, and the urgency of greater armament. Four years of warfare only made it more compelling for nationalists to justify the carnage. The Russian revolutions made it clear that the war was a wager for those in power, that defeat or mere exhaustion could destroy a regime. Ernst Troeltsch, the liberal German theologian and church historian, recognized in the aftermath that "from the military collapse at the front . . . resulted the collapse of our long undermined political system," while on the very day of triumph the French Ambassador in London, Paul Cambon, had written his brother Jules: "If we had been defeated our fate at home would have been terrible. Victory saves us within as without, but there will still be difficult moments to pass through."[1]

Cambon's warning of "difficult moments" suggests that no simple connection can be made between victory and stability, defeat and upheaval. The German defeat certainly helped topple a regime that had itself gambled on imposing a harsh conquest, but it did not overthrow capitalism. Conversely, Italy's final triumph could not in itself secure domestic stability. "Unless success be quick or, at all events, striking and clearly associated with the performance of the ruling stratum . . . ," Joseph Schumpeter later argued, "exhaustion, economic, physical and psychological may well produce, even in the case of victory, effects on the relative position of classes, groups and

---

[1] Ernst Troeltsch, *Spektator-Briefe. Aufsätze über die deutsche Revolution und die Weltpolitik, 1918/22* (Tübingen, 1924), p. 1; Paul Cambon, *Correspondance, 1870–1924*, 3 vols. (Paris, 1946), III, pp. 281–282; for the prewar socialist debates, see Milorad M. Drachkovitch, *Les socialismes français et allemand et le problème de la guerre, 1870–1914* (Geneva, 1953); also Richard Hostetter, "La questione della guerra nel Partito socialista francese," *Rivista Storica del Socialismo*, Nr. 10 (May–August 1960), pp. 357–389; Nr. 13/14 (May–December 1961), pp. 489–530; Nr. 20 (September–December 1963), pp. 433–465.

parties that do not differ from those of defeat."[2] As one of Salandra's adherents wrote his leader, "disintegration" and "decomposition" afflicted Italy even after the armistice: soldiers were singing anarchist anthems, while agitators were inciting to revolt. "After the victory! And if we had lost!"[3]

France and Italy really experienced sharply divergent outcomes despite their joint victory. True enough, Italian nationalists argued that their triumph was stolen, their victory "mutilated" at the Peace Conference because Rome did not win her Adriatic claims. This was a flawed perception: as Italian moderates pointed out, their country had won the fragmentation of her hereditary Habsburg foe, while France was left to face a resentful and united Germany.[4] Nationalist indignation, however, arose less from the disappointments at Paris than from social divisions at home. It represented a continuing reaction on the part of the right to the neutralism of the peasantry and working classes and to those Italian democrats who had accepted the war but renounced annexationism. French nationalism remained less fevered, because entry into the war was imposed and unanimously accepted, not manipulated and divisive. Her war effort, moreover, rested on a wealthier society with a bedrock of farm proprietors. Italian mobilization and conscription strained a semideveloped economy and wrenched into the field a land-starved, resentful, and bewildered peasantry. The final battlefield victory could not erase those structural differences.

These differences, moreover, contributed to the results of the parliamentary elections that took place simultaneously in each country a year after the Armistice. Renewal of the legislatures was overdue because of the war, and the tense wait for a new campaign dominated political calculations. Expectations diverged, however. Many Italian liberals, especially the active interventionists of the right, feared that resentment about the war, the surge of radicalism, and the emergence of a unified Catholic party would hurt them at the polls. French moderates and conservatives looked forward to a triumph over the left. In both

[2] Joseph Schumpeter, *Capitalism, Socialism and Democracy* [1943] (London, 1959), p. 354. For an emphasis on the interaction of defeat and unrest, see Arno J. Mayer, *Politics and Diplomacy of Peacemaking: Containment and Counterrevolution at Versailles, 1918–1919* (New York, 1967), and Mayer, *Political Origins of the New Diplomacy, 1917–1918* (New Haven, 1959); for a parallel argument in relation to World War II: Gabriel Kolko, *The Politics of War, 1943–1945* (New York, 1968), pp. 5–7, 428 ff.; and in general, Hannah Arendt, *On Revolution* (New York, 1965), pp. 5–11.

[3] Vincenzo Riccio to Salandra, December 15, 1918, in Lucera: Carte Salandra.

[4] *Corriere* attitudes in *RFP:APS*, 5, pp. 92, 169; also Alberto Albertini, *Vita di Luigi Albertini* (Rome, 1945), pp. 171–172; cf. Albertini to D'Annunzio, November 8, 1919 and to Gugliemo Emanuel, November 14, for the moralism and limits of non-annexationism, in Luigi Albertini, *Epistolario 1911–1926*, Ottavio Barié, ed., 4 vols. (Milan, 1968), pp. 1078, 1085.

nations, the results were to prove almost unprecedented—threatening the liberals' mastery of parliament at Rome, returning a conservative majority to Paris for the first time since the 1870's.

This meant that in France the voting confirmed a broad commitment to social conservatism and rough satisfaction with the outcome of the war. In Italy the results registered bourgeois disarray, division, and insecurity. Viewed comparatively, the elections prefigured the differing fate, not of each country's political elite, but of the rules by which they governed. The outcome suggested that defense of the bourgeois order was easy enough in a democratic France but perhaps impossible under the Italian liberal regime. What turned out to be at stake in the elections was not whether, but how the bourgeois forces might prevail: through votes or through violence.

Yet the elections brought no reversals that should not have been foreseen. They accurately reflected underlying political resentments and social concerns, which is one reason they reward study. It is also what liberal European statesmen claimed to desire. In both countries they had agreed to proportional representation, supposedly to allow each current of opinion to have a more effective voice. The electoral campaigns forced political leaders to feel out mass preoccupations and to articulate malaise. For middle-class voters there was resentment about inflation, sometimes about "radicals" who seemed to run down the war effort that had cost them sons or brothers, sometimes just about the fact that the same faces seemed always to run the system. Voters went to the polls in 1919 with mixed attitudes. On the one hand, they usually voted the slates that they traditionally had. They voted against the Church and the reactionaries, or against the Reds, or for the Republic or "decent" people. Despite the 1919 party realignments, the reactions of individual voters indicated that party choice was a traditional legacy, a choice of life style. Nonetheless, voters after the war seemed to have less patience for the rhetoric and ritual of the electoral process; they were sick of the clichés and the hacks. This reaction against politics was most likely to hurt the liberals of the center and left, the democrats and Radicals dependent upon the petit-bourgeois voters who had become the center of gravity of pre-1914 majorities. Now their supporters were less tolerant. Sensing this, skillful candidates shifted ground, exploited a harsher rhetoric of nationalism and antibolshevism, and sought to affiliate themselves with veterans' groups. (Similarly, working-class constituencies had become less patient with reformism and the praises of patient organizing, and their candidates became more stridently antibourgeois.) More significant than any ideological polarization was the new harshness and the

90

erosion of parliamentary courtesies. It would have been hard for the French wit who wrote *La république des camarades* a half-decade earlier to claim in 1919 that two deputies, one of whom was a revolutionary, had more in common than two revolutionaries one of whom was a deputy.[5] Both Italian and French elections, as the German and British ones had earlier, revealed the new impatience with the folklore of parliamentarism.

This impatience would add to the difficulties parliamentary government was to face throughout postwar Europe. Even if parliaments accurately reflected national divisions, they became less effective in resolving them. The coalitions that could win votes could not necessarily solve the grievances on which they had capitalized; during the 1920's majorities would become increasingly divided and unable to confront thorny economic and foreign-policy issues. This later futility suggests a further reason to examine the elections. It is precisely to illuminate the disjunction between campaign promise and coalition performance that the contests of 1919, and later those of 1924, merit attention. By contrasting the selection of programs and candidates with the subsequent parliamentary divisiveness, one may understand why parliaments fell gradually into eclipse and Europeans turned to more corporatist means of winning the consensus needed to govern.

Bourgeois Cohesion in France

By testing opinion in the wake of war and domestic unrest, the elections amounted to a referendum on the two-year political crisis that had gripped the warring countries since 1917. In that year, under the impetus of revolution in Russia and American intervention, the left had revived but failed to wrest decisive influence from the nationalist forces.[6] Despite the hope of democrats and Socialists for a negotiated settlement, there had been no real grounds for negotiations in the West in late 1917. The Austro-German offensive in Italy and the German Supreme Command's insistence on a harsh treaty with the Soviets undermined the Allied left once again.

[5] Robert de Jouvenel, *La république des camarades* (Paris, 1914), p. 17.

[6] For the effect of the Russian Revolution and American intervention, besides Mayer, *Political Origins of the New Diplomacy*, see Annie Kriegel, *Aux origines du communisme français, 1914–1920,* 2 vols. (Paris, 1964), I, pp. 54 ff.; German developments in Arthur Rosenberg, *Imperial Germany: The Birth of the German Republic, 1870–1918* (Boston, 1964), pp. 153 ff.; Klaus Epstein, *Matthias Erzberger and the Dilemma of German Democracy* (Princeton, N.J., 1959), pp. 153–213; cf. also Erich Matthias and Rudolf Morsey, eds., *Der Interfraktionelle Ausschuss: Quellen zur Geschichte des Parlamentarismus und der politischen Parteien,* I. Reihe, I (Düsseldorf, 1959), pp. xv–xxxix.

In France, the Assembly had entrusted power to Georges Clemenceau. Democratic representatives understood that the irascible "Jacobin" nationalist would rebuff the SFIO and left-wing Radical-Socialists, intimidate supposed "defeatists," and subdue parliament.[7] However, they despaired of any satisfactory alternative short of fighting for a clear military solution. Nationalists and conservatives welcomed the fragmentation of the left's 1914 electoral majority. By the end of the war the Radicals and center-left groups were reluctant to join the Socialists in an opposition stigmatized as antipatriotic and "soft" on Germany. At best they hoped for a return to the earlier parliamentary splintering that had allowed their own brokerage. Clemenceau, however, still basked in enough prestige from the victory and ruled firmly enough at home to preserve the support of center and right.[8]

What conservatives aspired to was the transformation of Clemenceau's personal mastery of parliament into a permanent majority of the right and center. They yearned for a nationalistic electoral campaign that would entrench, in the words of Le Temps, a republican "union" of all but "those on the right who dream of impossible monarchical restoration . . . those on the extreme left who dream only of overthrow." As it would signify throughout the 1920's, "union" thus meant a bourgeois coalition excluding not only the residues of Catholic traditionalism and monarchism on the far right, but the entire working-class representation on the left. As the year closed, Le Temps wistfully

[7] For the political implications of Clemenceau's accession, especially the concern with "defeatists": Georges Suarez, Clemenceau, 2 vols. (Paris, 1932), II, pp. 196 ff.; Jean J. H. Mordacq, Le ministère Clemenceau. Journal d'un témoin, 4 vols. (Paris, 1930–1931), I, pp. 49, 67–68; and the hostile Georges Michon, Clemenceau (Paris, 1931), pp. 168 ff.; on the antisocialist aspect, see Suarez, pp. 203–204; and Raymond Poincaré, Au service de la France, vol. IX, L'année trouble, 1917 (Paris, 1932), pp. 369–370. Clemenceau's status as political maverick was revealed by the continuing hostility of the far right up to his coming to power. See: L'Action Française, November 10, 1917, in RFP:APS, 3, p. 68; also Louis Marcellin, Politique et politiciens pendant la guerre, 3 vols. (Paris, 1923), II, pp. 217–221.

[8] For the confusion of the radical groups in the fall of 1918, see their vacillation over support for a resolution of the SFIO, CGT, and Ligue des Droits de l'Homme, indicting the right for trying to undermine Wilson's program: reported in "Avis aux républicains," Le Temps, October 28, 1918. For rightist accusations against the SFIO, see Serge de Chassin in L'Echo de Paris, November 17, 1918, p. 2; "Le parti de la paix sans victoire," Le Temps, October 4, 1918, and the editorials of October 8, "Une faute socialiste," October 12, "Contre la patrie," and October 13, "Les meneurs." Right-wing perception of potential opposition in Mordacq, Le ministère Clemenceau, III, pp. 52–53, 57–59; Marcellin, Politique et politiciens, III, p. 25; "L'agitation en faveur de Caillaux," L'Action Française, January 15, 1919. On Clemenceau's position at the end of the year, see the December 29 debate in the Chamber: JOC, 1918, pp. 3732 ff.; also Mayer, Politics and Diplomacy of Peacemaking, pp. 176–186.

eyed Lloyd George's Unionist and Liberal coalition trounce the dissenting left in the British coupon election.[9]

French elections, however, lay almost a year away, and initial *bien pensant* confidence dissipated before the domestic unrest and the wearying pace of the peace negotiations during the spring of 1919. "We are reaching the end of our civilization," the publisher of the respected *Journal des Débats* wrote privately, "and we are going to be destroyed not by the barbarians without but by those within."[10] As the Soviets seized power in Hungary and Bavaria in April, conservative spokesmen lost confidence that bolshevism would remain quarantined among the defeated peoples. "What value has the system of *cordon sanitaire*," asked *Le Temps*, "now that bolshevism is in Budapest?"[11] And after these revolutionary experiments collapsed, nationalists remained unhappy about the preliminary peace terms; Pertinax and Jacques Bainville pointed out that Germany would carry out the clauses only if subjected to perpetual compulsion, whereas France was protected only by limited occupation rights and ill-defined alliances.[12]

[9] "L'unité nationale," *Le Temps*, November 22, 1918, for republican union; satisfaction that a grouping of *modéré* forces had been formed in the Chamber in *Le Temps*, December 24, and "L'entente républicaine," December 25, 1918. Celebration of the coupon election in *Le Temps*, December 29, 1918, and by Pertinax in *L'Echo de Paris*, December 29, 1918. The theme continued by Emile Dupuy, "Un parti national industriel en Angleterre," *JI*, May 3, 1919.

[10] Pierre Miquel, " 'Le Journal des Débats' et la Paix de Versailles," *Revue Historique*, CXXXII, 2 (1964), p. 397. Miquel's *La Paix de Versailles et l'opinion publique française* (Paris, 1972), traces in detail the press and parliament through the first half of 1919. For the earlier post-Armistice confidence that disorder was confined to Eastern Europe, see "Réalités," *Le Temps*, November 19, 1918; also Pertinax in the same day's *Echo de Paris*; Charles Benoist, "Chronique de la quinzaine," *RDM*, January 1, 1919; Jacques Bainville in *L'Action Française*, November 10, 13, and 14, 1918.

[11] "Bulletin de Jour," *Le Temps*, March 25, 1919; cf. *RFP:APS*, 5, pp. 487–488; Auguste Gauvain's commentary for *Le Journal des Débats* collected in Gauvain, *L'Europe au jour le jour*, vol. XIV (Paris, 1922); Bainville's comments on the alliance of German and Magyar nationalism with bolshevism in *L'Action Française*, March 20 and 25; for general depression with the Peace negotiations, Bainville: "La victoire mutilée," *L'Action Française*, April 4, 1919; and *RFP:APS*, V, pp. 511–512; detailed coverage of the spring crisis in Mayer, *Politics and Diplomacy of Peacemaking*, pp. 599–603 on the repercussions of Hungary, and pp. 660–661 for right-wing efforts to secure tangible claims from Clemenceau.

[12] See Bainville's epigram that the peace was "trop douce pour ce qu'elle a de dur," in *L'Action Française*, May 8, 1919; also Charles Benoist, "Chronique de la Quinzaine," *RDM*, June 1, 1919, p. 719. *Modéré* papers, however, supported Clemenceau: Miquel, " 'Le Journal des Débats,' " p. 406 and Miquel, *La paix de Versailles et l'opinion publique française*, pp. 401–412; Gauvain, *L'Europe au jour le jour*, XIV, pp. 179–180 (May 8, 1919); "Ce que la paix avec l'Allemagne assure à la France," *Le Temps*, May 9, 1919.

Anxiety about radicalism at home accompanied the evaporation of euphoria on foreign issues. Urban inflation, the acquittal of Jean Jaurès' 1914 assassin Villain, worked to embitter French labor. From March to June 1919, a new wave of strikes shook the country. Although May 1 did not bring the social conflict that had been feared, the strike movement of June remained preoccupying, as Parisian metalworkers, Métro employees, and miners in the Pas de Calais all participated in mass walkouts.[13]

Yet the real significance lay in the limits of the movement. The CGT and the national Federation of Metalworkers refused to endorse the work stoppages, and the protests moderated in late June. One further test was scheduled for a month thereafter—the international strike that would protest Allied intervention in Russia—but on the eve of that imposing demonstration the CGT decided that French support was lacking and canceled its participation. In terms of their duration, mass involvement, and militancy, the successive strikes were impressive and perhaps frightening challenges. But the months of agitation yielded little that had not already been conceded. And with the ebbing of proletarian protest, bourgeois opponents recovered their confidence. By July, they condemned the projected international strike as designed to aid the enemy. "Everywhere today," signaled a correspondent for *Le Temps*, "there is becoming manifest a live, growing need for order," while *La Journée Industrielle* drew the lesson: "The hour has come to cede no more."[14] This reaction had naturally to be nationalist. After examining the failure of Italian socialist demonstrations in April, Bainville had written that the Allies' firmest force against disorder was national sentiment and the fear of sacrificing the hard earnings of victory. In the summer of 1919, preparations began for the electoral exploitation of these sentiments: the propaganda of the Bloc National unremittingly stressed the linked dangers of bolshevism and appeasement of Germany.[15]

[13] For labor unrest after January 1919, see Edouard Dolléans, *Histoire du mouvement ouvrier*, 3 vols. (Paris, 1953), II, pp. 298 ff.; Kriegel, *Aux origines du communisme français*, I, pp. 297–298 ff.; Georges Lefranc, *Le mouvement socialiste sous la Troisième République (1875–1940)* (Paris, 1963), pp. 222–223; Mayer, *Politics and Diplomacy of Peacemaking*, pp. 662–671; for right-wing comment on the acquittal of Vaillant—all the more rankling to the left since the unsuccessful assassin of Clemenceau was initially sentenced to death—see *RFP:APS*, 5, pp. 512–513; for attacks on the June strikes: *Le Temps*, June 4, 8, 14; *L'Echo de Paris*, June 15, 1919.

[14] "Opinions de province," *Le Temps*, June 24, 1919; "Ne plus céder," *JI*, June 4, 1919; denunciations of the planned international strike, *Le Temps*, July 12, 13; for planning and failure of the strike, Mayer, *Politics and Diplomacy of Peacemaking*, pp. 853–873.

[15] "L'échec de la grève générale en Italie," *L'Action Française*, April 19, 1919.

The results of the French voting depended upon the alignments with which candidates and parties entered the campaign. French parties had emerged as organized forces in the first decade of the century, but they still lacked the clear affiliations and disciplined organization of either the British or German parties. On the left, the French socialists, who had merged into the SFIO in 1905, formed the most cohesive alignment. They ran as Socialists and used the SFIO label for their designation in the Chamber. On the right, the party umbrellas—the prewar Action Libérale of the Catholics, the conservative Union Républicaine Démocratique, and the right-center Alliance Démocratique—represented little more than electoral bureaus for getting together slates and channeling finances. In the Chamber and Senate their candidates registered themselves among a congeries of small "groups." The unofficial description of *modéré* for the non-Catholic, but economically conservative legislators provided as useful a guide to their place in the spectrum as the particular labels chosen. The Radical Socialist Party fell between the *modérés* and the Socialists both in terms of ideology and party structure. Its organization remained important between elections, and its candidates usually chose to sit with the "Radical Socialist" group in the Chamber. Nonetheless, decisions about how to run a campaign were made at the local level, not by the Paris headquarters on the Rue Valois. Radicalism connoted a trend as well as a party, and many deputies who ran vaguely as radicals in their constituencies registered with nondescript Chamber groups of the center-left rather than with the Radical Socialist Chamber group itself. The discrepancy between electoral label and parliamentary grouping varied all the more in the Senate, where deputies were elected indirectly by Chamber deputies, mayors, and departmental councils and tended to blend their ideological stance into a vague defense of republican principles.[16]

For reasons both of ideology and structure, the behavior of the Radicals was critical to the electoral outcome. Radical Socialists had achieved dominance of the political system as champions of republican anticlericalism when the country split over the Dreyfus Affair. They were the pivot of the left bloc in 1902 and 1905, allying with Socialists and those centrist *modérés* of the Alliance Démocratique who also

[16] For an anatomy of the parties, see Georges Bourgin and J. Carrère, *Manuel des partis politiques en France* (Paris, 1924), a handbook of all groups organized in the political arena; for a discussion of major political forces: André Siegfried, *Tableau des partis en France* (Paris, 1930); for the breakdown of divisions in the Chamber: Alain Bomier-Landowski, "Les groupes parlementaires de l'Assemblée Nationale et de la Chambre des Deputés de 1871 à 1940," in François Goguel and Georges Dupeux, eds., *Esquisse d'un bilan de sociologie électorale* (Paris, 1951), pp. 75–89.

campaigned for the lay state against the right. The rhetoric and memory of that crusade were never to leave them. But Radical Socialism could not maintain its clear thrust and purpose after separation of Church and State in 1905. As the left of the Party moved on to propose a graduated income tax and greater unionization rights for state employees, the more loosely affiliated Radical Socialists veered toward an independent radicalism that made them allies of the *modérés*. As noted in the preceding chapters, the clear left-right divisions of the turn of the century eroded in the 1910 elections as French politics resumed the trend toward "concentration" majorities: the grouping of the left-center (fiscally conservative Radicals) and right-center (*modérés*) against the Socialists and left-wing Radical Socialists on the one side, against the proclerical conservatives on the other. 1914 interrupted the trend again, because most Radicals sniffed a good electoral opportunity in running alongside the SFIO on the plank of reduced military service. Indeed the Radical Socialist group in the Chamber returned 185 strong out of 600; but the majority gave signs of fragility as war intervened.

From the viewpoint of the *modérés* in 1919, the Radicals' option was critical: if the Radicals remained in their 1914 opposition to the center and right, the secular *modérés* would be isolated and politics would remain mired in the obsolete anticlerical issues. If, however, the radicals could be brought into a broad moderate, nationalist coalition, then the campaign would isolate the Socialists and reaffirm economic stability. The choice of the Radicals would determine the ideological trends and party alignments for French conservatism.[17]

What proved critical for the political development of the coming years was that the choice was never finally made—neither by the Radicals nor by the right. The Radicals oscillated between participation in coalitions of bourgeois union—never failing meanwhile to invoke the traditional pieties of left republicanism—and alliances with the Socialists. Conservatives and *modérés* oscillated, too: between

[17] On the Radical Socialists, see Daniel Bardonnet, *L'évolution de la structure du Parti Radical* (Paris, 1960); Daniel Halévy, *La république des comités: essai d'histoire contemporaine (1895–1934)* (Paris, 1934); Peter J. Larmour, *The French Radical Party in the 1930's* (Stanford, Calif., 1964), pp. 17–77. On party ideas and Herriot's role, François de Tarr, *The French Radical Party from Herriot to Mendès-France* (London, 1961), pp. 1–61; cf. Albert Thibaudet, *La république des professeurs* (Paris, 1927), and Thibaudet, *Les idées politiques de la France* (Paris, 1932), pp. 147–178; for insights into radicalism outside Paris: Jacques Fourcade, *La république de la province* (Paris, 1936); also Jacques Kayser, "Le presse de province sous la IIIe République," *Revue Française de Science Politique*, v, 3 (1955), pp. 547–571, for an important element of local Radical influence.

broad bourgeois coalitions that sought Radical participation on common economic stands and more sectarian right-wing formations that
sought to keep the Radicals away from key cabinet positions and
usually thrust them into opposition alongside the SFIO. From the
outset, the 1919 Bloc National equivocated between the older, more
reactionary and the newer, pragmatic impulses. Antisocialism and
nationalism brought the Bloc National together; the pre-1914 issues
of church and regime and the pre-1914 alignments remained political
sirens, ready to draw the coalition toward crack-up and foundering.[18]

The electoral system itself enhanced the pivotal influence of the
Radical Socialists. Opponents of the old single-member constituencies
argued for proportional election in multimember districts to minimize
patronage and let minority currents find representation. Underlying
the proposal was the expectation that reform would favor the centrist
coalition advocated by moderates and conservatives and undercut
the Radicals. The old districts or *arrondissements* provided the institutional base of Radical power; Radical candidates could usually
qualify for the run-off elections and inherit all the non-Catholic votes
against the rightist candidate; their famous committees arbitrated
between the prefect, the city hall, and the Masonic lodge, exerting
what Péguy, for instance, termed a multi-Caesarism. Proportional representation in multimember districts would enable Socialists, conservatives, and *modérés* to capitalize on their minorities to a far greater
extent than in the single-member districts.[19]

More than any other major politician, Aristide Briand identified
himself with the cause of electoral reform, denouncing the "stagnant
pools" of the *arrondissements* as early as 1910. Briand wove electoral
reform into his whole prewar effort to supersede the split between
Radicals and the right, to dissolve the Bloc des Gauches and create a
new centrist majority based on conciliation of Catholics and opposition
to syndicalist activity. In the spring of 1919, when the electoral reform
that seemed requisite for providing the Bloc National with a safe
majority bogged down, Briand devoted to it a supreme oratorical

[18] The best guide to the political trends of the period remains François Goguel,
La politique des partis sous la Troisième République, 3rd ed. (Paris, 1958), pp.
164 ff. For coalition trends 1919–1924, see Frederick W. Wurzburg, "The
Politics of the Bloc National," Diss. (New York, 1961); and for the evolution
of the right from clerical to antisocialist formation: Malcolm Anderson, "The
Parliamentary Right in France, 1905–1919," Diss. (Oxford, 1961).

[19] For arguments on behalf of proportional representation before the war:
Georges Lachapelle, *Élections législatives des 24 avril et 10 mai 1914: Résultats
officiels* (Paris, 1914), pp. 13–33. The Péguy judgment on the Radicals is cited
in Bardonnet, *L'évolution . . . du Parti Radical*, p. 33.

effort that helped to push it through the Chamber despite Clemenceau's own skepticism.[20]

The electoral system that emerged, however, minimized the extent of true proportional representation. At the first stage of vote tallying in each new multimember constituency, the candidates of any list who were named upon a majority of the ballots were automatically elected. Since voters often supported all the members of a given list, a slate that captured a small majority might win all the departmental seats much as United States presidential electors take individual states. Proportional allotment was resorted to only if there was no initial majority. Rather than benefit small parties, the new system logically encouraged the construction of broad coalitions whose candidates could attract a majority and capture all of a department's seats.[21]

The need to compose broad electoral slates immediately raised the question as to whether Radical Socialists would run with candidates of the center and right. Negotiations in the large Paris voting districts initially indicated that a basis for coalition might be found, then dashed that hope. The Radical Socialist left remained in eclipse after the wartime trials of Caillaux and Malvy. By the spring of 1919, under the leadership of Edouard Herriot, the Radicals subscribed to a vague antibolshevik program with the Alliance Démocratique. They seemed inclined to enter a coalition on the basis of "neither reaction nor revolution." Herriot, former literary historian, then the genial mayor of Lyons, enjoyed business as well as popular support for the annual city trade fair he assiduously promoted. Though understanding little of economics, he was impressed with the wartime organization of French industry as well as with new American management methods: in his book of 1919, *Créer*, he became an advocate of technological education and government by experts. In the fall of 1918 he successfully steered his party away from collaboration with the SFIO or

[20] Briand's speech, JOC, 1919, pp. 1389–91 (March 21); 1910 call for electoral reform and religious conciliation discussed in Georges Suarez, *Briand. Sa vie. Son oeuvre*, 6 vols. (Paris, 1938–1952), II, pp. 240 ff. Clemenceau's views in Georges Wormser, *La république de Clemenceau* (Paris, 1961), pp. 363–367.

[21] For a thorough explanation see Georges Lachapelle, *Élections législatives du 16 novembre 1919* (Paris, 1920), pp. 9–38. In brief: a voter in any district could name as many candidates as there were seats to fill. Candidates whose names appeared on a majority of valid ballots in the district were declared elected. Thus majorities, where accorded at all, usually went to all members of a list. But unlike the system in Germany, French rules allowed voters to choose candidates from different parties. When no majority list emerged and seats were then allocated proportionally, this popular ranking—and not the dictates of party headquarters—determined which candidates of a given list were elected. The "proportional" division of seats was carried out according to each slate's average vote per candidate. But the final calculations often decided one or even two seats per district by disproportional razor-thin margins.

CGT.[22] By late October 1919, encouraged by the businessmen's association affiliated with the Radical Socialists, the Comité Mascuraud, he reached agreement with the Alliance Démocratique on an electoral list. The electoral pact, however, stressed the formula of "absolute secularism," which appeased Radical Socialist consciences but offended Catholic ones. By the time Jacques Piou of the Action Libérale framed a compromise acceptable to Catholics, the Radicals had second thoughts and disavowed the original agreement, although outside Paris some Radicals pushed ahead with "union" lists on the basis of the October program.[23]

Old religious divisions rankled even when proclerical candidates dropped their most troublesome demand for a proportional Catholic share of state school funds. Denys Cochin rebuked the nationalist writer and deputy Maurice Barrès for his electoral alliance in the second Paris sector with ex-socialist Alexander Millerand and the equivocal position on Catholic school rights that it necessitated.[24] The Paris episcopate endorsed the union lists as preferable to separate clerical candidacies, which would split the right and "risk opening the doors to enemies of religion and the social order." But in the traditionalist West, right-wing Catholics either dominated the union lists or ran against them. Morbihan, the Vendée, the rural half of the Loire-Inférieure remained redoubts for Jean La Cour Grandmaison, Baudry d'Asson, and Tinguy de Pouët, palladins of the faith and monarchists by sentiment.[25]

Events in the Allier, north of the Auvergne, demonstrated how in rural areas old religious animosities conflicted with the priorities of a

[22] Edouard Herriot, *Créer*, 2 vols. (Paris, 1919), I, pp. 448–468, II, pp. 73 ff., 335; cf. Herriot, *Lyon pendant la Guerre* (Paris, 1924?); Michel Soulié, *La vie politique d'Edouard Herriot* (Paris, 1962), pp. 57–60.

[23] Robert Cornilleau, *Du bloc national au front populaire*, vol. I, *1919–1924* (Paris, 1939), pp. 19–20, 29–30; "L'hymne à l'union," *Le Temps*, October 25, 1919; on the components of the Bloc National, Bourgin et al., *Manuel des partis politiques*, pp. 54–56. For leading ideas of the Bloc National, see Edouard Soulier, *Le Bloc National Républicain* (Paris, 1924). Cornilleau was a Catholic democrat, Soulier a Protestant pastor.

[24] Diary notations in Maurice Barrès, *Mes cahiers*, vol. XII (Paris, 1949), pp. 178 ff., 188 ff., 198 ff., letters to Millerand, October 26 and 31, *ibid.*, pp. 325–329. Cochin to Barrès, September 19, *ibid.*, p. 321, and late October, pp. 331–332; also to Briand in Suarez, *Briand*, V, p. 50. Cf. "Pourquoi et comment nous faisons le Bloc National," *L'Echo de Paris*, November 8, 1919; and Raoul Persil, *Alexandre Millerand* (Paris, 1949), pp. 117–121.

[25] See Cardinal Amette, "Il faut voter et bien voter," *L'Echo de Paris*, November 9, 1919. *La Croix*, however, had to be rebuked by *Le Temps*, October 30, for its insistence that anticlericalism and not socialism remained the supreme danger. For conservative planks see: Chambre des Deputés, *Programmes, professions de foi et engagements électoraux de 1919* (Paris, 1920), pp. 469–471; 579, 911 ff. This volume, listing candidates, platforms, and results, and the equivalent for each election, were commonly cited as "Barodet."

broad antisocialist coalition. The local Radical senator, Albert Peyronnet, understood that under the new voting system the Allier's Radicals could not prevail in isolation. After winning the agreement of
centrist and right-wing leaders for a common list, he had then to
eliminate any conspicuous conservatives so that his usual Radical
Socialist voters would accept the slate. A place had to be reserved for
the local head of the Association Générale des Mutilés de Guerre,
while prudence dictated nominating an apolitical peasant respected
for his farm output rather than a wealthy and conservative landowner.
The local bishop, however, still threatened to sponsor a competing
conservative list if the Radicals did not drop their affirmation of the
regime's laic laws. Only the prefect, who was overseeing Peyronnet's
"electoral cuisine," could impose a compromise formula that substituted the term "republican laws" for "laic laws" so that Peyronnet
could finally muster his united list and carry the department.[26]

The vague call for "union" suggested right-wing concerns newer
than a reconciliation with Catholic sentiment. The 1919 Bloc National
often manifested a new impatience with the ritual parliamentarism of
the "Radicals' Republic." While the left's fear of Bonapartism exaggerated the sentiment, in 1919 many felt that victory was the proof
of military discipline, industrial organization, and the hard domination of a Clemenceau, not the oratory and mediation of the old ministerial class as represented, say, by Briand. Millerand was a good
representative of the new mood, and in many ways he typified the
thrust of the electoral coalition. In his campaign address at the Ba-ta-
clan theater, the deputy who two decades earlier had shocked the
socialist movement by joining a bourgeois government, now offended
the pieties of the republican left by asking that the French President
resume his abandoned power of dissolving the Chamber if he disagreed with its politics.[27] Brusque and impatient with what he viewed
as the intrigues and posturing of an excessive parliamentarism, Millerand had confirmed his antipathies during his tenure as War Minister,
first under Poincaré in 1912 and again in 1915–1916, when he felt that
politically motivated questioning in the Chamber was undermining
military confidence.[28] Never a traditionalist or clerical, Millerand none-

[26] Lucien Lamoureux, "Souvenirs politiques, 1919–1940," microfilmed MS at the
Bibliothèque de Documentation Internationale Contemporaine, pp. 465–486.
Other reminiscences in Paul Reynaud, *Mémoires*, vol. i, *Venu de ma montagne*
(Paris, 1960), pp. 130–133.

[27] Alexandre Millerand, *Union républicaine, sociale et nationale (Discours du
7 novembre 1919)* (Paris, 1919).

[28] Alexandre Millerand, "Mes souvenirs (1859–1941)," MS in possession of
Jacques Millerand, pp. 73–74.

theless celebrated virtues that under the Third Republic made conservative alignments natural: personal loyalty, leadership, firmness, a rigid notion of overriding national interest. Clemenceau exerted authority but scorned the orthodox right; Millerand accepted his supporters where he found them. Demanding authority in a system that confused authority and authoritarianism, Millerand gravitated toward rightist alignments. Even the old conservative Denys Cochin thought that a victory for Millerand's ideas in 1919 would mean "a perpetual 16th of May," a reference to the 1877 crisis when President MacMahon had dissolved and sought to cow the parliament.[29]

Millerand's demand for the restoration of the executive power last exercised by MacMahon touched a receptive nerve in 1919. Even those on the left celebrated expertise and technocratic leadership. On the right, Ernest Letailleur—Lysis, as he called himself—advocated a corporatist scheme he labeled La Démocratie Nouvelle: his Paris campaign attacked the political class as parasitic and, foreshadowing Poujade, he sloganeered, "Don't vote the incumbents." Paris did not answer Lysis' appeal, and La Démocratie Nouvelle went down to clear defeat.[30] Nor did the monarchist and authoritarian Action Française, which entered electoral competition for the first time, fare much better. Only Léon Daudet squeaked through with a seat, more because of his wartime denunciations of the enemy within than his sponsorship by Action Française. Here and there in the provinces the strident tone that Lysis established found an echo, sometimes from splinter candidates on the right, sometimes from local Bloc National slates themselves. As in other European countries, there was a residual anti-parliamentarism in 1919, but it reflected a war-born impatience with the *république des camarades*, a vague desire to end talk and institute business-like administration or an engineering efficiency rather than any commitment to archaic reactions. As such it could be accommodated within the Bloc National lists.[31]

[29] Cited, Suarez, *Briand*, vol. v, p. 50.

[30] Editorial of "La démocratie nouvelle," *La Presse de Paris*, November 12, a.m., p. 4. The *Presse de Paris* was a cooperative paper put out by the nonsocialist press during the newspaper strike of November 1919. On Lysis' organization see Bourgin et al., *Manuel des partis politiques*, pp. 95–97; also Lysis, *La démocratie nouvelle* (Paris, 1919); and on the technocratic appeal in 1919 my article: "Between Taylorism and Technocracy: European Ideologies and the Vision of Industrial Productivity in the 1920's," *Journal of Contemporary History*, 5, 2 (1970), pp. 38–39.

[31] For Daudet's campaign: Eugen Weber, *L'Action Française* (Stanford, Calif., 1962), pp. 127–129; also Daudet's article in *La Presse de Paris*, November 13, a.m., and for wartime stands: Léon Daudet, *La guerre totale* (Paris, 1918); *Le poignard dans le dos; notes sur l'affaire Malvy* (Paris, 1918). For authoritarian platforms outside Paris, see, for example, the Liste d'Union Républicaine et de Défense des Interêts Économiques in Indre-et-Loire, *Programmes, professions*

The majority of "union" slates in 1919 had no real intention of contesting the ground rules of the regime, but they were harshly anti-socialist. In the belt around Paris—the fourth and largest electoral sector of the Department of the Seine—a union list headed by Maurice Bokanowski fought and defeated a major SFIO roster with a candidate-by-candidate denunciation of the Socialists' alleged bolshevism and pro-German sympathies.[32] In Meurthe-et-Moselle in Lorraine, Louis Marin and the steel magnate François de Wendel constructed a slate of modérés that was to be elected with an absolute majority. Marin was unyieldingly anti-German and highly conservative on all social issues—a professor of anthropology turned politician among representatives of heavy industry, to whose economic interests he lent his own reputation for diligence and rigid honesty. In themes typical of the Bloc National, Marin advocated neutrality on religious issues and political ostracism of "the bad Frenchmen who are excited by the folly of revolutionary internationalism, who can admire only a bloody and scurrilous bolshevism, who can extend mercy only to the Boche."[33] The anti-Marxist orchestration of the campaign elsewhere varied in volume but little in tone. In his major campaign speech at Strasbourg two weeks before the vote, Clemenceau, too, attacked the socialists by association. "Between Bolsheviks and good Frenchmen," he said curtly, "it is only a question of force."[34]

It was the antisocialist theme that attracted business support. The Union des Intérêts Économiques, a pressure group formed to distribute electoral funds from business to appropriate candidates, was proud of the posters that it placarded throughout the country, especially its notorious evocation of the primeval bearded bolshevik: "the man with the knife between his teeth." Other inspired efforts showed the tentacles of the octopus of state control squeezing economic health out of the nation's hard-working producers or a harassed businessman unable to complete a telephone call through nationalized switchboards. The President of the UIE, Senator Ernest Billiet, took pride in these efforts; the left excitedly pointed to the role of business's occult financ-

---

de foi . . . 1919, pp. 380–383, and on the general antiparliamentarism of 1919: André Siegfried, *Tableau des partis en France*, pp. 131–132.

[32] *Programmes, professions de foi . . . 1919*, pp. 827–831. For the socialist side of the campaign, L. O. Frossard, *De Jaurès à Léon Blum. Souvenirs d'un militant* (Paris, 1943), pp. 76–88.

[33] *Entente républicaine et union nationale de la Meurthe-et-Moselle*, vol. I, nr. 1 (November 11, 1919). [A local broadside issue for the campaign, now in the collection of Marin press materials held by Mme Louis Marin, Paris.]

[34] Georges Clemenceau, *Discours prononcé à Strasbourg le 4 novembre, 1919* (Paris, 1919); commentary in Wormser, *La république de Clemenceau*, pp. 366, 384.

ing. The issue was overrated. The UIE, which had been founded to campaign against the government's match monopoly in 1910 and thereafter combated wartime tax legislation, remained old-fashioned in its concerns. It denounced bolshevism, but bolshevism meant the progressive tax and state monopolies. The UIE did become more effective in the spring of 1919, when it organized propaganda banquets and sent each legislator a questionnaire on his stance toward the association's programs. The results were well publicized as a criterion of support in the upcoming campaign, but the responses were predictable from prior affiliation. Many of the Radicals could give a platonic assent.[35]

The strategy of the UIE and business donors in general was to support not the right but the center, and to remove the clerical conservatives who would detract from the defense of *laissez-faire*. The UIE claimed that its support was apolitical, although more sophisticated industrial spokesmen such as Robert Pinot conceded that "industrialists cannot be indifferent to legislative tasks, and they have the right as citizens, a right never contested, to intervene at the moment of elections."[36] It was the passion for secrecy more than the support itself that contributed to the aura of conspiracy. After the 1924 elections, the victorious Cartel des Gauches sought to probe into the UIE's activities, but the major funds were untraceable. Billiet distributed electoral moneys personally and never entered them in the books of his organization, which dealt only with the costs of his office. The railroad companies provided large subventions in 1924 and perhaps in 1919 as well. But this money, levied on a quota basis, came from the companies' "publicity" budget, which legally did not have to be made public. Moreover, the funds never went directly to political campaigns, but first to the "Association of Stockholders and Bondholders of French Railways." Of the ultimate destination the railroad companies entrusted with the original collection claimed ignorance.

[35] For Billiet's view of the UIE, see the group's paper, *Le Réveil économique*, December 7, 1919: "Without our provincial groups, and our tracts, our conferences, our writers, without our posters which struck the mass imagination, we could not have obtained these results." On 1919 activities cf. also: L'Union des Intérêts Économiques et Confédération des Groupements Commerciaux et Industriels de France, *Le programme économique et l'action électorale* (Paris, 1920), p. 4. This publication, with its proud confession of influence, contrasts with the booklet that followed the 1924 investigation of the group: *La vérité sur l'Union des Intérêts Économiques* (Paris, 1926). See also Bourgin et al., *Manuel des partis politiques*, pp. 214–222.

[36] "Procès-Verbaux de la Commission d'Enquête sur les conditions dans lesquelles le Comité de l'Union des Intérêts Économiques est intervenu dans la dernière campagne électorale, ainsi que sur l'origine des fonds ayant servi à tous les partis en 1924." *Journal Officiel, Impressions*, tome XXXII, nr. 2098 (Paris, 1925), pp. 175–176.

In 1924 at least a million francs were thus silently transferred by the railroads. Insurance firms also provided money in this roundabout manner. Pinot insisted that the Comité des Forges never gave money as a group to the UIE, but that in 1924, and presumably in 1919, he had transmitted some funds from private industrialists. "I acted as if I met you on the street and your arms being loaded with packages, you asked me to call a taxi."[37]

The question of finances remains murky. Throughout Europe businessmen gave money to candidates, often across the board. Sometimes it went to those who could logically be expected to serve their interests; sometimes even to the far left to draw votes away from liberal democrats who otherwise stood a good chance of election. But the actual sums often proved disappointing—far below the implications of those on the left, who saw conspiracy, and perhaps less, too, than the mass levies trade unions might provide for their favored candidates. Political venality in postwar continental Europe, it must finally be emphasized, was a universal fact of life. It was assumed that newspapers and candidates would be supported by those who benefited: the right drew sustenance from business at home; the left was aided occasionally by powers abroad. Occasionally this money might purchase political convictions; more often it paid for the propagation of those already held.

The results of 1919 can be explained without reference to business influence; they followed logically from the antagonisms sharpened since 1917 and the operation of the new electoral law. Superficially, the prewar leftist trend was sharply reversed. The number of *modéré* deputies doubled. Socialists and Radicals suffered heavy losses in their representation; but despite the fact that the campaign was directed primarily against the SFIO, the Socialist popular vote still rose slightly. This may have reflected the wartime trend toward further urbanization and factory production.

Precise statistical analysis of the returns is difficult, however, because of the change in the method of voting as well as the vagueness of many candidates' party affiliation. The voting system, with its reward to majority coalitions, disproportionately weighted the Chamber to the right. In addition, the right and right-center, as comprised by the Bloc National, already included a wider spectrum of opinion than the right in prior elections.[38] To say that the strength of the old right

[37] *Ibid.*, p. 178; and on the railroad funds see the testimony by Marcel Peschaud, Secretary-General of the Paris-Orleans Company, pp. 150–156.

[38] Results most easily accessible in Lachapelle, *Élections législatives du 16 novembre 1919*, who estimates that the new system attributed 70 votes more to the Bloc National than would have one of "integral" proportional representation.

increased is less accurate than to indicate that the new right-wing coalition became less sectarian and more inclusive—an important qualitative observation but one that confounds quantitative comparison. The expansion of the conservative vote in 1919 reflected a broad antisocialist commitment, not any inherent traditionalist feeling on older issues.

Even in this respect, however, the conservative success achieved in 1919 was less imposing than it appeared. A comparison with the voting of 1910 is revealing—more so than with 1914, for in 1910 the Radical Socialist Party suffered some of the same fragmentation it did in 1919, as many of its members gravitated toward more nationalist and socially conservative principles. The vote on the Three Years' Law of 1913 has been suggested as a test issue for dividing the 1910 Chamber into a left and an enlarged right plus center-right. The military bill is, indeed, a convenient touchstone; for it not only offers the same type of national issue as was tested in 1919, but also the same line of division. In 1913 the vote for the army bill was 339 to 223, while in 1919 the Bloc National majority represented about 425 out of 620.[39] If one made corrections for the skewed results caused by the majority provisions of the electoral law, Bloc National adherents would probably have been reduced to about 350. Hence the growth in nationalist and conservative tendencies in 1919 is less startling than is sometimes presented. To go beyond these rough observations and attain a more precise national comparison, though, is virtually impossible.

In those regions that are susceptible to closer analysis, the campaign choice made by the Radical Socialists was apparently the critical factor in the diverse outcomes. Surveying those departments that revealed some significant rightward shift since the 1910 and 1914 elections, one finds, for instance, significant gains for the right in both the Yonne and the Côte-d'Or. The change did not lie at the door of the SFIO. In the Yonne the Socialist Party fared badly in comparison with 1914, while in the Côte-d'Or the SFIO vote rose by 13 percent of the electorate. The Radicals' merger with the Union slate in the Côte-d'Or was evidently critical; the customary supporters of the Radicals probably split to left and right, permitting both the SFIO and the Union lists to increase. The patterns of abstentions, where these have been followed, also shows the importance that the alignment chosen

[39] François Goguel, *Géographie des élections françaises de 1870 à 1951* (Paris, 1952), pp. 42–43. Goguel's computations for the Chambers of 1919 and 1914 measure rightist strength according to how elected deputies voted on key issues in parliament *following* the campaigns and elections. This makes comparison with the results of 1919 even more difficult.

by the Radicals could have had upon the results. In 1919, abstentions both in the Côte-d'Or and the Nièvre were significantly larger than in earlier or subsequent elections and apparently derived from the left. Since at the same time the Socialist vote hardly fell off in the Nièvre and rose significantly in the Côte-d'Or, the abstainers appear to have been left-center democrats disgruntled by the Radical Socialist alliance with the right. Hence the Radicals' decision perhaps created a homeless left in 1919 as well as moving many voters to approve the Bloc National.[40]

Were there underlying social changes that prompted the migration of left-center to right-center, as reflected in the Radicals' shift of 1919 or the more general growth in some departments of moderate right-wing allegiances? In general the shifts were so small in raw percentages or so transient that an answer for more than local situations is impossible. In any case one must look to the country and not the city for *modéré* gains. In the Côte-d'Or, votes that migrated with the Radical cadres to the right in 1919 stayed on the right thereafter, while the SFIO grew to become the major force on the left. Rural depopulation and the enrichment of those who remained on the land, the decrease in small holdings and a proportional rise in larger ones underlay a switch to social conservatism.[41] The absence of extreme social differentiation and of a reactionary right, hence the related absence of strong clerical conflict, allowed this consolidation of a moderate conservatism. In contrast, those areas that had historically been sharply polarized, or where agriculture remained more backwards—the bastions of the West and the hilly Cévennes, the Alps, and the East—often retained older patterns of conservatism and conflict. In the Ardèche, for instance, north of the Cévennes, the principal battle of 1919 remained that between clerical right and radical republicans, and socialism appeared merely as an advanced form of radicalism. In the Ardèche—as in Brittany and elsewhere—the old struggle between *curé* and school teacher continued; in the Côte-d'Or and the wealthier agricultural districts, prosperous rural entrepreneurs took a step toward the right.[42]

[40] Raymond Long, *Les élections législatives en Côte-d'Or depuis 1870* (Paris, 1958), p. 177; J. Pataut, "Les abstentions aux élections législatives dans la Nièvre (1902–1951)," in *Nouvelles études de sociologie électorale*, François Goguel, ed. (Paris, 1954), pp. 58–59. Alain Lancelot, *L'abstentionnisme électoral en France* (Paris, 1967), pp. 16, 42, 55 on the rate (28.9%) and special circumstances of 1919. For a discussion of how the SFIO vote in each department correlated with the radicalism or moderation of the local party, see Kriegel, *Aux origines du communisme français*, vol. I, pp. 334–339.

[41] Long, *Élections en Côte-d'Or*, pp. 114 ff., 174–178, 218–220.

[42] André Siegfried, *Géographie électorale de l'Ardèche sous la IIIe République* (Paris, 1949), pp. 65 ff., 95 ff. Cf. the enduring divisions in the Sarthe: Paul

The success of the bourgeois conservative effort, that is, of the Bloc National, did not come from wooing socialist voters, for class political lines were refractory. Its major accomplishment was convincing the usually democratic left to shun the Radical Socialist Party for the lists of "union." The Radical Socialists lost about 100 seats, and most of these came from the left wing, which sat as the "Group of the Radical Socialist Party" in the Chamber and now fell from 185 to 72. The groups of the center—if one includes among them the 60-odd deputies of loose Radical affiliation who chose not to sit with the Radical Socialist groups—rose from about 155 to 180. The bulk of 1919's gains went to the right-center, which now added about 75 new members for a doubling of their 1914 contingent. The far right gathered about 25 to 30 seats. Insofar as party groups were concerned, the conservative Entente Républicaine emerged as the nucleus of the new Chamber majority, with over 180 members. Most of these were *modéré* republicans, but many nationalists and clericals (Action Libérale), who in the previous legislature had preserved their own party identities, now chose to join the large rightist republican phalanx.[43]

The trends reflected in this lopsided result were less profound than initially appeared. In the following week Frenchmen elected new city councils, and despite the exhortations of the moderate and conservative press, the voting reverted to the old pattern with its strong Radical Socialist representation. In their turn, the indirectly elected Councils General of the departments and the new Senate also remained un-

---

Bois, *Paysans de l'Ouest* (Paris, 1960), pp. 44–50; and for the conservatism of Brittany and the Breton Marches, the classic, André Siegfried, *Tableau politique de la France de l'Ouest sous la Troisième République* (Paris, 1913).

[43] As taken basically from the *RPP*, CI (December 1919), p. 427, the changes according to general political tendencies were as follows:

Political Grouping	1914	1919
Far right (Conservateurs and Libéraux in 1914)	69	100
Progressiste republicans	59	133
Moderate republicans, measured by either		
(a) Républicains de gauche and other center groups or	77 or	133 or
(b) the same, plus independent Radicals	162	200
Radicals, including independent Radicals or	257 or	153 or
Radical Socialists (per Chamber affiliation)	172	86
Republican socialists	36	33
Socialists	104	68

For Chamber-of-Deputies divisions: Bomier Landowski, "Les groupes parlementaires de l'Assemblée Nationale et de la Chambre de Députés," pp. 81–82. In 1920 the Chamber, from right to left, included 29 Independents, 21 *non-inscrits*, prevailingly conservative in outlook, 183 of the Entente Républicaine, 200 from three center groups, the largest being the 93-member Gauche Républicaine, 86 Radical Socialists, 26 Republican Socialists, and 68 members of the SFIO.

regenerate. Whereas the Senate had been a conservative buffer before 1919, for the next five years it would serve as a left one.[44]

There was to be a prevailing image of the 1919 Chamber as a virtual reincarnation of the 1871 monarchist assembly or even the 1814 *Chambre introuvable*, a reactionary surprise brought in the wake of war, and taking its epithet of "blue horizon" from the color of the uniforms that seemed to predominate.[45] The Radical Socialists of 1924 were happy to depict the 1919 majority as usurpers exploiting a devious electoral system. Yet more revealing of the real political significance of the Bloc National Chamber was the malaise later felt by members of the new majority about their incomplete achievements.[46] Many of the conservatives were new and young, often soldiers. Seeking to sweep away the cliques and patronage so woven into *la république des camarades*, they collided with the intractability of more tolerant parliamentary practices. But the primary uneasiness of the Bloc National members derived from the fact that the 1919 majority was not so united in reactionary purpose as Radical critics later portrayed it. Indeed, the tension between those who yearned for harsh right-wing policies—resistance to labor demands, concessions to the Church, nationalist independence in foreign policy—and the moderates who gravitated toward the old comfortable centrist coalitions and pragmatic compromises led to many of the misunderstandings between future ministries and the "majority of November 16." In 1919 the far right had to cooperate with the center to secure a moderate, conservative direction for the country as a whole. The price of victory was the dilution of reaction. Authoritarianism and clericalism still beckoned to individual members of the far right, but the Bloc itself imposed constraints on their politics. There could be no further questioning of the ground rules of a regime that had won the Great War lest the new majority completely fly apart. Nonetheless, there was tension enough between right and center to undermine cohesiveness.

The controversy over Theodore Steeg's appointment to the sensitive Ministry of the Interior revealed this tension from the outset. Millerand himself raised the bellwether issue of Radical Socialist participation in the ministries of the 1919 legislature. As was readily foreseen from his prominence in the campaign, Millerand was called upon to form a government after Clemenceau resigned as premier immediately following the frustration of his bid to become president

[44] *RPP*, cii (February 1920), pp. 322–323.

[45] "It was reactionary and clerical, it was passionate, it was without political experience . . . ," Lamoureux, "Souvenirs politiques," p. 506.

[46] See for instance, Societé d'Études et d'Informations Économiques, ed., *Le Bilan de la XIIᵉ Législature, 1919–1924* (Paris, 1924), pp. xv–xvi.

of the Republic. The prevailing tone of Millerand's cabinet was conservative, but the nomination of his friend Steeg, a moderate Senate Radical, demonstrated his autonomy. Millerand's commitment was to executive independence, not right-wing traditionalism; moreover, the Steeg appointment demonstrated his commitment to an above-party "republican union."[47] Since the Radicals still remained crucial to the Senate majority, the appointment also represented a measure of political prudence. But the right had not won the elections to reward their old opponents, and Léon Daudet launched a fierce attack upon Steeg, which he apparently hoped would lead to Millerand's abandoning the nomination. The 180-strong Entente Républicaine also chose to abstain on the initial vote of confidence for the members of the new cabinet, although it did endorse Millerand's announced policies a week later.[48]

This premonitory skirmish suggested that a consistent rightist course was to remain beyond reach, hence the conservative and nationalist protests that would later develop into a right-wing *fronde* against ministries relying on the votes of the center. From the perspective of 1919 or 1924, the Bloc National represented a profound swing to reaction. The divisions of French opinion, however, permitted a bourgeois and nationalistic, but not a reactionary consensus to triumph at the polls. Ironically, this may have strengthened parliamentarism, not weakened it as the Radicals hinted. Happy with the outcome of the elections, French business interests did not yet take refuge in corporatist efforts for bypassing the Assembly or authoritarian dreams of suppressing it.

BOURGEOIS DISARRAY IN ITALY

Italians often viewed their political divisions in terms of those in France, and the model of government that the nationalists of 1918 urged upon their own leadership was that of Clemenceau.[49] But they could not impose such an uncontested pro-war stamp upon policy.

[47] For Millerand's view of the Steeg appointment, "Mes souvenirs," p. 93. On the "irresistible impulse" bringing Millerand to power, cf. *Le Temps*, January 20, 1920. For an account of how Clemenceau was foiled in his effort to win the presidency: Wormser, *La république de Clemenceau*, pp. 392–423; E. Beau de Loménie, *Les responsabilités des dynasties bourgeoises*, vol. III, *Sous la Troisième République, la guerre, et l'immédiat après-guerre* (Paris, 1954), pp. 202–212; also Barrès, *Cahiers*, XII, pp. 245–250.

[48] JOC, 1920, pp. 16 ff. (January 22), p. 91 (January 30).

[49] See the advice of the leaders of the Ansaldo firm to Nitti, in Alberto Monticone, *Nitti e la grande guerra (1914–1918)* (Milan, 1961), pp. 203–208; also the charge that Orlando was the Malvy of Italy, in Louis Hautecoeur, *L'Italie sous le ministère Orlando* (Paris, 1919), pp. 17 ff.

The consequence was that bourgeois political circles remained divided over war aims and support for successive governments. Bitterly hostile among themselves, Italian liberals were unprepared to maintain an effective electoral coalition. While in France the returns of November 16, 1919, confirmed bourgeois cohesion, the Italian results would recapitulate the paralysis of the Orlando and then the Nitti ministries.

The same national reflex that had finally brought Clemenceau to power made Orlando premier during the crisis of Caporetto. But while Clemenceau was to crack down upon wartime dissenters, Orlando pledged himself to maintaining an extensive degree of liberalism. His majority still comprised the deputies elected in 1913 under Giolitti's auspices. If by now they supported the war effort, many still resented the interventionist strong-arm tactics of 1915. Socialist moderates, moreover, now pledged their support in view of the Austrian invasion. While France commenced the war with a *union sacrée* government, Italy finally found a rough equivalent by the autumn of 1917.[50]

Pro-war activists, on the other hand, were distressed, especially after turmoil and bloody clashes with working-class demonstrators in northern Italian cities during August. The pro-war militants organized a new Fascio Parlamentare di Difesa Nazionale during the autumn crisis to strengthen interventionist influence. While the Fascio Parlamentare originally included those members of the left who had urged Italy's participation in the war, it became prevailingly conservative and authoritarian, increasingly impatient with Orlando for not moving against internal political criticism.[51] By November 1918, the right viewed all the ministers but Sonnino as "weak, cowardly, and incompetent owing to the fear deranging them" and looked to the Fascio as "defenders of

[50] For Orlando's position and political developments in the autumn of 1917, see Roberto Vivarelli, *Il dopoguerra in Italia e l'avvento del fascismo (1918–1922)*, I: *Dalle fine della guerra all'impresa di Fiume* (Naples, 1967), pp. 34–53, and Ivanoe Bonomi, *La politica italiana da Porta Pia a Vittorio Veneto* (Turin, 1946), pp. 406–415; Hautecoeur, *L'Italie sous le ministère Orlando*, pp. 12–58; also the portrait in Paolo Alatri, *Le origini del fascismo* (Rome, 1956), pp. 303–330. V. E. Orlando, *Memorie (1915–1919)*, R. Mosca, ed. (Milan, 1960), focuses on the controversies surrounding Caporetto.

[51] On the Fascio Parlamentare and interventionist sentiment, Luigi Albertini, *Venti anni di vita politica*, parte seconda, 3 vols. (Bologna, 1951–1953), II/2, pp. 581–584, II/3, pp. 86, 265; Renzo De Felice, "Giovanni Preziosi e le origini del fascismo," *Rivista storica del Socialismo*, nr. 17 (September–December 1962), pp. 502 ff.; F. L. Pullé and G. Celesia, *Memorie del Fascio Parlamentare di difesa nazionale (Senato e Camera)* (Bologna, 1932); Ferdinando Martini, *Diario, 1914–1918*, Gabriele De Rosa, ed. (Milan, 1966), pp. 1041–1087, passim. For the bitter debates between Giolittians and Fascio adherents on December 19–20, 1917, see AP: Camera, Legislatura XXIV, esp. pp. 15255 ff., 15280–15284, 15297–15320.

the anti-bolshevik order."[52] The Fascio, however, remained limited in scope. As Salandra, who hoped that the Fascio might renovate a "decadent" parliamentary order, later conceded, it was too divided internally to hold together after the war.[53] As a caucus of parliamentarians, it was also limited in its own antiparliamentarism. And when its young hotheads levied careless charges of treason against Giolitti during Camera debates in late 1918, it emerged discredited.[54]

The nationalist agitation, however, far transcended the Fascio. Nationalists demanded the annexation of the Istrian peninsula and portions of the eastern Adriatic shore which, in the 1915 Treaty of London, the Allies had told Italy she could carve from Austro-Hungarian territory. Nationalists also demanded annexation of the Istrian port city of Fiume, which Italy had neglected to stipulate in 1915 but whose center was ethnically Italian and more logically included than the Slavic areas that had been promised. Italy, claimed the nationalists, had actually saved the Allies at several critical moments in the war; she deserved her rewards, and without Fiume, Zara, the Adriatic islands off Dalmatia, and even the Dodecanese off Greece, she would remain perpetually menaced.[55] The Adriatic annexationists looked to Sonnino, who quietly and tenaciously sought to win Fiume and the eastern Adriatic together against the claims of the new, vigorous Serbo-Croatian kingdom. Inside the cabinet, Leonida Bissolati, the reformist socialist and democratic interventionist of 1915, advocated trading the secret promises of London in return for Fiume, but he collided with Sonnino and in December 1918 finally left the cabinet. In view of the nationalist clamor, Orlando backed his Foreign Minister. The conservative press claimed a triumph for Sonnino's views; Bissolati was condemned as a *rinunciatario*; and his own public justification—on behalf of Wilsonian principles—was shouted down by

[52] Pantaleoni to Salandra in Lucera: Carte Salandra, 1918; and Pantaleoni to Preziosi, cited De Felice, "Giovanni Preziosi," p. 506.

[53] Salandra address in Antonio Salandra, *I discorsi della guerra* (Milan, 1922), pp. 187–188; his later reservations on the role of the Fascio, *ibid.*, p. 122, n. 8. On Fascio disarray, see the report to the Ministry of the Interior, cited in Renzo De Felice, *Mussolini il rivoluzionario, 1883–1920* (Turin, 1965), p. 438.

[54] AP: Camera, Legislatura xxiv, pp. 17515 ff. (November 23), and pp. 17578–17579 (November 24) for demurral.

[55] Cf. Francesco Coppola, "La pace italiana," in the nationalist *Politica*, I, 1 (1918), pp. 55–86; also the summary of the nationalist press in: RFP:APS, 5 (November 19 and December 4), esp. p. 68. Also, Hautecoeur, *L'Italie sous le ministère Orlando*, pp. 32 ff.; Vivarelli, *Il dopoguerra in Italia*, pp. 169–211, covers the annexationist agitation from summer 1918, with extensive citations. For the diplomacy of the Italian-Yugoslav dispute: Ivo Lederer, *Yugoslavia at the Paris Peace Conference* (New Haven, 1963), pp. 54 ff.

Mussolini's adherents and Marinetti's Futurists at La Scala on January 11, 1919.[56]

The eclipse of Bissolati revealed that the nonannexationist interventionists, ranging from Albertini to the radical Salvemini, had no mass base.[57] The Socialists remained hostile to annexationism, but their domestic radicalism precluded any coalition with any of the liberals. Giolittians remained separated from Albertini, Bissolati, and Salvemini by the bitter memories of 1915, when their leader had been outmaneuvered by interventionists of left and right. Nitti, who also represented the left of the broad liberal spectrum, resigned from the cabinet along with Bissolati, but in no clear-cut protest over foreign policy. He claimed disagreement over economic issues and refused to endorse Bissolati's protest, maintaining a vague and nuanced opposition to preserve his own eventual candidacy for the succession. Meanwhile, without Bissolati, noted Giovanni Amendola for the *Corriere* at the end of 1918, the government was susceptible to "the worst nationalist instincts and the intoxication of victory." Italy, he wrote, was "the first of the countries where the crisis of conscience finds expression in a crisis of government."[58]

Soon the crisis was to engulf Orlando and Sonnino as well. In the feverish atmosphere created by nationalist rhetoric, the government had staked its position on the Adriatic gains that it could confirm in Paris. For conservative liberals all the influence won since 1915 seemed vulnerable. Salandra received warnings that "the parliamentary situation is degenerating badly. Not only the Giolittians, but all those elements who were largely checked and halted by the interven-

[56] Vivarelli, *Il dopoguerra in Italia*, pp. 212–218; and for the press, *RFP:APS*, 5, pp. 227, 273 (*GdI*, December 29 and 30, 1918, January 13, 1919). On Bissolati, Ivanoe Bonomi, *Leonida Bissolati e il movimento socialista in Italia* (Milan, 1929), pp. 192–193; Raffaele Colapietra, *Leonida Bissolati* (Milan, 1958), esp. pp. 232–279. Cf., too, the interviews recorded in Olindo Malagodi, *Conversazioni di guerra*, Brunello Vigezzi, ed., 2 vols. (Milan and Naples, 1960), II, pp. 460–461.

[57] The nonannexationist interventionists achieved their greatest success at the Congress of Rome in April 1918, which convened delegates of the nationalities in the Hapsburg Empire and extracted a promise of self-determination on their behalf from Orlando. Sonnino, however, repeatedly resisted any pledges to work for Austro-Hungarian dismemberment. For Albertini's clash with Sonnino, the *Corriere's* "New Mazzini" program of January 1918, the Congress of Rome, and renewed conflict in August 1918, see his *Venti Anni di Vita Politica*, II/2, pp. 235–239, 265–275, 369–371; also Colapietra, *Leonida Bissolati*, pp. 261–264; Vivarelli, *Il dopoguerra in Italia*, pp. 157–169, 185–195; René Albrecht-Carrié, *Italy at the Paris Peace Conference* (New York, 1938), pp. 44 ff. For Salvemini's articles in *Unità*, see *RFP:APS*, 5 (December 4, 1918), p. 93; also his 1918 pamphlet, "La questione Adriatica," now in Gaetano Salvemini, *Dalla guerra mondiale alla dittatura* (1916–1925) (Milan, 1964), pp. 283–483.

[58] *CdS*, December 29, 1918.

tionist forces before and during the war when the latter had government support, are reviving." Giolitti and the reformist socialists were just waiting for elections to lead a campaign against "the men of the war."[59] Outside parliament, the "maximalist" executive of the Socialist Party called for a general strike to win the immediate recall of Allied troops from Russia and complete demobilization at home. Social democratic leaders regretted the maximalist tactics and the chances it sacrificed for winning new support among middle-class elements disillusioned with the results of the war. But for reasons of party unity they felt constrained to accept the protests.[60]

Polarization was far graver than in France. On April 8, the *Corriere* asked Orlando to return from Paris to prevent impending civil war; and in a private letter to the premier, Albertini claimed that revolutionary propaganda had reached an "insurpassable pitch," and that prefectural reports indicated that a Leninist coup was being planned for Milan, as it had come to Munich and Budapest.[61] At the same time, antisocialist cadres were forming throughout the North. Mussolini had inaugurated his Fascio di Combattimento on March 23 "to channel revolutionary forces into the national camp," and a fortnight later a "Popular Antibolshevik Union" was announced in Milan, while similar formations and new fasci sprang up in Naples, Pavia, Trieste, Brescia, Bologna, Genoa, Parma, and elsewhere. The twenty-four-hour general strike in Rome on April 10 produced, not the leftist uprising Albertini feared, but militant nationalist counterdemonstrations in Rome and Milan, where the Socialist paper *Avanti!* was sacked on April 15, triggering in turn new strikes in Turin and Naples.[62]

[59] Nicola D'Atri to Salandra, March 22, 1919, and cf. also Vincenzo Riccio's warning of December 15, 1918 in Lucera: Carte Salandra. For Corradini's position, *CdS*, March 19, 1919.
[60] See Turati's letter to Anna Kuliscioff, March 22, 1919, in F. Turati and A. Kuliscioff, *Carteggio*, vol. v, *Dopoguerra e fascismo* (1919–1922) (Turin, 1953), pp. 61–62; also Kuliscioff's critique of the April strike, April 6, pp. 67–68. For the development of socialist attitudes in early 1919, Vivarelli, *Il dopoguerra in Italia*, pp. 312–320.
[61] "Affretare il passo," *CdS*, April 8, 1919; Albertini to Orlando, April 10 in ACS, Rome: Carte Orlando/1, f. "Fratelli Albertini." Now in Luigi Albertini, *Epistolario 1911–1926*, Ottavio Barié, ed., 4 vols. (Verona, 1968). III, pp. 1209–1211.
[62] De Felice, *Mussolini il rivoluzionario*, pp. 500–511 for the new Fascio di Combattimento; *CdS*, April 10, 1919, p. 5 for the Milan Unione Popolare Antibolscevico; reports of clashes on subsequent days; see too Vivarelli, *Il dopoguerra in Italia*, pp. 325–336 and 321, n. 45. Local groups in: N. S. Onofri, *La grande guerra nella città rossa. Socialismo e reazione a Bologna dal '14 al '18* (Milan, 1966), pp. 341 ff.; R. Muratore, "Il dopoguerra rosso e le origini del fascismo nel Novarese," *Rivista Storica del Socialismo*, 7–8 (July–December 1959), pp. 616–618 ff.; Mario Vaini, *Le origini del fascismo a Mantova (1914–1922)* (Rome, 1961), pp. 63–65.

The violence of Passion Week demonstrated how interwoven were foreign and domestic issues. The defense of revolution in Russia and the longing for a vague Wilsonian world order sent socialists into the streets, and not only in Milan and Rome, but also in Berlin, Munich, Budapest, and the great cities of the Western Allies during the April weeks of 1919. On the other side, however, there was real anger at those who supposedly rejected the ideals and sacrifices of the recent war. In the heated atmosphere of Italy, only a few flagging voices understood that "valorization" of the costly victory did not require the Dalmatian shore. But even those such as Albertini, who recognized that Italy had already "redeemed" Trent and Trieste, Istria and the Brenner, found maximalist denigration of the war effort repugnant. The underlying Socialist challenge to bourgeois society, the editor felt, was precisely its rejection of patriotic values, of "that sacred love of country that led [the bourgeoisie] to draw the nation into war, combatting all the utilitarianism and fears of the richest and poorest classes." Ominously, Albertini advised his readers there would be further strikes, but the rebellion in the heart of the bourgeoisie would surpass that among the workers.[63]

Still, if nationalist commitment was presently the touchstone of class division, Albertini did not wish to intensify the clash unnecessarily. If revolution threatened from the left, he warned Orlando, the government's tactics of stirring up nationalist fervor promised equal chaos. Walking out of the peace conference, he warned, would create at home the impression that the war had been pointless and would legitimize a revolution that might even sweep up the army:

> This people is exhausted. Its organism is threatened by all the infections that the war has caused to spread. Let the government not ask it to assume the weight and responsibility for a treaty of peace for which the government itself has created expectations destined to be disappointed. Let our plenipotentiaries have the courage to sign the best conventions they can get and return singing victory, not wailing or complaining.[64]

Orlando sensed the dangers of popular disillusionment. On March 1 he had told the Chamber that a vague unrest, "like a blind whirlwind of destruction and disordered violence," was threatening Europe.[65]

[63] "Per l'avvenire," *CdS*, April 19, 1919; also Vivarelli, *Il dopoguerra in Italia*, pp. 318–321.

[64] Albertini to Orlando, April 10, 1919, full citation: note 61.

[65] *Ibid.*, Orlando to Albertini, April 10; also Albertini's response that Orlando was encouraging the nationalist press, April 15, 1919: ACS, Rome: Carte Orlando/1, f. "Fratelli Albertini," and Albertini, *Epistolario*, III, pp. 1212–1215,

This danger did not stem from the left alone; to a private correspondent he stressed a "malaise spreading everywhere": "not a question of political agitation with given directions and ends, but of a vortex of varied tendencies. . . . we have a flowering of little Boulangers. . . . More than a political phenomenon it is a psychological phenomenon, almost universal and for that reason more disquieting."[66] But Orlando insisted that the nationalist ferment could not simply be rebuffed. As he answered Albertini, "I persist in believing that the most immediate danger . . . capable of overturning Italy would be constituted by a profound patriotic disillusionment." And he must have understood that the moralistic position of the *Corriere*'s editor was no basis for holding together a parliamentary coalition. Dumping Sonnino would have divided the liberals, whereas Bissolati's resignation produced scarcely a ripple.[67]

Unfortunately, clinging to Sonnino had disastrous results at Paris. The Foreign Minister's stubbornness on all possible Italian claims only intensified Wilson's determination to withhold Fiume. After the President's clumsy appeal in mid-April to the Italian people's sense of justice and self-determination over the heads of their government, Orlando and Sonnino returned home in a parade of self-righteousness. The press, patriotic societies, and Liberal Party associations denounced Wilson, often demanding annexation of all the territory attributed to Italy by the Pact of London and Fiume besides. But the gain for the ministry was only ephemeral. Orlando could not afford a definite rupture with the Peace Conference, whose work continued without Italy's delegates. Rather than risk exclusion from the treaties with Germany and Austria, Orlando and Sonnino quickly and unobtrusively returned to Paris by May 6 and encouraged more temperate reporting by the Italian press. Nevertheless, they could win no further concessions, and the moral support they had gained in Italy was dissipated by the fly-by-night return to the conference.[68]

1219–1220. For Sonnino's continuing strength: Vivarelli, *Il dopoguerra in Italia*, pp. 351–352; Mayer, *Politics and Diplomacy of Peacemaking*, p. 680.

[66] Malagodi, *Conversazioni di guerra*, II, pp. 649–650 (May 15, 1919).

[67] AP: Camera, Legislatura XXIV, p. 18075.

[68] Press summaries in *RFP:APS*, 6, pp. 9, 12–14, 36; Hautecoeur, *L'Italie sous Orlando*, pp. 222–230 ff.; see Vivarelli, *Il dopoguerra in Italia*, pp. 353–382; Albrecht-Carrié, *Italy at the Paris Peace Conference*, pp. 38–39, 181–194; Silvio Crespi, *Alla difesa d'Italia in guerra e a Versailles (Diario 1917–1919)* (Milan, 1937), pp. 471–531; Lederer, *Yugoslavia at the Paris Peace Conference*, pp. 203–217; Paolo Alatri, *Nitti, D'Annunzio e la questione adriatica (1919–1920)* (Milan, 1959), pp. 34–43 ff.; and Mayer, *Politics and Diplomacy of Peacemaking*, pp. 678–711 for the negotiations at Paris, Wilson's appeal, Orlando and Sonnino's return to Italy and then to the Peace Conference.

Dissatisfaction grew on left and right. Nationalists continued to demand annexation of the disputed territories; business groups remained annoyed with the continuing restrictions on commerce; Catholics, Socialists, and democratic liberals disliked Orlando's stand against proportional representation and finally forced him to withdraw a threatened veto. Major strikes continued, including 30,000 woolen workers in the Biellese region of northwest Piedmont during May, metalworkers in Rome, then tramway operators in early June, followed by hotel and restaurant employees. Adding additional tension, rumors of a contemplated *coup d'état* to be led by D'Annunzio, the Nationalist Party leader, Luigi Federzoni, Mussolini, and General Giardino— or at least the planned secession of Venezia, Venezia-Giulia, and Fiume under the Duke d'Aosta—reached the press around June 10. The final parliamentary crisis was heralded by Salandra's decision not to return to Paris as a negotiator and by the resignation of the Minister of Provisions, Silvio Crespi. Now, too, the *Corriere* turned against the government as "incompetent at Paris and incompetent at Rome," while the Fascio Parlamentare set a June 8 caucus to review its stance toward the ministry. Faced with multiplying defections, Orlando returned to Rome on June 14. In parliament he made a weak defense of his efforts at Paris, and choosing to fall on an issue of procedure rather than substance, he requested that further details and debate be confined to a secret session. The motion was defeated 262 to 78. From right to left, Salandra, Luzzatti, Giolitti, Nitti, and Bissolati all went into opposition.[69]

The adverse vote was more than a condemnation of Orlando's tactics. It confirmed a deeper failure on the part of all the liberals: failure to achieve the international stature for Italy that the liberals themselves believed she deserved, failure to pacify domestic opinion, failure ultimately to govern coherently. The question bequeathed by the crisis was whether any President of the Council could construct a durable majority in light of domestic polarization.

The logical candidate was Nitti. From the outset, however, Nitti drew harsh objections from the interventionist stalwarts. While he had accepted the entry into war, he had not been an enthusiast. On economic grounds he had counseled that Italy not undertake the final,

---

[69] For business discontent see Treasury Minister Filipo Meda to Orlando, telegram of April 22, 1919, in ACS, Rome: Carte Orlando/7, f. "F. Meda"; on the proportional representation issue, Hautecoeur, *L'Italie sous Orlando*, p. 253; for domestic unrest: *RFP:APS*, 6, pp. 210–211, 240; the alleged conspiracy in De Felice, *Mussolini il rivoluzionario*, p. 532; also Elio Apih, *Italia fascismo e antifascismo nella Venezia Giulia* (*1918–1943*) (Bari, 1966), pp. 87–88; *Corriere* criticism: *CdS*, June 7, 1919, "Alla deriva." Parliamentary debates in AP: Camera, Legislatura xxiv, pp. 18866–18867 (June 19, 1919).

triumphant offensive, but wait for a battlefield decision against the Central Powers in France. The nationalists resented the claims of a material calculus over heroism and patriotic valor, and many of the interventionists remained hostile. Nitti could still win over the customarily "ministerial" groupings of the liberal center, to which he added support from the Catholic deputies by his acceptance of proportional representation. Following the presentation of a sober, middle-of-the-road program, the new cabinet won a majority of 257 to 111—unresounding for a ministerial debut in the amorphous Italian party system. Moreover, the hostility of half the Fascio Parlamentare persisted, and little positive enthusiasm seemed generated. "The Nitti ministry," charged *Giornale d'Italia* in a warning of bitterness to come, "has an original sin: to be born outside and against the great currents of the country which campaigned for the war and were the true artificers of victory and wish to realize its fruits."[70]

Nitti's task became all the more difficult with the explosion of new labor violence. La Spezia, Genoa, and Carrara saw clashes between strikers and police in mid-June, while in Turin a mass walkout was held to commemorate Rosa Luxemburg's death a half-year earlier. At the end of June, riots, vandalism, and looting broke out in Forlì and radiated thence all over Italy in a desperate protest against the *carovivieri* or escalating prices. Local soviets sprang up in Tuscany and Liguria, and general strikes gripped Florence, Ancona, Bologna, and Palermo in early July. Eight were left dead in the small Apulian town of Lucera. Even Nenni, certainly sympathetic to the strikers if not the maximalists, described the action in retrospect as "tumultuous, anarchoid, bereft of direction, of overall concepts and clear and precise objectives."[71] In the wake of the agitation local authorities imposed price slashes of 50 percent on most essential goods, and Nitti gave official sanction to such emergency measures in a decree of July 6.

No sooner had price cuts restored some calm to the cities than bourgeois opinion was set on edge by Socialist plans for the two-day international general strike of July 20–21, which also so disturbed the

---

[70] For Nitti's weaknesses, Alberto Monticone, *Nitti e la grande guerra*, pp. 15–17, 289 ff.; and especially Roberto Vivarelli's extended review of Monticone in "A proposito di un libro recente su Francesco S. Nitti," *Rivista Storica Italiana*, 76, 1 (1964), pp. 172–192. The parliamentary debate and vote in AP: Camera, Legislatura xxiv, pp. 19315 ff. Reaction following in "Dopo il voto," *CdS*, July 16, 1919, and in *GdI*, July 23, 1919.

[71] Pietro Nenni, *Il diciannovismo*, pp. 38 ff.; the agitation can be followed in *CdS*, June 11/12, 1919, and following; Vivarelli, *Il dopoguerra in Italia*, pp. 412–418; Gaetano Salvemini, "Lezioni di Harvard: l'Italia dal 1919 al 1929," in Salvemini *Scritti sul fascismo*, i, Roberto Vivarelli, ed. (Milan, 1961), pp. 448–452, 465–468, now available as *The Origins of Fascism in Italy*, R. Vivarelli, ed. (New York, 1973), pp. 184–196, 209–221.

French right. Despite the fact that Italy awaited the climactic supreme strike—the *scioperissimo*—in great tension, the affair was a disappointment for the Socialists. After the French CGT canceled its participation, Italian railroad workers withdrew their support. *Avanti!* explained later that the strike had been meant as no more than a prelude to the real battle; but the result was working-class disillusionment and stiffened bourgeois resistance. With the failure of the *scioperissimo*, the wave of political strikes ended. August also saw spectacular walkouts, but on behalf of wage claims against inflation, no longer for Russia, socialism, or peace.[72]

The cresting and ebb of the 1919 strikes paralleled developments in France. But while in France the new bourgeois resistance worked to strengthen the government, in Italy it turned against it. Nitti was able to exploit the unrest of July 1919 for short-term advantage in winning his first votes of confidence.[73] But even when Nitti came out against the *scioperissimo*, the other groups that also condemned it—veterans' associations, *fasci*, and old conservatives—did not relinquish their hostility to the premier. Nitti's price cuts antagonized businessmen; and the right feared a possible coalition with the reformist socialists. "The real friends of Nitti are the Socialists. The boss of the Chamber is Modigliani who disposes of everything," Vincenzo Riccio wrote Salandra in early August.[74] In fact, Nitti's own need to stress "order" and the PSI's maximalism precluded any such alliance. Nor could Nitti arouse the enthusiasm of the nonannexationist liberals by any idealistic justification of wartime sacrifices. Nitti did not have the moral resources of a Bissolati: the heavy-set premier oscillated between fits of a Cassandran depression and facile optimism.

On the morrow of his installation Nitti was excessively cheerful and buoyed by the votes of confidence he had won only under the threat of a general strike. In reality his position was fundamentally unstable.[75] Nitti did not really possess a durable interest-oriented majority such

[72] Cf. *CdS*, July 22, 1919; Nenni, *Il diciannovismo*, pp. 44–46; Vivarelli *Il dopoguerra in Italia*, pp. 435–454.

[73] AP: Camera, Legislatura xxiv, pp. 19053–19059 (July 9, 1919), 19315–19316 (July 14); AP: Senato, pp. 5122 ff. (July 26); cf. Mayer, *Politics and Diplomacy of Peacemaking*, pp. 853–873.

[74] Riccio to Salandra, August 8, 1919, in Lucera, Carte Salanda. Giuseppe Emanuele Modigliani, brother of the painter, Amadeo, was one of the PSI parliamentary leaders, along with Turati and Claudio Treves.

[75] For Nitti's euphoria, see the wires to Foreign Minister Tittoni after parliamentary confirmation in: Paolo Altri, *Nitti, D'Annunzio e la questione adriatica*, pp. 84–85, 97. For the psychological defects of the new premier, cf. Ettore Conti, *Dal taccuino di un borghese* (Milan, 1946), p. 188: "a fear, I would say almost physical, prevents him from following a resolute line of conduct. . . ."

as Giolitti had forged, even though he was regarded as heir to the Giolittian coalition. According to Gramsci, *Nittismo* had two sources of support: the heavy-industry interests that benefitted from tariff protection and war orders, and the petit-bourgeois, Masonic "radicalism" of the Mezziogiorno. But it lacked a broad class base; and the very steel and chemical industries that had earlier looked to Nitti as a technocratic sponsor were now interlocked with the nationalist papers and politicians who despised him.[76] Unfortunately Nitti had little to give anyone. Before 1914 Giolitti had provided high tariffs and wages to the North plus guaranteed election to his Southern supporters; by 1920 even his right-wing foes believed that he alone could rescue social tranquillity and some of the territory promised by the Treaty of London. Nitti demanded renunciation, and not merely in the narrow, pejorative sense of giving up Adriatic objectives which the nationalists lent to the word. Produce more, consume less—in short, austerity—was the Nittian program, and he justified it by insistent reminders of Italy's abject dependence upon American credit and exports. As he wrote his Foreign Minister, Tommaso Tittoni, in early September, all countries now found themselves under U.S. financial control; a rupture with America over Fiume would bring economic distress, food shortages, and bolshevization.[77] In short, the Italian bourgeoisie wished to bask in the warm glow of Vittorio Veneto, and Nitti kept asking whence next winter's coal would come.

In the final analysis, however, the bitterness of Italy's political and social divisions, and not personal shortcomings, undermined Nitti's administration. The right attacked the premier for encouraging disorder at a moment when it was itself a major force for sedition. Nitti was correctly concerned with the subversive potential of the Arditi and the new *fasci*. He also inherited an impatient army of about 1.7 million undemobilized officers and men, which remained in administrative control of the contested ex-Hapsburg areas in Venezia-Giulia, Istria, and Dalmatia. Preoccupied by the political dangers and the financial burdens, Nitti pressed ahead with demobilization. To conciliate the military in return, Nitti selected a general as Minister of War, and in August he sought to curtail any inflammatory debate of the

[76] Antonio Gramsci, *Passato e presente* (Turin, 1951), p. 48. For the industrial tie see also Roberto Vivarelli, *Il dopoguerra in Italia*, pp. 427–428; and for the weakness of Nitti's position, pp. 429–431; also, on the connections with industry: Alberto Monticone, *Nitti e la grande guerra*, pp. 208 ff.; Raffaele Colapietra, *Napoli tra dopoguerra e fascismo* (Milan, 1962), pp. 40 ff.; on the protectionist program: Franco Catalano, *Potere economico e fascismo. La crisi del dopoguerra, 1919–1921* (Milan, 1964), pp. 39–57.

[77] Alatri, *Nitti, D'Annunzio e la questione adriatica*, p. 173.

official report on Caporetto which laid heavy blame on General Cadorna.[78]

Nitti's effort to keep the military under control and mollify nationalist demands was shattered, when, with the connivance of nationalist political leaders and army units in the area, D'Annunzio seized Fiume on September 12. Allied criticism of Rome's provisional occupation of the city after clashes between Italians and Slavs, and right-wing fears that Nitti was prepared to withdraw troops and reach a quick settlement, probably determined D'Annunzio's take-over.[79] The underlying objective was the fall of the Nitti ministry and a change of policy in Rome. Only after this failed did D'Annunzio move to institutionalize his administration of the "Free State of the Quarnaro." Rather than serving as a dress rehearsal for the March on Rome, the descent on Fiume was a precursor of the military coup on the periphery designed to blackmail the capital, such as the Manchurian Incident of 1931 or the 1958 Committee of Public Safety in Algiers.

Conservatives who felt uneasy about supporting a mutinous direct action were still quick to condemn Nitti's handling of the ensuing crisis.[80] What infuriated the right was less Nitti's response to D'Annunzio's expedition than the leftist alignments he brandished. Nitti understood that the army was not reliable enough to be used in suppressing the insurgents at Fiume. Unlike Giolitti fifteen months

[78] On the army, see Giorgio Rochat, *L'esercito italiano da Vittorio Veneto a Mussolini* (*1919–1925*), pp. 47–51; for Nitti's view of a military conspiracy, see his *Rivelazioni, Dramatis personae* (Naples, 1948), pp. 327–330; Alatri, *Nitti, D'Annunzio e la questione adriatica*, p. 108. For Nitti's moves toward suppressing the Arditi, see the exchange of letters with Albricci in ACS, Rome: Min. Int., Dir. P.S. Div. aff. gen. e ris. (1914–1926), 1919, B. 44, f. "Arditi"; Albricci to Nitti, August 19; Nitti to Albricci, September 16, 1919. Albricci did issue orders on September 25 against uniformed officers participating in fascist assemblies. See Giorgio A. Chiurco, *Storia della rivoluzione fascista*, 5 vols. (Florence, 1929), I, *Anno 1919*, p. 189. On the Caporetto report, Rochat, *L'esercito italiano*, pp. 67–119, for a résumé of the controversy; cf. also Alatri, *Nitti, D'Annunzio e la questione adriatica*, pp. 150–156, and Luigi Salvatorelli e Giovanni Mira, *Storia d'Italia nel periodo fascista* (Turin, 1956), pp. 89–91.

[79] For the development of the Fiume expedition, see Vivarelli, *Il dopoguerra in Italia*, pp. 500–530; cf. also Eduardo Susmel, *La marcia di Ronchi* (Milan, 1941); Alatri, *Nitti, D'Annunzio e la questione adriatica*, pp. 178–205; Nino Valeri, *Da Giolitti a Mussolini, Momenti della crisi del liberalismo italiano* (Florence, 1956), pp. 34–67, which spotlights the government's half-measures before the coup (reminiscent in many ways of the SPD's behavior in the days before the Kapp Putsch nine months later).

[80] For nationalist hopes to reverse Nitti: Giovanni Giuriati, *Con D'Annunzio e Millo in difesa dell'Adriatico* (Florence, 1954), p. 40; Vivarelli, *Il dopoguerra in Italia*, p. 350; also Turati's report of the nationalist Sinigaglia's bid for "Nitti's head in exchange for the surrender of D'Annunzio" and perhaps even a cabinet position for Turati, in Turati and Kuliscioff, *Carteggio*, v, pp. 147–148 (but Sinigaglia's démenti, p. 165, n. 2). For the parliamentary opposition cf. the letters published in Colapietra, *Bissolati*, pp. 302–303.

later, Nitti had no internationally agreed-upon alternative. Essentially, Nitti accepted General Badoglio's advice to temporize;[81] still, the right could not forgive his angry speech to the Chamber, which condemned the army's sedition and appealed to the masses: "The people do not want a new war; the people with their grim and austere conduct will prevent any perilous adventure. I turn, therefore, to the anonymous masses, to the workers and peasants so that the great voice of the people can emerge as an admonition to all to keep to the path of renunciation and duty."[82] Nitti clearly was not an Italian Lenin, but liberals and nationalists feared that he might prove another Kerensky. From overconfidence—on August 27 he had told Tittoni that the agitation over Fiume was insignificant—he veered toward alarm. Two days after the coup, he warned the journalist Malagodi that Italy faced disintegration and famine: "Italy is on its way to becoming a big Nicaragua. And that because of the will and work of the classes that claim to be in charge. This stupid and idiotic bourgeoisie does not have the slightest sense of the mortal danger we are in and works happily to speed up the catastrophe."[83] Some liberals sensed the same danger; many just resented the appeal to workers and peasants. The nationalist press depicted Nitti as a tyrant; even the *Corriere della Sera* criticized Nitti's plea as "unworthy of the country or the hour." Nonetheless, Albertini refused to oppose the government outright. In response to Salandra's urging of a harsher position, he wrote privately that Orlando and Sonnino had brought on the difficulties and that nationalist virulence was largely responsible for Wilson's refusal to cede Fiume. "To me the situation seems such that even were Giolitti in power, I would help him to overcome the terrifying difficulty of this hour."[84]

To strengthen his position Nitti took the unprecedented step of summoning a Crown Council for September 26: a conclave of cabinet,

[81] Pietro Badoglio, *Rivelazioni su Fiume* (Rome, 1946), pp. 158–161, esp. the wires of September 15 and 29; Valeri, *Da Giolitti a Mussolini*, pp. 61–67. For a view that the government might have suppressed the uprising, see Badoglio's successor: Enrico Caviglia, *Il conflitto di Fiume* (Florence, 1948), p. 142; Vivarelli, *Il dopoguerra in Italia*, pp. 541–545.

[82] AP: Camera, Legislatura XXIV, 924, p. 21092, September 13. But see the rebuff in *Avanti!* that one man of order just wished to use the proletariat as cannon fodder against other men of order. Cf. Valeri, *Da Giolitti a Mussolini*, p. 41; and Turati's favorable but isolated reaction in Turati-Kuliscioff, *Carteggio*, v, p. 138.

[83] Wire of August 27 in Valeri, *Da Giolitti a Mussolini*, p. 67; the fear of Nicaragua in Malagodi, *Conversazioni di guerra*, II, p. 715.

[84] *CdS*, September 14, 1919. For rightist reactions: "Cinicismo cieco," *L'Idea Nazionale*, September 17, 19, and after; *GdI*, September 17, 1919. Albertini's strictures in *CdS*, September 14, 1919; letter to Salandra, September 25, 1919, in Lucera: Carte Salandra. Now in Luigi Albertini, *Epistolario*, III, p. 1292.

monarch, military commanders, and ex-premiers to review the situation. Supporting Nitti, as the opposition argued it was calculated to do, the Council did reject the hawkish alternative of an immediate Italian annexation of Fiume. Feeling bolstered by the meeting, the government went on to face the Chamber on the following two days in the stormiest sessions since parliament's 1899 confrontation with the reactionary General Pelloux. Despite a bitter attack by the spokesman for the Fascio Parlamentare, the ministry emerged with a narrow vote of confidence. Nitti promised that the Versailles Treaty would be debated in the Chamber two days later—but in a surprise move the same evening he dissolved parliament and provided for new elections.[85]

The opposition was furious, for it had awaited an early overthrow of the government. In the Crown Council, Salandra had opposed early elections, and the decision, fumed the *Giornale d'Italia*, was "unconstitutional, antidemocratic, authoritarian, factious and Bourbon." Afraid to confront parliament again, Nitti was going to the country flanked by socialists and Giolittians, who would exploit the campaign to ask what purpose the bloodshed of 1915–1918 had served if Fiume was still unattainable.[86]

The nationalists had a point when they charged that Nitti dissolved parliament in order to stay in power. He could not have survived more than another session or two. The margin of 60 votes he won on September 28 was a thin one for Italian governments, which usually cajoled all but the extremes of the Chamber into the majority or resigned. Moderate spokesmen, however, realized that Nitti had valid reasons for not confronting the Chamber and endangering Treaty ratification. The *Corriere* declared that it would support the government as the representatives of civil order, and it attacked the liberal "governing class" for overlooking the perils of militarist rebellion. The discerning editor of Turin's pro-Giolitti *La Stampa*, Alfredo Frassati, condemned the parliamentary Fascio for its bitter opposition. "Take away from the Fascio their violence and you have nothing." The true anarchists of the day, he wrote, were the nationalists—all the more dangerous since they were not mere theorists but sought to control the streets.[87]

[85] Attack on Nitti's moves in "Crisi latente," *GdI*, September 21; cf. also *L'Idea Nazionale*, September 24, 1919. For the Council, see the report in *CdS*, September 26, 1919; also Alatri, *Nitti, D'Annunzio e la questione adriatica*, pp. 239–242, with the minutes of the conclave. On the parliamentary session, see the report in *CdS*, September 29, 1919; also AP: Camera, Legislatura XXIV, pp. 21379–21428.

[86] See "La caotica battaglia elettorale," *GdI*, October 1, 1919; and on the nationalist moves: Giuriati, *Con D'Annunzio e Millo*, p. 53; for reactions in Fiume: Vivarelli, *Il dopoguerra in Italia*, pp. 538–540.

[87] *CdS*, October 1, 1919; *La Stampa*, September 30/October 1.

Divisions within the old governing class precipitated the elections. Nitti and the nationalists both represented bourgeois Italy, but an Italy fractured between liberal left and liberal right, neutralists and interventionists, *rinunciatari* and annexationists—all overlapping though not exactly equivalent splits. Yet if the causes of the early election involved liberal schism, the result might well be the eclipse of liberals as a whole before the new mass-party challenges. Would liberals organize against each other, or against Socialists and Catholics?

For Italian liberals the upcoming elections would be only the second held under universal male suffrage and the first under proportional representation. They were at home with neither. In 1912 the opening of the ballot to all male adults had come about as a result of a political bidding for a parliamentary majority: Giolitti had carried the measure, but Salandra made it clear that he assented, and Sonnino had even proposed granting the vote to women. The presence of single-member constituencies and the persistence of clientele politics in the South seemed likely to damp down any electoral shock waves. Without proportional representation the socialists could be limited to about forty deputies. A Catholic party had little hope of capturing majorities in any significant number of districts, so Catholic political leaders were willing to bargain with Giolitti in 1913 and trade the votes of the faithful for pledges against anticlerical initiatives and divorce. Six years later, however, proportional representation was in effect; an assertive party of Catholics had emerged; and liberals were bitterly divided among themselves over the issues of war and peace. New elections were bound to yield rude and unpleasant results no matter who "made" them.[88]

As in France, party organization took on new urgency in light of the system of proportional representation voted in the summer of 1919. But while in France, the Bloc National was constructed to magnify the expected majority, in Italy coalition was required simply to forestall electoral disaster. The Italian system of proportional representation offered no majority-take-all provision; its complex counting of preference votes for candidates and slates would not exaggeratedly skew the distribution of seats or unduly reward a coalition. Proportional representation in France had been aimed at undercutting Radical Socialist supremacy on behalf of the *modérés*; in Italy the equivalent of the *modérés* feared its effect because they understood its

---

[88] For the suffrage requirements and participation in earlier elections, see the official *Compendio delle statistiche elettorali dal 1848 al 1934*, 2 vols. (Rome, 1946), I; for the impact of the issue in 1911–1914: Brunello Vigezzi, "Il suffragio universale e la 'crisi' del liberalismo in Italia (dicembre 1913–aprile 1914)," *Nuova Rivista Storica*, 48, 5–6 (1964), pp. 529–570.

benefits for the Socialists and, above all, for the new Catholic Partito Popolare Italiano. Without proportional representation, anticlerical alliances would nullify the widespread and significant minority support the Popolari seemed destined to receive. With the new system, however, liberals had to coalesce or face sharp reverses.

Despite the peril, liberals could not magically overcome their internecine hostility. The right summoned a nationalist front against what the *Giornale d'Italia* chimerically depicted as the "socialist-neutralist" or "Bolshevik-Giolittian" bloc.[89] Interventionist moderates such as Albertini sought to renew the coalition of 1915 by merging left-wing republicans, radical pro-war leaders, Bissolatian Reformist Socialists, and liberals in a National Bloc. The *combattenti*, or veterans, organized as the Rinnovamento for the campaign, it was hoped, would enter these interventionist alliances. Such an extensive degree of unity, however, was difficult to achieve. *Combattenti*, Republicans, and Reformist Socialists stressed their domestic radicalism and often scorned the old ruling groups. In the South, moreover, where Nitti remained strong and elections always pitted supporters of the ministry in power against opponents, rival liberal slates were inevitable.[90]

There were other hindrances to unity even among interventionists. Italian liberalism rested upon a fragmented, archaic organizational base. Local associations and clubs might have ensured liberal cohesiveness when Italy had a restricted electorate, but they were antiquated in a world of mass suffrage. In Milan a half-year after the elections, the prefect could list the Liberal Association, the Lombard Democratic Society, the Lombard Democratic Association, and the Economic Union, all of which were in "complete disarray":

> The said parties are divided, distinct, in multiple gradations that represent no diversity of program but only of personal ambition— what is worse, the ambitions of men formerly in public life who left a bad name for their administrations, who were passed over, and who wish to make a comeback today exclusively for their own particular interests.[91]

[89] *GdI*, October 1, 1919; *CdS* and other papers on October 3.

[90] The material on the electoral competition is derived primarily from *Corriere della Sera* and *Giornale d'Italia* from October 1 on. Both papers carried frequent reports on the different districts.

[91] ACS, Rome: Min. Int., Dir. gen. P.S. Div. aff. gen. e ris. (1914–1926), 1920, B. 54, f. Milano, sf. "Spirito Publico," report of Prefect Flores to the President of the Council, June 18, 1920, 15981. The effective size of these groups was apparently small: see the report to Salandra by the conservative Milanese banker De Capitani D'Arzago, October 9, 1924—admittedly a date when defections to fascism may already have hit hard—in Lucera, Carte Salandra. The Associazione Liberale was credited with 2000 members; the smallest and most prestigious of the local political groupings was then La Costituzionale with only 280 members.

Liberal survival in the twenty-six new electoral districts required imposing some discipline on these party fragments. In the absence of central organization, success varied according to local leadership or jealousies. In Milan, the largest of the new constituencies with twenty deputies to choose, the *Corriere* urged consolidation for "those principles of order and evolution . . . common to all constitutionalists of the most diverse origins." Yet for Albertini, liberal reunion must stop short of the neutralists, despite his denial that he wished to prolong the schism of 1915.[92] Even left and right interventionists could not close ranks. The Agricultural Association of Upper Italy, the nationalists, and the Merchants' Association organized a Fascio Patriottico to select a slate of right-wing "constitutionalists." *Combattenti*, Reformist Socialists, Radicals (a party designation inherited from before 1915 and now obsolescent), and Republicans (an embattled minority conventicle) nominated a Left Bloc. Mussolini sought some places on the latter slate for his own Fascio di Combattimento, but was rejected by the left-wing interventionists, who feared that including him would eliminate any chance of winning support from discontented Socialists. Fascists, along with *arditi* and Futurists, thus had to run their own slate —the final failure of Mussolini to take over the forces of radical interventionism.[93]

Outside the northern metropolis, alignments were simpler. In Lombardy, interventionists managed to impose a high degree of liberal unity under their own auspices. In Bergamo, all non-Catholic and nonsocialist forces agreed on a single slate, while in Mantua, Bonomi's personal ascendancy let him form a Blocco Democratico uniting all liberals, democrats, and reformist socialists. Lombardy, however, was a traditional stronghold for conservative liberalism, and its deputies had voted almost unanimously against Nitti on September 28. Neighboring Piedmont, in contrast, remained Giolitti's fief, hence favorable for noninterventionists. In Cuneo, Giolitti's home province, conservatives and nationalists did not even mount a campaign. In Turin, however, "constitutional interventionists" under the aged Paolo Boselli challenged a Giolittian list headed by Luigi Facta, who was to precede Mussolini as premier in 1922. Given the size of Turin, interventionists themselves divided, and Boselli's conservative slate had to face a "Radical Alliance" of Reformist Socialists, Republicans, and other leftist supporters of the war. In rough balance, interventionists and Giolittians controlled the liberal organizations of Lombardy and Pied-

[92] "La formazione delle liste," *CdS*, October 6, 1919.
[93] Renzo De Felice, *Mussolini il rivoluzionario*, p. 543. On the other hand, rightist liberals still believed the Arditi and Fascists too radical. De Capitani wrote Salandra on October 9 that they were too antimonarchical for inclusion in the Blocco Nazionale: Lucera, Carte Salandra.

mont, respectively—but challenged in large urban areas by the veterans and young radical nationalists impatient with the old politics and local "establishments."[94] In Tuscany, liberal associations quarreled even more bitterly over candidates and the issues of the war and peace, such that Florence ended up with neutralists, nationalists, and radical interventionists in hostile competition.[95]

South of Rome, the pattern was altered by the tendency of candidates to identify themselves with the ministry or to challenge it in a venerable contest of "in's" and "out's." Often the division had little ideological rationale. Usually, however, the Nittians were liberal-democrats while the "constitutionalists" in opposition were more conservative. This made an unwelcome choice for veterans and left-interventionists. They found the pro-Nitti slates tainted with neutralism and the anti-Nitti candidates identified with the local, often reactionary elites. Hence, south of Rome the *combattenti* generally nominated their own slates, of which Salvemini's was the most notable.

The two largest cities of the kingdom offered their own distinct alignments. In the capital, liberals and the right drew their strength less from a business leadership as in Milan than from the milieu of bureaucrats, politicians, and intellectuals. This allowed the Nationalist Party of Luigi Federzoni to exert a strong influence over a "National Alliance" formed with liberals, *arditi*, and the Roman Fascio di Combattimento. In Naples there were no fewer than eleven slates, including three socialist groups, *combattenti*, a list of "employees and trade unionists," and Arturo Labriola's vaguely syndicalist Party of the Avant-Garde. Bourgeois liberals divided, not over their stance toward the government—for Nitti won endorsement from three slates—but according to nuances of conservatism and local considerations.[96]

Despite the persistence of clientele loyalties, parochial feuds, and irrepressible ambitions, some rough pattern was discernible. Socialists ran candidates in each of the twenty-six districts, and the Popolari did so in all but one. If the district was remote from urban turmoil or safely in the vestpocket of a local *notable*, "constitutionalists" might unite, so the minimal contest would be among three parties. More often liberals divided, often over intervention, making the battle at least four-sided. *Combattenti* slates, however, also entered many of the southern constituencies, while left interventionists vied in the more urban northern ones. This created a five-party campaign in which,

[94] Lists taken from preelection issues of *Corriere della Sera*. See also Ugo Giusti, *Le correnti politiche in Italia attraverso due riforme elettorali dal 1909 al 1921* (Florence, 1922), pp. 67–70.

[95] "La baraonda elettorale a Firenze," *GdI*, October 24, 1919, p. 3.

[96] Colapietra, *Napoli tra dopoguerra e fascismo*, pp. 81 ff. For Rome: *CdS* report, October 22, 1919.

besides PSI and PPI candidates, Giolittians faced conservatives and pro-war radicals in the North while Nittians battled conservatives and combattenti in parallel contests below Rome.

For a liberal such as Albertini, party rivalry discredited the political elite. If liberals could not forge local organizations as cohesive as those of the Socialists, Popolari, or *combattenti*, he wrote, they deserved political extinction.[97] But Albertini did not wish to recognize how deep the ideological fissures ran. On the right, for example, the *Giornale d'Italia* supported Federzoni's slate in Rome—indeed its editor, Bergamini, had privately sought Salandra's candidacy in the capital— and condemned Giolittian liberal democracy as the "dream of the weak, the lazy, the inept," as no more than a search for "benefits and privileges for the class of manual workers against the directing elite." Nitti's politics, the paper felt, were much the same: vestiges of Giolittianism blended with southern Freemasonry and representative of a new parvenu plutocracy.[98]

On the other side, Giolitti enunciated the most reformist liberal program of 1919 in his major election address at Dronero on October 12. He condemned the "reactionary parties" who had exploited intervention because they could not achieve a parliamentary majority under peacetime conditions. He also urged adoption of a rigorous financial program, including heavier taxes on wartime profits and the conversion of bearer securities, which evaded taxation, into stocks and bonds registered by name. Nitti, on the other hand, contented himself with an anodyne letter to his Basilicata constituents that stressed hard work, public construction (always a plum for the South), and a vague economic justice. Where Nitti wanted the war to be treated as a closed chapter, Giolitti asked for an investigation of how Italy had become involved. This polemical demand, plus the vehemence with which he attacked pro-war groups, even hinted at the possibility of a future coalition with moderate Socialists and Popolari.[99]

In effect, each major liberal spokesman outlined an election alternative that suited his own ideological and tactical position. Albertini envisioned a choice among four movements: socialism, clericalism, Giolittian neutralism, and a reformist, interventionist liberalism. Albertini's was an elitist utopia of the moderates, its narrow political base demonstrated by the failure of Bissolati nine months earlier. In

[97] "Partiti e liste," *CdS*, October 29, 1919.

[98] "I partiti e la lotta elettorale," *GdI*, November 13, 1919. For Bergamini's invitation to Salandra, see Lucera, Carte Salandra, October 20, 1919.

[99] Dronero address in Giovanni Giolitti, *Discorsi extraparlamentari*, Nino Valeri, ed. (Turin, 1952), pp. 294–327. *CdS* reaction in "A Ritosa della storia," October 13, 1919. For the contrast between Giolitti and Nitti at this point, cf. Giampiero Carocci, *Giolitti e l'età giolittiana* (Turin, 1961), pp. 181–183.

reality, the right had come to dominate the liberal interventionist slates and precluded their reformist potential. Right-wing liberals and nationalists sought to impose a terribly simple alternative: one between supporters of the war and supposed defeatists, which evaded any issue of domestic reform. Anarchy and neutralism were equivalent from the nationalist perspective. Giolittians clearly rejected the Manichaean conception of their nationalist foes. *La Stampa* condemned instead fascism and bolshevism as twin evils. Each prevented needed reform, drove Italy toward civil strife, and precluded the reconciliation of classes that was always central to Giolitti's political strategy. Thus there were at least three major ideological orientations of Italian liberalism on the eve of the elections: the Giolittian mix of reformism and hostility to the men of the war; the interventionist myth of an Albertini that a majority existed both to support domestic reform and defend the war effort; finally, a nationalist reaction as represented by the Rome coalition and the editorials, typically, of the *Giornale d'Italia*. Despite the pressures of proportional representation and the sharper competition from Catholics and Socialists, these positions remained unreconciled.[100]

The elections, which Nitti rashly conducted without the usual prefectoral intervention,[101] marked the end of liberal parliamentary hegemony. With his recurrent overoptimism, Nitti had predicted the return of a safe constitutionalist majority and the election of no more than 60-odd Socialists. In fact, the PSI, which had 52 seats in the 1913 legislature (undoubtedly an underrepresentation of its popular vote) now returned with 156 deputies. Catholic representation leapt from 29 deputies vaguely designated as clericals to 100 members of the new Partito Popolare. The constitutional parties—nationalists, conservative and democratic liberals, radicals—returned with 239 of their earlier 410 seats. The newspapers blamed the defeat on high abstentions, which was a contributory factor, but could account only partially for the setback. As *La Stampa* headlined the result, it was the revenge of those who had not wanted the war over those who had made it.[102]

[100] "L'assurdo dei blocchi," *La Stampa*, October 16–17; "La piattaforma elettorale," October 29–30; "Fascismo e bolscevismo," November 15–16, p. 2. For the general position of the press in this period see, Piero Melograni, ed., *Corriere della Sera (1919–1943)* (Bologna, 1965), pp. xxi ff., 13–29; Franco Gaeta, ed., *La stampa nazionalista* (Bologna, 1965), pp. lv–lviii, 227–232; Brunello Vigezzi, ed., *1919–1925. Dopoguerra e fascismo. Politica e stampa in Italia* (Bari, 1965), pp. 274–286 for *La Stampa*, 180–191 for *Il Corriere della Sera*, 18–28 for *Il Giornale d'Italia*, 439–448 for *Il popolo d'Italia*.
[101] Enrico Flores, *Eredità di guerra* (Rome, 1925), p. 36.
[102] *La Stampa*, November 18, 1919.

The percentages of the popular vote changed in much the same way as the final allotment of seats. Unlike France, there were important political migrations. In 1909 the Socialists had won 19.0 percent, and in 1913, with Giolitti managing the elections, 17.7; in 1919 they jumped to 32.4 percent. Catholic candidates in the earlier elections had won 4 to 6 percent, whereas now they gathered 20.5. This phenomenal rise resulted primarily from their new mass political organization. "Constitutionals" fell from 72.5 percent in 1909, to 67.6 in 1913, to 36.9 in 1919. Socialist independents and Republicans, who sometimes ran together, sometimes separately, rose to 10.2 percent from 8.7 percent in 1913 and 4.5 percent in 1909.[103]

The decline of the liberals was not merely a function of their own divisions. The progress of Italian socialism was an index of a continuing transformation of the society. Not surprisingly, the Socialists performed best north of Rome and generally in the urban centers. Special provincial strength showed up in Emilia-Romagna (60.1 percent of the vote), Piedmont (50.2), Umbria (46.8), Lombardy (46.0), and Tuscany (43.9). The major cities that the PSI dominated included Bologna (63.1 percent), Turin (62.8), Milan (53.9), Livorno (52.0), and Venice (50.4). In general, the urban centers of the electoral districts were more strongly Socialist than the rural surroundings; for the kingdom as a whole the PSI won 40.2 percent of the cities and 30.4 percent of the countryside. But important exceptions existed where the Federterra, the agrarian labor foundation, had organized farm workers. The province of Bologna had almost three-quarters of the rural voters—those outside Bologna and Imola—cast Socialist ballots (72.3 percent), as did the district of Ferrara-Rovigo (74.7). The

---

[103] Giusti, *Correnti politiche*, p. 21. The government's statistics permit a slightly finer breakdown of tendencies within the amorphous "constitutional" or liberal category. (Because of slightly different reckonings, minor differences appear with respect to Giusti's figures.)

	1913	1919
Liberals, Democrats, and combinations	55.9%	36.9%
Catholics	6.1	PPI 20.5
Radicals	11.7	Combined leftist lists* 7.7
(1913 Ministerial majority = 73.7%)		
Republicans	3.5	
Socialists (all shades)	22.8	Official Socialists 32.3

* Includes slates combining Radicals, Republicans, independent Socialists and/ or Combattenti; Combattenti lists alone; Republicans alone. Tables from *Compendio delle statistiche elettorali*. This breakdown, however, cannot illuminate the critical interventionist–neutralist split.

overwhelming Socialist domination of the Emilian countryside must be remembered in light of the fact that a year later the Fascist offensive exploded from the same area, quickly decimating the Federterra's patiently woven organization. The high rural vote also illuminates the bitter antisocialism and interventionism of the Republican Party, whose strongholds lay in the towns of the same region. Republicanism as an older and competing radicalism had long since been overtaken by the Socialists, except for its besieged petit-bourgeois strongholds in the towns of the Romagna.[104]

The increase in Socialist strength depended upon continuing industrialization and the organization of agrarian labor in the North. The South and the islands formed an almost unconquerable area, and returned only 10 of the 156 Socialist deputies.[105] Apulia, the heel of the peninsula, was a partial exception; for there a capitalist agriculture had aided the growth of the Federterra and the major cities showed substantial Socialist strength. It is revealing that in the Mezzogiorno, which generally proved such an arid land for the PSI, the Apulian cities (Brindisi, Taranto, Barletta, Bari, Andria, Cerignola, Foggia) returned significantly higher Socialist votes than the larger metropolises

---

[104] Giusti, *Correnti politiche*, pp. 60–61. In 1919, the left blocs that were dominated by Republicans achieved their best results by far in the district of Ravenna-Forlì with 28 percent. In the cities of Ravenna, Forlì, and Cesena they formed almost half the electorate; in the countryside a shade under 20 percent. In the same district the Socialists held 56.2 percent of the countryside, 40.4 percent of Ravenna and about one-third of Cesena and Forlì. The Socialists dominated Rimini (61.3), but in general the political picture appears to be that of an urban bourgeois Republicanism versus an agrarian proletariat—the former vociferously pro-war and latter neutralist. The hostility of the confrontation was perhaps exacerbated by the long-term decline of the Republicans in the area as Socialist strength rose. Although the picture is necessarily diluted by having here only the figures for Emilia-Romagna as a whole, instead of just Ravenna-Forlì, the trend is still visible from this table.

	1895	1900	1904	1909	1913	1919
Republicans	26%	13.9%	9.0%	10.5%	7.1%	4.7%
Socialists	21	26.5	37.0	39.6	38.2	60.0
Ratio of Republican to Socialist votes	1.19	0.52	0.24	0.26	0.19	0.08

[105]   SHARE OF TOTAL VOTES OBTAINED BY SOCIALISTS

	1909	1913	1919
North	26.18%	29.6%	42.5%
Center	18.31	24.3	56.0
South	3.31	11.6	8.9
Islands	9.04	15.8	6.7
(Apulia alone)	(3.0)	(17.4)	(18.2)

of the Campagna (Naples, Salerno, Caserta).[106] In the Campagna cities, ministerial candidates usually dominated, and radicalism expressed itself more in individualist leftist positions, such as Labriola's syndicalism or even Bordiga's "abstentionism," than through a disciplined Socialist Party.

Explanation must be tentative, but the difference between the partial success of socialism in the Apulian urban centers (29.7 percent) and its stagnation on the other side of the Apennines seems linked with the more dynamic growth of Apulia since unification. Between 1870 and 1911, population increase for the Apulian cities far outpaced that of the urban centers on the opposite coast. Apulia's new growth probably brought with it the dynamism and organization of industrial politics, whereas in Naples a nineteenth-century radicalism could subsist in a teeming but more stable environment. As Gramsci was to point out, the urban centers of Italy outside the North remained in large part preindustrial conglomerations.[107] In general, therefore, the South remained a reservoir of conservative strength. As a statistician had observed in 1904, for a phenomenon even then traditional, the Mezzogiorno was "the promised land for any ministry, whatever its politics."[108]

106

	Population in Thousands				Population Growth			
	1871	1901	1911	1921	1871–1911	1901–1911	1901–1921	PSI Vote 1919
Apulia								
Bari	49.4	72.3	95.6	110	94%	32%	52%	26.6%
Brindisi	12.1	21.0	22.6	31.1	87	8	34	29.2
Foggia	34.2	49.9	71.6	c. 70	110	44	c. 40	20.7
Taranto	20.5	60.7	69.7	103.9	239	15	72	25.4
Campania								
Naples	1000	1250	1400	1550	40	12.5	24	8.1
Salerno	550	590	600	610	9	1.7	3.4	0.7
Caserta	370	420	430	450	14	2.4	7.1	0.9

The coefficient of correlation (R) between the percentage growth in population from 1901 to 1921 and the 1919 PSI vote = 0.84. Population figures from Domenico Ruocco, *Campania* (Turin, 1965), and Osvaldo Baldacci, *Puglia* (Turin, 1962), *passim*; vols. XIII and XIV of the series *Le regioni d'Italia*.

[107] Antonio Gramsci, *Il Risorgimento* (Turin, 1955), p. 95.

[108] A. Schiavi, "Le ultime elezioni politiche italiane," *La riforma sociale*, XV, 12 (1904), and XVI, 2 (1905), cited in *Compendio delle statistiche elettorali*, II, p. 112. The following table illustrates this remarkable ministerial or "constitutional" support in the South. (The category of "constitutional" has been used throughout because it permits a more consistent comparison between 1919 and 1913.) The 1919 results did not break down in terms of pro- or antiministerial

The geographical patterns of liberal trends were less marked. Giolittians enjoyed obvious prominence in Piedmont. Nationalist candidates were strongest in Milan and white-collar Rome, where the "constitutionals" led other lists with almost 38 percent of the vote. One interesting development is unfortunately obscured by the available figures: the evolution of the Radicals. In 1919 many avowed Radicals campaigned in common slates with liberals or with Republicans and Reformist Socialists, which prevents a precise comparison with earlier contests. Nonetheless, the results revealed a continued migration of Radical strength from the North and Center toward the South.[109] This movement suggests that in contrast to Italian republicanism, radicalism was a fringe of the liberal spectrum—effaced in the North by competing leftist alternatives, preserved in the South as a reformist or merely regional outlet where clientelism and backwardness retarded the growth of socialism. Republicanism, on the other hand, remained a carefully delineated tradition both by virtue of its geographical roots and by its spiritual rejection of the monarchical regime.

Liberals knew that the Socialists were their political foes; they were uncertain about the Popolari, who emerged as a well-dispersed party throughout the North. The Bergamo constituency of the radical priest and agrarian organizer, Guido Miglioli, voted two-thirds Popolare; Brescia, 46 percent; Como-Sondrio, one-third. Venetia proved another Catholic stronghold (35.8 percent) thanks to the "white" organizations of the independent peasants; the Marches had a strong Catholic showing (27.3), as did Rome and its region (26.3). Despite respectable strength in Naples (20.9 percent), and Bari (18.5), political catholi-

positions. The "Constitutional Catholics" have been subtracted from 1913's figures, for they later flowed into the PPI.

	North	Center	South	Islands	Kingdom
1904	56.2%	55.4%	83.1%	74.8%	64.8%
1909	53.9	56.4	87.1	76.1	62.6
1913	67.8	66.5	86.7	82.3	73.7
1919	22.3	35.9	65.0	57.6	36.9

[109]   RADICAL AND RELATED VOTE

Region	1904	1909	1913 (incl. dissident Radicals)	1919 (Separate Radical lists)
North	8.73%	10.13%	8.9%	No separate northern results.
Center	9.21	11.77	9.6	2.4%
South	7.17	7.32	15.7	4.1
Islands	7.46	11.07	18.5	5.2
Total	8.38	9.92	11.7	1.9

cism failed to take hold in the backward areas of the South: Christian Democracy stopped at Eboli. In Basilicata no Popolari ran; in the hilly impoverished Abruzzi they won only 3.5 percent. In Apulia and the islands their vote ranged from 10 to 12 percent. In Calabria and Campagna the results were a bit stronger; but generally in 1919 Popolare support required an assertion of rural peasant consciousness that could not prevail against the South's poverty and patronage.[110]

The Popolari came to Rome as a source of uneasiness for the liberals. They were tainted with neutralism and offended the secularism that still marked the heirs of the Old Right. Most important, their future political course was unpredictable in view of the great split between Catholic radicals such as Miglioli and clerical reactionaries. In the confrontation with the Socialist deputies, liberals would have to win PPI support if they were to retain parliamentary control. But could the Popolari be counted on to vote as good "constitutionalists?" In their convention of December 1919 they divided into a Miglioli faction hostile to Nitti, a group led by the veteran parliamentarian Filippo Meda, who advocated provisional and wary support, and finally a ministerial current that wanted to participate in the government. The Party Secretary, Father Luigi Sturzo, was not so radical as Miglioli, yet he emphatically refused to let the PPI join any antisocialist bloc or merely second the old liberal establishment. Eventually the Popolari gave their votes to the postelection Nitti government, but they insisted on freedom of action. If labor and the Socialists could paralyze the country through strikes, the Popolari could paralyze the parliament by preventing the emergence of a majority. While pacifying the country at large, any government had also to keep on good terms with the Catholics for the sake of retaining its majority. To accomplish both was to exceed the capacity of any liberal premier.[111]

As of the end of 1919, many observers feared that it certainly was beyond the capacity of the incumbent premier. The day after the elections, Socialists and Fascists clashed in Milan and an explosion wounded eight demonstrators. At the opening of the new legislature, the massive PSI contingent that had originally planned to withdraw before the speech from the throne stayed instead to cheer for the

[110] Popolare results in Giusti, *Correnti politiche*. Giusti has worked out for Florence (14 deputies) how the election would have looked if old-style single-member districts had been retained. The Popolari who won 22 percent of the vote and elected three deputies would have been able to seat none of them under the old system. *Correnti politiche*, p. 41.

[111] For PPI attitudes in December 1919 and early 1920, see the reports in *CdS*, December 11, 12, and following, 1919. Also Giulio di Rossi, *Il primo anno di vita del Partito Popolare Italiano* (Rome, 1920), pp. 315 ff.; Gabriele de Rosa, *Il Partito Popolare Italiano* (Bari, 1966), pp. 84–89; Edith Pratt Howard, *Il Partito Popolare Italiano* (Florence, 1957), pp. 199–204.

socialist republic. In the wake of the demonstration in the Chamber, students and officers paraded to the Quirinal palace to manifest their monarchical loyalties. Socialist deputies were attacked in the streets, and in response the party called for two-day general strikes in Milan, Turin, Naples, Genoa, and elsewhere—the advent of a new wave of "strike mania." Nitti seemed unable to control the Chamber or the streets; furthermore, he remained paralyzed over Fiume, where D'Annunzio refused to accept the *modus vivendi* offered by Badoglio on behalf of the government in December.[112]

The Italian elections thus bequeathed to a leader with few friends on the right a situation of peril on the left as well. Henceforth the Chamber reflected the larger social divisions throughout the country; no longer would it serve as a local liberal association writ large. Its transformation signaled that the crisis *within* liberalism was to become a crisis *of* liberalism.

On both sides of the Alps the elections of November 16, 1919, acted as a political burning glass to focus and intensify the developments already underway. In France the voting confirmed a broad antisocialist and nationalist consensus clearly emergent under Clemenceau. In Italy neither Orlando nor Nitti provided consistent bourgeois directives, nor could the electoral mandate furnish them as a surrogate. Hence French bourgeois security seemed consolidated by the results of November 16, whereas Italian conservatives would have to resist the logic of the new parliamentary alignments—or, alternatively, reduce the role of parliament itself. Nationalists had already despaired of democratic procedures to subdue the left and enhance Rome's power; but their solution so far consisted of rebellion at the periphery, not sustained violence at the center. Other conservatives despaired of Nitti's policies, but not of liberal institutions. Within two years each group would move to the more radical conclusion or course of action, because neither was willing to live with the balance of political power reflected by the 1919 election.

Finally, there were sources of instability concealed by even the superficially decisive French mandate. Bourgeois voters might resoundingly condemn working class militance, but they could not make Germany pay or painlessly distribute the costs of the war by casting ballots for conservative candidates. Reparations and the internal distribution of debts and taxes had hardly intruded into a campaign where every nonsocialist candidate had suggested that Germany must pay. But these issues would remain to vex and ultimately to fragment electoral coalitions whether of the right, or later, of the left.

[112] See *CdS*, November, December, 2, 3, and following. Alatri, *Nitti, D'Annunzio e la questione adriatica*, pp. 323 ff. for negotiations on Fiume.

· 3 ·

THE LIMITS OF ECONOMIC
RESTRUCTURING

In the fortnight before the November elections, Europeans commemorated the ending of the great war. On the anniversary of the Armistice, November 11, Marshal Foch attended a solemn high mass at the Invalides and there were banquets in the provinces. President Poincaré enjoyed a brilliant reception in London and marked the Allied triumph at the memorial cenotaph in Whitehall. These sober but confident celebrations contrasted with the tense mood in Italy where the government weighed postponing the anniversary of Vittorio Veneto, November 4, and Nitti discouraged any public wearing of uniforms for fear of provoking street clashes. Berlin clearly took no public note of these events. It snowed on the anniversary of the Revolution, and sympathetic demonstrators thronged around Hindenburg and Ludendorff when they appeared on November 15 as supercilious witnesses before the National Assembly committee investigating the causes of Germany's collapse a year earlier. The differing receptions given the military revealed the wider state of public opinion: the security of bourgeois institutions in France (and England), the sense of their vulnerability in Italy, the hollowness of social democratic power in the German Republic.[1]

A year later there would be less discrepancy. In the interval, working-class and social democratic aspirations would meet decisive setbacks in each country. The reversals were sometimes spectacular, as with the CGT's massive but unsuccessful strikes of spring 1920; sometimes disguised under such evanescent and illusory triumphs as the Italian Occupation of the Factories; sometimes discernible only as the slow dissipation of social democratic authority as in Weimar Germany. By the end of 1920 and early 1921 the left was in retreat everywhere. European governments had become ministries of the center ruling for the center. In Germany the SPD renounced a cabinet role in June 1920; a month later the Nitti ministry was swept away. A new bourgeois equilibrium seemed attainable in Germany and Italy as well as France; it rested on a consensus that united elites and middle

---

[1] "La celebrazione della vittoria rinviata," *CdS*, October 22, 1919; "L'anniversaire de l'armistice," *La Presse de Paris*, November 11, 1919; "L'anniversaire de la révolution allemande," *Le Temps*, November 11, p. 4; *BT*, November 15, 1919. Cf. Ernst Troeltsch, *Spektator–Briefe. Aufsätze über die deutsche Revolution und Politik 1918/22* (Tübingen, 1924), pp. 88–92.

classes against militant working-class claims. Capitalism and bourgeois hierarchies proved more resilient than either defenders or attackers had originally believed.

The movement of restoration, moreover, was wider than the three societies examined here. Across the Atlantic, "red scare" and recession were ushering in the era of normalcy; in Britain the trade unions' campaign for public control of the coal industry, then for defensive wage stabilization, collapsed on Black Friday in April 1921; in Spain radical ferment in the army and the labor movement was receding in a series of violent skirmishes; Social Democrats withdrew from the Austrian coalition; an authoritarian and conservative regime was clamped on truncated Hungary; Lenin inaugurated the New Economic Policy in a partial compromise with private enterprise. In short, the developments analyzed here formed only part of a world-wide Thermidor.

The Evolution of Leftist Objectives

The transition from the turmoil of 1918–1919 to the bourgeois recovery of 1920–1921 was not just an episode of socialist and left-wing defeat. It was also a crisis of transformation and redirection. With some oversimplification, we can distinguish three phases: late 1918 and early 1919 brought a wave of apocalyptic militance punctuated by general strikes. Attackers and defenders alike shared moments of belief that the bourgeois order was near collapse. The year or so after Versailles brought equally militant agitation, but now targeted on more specific economic objectives. With the breaking of the second wave, finally, there emerged a period of internal reorganization for the "long period," marked by working-class schism and the formation of communist parties. Each period brought an intensification of radical commitment—but a narrowing of radical objectives. Usually these developments are examined from the vantage of the left alone; yet each phase reflected not only the internal dynamics of the working-class movement, but the reorganization of West European industrial society as a whole.[2]

In the spring of 1919 the organized working class demonstrated on behalf of a vague Wilsonianism that promised a new international order. But the social democratic left felt betrayed by Wilson himself, as the political leaders in Paris imposed reparations on Germany, rati-

[2] This sequence is suggested by Annie Kriegel, *Aux origines du communisme français*, 2 vols. (Paris and the Hague, 1964), I, pp. 339–340, 539–547; II, pp. 752–754.

fied territorial cessions, and struggled to destroy the bolshevik regime. Disillusioned democrats forgot that Wilson's ideas had clear limits to the left from the outset. Wilson envisaged a confederation of liberal-democratic and noncommunist countries. Like the socialists, he believed that certain regimes were prone to aggressive drives; but while socialists connected capitalism and imperialism, Wilson, as a liberal, linked militarism with unchecked executive power. The armistice demands that he thrust upon Germany were designed to impel the defeated country to change its governing system and to eliminate autocratic power. The treaties he helped frame were meant to associate nation-states that shared the democratic and pluralist politics he defended. The need for American intervention produced a general agreement among European political leaders of the center that self-determination, international organization, German democratization, and the preservation of capitalism and entrepreneurship should remain the baselines for international and domestic settlement. Those elements who did not consent were intended to remain outside the new comity: on one side, the unreconstructed right, represented, for instance, by the Prussian-German ruling class, or on the other side, the revolutionary left.

Wilson's convictions and American power deeply influenced the goals and strategies of all segments of the left during 1918–1919. In effect, Wilson persuaded Western socialists to acquiesce for over a year in a relatively unfavorable political *status quo* for the sake of a supposedly world-transforming peace. This socialist cooperation helped to isolate the pro-Leninist left in the West and kept bourgeois institutions more immune from attack than they might have been otherwise.[3]

The signing of the Versailles Treaty on June 28, 1919, the failure of the *scioperissimo* in July, and the completion of the Weimar Constitution in August indicated a new stabilization. Leftist aspirations reflected this change as well. No longer did European labor demonstrate for a vast but vague democratization. It sought definite guarantees for the working class by restructuring economic institutions. This meant that social democratic parties focused on social transformation— and when this, too, was frustrated, a remnant looked for new political discipline through the Third International. In the evolution, ironically enough, the left discovered the same advantages of corporate organ-

[3] For these themes, see N. Gordon Levin, Jr., *Woodrow Wilson and World Politics, America's Response to War and Revolution* (New York, 1970); Arno J. Mayer, *Political Origins of the New Diplomacy, 1917–1918* (New Haven, 1959); and Mayer, *Politics and Diplomacy of Peace-making: Containment and Counterrevolution at Versailles, 1918–1919* (New York, 1967).

ization that business and the right were learning. Its own proposals came to focus less on transforming society as a whole than upon preserving a quota of working-class power in that society. In light of the resilience of the capitalist order in the West, working-class parties unconsciously changed their strategy to one appropriate for pluralist competition rather than radical restructuring. The Thermidor of 1919–1920 was a period of reeducation as much as repression.

The major proposals of the socialist left during 1919–1920 centered around factory councils, nationalization, and economic planning. It was the council movement that embodied the most radical potential; for (as seen in Chapter One) it threatened to undermine established union hierarchies as well as authority patterns of industry. But the councils' proposals did not have to be radical. They could evolve into schemes of working-class representation at the plant level. They could become just new means for cooptation and enhancing entrepreneurial authority. What actual political and economic thrust the councils would have remained to be worked out.

In Germany the councils underwent several stages of development. The workers' councils and soldiers' councils that mushroomed in the revolution were intended as emanations of direct public will designed to undercut old hierarchies and authorities. Despite the borrowing of the name from the Russian experience, their membership was not always socialist or radical; they aspired to representative democracy; and their delegates voted to reestablish and strengthen parliamentary institutions in December 1918. As workers' and soldiers' councils lost their political power during early 1919 with the restoration of a new central authority, focus shifted to factory councils and workers' chambers. These organs were intended by their advocates to have extensive power in overseeing the economic order; they would plan production and make the worker a part of the planning process. As one enthusiast wrote, "The council system means (for the class-conscious working class) hope for earthly goods in the material realm, and in the spiritual, the transcendence of parties and parliamentarism and the resurrection of the free man out of oppressive need."[4] After repeated strikes and clashes, as seen above, the workers of the Ruhr, Berlin, and central Germany secured the inclusion of councils in the constitution. But the fight over the prerogatives and structure that these councils were actually to have was protracted and bitter.

[4] Ernst Jacobi, "Wesen und Bedeutung des Rätesystems," *Wirtschaftliches Kampfbuch für Betriebsräte* (Berlin, 1920), now in Günter Hillmann, ed., *Die Rätebewegung*, i (Reinbeck bei Hamburg, 1967), p. 173.

When did the call for factory councils represent a radical demand? When did it advance the socialist transformation of society? These remained critical but unanswered questions, not only in Germany, but in Italy and to a lesser degree in Austria and in England as well. For the concept of the factory council was malleable. Those who led the movement saw the *Räte* as the cutting edge of socialism or even proletarian revolution. In the winter and spring of 1919, the radicals of the Berlin labor movement, especially Ernst Däumig and Richard Müller, looked to the factory councils as transforming agents within capitalist society. Political parties such as the SPD or USP, agreed the Second *Räte* Congress of April 1919, had matured within the bourgeois state and were inappropriate organs for socialization. Instead the *Räte* theorists planned a pyramid of regional workers' councils and an overlapping hierarchy of factory and industry-wide councils. Regional workers' councils would arbitrate disputes between factory councils and factory owners. Each level of the two hierarchies would exert a broader overseeing function up to a general economic parliament and/or Central Council. The councils would thus serve as instruments for socialization; they would allow the working class to exercise a nonbureaucratic public control on behalf of the community. From factory control one could get to *Sozialisierung*.[5]

But was the path to socialism really clear? In his columns of March and April 1919, Marxist critic Karl Korsch complained that the idea of socialism remained undefined among Social Democrats. Like other *Räte* advocates, Korsch feared that nationalization alone could not alter the position of the worker. Rather than simply changing the ownership of the means of production, one had to transform the process of production from within. On the other hand, syndicalist efforts simply to place workers in control of their factories could work to the detriment of the wider community and would merely create a new "special property." The real task was to evolve from private property via an intermediate "group egoism" to common ownership. Korsch's own suggestion for reconciling workers' control with the economic needs of the whole society was "industrial autonomy"—the socialization of specific branches of economic activity or, as he wrote in April, "industrial democracy" and "control from below." Ownership

---

[5] Peter von Oertzen, *Betriebsräte in der Novemberrevolution* (Düsseldorf, 1963), pp. 86–94, 100–102, and cf. 149–150; Richard Müller, *Was die Arbeiterräte wollen und sollen* (Berlin, 1919), and Müller, *Vom Kaiserreich zur Republik*, 2 vols. (Vienna, 1924–1925), II, pp. 107–111; Ernst Däumig's report to the Second Congress of *Räte* was printed as *Der Aufbau der Rätegedanke* (April 1919), and his report after the conference is excerpted as "Die Bilanz des[2.] Räte Kongresses," in Hillmann, ed., *Die Rätebewegung*, esp. pp. 127–128.

would be vested in the state, while through their councils, workers and managers together would run their own industry without class conflict over property rights. The *Räte* system was crucial to this sector-by-sector transformation of decision making and ownership, since it alone could combine the goals of workers' control from below with those of socialization from above.[6]

Korsch's concepts of industrial autonomy, industrial democracy, and control from below partook of the guild-socialist and works-councils schemes discussed in the British Labour Party.[7] But while British intellectuals and trade unionists vigorously demanded a new economic order, they did not benefit from the collapse of traditional power. In Germany the revolution provided far greater opportunity for reconstruction, but the occasion was lost, in part because socialism remained an elusive and ill-defined objective. SPD leaders generally distrusted any attack upon the hierarchies of modern industry and defined socialism as the maximization of the general welfare. This allowed even conservatives and business leaders to design a socialism that they could accept.

Both the original coal socialization effort of 1919 and the evolution of *Gemeinwirtschaft* plans in the Economics Ministry revealed how plastic were the notions of socialism in play. The USP-SPD provisional revolutionary government had proclaimed the principle of socialization in December 1918 and had established a study committee composed, among others, of Emil Lederer, the editor of the *Archiv für Sozialwissenschaft und Sozialpolitik*, Kautsky and Hilferding, union leaders Hue and Umbreit, and the unorthodox conservative, Joseph Schumpeter. Its functions were not clear, and it clashed with the conservative Wirtschaftsamt (RWA) under Colonel Koeth and the old SPD leader August Müller. Its majority called for collective exploitation of the coal mines under a supervisory organ representing company directors, workers, coal consumers, and the Reich. Instead, the govern-

---

[6] Karl Korsch, "Die Sozialisierungsfrage vor und nach der Revolution" [1919], in: Korsch, *Schriften zur Sozialisierung*, Erich Gerlach, ed. (Frankfurt am Main, 1969), pp. 50–54; also "Was ist Sozialisierung?" [March 1919], *ibid.*, esp. pp. 15–21, 26–27, 32–41. On Korsch in this period, see Hedda Korsch, "Memories of Karl Korsch," *New Left Review*, 76 (November–December 1972), pp. 39–40. Cf. Heinrich Ströbel, *Socialisation in Theory and Practice*, H. J. Stenning, trans. (London, 1922), for a review of current socialization concepts.

[7] See, for example, Arthur Gleason, *What the Workers Want* (New York, 1920), esp. pp. 169 ff., 185 ff.; G.D.H. Cole, *Workshop Organization* (Oxford, 1923); L. P. Carpenter, *G.D.H. Cole: An Intellectual Biography* (Cambridge, 1973), pp. 77–111; Walter Kendall, *The Revolutionary Movement in Britain, 1900–1921. The Origins of British Communism* (London, 1969), pp. 142–169 on shop stewards, pp. 278 ff. on guild socialism.

ment's bill disregarded the report and provoked the resignation of the
First Socialization Commission, which felt that it fell short of any
meaningful transfer of German coal resources to the public.[8]

The principles behind the bill were similar to those of the planning
precedents of the war and to those concurrently under consideration
for regulation of the entire national economy. The law erected a compulsory Coal Association (RKV) out of eleven regional coal syndicates
and crowned the structure with a Coal Council (RKR) that could
regulate prices and market quotas. The state kept a right of veto
over Coal Council price decisions; but within the new Council, real
influence reverted to the mine owners while the planned participation
of workers' and consumers' representatives remained only theoretical.
In large measure the new structure degenerated quickly into a new
cartel, all the more formidable because it was state sponsored. The
Coal Council merely passed along to the Ministry the managers' requests from the regional syndicates and from the Coal Association,
where real policy continued to be made.[9]

The plan behind the Coal Council and Coal Association stemmed
not from the left but from the State Secretary at the Economics Ministry, Moellendorff, and Economics Minister Wissell. Moellendorff in
turn had assisted Rathenau, first at General Electric (AEG), then in
the critical Raw Materials Division of the Prussian War Ministry. The
practical model for the proposed "common economy" was the war experience, with economic supervision by boards of businessmen and
officials and mixed governmental and private companies. Both men,
however, pushed beyond this precedent to design a future "organic"
economic order in which wasteful competition was to be eliminated
by industrial self-government based upon regional and industry-wide
associations. The collaboration of labor and management, producers

[8] Clash of the Socialization Commission with Koeth, in Wolfgang Elben, *Das
Problem der Kontinuität in der deutschen Revolution. Die Politik der Staats-
sekretäre und der militarischen Führung vom November 1918 bis Februar 1919*
(Düsseldorf, 1965), pp. 81–83; Oertzen, *Betriebsräte*, p. 248; Hans Schieck, "Der
Kampf um die deutsche Wirtschaftspolitik nach dem Novemberumsturz 1918,"
Diss. (Heidelberg, 1958), pp. 58 ff.; reports of the Commission reprinted as
"Anhang" to *Verhandlungen der [zweiten] Sozialisierungs-Kommission für den
Bergbau im Jahre 1920*, 2 vols. (Berlin, 1920). Legislative debates on the bills,
March 7, 8, and 13, in VNV: SB, 326, pp. 541 ff., 565 ff., 697 ff., and 327, pp.
746 ff., 775 ff. Cf. comparable plans in the concurrent Austrian debates in Charles
A. Gulick, *Austria from Habsburg to Hitler*, 2 vols. (Berkeley, Calif., 1948), p. 136.

[9] Maurice Baumont, *La grosse industrie allemande et le charbon* (Paris, 1928),
pp. 125–128; also Heinrich Göppert, "Die Sozialisierungsbestrebungen in Deutschland nach der Revolution," *Schmollers Jahrbuch für Gesetzgebung, Verwaltung,
und Volkswirtschaft im deutschen Reich*, 45/2 (1921), p. 329, for general criticism of German socialization effort.

and consumers, and appointees representing the public interest or the state, would allegedly make these associations the interlocking basis for a true industrial commonwealth.

These ideas had a wide resonance. They found favor among younger bureaucrats and left-liberals who wanted to bridge the gap between socialist and bourgeois concepts: men such as Rathenau himself and the editor of the liberal *Vossische Zeitung*, Georg Bernhard, friendly to the new Democratic Party and ebullient advocate for all the parity-council networks.

These themes also found an echo deep in the German right, as evidenced, for example, by Spengler's 1920 vision of a conservative Prussian socialism. They harked back to Fichte's idea of the closed commercial state; and the wartime encirclement of Germany only intensified their emotional resonance.[10]

Moellendorff carried his ideas from the Prussian War Ministry to Weimar's Ministry of Economics, where they served as the basis for the coal socialization bill and then for the memorandum of May 7, 1919: "The Construction of the Common Economy." The coal nationalization bill was intended as a pilot for the general economic restructuring envisaged by the Ministry's controversial memorandum. As mentioned above, the Moellendorff-Wissell proposal called for planning and supervisory organs for each branch of production—e.g., iron, coal, paper, chemicals—ranging from the local and regional level up to industry-wide national councils. Overlapping advisory bodies, which would weigh regional economic needs, would culminate in a National Council of Labor to serve as an economic parliament for Germany. A firm such as German General Electric might thus have delegates among the consumer representatives of a steel industry board, among the producer delegates of a machinery board, and finally on a Berlin regional council. The network of economic advisory bodies would seek to minimize wasteful competition and plan production by assigning raw materials, output quotas, and prices.[11]

[10] For the connection between war measures and "common economy" ideas, see W. F. Bruck, "Die Kriegsunternehmung. Versuch einer Systematik," *Archiv für Sozialwissenschaft und Sozialpolitik*, 48, 3 (1921), pp. 547–595. For the theoretical writings: Walther Rathenau, *Die neue Wirtschaft* (Berlin, 1918); *Von kommenden Dingen* (Berlin, 1917); Wichard von Moellendorff, *Konservativer Sozialismus* (Berlin, 1932), pp. 166–195; Ralph H. Bowen, *German Ideas of the Corporative State with Special Reference to the Period 1870–1918* (New York, 1947). For the attractiveness to conservative circles, Oswald Spengler, "Prussianism and Socialism" [1920], in *Selected Essays*, Donald O. White, ed. (Chicago, 1967). A trenchant critique of conservative tendencies in Rathenau's post-1918 writings is in Emil Lederer, "Randglossen der neuesten Schriften Walther Rathenaus," *Archiv für Sozialwissenschaft und Sozialpolitik*, 47, 1 (1921), pp. 286–303.
[11] Wichard von Moellendorff, *Der Aufbau der Gemeinwirtschaft. Denkschrift des Reichswirtschaftsministeriums vom 8. [sic] Mai, 1919* (Jena, 1919); unpub-

This blueprint for "economic self-administration" had some similarity to the *Räte* networks that the SPD was reluctantly prepared to "anchor" in the new constitution. But its political thrust diverged from the plans that USPD leaders and shop stewards advocated. Where the theorists of the left wanted factory councils and regional workers' councils to exercise key decision-making power, the Moellendorff-Wissell scheme involved parity representation with management delegates at all levels. Working-class power exercised from the factory— the heart of the councils idea—yielded to a class-neutral technocratic concept.

In this format the "Common Economy" plans really appealed only to relatively conservative Social Democrats, especially the revisionist and corporative thinkers around Max Cohen, Julius Kaliski, and the *Sozialistische Monatshefte*. First at the second national Congress of *Räte* in April, then at the SPD Party Congress in June 1919, Cohen warmly advocated a network of local Production Councils crowned by a Chamber of Labor, which would serve as an economic parliament alongside the Reichstag. In appearance the scheme was close to the left's *Räte* proposals, and the *Räte* Congress had accepted a resolution along Cohen's lines. But like the Moellendorff-Wissell concept, the Cohen-Kaliski proposal rested upon a parity basis, not upon workers' delegations. By stressing efficiency instead of working-class power—by emphasizing aggregate output rather than redistribution—the Cohen-Kaliski ideas added to the rhetoric of production that the right turned to its own uses throughout postwar Europe. Socialization as an enhancement of productivity for the community might be worthy in the abstract. Still, it remained an objective that was likely to end up reinforcing the traditional hierarchies of capitalism.[12]

Cohen's ideas awoke no enthusiasm at the 1919 Party Congress. But this did not mean that the SPD was prepared to take a more radical stance. Hugo Sinzheimer defended the workers' councils with great

---

lished form now included in Hagen Schulze, ed., *Das Kabinett Scheidemann. 13. Februar bis 20. Juni 1919.* In *Akten der Reichskanzlei: Weimarer Republik* (Boppard am Rhein, 1971), pp. 272–283, and accompanying "Wirtschaftsprogramm," pp. 284–289.

[12] Cohen-Kaliski proposal in *Dokumenten und Materialen zur deutschen Arbeiterbewegung*, vi/vii (Berlin, 1966), pp. 64–65. April *Räte* Congress summarized in Oertzen, *Betriebsräte*, pp. 261–262; excerpts in Eberhard Kolb and Reinhard Rürup, eds., *Der Zentralrat der deutschen Sozialistischen Republik 19. 12. 1918–8. 4. 1919* (Leiden, 1968), pp. 790–805. For a sharp distinction between economic measures aimed at productivity and development and those aiming at socialism as the replacement of private property, see Emanuel Hugh Vogel, "Die Sozialisierungsgesetzgebung Deutsch-Österreichs in ihrer volkswirtschaftlichen Bedeutung," *Archiv für Sozialwissenschaft und Sozialpolitik*, 48, 1 (1921), pp. 75–76.

verve as being compatible with democracy. He successfully attacked the idea of an economic parliament as being just a new form of estatist representation, which would entrench the big "interests." The congress' resolutions supported Sinzheimer's vindication of the *Räte*, but probably the party leadership most appreciated his insistence that only the state, not the councils, could socialize industry. Despite the resolutions, the party leadership still shared Cohen's belief that socialism meant a vague furthering of community welfare through more efficient production, not a redistribution of power from capitalists to workers. Chancellor Bauer distrusted workers' and factory councils and "wildcat socialization" such as had marked the Ruhr agitation of March. Workers, Theodore Leipart told fellow union leaders at their Nuremberg Congress, could not socialize on their own. Like Cohen, the SPD leaders were more comfortable with parity institutions than with working-class power.[13]

What is more, SPD leaders refused to endorse the project of their own Ministry of Economics. Robert Schmidt, who held the portfolio of food and agriculture, complained that Wissell's *Gemeinwirtschaft* did not advance the collectivist ownership that the old Erfurt Program had envisioned; instead, he urged, the SPD should press its traditional objective of nationalizing particular monopolistic industries.[14] The Democratic Party coalition partners of the SPD also disliked the planning concepts. Still, they would have acquiesced; and the SPD could no doubt have pushed nationalization of a few major industries through the Reichstag by threatening to unleash working-class demonstrations.[15] But the party leaders were legalistic. As craft-union veterans, they remained uneasy with the spontaneity of younger industrial workers not safely organized in their own venerable cadres; and as cabinet ministers, Wissell and his SPD colleagues remained at odds over their respective bureaucratic fiefs.

[13] For the Sinzheimer-Cohen debate, see *Protokoll über die Verhandlungen des Parteitages der Sozialdemokratischen Partei Deutschlands, abgehalten in Weimar vom 10 bis 15. Juni 1919* (Berlin, 1919), pp. 406–455; resolution along Sinzheimer lines, pp. 113, 126–127. Cf. renewed debate: *Protokoll . . . des Parteitages . . . in Kassell vom 10. bis 16. Oktober 1920* (Berlin, 1920), pp. 120–143. Leipart's caution to Free Trade Union (ADGB) congress in Nuremberg, cited in Oertzen, *Betriebsräte*, p. 262. For union attitudes, see Emil Lederer, "Die Gewerkschaftsbewegung 1918/1919 und die Entfaltung der wirtschaftlichen Ideologien in der Arbeiterklasse," *Archiv für Sozialwissenschaft und Sozialpolitik*, 47, 1 (1920), esp. pp. 244–260.
[14] See Robert Schmidt's memo as SPD Minister of Food and Agriculture, May 7, 1919, in Schultze, ed., *Akten: Scheidemann*, pp. 289–297; also his comments at the Weimar SPD debates: *Protokoll über die Verhandlungen des Parteitages*, p. 383.
[15] Cf. Friedberg at the DDP Executive session April 12 and 13, 1919: "If we topple the government, where will be the bayonets with which the bourgeois parties can maintain themselves?" NSDAP Hauptarchiv/f. 723.

Bourgeois attitudes toward economic self-administration and planning were also mixed, but for reasons different from those of the SPD. The underlying issue, many realized, was to what extent the proposals would actually strengthen capitalist power while nominally controlling it. Felix Pinner, the astute economic columnist for the left-liberal *Berliner Tageblatt*, saw the plans of the Economics Ministry as a new license for the largest and most ruthless enterprises to enhance their own market preeminence. "Behind a lovely, painted, precious facade, behind a tangle of front and rear entrances is hidden what looks like a duplicate of the old cartel spirit." The Moellendorff-Wissell draft would only fetter healthy entrepreneurial innovation on behalf of the old, oppressive cartels.[16]

The attitude of businessmen also remained mixed. Traditional-minded industrialists tended to reject the proposals angrily, as did one spokesman at the June meeting of the Reichsverband der deutschen Industrie, who claimed "that supply and demand and the market economy will continue to rule the world, and no resolutions and manipulation from any advisory bodies and green baize tables will eliminate them in the conceivable future."[17] Others became more flexible. Jakob Reichert originally claimed in early 1919 that he would prefer naked government coercion to the half-truths of Moellendorff's "self-administration." But by June he was ready to accept a compromise that could be exploited by heavy industry in its search for cartels: "The given factor is industry's great desire to build horizontally and not vertically with consumer and commercial interests."[18] The major objection for the Ruhr coal and steel producers was their having to share power over prices and distribution with the purchasers of their plate and pipe.

In one way, the Wissell-Moellendorff plans were more dangerous than proposals for outright socialization: they promised a more feasible, hence more menacing degree of government control. Nevertheless, as events were to prove, they could be exploited by business interests. Whether state supervision would strengthen the "common good" or the power of industry was uncertain. Back in 1910, Hilferding himself had predicted that the development of *Finanzkapital*—the emergence of cartels and of interlocking industry and banking combinations—

[16] Felix Pinner, "Planmässige Wirtschaft," *BT*, May 31, 1919, p.m. Other criticisms in Bowen, *German Theories of the Corporative State*, pp. 196–203.

[17] "Beratungen über die Frage der Selbstverwaltungskörper, 12. Juni 1919," *Veröffentlichungen des Reichsverbandes der deutschen Industrie*, 3. Heft (July 1919), p. 19.

[18] "Aufzeichnung über eine Besprechung am 15. Mai 1919 im Reichswirtschafts-amt . . . ," p. 18 in BA, Koblenz: R 13 I (VdESI)/191, p. 191. Later statement in "Beratungen über . . . Selbstverwaltungskörper," *Veröffentlichungen*, pp. 29–30.

effectively prepared the way for socialism. All that would be needed would be the public take-over of the new organizations gestated by capitalism itself. Socialism by this route, however, presupposed that working-class delegates were in prior political control, whereas German Social Democracy shrank from exercising decisive power. Under these conditions, planning might merely rationalize capitalism.[19]

Planning ideas and the call for councils had the same ambiguities elsewhere in Europe. In Great Britain by the late nineteenth century, the Fabian Society was advocating industrial self-government, which envisioned a parliament of industrial representatives alongside Westminster. Less statist in orientation, the Guild Socialist movement advocated rule by producer groups, while by the end of the war, the demands of the shop stewards recalled much of the German Factory Council movement. But in Britain as in Germany, workers' councils could quietly be defused into grievance committees or the new "Whitley Councils" designed to secure better harmony between management and labor. The Labour Party and unions' demand for take-over of the coal industry would also be deflected—in this case by Lloyd George, who established a commission of workers, owners, and jurists to study nationalization, and then discarded its recommendations in a development comparable to the fate of Weimar's Socialization Committee. By the fall of 1919 both the pressure of nationalization and the powerful shop stewards' movement had dissipated. The year that began with a Red Flag hoisted over Glasgow City Hall ended with a trade union movement frustrated by Lloyd George's skillful parrying of nationalization and workers' control.[20]

The other major testing ground for the councils of 1919–1920 was Italy.[21] There, too, the movement was fragile; but for a brief year, indefatigably encouraged by Antonio Gramsci's essays in *L'Ordine*

[19] Rudolf Hilferding, *Das Finanzkapital* [1910] (Frankfurt/Main, 1968), p. 47; cf. Charles S. Maier, "Between Taylorism and Technocracy: European Ideologies and the Vision of Industrial Productivity in the 1920's," *Journal of Contemporary History*, 5, 2 (1970), pp. 27–60.

[20] See Charles L. Mowat, *Britain between the Wars, 1918–1940* (Chicago, 1955), pp. 17–43; Gleason, *What the Workers Want*, pp. 394–440; Alan Bullock, *The Life and Times of Ernest Bevin*, I, *Trade Union Leader, 1881–1940* (London, 1960), pp. 68–72, 98 ff. G. D. H. Cole, *Labour in the Coal-Mining Industry (1914-1921)* (Oxford, 1923), pp. 77–121.

[21] It is worth noting the relative weakness of this movement in France despite a tradition of syndicalist organization. Workers' delegates had not wrested the wartime prerogatives they had elsewhere; nor, apparently was the idea of factory delegations easily reconciled with the stratification that French authority patterns inculcated. See, William Oualid and Charles Picquenard, *Salaires et tariffes, conventions collectives et grèves: la politique du Ministère de l'Armament* (Paris and New Haven, 1928), pp. 420–440, 502–509; Roger Picard, *Le mouvement syndical durant la guerre* (Paris and New Haven, 1927), pp. 118–131.

Nuovo, it provided a focus for working-class aspirations. Gramsci and his young Turin collaborators seized on the factory council in early 1919 as an Italian equivalent of the Russian soviets. Despite the strictures of colleagues such as Angelo Tasca, who charged that *L'Ordine Nuovo* was seeking to emulate an inappropriate model for Italy, Gramsci's factory councils enjoyed a brief and turbulent recruitment in Turin. The Piedmontese metropolis of 500,000 offered a special, favorable terrain: it was dominated by the new engineering and automobile industry, which had developed since the turn of the century and expanded enormously during the war. As in Germany, wartime legislation authorized new worker delegations or *commissioni interne*. For the enthusiastic Gramsci the new councils that were emerging could serve as a revolutionary crucible, the "national territory" for the class that had no fatherland. Through the councils workers would educate themselves to a new consciousness of their position as producers and as objects of exploitation. More directly than trade union or party, the council would emanate directly from the workers' position in the factory, without the need for a mediating bureaucracy or the danger of cooptation.[22]

Gramsci's journalistic efforts were inspired by and in turn influenced the struggles at Turin's Fiat works. But as in Germany, the trade unions distrusted the new emphasis on the plant, while Socialist Party leaders suspected the councils of anarchosyndical tendencies. Even fellow radicals and future communists such as Amadeo Bordiga felt that Gramsci underestimated the political momentum needed for revolution. Tasca accused him of succumbing to his own intellectualism and "idealism" in the very preoccupation with undermining Crocean culture. The elan of the movement, however, could not simply be ignored. The Socialist Party and the CGL were forced to take account of the workplace demands during the labor agitation of spring 1920, as workers began to commandeer their plants and carry on production rather than submit to proprietors' lockouts. By the time of the massive occupation of the factories, when workers took over plants throughout northern Italy, Gramsci wrote, "Every factory is an illegal state, a proletarian republic that lives day to day, awaiting the unfolding of

[22] For major statements on councils see Antonio Gramsci, *L'Ordine Nuovo* (Turin, 1955), pp. 123–135, 176–186; and for the polemic with Tasca, pp. 127–131, 146–153; also Angelo Tasca, *Nascita e avvento del fascismo*, 2 vols. (Bari, 1965), I, pp. 25–26, 37 (n. 42), 122. Cf. Paolo Spriano, *Torino operaia nella grande guerra (1914–1918)* (Turin, 1960), pp. 297–302 on the *commissioni interne* or factory delegations and pp. 315–335 for Gramsci's concepts during 1917–1918. For socioeconomic conditions: Giuseppe Prato, *Il Piemonte e gli effetti della guerra sulla sua vita economica e sociale* (Bari and New Haven, 1925), pp. 166–210.

events."[23] As in Germany, however, originally radical organizational forms could lose their radical impetus. At the apparent zenith of labor upheaval the radical thrust of the workers' councils proposals was blunted. What the metalworkers initiated as a strike to defend wages became a spontaneous seizure of factories and impelled the CGL leadership to adopt the demand for workers' control. But under CGL leadership, "syndical control" changed from a revolutionary claim to a demand for a union voice in overseeing factory conditions.

This evolution, it turned out, was a common pattern. In both Italy and Germany the councils' movement became domesticated under the persuasion of traditional working-class leaders and perspicacious bourgeois statesmen. Workers' control, which originated as a wedge for revolution, ended by heralding a new approach to industrial relations. Indeed, both possibilities had been present from the outset. For Gramsci the councils had been intended to prepare a Leninist revolution as well as a reorientation of culture and values. For Austrian Marxists such as Max Adler, the councils would anchor a working-class democracy. For those trade union leaders who could overcome their initial suspicions, the councils offered a new self-determination for factory labor. The councils could thus hold either old union beer or new revolutionary liquor. Bourgeois leaders were prepared to drain a glass if the workers agreed to the weaker potion.[24]

Now, too, socialists presented other ostensibly advanced proposals, not so much as assaults upon capitalism but as measures by which society could recover the trust of its working classes and enhance productivity. Albert Thomas on the right of the SFIO and other French socialists urged nationalization of the French railroads on nonradical grounds. Since the 1880's, private firms had developed French railway lines in return for state guarantees of a profitable rate of return on railroad bonds. The aim was to encourage investors to finance a railroad network for low-traffic regions in the interior that would yield only meager income. The state was scheduled to receive a share of all revenues that exceeded the guaranteed interest and dividends, but this return proved a mirage except for the heavily traveled lines of the

---

[23] "Domenica Rossa," from *Avanti!* (Turin), September 5, 1920, now in *L'Ordine Nuovo*, p. 165. The PSI's maximalists praised the councils at the Party's Congress of Bologna in October 1919, but after the April 1920 strike in Turin, the metalworkers' union (FIOM) asked for more effective trade-union control over the movement. See Tasca, *Nascita e avvento del fascismo*, I, p. 134; for the strike movement, see part two, below, and Paolo Spriano, *Storia del Partito Comunista Italiano*, I. *Da Bordiga a Gramsci* (Turin, 1967), pp. 50–63.

[24] Workers' councils had been consciously adopted in Austria as a control measure designed to limit "wildcat socialization": Gulick, *Austria from Habsburg to Hitler*, I, p. 137; Karl Pribram, "Die Sozialpolitik im neuen Österreich," *Archiv für Sozialwissenschaft und Sozialpolitik*, 48, 3 (1920–1921), pp. 647–649.

North and the "PLM," or Paris-Lyon-Méditerranée. During the war the government took over the roads; and advocates of nationalization saw no reason to revert to the old system with its subsidies of what they claimed was an inefficient private management. On the other hand, the owners and managers, who had united as the Association of Stock and Bondholders in French Railways, argued that heavy wartime use justified new massive assistance. Rejecting nationalization, they asked instead that the state pay for their rolling stock and assume their indebtedness, which by 1919 totaled 22 billion francs.[25]

As the railroad system became the focal point of large-scale labor disputes in 1920, the CGT adopted a plan for nationalization that Léon Blum introduced in parliament. This proposal called for an autonomous public railroad corporation to be directed by consumer representatives, workers, and management. In its sharing of control with the existing entrepreneurs the plan was a moderate one, recalling the German coal scheme of 1919. The timing of the measure, moreover, which came as the unions were under attack, made it more defensive than otherwise. Nationalization, the deputy Lobet explained in the Chamber debate, was the only way of restoring to the allegedly demoralized personnel of the railroads a confidence that their welfare and that of the public were heeded by management.[26] In short, nationalization was advanced as an efficient remedy for a wasteful industry and a way of restoring morale and commitment to the workers. Nationalization, the socialists and CGT claimed, would give the workers a stake in their workplace. These were important aims for any labor movement, but certainly more limited and focused than the strikers' demands of 1919. The change reflected the stabilization of the wider bourgeois society that the elections of November 1919 had already confirmed. The working class did not abandon its militancy but went on from apocalyptic to professional objectives.

By 1920, therefore, the aspirations of the radical left were taken up by labor-union leaders and reformist socialists across Europe. Workers who had struck for a Wilsonian peace, against intervention in Russia,

[25] On the railroad problem: Kimon A. Doukas, *The French Railroads and the State* (New York, 1945), pp. 94–95; socialist views in Georges Lefranc, *Le mouvement socialiste sous la Troisième République* (Paris, 1963), pp. 226–227; Edgard Milhaud, *Les fermiers généraux du rail* (Paris, 1920), pp. 371–372; railroad managers' and related views: JOC, 1920, p. 268 (Noblemaire speech); "La crise des chemins de fer," *Le Temps*, February 26, 1920; Georges Allix, "Sur les chemins de fer français," *RPP*, cv (November 1920). Cf. also Harvey J. Bressler, "The French Railway Problem," *Political Science Quarterly*, 37, 2 (June 1922).

[26] Lobet in JOC, 1920, p. 292 (February 24). See renewed debate over Le Troquer project, December 7, 14–15 and following: *ibid.*, pp. 3496 ff., 3617–3634 (including Blum-CGT alternative, p. 3630), 3647–3656.

or, more limitedly, for the long-sought eight hours, compelled working-class spokesmen to press for nationalization or factory-council power. Yet even as working-class leaders nominally took up the cause of economic restructuring, they altered it: the measures they urged were really intended not to transform capitalism but to protect working-class enclaves within it. In effect, this meant merely that the organized working class adapted itself to the corporatist strategy of the wider society. The power of the working class ebbed in 1920 and 1921. Wartime production needs and deferred postwar demand declined. Instead, postwar recession created gluts of coal and steel and a slack labor market. Proposals for nationalization and factory councils thus took on a defensive aspect; they would entrench the working class in capitalist power structures and consolidate the social guarantees won in World War I, like proletarian La Rochelles confronting a bourgeois hinterland.

It was not merely the social democrats who responded in this way. The next step in the evolution of working-class politics was the transformation of the revolutionary left, which now sought to consolidate its inner capacity of resistance. Having failed to shake capitalist power by general militancy in 1919, the socialists also failed to transform the capitalist economy by more professional and targeted economic demands in 1920. By the end of 1920, the working-class movements themselves were on the defensive. For the radicals in the European socialist parties, only Soviet Russia remained a homeland for revolution. Their aim narrowed once again, now into one of support for Moscow's communists. Simultaneously, the Soviet leaders defined their own aims outside Russia in terms of creating a disciplined phalanx of supporters and of forcing a break with the compromising elements of the Second International.

A word is needed about that development and its timing: the impetus for the formation of the Western communist parties came from the second congress of the Third International, convened at Moscow during the summer of 1920. The congress coincided with the Red Army's exhilarating advance on Warsaw during the Russo-Polish war, which the Poles had launched with the encouragement of French officials the preceding spring. For a brief mid-summer month the hope of igniting Central European revolution by military success kindled communist elan and a harsh fervor. Delegates of the left who came to Moscow were caught up in an atmosphere of radical intoxication. As L. O. Frossard noted, "The current is carrying us away."[27]

[27] Cited in Robert Wohl, *French Communism in the Making, 1914–1924* (Stanford, Calif., 1966), p. 178; the international situation: Piotr S. Wandycz, *France*

The current was strong and cold, however. For adherence to the Third International, Soviet leaders levied their famous twenty-one conditions, which required that socialist parties adopt the name Communist and expel their "opportunists," including some singled out by name, such as Turati, Kautsky, Hilferding, and Longuet. What Moscow demanded at a moment of triumph, however, had to be executed at the advent of a more sober era. By autumn the Poles had pushed the Soviets back inside their old frontiers, and within each Western country plans for a radical change of economic structure had darkened. The defeat of the French strike in May 1920, the electoral reversal in Germany, and the meager upshot of the occupation of the factories suggested that working-class power had already peaked. As the USPD majority voted to join the small German Communist Party, as the French and Italian socialist parties moved toward the schisms of Tours in late December and of Livorno three weeks later, the emphasis on revolutionary purity itself became defensive.

Not that working-class "alienation" was diminished. Disgust with bourgeois institutions intensified during the course of the conflicts and setbacks of 1920. The rebuffs of 1919 and 1920, resentments at war and inflation, and the very resilience of capitalism only convinced many in the old parties that a break must be made, that the equivocal stance of social democracy was bankrupt. The prospect of losing large masses did not dismay the supporters of the twenty-one demands. "There is no need to be many," Gramsci argued, citing the Soviet experience. The adherents of the twenty-one demands won a majority of the SFIO and USPD, but only a minority of the Italian Socialist Party, which declared adhesion to the Third International yet reserved interpretation of contested points according to local conditions. In each country the communists distilled out a party of revolutionary dedication but at a moment of working-class setback.[28]

The constituting of disciplined Marxist parties, defined on the basis of schism and stringent criteria of loyalty, suggested, in fact, the toughness of European bourgeois society and not its fragility. The Third International emerged from the revolutionary left's own recognition of the ascendant conservative recovery of 1920–1921, including the society's ability to blunt labor militancy and absorb some working-class representatives into a new structure of interest-group bargaining. The adherents of the Third International regrouped to preserve a

and Her Eastern Allies, 1919–1925 (Minneapolis, 1962), pp. 135–185; Richard H. Ullman, Anglo-Soviet Relations, 1917–1921, vol. III, The Anglo-Soviet Accord (Princeton, N.J., 1972), pp. 135–264; E. H. Carr, A History of Soviet Russia: The Bolshevik Revolution, 1917–1923, 3 vols. (London, 1950–1953), III, pp. 209–228.
[28] On the concept of a communist party, Kriegel, Aux origines, II, pp. 702–712; Spriano, Storia del PCI, I, p. 58, for Gramsci citation.

working-class nucleus against the "opportunist" brokerage encouraged by the war. Simultaneously, however, their new discipline responded to the same imperatives of organized political and economic competition to which successful bourgeois groups were adapting. The communists were not prepared to play the game of interest-group politics, but unyielding opposition to the system required preserving a party that was at least as centralized and cohesive as those participating.

The major Western theorists of communism during this transformation—the German-Hungarian Lukács and the Italian Gramsci—themselves testified to the new demands of party discipline when they linked their renewed emphasis on socialist humanism to the Third International's claim for orthodoxy. In essays between 1919 and 1923, Lukács argued that rationality and freedom depended upon commitment to the Party. Paying tribute to Rosa Luxemburg in early 1921, Lukács wrote, "The form taken by the class consciousness of the proletariat is the *Party*."[29] The communists' confrontation with Luxemburg was revealing of their general dilemma in 1921. Even while redeeming Luxemburg as a theorist of the proletarian vanguard, Lukács altered her emphasis upon action from below to one of direction from above. He silently but significantly expurgated Luxemburg's criticism of bolshevism and glossed over the difference between the two forms of working-class movement: the mass strike and the centralized party. Lukács's interpretation, however, was not just a willful distortion. Although Luxemburg's stress on spontaneous mass action had perhaps served as an appropriate leftist strategy for the turbulent period from 1917 through 1919, the end of the red biennium rendered her prescriptions obsolete.

This held, above all, for Luxemburg's concept of spontaneity, which Gramsci and Lukács (and Lenin) rejected. Gramsci argued that a stress on spontaneity fostered passiveness: a defect besetting Serrati's maximalists as gravely as Turati's reformists, for the maximalists provoked the bourgeoisie without preparing a revolutionary program to deprive them of power. Although in 1920 Gramsci stressed the factory councils as workshops for revolution and heralded Turin as Italy's Petrograd, after the occupation of the factories and the Congress of Livorno, he changed his emphasis to the role of the new Communist Party. The Party would unite peasants and workers, the oppressed of the South as well as the North. This was critical, for as Gramsci was just beginning to learn from the failures of 1920 and after, the hege-

[29] Georg Lukács, "The Marxism of Rosa Luxemburg," in *History and Class Consciousness*, Rodney Livingstone, trans. (Cambridge, Mass., 1971), p. 41. Cf. "Critical Observations on Rosa Luxemburg's 'Critique of the Russian Revolution,'" [January 1922], *ibid.*, pp. 272–293.

monic structure of bourgeois Italy depended upon a coalition of urban and rural elites that only a national, revolutionary party could displace.[30]

Gramsci and Lukács in 1920–1921 thus associated socialist voluntarism and rationality with the stringent new demands of loyalty to the Third International. With different argumentation each updated communist theory for an era of party centralization and, in turn, for the advent of a new European stability resting upon powerful interests whose political influence depended upon inner cohesion. By 1921 communism became stricter in Russia itself. With the partial suppression of the Workers' Opposition of Kolontai and Shlyapnikov, the vision of factory representation temporarily faded in Eastern as well as Western Europe.[31] This was not surprising. Throughout the continent, power gravitated to bureaucratically organized interests, not the fragile associations thrown up by anarchists or syndicalists or even bourgeois democrats.

The shaking of the European political order by war and revolution between 1917 and 1919 had aroused the dream of spontaneous reform from below—a dream that Wilson as well as Lenin had sponsored. As that vision failed to find confirmation in institutional developments or the new peace treaties, the left sought to build enclaves of working-class power in the capitalist economies of the West. But as this strategy seemed to yield little except a more supple pattern of private control, the most uncompromising elements on the left regrouped into a new party that sought to negate the system more resolutely. Hence radical movements grew narrower in goal, more focused in action, and more demanding in discipline, reflecting the competition of interests in which they unwillingly had to participate, if only to recruit their membership. The lesson of the years between 1917 and 1921 was that the left absorbed, as much as it rejected, the new organizing principles of bourgeois Europe.

STRATEGIES OF BOURGEOIS DEFENSE

Beneath the demands for economic change lay less the question of wealth than that of power. Bourgeois forces interpreted working-class demands as an issue of who was going to be master. Businessmen

[30] Cf. Gramsci, *L'Ordine Nuovo*, pp. 116–123; also Diana O. Pinto, "Antonio Gramsci and the Search for an Italian Revolutionary Movement," Honors Thesis (Cambridge, Mass., 1970); for biographical data: Giuseppe Fiori, *Antonio Gramsci* (Bari, 1966).

[31] Carr, *Bolshevik Revolution*, I, pp. 176 ff., 196–198 ff., and II, 222–226; Leonard Schapiro, *The Origin of the Communist Autocracy* (London, 1955), pp. 296 ff., 314–336; cf. Daniel Bell, "Two Roads from Marx," in *The End of Ideology* (Glencoe, Ill., 1960), pp. 359–363.

viewed schemes for workers' councils and nationalization as attempts to eliminate their control over their enterprises. Agrarian proprietors and "respectable" people in the Po Valley resented new labor claims as an effort to impose working-class dictatorship over their estates and towns. Members of the Bloc National felt that the CGT was trying to dictate to industry and even the nation. In all areas, conservatives believed that the basic hierarchies of bourgeois society were under attack in 1919–1920, and that efficient and relatively just social arrangements were being undermined.

They were partly correct. The proposals for economic restructuring cited above were part of a fundamental challenge to existing hierarchies. So too were the strikes and violence that made 1920 an unprecedented year of labor unrest in Italy and France. Generally, however, working-class spokesmen were not asking to be master of Europe's governments and economies. They were seeking their own share of political influence. They were pressing to make permanent the system of wartime bargaining that conservatives had accepted for the duration but now felt strong enough to challenge.

Bourgeois groups who fought to strengthen their own collective influence over policy now branded the working class's effort at the same result as revolutionary. While business leaders were forming new industrial associations and marketing arrangements, they still dreamed of industrial relations as they had existed previous to World War I, before the needs of patriotic collaboration had elevated labor leaders to the level of social partners. Businessmen, and elites in general, wanted to go back even as they reorganized for new competition; hence they found labor's claims of 1920—whether the demands of the conference table for nationalization schemes, or the demands of strikers for organization and power in the workplace—radical and unacceptable. But the tactics chosen for the workplace or the conference table differed according to the strength of the challenges, the underlying sense of bourgeois security or anxiety, and the political temperaments of men in power.

The French labor movement met the most decisive and predictable rebuff in the spring of 1920. The state railroads were destined to be the arena of social conflict because of their chronic unprofitability, the strains placed on men and matériel by the war, and the massive unionization efforts achieved by railroad workers, whose national federation leapt from 65,000 members in 1917 to 221,000 by January 1919 and 352,000 a year later.[32] When SFIO delegates and the CGT de-

[32] Kriegel, *Aux origines du communisme français*, I, pp. 375–376.

manded nationalization, however, the owners asked for subsidies. The head of the PLM company, Noblemaire, who sat as Bloc National deputy for Lyon, demanded increased state guarantees for the present management and their "patriotic" bondholders: "Small savers have committed about twenty billions to the French railroad industry. It must be fully safeguarded." While there were reasonable arguments in favor of public assistance to the war-tried industry, management claimed that their troubles were rooted in demagogic union leadership. When in January 1919 the Minister of Public Works had asked for extra diligence from the unions, they had demanded nationalization in return. For railroad executives, as Noblemaire claimed, "this was a revolutionary and anarchic demonstration."[33] Managers pleaded for "a minimum of loyalty," or as Marcel Peschaud, Secretary-General of the P.O. (Paris-Orléans) company wrote, "The best remedy for the fall in output of railroad equipment would be the restoration of legally accepted discipline, respect for authority and devotion to the common weal."[34] Within the government, too, preoccupation with discipline emerged: as Minister Yves Le Trocquer told the Chamber during an early clash with the *cheminots*, "I am here to have discipline respected. I shall never commit an act that could have as a consequence the weakening or suspension of sanctions pronounced by responsible chiefs for acts of indiscipline."[35]

If basic industrial authority were to be the issue, there could be little ground for compromise. Although Millerand hoped to limit the dispute and sought to patch up the January clash, he was soon pushed into support of the companies' position. In February the PLM (Paris-Lyon-Méditerranée) line suspended a carpenter who had taken what he claimed as a justified absence to attend a union meeting. After union negotiations with the government failed to secure his reinstatement, the national federation of railroad workers called a strike against all the railroads at the end of February. The union refused to negotiate before reinstatement of their worker; Millerand refused to arbitrate before the union returned to work. A mere matter of "interior discipline," as *Le Temps* put it on the eve of the strike, had become a fundamental test of power. "We are in truth faced with a political movement," Millerand told the Chamber as he supported an emergency bill authorizing the requisition of all nonrail transport. "There

[33] Noblemaire in JOC, 1920, pp. 268–270 (February 20); "small savers" defended in *Le Temps*, February 26, 1920.

[34] Marcel Peschaud, "La crise des transports," *RPP*, cxii, February 1920, p. 177. Cf. Le Troquer on the contribution of run-down equipment to the lower output of the yards, JOC, 1920, pp. 282–283 (February 24).

[35] JOC, 1920, p. 285 (February 24).

is no corporation, whatever its private interests, that has the right to set itself up against the nation."[36]

Despite the proclamation of a total work stoppage on the railroads negotiations did continue, and produced a settlement basically satisfactory to the workers within two days. Both sides, however, emerged embittered. The railroads imposed fines and suspensions that the workers felt violated the accord. At this juncture the CGT raised the stakes of the dispute by demanding nationalization of the rail lines. By the end of March the national labor federation decided to make their May Day strike a demonstration for nationalization. The *cheminots* resolved that on May 1 they would walk out for as long as it took to secure the rehiring of the workers who had been suspended.[37]

Government and industry prepared to resist and readied themselves for a "civic battle of the Marne." Peschaud consulted with Robert Pinot of the Comité des Forges about mobilizing Chambers of Commerce and professional groups to demand legislation that would prohibit strikes against public services. The railroads planned scenarios of conflict and reprisal; the government gave the Union Nationale des Combattants 100,000 francs for its expenses in helping to protect public order; and Millerand approved a volunteer militia under the prefects. Local formations of volunteer strike breakers were organized as Unions Civiques. By mid-May there were 15,000 would-be tram drivers or Métro conductors organized in 65 sections in addition to those of Paris.[38] Except in Marseilles, their proffered services found little employment. Rhetoric also escalated. While *Le Temps* initially exempted the CGT from its condemnation of the strike leaders as revolutionary, political, and criminal, it soon decided that "the CGT is revolutionary in its essence." Ministers and deputies developed the same theme before the Chamber when it returned from recess on May 28, and the young Parisian representative, Pierre Taittinger, called on the government "to consider the modest, the humble, the submissive, those who always work and obey." Nonstrikers, Taittinger said, should be rewarded by raises and advancement; strikers should be penalized. In fact, this was the tactic of the companies, as they doled out bonuses to faithful workers and punished recalcitrants on a scale of increasing severity from delays in promotion to cuts in pay, rank, or outright dismissal.[39]

[36] JOC, 1920, pp. 367–368 (February 27).
[37] Kriegel, *Aux origines du communisme français*, I, pp. 396–397, 411–412.
[38] *Ibid.*, pp. 432–434, 455. On the Unions Civiques, cf. *L'Echo de Paris*, May 11, 1920, and *Le Temps*, May 14, 1920, p. 2, for estimate of membership.
[39] *Le Temps* on the CGT, May 1 and 5, 1920; Taittinger in JOC, 1920, p. 1531 (May 18).

The key to the conflict was the government's attitude. As Peschaud said, "if the government does its duty, that is, if it has the right to work respected and if it leaves the companies free to restore the discipline without which good management cannot exist . . . the revolutionary movement threatening us will end with the defeat of French and foreign bolsheviks." The government did its duty. Urged on by Auguste Isaac, Minister of Commerce and himself a railroad executive, and by André Maginot, Minister of War and forceful hero of nationalist groups, Millerand decided to ask the courts to dissolve the CGT for having exceeded the corporate objectives granted by the 1884 Law of Associations. Legal dissolution, which followed in January 1921, meant little, however; the CGT won an indefinite stay upon appeal and continued *de facto* existence throughout the proceedings. Nonetheless, judicial harassments persisted, as in early May union leaders and others connected with radical groups were arrested on conspiracy charges based upon encouragement sent from communists abroad. The legal moves won applause from the right. As Léon Daudet declared, "we have been sent here to bar the road to revolutionaries. M. Millerand seems decided to bar the road to revolution; we approve him wholeheartedly."[40]

More than judicial harassment, it was the failure of the strike itself that broke the labor challenge. The CGT committed its efforts and prestige too deeply not to suffer. If the railroad companies employed a strategy of graduated reprisals, the CGT originally had its own plan for successive "waves of assault." Miners in the Nord and Pas de Calais as well as Paris metalworkers left work on May 10, but not without hesitation. The Paris Métro stoppage was a failure that lasted only a day. On May 20, the Confederation of Labor decided to have nonrail workers return to their jobs; on the twenty-ninth the *cheminots* themselves gave in, to face wholesale suspensions and dismissals. Demoralization followed not only from defeat but from suspicions of mutual betrayal. Radical "minoritarians" condemned the CGT's readiness to capitulate; "majoritarians" resented being dragged into a foolish attempt at revolution. The defeat of the union meant adjournment of any plan for nationalization. The railroads signed an agreement with Le Trocquer and won legislation in 1921 that consolidated their debt and continued the guarantee to bondholders for another five

[40] Peschaud interview in *Le Temps*, May 1, 1920; Millerand's judicial moves in Kriegel, *Aux origines du communisme français*, I, pp. 470–475; cf. Alexandre Millerand, "Mes souvenirs," MS, p. 94. For conspiratorial views: Marcel Hutin, "Le complot révolutionnaire," in *L'Echo de Paris*, May 4, 1920, and similar warnings in subsequent issues; also *Le Temps'* guarded discussion of foreign influence, June 11. For Daudet, see: JOC, 1920, p. 1564 (May 19).

years. Thereafter, a "common fund" to subsidize the poorer lines—in part, from future profits of the richer networks—would take over. It was a scheme destined to work little better than the earlier one, and the socialists would have a chance at nationalization under the Popular Front government. The fortunes of the labor movement suffered more from the blow to the unions than defeat of nationalization. Membership and support ebbed; the circulation of L'Humanité, which had reached a May circulation record of 8.5 million for the month, relapsed to under 6 million in June. As a prefect in Bordeaux reported three years later, when he had arrived in February 1920 he had found a powerful syndical organization, a workers' party led with vigor and intelligence, and a membership conscious that they had profited from their previous strikes.

> Then occurred the general strike of May 1920. I need not recall what the results were; I limit myself to noting that in the Gironde there was a veritable collapse of the Bourse du Travail [the labor headquarters] and of the union organizations. Their omnipotence had undergone a grave check; severe sanctions were pronounced and neither threats nor pleading could obtain the slightest attenuation.

Thereafter there was a decline in contributions and schism in the movement; "after that, the debacle, the impossibility of holding any serious public meeting, or discussing any question whatsoever without insults or even blows. . . ." This was the hangover of labor's postwar intoxication. Followed by the recession of 1921, it effectively subdued proletarian militancy for a decade and a half.[41]

By mid-1919 the battle with the left in the streets of Germany was largely over. With the suppression of the Munich Räterepublik there was to be no further revolutionary challenge. Nonetheless, there were still legislative proposals for councils and nationalization that had to be considered. Their disposition depended upon the exigencies of coalition politics as well as upon the commitment of the Majority Socialists. While the Center Party—influenced by Matthias Erzberger's important cabinet role and its own Catholic labor movement—did not seriously contest socialization plans, the other government partner, the Democratic Party, with 100 Reichstag votes, was far more concerned. At the Party's executive committee meetings on April 12 and

[41] Strike chronology in Kriegel, *Aux origines du communisme français*, I, pp. 476–494, and in daily press. Prefect's report in AN, Paris: F I C III (Esprit public et élections)/1128, f. Gironde. Report of March 17, 1923. See Picard, *Le mouvement syndical durant la guerre*, pp. 214–232 for a summary of the strike and its consequences.

13, 1919, there were sharp complaints that the DDP's own National Assembly delegates were too subservient to the Socialists. The Democrats worried about their own *Mittelstand* constituency; and as one member argued, further concessions would produce only another shift to the left and the "collapse of the economic system."[42] The Democrats were to leave the government for five months over the issue of accepting the Versailles Treaty. But it was evident from the socialization question that many members were already unhappy with the collaboration and that the Treaty merely provided an opportunity for abandoning a difficult cabinet responsibility.

Within the cabinet, meanwhile, DDP Treasury Minister Georg Gothein resisted Wissell's measures for planning and economic regulation. Gothein, his party colleague Bernhard Dernburg, the banker and prewar Colonial Minister who took over the Finance Ministry in April, and Robert Schmidt, the SPD Minister of Food and Agriculture, pushed through an inner cabinet committee ostensibly designed to control all foreign currency movements. In fact, the mandate of this "dictatorial economic committee" was broad enough to allow a constant veto power over Wissell's planning initiatives under the pretext of facilitating food imports. In the face of this bureaucratic maneuver, Wissell quickly submitted his and Moellendorff's Common Economy Memorandum of May 7—only to provoke a strong counterattack. Gothein demanded an end to economic restrictions as the only path to recovery. He attacked the Economics Ministry of trying to perpetuate wartime regulation (*Zwangswirtschaft*) in "a capitalist-guildlike form." From an alternative perspective, Schmidt defended selective nationalization against the Common Economy idea both in the cabinet and at the SPD Party Congress in June. Finally, outside the cabinet, Rathenau himself sharply attacked Moellendorff's scheme for supposedly departing from the earlier conceptions they had developed together.[43]

[42] DDP Hauptvorstand conference of April 12–13, 1919, in NSDAP Hauptarchiv/36, f. 723.

[43] On the "dictatorial economic committee," see the cabinet meeting of May 6, 1919 in *Akten: Scheidemann*, pp. 264–265; also Wissell's complaints to the Chancellor, pp. 268–269; and Gothein's notes in BA, Koblenz: Gothein Nachlass/12, "Aus meiner politischen Arbeit." Gothein's formal rejoinder to the Wissell-Moellendorff memorandum is in the "Denkschrift des Reichsschatzministeriums," *Akten: Scheidemann*, pp. 297–303; Schmidt's rejoinder is in the "Denkschrift des Reichsernährungsministers . . . 7 Mai 1919," pp. 289–297. His later critique at the Weimar Congress is in: *Protokoll über die Verhandlungen des Parteitages . . . vom 10. bis 15. Juni 1919*, p. 383; for the entire debate see pp. 363–404. For Rathenau's critique, see Walther Rathenau, *Die autonome Wirtschaft* (Jena, 1919). The exchange of letters in the press between Rathenau and Wissell and Moellendorff available in BA, Koblenz: R 43 I/2111.

It was Wissell's own party colleagues who finally undid his projects. Despite a vote of approval from the rank and file at the SPD Congress, Wissell's plans faced renewed attacks at the Free Trade Union Congress in Nuremberg and then outright rejection in a hotly argued cabinet session on July 7 and 8.[44] Isolated, Wissell resigned in midsummer. As Chancellor Bauer indicated to the National Assembly on July 23, little remained of any comprehensive socialization plans besides the weak coal and potash administrations, an export office, and some old demobilization orders limiting prices. Only after the unions themselves raised the issue of nationalization again in the wake of the Kapp Putsch would a stronger coal socialization measure receive consideration.

The *Räte* question, however, could not be interred so quickly. The Social Democrats had promised to "anchor" the councils in the constitution. Yet bourgeois forces found the trade-union leadership implicit allies in their rearguard resistance to effective councils. The regional councils that the original draft legislation provided threatened to become powerful competitors to the traditional labor organizations. During May and June 1919, the Ministry of Labor worked out new and more limited projects with employees' and employers' representatives. But factory council delegates who examined the latest draft in Berlin on July 9 and 10 decided that it reduced the proposed councils to mere grievance and arbitration committees such as had been established during the war. Once again the government draft was reworked, to emerge before the National Assembly only in September.[45]

By this time it was under fire from the *Räte* theorists among the Independent Socialists as a capitalist sham, while at the same time it seemed too radical for business groups. The legislation provided that in factories with more than 100 salaried employees or 500 wage workers, *Räte* representatives were entitled to sit on the boards of directors and to examine the balance sheets. This, however, had traditionally been the function only of management: a corporation, employers emphasized, belonged to the stockholders, and its directors had no special responsibility to the men who accepted employment; the workers perhaps enjoyed the right to fair and generous conditions, but not a voice in company policy.

[44] *Protokoll der Verhandlungen der Freien Gewerkschaften Deutschlands 1919*, pp. 523–561. For the cabinet discussion of July, see GFM: ARK, Kabinettsprotokolle, 3438/1666/742683, 742726–742731. For the socialist debate on *Planwirtschaft*, I am indebted to Richard Breitman's manuscript study of SPD policy in the Weimar Republic.
[45] Oertzen, *Betriebsräte in der Novemberrevolution*, pp. 153 ff. traces the vicissitudes of the bill.

As was the case with socialization, the Democratic Party remained especially divided over policy. Opposition from the rightist parties was a matter of course; but while the DDP had left the government, it did not really feel that it could join the Nationalists and the People's Party in antirepublican opposition. And although the Center and Socialists enjoyed a parliamentary majority in their own right, they felt that they needed support from representatives of the non-Catholic middle class. In late September they asked the Democrats about rejoining the coalition, but DDP delegates feared working with Erzberger, who was the special target of Nationalist slander. The DDP also worried about the factory council issue. Most Democrats felt that some form of factory council law must be accepted, and according to Erich Koch Weser, the industrialists affiliated with the Party were also ready for concessions.[46] Still, there remained bitter opponents: Gothein, who also objected to Erzberger's new tax reforms, condemned the factory bill as "simply monstrous" since it required that a company's books be opened to workers or stockholders who might then demand higher wages or dividends. German companies, he argued frankly, stashed away hidden reserves under camouflaged headings, concealed earnings needed for competition and investment. "German industry has become great not on the profits it has displayed but on those it has hidden."[47]

Since the Center and Socialists wanted the Democrats back in the cabinet, the party hoped to win modification of the factory council law in return. In the key interparty meetings, which convened before the legislative committee sessions set to draft the legislation in late November, the Democrats suggested limiting the role of factory council representatives on the board of directors to discussion of plant operations. They further wished to exempt firms from even this requirement if they engaged in international business and if disclosure of their operations—presumably by untrustworthy council delegates— might hurt the German economy. Finally, the DDP members felt that the councils should enjoy the right only to see public balance sheets,

[46] BA, Koblenz: Koch Weser Nachlass/16, pp. 261–263.

[47] Georg Gothein, "Unannehmbares in Betriebsräte Gesetzentwürfe," *BT*, October 30, 1919, a.m. The Factory Council Law was discussed during the same months as Erzberger's stiff tax reform, especially his emergency capital levy (*Reichsnotopfer*). For DDP opposition to these needed reforms see Gothein, "Erzbergers Steuerprogramm," *BT*, December 6, 1919, which described the tax as a "concession to the streets"; also Lujo Brentano's critique, "Das Reichsnotopfer und unsere Valuta," *BT*, December 5, 1919; and the arguments in VNV: SB, 331, pp. 3927 ff. (December 9 and 10, 1919). On the general problem: Erwin Respondek, *Die Reichsfinanzen auf Grund der Reform von 1919/1920* (Berlin and Leipzig, 1921); Klaus Epstein, *Matthias Erzberger and the Dilemma of German Democracy* (Princeton, N.J., 1959), pp. 328–348.

not the unpublished ledgers. Apparently the SPD was willing to make some compromises so long as their concessions were not too patent. If they had threatened to abandon the government, the Social Democrats could probably have forced the Center, perhaps even the Democrats, to accept their draft proposals. Instead, in late November they allowed themselves to be quietly outvoted in the parliamentary committee alongside the Independent Socialists. Consequently, the factory councils that would be established in large companies won the right to get quarterly reports from management as well as yearly glimpses into the balance sheets; but council delegates still remained barred from the books used to prepare the summary statements.[48]

The DDP-affiliated *Berliner Tageblatt* represented these compromises as a victory in minimizing the *Räte* role. To the right, however, the powers that the legislative committee had granted the councils still seemed excessive. Moreover, at a subsequent session the committee lowered the voting age in *Räte* elections from 20 to 18—presumably a goad to radicalism—and imposed the obligation to "explain" the balance sheets upon smaller firms than previously stipulated. At the Reichsverband der deutschen Industrie meeting on December 11, industry leaders charged that compromise had led to a more outrageous bill. Walter Simons, who had been a leader of the German delegation at Versailles and who was close to the DDP, admitted that DDP members were disappointed that more concessions had not been secured as a price for reentering the goverment. Ernst Borsig charged that by the right to demand quarterly reports on company finances, "the worker can question the soul out of our bodies. . . ." The Berlin industrialist warned "that schools have already been set up where these people are being taught how to read a balance sheet, or rather what they should read out of a balance sheet." In response, he suggested the possibility of organizing a mass lockout if the legislation were passed.[49]

As in the case of French reaction to the 1920 strikes, German business protested with exaggerated denunciation of a supposed revolutionary menace. But industrialists could unbridle their anger more than could the politicians of the parliamentary right, who realized that some factory council law was inevitable, indeed necessary to pre-

[48] "Das Kompromiss im Betriebsrätegesetz angenommen," *BT*, November 28, 1919, p.m. For the final provisions: J. Feig and F. Sitzler, *Das Betriebsrätegesetz vom 4. February 1920* . . . (Berlin, 1920).
[49] "Protestkundgebung der deutschen Industrie gegen das Betriebsrätegesetz, 11. Dezember 1919," *Veröffentlichungen des Reichsverbandes der deutschen Industrie*, Heft 9 (January 1920), pp. 5–7, 12–14. For financial pressure and DDP tacking see Lothar Albertin, *Liberalismus und Demokratie am Aufang der Weimarer Republik* (Düsseldorf, 1972), pp. 181–185.

vent a new polarization of bourgeois and socialist forces. Throughout November 1919, the SPD had wavered in the coalition; were they to be rebuffed by a bourgeois majority in the Reichstag, they might go into opposition and unleash working-class demonstrations. On the other hand, moderate political leaders could calculate that passage of this particular bill, which remained so unsatisfactory to radicals and Independent Socialists, might widen the divisions among the working class.

Such an outcome seemed tragically confirmed during the decisive second reading of mid-January 1920, when a massive radical demonstration called out by the USPD newspaper, *Freiheit*, to protest the bill clashed with police before the Reichstag. To the Independent Socialists the factory councils law appeared a pious fraud.[50] As pro-USPD demonstrators assaulted the parliament building while inside the bill was being reported from committee, they met machine gun fire that killed 42 and wounded 105. Learning of the demonstrators outside but not yet aware of the massive toll taken among them, the Majority Socialists turned their anger more upon their challengers to the left than upon the conservative opponents of the bill.[51] On the second day of debate the conservative parties contented themselves with formal statements of opposition, while the Democrats sought to justify their own ambivalent position. Although they were unhappy with much of the bill, the DDP spokesman explained, rejecting it outright would just intensify working-class radicalism. The bill ultimately had to be swallowed as the final consequence of November 1918. Nationalist speaker Martin Schiele scornfully rejected the DDP attitude as a useless "dancing on eggs." Albert Vögler, who spoke for the DVP, warned of mechanically seeking to institute majority rule in a sphere where objective economic laws held sway and charged the law meant "the denial of the idea of capitalism." But the speeches were merely statements for the record, not live debate. The grim violence of the preceding day had demonstrated that the new law, which was viewed so hostilely by the far left, hardly represented the last word in radicalism.[52]

What did the factory councils legislation really amount to? To industrialists the *Räte* idea subverted the necessary institutional structure for giving talented and qualified leadership the freedom of action it merited. It undercut all existent and rational channels of authority; it awarded a premium to those radical demagogues who could most

---

[50] See Geyer's speech, VNV: SB, 331, pp. 4249 ff. (January 14, 1920). Cf. Wolfgang Noske, *Von Kiel bis Kapp* (Berlin, 1920), pp. 192–193.

[51] VNV: SB, 331, pp. 4203 ff.

[52] *Ibid.*, pp. 4226, 4232–4239, 4243–4245.

successfully coerce otherwise loyal workers to follow their leadership. In fact, the limited councils that the new law sanctioned could not fulfill such dire expectations, as even the right sometimes admitted: the *Kreuzzeitung* itself recognized that the law was an effort to rectify old grievances and not to impose a dictatorship over industry.[53] Instead of a harbinger of more radical experiments, the final Factory Councils Act represented the meager realization of the social hopes and expectations that had accompanied the November revolution. A year earlier the councils had been the theoretic source of revolutionary authority; by late 1919 they barely won the right to inspect private industry's published accounts. The agitation on behalf of the bill impressed its opponents, much as the wave of strikes in France and Italy so disturbed bourgeois elements. But the real significance of the legislation consisted in its moderation and attrition along the legislative path— just as in France and later Italy the limits upon radicalism were what finally counted.

The clash between Majority and Independent Socialists in January 1920—much like Spartacist week a year earlier—convinced sensitive bourgeois observers that they still needed a viable social democracy to guarantee a moderate regime. The question was how much had to be conceded. To resist the factory council law might radicalize the working class; but as it turned out, that moderate bill proved the last real Social Democratic achievement. Early 1920 was to confirm a new balance of forces established between bourgeois groups and the Social Democrats. The new balance effectively sealed the brief period of efforts at structural reform. The steps in attaining and then testing the new equilibrium would include the abortive Kapp Putsch of March 1920, the parliamentary elections three months later, and the coal socialization controversy later in the year. Each of these events revealed the modest degree of change the German pluralist system would absorb.

Some conservatives were reassessing their opposition to the SPD in late 1919, but calls for cooperation on the right were still infrequent. Nationalist opinion remained inflamed by the bitter defamatory attacks of Karl Helfferich on Erzberger in the wake of the signature of the peace treaty. Helfferich accused the Centrist minister of undermining the German war effort, and later of financial malfeasance. Nationalists mobilized again with demonstrations in mid-November as Hindenburg, Ludendorff, and Helfferich came to Berlin for the hearings on the causes of the collapse in 1918. Westarp heralded a nation-

[53] "Vor der Entscheidung über das Betriebsrätegesetz, *NP(K)Z*, January 12, 1920.

alist comeback in his *Kreuzzeitung* column, while Theodor Wolff of the *Berliner Tageblatt* confirmed the diagnosis from a worried democratic perspective, and the SPD Minister-President of Prussia, Hirsch, denounced "reactionary drives of violence" before the Landtag. Foreigners retailed rumors of military conspiracy, while Troeltsch noted in mid-December that "The Wave from the Right" was now a common headline: by exploiting the slogan of the stab in the back, "the old patriotic circles of the social order, for a long while surprised, overtaken, and rendered completely helpless are emerging again."[54]

Nonetheless, occasional conservative countercurrents were also emerging as Weimar seemed headed toward bitter polarization. In late September, the chairman of the DNVP, Oskar Hergt, presented his so-called Program of Order before the Prussian Landtag, which envisioned eventual collaboration with moderate Socialists in a national government. Such a notion, however, really was out of place in the DNVP, and Hergt ran up against the more authoritative view of Westarp, who wished to remain out of the government "and if unavoidable certainly not with the Social Democrats."[55] Nor could the SPD have responded to any such overtures at this time. They were preoccupied with preserving the loyalty of their supporters *vis-à-vis* the Independent Socialists. This required a militant pose, such as marked Scheidemann's mid-November appeal for proletarian union and his declaration that "the enemy stands on the Right."[56] The emotional storms surrounding the Investigation on the Causes of the Collapse of November 1918 permitted a reunion among all shades of Socialists, especially during the fortnight that spanned Helfferich's and Hindenburg's appearances, the accompanying nationalist street demonstrations, and the decisive interparty disputes between Democrats and the SPD over the prerogatives of factory council representation.

This crisis raised the possibility that the SPD might join the USPD in an opposition punctuated by mass demonstrations and general strikes. For a moment such a prospect might seem to offer a welcome occasion to unite Democrats, Center, People's Party, and Nationalists into a bourgeois-bloc ministry: "from Gothein to Graefe," as Stresemann expressed it before the Executive Committee of the DVP Novem-

[54] See Epstein, *Matthias Erzberger*, pp. 349–69; Karl Helfferich, *Fort mit Erzberger* (Berlin, 1919); Erich Eyck, *A History of the Weimar Republic*, 2 vols. (Cambridge, Mass., 1962–1963), I, pp. 134–139 on the hearings; Westarp in *NP(K)Z*, November 15, 1919; Theodore Wolff in *BT*, November 17, 1919; Hirsch reported in *BT*, November 15, 1919; Troeltsch, *Spektator-Briefe*, pp. 88–92.

[55] Westarp to Hergt, October 1, 1919, in Westarp Nachlass, Gaertringen; cf. Lewis Hertzman, *DNVP: Right-Wing Opposition in the Weimar Republic* (Lincoln, Neb., 1963), pp. 79–83.

[56] VNV: SB, 330, pp. 2886–2888 (October 7, 1919).

ber 24. A day's sober reflection led Stresemann to conclude that those Social Democrats who sought to forestall a reunion with the Independents, such as Noske, would prevail over Scheidemann and those who wanted a common left-wing opposition. In fact, within two days an acceptable factory compromise was reached between the DDP and the SPD. Perhaps Stresemann already sensed that a government with the SPD was still healthier than an all-bourgeois cabinet arrayed against an all-socialist opposition: "The bourgeoisie is often going far to the right and the workers frequently all the way to the left," he wrote on November 25, and regretted that no statesmen had yet emerged to heal the rift.[57]

Throughout the coming months Stresemann remained torn between his growing realization that Social Democracy had to remain a governmental force and his desire to capitalize on short-term right-wing gains. Erzberger's role in the cabinet and his plans for an emergency capital levy precluded DVP participation in the government.[58] Joint DVP-DNVP support for Hindenburg's presidential candidacy (the presidential elections were thought to be imminent) appeared a more promising tactic, especially since laborious preparation had already taken place.[59] For the moment the DVP decided to preserve a jealous independence from the Nationalists while still maintaining a common rightist opposition. This would allow the People's Party to remain attractive to conservative Germans who had voted prudently for the Democrats in 1919, and who were now returning to right-wing liberalism but could not stomach the Nationalists' extremism or anti-Semitism.

Still, the idea of an approach to the Socialists became more central in Stresemann's calculations as a result of his bitter polemic in early 1920 with Albrecht von Graefe of the German Nationalists. Graefe charged publicly that Stresemann ought to have committed the DVP to a militant right-wing fusion against the Weimar coalition, ultimately to unite all bourgeois parties and drive all socialists into opposition. In addition to his public rebuttals, Stresemann replied privately that Germany could not have a government without Social Democrats for two to three years lest the country stagger from one general strike to another. By early February he was writing that in principle he would not shy from working with those Socialists who agreed to an orderly rebuilding of the economy. To drive the SPD into the arms of the

[57] GFM: Stresemann Nachlass, 6922 = 207/3088/138051–138064 for November 24 speech, and 138031–138033 for November 25 letter.

[58] Stresemann to Rose, December 3, 1919, in *ibid.*, 6922 = 207/3088/138104–138105.

[59] Cf. Henry A. Turner, Jr., *Stresemann and the Politics of the Weimar Republic* (Princeton, N.J. 1963), pp. 43–44; Andreas Dorpalen, *Hindenburg and the Weimar Republic* (Princeton, N.J., 1964), pp. 53–54.

Communists and Independents would be irresponsible; one had to attenuate their "predominant influence," perhaps through a wider coalition. At the March executive meeting of the party he reiterated these concerns.[60] Graefe answered that he believed the DVP must choose between collaboration with the Nationalists or enmity. Businessmen within the DVP, such as Vögler, tended to agree and condemned Stresemann for indulging in the press feud with a friendly party.[61] The basic issues, however, became obscured by personal hostility, and the controversy degenerated as the Nationalists condemned the Volkspartei for its Jewish membership. Given the pathological anti-Semitic undercurrent of German conservative politics, this issue had to be debated on its own degrading terms.[62]

Nonetheless, the debate did raise the central issue of the Social Democratic role in Weimar politics. What was essential for Stresemann's later renowned role in stabilizing the Republic was less his attitude toward the legal form of the regime than his acceptance of collaboration with the Socialists. To contemplate cooperation with even moderate Social Democrats meant making one's peace with the revolution. And it had been the act of revolution, more than the form of government that had emerged from it, which prevented support for the regime of November 1918. Disturbed by the resurgent polarization between November 1919 and February 1920, comprehending that class war would be disastrous, Stresemann edged toward collaboration with the Socialists, and thus eventually toward republican statesmanship.

This did not mean that Stresemann's party abandoned its own bourgeois mission and antisocialism at the polls. To win as wide a constituency of nonsocialists as possible, the DVP had to avoid too sectarian an alliance with the Nationalists or too conciliatory a stance toward the Socialists.[63] Moreover, Stresemann's growing acceptance of SPD power in 1920 did not prevent him from showing great sympathy for the Kapp Putsch a month later. Kapp's *fait accompli* would tempt Stresemann as an easy way out of republican confusion and dif-

[60] GFM: Stresemann Nachlass, 6935 = 220/3091/140028–140032, 140076–140077; 6936 = 221/3091/140297–140300.

[61] Graefe to Stresemann, February 3, 1920, *ibid.*, 6935 = 220/3091/140033–140036; Vögler's earlier views of June 1919: 6920 = 205/3079/137579–137609 (DVP Executive Committee); letter to Stresemann, February 9, 1920: 6935 = 220/3091/140014–140016, and Stresemann response, February 12: 140017–140018. Cf. Wolfgang Hartenstein, *Die Anfänge der deutschen Volkspartei 1918–1920* (Düsseldorf, 1952), pp. 139–140.

[62] On the anti-Semitic issue see Executive Committee March 4, 1920, in GFM: Stresemann Nachlass, 6936 = 221/3091/140297–140300; also letters to Jewish DVP members in January 1920 from Stresemann's secretary: 6936 = 220/3091/140002–140003, 140013–140018, 140050–140053.

[63] Cf. Hartenstein, *Anfänge der DVP*, p. 144.

ficulties. Yet this attitude was really a regression, and not a mere continuation of his earlier right-wing views.

Stresemann's confused attitude toward the Kapp Putsch, in fact, was symptomatic of many bourgeois groups. It did not reveal a concerted counterrevolutionary mentality on the part of important business or political leaders, but it did confirm the underlying lack of commitment to the republican order. Industry's leaders looked to the "economy" as the asset that must be preserved whatever the political result, yet also as a source of power that might dictate a compromise. Political groups looked nervously at who was likely to win without commitment to the constitutional order.

From the perspective of the central contest between bourgeois and socialist parties, the Kapp Putsch had only tangential significance. Despite prior knowledge of the plotting by right-wing leaders, and the suspicions of many others, few foresaw a serious *coup* attempt. The origins of the Putsch lay in a final gamble by the politically displaced: Free Corps officers to whom political activity meant only the crushing of local communist insurrections, isolated East Elbian circles of Pan-German reactionaries, including old bureaucrats, such as Wolfgang Kapp himself. But for the rightist forces that were more involved with Berlin politics, the Putsch did not appear beforehand as a rational tactic.[64]

Kapp in Berlin, however, represented a windfall opportunity. While some conservative politicians and industrialists feared radicalization of the working classes, others were tempted—whether for a day, like Stinnes, or longer, like Stresemann—into rash pronouncements of support or compromising negotiations. Kapp's chief attraction was his promise of new elections, which the SPD had threatened to postpone. Both right-wing parties had been angered in early 1920 when Chancellor Bauer indicated that the Reichstag vote might be delayed until autumn and that the presidential office might be made the choice of the Reichstag—a constitutional change that would eliminate any chance for Hindenburg. The Kappists who seized Berlin declared their loyalty to the President, and both right-wing parties recognized them as a new ministry, blaming the old cabinet for provoking the Putsch

[64] Cf. Johannes Erger, *Der Kapp-Lüttwitz Putsch. Ein Beitrag zur deutschen Innenpolitik 1919/20* (Düsseldorf, 1967) for a general survey; also Harold J. Gordon, Jr., *The Reichswehr and the German Republic* (Princeton, N.J., 1957), pp. 90–143. These contain full bibliographies. For a rightist view see Ludwig Schemann, *Wolfgang Kapp und das Märzunternehmen vom Jahre 1920* (Munich and Berlin, 1937). For right-wing involvement see Westarp's admission in his memoirs that he stood closer to the Putsch than publicly believed, Westarp Manuscript, Gaertringen, p. 74; also Werner Liebe, *Die deutschnationale Volkspartei 1918–1924* (Düsseldorf, 1956), p. 54.

by usurping authority. Similarly, after the Putsch collapsed, the DNVP leadership blamed it upon "the unconstitutional desire for power by an incompetent party government." Nor were the rightists unsuccessful: despite their need to falsify their own compromised role and their tortuous efforts to arrange amnesties and compromises as the Putsch fell apart, the two parties did win a guarantee of new elections from the legal government which had fled to Stuttgart.[65]

Industrialists outside the capital were also torn, but the need to keep open communications with labor leaders prevented significant support for Kapp. Business leaders protested against the Central Arbeitsgemeinschaft taking a stand one way or another. When Stinnes met with Catholic and socialist union leaders in the local Arbeitsgemeinschaft for the coal industry at Essen on March 14, he urged that in common they exploit their control of scarce coal resources to dictate a settlement. But, he pleaded with Hue and Imbusch, "do not demand that we take sides for one party or the other in a political strike." In fact, the union leaders won a resolution that did distinguish between the legitimate government and the putschists. It also called upon industry to cover wages for the general strike that the Social Democrats had invoked against the Putsch. The leaders of the more progressive chemical industry also readily agreed to condemn any effort at violent changes of government.[66]

Once the Kappists collapsed, however, many industrialists protested that the officially sanctioned strike represented an intolerable instance of partisanship and class warfare. They were especially irate that Karl Legien, the leader of the Socialist Federation of Trade Unions (ADGB), prolonged the general strike two days beyond the Putsch to win promises of "decisive union influence" over the formation of a new cabinet as well as reforms such as a purge of the military and resumption of nationalization measures. In the Ruhr, the general strike rekindled aspirations of a year earlier and developed into a major insurrectionary movement, which the SPD moved to suppress with military units. Industrial leaders did not limit their concern, however, to the turmoil in the Ruhr. The unions' political demands prompted

[65] See the account in Hartenstein, *Anfänge der deutschen Volkspartei*, pp. 149–193; Liebe, *Die deutschnationale Volkspartei*, p. 58; Erger, *Der Kapp-Lüttwitz Putsch*, pp. 219–225, 238–244; Albertin, *Liberalismus und Demokratie*, pp. 367–375.

[66] For business attitudes, see Gerald D. Feldman, "Big Business and the Kapp Putsch," *Central European History*, IV, 2 (1971), pp. 99–131. This is based on a major memorandum by Kurt Sorge to Wiedfeldt, March 19, 1920, now in Fr. Krupp, A.G.: WA III 227. The Stinnes quote is from the record in the archive of the Phoenix-Rheinrohr company (Thyssen) in Düsseldorf: P 1/25/39: "Verhandlung der Arbeitsgemeinschaft Kohlenbergbau Essen," and kindly transmitted by Henry A. Turner, Jr.

harsh attacks from conservatives, an anger that contrasted sharply with the neutrality shown during the Putsch.[67] The pay issue became especially bitter: the Westphalian leaders in the Arbeitsgemeinschaft who consented to payment for the strike days came under heavy criticism from more intransigent colleagues. The Central Arbeitsgemeinschaft emerged badly strained: first because of trade-union insistence on resistance to the Putsch, then because of the bitter pay issue—and Vögler, for one, had to defend the ZAG's role against angry industrialists such as Borsig.[68]

Unfortunately for German democracy, what the unions gained from their efforts proved insubstantial. Legien himself declined to take over what might have proved a reform-minded government. Decisive union pressure could not easily be made permanent; the results of renewed socialization discussions, it will be seen, proved trivial; and the purge of army and volunteer units that might have been significant for the Republic was largely frustrated.[69] Whatever healthy reassessment might have occurred among the far-right German Nationalists was cut short when the party's liberal gadfly Siegfried von Kardorff, went over to the DVP—in part from principle, but also from hurt pride that no local groups would sponsor his candidacy in the coming elections and from resentment at Westarp's dominance.[70] Finally, as wags said, the Kapp Putsch did succeed in Munich. The uneasy SPD-Catholic coalition that had governed since the suppression of the Munich Revolution in April 1919 collapsed, as the SPD went into opposition and a conservative Catholic official, Gustav von Kahr, became Minister-President.[71]

[67] Feldman, "Big Business and the Kapp Putsch," pp. 108 ff. For Legien: Hans J. Varain, *Freie Gewerkschaften, Sozialdemokratie und Staat. Die Politik der Generalkommission unter der Führung Karl Legiens (1890–1920)* (Düsseldorf, 1956), pp. 172–184. For the imposing dimensions of the working-class action in the Ruhr, see the left's view in Erhard Lucas, *Märzrevolution im Ruhrgebiet. Vom Generalstreik gegen dem Militärputsch zum bewaffneten Arbeiteraufstand. März-April, 1920*, vol. I (Frankfurt, 1970), pp. 248 ff.; and a pro-industry account in Hans Spethmann, *Zwölf Jahre Ruhrbergbau*, 4 vols. (Berlin, 1928), II, pp. 76–275.
[68] On the pay controversy see BA, Koblenz: R 13 I (VdESI)/158, p. 38. DZA, Potsdam: ZAG Akten/29, pp. 129–140; Feldman, "Big Business and the Kapp Putsch," pp. 126–128.
[69] Cf. here DZA, Potsdam: Reichspräsidialkanzlei/219 for exchanges on purges between Ebert and the new Defense Minister, Otto Gessler; also Otto Gessler, *Reichswehrpolitik in der Weimarer Republik* (Stuttgart, 1958), p. 129 ff. Francis L. Carsten *Reichswehr und Politik (1918–1933)* (Cologne-Berlin, 1965), pp. 104–111.
[70] For dissension in the DNVP see Otto Hoetzsch to Hergt, April 25, 1920, in DZA, Potsdam: DNVP Akten/3, "Strömungen in der Partei." Also Kardorff letter in GFM: Stresemann Nachlass, 6936 = 221/3091/140222–140231; and Westarp to Heydebrand in Westarp Nachlass, Gaertringen.
[71] Bavarian events in Herbert Speckner, "Die Ordnungszelle Bayern," Diss. (Erlangen, 1955), pp. 90–120; Ernst Müller-Meiningen, *Aus Bayerns schwersten*

If the Kapp Putsch, therefore, discredited the *coup* as a rightist alternative, it did little to impede any conservative revival through institutional channels. It goaded socialists into demanding new reforms, but designed more to secure the republican constitution against concentrations of economic power than to institute socialism itself. And because of the disrepute it cast upon the unprepared Bauer government, as well as the resentment of many moderates at the general strike, the Kapp Putsch hurt the SPD even as a party of legality.

The elections of June 1920 confirmed the social democratic reversal, as voters turned toward the extremes of the political spectrum at the cost of the democratic left and center in the Weimar coalition. The coalition parties (SPD-DDP-Center) fell from just over three-quarters of the popular vote of 1919 to slightly under half. Voters throughout Germany reverted to prewar preferences, revealing the results of 1919 as an abnormal swing to the left. While the socialist left dropped as a whole from 45.5 percent to 42.1 percent, even more significant was the passage of many Majority Socialist voters into the Independent and Communist Party columns. The left opposition thus almost tripled its previous strength. The right opposition (DVP and DNVP) rose from 14.7 to 28.3 percent, a virtual doubling of its hold on the electorate. Eventually, when the later partial elections were counted, the Nationalists came back with 71 seats instead of 47, the Volkspartei with 62 seats instead of their previous 19. Along with the Independent Socialists, the People's Party had most strikingly improved its showing—a fact Stresemann used to justify his maintenance of independence from the DNVP.[72]

Tagen (Berlin, 1924), pp. 233–238; Hans J. Hofmann, *Der Hitlerputsch* (Nymphenburg, 1960), pp. 45–48.

[72] Official results in *Statistik des deutschen Reiches*, Bd. 291; Bernhard Vogel, Dieter Nohlen, R.-O. Schultze, *Wahlen in Deutschland* (Berlin, 1971), pp. 293 (Table A 8) and 296–297 (A 11), allows the following comparison:

	1912 Percent of vote	Seats		1919 Percent of vote	Seats	1920 Percent of vote	Seats
Cons./Free Cons.	12.2	57	DNVP	10.3	44	15.1	71
Nat. Lib.	13.6	45	DVP	4.4	19	13.9	65
Progressives	12.2	42	DDP	18.5	75	8.3	39
Catholics	16.4	91	Center	19.7	91	18.0	64 (& 21 BVP)
SPD	34.8	110	SPD	37.9	165	21.7	102
Misc.	10.8	52	USPD	7.6	22	17.9	84
			KPD			2.1	4
			Misc.	1.6	7	3.0	9
	100.0	397		100.0	423	100.0	459

Many of the Democratic voters, perhaps those who had originally been National Liberals, obviously returned to the right-liberal fold. The DDP lost as a percentage of the electorate about what the People's Party gained. In some rural districts, moreover, SPD votes among agrarian laborers may even have migrated directly to the Nationalists. The right in general fared well. Nor were the gains merely the visible quantitative ones. The Nationalist parliamentary party that returned to Berlin was a more disciplined right-wing group, and even the Democrats had grown more conservative. Koch-Weser noted the presence of "quite a few industrialists and financiers who are distinct from the People's Party only by virtue of a stronger degree of insight into political necessities." The new tone of the party was set by Otto Gessler, the tough-minded Defense Minister, by Koch-Weser himself, and by conservatives such as Gothein.[73]

Given the DDP losses and its shift to the right as well as the reduction of the Majority Socialist delegation, a different ruling coalition was likely to result. But obtaining any cohesive majority for a new cabinet could not be easy. The SPD was still the strongest party, but it did not wish to enter a government without the Independent Socialists who had been able earlier to snipe profitably from the left. The Independents, though, would not collaborate with the nonsocialist parties. Once the efforts of Chancellor Herman Müller failed to win USPD participation, President Ebert called upon the floor leader of the DVP, Rudolf Heinze. Heinze sought to construct a "Great Coalition" that would include Social Democrats, Democrats, Center, and his own People's Party —a solution Stresemann had earlier suggested. But the Social Democrats were unwilling to collaborate with the DVP after the People's Party had haggled with Kapp in Berlin. Heinze's alternative suggestion of including the Nationalists was rejected by the Center and Democrats. Ultimately the SPD agreed to support a minority government, which the old Centrist leader Konstantin Fehrenbach assembled from the three bourgeois center parties: Democrats, Center, and DVP. Discussion over specific ministries proved especially painful. Fehrenbach hoped to name a representative of Ruhr industry to one of the economic posts but was rejected by Stinnes, Vögler, and Otto Wiedfeldt, one of Krupp's principal directors. In view of the upcoming Spa Conference industrialists did not wish to take responsibility for reparations decisions that were likely to involve sacrifices for the Ruhr business community. Fehrenbach's final appointment of Hans von Raumer of the electrical industry was not calculated to win their loyalty. They

---

[73] BA, Koblenz: Koch-Weser, Nachlass/27, p. 131. Cf. analysis of DVP-DDP voter changes between 1919 and 1920 in Hartenstein, *Anfänge der deutschen Volkspartei*, pp. 224–253.

distrusted Raumer's compliance toward labor, while the electrical producers had long opposed the hegemony of the metal producers. The business-affiliated People's Party also lost the Ministry of Transportation portfolio to General Groener, who had resisted industry's wishes when he had managed the railroads during the war. Finally, they had to accept the continuing presence of the apparently left-wing Catholic, Joseph Wirth, at Finances.[74]

The composition of the Fehrenbach cabinet epitomized the political stalemate that the Weimar Republic had attained. In truth it was a caretaker cabinet, chosen because the Socialists preferred relinquishing power to entering the government or running the risk of new elections. Yet who would have thought in the winter of 1918–1919 that the Socialists would be on the sidelines of power eighteen months later! Stresemann had recognized that his country could not be governed against the will of the SPD, and that any cabinet required Social Democratic support until that calmer day when a coalition of Nationalists and middle parties might be feasible. If the SPD's absence from power was their own choice, it also reflected the heavy losses they had suffered in the elections. Stresemann had also believed that a cabinet without SPD participation was impossible—but here he was wrong: by the summer of 1920 the working-class parties were excluded from federal office and the Fehrenbach government was prepared to bury the last projects for economic restructuring that they had left behind.

The tempo of Italian reaction lagged behind the German and French, and when bourgeois recovery was at hand it went unrecognized. By early 1920 the restoration of order in conservative eyes depended upon ousting Nitti. The convocation of the new legislature removed none of the premier's problems. Financial difficulties, upheaval on the part of peasantry and urban labor, and the continuing ulcerating nationalism that focused on Fiume all continued to weaken the ministry. Budget deficits fed an inflation that contributed to the widespread agitation and turmoil. While special committees worked on progressive reforms that would tax dividends and war profits, the right looked only at the costly bread subsidy as an unjustified social luxury.[75]

Financial discontents, though, still remained less preoccupying than

[74] On the formation of the government, GFM: ARK, Kabinettsbildung, K2283/5744/642732–642739; Albertin, *Liberalismus und Demokratie*, pp. 392–400. On the question of industrialist participation in the new cabinet see: Wiedfeldt to Sorge, June 17, 1920 (two letters) and June 21, 1920, and Sorge to Wiedfeldt, June 22, 23, and 24, 1920, in Fr. Krupp, A.G.: WA IV 2574, 2565.
[75] Luigi Einaudi, *La guerra e il sistema tributario italiano* (Bari and New Haven, 1927), pp. 231 ff.

agrarian and urban social unrest. In July and August 1919, peasants in the province of Rome had begun a series of land invasions, appropriating the uncultivated portions of state, church, and private estates in almost half the communes. Thereafter, the occupations of the soil spread southward until in the autumn of 1920 almost all the Sicilian *latifondi* were invaded. Faced with a movement it could not effectively halt, the government issued the Visocchi Decrees of November 1919 in an attempt to systematize the transfer of unused land to legally constituted cooperatives. Even as land invasions multiplied in the South, renewed agrarian strikes threatened to disrupt farm production in the North throughout 1920. Membership in the "red" and "white" agricultural leagues would more than double; sharecroppers and even leaseholding peasants would join day laborers in protest; and strike days lost would quadruple from 1919's already imposing total of 3.5 million.[76] With wartime agricultural contracts finally on the table for renegotiation, *braccianti* were to ask higher wages; peasants who shared the harvest would demand larger quotas of the crop or to become rent payers. Even more controversial was the quota of hirings or compensatory indemnity imposed upon the landlord when no work was available—a roughshod method of minimizing the hardship of seasonal unemployment that infuriated proprietors. The temporarily powerful Socialist unions resorted to boycotts, intimidation, and assault not only against proprietors but against dissident laborers or priests seeking to organize competing white leagues.[77] The harsh labor organizing conflicts were a major reason Catholic peasant leaders tried to extract an advanced agrarian reform plank from the Popolari. They also angered agriculturalists who had to come to terms. The resentment was not to be confined to large landowners: small proprietors who felt that they could not meet the new demands of the *braccianti* warned the government that they would cultivate only the land their own families could work.[78]

[76] Arrigo Serpieri, *La guerra e le classi rurali italiane* (Bari and New Haven, 1930), pp. 190–210, 260–265, 276. For the "white" leagues: Amos Zanibelli, *Le leghe "bianche" nel Cremonese* (*dal 1900 al "lodo Bianchi"*) (Rome, 1961), pp. 57–64 on the conflicts of early 1920 in the Soresinese, the plain north of Cremona.

[77] "Elenco numerico e dimostrativo di reati dipendenti dall'agitazione agraria . . . ," in ACS, Rome: Min. Int., Dir. gen. P.S., Div. Aff. gen. e ris. (1920), B. 48, f. "Bologna, Agitazione agraria II°." Cf. Angelo Tasca, *Nascita e avvento del fascimo*, 2 vols. (Florence, 1965), I, pp. 153 ff. and Mario Missiroli, "Il fascismo e la crisi italiana," now in *Il fascismo e il colpo di stato dell'ottobre 1922* (Rocca San Casciano, 1966), pp. 95 ff.

[78] Report from Prefect of Ferrara, June 16, 1920, in ACS, Rome: Min. Int., Dir. gen. P.S., Div. Aff. gen. e ris. (1920), B. 51, f. "Ferrara, Agitazione agraria."

Later, we shall see that this harsh offensive inwardly weakened the Socialists in the countryside. But for a year it appeared as if property and labor relations in agriculture might be durably transformed. Against the Federterra's offensive in 1919 and 1920, "agrarian bourgeois" reaction was fragmented and ineffective. In 1914, 60 percent of the agrarian strikes in Italy had resulted in a halfway compromise or better for the workers; 30 percent brought a largely favorable decision, 40 percent had been frustrated. In 1918, 1919, and 1920 almost half the strikes yielded largely favorable decisions to the workers and fewer than 20 percent met only minimal satisfaction or defeat. The large strikes almost all brought some measure of success, and only one-tenth of the strikers of 1919 and 1920 returned to work with less than a halfway settlement. For now the proprietors could do little more than nurse their grievances and charge them against government weakness.[79]

In the cities, the general strikes of December 2 and 3, 1919, opened a renewed wave of "strike mania." Public-service walkouts most disturbed middle-class opinion. Socialist telegraphers and telephone employees left their jobs in mid-January 1920, but the government appeared to be able to count on the "white" workers affiliated with the Popolari, who remained at their post. Nonetheless, in the absence of Nitti at the Conference of London, Postal Minister Pietro Chimienti conceded the strikers' requests, promised no punitive action, and paid the employees for their strike days. Liberals and Popolari attacked these concessions as a shameful abdication of state authority. Railroad workers struck on January 20, but at least were won back to work without extensive concessions. Nonetheless, the PPI felt injured anew; for contrary to implied government promises their own labor representatives, who again had refrained from striking, were excluded from the negotiations. The rebuffed Catholics were to force a ministerial reorganization when Nitti returned from abroad.[80]

In the wake of the public-service strike there followed new and alarming factory take-overs. At the end of February, workers occupied the Mazzonis cotton mills in the Turin region after a month-long labor dispute. Gino Olivetti and other industrial leaders were annoyed with the Mazzonis' refusal to join the industry-wide and regional business associations and disapproved of their refusal to accept collective bargaining. Still, they closed ranks when the prefect requisitioned the mills in early March and dictated a settlement that required recog-

---

[79] Serpieri, *La guerra e le classi rurali italiane*, p. 279.
[80] Strikes followed in *CdS*; for PPI attitude cf. Luigi Sturzo, *Popolarismo e fascismo* (Turin, 1924), pp. 27–28.

nition of the union, conformity with national pay standards, and payment of strike days. At a conference of Confindustria delegates in Milan on March 6 and 7, Olivetti demanded resistance to the new factory councils that were preparing for revolution and claiming rival authority in the plant.[81] Three weeks later, the "strike of the clock hands," triggered by Fiat's decision to enforce unpopular daylight saving time, developed into a full-blown clash over the prerogatives of the "internal commissions" established in the war and the newer councils. The specific dispute came to center on the right of the councils to recruit among workers during factory hours. Piedmontese industrial leaders, including Fiat's Agnelli, decided that their interference must be suppressed even if it required a major shutdown of the plants. Efforts to arrange a compromise in the Fiat dispute failed, and by mid-April the work stoppage spread to other firms, then to newspaper workers and public services throughout the province of Turin. Olivetti and other industrialists designated a group of Turin business leaders, including Agnelli and the old Benedetto Craponne, who organized a Committee for Civic Organization that arranged substitute services for distribution and public order. While industry's response was coordinated labor's was not. Turin's working-class militants failed to persuade the national CGL leadership to join the movement, which finally collapsed by April 23. The Socialist Party leaders and CGL officials lacked sympathy for the Gramscian objectives pursued in Turin. This enabled the industrialists to override the prefect's recommendations for a compromise settlement and to secure a victory for what Olivetti summarized as the principle that "in working hours, one will work and not talk and authority shall remain undivided in the factory." As Agnelli concluded, "Turin's industrialists fought a real struggle for defense of the state and social order against a clear attempt at revolution."[82] Yet while in France the government had been actively associated with the victory over labor, in Italy the state's rep-

[81] Mario Abrate, *La lotta sindacale nella industrializzazione in Italia 1906–1926* (Turin, 1967), pp. 249–258. Einaudi's coverage of the Mazzonis cotton factory occupation in *CdS*, March 1–3, 1920; included in Einaudi, *Chronache economiche e politiche di un trentennio (1893–1925)*, series II, vol. V (Turin, 1961), pp. 672–682; report of Miani-Silvestri factory take-over in Raffaele Colapietra, *Napoli tra dopoguerra e fascismo* (Milan, 1962), pp. 103–105.

[82] See Abrate, *La lotta sindacale*, pp. 258–269; Tasca, *Nascita e avvento*, pp. 116–119; and Gramsci's report on the strike, in Gramsci, *L'Ordine Nuovo, 1919–1920*, pp. 176–186. Cf. also Paolo Spriano, *L'occupazione delle fabbriche, settembre 1920* (Turin, 1964), pp. 22–30; and a conservative evaluation in Prato, *Il Piemonte e gli effetti della guerra*, pp. 147–149. For the most recent synthesis: Giuseppe Maione, "Il biennio rosso: lo sciopero delle lancette," *Storia Contemporanea*, III, 2 (1972), pp. 239–304. Fiat, in fact was willing to move its work-day back an hour so the legal hour did not diminish the morning light. But summer time was associated with the discipline of wartime production and disliked everywhere.

resentatives appeared fainthearted and inept. The employers won, but, as they saw, by their own resistance.

The strike assaults continued, however. Still quarreling over disciplinary questions and pay, the post and telegraph workers resumed their slow-down in April. Nitti wished to suppress the movement, but could not secure a lasting return to work. From the Conference of San Remo he wired his Treasury Minister, Carlo Schanzer, "to hold firm . . . above all never concede payment of strike days," and he won a resumption of work without important concessions. Nevertheless, telegraph service was again interrupted, and by the first week in May unrest among postal workers seemed about to explode again. At the same time railroad employees were refusing to carry soldiers to the disturbed Piedmont area, while sizable clashes left several dozen dead and wounded. Viareggio was seized by "insurrection" on May 2; everywhere the liberal press reported violence, lawlessness, and apparent social dissolution.[83]

In the Socialist-administered cities above Rome or in the smaller towns surrounded by powerful agrarian unions, revolution already appeared underway. The well-born or the educated, who had basked in the deference extended by the *basso popolo*, found their world of social expectations crumbling. In everyday life a hundred reminders pressed home the fragility of bourgeois attainments: a successful election for the left or an uncomprehended grievance brought forth a parade of workers willing to exchange blows with opponents in their way. Trolley-car service was subject now to interruptions for days at a time, and when the trams finally rolled from the yards, their crews might bedeck them with red flags of triumph. In Bologna and elsewhere the tower of the medieval city hall glowered down as a Socialist stronghold. If the town dweller owned land in the countryside, he had to bargain with his laborers' powerful union, pay higher wages, or accept lower rents. He had to promise to keep a quota of men employed even when there was no work for them; and should he quibble, or should his own organization attempt resistance, then the wheat might rot in the fields, the grapes wither before harvest, and his haystacks go ablaze. The government seemed unwilling or unable to defend his most accustomed property rights. Nitti had organized a *regia guardia* for better public order in autumn 1919; but although this new security force angered the Socialists, it seemed to offer the middle classes insufficient aid. Nor was it easy to be a policeman; one could expect violence in any confrontation with an unruly demonstration, and for a *carabiniere* in a rural outpost, attack by local peasants

[83] Nitti to Schanzer, April 20, 1920, in ACS, Rome: Carte Schanzer/29. Press reports in *CdS*.

or workers was often a possibility. A letter to Nitti's Minister of Finances, Carlo Schanzer, from a friend in Bologna offers eloquent testimony to conditions as they were perceived by the upper classes:

> It is not a mere phrase when I write that the province of Bologna today is only nominally a part of the kingdom of Italy . . . the Camera del Lavoro [local socialist headquarters] rules and no one dares disobey its orders because everyone has become convinced that the government will not help anyone who takes the initiative in resisting socialist tyranny. This is what the bourgeoisie and the sound people believe, after they see how open and ever more frequent violations of the prefectural ordinances go unpunished—be it by the city administration or by the Camera del Lavoro. And they note that with every renewed general strike the power of the authorities, so it seems at least, wanes further. . . .
>
> Your Excellency knows that great tracts of land in this province— and not previously uncultivated ones, but those belonging to one proprietor or another—have been invaded with impunity by the laborers. . . . Be it added that crimes against property, fires, armed attacks, thefts . . . follow with frightening frequency. . . . Believing themselves unprotected by the government, the sound part of the population does not dare react, but instead, motivated by the legitimate instinct of self-defense and the desire to safeguard as best it can its own interests in the absence of state aid, is beginning to make arrangements with the extremist elements. Thus the authority of this anonymous socialist government is increasingly reinforced and in fact is the only one recognized in this province. The population is divided in two parts: one threatens with arrogance and self-confidence; the other lives oppressed by terror. We cannot go on in this manner.[84]

For the right the major step in reasserting bourgeois will was getting rid of Nitti. But conservatives no longer wished to play the D'Annunzian card. The poet's madcap landing at Zara, his rejection of Badoglio's *modus vivendi,* and his increasing connection with syndicalist advisers lost him conventional right-wing sympathy. Even Mussolini indicated uneasiness when D'Annunzio appeared ready to consider anarchist and republican plots for taking over the mainland. The conventional forces of the right refocused, therefore, on parliamentary tactics.[85]

[84] Aldobrandino Malvezzi to Carlo Schanzer, April 10, 1920, in ACS, Rome: Carte Schanzer/22. For the general ambiance see Tasca, *Nascita e Avvento,* i, pp. 151 ff.

[85] Paolo Alatri, *Nitti, D'Annunzio e la questione adriatica* (Milan, 1959), pp. 313 ff. Giovanni Giuriati, *Con D'Annunzio e Millo in difesa dell'Adriatico* (Florence, 1954), pp. 65–85, 115–123; Umberto Foscanelli, *Gabriele D'Annunzio e*

When opponents of Nitti looked to parliament, however, they collided with the Popolari, who held the keys to a stable majority but were internally divided and unpredictable. On the other hand liberals themselves had little sympathy for political Catholicism. The resulting dissension led to a series of confused cabinet crises which totally eroded Nitti's only possible centrist coalition. In early March 1920, it seemed that the Popolari would no longer tolerate a ministry that had bargained with the Socialist railway workers at the expense of the "white" labor organizations. But in the first cabinet crisis, the PPI initially set such a high price for their renewed support with their clerical demands that they actually helped Nitti to return with stronger liberal backing. And despite a week's hesitation, the PPI finally delivered the votes Nitti needed for a new majority (250–195).[86]

The Catholics went along with the government in part because it was the easiest way to avoid rupture in their own ranks. On the left of the Party, Guido Miglioli and his radicals in Bergamo pressed for a radical social program, so they might hold their own against the Socialists in the competition for peasant loyalties. The PPI Congress of Naples in mid-April put aside Miglioli's passionate plea on behalf of the transfer of land to those who worked it for a more moderate but still reformist platform. Given the deep divisions on social policy, and even the old interventionist issue, the Popolari united their ranks by emphasizing their own political militance and disdaining to provide merely a package of votes for the liberals. Nitti, it was felt, had no understanding either of real peasant needs, or of the aspirations of the Catholic political movement; he allegedly believed that Vatican pressure would always deliver the PPI votes he needed.[87] Finally, by April 30, when further violent clashes set Popolari against Socialists, the PPI's National Council again withdrew its confidence in the Ministry

---

l'ora sociale (Milan, 1952), pp. 120 ff.; Nino Valeri, *Da Giolitti a Mussolini. Momenti della crisi del liberalismo italiano* (Florence, 1956), pp. 57 ff., 78 ff., 89–91 on the conspiracies around D'Annunzio and connections with the mainland. See the offer of funds from the Perrone brothers of Ansaldo, perhaps motivated by their relationship to the Genoese maritime workers: ACS, Rome: Min. Int., Dir. gen. P.S., Div. Aff. gen. e ris. (1903–1949), Serie A5, B.6, "Agitazione pro Fiume e Dalmatia," f. 49, sf. 2. Conversation of December 20, 1920. Mussolini's turn away from D'Annunzio, in Renzo De Felice, *Mussolini il rivoluzionario, 1883–1920* (Turin, 1965), pp. 557 ff.

[86] Reports in *CdS*, March 10, 14, 23, and 31, 1920. Cf. especially Giovanni Amendola, "La crisi ministeriale aperta," of March 10 for liberal views. Cf. Sturzo, *Popolarismo e fascismo*, pp. 29–30; Elizabeth Pratt Howard, *Il Partito Popolare Italiano* (Florence, 1957), pp. 216–219; Gabriele de Rosa, *Storia del Partito Popolare* (Bari, 1958), pp. 97–102.

[87] Francesco Malgeri, ed., *Gli atti dei congressi del Partito Popolare Italiano* (Brescia, 1969), pp. 148–160, 179–192, 203–215; De Rosa, *Storia del PPI*, pp. 104–126; Pratt Howard, *Partito Popolare Italiano*, pp. 222–234.

and the King turned to a Catholic politician, Filippo Meda. But Meda, who was the closest habitué of the liberals among the Popolari, never really felt at home in a militant Catholic party. Self-deprecating and cautious, he had not wanted to oppose Nitti, and suggested now a Nitti-Giolitti combination. The Secretary of the Popolari, Don Sturzo, hoped to avoid the old liberal stalwarts and looked favorably on Bonomi, but Bonomi's interventionist affiliation made him unwelcome among those PPI delegates who represented the neutralist sentiments of the Catholic peasantry. With Meda reluctant, Bonomi excluded, and Giolitti not quite ready, only another Nitti "reincarnation" seemed feasible—this time with the participation of Popolari ministers.[88]

Nonetheless, Nitti's support was rapidly dwindling. Albertini's old loathing of Giolitti made the *Corriere* one of the premier's last supporters. "Giolitti is at the door," warned the Milan newspaper, as it accepted a third Nitti ministry.[89] Nonetheless, the *Corriere's* stance exasperated much of the right, which wanted only to remove the premier. The conservative Milan banker, De Capitani, wrote to Salandra that "the Nitti-ism of the *Corriere della Sera* is assuming mastodonic proportions." Through private meetings the Salandrans sought to woo the Popolari away from Nitti and to overcome their reticence about an alliance with conservative Liberals.[90] Indeed, barely had agreement been reached on a third Nitti government when the cabinet was thrown again into deepest crisis. On May 24, nationalist student demonstrators paraded toward the Quirinal in commemoration of the fifth anniversary of the Intervention. They clashed with the police, shots were fired, and eight were left dead to be exploited as martyrs by the nationalist press. Three days later Giolitti released an interview in the friendly *Tribuna* which amounted to his own declaration of availability. The former premier stressed the necessity of reform: to recover unjustified profits he demanded the compulsory registration of bearer securities (which the Nitti government had dealt with only hesitantly) and he asked an end to the proliferation of decree laws

[88] The defeat of the Ministry proved an embarrassment for Sturzo. While his Party's resolution in parliament called for toughness against Socialist strikers, the PPI still voted with the Socialists against Nitti's demand to postpone debate and defeated the ministry. For the view of Bonomi, "Bonomi ed i popolari" *CdS*, May 18, 1920. On Meda, see De Rosa, *Storia del PPI*, pp. 105 ff. also De Rosa's biography: *Filippo Meda e l'età liberale* (Florence, 1959). Cf. Sturzo, *Popolarismo e fascismo*, pp. 31–33.

[89] "Dopo la crisi," *CdS*, May 23, 1920.

[90] De Capitani to Salandra, May 23, in Lucera: Carte Salandra, 1920. On the meetings see G. B. Gifuni, ed., "Salandra, Pantaleoni e Sturzo (Da un diario di Antonio Salandra)," *Risorgimento*, XII, 3 (October 1960), pp. 210–216—now included in *Il diario di Salandra*, G. B. Gifuni, ed. (Milan, 1969), pp. 235–240; also Maffeo Pantaleoni to Salandra, May 3, 1920, in Lucera: Carte Salandra.

bypassing parliament. Despite the reform-minded program, the same nationalists, the *Corriere* recognized, who in 1915 had shouted "Death to Giolitti" were now proclaiming "Better Giolitti than Nitti!" As the *Idea Nazionale* argued, a government that had devalued and dishonored Vittorio Veneto was no more acceptable than one headed by a man who had merely failed to understand the need for intervention.[91]

Nitti sealed his fate with a premature attempt to resolve the wheat subsidy issue. To raise taxes seemed impossible in the spring of 1920, especially since Nitti had added conservatives such as Luzzatti to his cabinet. Instead the government sought to terminate cheap grain sales.[92] Although employers were directed to provide family wage supplements that would ultimately be drawn from a new progressive surtax, the Socialists objected that Nitti had pledged himself to consult the Chamber before acting on the grain question. The complexity of the scheme made it appear that the government was merely removing the subsidy. Riots erupted in Milan and Bari, the second major series of disorders in a fortnight. Socialists, Radicals, and right-wing Liberals announced their opposition to the grain measure. Faced with a third cabinet crisis, facing attacks from both left and right, Nitti appeared before the Chamber June 9 to withdraw the grain decree and offer his resignation.[93]

Conservatives now welcomed Giolitti as a champion of law and order. "If Giolitti and *only, only Giolitti* is in condition to try to reestablish a government he cannot be opposed, and one must stand ready to suspend judgment," wrote De Capitani to Salandra urging the latter's support. Even Mussolini wrote that Giolitti was more likely than Nitti to "realize" the victory; the *Idea Nazionale* viewed the new cabinet as a last "surviving will to resistance on the part of state and nation, resistance not to revolution as conscious violence . . . but to a suicidal mania, a medieval will of dissolution as personified by Nitti."[94] Despite his 78 years Giolitti seemed to possess the surest control over the bureaucracy and strike-prone functionaries; despite his calls for radical economic measures, the world of affairs seemed comforted. Agnelli telegraphed his confidence "in the only man who can resolve the grave

[91] Giolitti interview reprinted in *CdS*, May 28, 1920; comment in "Il presente e il trapasato," May 29, 1920; nationalists in "Giolitti," *Idea Nazionale*, May 29, 1920.

[92] On intracabinet tax controversies, see Schanzer to Nitti, March 11, 1920, in ACS, Rome: Carte Schanzer/B. 32. On the grain issue, "La politica degli approvvigionamenti," *CdS*, March 19, 1920; also Einaudi's report on tax plans, *CdS*, April 17, 1920, and June 5, 1920.

[93] AP: Camera, Legislatura xxv, 951, pp. 2196–2205 (May 12, 1920), 2207–2218 (June 9, 1920).

[94] De Capitani to Salandra, June 13, 1920, in Lucera: Carte Salandra, 1920; *Idea Nazionale*, June 16, 1920.

crisis the country is traversing," and the officers of the Banca Commerciale reassured each other on the phone: "Giolitti has definitely tranquilized opinion despite his draconian laws . . . because it is better to lose a certain amount than to lose everything at the hands of bolshevism, which we would be approaching irremediably without an energetic man in the government."[95]

In fact, as Nitti fell, the debilitating rebellion of the post and telegraph workers was nearing a solution, and Yugoslav and Italian delegates—in a move sanctioned by the Allies—were about to begin the direct negotiations that would lead to agreement in November. On the left and right, occasional moderates were able to credit Nitti with some achievements: Turati, who in the previous crisis had called for a Nitti-Giolitti combination, wrote to Anna Kuliscioff that voting against Nitti meant playing into the hands of the right.[96] Meda had never shared the PPI hostility toward the government; Albertini had offended his political associates by offering the Corriere's support. Still, the fate of Nitti seemed beyond the good will of the moderates, for neither left nor right nor Catholics were willing to extend collaboration.

The spring of 1920 brought in fact a turning point in the postwar development of Italy: the gradual passage of political impetus from left to right as the divisions inherited from the Intervention became less preoccupying than domestic social unrest. Moreover, Giolitti's studied silence on the Treaty of London counted for more with the right than his earlier reluctance to accept entering the war; Nitti's failure to win Fiume condemned him no matter what he had done between 1915 and 1918. No doubt Nitti contributed to his failure by his inability to be warm and enthusiastic about Italian national aspirations and to project a vision beyond austerity. But more important was the legacy of almost unbridgeable sociopolitical divisions: political order was hostage on one side to a nonproductive maximalism, and on the other, to an angry, elitist liberalism. By the summer of 1920, the old elite enjoyed its first postwar political success in ousting Nitti. But while Giolitti's accession appeared a victory, Giolitti would offend the right in turn by his own compromises with labor.

The reorganization of industrial pressure groups, the fall of Nitti, later the municipal election returns of November 1920, indicated that

[95] Agnelli wire in Quarant'anni di politica italiana. Dalle carte di Giovanni Giolitti, Claudio Pavone, ed., 3 vols. (Milan, 1962), III, pp. 272–273; Banca Commerciale wiretap in ACS Rome: Min. Int., Dir. gen. P.S., Div. Aff. gen. e ris. (1921), B. 45, "Vigilanzi sui cambi," N. 2345, Rome (July 5, 1920).

[96] Filippo Turati and Anna Kuliscioff, Carteggio, vol. v, Dopoguerra e fascismo (1919–1922) (Turin, 1953), p. 332.

the leftward thrust of Italian politics was ending. As elsewhere, plans for radical reconstruction ran into inherent limits imposed by divisions within the working classes, the advent of economic recession, and finally the very vagueness of socialist programs.

But while Giolitti superintended the process of exhausting the left, he did not know how to make himself or liberal institutions the beneficiary. The premier would seek to reestablish the viability of the center by his traditional means of working obstreperous groups into broad electoral coalitions and new parliamentary majorities. Precarious before 1914, this approach now proved inadequate. The reformist Socialists resisted Giolitti's blandishments, while the Fascists accepted his measures of appeasement but exploited them to increase their own independent power. Even as the old statesman sought to play the game of *trasformismo* to undercut the left, it was the right that was evading control. By the end of November Fascist squads would be wresting *de facto* mastery of the Po Valley from the Socialists by brutal attacks on local union and Socialist Party headquarters. At the very moment the strength of the left had crested, an angered right bypassed the government in its own search for reaction.[97]

What is revealing about the situation of 1920 was not just the new Fascist onslaught, but the limits of what Giolittian liberalism could achieve in its own right. Giolitti offered a reformist program comparable to the Social Democratic alternative in Weimar Germany. He planned a course that would satisfy legitimate reform aspirations, blunt the more radical demands of the left, and secure a parliamentary consensus. But because of underlying polarization as well as tactical errors, he failed to stabilize this centrist option.

Giolitti's cabinet choices and his program reflected from the outset the direction of his political effort and where he was likely to fail. In the familiar effort to domesticate the reformist left, Giolitti offered Turati a cabinet post. The Socialist leader felt that he would be disavowed by his party colleagues and declined. To cement Catholic support Meda was installed at the Treasury, while Giolitti and Croce— an imaginative choice for Minister of Education—promised pro-Catholic concessions on teachers' examinations. Giolitti also promised to meet PPI demands for the extension of proportional representation to local elections. Despite all, however, Catholic support remained

[97] For harsh judgments on Giolitti, see Tasca, *Nascita e avvento*, I, pp. 146 ff.; Paolo Alatri, *Le origini del fascismo* (Rome, 1962), pp. 58 ff.; also the contemporary judgment by Gramsci reproduced in *L'Ordine Nuovo, 1919–1920*, pp. 333–338. Less damaging assessments in Valeri, *Da Giolitti e Mussolini*, pp. 103, 191–193; Gabriele De Rosa, *Giolitti e il fascismo in alcune sue lettere inedite* (Rome, 1957), pp. 72–73.

precarious: in part because of the Popolari's own inner divisions; perhaps, too, because Giolitti's proposed registration of bearer securities seemed to threaten Church wealth.[98]

Conservatives seemed ready to accept the premier's economic program, which included revision of war contracts and higher inheritance taxes along with the effort to seek out the 70 billion lire of fugitive securities that evaded taxation. To emphasize the bargain he wanted from the right, Giolitti deftly brandished the threat of radical protest. Nationalist demonstrators injured the Socialist deputy Modigliani in a new clash following a week of tram strikes and demonstrations, and Giolitti promised punishment of the guilty. As simultaneously Ansaldo laid off several thousand workers in what the left saw as a threat to the new fiscal proposals, the premier told the Chamber, "If anyone believes that with his billions in profit he can influence the political life of the country he is mistaken." The legislation passed quickly by the end of July, but the well-off did not lose. Application was postponed repeatedly until the March on Rome and then finally annulled.[99]

The real value of the Giolittian tax program was problematic in any case. Einaudi argued that government policy oscillated between "timidity" and "charlatanry": charlatanry, in that conversion of bearer bonds would yield only a few hundred million in new taxes at a time when the projected deficit was already 14 billion lire; timidity, in the refusal to eliminate the costly bread subsidies. This critique ignored the political factors behind the tax program. Given Giolitti's constant balance of left and right, the new levies and registration of bearer bonds were a necessary prelude to action on the grain subsidy: a demonstration to the left that the state did not belong to the privileged. Nor did business leaders protest heavily at first. Only when conservatives became dischanted about the government's overall performance did opposition focus on the financial innovations.[100]

What effectively mobilized the resentment of industrialists and conservatives was the Occupation of the Factories, which saw half a million metalworkers seize and organize production in plants through-

[98] Cf. De Rosa, *Storia del Partito Popolare*, pp. 127 ff., 156–157. On Vatican reservations: see the revealing interview with the editor of *Civiltà Cattolica*, January 25, 1921, in *Carte Giolitti*, iii, pp. 322–323. For the overall political configuration: Carlo Valauri, "Il ritorno al potere di Giolitti nel 1920," *Storia e Politica*, ii, 1 (1963), p. 85.

[99] Giovanni Giolitti *Discorsi parlamentari*, 4 vols. (Rome, 1953–1956), iv, p. 1771 for the speech; strike events in *CdS*. On the fate of the legislation see Luigi Einaudi, *La guerra e il sistema tributario italiano* (Bari and New Haven, 1927), pp. 366–374.

[100] Einaudi criticism: *CdS*, August 3, 1920, reproduced in *Chronache economiche e politiche di un trentennio*, series ii, vol. v, p. 773; cf. article of June 25 in *Chronache*, pp. 762–767. For consensus on bills: Valauri, "Il ritorno di Giolitti," pp. 89–90.

out the peninsula. The dispute crystallized over wage claims which the more intransigent employers insisted they must finally resist. As the Tuscan negotiator told Bruno Buozzi, the chief of the metalworkers (FIOM): "Ever since the war ended we've had to strip bare. Now we've hit the limit and you can begin."[101] Economic difficulties as well as political calculation motivated the showdown. The first signs of recession troubled industry; moreover, the cutthroat rivalry for control of the major banks in early 1920 had left the finances of the giant iron and steel producers shaky and overextended. To a cautious observer such as Einaudi, the metalworkers' wage demands were justified: iron and steel were not entitled to plead special hardships; they were industries unsuited for Italy given her lack of raw material and existed only by virtue of heavy tariffs and massive war orders. Buozzi was correct, Einaudi agreed, in arguing that labor should not subsidize this uneconomic arrangement.[102]

But the labor cause alienated Einaudi once the dispute widened to include workers' control, which the CGL felt impelled to champion in light of the spontaneity and extensiveness of the sit-in movement. Both sides, moreover, escalated their tactics to force government intervention and an early settlement. Among industrialists, apparent confusion existed over Rome's real stance. They understood that Giolitti was unwilling to provide security forces for any confrontation with labor. Still, on August 31, Agnelli seemed to feel that Giolitti had given silent approval for a lock-out, while Giolitti insisted that he had advised against one.[103] Despite earlier assurances to Camillo Corradini, Giolitti's Under Secretary of the Interior, the industrialists precipitated the sit-in movement by resorting to a lock-out on September 1. Corradini was angered, and in his report to Giolitti, who was vacationing and conferring with Millerand in France, the Under Secretary accused industry's leaders of "intransigence," a "refusal to discuss" issues, and a willingness to go to extremes.[104] On labor's side, the occupation of the factories was also calculated to force a quick settlement by pro-

[101] Cited in Spriano, *L'occupazione delle fabbriche*, p. 42. Valerio Castronovo, "La grande industria: giochi interni e linea de fondo," in *1920. La grande speranza* (special issue of *Il Ponte*, October 31, 1970), pp. 1207 ff. brings out the economic and financial stakes for industry in 1920.

[102] For the recession: Riccardo Bachi, *L'Italia economica nel 1920* (Città di Castello, 1921), pp. vii–viii; Einaudi judgment in "La contesa metallurgica. Principi fondamentali," *CdS*, September 2, 1920. Cf. Ivan Togneri, "Crisi siderurgiche e potere in fabbrica," in *1920. La grande speranza*, pp. 1325–1358.

[103] For this claim, Abrate, *La lotta sindacale*, pp. 293–294; but see the argument in Valerio Castronovo, *Giovanni Agnelli* (Turin, 1971), pp. 246–248. Cf. also Spriano, *L'occupazione delle fabbriche*, p. 54; Tasca, *Nascita e avvento del fascismo*, I, pp. 124–130.

[104] Corradini report reproduced in Spriano, *L'occupazione delle fabbriche*, p. 172.

voking government intervention. Giolitti, however, decided upon conspicuous noninvolvement. The premier allegedly told an excited Agnelli that he could, of course, clear Fiat with artillery, but the industrialist was not prepared to accept the assistance.[105] The Giolittian strategy was to keep open lines of possible communication, preserve civil peace, and suggest a compromise when both sides felt at an impasse. His calculation depended in part upon the tensions between those maximalists and radicals who hoped for some vague revolutionary outcome and the CGL directorate, especially Bruno Buozzi and Ludovico D'Aragona, which sought a tangible but limited labor victory.

The CGL demanded "recognition on the part of the employers of the principle of syndical control of the plants," which would lead in turn toward socialization of the economy as a whole. This sounded radical but left room for compromise. Although most businessmen remained hostile, after a week of sit-down strikes Confindustria leaders decided that they could live with the CGL demands. When Giolitti returned from abroad, he summoned CGL and Confindustria leaders to Turin on September 15 and finally dictated a scheme for a mixed commission of CGL and industry delegates that would work out factory council legislation. As in Germany, such legislation would allow workers' delegates to sit with the directors and view their firm's accounts. Ettore Conti, the Milan electrical magnate and recently elected President of Confindustria, claimed to a later historian that despite instructions to resist, he in fact drafted the outlines of the proposal Giolitti decreed as a compromise. Certainly Conti and Silvio Crespi, a director of the Banca Commerciale whose family owned textile mills and the *Corriere della Sera*, recommended the Giolittian scheme to angry Confindustria delegates in Milan the next day. Official public announcement of the mixed commission reached the businessmen at the same time, and provoked a bitter debate which finally resulted in reluctant acceptance of the decree. Three days later, labor contracts that settled the dispute with the metalworkers were finally signed as well.[106]

For the workers the result proved inconclusive. Although they marched from the factories in triumph, there was a quick onset of disillusion. Giolittians saw a victory for compromise and gradualism; as Frassati wrote in *La Stampa*, the settlement would lead the reform-

[105] Alfredo Frassati, *Giolitti* (Florence, 1959), p. 30. Cf. Carlo Vallauri, "L'atteggiamento del governo Giolitti di fronte all'occupazione delle fabbriche (settembre 1920)," *Storia e politica*, VI, 1 (1965).

[106] Spriano, *L'occupazione delle fabbriche*, pp. 100, 108–124; Abrate, *La lotta sindacale*, pp. 297–298, based on a discussion with Conti; cf. Ettore Conti, *Dal taccuino di un borghese* (Milan, 1946), p. 239.

ist Socialists toward collaboration with the government and would demonstrate the bankruptcy of maximalism. Confindustria's secretary, Olivetti, also believed that the premier was trying to buttress the CGL leadership against the extremists.[107] But in fact, the settlement brought no victory for any Giolittian opening to the left. The moderate union leadership remained subject to accusations of bad faith in the wake of subsequent setbacks. When the Socialist Party split at Livorno in January 1921, not the reformists but the communist left walked out, so that Turati and Treves still remained constrained by the maximalist leaders whom they refused to disavow. Giolittian hopes that the Socialists would quickly collaborate proved vain.

Just as significantly, Giolitti's decree provoked an angry reaction in the bourgeois camp. Conti and Crespi, Olivetti, and ultimately Agnelli, had been most willing to seek agreement. Conti calculated that the mixed commission would never work out effective draft legislation; moreover, under the pressure of the growing unemployment, employers could gradually undermine the scope of workers' control. Other industrialists, however, remained more agitated and defiant. When the Perrone brothers of Ansaldo spoke to each other on September 16, the day they learned of Giolitti's decree, they predicted in panic that Conti's acquiescence would end up having them all expropriated. Once Conti and Crespi convinced their colleagues that they must accept some principles of syndical control, they were accused of a craven retreat by the Ansaldo-financed *Idea Nazionale*.[108] Under pressure from government or labor, the business community split according to its internal rivalries. The iron and steel concerns, especially Ansaldo and Ilva, seemed especially hostile to any compromise. But other branches of production demonstrated little consistency. Local rivalries, such as the resentment of Turin businessmen at Milan's domination of Confindustria, led to differing reactions. So too did personal make-up, whether the tactical subtlety of a Conti or the independence of a *grand seigneur* such as Agnelli.

Nonetheless, the industrial disputes of 1920 were gradually forging a cohesive and militant organization of Italian industry. Olivetti seized upon the April strikes to argue for a more disciplined and cen-

[107] *La Stampa*, September 21/22, 1920, cited in Spriano, *L'occupazione*, pp. 133–134. Olivetti's view in Abrate, *La lotta sindacale*, p. 305.

[108] Perrone brothers conversation in ACS, Rome: Min. Int., Dir. gen. P.S., Div. Aff. gen. e ris. (1920), B. 74, "Agitazione metallurgica," Milano, f. II°, N. 2947. For the attack on Conti and Crespi, see Italo Minunni, "Il retroscena di una capitolazione," and "Storia della capitolazione industriale," *Idea Nazionale*, September 18 and 19, 1920. On the planning for this journalistic approach; ACS, Rome: Min. Int., Dir. gen. P.S., Div. Aff. gen. e ris. (1920), B. 74, Milano, f. II°, N. 2939; cf. Spriano, *L'occupazione*, pp. 121–122, 184–186; Abrate, *La lotta sindacale*, pp. 297–302.

tralized confederation of industry. The magnitude of the September crisis enforced centralized bargaining; and the very neutrality of the government led to desperate efforts to find a common negotiating position. Despite the rifts among businessmen, concerted bargaining and industry-wide pressure upon central authority had proceeded further than before. While Giolitti's summoning of Confindustria delegates remained an *ad hoc* response, Mussolini would later work the industrial leadership into the permanent councils of government.

Yet industry's corporatist reaction was only one outcome of the occupation of the factories. Just as decisive was the general upper-class reaction to what was viewed as a crisis of regime and an onset of anarchy. Phoning to Amendola on September 15, Albertini complained that "the most elementary functions of government no longer exist in Milan. . . . There is nothing, nothing, absolutely nothing that resembles a government. . . . People are being seized, there are thefts and homicides; everything, everything is permitted!" Albertini suggested that the only way to avert complete anarchy was actually to give power to the CGL. Amendola feared that this would stimulate a Soviet-style uprising, but wrote two days later that government action was mandatory, that "nothing is more miserable than the frivolous and unconscious agony in which some societies decline." Again a few days later Albertini called on the Socialists to rescue a bankrupt ruling class from disorder:

> By this time we have nothing further to concede. What else can be desired from this bourgeoisie? The regime is dying not so much because its enemies desire it as because the political formula that its governments obey is mortal. The time for decision has arrived: either the bourgeoisie will give itself a government if there is still time and if a man can be found, if the man finds a following; or it will give the responsibility of power to the Socialists and to the heads of the Confederation of Labor.[109]

In their sense of abandonment, isolation, and weakness, bourgeois spokesmen overlooked the victory that they had really achieved. The working class, after all, had given up its potentially revolutionary hold on industry for vague promises of workers' participation in management. The left was not really prepared to face a showdown with either industry or the state. But few liberals drew this lesson from the contest; instead, within the next weeks many began to look to fascist help. Giolitti and his supporters, on the other hand, yielded to overoptimism.

[109] Albertini conversation, ACS, Rome, *ibid.*, N. 2936; reproduced in Spriano, *L'occupazione*, pp. 187, 189; G. A[mendola]., "Il governo e la situazione," *CdS*, September 17, 1920; Albertini: "Come uscirne?" *CdS*, September 19, 1920.

The premier viewed his handling of the occupation of the factories as a repetition of his successful Fabian tactics during the 1904 general strike, and of waiting until the masses were convinced that extreme measures were futile. To the Senate, Giolitti gave a justification of his actions that calmly looked back on the accession of the working class to growing wealth and power since the turn of the century. He still believed that the left would disintegrate, while the right could be appeased and domesticated. In 1913, Arturo Labriola had already warned Giolitti that this traditional approach had broken down: "On the one side there is an Italy that is nationalist and revolutionary, and on the other a socialist Italy; but there is no longer a Giolittian Italy." Certainly the situation had not improved.[110]

Nevertheless, if the right wanted only to contain radicalism, it did not need to abandon liberal politics. This was shown by the municipal elections of late October and early November, which revealed that conservative strength was reviving. The "constitutional" forces worked to overcome their earlier fragmentation and under government and prefect sponsorship organized cohesive electoral alliances. These captured the major cities except for Bologna and Milan, although the Socialists still held slightly under one-quarter of all the communes. Increased electoral participation testified to a growing political mobilization among the bourgeoisie of the major urban centers, for it had been the liberals that had been hurt by the abstentions of the previous autumn. Only Bologna's voting percentage dropped off among the cities over 100,000 on the mainland—perhaps a consequence of the apparently overwhelming strength of Emilian socialism and the discouragement it may have produced. Elsewhere, increased numbers of nonsocialist voters trooped to the polls to wrest their municipal palaces from red control. In Turin 58 percent of the eligible voters had participated in the legislative elections of 1919 and now 65 percent cast ballots; in Genoa the percentage jumped from 45 to 55, in Milan from 59 to 74, in Florence from 52 to 62, in Rome from 30 to 48. Most revealingly, the total "constitutional" vote—spanning Radicals to Nationalists—rose from its 1919 total of 47 percent to 56 percent, while the Socialists dropped from 32 to 24 percent.[111]

The municipal elections of 1920 disclosed, in short, that bourgeois revival was underway in Italy as elsewhere. However, too many groups

[110] Giolitti's justification in AP, Senato: and *Discorsi parlamentari*, IV, pp. 1784 ff. Cf. Giovanni Giolitti, *Memorie della mia vita*, 2 vols. (Milan, 1922), pp. 597–599. Labriola cited in Nino Valeri, *Da Giolitti a Mussolini*, p. 20.

[111] Electoral returns in Ugo Giusti, *Le correnti politiche italiane attraverso due riforme dal 1909 al 1921* (Florence, 1922), pp. 31, 34; and *Compendio delle statistiche elettorali italiane dal 1848 al 1934*, 2 vols. (Rome, 1947), II, pp. 164, 167, and Table 58.

were outraged to be content with only a recovery of influence within a liberal system. This meant that by the end of 1920, despite notable successes, the Giolittian attempt at equilibrium remained prey to harsh strains. New economic pressures undermined the reformist financial legislation Giolitti had hoped would serve to hold together business and labor leaders. The deepening recession led government officials to urge abandoning the promised economic reforms. After receiving an alarming report on the falling rate of government bonds from the Director General of the Bank of Italy, Giolitti's Minister of Commerce, Alessio, suggested suspending the registration of bearer securities, at least of long-term government bonds. The four major banks and the Banking Association also asked for a postponement of the conversion of bearer securities, postponement of projected tax increases, quick action to eliminate the grain subsidy, and more generous support from the state-sponsored consortium in charge of subsidies to industry. Giolitti still pushed ahead with the tax on excess war profits and sent the government bills to an intraparliamentary committee in February 1921; but the proposed legislation drew anguished complaints throughout the spring and estimates that perhaps 500 firms would go bankrupt.[112]

The other major economic complaint was the overhanging legislation on workers' control. The CGL and Confindustria each presented alternative plans to the parity commission Giolitti had established. The CGL project would have given the factory councils a voice in hiring and firing and envisaged restrictions on future lay-offs; the industrialist proposal called merely for discussion of common problems between entrepreneurs and councils. When no single proposal emerged from the parity committee, Giolitti presented his own compromise legislation to the Chamber in February. Industrialists, who had short memories, blasted the bill for "surpassing even those extreme concessions extorted from certain classes of industrialists in their gravest moment." Although the project remained dormant, the biweekly Confindustria newspaper, L'Organizzazione Industriale, remained filled in early 1921 with the records of countless local meetings held to protest the project for syndical control as well as accounts of how such schemes always failed elsewhere.[113]

So far as labor-management relations were concerned, the industrialists did not really have to worry. The very economic downturn

[112] Alessio and bankers' pleas, in Carte Giolitti, III, pp. 297–298, 299–309; complaints in Catalano, Potere economico e fascismo, pp. 176–179.

[113] Alternative industry proposals in Carte Giolitti, III, pp. 290–297; Catalano, Potere economico, p. 54; "L'agitazione contro il progetto di legge per il controllo," L'Organizzazione Industriale, I, 1 (March 15, 1921), and subsequent issues.

that caused them difficulty led to lay-offs, unemployment, and a new vulnerability for labor. The crisis was especially severe in the primary producing industries, above all in the giant steel firms "pathologically" overextended by war contracts and postwar speculation.[114] In short, economic stringency struck those sectors of the economy where labor organization had been most vigorous: agriculture and heavy industry. Strikes diminished progressively throughout 1921, and where they occurred they were often waged to protest pay cuts or firings. Long strikes seemed especially likely to lead to the defeat of the workers, for given slack demand there was little leverage to exert on the employers. Giolitti's prewar conciliation of labor and industry had always depended upon rising productivity and economic growth, but the reversal of 1921 eliminated this prerequisite.

The disarray of the right had helped to return Giolitti to power; now the success of the right would frustrate his use of it. The right had been angered because Giolitti in effect stripped away what might be called the illusion of sovereignty. At the end of July 1920, Gramsci had written that the state was dissolving under class pressure. "The bourgeois state . . . is decomposing into the two parts that constitute it: The capitalists are forming their own private state just like the proletariat. . . . The state is vainly attempting to maintain the contest within the framework of its own legal order."[115] Many liberals would have agreed. Earlier they had valued a supposedly transcendent authority— in reality a state they had dominated without serious challenge. Now they could turn at best to the contested power of a broker state mediating among jealous interests. Giolitti himself, however, did not seem to realize the erosion of authority. He understood interest-group politics as well as anyone, but he still believed he could maintain the role of the state as a superior arbitrating force. He inherited enough of the Piedmontese liberal assumptions and had sufficient experience with the bureaucracy to remain convinced that his brokerage among social classes would in the long run enhance and not diminish public authority. But by 1920, only the precarious balance between social forces—the fragile equilibrium in the countryside and cities—preserved public authority, not the inherent strength of the political and administrative system. Giolitti mistook the momentary balance between left and right for a durable recovery of sovereignty. As he worked to demonstrate that the left could not master the state, he was helping to undermine the only social force that might counter-

[114] Bachi, *L'Italia economica nel 1921* (Citta di Castello, 1922), pp. 200 ff., 223–230.

[115] *L'Ordine Nuovo*, July 31, 1920, reproduced in Gramsci, *L'Ordine Nuovo*, pp. 346–347.

balance the militant right, not, as he believed, restoring the legal order. Montecitorio and even the Viminale—parliament and prefects—had become shadow powers.

Late 1920 and early 1921 thus saw the end of the postwar working-class offensive throughout Europe. In France and Italy the unions had suffered or were shortly to suffer serious setbacks; in Germany their Republic seemed stalemated and in bourgeois custody. Major changes in the ownership or control of the economy had failed to come about: French railroad nationalization was a dead letter; German coal mines remained under private auspices (as did English ones). Workers' councils—about which a year earlier the Austrian Socialist Max Adler had written, "They are presently the dearest concept in the hearts and spirit of the revolutionary proletariat"[116]—had lost their radical impetus, and Italian labor had given up its hold on the nation's factories for the promise of a study committee. The inflationary cycle upon which much of the labor ebullience rested was ending, as the postwar recession originating in America in 1920 struck England and the Continent by the winter of 1920–1921. With the exception perhaps of Weimar's Labor Ministry, the organized working class did not even have the protection of a social Maginot line by the end of 1920.

Radical change had also threatened property relations in the countryside—a more backward and reactionary battleground. Here, too, the wave of agrarian agitation left little impress outside Emilia Romagna. Faced with disturbing farm-worker unrest, East Prussian landlords in the summer of 1919 had contemplated secession from Red Berlin rather than capitulate, as they saw it, to Social Democratic rule. The military commander of Stettin had helped landlords arm to suppress a general strike; the President of the Agrarian League, Conrad Wangenheim, sought a military hero to lead an East Prussia that might temporarily go its own way as a refuge for landlords.[117] But even without secession, Social Democratic agricultural organization was safely extirpated: the 1920 parliamentary electoral statistics revealed that agricultural workers had fallen back under the patrimonial influence of their landlords, much as the 1921 vote in Romagna would disclose that the *braccianti* were being pressed into fascist cohorts. In the agrarian regions of Europe the paternalistic conceptions of land-

[116] Cited in Max Adler, *Démocratie et conseils ouvriers*, Yvon Bourdet, ed. and trans. (Paris, 1967), p. 77.

[117] See Wangenheim to Roesicke, December 9, 12, and 16, 1918, in DZA, Potsdam: Wangenheim Nachlass/Bd. 13; Eberhard Kolb, *Arbeiterräte*, pp. 398–400; Otto Braun, *Von Weimar zu Hitler* (New York, 1940), pp. 52–56, and Braun in VNV: SB, 165, pp. 1899 ff. (July 24, 1919). See, too, the petition in DZA, Potsdam: Reichspräsidialkanzlei/327.

lords remained unyielding. Landlords in the Landes along the Bay of Biscay complained to Millerand that their sharecroppers were being stirred up by revolutionary workers: concessions would lead ultimately "to the very abandonment of the land . . . the sharecropping syndicates are only a pretext, only a camouflage for the agrarian socialism" that would reduce the French peasant to the condition of the Russian.[118] From Lecce, on the heel of Italy, Nitti was warned by the president of the Agricultural Association that the peasant who gets his own land "will be a bourgeois, avid and greedy, a natural enemy of any country and of Italy. . . . Undoubtedly if one wants to come to civil war— everybody's patience has limits; if yesterday the bourgeois has been slothful, tomorrow, if need be, he can become even revolutionary."[119]

Outside these peripheral agrarian redoubts, however, class relations could not remain frozen in the patriarchal mold. East Prussian reactionaries could hatch the Kapp enterprise, but not a serious counterrevolution. Most conservatives in urban centers understood the need for some compromise with the demands of the working class. Increasingly, a new rift emerged between moderates and hard-line reactionaries. Stresemann's argument with the Nationalists centered on his vision of future collaboration with the SPD. On the right of the French chamber Paul de Cassagnac, Pierre Taittinger, and others wanted legislation that would dissolve public-service unions which organized strikes and would prevent strike leaders from holding labor office for up to a decade. Millerand would not go along with these yearnings. Similarly, Millerand ultimately had to accept the final defeat of the white armies in Russia, despite his instructions to Foch to support Wrangel to the greatest degree possible.[120] Similarly, Giolitti—far more supple than Millerand—made it clear that he wished to bring labor to heel, not eliminate its influence; as always, he sought to balance the political forces at hand.

By the end of 1920 conservatives and moderates had defeated the last serious efforts for almost a decade to democratize the economic

[118] Proprietors of Dax to the Président du Conseil, February 1920, in Bibliothèque Nationale, Fonds Millerand, Carton: "Grèves: 1920 et 1921."

[119] Associazione dei Proprietari della Provincia di Lecce to Nitti, December 1919, in ACS, Rome: Archivio della Presidenza del Consiglio, Gabinetto: Atti, 1919, f. 3/8.

[120] Paul Cassagnac, "Pour maintenir l'ordre," L'Echo de Paris, June 10, 1920. French attitudes toward Soviet Russia in 1920 emerge from Richard Ullman, The Anglo-Soviet Accord (Princeton, N.J., 1972), pp. 135 ff., 189 ff., 237 ff., 312–313; E. Malcolm Carroll, Soviet Communism and Western Opinion, 1919–1921 (Chapel Hill, N.C., 1964); Alexandre Millerand, "Au secours de la Pologne," Revue de France, xii, 16 (August 15, 1932); also exchanges with Lloyd George at Spa, Boulogne, and Hythe, July 9–10, 27, and August 8–9 in Documents on British Foreign Policy, First Series, viii, pp. 502-755 passim.

relationships of bourgeois society. But while the pendulum of political and economic change had come to the center, it had not come to rest. New strains and social burdens lay upon the centrist and conservative coalitions. In Italy middle-class groups given a new prosperity or sense of national importance by the war were angered by the working-class challenges to their enhanced status. In Germany and France the costs of the war were still to be apportioned by means of relative expropriation through inflation and taxes. In short, the consensus built around antisocialism, which had successfully prevented any durable transformation of economic power, was not necessarily a basis for governing. The question now at hand was whether the parliamentary center could rule.

THE COAL CRISIS

One particular episode in the meager performance of the left is especially instructive. The resumption and failure of efforts to socialize the German coal industry marked the end of any fundamental attempt to alter the distribution of economic power in Germany. The failure left intact the property and political influence of the great Ruhr industrialists, with weighty consequences for the future of Weimar democracy. It illustrated how social democrats became constrained by their own commitments to productivity and the general welfare—ultimately to the detriment of the "community." It further showed how the economic dilemmas left by World War I—the exaggerated development of heavy industry, and the thorny reparation issue—undermined even moderate socialist reforms.

The failure of socialization in Germany was affected in turn by the European coal crisis of 1920. Scarcity made coal a major stake of domestic conflict in France, Germany, and Great Britain. In Britain, as in Germany, nationalization was handily defeated in 1919, and the labor unions faced demoralizing reversals in 1920 and early 1921. In France, the counterpart to the failure of socialization was the inability to devise a public solution for coal distribution that could harmonize the interests of the large steel firms and the smaller metal producers. The coal shortage, it will be seen, set the interests of big industry against those of smaller companies, protected in the French case by government agencies and policies. Although socialization was not under discussion, public regulation on behalf of the smaller firms was undercut by the constraints of scarcity.

Thus even as a general "bourgeois" recovery frustrated plans for economic restructuring, the postwar coal crisis also worked against public control and planning. But the coal crisis did not do so by evoking a political reaction. Instead it gave large-scale industry the incentive to assert its own corporate objectives and identity and to claim trustee-ship of national economic interests. Public control of Europe's key in-dustry faltered in France and Germany because in a time of critical fuel shortage big industry made economic survival appear to ride upon its own independence.

From autumn 1919, "*la crise de charbon*" became a regular news headline. Naturally the winter brought the most acute coal famine. Wartime destruction of mines, depreciation of equipment and ex-haustion of veins, the shortening of the working day, and the frequent strikes of 1919 hurt production badly. Coal transport suffered from shortages of the very fuel it was needed to carry. Railroad wagons were dispersed or in need of repair. Water haulage languished: the Seine and the Rhine flooded, and in northern France the barges that plied rivers and canals had been destroyed. Coal was bottled up at Rouen while Paris urgently required it. In January 1920 the Lille Chamber of Commerce told Loucheur that "the crisis of coal is cre-ating impossible difficulties for us; you will understand that our nerves are strained." Better to shut down the factories for a time than suffer "anguish every instant." A month later the coal question arose in the Chamber to trouble the new Millerand government. "Without coal, no industry, no transport, no light, no heat, no life," warned one deputy; and it was indeed this peril which, after the labor issue, most challenged the government.[121]

How much coal was required? Minister of Public Works Yves Le Trocquer counted French annual needs at 70 million tons; French pro-duction in 1919 was about 20 million, and from its damaged northern mines the country had reached the limit of what could be extracted at present. England, Le Trocquer indicated, could provide only limited help. Great Britain exported only 33 million tons out of 240 million—of which France received 18 million—whereas before the war she had been able to produce 290 million and to export almost 80 million. For Le Trocquer, as for other members of the new majority, German coal was the only way to meet the French coal crisis.[122]

Price considerations also made German coal fields a black Eldorado. By 1919 the average price for French coal was seven times that of

[121] *Archives de la Chambre de Commerce de Lille*, 55 (1920), p. 43. For the debate in the Chamber: JOC, 1920, p. 211 (February 17).

[122] Le Troquer in JOC, 1920, pp. 233–234 (February 19). Also Le Troquer to Millerand, March 19, 1920, in Min. Aff. Etr.: Série A. Paix/1374, Dossier 3.

1913, while the overall cost-of-living index had risen only one-third to one-half that amount. German coal would be provided without cost to the French government and merely credited against Germany's ultimate reparations debt. Even the amount that France had to credit toward German reparations payments would be based on the German inland price, which was the lowest in Europe. The terms on which France acquired British coal were far more adverse. To favor its own industry and keep down the cost of living, after May 1919 the English government imposed far higher prices on foreign purchasers than on domestic consumers. During 1919 export prices rose from 40 shillings per ton (60–80 francs) to 100 shillings (then 200 francs) at the end of the year. Freight prices, too, were freed from British ceilings in the summer of 1919 and jumped about fourfold in early 1920. For the Cardiff-Le Havre passage the price per ton jumped from about 35 to 140 francs. Deputies charged in February that Frenchmen had to pay up to 380 francs for coal in French ports. At Paris later in the year, small businesses paid as much as 400 francs, and the Minister of Commerce cited coal prices up to 550 to 600 francs. At the same time the equivalent price in Stuttgart or Berlin was about 300 marks or 100 francs.[123]

Inside France the government sought to minimize the difference in prices between domestic and foreign coal. During the war it had established a *péréquation* system under which the state purchased and sold fuel at prices calculated to subsidize users of the expensive foreign coal and tax the cheaper domestic production. This system was designed to protect smaller firms that did not have favored access to large-scale domestic orders.[124] Perequation did not go far enough, however, to satisfy the small steel companies, whereas large interests who controlled their own coal supplies wanted to evade it. Wendel asked that perequation be transferred from the state-run National Coal Bureau to a consortium of coal and steel manufacturers organized by the Comité des Forges, while smaller producers feared that

[123] Ferdinand Friedensburg, *Kohle und Eisen im Weltkriege und in den Friedensschlüssen* (Munich and Berlin, 1934), pp. 189–201; M. Olivier, *La politique du charbon 1914–1921* (Paris, 1922), pp. 69–70, 78–80, and charts pp. 291–293; Sir Richard Redmayne, *The British Coal Mining Industry during the War* (New Haven, 1923), pp. 224–228, 235–237, and table, p. 315. Minister of Commerce's estimate is in AN, Paris: F[12] (Ministère du Commerce)/8860, "Note pour M. le Président du Conseil," March 4, 1920. Stuttgart and Berlin prices as of the summer of 1920 are in the report of the Reich Coal Council manager, Köngetter, September 24, 1920, in BA, Koblenz: Paul Silverberg Nachlass/135.

[124] System described in Olivier, *La politique du charbon*, pp. 113–116, 140–162, 198–206. See the price controversies of 1920–1921, in AN, Paris: AJ[26] (Bureau National du Charbon)/2.

this step would only perpetuate the advantages of the large firms at their expense.[125]

This disagreement was part of a wider divergence of approach to the coal and reparation questions. By the spring of 1920, small producers emphasized that German coke and coal, delivered free and credited against German reparations at the low German inland price, was the only solution to French shortages. To compensate for German destruction of French coal mines in occupied territory and to assure the continued provisioning of the Lorraine iron industry, the Allies had demanded at Versailles that Germany furnish up to 27 million tons of coal per year to France alone and from 40 to 43 million tons to all the victors. At first this seemed barely feasible: inside its 1920 frontiers, which excluded the Saar but did still incorporate Upper Silesia for another two years, the Reich had produced 140 million tons of coal in 1913 and consumed 124 million tons. But in fact the treaty stipulated only a theoretical maximum or a legal "option." The Reparation Commission, which set the actual levies, was never to ask more than a yearly total of 24 million tons. Coal output, moreover, was not fixed; by 1929 the Germans were extracting more without the Saar and Upper Silesia than they had within their 1913 borders.[126]

For the Germans, however, the shortages of 1919–1920 as well as longer-run economic developments made the reparation claims intolerable. By November 1919 coal reserves for the railroads had dropped to a mere four- to five-day supply; municipalities and public institutions were scrambling for stockpiles; passenger train service was interrupted and restrictions placed on home heating and city lighting.[127] By early 1920 industry was picking up tempo and demanding coal, but there were strikes, Ruhr disorders, railroad delays, and run-down mines. Once the most acute winter shortages eased, German producers still resented the low inland prices stipulated for reparation coal. But as the French learned by March 1920, and as Stinnes in-

[125] Cf. Wendel to the Ministre des Régions Libérées, February 1921, AN, Paris: AJ[26]/90, F. Ind. 63; Pinot report, January 25, 1921, F. Ind. 90; opposition expressed by Syndicat Général des Fondeurs en Fer de France to the Ministre de Commerce, March 8, 1921, and by diverse steel companies March 18, 1921, both in F. Ind. 63. Cf. also PAM/7250: f. Combustibles 1919. "Compte Rendu de la Réunion 'Coke' à Metz, le 13 novembre 1919."

[126] On conflicting reparation claims: André Tardieu, *La Paix* (Paris, 1921), pp. 284–285, 308–313; Friedensburg, *Kohle und Eisen*, pp. 98–104; for the dependence of Lorraine iron and its role in calculating reparation needs: Guy Greer, *The Ruhr-Lorraine Industrial Problem* (New York, 1925), pp. 101–103; for overall output figures, Baumont, *La grosse industrie allemande et le charbon*, pp. 21–23, 362–363.

[127] Reichsverkehrsminister to Foreign Ministry, June 21, 1920, in: GFM 9125/3469/H243207-243208; Baumont, *La grosse industrie allemande et le charbon*, pp. 322–323.

dicated in May, the Germans were willing to sell for cash at premium prices.[128]

Initially after the war the French hoped that the Germans would continue their exchange of Ruhr coke for the ore of formerly German Lorraine, despite French take-over. In the decade before 1914 Ruhr producers had developed their own smelting facilities in German Lorraine, where there was more room for blast furnace expansion than in the Ruhr. The freight cars that brought ore to the Ruhr would bring coke to Lorraine. The optimal carload ratios suggested that two-thirds of the local ore should be converted into raw or pig iron on the spot and about one-third of the iron returned to the Ruhr with the extra Lorraine ore for further processing into steel products. Because of the high heat needed per unit of steel output, this operation was logically carried on close to the source of the coke. Other Lorraine iron products went to the machine and engineering firms of South Germany.[129]

This pattern of exchanges left Lorraine vulnerable to market demands inside Germany; like a colony, the province contributed more to the raw-material stage than to the final product of industry. The war, moreover, disrupted the exchanges with Germany proper. Ruhr producers relied less on the bulky and low-yield minette ore of Lorraine and imported high-quality Swedish ore instead. The proximity of the Western front led to a curtailment of pig iron production in

[128] See Président du Conseil to French delegate on the Reparations Commission, March 1, 1920, in Min. Aff. Etr.: Série A. Paix/1374, dossier 3; also AN, Paris: F^{12}/8860, "Note pour M. le Ministre: Négociations franco-allemandes," May 12, 1920.

[129] See Greer, *Ruhr-Lorraine Industrial Problem*, pp. 39–42; also Ausschuss zur Untersuchung der Erzeugungs- und Absatzbedingungen der deutschen Wirtschaft, (Enquête-Ausschuss), III. Unterausschuss, *Die deutsche eisenerzeugende Industrie* (Berlin, 1930), pp. 12 ff. Friedensburg, *Kohle und Eisen*, pp. 12, 41; Henry Laufenberger, *L'industrie sidérurgique de la Lorraine désannexée et la France* (Strasbourg, 1924), pp. 45–64. Coke shortages were even more worrisome for France, for even when French coal output rose, she had a far lower coking furnace capacity than did Germany. See also Paul Berkenkopf, *Die Entwicklung und die Lage der lothringisch-luxemburgischen Grosseisenindustrie* (Essen, 1928), pp. 102–134. Cf. table:

Year	Coke Produced in Ruhr (tons)	Coke Produced in Saar and Lorraine (tons)	Coke Consumed in Lorraine (tons)
1913	24,496,000	1,797,000 (German) 171,000 (French)	4,458,000
1920	19,891,000	<1,300,000	1,818,387

The fall in coke consumption reflected the depressed state of the French iron industry, whose production in 1920 dropped to 30 percent capacity.

Lorraine and likewise in Zollverein-partner Luxembourg, while the Ruhr increased its own iron output. During and after the war, moreover, German manufacturers switched to the Siemens-Martin steel process, which substituted scrap steel in the open-hearth furnace for iron ore and raw iron.[130]

The consequence was that after France recovered Lorraine and took over the German-built blast furnaces, the Ruhr magnates were happy to let the French "smother" in their new ore.[131] By 1922, Germany was taking only 160,000 tons of pig iron from Lorraine, whereas before the war the Ruhr alone had absorbed almost ten times this amount. Even as the conversion to Martin steel cut down the German need for ore and raw iron, the destruction of war matériel in the early 1920's increased her supply of scrap steel. As Robert Pinot was to explain to Camille Cavallier of Pont-à-Mousson in early 1922, the German use of scrap had "permitted a boycotting of our minette ores these past years." Whereas before the war the ratio of Martin to Thomas steel output was 50:50, by 1920 it was 60:40, and by 1921, probably 70:30.[132] Only after the mid-decade trade agreements with France did the percentage of raw iron begin to rise again slightly.

After 1919 French steel producers often cited the old complementary roles of Lorraine ore and Ruhr coal. They needed to reinstitute the

[130] Friedensburg, *Kohle und Eisen*, pp. 134–137, 169 for wartime decline in Lorraine and Luxembourg production. Enquête-Ausschuss, III. Unterausschuss, *Die Rohstoffversorgung der deutschen eisenerzeugenden Industrie* (Berlin, 1928), pp. 8 ff., 23 ff.; Étienne Weill-Raynal, *Les réparations allemandes*, 3 vols. (Paris, 1947), I, pp. 420–421, and the Mission Interalliée de Contrôle des Usines et des Mines (MICUM), *Enquêtes générales faites dans la Ruhr en 1923 et 1924*, 10 vols. (Brussels, 1924), vols. III and IV, *L'industrie de fer dans la Ruhr*, III, pp. 65 ff.; IV, pp. 7 ff. reveal the shift away from French ores and the changing technologies of steel making. The Enquête-Ausschuss, III. Unterausschuss, *Die deutsche Eisenerzeugende Industrie*, p. 16, provides the following table:

PERCENTAGE OF IRON ORE SUPPLIED
(MEASURED BY METAL CONTENT)

Year	Inland	France	Sweden/Norway	Spain	Luxembourg and others
1920	38.5	9.4	35.0	4.2	12.9
1922	27.1	9.2	36.8	8.8	18.1
1925	22.3	5.2	47.6	9.7	15.2
1927	20.6	9.6	46.3	9.6	14.5
1929	18.5	11.3	42.7	11.7	15.8

See, too, the map of iron and steel flows, below, p. 518.

[131] See Reichert to Foreign Minister Simons, February 24, 1921, in GFM: Büro des Reichsministers 5, Reparation, 3243/1642/716332–716335. Cf. the industrialists' discussion of February 21, 1921, in BA, Koblenz: R 13 I (VdESI)/158.

[132] Letter of February 3, 1922, in PAM/7246, f. 122.

connection to fill their own coke needs and reconquer a market for their now excess ore and raw iron capacity. But Comité des Forges spokesmen and government officials quietly admitted by the spring of 1920 that the Germans hardly required French ore.[133] Why should they exchange their precious coke for it? Nor did reparations reliably secure the coal and coke that were needed. As the first six months under the regulations stipulated by the Versailles Treaty revealed, the Germans could quietly sabotage delivery.

Because of delayed treaty ratification, coal reparations would not legally have come due before spring 1920. But to get badly needed shipments in the winter of 1919–1920, the Allies had signed further coal agreements at Luxembourg and, more important, again at Versailles. In these they had promised to delay imposing the maximum reparation demands that might be levied in return for advance German coal deliveries.[134] But the French were soon disillusioned. Over the fall of 1919, the Germans delivered only between 350,000 and 650,000 tons per month, while the French claimed that they had been informally promised at least a million. At Essen in early December the Germans promised a million tons for the month ahead but failed to meet their pledge. January was to be the first month to apply the quotas determined by the Versailles protocol, which provided that on the basis of their monthly output the Germans should deliver 2.5 million tons. The allies received only what appeared to be a paltry 300,000 tons.[135]

While parliamentary opinion grew angry, the major French steel industrialists came to feel that it would be more fruitful to abandon the approach of rigid exactions. Various schemes arose for getting around the German resistance. Léon-Lévy of the Commentry foun-

[133] For Comité des Forges admission see Min. Aff. Etr.: Europe, 1918–1929, Allemagne/522. f. I. 1919–1923, pp. 184–187, "Note pour le Président du Conseil, N° 1: Négotiations Allemandes, Réunion avec les délégués français 19 mai 1920." Cf. Serruys' estimate that France's ore assets were nugatory. AN, Paris: F¹²/8860, "Note pour M. le Ministre, Négotiations Franco-Allemandes," May 12, 1920.

[134] Karl Bergmann, *The History of Reparations* (Boston and New York, 1927), pp. 26–28; Weill-Raynal, *Les réparations allemandes*, I, pp. 428–430; Friedensburg, *Kohle und Eisen*, pp. 206–207; text in *Documents on British Foreign Policy* (henceforth: DBFP), series I, vol. v, p. 336. The Versailles Protocol of August 1919 provided 1.66 million tons per month plus a fraction of surplus production; the Treaty itself authorized Allied demands of up to 3.5 million tons.

[135] "Report on the Coal Situation in Occupied Territories," by the British Deputy of the Interallied Rhineland High Commission, Koblenz (February 14, 1920), in DBFP, series I, vol. x, p. 185. For the estimate of French experts as to respective French and German coal conditions, see: AN, Paris: AJ⁶ (Commission interalliée des Réparations)/203, Procès-Verbaux, Annèxe 77 bis.

dries urged paying a cash premium to the Germans beyond the reparations credit; the cost would still be far below that of British coal.[136] As early as February 1920, Humbert de Wendel told the Ministry of Commerce that the prospect of reparation coal was illusory. Instead, the government should pressure the Germans into selling "significant and perhaps preponderant" stock shares in those old Ruhr firms that had earlier been linked to the Lorraine smelters. The French companies putting up the money for German shares would have the "right" to buy coal and coke for cash payments, which would be higher than the Germans' internal price but at least would encourage Germans to deliver to the French. In return the French purchasers would turn over half the coal, free, to their own National Coal Office for distribution to other companies through the *péréquation* system. Allegedly everybody would benefit: German firms would supply more coal; the German government would not have to pay its own domestic firms (as it did for reparations deliveries) but would still have half the French purchases credited toward reparations requirements; the French National Coal Office would get free coal; and as Wendel's memo explained, the French companies that took the "risk" of buying into German mines would keep half the coal for their own use. Although they would be paying in effect twice the commercial price for the tonnage they retained, they would still avoid the soaring English prices and the shortages of *péréquation*. Not surprisingly, Wendel especially stood to profit, since his family's interests had enjoyed the most extensive prewar holdings in German coal firms.[137]

The alignment of economic interests and government agencies resembled that of a year earlier. Large steel producers wanted government sanction for advantageous private arrangements; smaller firms sought to hold the big firms to public arrangements that entailed a wider spreading of profit opportunities or of exceptional costs. For the major companies reparations and *péréquation* were more burdens than gifts; for the smaller producers they appeared as absolute necessities. As in 1919, the large firms apparently found the support of Louis Loucheur who, according to Wendel, supported the proposals for special arrangements with German industry. The smaller steel producers still enjoyed protection at the Ministry of Commerce, where a year earlier Clémentel had run into the silent opposition of the Comité des Forges in inaugurating his planning bodies. Now under Minister

---

[136] Min. Aff. Etr.: Europe, 1918–1929, Allemagne/522. f. 1919–1923, pp. 188–189, "Note . . . N° 2: Négotiations Allemandes, 19 mai 1920."

[137] AN, Paris: F[12]/8860, F. Note Wendel. "Note relative à l'approvisionnement du Bassin métallurgique lorrain en coke allemand," February 1920.

Isaac—who as a major executive of the PLM railroad company understood the needs of coal and steel consumers—and the permanent Under Secretary for Foreign Commercial Relations, Serruys, the Ministry of Commerce advised buying all the English coal available even at exorbitant prices: better inflation than shutdowns of industry.[138]

As premier and Foreign Minister, Millerand thus faced contradictory needs. He initially rejected the Minister of Commerce's counsel that France should simply continue to buy huge quantities of expensive British coal; for he felt this would only give London an incentive in helping Germany evade reparations.[139] As early as February 1920 he insisted vigorously that the Allies plan upon occupation of the Ruhr to compel Germany to deliver the coal she owed.[140] Nonetheless, Millerand's instructions to his *chargé d'affaires* in Berlin in April indicated that he hoped to exploit France's treaty position to extract interindustry arrangements between the two countries which transcended the narrow framework of reparations.[141]

This approach should have encouraged the Wendels and other industrialists who sought to have the state win them important concessions. In May 1920, Robert Pinot of the Comité des Forges asked the premier to seek up to 75 percent of the stock in the German companies formerly linked to the Lorraine steel mills.[142] Nonetheless, until Loucheur returned as minister under Briand in 1921, the state was evidently hesitant to adopt industry's plan for pressing the Germans to turn over stock shares. Millerand's advisers, moreover, were leery even about the steel industry's plans for private coal purchases outside the reparations framework. As officials pointed out, if the Germans pleaded that they could not provide reparation coal precisely because French industry was buying it privately, the French government would be in a difficult position to raise a protest. Jacques Seydoux, the major

[138] AN, Paris: F¹²/8860, "Note pour M. le Président du Conseil," March 4, 1920.

[139] *Ibid.*, Président du Conseil to Ministre du Commerce, March 11, 1920.

[140] See the February 2 conference of ambassadors as reported by the Earl of Derby to Curzon in DBFP, series i, vol. x, p. 183; also Millerand's London Conference statement in DBFP, series i, vol. vii, pp. 32–37.

[141] Min. Aff. Etr.: Europe 1918–1929. Allemagne/522, pp. 137–145, Millerand to Marcilly, April 14, 1920. Cf., too, Millerand's encouragement of abortive Krupp-Schneider negotiations (June–October 1920), reported in Allemagne/540, Note of October 26, 1920, from Sous-Direction des Relations Commerciales [Seydoux]. Also Georges Soutot, MS on the French government's economic diplomacy in early 1920.

[142] Bibliothèque Nationale: Fonds Millerand. Robert Pinot, "Note aux approvisionnements de charbon et de coke qui pourraient être assurés à la métallurgie française lors des négociations de Spa." Also in AN, Paris: AJ²⁶/58, f. Conférence de Spa.

reparations adviser at the Quai, also feared that France would be open to charges of bad faith. Seydoux and Millerand preferred that French coal purchasers negotiate their own contracts and send the bills to the French government and Reparations Commission for crediting to the Germans, even if the price was higher than what Berlin was supposed to be allowed.[143] No solution was satisfactory, however: as Le Trocquer told Millerand in mid-March, the Germans were not delivering at a time when "the whole job of economic recovery is dominated by the solution that one can find for this agonizing coal question."[144] The Germans, moreover, had the coal; and, according to the British delegate to the Rhineland High Commission, there were "no conclusive reasons apparent why the already much reduced demands of the Allies under the Peace Treaty should not be met."[145]

By late March, however, the Germans declared that they could not meet the new quotas set by the Reparations Commission and pleaded the Kapp Putsch and the general strike as mitigating circumstances. The coal requirements were lowered in April and May but still could not be fulfilled to any significant degree. In April, moreover, the Reparations Commission demanded that deliveries to Poland from the Upper Silesian mines be raised from 200,000 to 450,000 tons monthly, a disposition evidently urged by France to help the Polish war effort. To the anger of the Allies, the Germans unilaterally decided to reduce their Ruhr coal deliveries by 300,000 tons per month as compensation. By the end of June the Reparations Commission announced that Germany was formally in default on coal deliveries: for the last three months she had met only 51 percent of the reparations demands.[146]

The prolonged conflict over coal came to a climax at the Spa Conference of July 1920, the first major postwar discussion with the Germans on disputed issues. For Lloyd George, Spa presented the chance to reopen basic peace treaty questions in hopes of reintegrating Germany and Russia into the European economy. For the French it was an unwelcome risk. By the spring of 1920 spokesmen for French bour-

---

[143] See "Observations de M. Fromageot [legal adviser at the Quai d'Orsay] . . . ," February 11, 1920; Seydoux to Laroche, February 21, 1920; Président du Conseil to French Delegate on Reparation Commission, March 1, 1920," in Min. Aff. Etr.: A. Paix/1374, dossier 3. Cf. AN, Paris: F¹²/8860, "Note pour M. le Ministre," May 12, 1920.

[144] Le Troquer to Millerand, March 19, 1920, in Min. Aff. Etr.: A. Paix/1374, dossier 3.

[145] "Report on the Coal Situation . . . ," February 14, 1920, in DBFP, series I, vol. x, pp. 185, 194–195.

[146] Weill-Raynal, Les réparations allemandes, I, pp. 430–431; Bergmann, Reparations, pp. 30–31; also Millerand's statement at Spa, July 9, 1920, DBFP, series I, vol. VIII, pp. 509–511.

geois opinion such as Clemenceau's former aide, André Tardieu, and the Chairman of the Reparations Commission, ex-President Poincaré, were disillusioned with the meager fruits of victory and fearful of being victimized by German deception, English disengagement, and Italian Francophobia. Poincaré was doubly annoyed in the spring of 1920 as the heads of government increasingly removed reparations policy from the competence of the International Reparations Commission that he chaired. He also feared that the final setting of a reparation sum would be based on Germany's present capacity to pay, not the real extent of French damages. The upcoming conference of Spa, he warned, threatened "to become the most dangerous of adventures."[147] Millerand shared many of these nationalist forebodings. He had consented only reluctantly to the discussion with the Germans, and insisted that the Allies agree beforehand to plan definite sanctions if the proposed conference failed. Ultimately, despite the dangers of revision, he hoped to get British help in halting German weaseling on the Treaty terms.[148]

The German delegates recognized reparations in coal as the pre-eminent issue at Spa, superior even to the bitterly disputed disarmament question, on which they finally submitted for the sake of economic concessions.[149] Yet the coal question produced even more difficult disputes. The underlying fact was that most Germans did not believe they could fulfill the Treaty, and differed among themselves primarily over the strategies of revision. Social Democrats, moderates among the middle parties, and finally some of the economic advisers of the Foreign Ministry believed that Germany must attempt temporary fulfillment, if only to demonstrate that in the long run the Treaty demands were harsh and beyond Germany's capacity. Nationalists counted on immediate defiance of the Allies to bring the latter to their senses. As early as March some German advisers recommended simply refusing to deliver more than a million tons of coal per month. Carl Bergmann, head of the German War Charges Commission (Kriegslastenkommission) and chief negotiator with the Allies, insisted upon a more moderate approach, arguing that "The Peace Treaty is not yet ripe for being overturned." Still, Bergmann's own suggestion that under certain favorable conditions, such as retaining all of Silesia, Germany might

[147] Raymond Poincaré, "Chronique de la Quinzaine," *RDM*, June 1, 1920, pp. 717–718; cf. "Chronique," May 15, 1920, p. 477. For Tardieu's position, see the May 28 debate on the Hythe Conference in JOC, 1920, pp. 1711–1712.

[148] For Millerand's attitude see the San Remo Conference of April 18 and after: DBFP, series I, vol. VIII, pp. 10–20, 144–155.

[149] For German views on the military issue, see: GFM, Büro des Reichsministers, Spa 4a: 3243/1642/716047–716050. Also DBFP, series I, vol. VIII, pp. 435–441, 470–495.

eventually work up 1.4 million tons monthly offered the Allies only a little more than Berlin's defiant nationalists.[150]

Bergmann at least negotiated without histrionics. Stinnes, however, set the initial tone of the coal discussions at Spa with a gratuitously aggressive speech, while the German delegation repeatedly postponed submitting their own estimate of feasible coal deliveries. Lloyd George obtained Millerand's agreement that getting the Germans to consent to 2 million tons per month would be preferable to trying to impose a higher sum by duress. But Berlin's representatives offered only 1.1 million tons at the outset, 1.4 million within a month or two, and finally 1.7 to 1.8 million tons monthly in another year. Even Lloyd George, who yearned for any accommodation, thought glumly that the Allies might have to resort to occupation of the Ruhr.[151]

During the final two days of the conference Lloyd George frantically pursued some settlement, trying to dissuade Millerand and Foch from sanctions while seeking to convince Simons that he really was courting occupation of the Ruhr.[152] While the Germans were debating among themselves over how much coal they could offer, the two Allies also came to harsh words over the troublesome issue of the price of reparation coal. British labor and industry would not tolerate London's participation in any occupation of the Ruhr, Lloyd George insisted, just so French competitors could get coal at about four-fifths the price that British businessmen had to pay for their own fuel. For English participation in any Ruhr sanctions, the coal that was obtained thereby must be credited to reparations at the high world-market or British export price. Millerand reminded the Prime Minister that the average price of coal in France was far higher than in Britain, but he still felt that joint action was mandatory. He had consented to the Spa Conference in part to win the promise of British cooperation if coercion finally proved necessary. To preserve London's agreement, he gave in to the British on the price issue; what is more, he agreed to supplement the reparation credit for coal with a cash payment to Germany of 5 gold marks (13.75 francs) per ton. The ostensible justification for this concession was to subsidize food for the Ruhr miners, whose undernourishment, the Germans claimed, contributed to their laggard coal deliveries.[153]

[150] Bergmann to Simons, March 30, 1920, in GFM: Wirtschaft Reparation, K 2189/5585/603215–603218.

[151] DBFP, series I, vol. VIII, pp. 521–523, 562–570, 576.

[152] *Ibid.*, pp. 582 ff., 597 ff., 617–620.

[153] *Ibid.*, pp. 621–632. Lloyd George claimed that the difference between German coal prices and British export prices was 45 shillings (about 110 francs). In fact, current English export prices were 115 shillings (or 280 francs) and the difference closer to 80 shillings (or 200 francs). On the issue of the 5-mark advance, cf. AN, Paris: AJ²⁶/58, f. Conférence de Spa. "Note pour le Président du Conseil," Spa, July 8, 1920. See also the Ministre des Travaux Publics (Le

Against the advice of Stinnes, Ewald Hilger, and the other coal experts from private industry, the German delegation, urged by Rathenau and Carl Melchior, finally decided to close the gap between the 1.8 million tons they indicated might be produced ultimately and the 2 million tons demanded by the Allies immediately. But now the Germans demanded that the difference between their inland price credited toward reparation and the high world-market price be paid to them in cash. This ran counter to Treaty provisions; but since Berlin was prepared to yield on the quantity of coal demanded, it was a hard issue for Paris to contest. Was a Ruhr occupation to be embarked upon only because of what Lloyd George charged was merely a question of 40 shillings per ton? Millerand had already agreed to accept British price levels if a Ruhr occupation were actually needed. It appeared irrational to demand that very occupation because Germany now insisted on the British price. Millerand was angry but cornered. Ultimately the Allies reached a compromise by which a so-called loan was extended to Germany for each ton of coal it delivered. The loan actually represented a back-door way of meeting German demands: it just made up the difference between the internal German price (plus freight and the 5-gold-mark premium) and the British export price. In short, it raised the cost of German coal to French consumers and cut its competitiveness with British fuel. The loan was never repaid but taken off the credits accumulated by Germany toward reparation as of May 1921—essentially annulled. On the basis of this compromise a six-month Spa Protocol was finally signed July 16, 1920.[154]

Troquer), "Notes pour le Président du Conseil," July 23 and 30, 1920, in Bibliothèque Nationale: Fonds Millerand, f. "La question des avances." Also Seydoux to Millerand, June 23, 1920, in Min. Aff. Etr.: A. Paix/1374, dossier 3.

[154] Not only was the "loan" never repaid, but in the wake of the collapse of coal prices it was more than high enough to cover the costs to the German government of buying reparation coal from its producers for shipment abroad. See Greer, The Ruhr-Lorraine Industrial Problem, p. 138. England, it should be noted, made a hidden concession. The cost of the loan to Germany was proportioned according to the overall agreed-upon Allied shares in reparation, not the quota of coal received. France thus paid 55 percent of the advance and received 80 percent of the coal while Britain paid about a quarter of the advance and got no coal. Finally, one dispute was resolved in favor of France a year and half later: the one-third of coal sent to France from Germany that left via Rhenish ports and Rotterdam was credited at inland prices. The British had originally wanted it credited at world-market prices, which was what was allowed for coal shipped from German ocean ports. All these disputes over costs, it might be objected, were arguments over a bit more or less on a huge charge account to be liquidated in the remote future if at all. But the reparation price levels did determine what price German coal magnates claimed from their own government in current marks as well as the costs of *péréquation* coal to French industry. Hence, the price levels could deeply influence relative profitability and competitiveness.

The Spa agreement brought immediate recriminations on both sides. French critics criticized its diminished coal yield again in light of the theoretical limits offered by the Versailles Treaty. In the Assembly, Tardieu charged that the government had embarked upon a dangerous course of revising the Treaty. In his fortnightly political column, Poincaré declared that the conference results justified all his forebodings. Millerand, however, defended his actions as the necessary price for assuring continued execution of the Treaty, and the only way to rescue any effective coal reparation whatsoever. Other men had made the Treaty, he reminded Tardieu, but left him to execute it. If there were more capable hands for this latter task, then the Chamber should summon them. Millerand won his vote by 445 to 136.[155] In addition to the Socialists, the opposition comprised some dissatisfied nationalists and most conspicuously Tardieu and other "Clémencistes" who had worked for Millerand's predecessor. Malaise, however, was more widespread in conservative circles than the vote indicated; as *Le Temps* wrote, Spa presented a mixed balance sheet. Final judgment depended upon what would finally be extracted from the agreements and how they influenced the future course of reparations. Without vigilance, however, "the illusions of today would engender the disappointments of tomorrow."[156]

In Germany Spa opened up the bitter divisions over the question of fulfillment. The DVP, especially, found itself internally divided: its members Heinze and Scholz were serving as Vice Chancellor and Minister of Economics in the Fehrenbach government even while its prominent economic spokesman, Stinnes, was attacking the agreement and thereafter urging its rejection. Stresemann, however, feared a return of the old Weimar Coalition, and refused to take the DVP out of the ministry over Spa. Ultimately the Party voted with the government for ratification.[157]

During the German debates the coal protocol actually received closer attention before the new Provisional Reich Economic Council than before the Reichstag. The Economic Council (Reichswirtschaftsrat or RWR) was the meager upshot of the schemes for national economic councils that had been "anchored" in the constitution during 1919. After plans for an extensive pyramid of councils frittered away,

[155] Tardieu's critique, JOC, 1920, ii, pp. 2980–2984 (July 20), and Millerand's response, pp. 3005–3006. Poincaré's views in *RDM*, August 1, 1920, p. 667.
[156] "Le Bilan de Spa," *Le Temps*, July 17, 1920.
[157] For the DVP's concern with Heinze and Scholz's participation at Spa, see the wires in GFM: Stresemann Nachlass, 6930 = 215/3090/139301–139302. For Stresemann's calculations about voting for the agreements: 6934 = 219/3091/139893–139905. Cf. advice from the progressive Hamburg leader, Rose, July 24, 1920: 6929 = 214/3090/139026–139027.

the provisional Reich Economic Council was instituted by decree in May 1920 along the customary "parity" lines. It soon fell into a talkative advisory role bereft of any real power; nonetheless, for a few years it offered a significant forum for the airing of important issues. In its hearings on Spa, Stinnes reiterated his view that the coal agreement was "intolerable for the German economy," and he charged that the amount that Berlin had finally had to agree to beyond its first offer (900,000 tons monthly) would reduce the coal for German industry by 20 percent. Bernhard Dernburg, the Democratic Party's banking expert and friend of Rathenau, Colonial Secretary from 1906 to 1909 and another consultant at Spa, told Simons that the coal magnates' evaluations were distorted, that in effect they were lying through misleading statistics. Stinnes in fact presupposed that coal production was stationary at 10 million tons per month when it actually averaged 13 million tons through 1920, and he assumed further that all deliveries would be at the cost of industry's rough half-share of German output. In general, however, the arguments for Spa as advanced by Simons, Rathenau, and others rested upon the political necessity of the agreements and upon the fact, as Rathenau stressed, that a Franco-German dialogue on reconstruction had been initiated.[158]

Naturally, what German defenders praised about Spa were the aspects that offended French critics and vice versa. On both sides reparation was now emerging as an ulcerating political and social issue. For the French, the Versailles Treaty represented an effort to guarantee a security and prosperity fought for at great cost. The Treaty was designed to compensate for the shocks to the economic and social order that war had imposed, as well as to provide for territorial security. Reparation—through coal or money—formed part of the Bloc National's attempt to rebuild the financial solidarity of prewar years, restore the industrial establishment, and secure a rewarding social stability. Spa, however, revealed that defense of the Treaty was a principle that did not offer ready-made answers for every problem. It left as many bitter choices as it settled.

For Germans the Treaty problem was somewhat different. From left to right, Germans thought themselves victimized by Versailles, and a ready acceptance of Treaty demands was political poison for any government. Nonetheless, the Spa accord—like the Revolution— could be exploited by many different groups: by nationalist critics, yes; but also by the organized working class who had reopened the

---

[158] Stinnes, Rathenau, and Simons testimony in DZA, Potsdam: RWR/6, pp. 58 ff. (Sitzungsprotokolle, vol. 1, July 24, 1920). On the Economic Council see Dr. Hauschild, *Der vorläufige Reichswirtschaftsrat, 1920–1926* (Berlin, 1926). Dernburg views in GFM: Büro des Reichsministers: Spa, Kohlenfrage 4e: 3243/1642/716268–716270.

question of socialization; and, of course, by heavy industry, who could claim that their expertise was all the more necessary in light of Allied exactions. Thus Spa raised the stakes of social conflict within Germany and provided new arguments for the respective economic solutions of each side: nationalization for SPD and the unions, further corporatist organization for heavy industry.

Spa refocused attention on the power of the German coal and steel industry, which the Allies rightly recognized as the key determinant of German reparations policy. It provided a new impulse for dispute between industry and labor; it opened the question as to which groups would pay the price of the coal deliveries—miners or owners. More generally, it raised the issue of the continuing political role of heavy industry within the German state.

In the summer of 1920 that role was epitomized by Hugo Stinnes. He awed even those who distrusted heavy industry: in May 1920, the editor of the liberal *Vossische Zeitung*, Georg Bernhard, wrote:

> It would be false to see in Stinnes a parasite upon human society or simply a profiteer. . . . Hugo Stinnes is a man of persuasive understanding and simplicity of thought, such as is to be observed only in natures of genius. He has a largely constructive imagination. . . . In short, he is the most brilliant organizer that Germany possesses.[159]

There was much truth in this assessment. Inheriting a family firm laid down by his grandfather and father, by 1914 Stinnes himself had built up mining, smelting, electrical, and shipping industries. The end of the war provided new incentives for a fabulous parlaying of enterprises. French steel concerns provided relatively "hard" money as they formed new holding companies such as Hagondage to buy early control of the Lorraine firms that Germans were slated to surrender in any case. Provided with ready money, spurred on by a depreciating currency to borrow more, the coal and steel industrialists accumulated enterprises and integrated firms backward and forward.[160] Stinnes

[159] *Vossische Zeitung*, May 7, 1920, Nr. 237. Included in BA, Koblenz: R 43 I (Reichskanzlei)/2469. For biographical treatments see Hermann Brinckmann, *Hugo Stinnes* (Munich, 1920); Gaston Raphaël, *Le roi de la Ruhr, Stinnes* (Paris, 1924); the essay in Felix Pinner, *Deutsche Wirtschaftsführer* (Charlottenburg, 1925 ed.), pp. 28–42; Gert von Klass, *Hugo Stinnes* (Tübingen, 1958); and for Stinnes' holdings see the publication of the Deutscher Metallarbeiter–Verband, *Konzerne der Metallindustrie* (Stuttgart, 1924), pp. 71–151: a schematic presentation of the scores of firms in this corporate empire.

[160] Richard Lewinsohn, *Die Umschichtung des europäischen Vermögens* (Berlin, 1925), pp. 117–120, 123 ff.; also from the French viewpoint the references in chapter one, note 123. Insights into the transfer process available from the reports of Haguenin mission in Germany in 1919. See Min. Aff. Etr., Europe 1918–1929, Allemagne/522, pp. 5–12, 23–28.

owned and controlled perhaps 500 companies at his death in 1924: the German-Luxemburg Mining and Smelting Company was the pivot, and it joined the Kirdorf family's Gelsenkirchen Mining Firm to form the Rhein-Elbe Union. Shortly thereafter even the Siemens-Schukert network of electrical enterprises and tramway networks was temporarily woven into the combination as each side sought new sources of precious liquidity.

The rewards were not luxury or leisure—Stinnes pretentiously shuffled around in inelegant clothing with calling cards that announced "Merchant from Mühlheim"—but unprecedented public influence. Stinnes never became an *éminence grise* behind politicians; to the DVP he granted only disdainful participation and disappointing financial support; Reichstag prominence was not a real goal. What he personified was an oracular economic expertise desperately sought by his peers and the middle-class public in the failure of the traditional political leadership. Inside the DVP Stresemann often held his tongue; other industrialists ruefully realized that their proposals all needed his imprimatur.[161]

The remedies Stinnes proposed all involved restoring German productivity by removing the handicaps imposed by defeat and revolution. Reparations allegedly crippled the economy by their hovering uncertainty; Stinnes wanted a fixed sum set, but only when it represented a massive write-off of the reparations debt. Until then, efforts to stabilize the German exchange rate and halt the inflation, he insisted, were impossible. German labor had to work more: whatever reparations demands were finally imposed, they could be met only by restoring a ten-hour day, or, as he suggested in 1922, an agreement on overtime work for the next decade. Stinnes cooperated with Carl Legien, prided himself on the lack of social distance from his workers, but insisted that they abandon the one tangible reward they had gained in the Revolution. It was an unchanging line over a four-year period: before he left for Spa he asked union delegates to return from the seven- to the eight-and-a-half-hour day for miners to forestall a Ruhr occupation. When he returned, he told the Reich Economic Council that only

[161] Internal DVP conflict on the role of heavy industry reflected in August 5 debate between Stresemann and Stinnes' associate Quaatz, GFM: Stresemann Nachlass, 6929 = 214/3090/139093–139098; also letter to Vögler and Stinnes same date, 139099–139100, 139103; Stinnes' answer to Stresemann, August 7, 139113–139115; and Stresemann to Stinnes, August 16, in 6924 = 209/3088/138174–138175. For influence within the industry community, see Silverberg to Generaldirektor Kruse, September 17, 1920: "It is really apparent how foolish the Ruhr men are, as they cannot arrive at any decision or clear position. They make no utterance before they've obtained the blessing of Stinnes or Vögler." BA, Koblenz: Silverberg Nachlass/136.

overtime work can "rescue us from immediate collapse."[162] In 1922 he said that he could double or triple miners' salaries if they consented to only two hours more labor per day. In 1923 he flirted with dictatorship to effect the same goal. There were perhaps other roads to higher production, but Stinnes never saw them as being immediately effective. He could pose insuperable objections to intensified capital investment in coal mines within the Reich, even as in 1921 and 1922 he invested in new Austrian acquisitions.

Eventually, Stinnes believed, Germany would turn to her economic organizers to pull herself from the postwar morass. The dynasties had departed, the army was diminished, the bureaucrats demoralized by revolution and inflation; the state itself was a pale and ghostly entity allegedly forced to bend only to Social Democratic or Allied pressure. Combined with Stinnes' personal outward sobriety and would-be simplicity was an inward impulse toward the fantastic and megalomaniac. Georg Bernhard compared him to Ludendorff in this respect; another comparison might be made with General Schleicher, who later, in 1932, sought to see himself as "the Social General" and to arrogate for the Reichswehr the role Stinnes allotted to industry. Felix Pinner of the *Berliner Tageblatt* spoke of an entrepreneurial mentality that was "overdeveloped, naively sovereign, totally egocentric and oriented toward private economic gain."[163] Stinnes, however, believed that Germany and his firms prospered together, in fact, that political questions were only problems of coal, steel, and disciplined labor, that Germany's power would flow from her industrial productivity, and the latter from the remedies he prescribed. He and his colleagues, Pinner charged, felt that ultimately the state could perish if the economy continued; industry alone, Stinnes once told Rathenau, had the right to lead Germany politically, because industry alone had known how to survive and indeed thrive in the general catastrophe that overtook Germany.

To Bernhard this baroque energy seemed creative but harmful, be-

[162] For Stinnes' appeal before Spa see the report from Berlin, June 29, 1920, in AN, Paris: AJ²⁶/58, f., Conférence de Spa, "La question de charbon." For Stinnes' subsequent appeal, see DZA, Potsdam: RWR/6, p. 60 (Sitzungsprotokolle, July 24, 1920). Overtime work of seven hours per week had been instituted in February 1920 in return for special food and pay. The workers did not distribute it over each day but performed it in two extra sessions for fear of undermining the eight-hour principle. The agreement was confirmed on August 19 in the wake of Spa, but denounced by the miners in March 1921 because the extra rations had not been provided. In September and October 1922 a new six-hour overtime agreement was initiated but interrupted by the Ruhr occupation. See Baumont, *La grosse industrie allemande et le charbon*, pp. 562–563.
[163] Pinner, *Deutsche Wirtschaftsführer*, p. 36.

211

cause in Germany it could not be harnessed for the common welfare. Dissolution of the *res publica* might mean to Stinnes that his enterprises were of supreme value for the country, but to Bernhard the same dissolution meant that Stinnes was inevitably appropriating more and more of Germany as a private business. Stinnes did not contest this fact; indeed he complained only about being characterized merely as a Rhenish-Westphalian magnate.[164] The confusion between public and private welfare was central to the ambiguity in Stinnes' role; and this was the very ambiguity engendered by the new corporatist tendencies which a Stinnes both advanced and exploited. The opposed concepts of the public welfare that Stinnes and Bernhard held embodied a fundamental alternative for the Weimar Republic. In general the coal socialization controversy, made more pressing by Spa, was basically a dispute over these very conceptions. Consequently, it is worth following closely.

The agreements signed at Spa focused German concern on enhancing coal productivity. Union representatives pointed out how ill-housed and undernourished the miners were. They also demanded prompt renewed action on public take-over. Coal miners, said the Catholic labor leader, Imbusch, would contribute to the growth in production needed to fulfill the Spa obligations only with further socialization measures; they could not feel that their extra efforts went to the profits of capitalists alone. The French railroad workers had presented the same arguments: socialization provided a stake in society for its laborers, a guarantee that efforts went to socially useful and equitable causes and not merely to the pockets of a distrusted management. Georg Bernhard concurred with this view when he stressed that socialization was a moral or psychological prerequisite for winning extra productivity. In the Reichstag, Breitscheid for the USP and Stampfer for the SPD also called for socialization, although the latter delegate talked guardedly about an "understanding way" toward this goal. Foreign Minister Simons did not contest the objective, but he offered an indication of how affairs might go when he said that he, too, approved of socialism, "rightly understood." Not the removal of private entrepreneurs, "socialism is the cooperation between capital and labor."[165] All seemed, therefore, to hang upon the content of socialism, rightly understood. Of what would German socialism really consist?

Hitherto it had consisted of precious little. The Kapp Putsch had

[164] Letter of August 8, 1920, in GFM: Stresemann Nachlass, 6929 = 214/3090/139114.

[165] Imbusch and Bernhard in DZA, Potsdam: RWR/6, pp. 53–58 (Sitzungsprotokolle, July 23, 1920). Breitscheid, Stampfer, and Simons in VDR: SB, 344, pp. 272–286 (July 27, 1920).

led the unions to demand the resumption of meaningful socialization procedures as one objective of the General Strike. The agencies designed by Wissell and instituted in 1919—the Reich Coal Association and the Reich Coal Council—had failed to produce a real public control, but just provided a public authority to voice the wishes of the mine owners.

The critical issue that had revealed the shortcomings of the Coal Council was that of price. The question of coal prices concealed political and economic implications crucial to the whole socialization question. The price of inland coal was low in Germany, lower than even the price of inland coal in England. The mine entrepreneurs kept pushing for price increases beyond those acceded to at intervals by the Economics Ministry, which could veto the recommendations of the Coal Council, generally favorable to the mine owners. Stinnes held the view that the German coal price should approach that of the English inland coal price; German coal had risen since 1913 only from the equivalent of 12 shillings to 16 or more, while domestic British coal prices had doubled. On the other hand, German costs of production in real terms had risen little, and the Economics Ministry sought to determine prices by reckoning production costs and allowing a certain margin for amortization, interest payments, and "pure profit."[166]

These costs and charges were bitterly disputed. Here, in fact, seemed to be the nub of the early socialization dispute, for without clarity on the costs of coal production no equitable prices could be determined and the public interest could not be preserved. Hitherto the Economics Ministry had not been able to obtain a clear view into costs by means of the Coal Council, and this was one reason for desiring a more effective agency. Two major components entered into cost calculations and became objects of intense controversy: the price of labor and the charges for capital repair and new investment. Stinnes and others pointed to the rising cost of mine labor; and they desired still higher salaries for underground workers. Otherwise the miners were lost to the high-paying state railroads, which supposedly hired many redun-

[166] Stinnes' statistics were exaggerated: 33 shillings and not 45 was the current base price for British coal. But the argument was also misleading. The Ruhr spokesmen implied that British and German prices had been equal before the war, hence German coal prices should be set equal to current British prices according to the current exchange rate between mark and pound. In fact, German internal price levels in 1920 had inflated far less than the mark had depreciated in terms of stable currencies; and costs to the coal producers were a function primarily of internal German prices and not external depreciation. For Stinnes' views see: *Verhandlungen der Sozialisierungs-Kommission für den Bergbau im Jahre 1920*, 2 vols. (Berlin, 1920), i, pp. 16–17, 31, 39. On the divergence of price index and exchange rate: Costantino Bresciani-Turroni, *The Economics of Inflation* (London, 1937), pp. 131–132.

dant men.[167] The coal owners, though, wanted any wage increase compensated for by a price rise in coal. The Economics Ministry accepted this claim, but remained more skeptical when owners demanded that a further 60 percent of the wage increase per ton be added on the new price, supposedly because all other costs rose in tempo with wage increases.[168]

Julius Hirsch, the representative of the Economics Ministry at the opening sessions of the 1920 Socialization Commission discussions on April 22 and 23, contested this correlation. A Socialist member also pointed out that despite higher money wages the real price of labor formed a lower percentage of the coal price than before the war.[169] The Economics Ministry officials complained, too, that they had never been furnished with adequate information as legally required and had had to make their own investigations. They contended that as of September 1919, their price allowances had permitted a pure profit, even after payment of interest and amortization, of 4.5 marks per ton (then about 3 percent). And when the profit had fallen in November to half the amount, the Economics Ministry had sanctioned a price rise; moreover, they had consented thereafter to further increases because the coal owners said that these would be passed on proportionally in wages. But the wage increases, the Ministry charged, had not been granted. Up to February 1, 1920, when the deadlock over pricing with the coal owners hardened, the Ministry calculated its prices to include a profit of 5 to 8 marks per ton, and it was probable that the Ministry erred, if at all, on the side of generosity. Rathenau, who sat on the new Committee, believed that in the spring of 1920 the coal entrepreneurs were in reality earning about a 25 percent profit.[170]

Just as indicative of the conflicting interests at stake was the thorny question of "write-offs." The coal owners argued that the prices allowed by the government were insufficient to permit adequate depreciation allowances or investment reserves. By early 1920 the coal mine owners desired that an 85 percent amortization allowance for new investment be included in the price of coal! Any capital improvement should pay for itself in little over a year. To justify this exaggerated incentive, Stinnes and Paul Silverberg of the Stinnes-affiliated Rhenish Lignite Company argued that the mark would probably appreciate back toward its prewar value. Future paying back of present investments would thus represent an intolerable burden on the com-

[167] *Verhandlungen der Sozialisierungs-Kommission . . . 1920*, i, p. 18.
[168] *Ibid.*, i, pp. 72 ff., 78.
[169] Richard Kuczynski in *ibid.*, i, pp. 21–22.
[170] *Ibid.*, i, pp. 33, 50, 75–76; Rathenau estimates, pp. 82, 318–320. The British, to give some standard of comparison, allowed a statutory profit of 1s/2d, or about 4 percent of the prices at the mine.

panies unless they were given huge write-offs. Rathenau argued that a government guarantee of future assistance in case the mark really did rise would be sufficient. Stinnes wanted the guarantees built into the price of coal and present profits.[171]

The problem of price emphasized the issue of public control. Without an agency capable of probing the secrets of the coal firms' accounts, the public could never know what exaggerated incentives might be built into their alleged costs. What, in sum, were the coal magnates demanding? Stinnes called first for a large price increase to tie German coal prices to British ones when his domestic costs had risen less. He then reiterated the necessity of a growth in productivity, but one that would rest on the workers' increased labor contribution. (As a spur to productivity, Stinnes even asked the Allies at Spa to help in evicting nonminers from scarce Ruhr housing.)[172] Finally, he seemed willing to invest only when granted a huge guaranteed return.

The Economics Ministry had sought to combine investment incentives with a greater degree of public control. Even before the Kapp Putsch, Hirsch had proposed allowing price rises if the increase (or a demonstrated 50 percent of it) was applied to capital outlay, and the coal agency was given a supervisory power over these investments. The mine owners had rejected the idea as an indirect road to socialization, and consequently the Ministry sanctioned no price increases. Profits were limited, but so was desirable expansion, and the mine owners' bitterness continued. Stinnes characteristically condemned the Economics Ministry for its "criminal policy."[173]

While price policy remained deadlocked, the question of national reorganization showed some progress. After the Kapp Putsch, the SPD government promised the unions a renewed effort at nationalization; and in view of the upcoming elections it established a new Socialization Commission and drafted a preliminary bill to amend the March 1919 Act that had established the Coal Association and Coal Council. The unions sought to socialize the regional coal syndicates which were dominated by the coal firms and remained the real decision-making bodies for price, investment, and allocation. As an interim step, the Economics Ministry suggested doing away with the Reich Coal Association, which comprised the regional syndicates of mining interests, and transferring its powers to the hitherto feeble Coal Council, potentially more responsive to public and consumer interests.[174] The new

[171] *Ibid.*, I, pp. 76–77, 90–107.
[172] See DBFP, series I, vol. VIII, pp. 591–593.
[173] Hirsch proposal: *Verhandlungen der Sozialisierungs-Kommission . . . 1920*, I, pp. 1–6; Stinnes accusation, I, p. 35.
[174] Discussion and criticism of this alleged half-measure at the Socialization Commission session of April 30, 1920, in *ibid.*, pp. 179–207.

Socialization Commission turned the government bill over to the critical Rathenau for an introductory study and report. Rathenau went beyond his mandate and prepared an alternative scheme for what he called socialization.[175] What he came up with formed the new basis of discussion, but it also meant a major step toward diluting socialization of real meaning. Stinnes may have detested Rathenau, especially after Spa, when he said that the Jewish expert's "alien psyche" had weakened German resistance;[176] nevertheless, Rathenau helped save Stinnes' coal mines. As an industrialist and self-styled philosopher, Rathenau was convinced of the virtues of individual entrepreneurship, yet filled with vague *gemeinschaft* longings. Underlying all the common economy schemes he articulated with Moellendorff was the belief that by setting together manufacturers and their workers, or producers and the consumers of their products, and endowing them with self-regulatory power, a real commitment to the public welfare would follow as well. Even Rathenau admitted that it had not worked so far, but he believed his new scheme would remedy the defects.

This conviction stemmed in good part from his personal make-up. Rathenau always felt that his ideas were striking and revolutionary innovations, when often they were restatements of older views. In economic discussions he intervened most impressively in summarizing and clarifying the policy alternatives under consideration. His was an analytical faculty that could crystallize a group's unarticulated concerns or nail down an opponent's slippery reasoning and impress participants by its lucidity. (The reverse was true in his pretentious philosophical writings.) Accompanying his schemes, however, was a transparent veneer of artificial modesty that often covered the vanity of a brilliant and pampered child.[177]

Rathenau introduced his proposals by claiming that he would endow the industry-dominated coal syndicates with responsibility to match their great power, rather than removing their authority as the government bill proposed. The essential, he said, was "transparency"— transparency of the cost structure so that equitable coal prices could

[175] *Ibid.*, i, pp. 223–225, 240.

[176] For Stinnes' complaint, which reflected more an off-hand than a deeply considered anti-Semitism, and the resulting controversy, see: GFM Stresemann Nachlass, diary notes, 7351 = 141/3171/165727–165731; also Max Warburg to Stresemann, July 22, 1920: 6929 = 214/3090/139015–139018; Max Warburg papers/140a, "Jahresbericht"; and the Stinnes-Melchior exchange in GFM: 3398/1731/736764–736768.

[177] For a recent discussion of Rathenau's ideas: Peter Berglar, *Walther Rathenau* (Bremen, 1970). A perceptive portrait is in James Joll, *Three Intellectuals in Politics* (London, 1955); and a hostile but not unjust literary portrayal is provided by the character Arnheim in Robert Musil's *The Man without Qualities*.

be determined in the public interest. There were to be guarantees for the presentation of meaningful accounts by individual firms. The new Coal Council would also have the power to require new investment, but investment for which firms could demand reimbursement should they not accept the risk and potential profits themselves. Finally, Rathenau's plans stipulated that the companies could be bought out by the end of a thirty-year period by virtue of an annual 1.5 percent of their capital value to be calculated in the price of coal. In the interim three decades, however, no property rights or control would accrue to the state.[178]

Socialists on the Committee objected to Rathenau's thirty-year postponement of nationalization. Hilferding complained that the Rathenau proposals might ensure more effective assessment of real production costs, but they meant no real socialization.[179] Characteristically, Rathenau replied:

> I feel my conscience a little unburdened by Messrs. Hilferding and Kuczynski [another Socialist critic], for I had believed that what I was proposing was so revolutionary that it would stir up a great deal of indignation. . . . My proposal is a question of absolute socialization; perhaps not in the sense of party programs, I concede that; state ownership is not mentioned at all, and the entrepreneurs are retained at first. . . . I do not believe any socialist form can go further.

For the present, however, public ownership would stifle the virtues of individual entrepreneurship: "If today you immediately exclude the entrepreneur from the mining industry, the coal mines of the country will collapse."[180]

Rathenau's opponents wanted an earlier take-over. The Socialist union leader Umbreit warned that his miners would be unhappy with a thirty-year delay. Either immediate transferral of ownership with indemnification through interest-bearing bonds, or progressive acquisition of control in yearly installments (originally the suggestion of mine supervisor Georg Werner) was required. Without transfer of ownership, the Socialists felt, Rathenau's scheme would change no more than had the earlier system of "self-administration" and the Arbeitsgemeinschaft. As Hilferding observed, there would be reorganization in any case, but the question was whether it would be capitalist and hierarchical, or socialist and allegedly democratic. Earlier "self-

[178] *Verhandlungen der Sozialisierungs-Kommission* . . . *1920*, I, pp. 212–220, 250–256, 322–326, 499–500, 557–558.
[179] *Ibid.*, I, pp. 227–230.   [180] *Ibid.*, I, pp. 235–236, 271, 345.

administration" schemes, such as the Coal Council, had "only resulted in a certain strengthening of capitalist organizational tendencies."[181]

The conflicting views were both presented to the full Socialization Commission at the end of June. Those who had united behind the majority report of the 1919 Socialization Commission, which had recommended nationalization, now supported the formal proposals drafted by the Heidelberg economist, Emil Lederer. The 1919 minority now rallied to Rathenau's plan. Lederer attacked Rathenau's scheme for its virtual abandonment of nationalization; it offered "only a new organization . . . without any of its own influence, without any initiative. . . ." And until coal owners were actually bought out after three decades, socialism would remain under constant debate, or, as Hilferding noted, the stake of a new Thirty Years War.[182] The Lederer-Rathenau antagonism could not be reconciled in the full Socialization Commission. Parity representation of labor and capital, it was revealed again, meant stalemate as well as fairness. At the conclusion of its meetings on July 31, the Commission presented both reports. Lederer's was approved by ten members, of whom half—including Hue, Umbreit, and Werner—expressed willingness to accept the Rathenau scheme should it ultimately be adopted. Rathenau's ideas won the support of eleven members, including Wissell, moderates among the business representatives such as Carl Melchior and Carl Siemens, and the agrarian spokesman von Batocki.

Up to this point Rathenau's proposals had helped to blunt labor's renewed thrust for socialization. But now alarmed industrialists moved to intervene as well. Otto Wiedfeldt of Krupp pressed for an official industry proposal, because he feared that the Fehrenbach government was committed to bring in some socialization scheme. Warning colleagues in the coal syndicate that they must build sluices and levees before the flood, Wiedfeldt especially urged Vögler and Stinnes to come forward with a credible alternative.[183] Siemens, who had subscribed to the Rathenau proposals, also asked Vögler whether the bourgeois parties could not unite behind a scheme that would enact a theoretical state take-over of the coal mines and equipment but

[181] *Ibid.*, I, p. 507; II, p. 399.

[182] *Ibid.*, II, p. 559, 591. Lederer extended his criticism to Rathenau's recent theoretical articles, noting the author's new trust in the entrepreneur and his cultural justification of inequality. See "Randglossen der neuesten Schriften Walther Rathenaus," *Archiv für Sozialwissenschaft und Sozialpolitik*, 48, 1 (1921), pp. 286–303.

[183] Wiedfeldt to Vögler, August 3, 1920, in Fr. Krupp, A.G., WA IV 1999. Nachlass Wiedfeldt, "Sozialisierungsbestrebungen." Cf. also Ernst Schröder, *Otto Wiedfeldt, Eine Biographie* (Essen, 1964), for an account of Wiedfeldt's political activity.

allow a long-term leasing back to the companies. Siemens planned to sell the project to his own Democratic Party if Vögler could win over the People's Party. "With this sort of proposal," he conceded, "obviously we cannot get by according to the old saying: 'Wash me but don't get me wet.' Mine owners must be especially sensitive in adjusting to the new circumstances."[184] Vögler partially agreed with Wiedfeldt and Siemens; his original thought was to change the legal form of the mines into a "union" and allow the government a participatory share. Sorge, another Krupp manager and Chairman of the Reichsverband, and Köngeter of the Phönix concern also agreed that industry must generate a counterproject. Thereafter, the DVP could adopt it for its own and present it in the cabinet. At a meeting of the Mine Association on August 21, Vögler claimed to be "very pessimistic" about halting socialization unless industry brought forth its own scheme. Despite the fact that Stinnes allegedly wanted to wait, Vögler won approval to prepare a proposal for "participation of employees and workers in the ownership of the factories."[185]

This vague mandate may well have been designed primarily to appease Krupp's spokesmen, such as Wiedfeldt, who were pressing for positive industry action. Wiedfeldt's own scheme envisioned giving the local Arbeitsgemeinschaft for the mining industry a 20 percent share in each coal mine and the right to nominate one-fifth of each board of directors.[186] But Vögler's authorization was for a less binding plan. Indeed, following upon the August 21 meeting, Stinnes and Paul Silverberg presented a very elusive concept for socialization to the newest government forum, a Subcommittee on the Socialization Question that was established by the Reichswirtschaftsrat and the Reich Coal Council. In line with Vögler's suggestion, Silverberg amplified the idea of issuing small shares as a supposed path to workers' participation in the enterprise. Stinnes presented a socialization plan that envisioned regional groupings of producers and consumers to increase production and efficiency.

[184] Carbon of Siemens letter, September 21, 1920, in BA, Koblenz: Nachlass Paul Silverberg/135, pp. 38–40. Ultimately, Siemens was reported as rallying to a more conservative DDP project elaborated by Gothein, which guaranteed private ownership of the coal fields for at least a generation. See Report of Fachgruppe Bergbau of the Reichsverband der deutschen Industrie, *ibid.*, p. 75.

[185] Vögler idea for "Gewerkschaft" in letter to Wiedfeldt, August 4, 1920; Sorge and Köngeter attitudes described in Wiedfeldt letter to Krupp von Bohlen und Halbach, August 12, 1920, detailing discussion among Ruhr leaders; both in Fr. Krupp, A.G., WA IV 1999. August 21 meeting of the Zechenverband in GHH: 301043.

[186] Wiedfeldt's project outlined to Vögler, August 13, 1920, Fr. Krupp, A.G., WA IV 1999.

It was not surprising that Stinnes' notion of a socialist economy resembled his own industrial empire. He cited the connections among his own large coal, steel, and electrical interests as a model for the future German economic community. Local producers and consumers of coal would be endowed with public authority to strengthen their cooperative planning. Since almost half of German coal was consumed by the corporately linked iron and steel firms, Stinnes the producer and Stinnes the consumer of coal could jointly regulate the industry in the public interest. Making the new coal authorities regional, moreover, would eliminate Berlin's authority over Rheinland-Westphalia. In reality the plan meant little more than the removal of state supervision and new sanctions for trustification. Although the Reich and municipalities were to have majority shares, freedom from outside control was to be guaranteed. Moreover, Stinnes stipulated, "the false price policy of the Economics Ministry and the purely private interests of a few single workers or stockholders" had to be eliminated on behalf of the community, which meant *carte blanche* for price hikes and takeovers. Finally, the new "socialized" industry would retain 90 percent of profits; only a tithe would be available for state needs.[187]

For the traditionalist industrialists of Silesia, Stinnes' proposal seemed a "lame compromise" and "objectionably close to Wissell's ideas for a planned economy."[188] On the other side, Wiedfeldt felt that the new plan was politically doomed. The proposal to make coal distribution rational and efficient, he told Stinnes, was acceptable for those who had a sense of the general welfare and some economic expertise. But in political terms there existed a coalition of householders, mine workers, socialistic thinkers and planners, as well as a government subject to popular pressure that would all find the measure insufficient. "With your plan alone," Wiedfeldt insisted "we cannot come through"; one had to satisfy "the dark feelings of the workers which are hidden more or less behind the slogan of socialization." Wiedfeldt, however, recognized that he was in a minority; as he wrote to another Krupp manager, Vielhaber, "Reusch is raving like a lunatic against [my socialization proposal] from his castle in Württemberg," and most other industrialists such as Thyssen were also opposed. In fact, Wiedfeldt was too fearful. Ultimately, the Fehrenbach government would survive

[187] *Verhandlungen des Unterausschusses der Sozialisierungsfrage*, p. 40 (October 25, 1920); protocols found in BA, Koblenz: R 43 I/2114.
[188] Executive of the Oberschlesische Berg- und Hüttenmännische Verein, E.V., Kattowitz to Verein für die bergbaulichen Interessen . . . Dortmund, November 12, 1920, in BA, Koblenz: Silverberg Nachlass/135, pp. 280–281. Ultimately the Union of German Iron and Steel Industrialists accepted the Stinnes concept: BA, Koblenz: R 13 I (VdESI)/96 (Executive Committee session, November 18, 1920).

without bringing in socialization laws, and Stinnes' utopia would prolong the discussions beyond the danger point.[189] By October 26, Vögler could tell the DVP's industrialist committee that he was no longer pessimistic. The workers were less enthusiastic about nationalization, while the bourgeoisie would rather unleash a civil war than let the economy be "socialized *kaputt.*"[190]

Naturally, the Socialists on the new Subcommittee opposed Silverberg's plan for "small shares" and Stinnes' new vertical integration.[191] No agreement seemed any more likely in the new Subcommittee than in the original Socialization Committee, so it was decided to establish a "Reconciliation Committee" (*Verständigungskommission*) of seven members. Stinnes, Silverberg, and Vögler represented the industrialists; Georg Werner, Imbusch, and Wagner, the editor of the socialist *Bergarbeiterzeitung*, spoke for the miners, and a "consumer representative" of the Economic Council, Franz Berthold, was nominated as nonpartisan. Stinnes and Silverberg dominated the work of the Reconciliation Committee, which met in Essen in early November and accepted the industrialists' plans in its majority report to the Subcommittee on November 10. Nationalization, Silverberg's draft affirmed, was not to be confused with true socialism. Socialism really meant "the security that all means of production are used in the highest economical and communal interest of the whole nation as rationally as possible, and under the equal and complete participation, co-determination and co-responsibility of all the participants in the productive process." No interference in existing legal relationships was justified for the present; the productive process had to become as efficient as possible. Although disclaiming any ideas of trustification, the report looked toward "the construction of natural communities of interest between coal mining and secondary industry." Any centralizing administration was rejected. Small shares—with an issue value now specified at 100 marks (a few dollars worth)—would allegedly bind the workers' loyalties to the fate of the enterprise.[192]

[189] Wiedfeldt to Stinnes, September 9 and 14, 1920; Wiedfeldt to Vielhaber, September 9, 1920, offers valuable if partial insight into industry-wide alignments: "That you regard my socialization proposal as a mild salve pleases me. . . . In the whole mining industry except for us and Tengelmann there is no one, I believe, who understands it at all. Becker of Rheinstahl and Thyssen are certainly of another mind. But because Hugenberg unfortunately is ill in Rohbraken and we, with our 2 to 2½ percent of German coal properties, in contrast to Stinnes who controls 12–15, certainly cannot claim leadership, nothing will be done. Fate will take its course." Fr. Krupp, A.G., WA IV 1999.

[190] GFM: Streseman Nachlass, 7351 = 141/3171/165781–165788.

[191] See Werner statement in October 26 session: *Verhandlungen des Unterausschusses*, p. 45.

[192] *Ibid.*, pp. 90–93.

Here was a socialism cut for the entrepreneur! On the Reconciliation Committee, two of the working-class representatives, Wagner and Imbusch, had adopted a conditional wait-and-see stance toward the Silverberg-Stinnes plans without rejecting them entirely. But Georg Werner, who throughout the controversy defended the original, 1919 concept of socialism, presented a counterplan. Borrowing the common rhetoric about the need to increase production, he still offered a genuine alternative for public control. His plan called for a complex hierarchy of organizations, but one that had public directors who could appoint company directors and would in turn be accountable to larger public supervisory bodies. The present owners would be removed and compensated by special 4-percent bonds. One-third of any net profit from coal—after payment of the coal tax to the Reich—would go toward redeeming these bonds, one-third for investment reserves, and one-third for educational projects among the mining population.[193]

Yet Werner stood alone, for the other Socialists disliked the tendencies toward centralization in his scheme. The critics of Silverberg's report, moreover, were those who favored the earlier Rathenau proposals; they were not advocates of outright public take-over. Bernhard, for instance, admitted that the Stinnes-Silverberg plan involved no meaningful socialization; it would merely provide Stinnes and his colleagues with enormous authority for assigning quotas and profits and freezing out unwelcome competition. No man, Bernhard said, could be trusted to make his private interests into a guiding star for the needs of the community.[194] Rathenau contented himself with a Delphic critique. He accused Stinnes of creating "industrial duchies" by regional patterns of vertical integration, and he recommended horizontal integration instead. But he withdrew from the conflict as his proposals were bypassed, merely expressing satisfaction that his original ideas for a planned economy had won acceptance even in industry, and largely by dint of his own pioneering writings. As the guru of the "common economy," Rathenau could claim credit for any more communal ordering of the coal mines that might emerge. But once again there was no decision; the Subcommittee enlarged its Reconciliation Committee from seven to fifteen and sent them off anew to Essen.[195]

How long could the delays continue? The Reconciliation Committee bogged down in December over the issue of whether the Allies might sequester socialized mines for reparation guarantees. Throughout the winter of 1920–1921 socialization remained stalled. Some of the political parties were happy; the DVP had praised the Stinnes road to socialism but really desired only further delay. Frustration on the left

193 *Ibid.*, pp. 98–102.   194 *Ibid.*, pp. 124–130.
195 *Ibid.*, pp. 132–138.

erupted in a Reichstag debate November 20, as SPD speakers asked the Fehrenbach government if it still planned to fulfill its repeated promise to offer socialization bills. Economics Minister Scholz of the DVP said yes, but pointed out that the expert committees were still meeting, and reminded the Socialists that for their own year-and-a-half in power they had instituted no substantial socialization measures. Speaking for the DVP from the floor, Julius Curtius praised the Economic Council with its protracted and inconclusive debates as the guarantor of objectivity, and depicted the Socialization Commission as a creature imposed only by union pressure in the wake of the Kapp Putsch. Perhaps the Independent Socialists' delegate, Henke, was the most truthful when he conceded that socialization was indeed a partisan demand: "It is a recognized truth that the question of socialization is a question of political power."[196]

But it was a question the Socialists could not win. Further hurting their cause was a split with the Center Party. Throughout the spring and summer of 1920 the Catholic unions and their spokesman Imbusch had supported Social Democratic pressure for a meaningful socialism and even state ownership of the mines. But by late autumn the Catholic and SPD unions diverged, as Otto Hue of the SPD-affiliated mineworkers became more defiant and radical, and the socialist *Bergarbeiterzeitung* threatened civil strife if the Lederer proposals were not enacted. Imbusch, however, was under pressure to preserve the unity of the ideologically disparate Center Party and the shaky equilibrium of the Fehrenbach cabinet, which was torn between the demands of the Catholic unions and the business interests of the People's Party. Imbusch told his union leaders on January 9, 1921, that he desired some state claim over underground coal reserves but otherwise could live with the old system. The Coal Council could take the power of pricing from the Coal Association; but this was an insignificant change, for in fact the Economics Ministry and Cabinet had been vetoing prices throughout the past nine months. Profits should be limited and the role of factory councils strengthened; small shares would be welcomed.[197]

Apparently the cabinet, despite all its backing and filling, still felt some need to present legislation. Nevertheless, the dilatory proceedings of the Reconciliation Committee and the resistance of the Volkspartei within the coalition impeded further action. Economics Minister Scholz told the cabinet in February that the Reconciliation Committee wanted experts to determine whether the Allies would enjoy stronger

[196] VDR: SB, 345, pp. 1133–1144.
[197] Reports in *Kölnische Volkszeitung*, January 10, 1921, and *Frankfurter Zeitung*, January 11, 1921, both included in BA, Koblenz: Silverberg Nachlass/138.

claims over a nationalized industry, and he recommended that the government wait for such a report.[198] In February 1921 the DVP asked that further action wait until after the March elections for the Prussian Landtag in order to remove the issue from the political campaign.[199] In April the experts decided that Allied claims were not sufficient reason to halt socialization; but the project was long since dead. The enlarged Reconciliation Committee returned with a compromise proposal that would place ultimate domain of coal resources in the hands of the state, but otherwise leave the system as it stood. Nothing resulted, and the terms of the whole coal question were to change in the recession and reparations crisis that followed.

With the advent of 1921 the world-market price fell drastically; and the issues that had revolved around the price question were muted. German and French production was up, while America, suffering recession, shipped coal to Europe in larger quantities. The whole artificial structure of British export prices collapsed, and free markets in coal were restored on both sides of the Channel. English coal went from 115 shillings in summer 1920 to about 25 shillings by the end of 1921. Germany fulfilled the Spa agreements sufficiently to satisfy the French, who, although they complained about quality, could even release small quantities of reparation coal for sale to neutrals. Scarcity had politicized the coal question; and plenty now assuaged it.[200]

The victory of the bourgeois groups could be attributed to many factors. Some of the faults lay with the Socialists themselves. They did not have the power legally to force expropriation, but could not unite on meaningful public control in another form. Many among them did not really want to disturb the capitalist system—witness the haste with which the cabinet had retreated from the socialization question in the summer of 1919. Kautsky and other Socialists felt that to nationalize in the midst of economic difficulties might saddle the SPD with responsibility for what could be an economic catastrophe. Finally, the Social Democrats were too committed to the system of parity committees, now embodied in the Reich Economic Council and its organs, to push through their own ideas. Every parity committee broke down into at least two sides, and controversies were thereupon sent to parity subcommittees where no further decision was forthcoming.

The term socialization, moreover, remained so murky that opponents could seize it for their own meaning. Rathenau's personality played a role here: although sincere in desiring a true "community" control over

[198] GFM: ARK: Kabinettsprotokolle, 3438/1671/746761–746762.

[199] Interparty meeting, January 21, 1920, BA, Koblenz: R 43 I/2115.

[200] Baumont, *La grosse industrie allemande et le charbon*, p. 135. AN, Paris: AJ²⁶/58, f. Nouveaux Accords après Spa. "Note pour M. le Ministre," January 26, 1921.

abuses, he was too entranced with his own schemes to see that they might be ineffective. He, at least, diluted socialism in good faith. The Silverberg-Stinnes phase of the debate saw a more conscious manipulation of ideas; inexpensive shares could hopefully prove dust in the eyes of the workers and perhaps exert a special appeal to the Catholic unions with their ideals of small, diffused property. But Stinnes was not fundamentally insincere either, and he no doubt believed that the "industrial duchies" that would give public authority to the Stinnes empire in Rhineland-Westphalia would best serve Germany. Finally, the stress on brute production made urgent by the Spa demands helped industry defeat nationalization by an appeal to the requisites of productivity itself: since November 1918 Germany retained one asset, her economic power—why risk squandering it?

Yet socialization as an issue for Germany transcended the merits of any particular scheme. In no other country were the major industrialists so great a power factor. Some control over their economic preponderance was needed if Germany was to make democracy function; and coal was the logical point at which to start making the structure more responsive to community considerations. Industrial leaders throughout the early 1920's would often demur from tax contributions for reparations or currency stabilization by pleading constant economic and financial distress. Into their peculiar ledgers, with exaggerated amortizations, obligations, and costs, was constructed a constant demonstration of impecuniousness, uncontestable by public authority. The conflicts over reparations and credits in 1921 and 1922 would demonstrate this anew. Was there a way to exert sufficient control short of outright nationalization, or were all compromises ineffectual? This question provoked a division between socialists and democrats that undermined any change. Stinnes, nonetheless, had not won a total victory. Throughout the summer and fall of 1920 the government sought to maintain equity by holding firm against coal price rises.[201] Spa was signed and carried out. Stinnes' plans for cartel socialism did not materialize. Yet by the winter of 1921 the foundations of industrial power still remained beyond public control, and the last concerted effort to tame that power had dissipated in endless discussion.

[201] This issue arose frequently in the cabinet. On July 29, 1920, the Economics Ministry finally supported a rise in the coal price after Spa, but the Ministers of Labor, Railroads, Interior, and Finance opposed it as inflationary and especially hard on the railroads. Stinnes termed the decision false savings. On October 27, an increase was rejected and again on January 26, 1921, when it was feared that such an increase would reignite the socialization question. A price rise was finally sanctioned on March 23, 1921. See GFM: ARK, Kabinettsprotokolle: 3438/1669/ 745304, 745320–745321, 745892–745893; 3438/1671/746708–746709; 3438/ 1672/747616.

PART II

THE FAILURE OF

THE PARLIAMENTARY

CENTER

To apply Yeats to politics, the center was not to hold. While bourgeois groups could stalemate radical initiatives, no effective majority yet held together to govern. Even before the war European parliamentary systems were entering a period of crisis. Arms races and stiffer tax burdens, new working-class militancy and socialist party challenges, the skillful reassertion of political Catholicism and bitter ethnic antagonisms from Ireland to Austria-Hungary were all fragmenting political majorities. Coherent policy, whether formulated by parliamentary cabinets as in Britain, France, and Italy, or by ministers who were only minimally dependent upon parliamentary votes as in Germany and Austria, became increasingly difficult. The advent of war temporarily helped conservative forces to reshape effective coalitions, but the crisis of 1917 opened a new period of left-wing challenge. Finally, after the dissipation of the left's offensive during the course of 1920, it seemed feasible once again to reconstruct centrist coalitions that might achieve a stable balance among contending interests through parliamentary bargaining. This centrist stability, however, was to prove evasive. Why?

Most obviously, the developments of the decade before 1920 reduced the relative electoral strength of bourgeois parties. Just as critically, they also made it more difficult to unite the middle-class elements needed for moderate coalitions. Naturally, as the radical challenges ebbed, the motive of antisocialist unity became less compelling. The bourgeois consensus of 1920 tended to disintegrate over questions of foreign policy, working-class protest, and taxes. The right, in short, became impatient with the centrist policies of those who had inherited power in 1920. Within two years they were to turn against policies of social and international compromise.

The economic problems left by the war aggravated bourgeois disunity. European societies had expended vast resources on the war and reconstruction, but they had postponed tough decisions on how to allocate these costs among their different social groups. They had multiplied paper claims on wealth and national income which could not all be honored at their original value. Throughout much of the decade to come they faced the dilemma of how to meet debt charges and fix currency values through varying dosages of taxation and inflation. Even had there been no external debts, just the fight over internal transfers would have been bitter and protracted. But the choices were all the more agonizing because of the interlocked debt and reparation system.

Until 1924, at least, French political leaders acted as if German reparation payments would cover the debt service that they owed both the Anglo-American allies and their own citizens. On the other hand, Germans avoided the withholding from consumption needed to make reparation transfers, in part because of the resentments of defeat and the Peace Treaty, in part because of the interests of key German pressure groups, heavy industry above all. The resulting disputes divided the bourgeois majorities in each country. The financial aspects (which we will examine closely in Part III) separated middle-class elements according to the fixity of their incomes or the nature of their personal savings. The political aspect (analyzed immediately following) separated the liberal democratic left from those who advocated nationalistic policies to compel, or in the German case, to resist, reparation payments. The French right chafed at the failure to enforce the Treaty of Versailles; the German right attacked the failure to renounce its burdens entirely.

While French and German coalitions of the center fell apart over reparations, the Italian liberal establishment fragmented before the mass political movements represented by the Catholic Popolari, the Socialists, and ultimately the Fascists. Although the working-class challenge led to a heated rhetoric of bourgeois defense, it also divided liberals between moderates and those who turned toward militant reaction. The Popolari added to the confusion of arranging party combinations at the center of the political system, even as the Fascists extended their guerrilla-like control over the Po Valley. Liberals, including Giolitti, did not realize the full extent of subversion for a critical year between late 1920 and 1921 because they found it hard to abandon their central political myth: the identification of parliament with the country, such that to muster a majority was supposedly to ensure control of the social forces at large. By 1922 even a durable majority seemed beyond the reach of any liberal prime minister. As in France and Germany, the Italian middle-class parliamentary representation could no longer provide coherent solutions for the group conflicts which the war had ripened.

The prime ministers of 1921–1922—Briand, Wirth, and Giolitti (with his successors, Bonomi and Facta)—testify in common to the predicament of democratic parliamentarism. They all sought support on the basis of a reformist or moderate position and found themselves stalemated. To be sure, defects of character and circumstance played a role: Briand's lackadaisical administration and his "softness" made him appear subservient to Great Britain and a poor defender of French interests. Wirth, too, depended upon rhetoric to cover over harsh alternatives and was deprived of his strongest collaborator, Rathenau, by assassination. Giolitti faced a movement unprecedented in its willingness to apply political brutality, and he was unprepared to assess its novel dangers. Still, even more skillful or vigorous men might have failed to meet the political challenge these three leaders set themselves: governance on the basis of centrist coalitions as if the prewar crises and the subsequent social transformations—the strengthening of the organized working class, the expenditure of European savings, and the arousal of nationalist passions—had no political consequences.

These factors did not have to destroy liberal government—although they did so in Italy. But they did prevent parliamentary coalitions and assemblies from becoming the true *loci* of bourgeois power after the war. They helped shift decision making to private militias or to powerful interests. Had they come from these milieux, Briand, Wirth, and Giolitti might have more skillfully mediated among interest groups. They might have arranged a smoother transition from parliamentary forms to the corporatist bargaining that was to prevail later in the decade. But Briand had been a provincial lawyer and Giolitti a bureaucrat before both became long-term professional parliamentarians; Wirth was a school teacher before being drawn into the Catholic political apparatus. And as political moderates they did not realize how inwardly weakened the old coalitions had become. Inheriting power when the socialist left had lost its political initiative, they staked their offices on the hope that coalitions of the center, which united liberal democrats and conservatives, could rally consensus enough to govern. In France and Germany, however, this consensus would have required removing foreign policy as a source of friction among the bourgeois parties, and this was impossible in light of the reparation issue. It would also have depended upon financial compromises that would reconcile the differing interests among middle-class constituencies. This also proved beyond reach until Europe's overall balance-of-payments problems were resolved at mid-decade. In Italy broad bourgeois support would have depended upon winning over Christian democracy and simultaneously restoring to the liberals the assurance of parliamentary hegemony they had enjoyed before 1919—another impossibility. As of 1921, liberal ministers had too many circles to square. The result was a fruitless search to appease different obstructionist groups —increasingly, now, on the right—such that finally all three experiments faced defeat.

· 4 ·

THE POLITICS OF
REPARATION

The Wager on "Fulfillment"

The reparation issue was not settled at the Paris Peace Conference. Wilson resisted the most extensive demands of the European allies, but recompense for civilian damages, which he did sanction, was bound to be enormous. Britain, moreover, won the principle that separation allowances and pensions for veterans or dependents must also be borne by Germany. To forestall divisive argument, it was agreed that a Reparations Commission would determine the total damages and levy a final bill by May 1, 1921. By that date Germany would also be required to pay an initial 20 billion gold marks plus the running costs of the Allied armies of occupation. Payments in kind could be credited against either the 20 billion or the final sum. Throughout early 1920 coal obligations remained the most disputed aspect of reparation. But by the end of 1920 the Spa arrangements were generally working, while economic recession made coal for a laggard industry plentiful and cheap. The focus shifted from coal to cash. Once the Allies agreed at Boulogne and Spa in mid-1920 how to divide the reparation shares among themselves, the question of what payments to wrest from Berlin became the central issue. Yet even as Allied ministers and technical experts went from discussion to discussion, the French continued to float reconstruction loans, the mounting interest charges of which were budgeted against eventual German payments. On the other side, the Germans protested against any meaningful reparation assessment, especially since the obligation to pay was theoretically based upon the so-called war-guilt clause of the Treaty (art. 231). While Berlin's technical experts discussed provisional schemes, the German government refused to consider any realistic alternatives that they might themselves propose to the Allies.[1]

[1] For the reparation issue from 1919 to 1921 see Étienne Weill-Raynal, *Les réparations allemandes et la France*, 3 vols. (Paris, 1947), vol. i, *Des origines jusqu'à l'institution de l'état des paiements (novembre 1918–mai 1921)*; Carl Bergmann, *The History of Reparations* (London, 1927), pp. 3–62; Phillip M. Burnett, *Reparation at the Paris Peace Conference*, 2 vols. (New York, 1940); for polemical discussions: John Maynard Keynes, *The Economic Consequences of the Peace* (New York, 1920); Étienne Mantoux, *The Carthaginian Peace or the Economic Consequences of Mr. Keynes* (London, 1946); André Tardieu, *La Paix* (Paris, 1921), pp. 314 ff.; and for documents: Germain Calmette, *Recueil de documents*

The political context was bound to imperil any compromise policies. Both before and after May 1921, hawks on both sides viewed their respective governments as too submissive. But neither government could dispense with the hawks. Any French premier still had to face the majority of November 16, 1919. Although he might make up some nationalist defections with votes from the Radical Socialists, too obvious a reliance on the Radicals would alienate all conservative support. In Germany, Wirth's cabinet began as a ministry of the Weimar coalition —Social Democrats, Center, and Democrats—but Wirth required support from the powers of industry and from the People's Party to push through the tax legislation needed for reparation payments. Both governments were hostage to conservative representatives, which made agreement on reparations almost impossible, yet both governments staked their power on achieving some satisfactory settlement. Nor was it only right-wing and nationalistic elements in Paris and Berlin who feared a sell-out. Virtually the mass of German opinion felt that Allied demands were unrealistic and unfair; almost all French spokesmen felt that Germany would pay no reparations unless threatened with sanctions. Briand and Wirth wagered their offices on finding a common ground with which they could rally moderate opinion at home. But even men of relative good will were far apart on the reparation issue.

Briand inherited a Chamber of Deputies that since Spa had been chafing at alleged mollycoddling on reparations. While the Bloc National welcomed Millerand's toughness toward labor and his salvation of Poland, they remained uneasy about the complexities of the reparation issue, troubled in part by Poincaré's repeated forebodings, which were circulated in the *Revue des Deux Mondes*. Anxiety about French weakness in the upcoming Paris conferences on reparations helped destroy the cabinet of George Leygues in January 1921. The amiable but unimposing Leygues had been selected by Millerand after his succession to the presidency in an effort to retain as much political control as possible. After various efforts were made to construct cabinet combinations with Poincaré, whom Millerand still resented for his brushfire criticism during 1920, the President selected Aristide Briand.[2]

sur l'histoire de la question des réparations, 1919–5 mai 1921 (Paris, 1924). Peter Krüger, *Deutschland und die Reparationen 1918/19* (Stuttgart, 1973), offers shrewd and critical judgments on the connections with domestic issues.

[2] For the weakness and collapse of the Leygues government, see the debates over internal politics, December 22, 1920, and military service, December 23–24, 1920, in JOC, 1920, pp. 3869 ff., 3889 ff., 3939–3949, 3976–3990, and final defeat at the hands of the right, JOC, 1921, pp. 8, 25 (January 21). Coverage by François Albert in "Chronique parlementaire," *RPP*, cvi, January 10, 1921, pp. 109–112, and February 10, 1921, pp. 280–289. Poincaré criticism in "Chronique

Briand had been patiently preparing the terrain for a comeback; he had helped defeat Clemenceau's bid for the presidency and, after the short administration of Deschanel, worked to get Millerand elected despite the left's hesitations. Briand sensed that the Chamber wanted a display of firmness and put together a team designed to appeal to conservatives. Louis Barthou came in at the War Ministry; Steeg left the sensitive Ministry of the Interior, and the 183-member Entente Républicaine was partially appeased with some secondary ministries.

The reparation issue arose immediately as Pierre Forgeot, the newly elected, blunt, and conservative deputy for Rheims, asked whether Briand would follow the approach of Poincaré or Millerand. Poincaré, claimed Forgeot, wanted all damages to be fully computed before any reparation bill was handed to Germany, even at the cost of delay; Millerand had shown at Hythe and Boulogne that he was willing to settle quickly for what might be a smaller sum determined arbitrarily (the so-called *forfait*). Briand, as usual, sought to avoid a stark alternative and outlined a moderate course. In contrast to Poincaré's insistence on total compensation, he referred to the limits on Germany's current capacity to pay. (The Treaty had called for a reparations settlement that somehow took account of both considerations.) At the same time he rejected settling for a mere *forfait* and, in line with the Avenol scheme of April 1920, advocated flexible payments that would rise with future increases in German productivity.[3] With his usual equivocations and rhetorical flourishes, Briand stressed the open-ended situation that France faced, showed sympathy for what might be genuine in the German economic

---

de la quinzaine," *RDM*, January 1921, pp. 217–222. For construction of the new government, see *ibid.*, and Georges Suarez, *Briand. Sa vie. Son oeuvre*, 6 vols. (Paris, 1938–1952), v, pp. 99–107; Edouard Bonnefous, *Histoire politique de la Troisième République*, iii, *L'après-guerre (1919–1924)* (Paris, 1959), pp. 206–209.

[3] JOC, 1921, pp. 80–85 (January 21); also Suarez, *Briand*, v, pp. 111–116; and on Forgeot, see François Albert, "Chronique Politique," *RPP*, cvii, June 1921, pp. 449–451. See Weill-Raynal, *Les réparations allemandes*, i, pp. 547–560, for the plans of Millerand and Joseph Avenol—financial officer at the London Embassy—for a minimal *forfait* of 3 billion marks annually plus increments keyed to German growth. At Hythe (May 15–16, 1920), the French asked further that the overall reparations bill be set at 120 billion gold marks in present discounted value, of which they would get 55 percent (66 billion gold marks or 80 billion gold francs) to cover estimated damages and pension demands of 200 billion paper francs. At Boulogne and Brussels on June 21 and July 2, however, the French reluctantly accepted a *forfait* plan involving two parallel series of German payments with a total present value of 102.5 billion gold marks. (The calculation of present discounted value amounts to asking what one would pay immediately for a stream of future payments, given a certain rate of interest. The later payments are made, the lower their present value: to withdraw $100 in a year's time from a savings bank that gives 5 percent interest requires a deposit of about $95 now; to withdraw $100 in two years requires a present deposit of only about $90.)

predicament, and asked for freedom of action to exploit the possibilities of sanctions in the Treaty. There was toughness enough to hold the right, while the evocations of secularism, the subtle dissociation from Millerand's judicial proceedings against the CGT, and finally the memory of 1917—when Briand had been attacked by the nationalists—disarmed the left and softened even the SFIO's opposition.

Briand was essentially evasive, and his handling of reparations would be of a piece with his overall political approach. He composed a ministry that seemed to promise more influence for conservatives but without specifying a conservative policy. He was lazy in administrative practice, and uninterested in technical questions. With his Permanent Undersecretary of the Quai d'Orsay, Philippe Berthelot, he could seem almost frivolous in his approach to the detailed rights that provided France's protection under Versailles. Later in the 1920's Briand and Berthelot would offer to reduce French occupation forces in the Rhineland in exchange for German tariff concessions on wine so that the government could silence troublesome protests in the Chamber of Deputies. Still, Briand usually defended essentials: at no point did he concede fundamental and real advantages, although he overlooked German violations of Treaty stipulations that not even a policy of force seemed capable of redressing. (For all of Poincaré's hawkish rhetoric, the slow ebbing of France's strength after Versailles continued as much under his supervision as under Briand's: ultimately the two worked together in the later 1920's as they passed the defense of French continental interests from the General Staff to the Bank of France.) There were, moreover, real strengths in Briand's approach, given the power of the legislature and the importance of ideological ritual. Briand understood the continuing responsiveness of the 600 deputies to inherited formulas, and he could disguise ambiguous policies under Republican pathos. He had helped to engineer first the separation of Church and State and then the conciliation of Catholics. With Louis Barthou in 1914 he had constructed a right-center coalition that gave itself the name Fédération des Gauches and made a fuss about opposing clericals while really competing against Radicals and Socialists. In 1919 he served up proportional representation, which could appeal to left and right, as the culmination of democracy. In many ways Briand resembled his fellow "Celt," Lloyd George, but without the latter's populistic initiative and scrappiness. Lloyd George never lost his creative demagogy; in negotiating with the French he would repeatedly draw upon his old Limehouse rhetoric, substituting a niggardly Paris for rapacious coal barons. Briand's *bonhomie* and *pathétique* remained less effective. Lloyd George, too, sought to mold the public opinion to which he was so attuned, while Briand served as a more passive oracle for the middle-class moods that he divined.[4]

The course of the reparations conferences during the early months of 1921 illustrated Briand's methods and its limits. Briand had not outlined a firm plan for the imminent Paris conference, where the Allies were scheduled to determine a reparations scheme that they could present to the Germans. During late 1920 their technical experts had been considering postponement of a decision on a total and probably inflammatory reparations bill. After the Brussels conference of December, 1920, which brought together German and Allied financial teams, the experts suggested settling on a provisional plan for five annual payments of 3 billion gold marks each, or even an indefinitely prolonged series of rising annuities.[5] But no one was enthusiastic: the Germans wanted a 2 billion mark base and retention of Upper Silesia; Lloyd George preferred to keep the Boulogne proposals of the preceding summer; while Briand felt that the Chamber needed to be reassured that he would hold out for massive payments. At the first session of the Paris conference devoted to reparations, on January 26, Briand's Finance Minister, Paul Doumer, estimated French claims at 110 billion gold marks and total Allied needs at 200 billion gold marks. To yield this present value he demanded that Germany pay 12 billion gold marks annually for 42 years. For Lloyd George such staggering sums could not be meant seriously; indeed the French apparently intended primarily to overthrow the Boulogne payments plan and win a larger sum. Lloyd George argued that the Allies must return to the Boulogne accord; Briand insisted that this would doom his government, and he fell back upon the provisional five-year annuity scheme. Lloyd George threatened finally to break up the conference until the Belgian premier won a compromise package.

The British held the basic payment down to 42 annuities rising from 2 to 6 billion gold marks and the French won a second, concurrent series of payments amounting to 12 percent of German exports and thus keyed to German economic growth. The result was a paper victory for Briand. If the awesome predictions for German foreign trade offered by Louis Loucheur, Briand's Minister of Liberated Regions,

[4] For Briand, besides the essential and sympathetic Suarez, see Charles Daniélou, *Le vrai visage de Briand* (Paris, 1935) and for the operations of his and Philippe Berthelot's foreign policy: Jules Laroche, *Au Quai d'Orsay avec Briand et Poincaré 1913–1926* (Paris, 1957), esp. pp. 136, 229. For the wine-tariff bargaining in 1926, see below, pp. 541–542.

[5] See the report of March 3, 1921, on the Bergmann-Seydoux talks of January 16 and 18, 1921, in Min. Aff. Etr.: Europe, 1918–1929, Allemagne/460, pp. 97–98; also Bergmann, *Reparations*, pp. 50 ff.; Weill-Raynal, *Les réparations allemandes*, I, pp. 583–592.

did materialize, the Paris plan would yield a present value of 124 billion gold marks. Paris's share would be about 70 billion, which meant that Briand could show the Chamber an apparent increase over the total Millerand had brought back from Boulogne and Brussels in July 1920. Briand also reaffirmed the theoretical right to seize German customs and the promise of Anglo-French cooperation in further sanctions if the Reich did not negotiate on the basis of the Paris plan. For in fact, the Paris scheme was not final but considered merely a basis for further discussions with Berlin. The paper totals thus depended first upon German agreement and thereafter upon Germany's flourishing as an exporting nation.[6]

Both sides felt grieved, however. The total sums that were brandished in the German press struck all parties as arbitrary and impossible to fulfill. French nationalists, on the other hand, judged the plan on the basis of its minimal yield. Briand expected unrest among the Chamber majority. Rather than waiting for the committees of the Assembly to consider the project in a detailed study, he laid the results before the deputies as a whole a few days later, stressing that he now brought back the promise of effective execution. In response, André Tardieu observed that the sanctions for enforcement were already in the Treaty and sought to demonstrate that the plan would yield less than the rejected German offer of 92 billion gold marks made at the Peace Conference. "The Treaty of Versailles," he complained, "is now a matter of continuous revision." Loucheur responded to Tardieu with more complicated figures, but to prove that France would get her due he had to predict a resurgence of German exports that was worrying in its own right. Moreover, Loucheur was suspect; at the Paris Peace Conference he had originally demanded 800 billion gold marks, then recommended 120 billion, then just the previous summer had supported Tardieu against Millerand. The Chamber majority was uneasy. Tardieu was pedantic, arrogant, and supercilious, but his objections seemed solidly grounded. Forgeot, too, spoke for the majority's concerns and asked the blunt question: Would Briand be willing to act alone if need be to force German acquiescence at the upcoming London conference? Briand refused to be pinned down, declaring that it would be imprudent to commit the government. Forgeot derided his indecision.[7]

6 DBFP, first series, vol. xv, pp. 39–48, 56–57, 59–94. Weill-Raynal, *Les réparations allemandes*, i, pp. 593–605; see also Thomas Lamont's analysis written as "a Member of the American Commission to Negotiate Peace," *Evening Post*, February 3, 1921, now in Baker Library: TWL 172–16.

7 JOC, 1921, pp. 286 ff., 295 ff. (February 3), 313 ff. (February 4), 412 ff. (February 9, 2nd session). Cf. François Albert, *RPP*, cvi, March 1921, pp. 500–503. Tardieu's claim was misleading; for the German offer at Versailles envisaged

Briand won a resolution of confidence, 387 to 125, but the abstentions and the negative votes cast by the Clémencistes and even others of the Bloc National demonstrated the anxieties of moderates and conservatives. So too did the decision among the Senators to replace Selves by Poincaré as head of the key Foreign Affairs Commission. Briand sensed that his majority might evaporate as it had for Leygues. He was rescued in February, however, by an upsurge of German nationalist feeling nurtured by Berlin's Foreign Minister Walter Simons. Summoned to London in February to discuss their own reparation proposals, the Germans reverted to their evasive stance of the previous summer. Berlin was expected to suggest a scheme of payments based upon the Paris resolutions. By dropping the variable annuities, claiming large payments already made, capitalizing future installments at 8 percent, and borrowing at 5 percent, Simons attempted to shave the Paris total of 130 billion gold marks down to only 22 billions. Lloyd George angrily ended the discussion, supposedly observing that in another few minutes the Allies would be owing money to Germany. Sent home for a counterproposal, Simons offered to follow the Paris schedule but only for the first five years, and only if Upper Silesia remained German. Thereafter new agreements would be required; meanwhile no final minimum could be promised; perhaps the whole warguilt clause would be put up for review. Even Lloyd George could not accept the Germans' unwillingness to envisage a long-term settlement. On March 9, the Allies occupied Düsseldorf, Duisburg, and Ruhrort on the right bank of the Rhine.[8]

The following month afforded Briand the chance to pose as strict

at best somewhere between 80 and 100 million gold marks of total annuities spread out over an undefined term without interest, hence possessing a present value of perhaps half their nominal value. See Weill-Raynal, *Les réparations allemandes*, i, pp. 108–112, and Krüger, *Deutschland und die Reparationen*, pp. 181–209, for the origins of the German counteroffer of a nominal 100 billion gold marks.

[8] DBFP, first series, xv, pp. 216–223, 223–225, 225–265, 286–332. Weill-Raynal, *Les réparations allemandes*, i, pp. 607–617; Bergmann, *Reparations*, pp. 62–67. Lloyd George did not like the occupation, and as his price for cooperation forced the allies to pass "reparation recovery acts." These required each importer to pay his national government up to 50 percent of the value of the German goods he purchased. The theory was that the German exporter would give his customer an equivalent discount and reclaim it from the German government. The French were unhappy over the concept. At first they feared that it would allow Britain to keep yearly reparation revenues above and beyond the shares allotted at Spa. Some suspected that the British wanted it as much to impede German imports as to facilitate payment of reparations. While Paris passed the law as a discretionary measure, it remained unapplied until September 1924, when it was used to exert pressure in trade negotiations. See DBFP, pp. 335–341, 349–353, and the report on the French legislation and debate in JOC, 1921, pp. 1593 ff. (April 13, 1st session); pp. 1610 ff. (April 14, 1st session); also GFM: 4482H/2222/E092900–092901 (memo to French consuls, November 13, 1924).

executor of the Peace Treaty. Although he left a Paris rife with rumors of a cabinet crisis, all seemed transformed when the news of German obstinacy and Lloyd George's reaction arrived. In the parliamentary debate in mid-March, Forgeot and Tardieu did not speak, a veiled attack by Mandel had little resonance, and only the Socialists and Léon Daudet voted against the government. To the Senate Briand promised that if Germany sought to evade her obligations, "it will be a firm hand that strikes her collar."[9]

The French hard line continued through April as Germans and Allies quarreled over the initial 20 billion marks due by May 1. The Germans claimed, frankly disingenuously, to have met this obligation; the Reparations Commission credited only the equivalent of 8 billion marks. Briand felt that he had to demonstrate firmness both with respect to the remaining 12 billion marks as well as the future reparation totals still to be determined. At a new conference at Hythe on April 24, the French government suggested immediate occupation of the Ruhr to force Germany to produce a plan for payment. The English resisted, pointing out that the Treaty permitted occupation only as a "sanction" for default, not as a means of pressure. But so long as the Germans disputed their debt, Briand was committed to the policy of the firm hand. After Hythe, he promised the Chamber and Senate that France would indeed occupy the Ruhr if, by the end of April, there was no satisfactory assurance that the 12 billion marks would be paid in time. Foreign Ministry officials coordinated plans for the occupation of Essen. Seydoux explained how France could impose an export tax, seize majority shares of stock in German companies able to manufacture war matériel as well as two-thirds of the shares in commercial aviation firms, and raise a 5 to 6 billion gold mark loan for reparations by pledging German customs and coal-tax receipts. Loucheur and Berthelot presented proposals to the British for a take-over of Ruhr coal distribution and a levy of 40 gold marks per ton.[10] Returning to London at the end of the month, Briand announced mobilization of a class of conscripts for early May.

[9] JOC, 1921, pp. 1270 ff., 1305 (March 16–17); JOS, 1921, p. 612 (April 5).

[10] For French planning for a Ruhr occupation see Seydoux's note for the Président du Conseil, April 1921, and the unsigned plan for the take-over of German customs, etc., April 21, 1921, in Min. Aff. Etr.: Europe, 1918–1929, Allemagne/462, pp. 203–211, and 166–183; also the proposals submitted by Loucheur and Berthelot in C8632/2740/18 and C8853/2740/18 in FO 371/6025–6026. Although Lloyd George protested at Hythe, the British were reluctantly prepared to participate in a temporary Ruhr occupation if France accepted the Paris plan of January as a maximum demand and, moreover, was willing to acknowledge proposals for using German material and labor in reconstructing the devastated areas. See FO 371/6024: C8190/2740/18; also C8360/2740/18. For the arguments at the Hythe (Lympne) Conference on April 23–24 see DBFP, first series, vol. xv, pp. 453–486.

In fact, there was no chance that Berlin could raise and transfer 12 billion gold marks within a few days; and London insisted that sanctions would be improper unless the Reparations Commission presented and Germany rejected a final bill. Briand was caught between the frustrations of the Bloc National, the delays of the Germans, and the reluctance of the British to force a crisis. On April 27, though, the Reparations Commission finally decided on an overall estimate of claims of 132 billion gold marks. The figure was a compromise: perhaps a quarter lower than what the French preferred, but still acceptable. By virtue of a Belgian and Italian suggestion, moreover, Briand was able to keep the count-down going on his ultimatum. "The kettledrum," admitted Lloyd George, "should stay in the Place de la Concorde."[11] Germany was to be charged with defaulting on earlier obligations but sanctions would be suspended if she accepted the new Reparations Commission findings. The Reparations Commission, however, had to present a schedule of payments as well as a global total. Allied finance experts worked out a schedule of annuities by May 3, which the Commission endorsed as an alternative to harsher Treaty provisions. The new demands tacitly ignored the fact that 12 billion gold marks had been due two days earlier and asked instead for 1 billion gold marks' worth of acceptable currencies or gold by September.

France had to accept a second and more serious sacrifice. The 132 billion mark total turned out to be only a paper calculation, and the schedule of payments amputated more than half its value by virtue of a delayed funding scheme. Reparation payments were to take the form of interest and amortization of special bonds that Germany would issue. Over French resistance, Belgian and Italian delegates agreed with the British that Berlin simply could not service the entire 132 billion mark debt: this would have exacted an impossible 8 billion gold marks yearly. Instead, Berlin was initially required to defray the interest and amortization on 50 billion marks worth of so-called "A" and "B" bonds by paying a fixed annuity of 2 billion gold marks plus a variable payment equal in value to 26 percent of German exports. Only when the proceeds of German foreign trade climbed sufficiently to amortize the "A" and "B" bonds as well as pay interest on the remaining 82 billion marks would the "C" bonds actually be issued. Many experts felt that the "C" bonds were a sham commitment designed to appease those who still insisted on a large total. Even if Loucheur's projections were correct, Germany would not float the "C" bonds before the end of the decade. This meant lowering the present value of the reparations' debt to 108 billion marks, less than the Paris resolutions of January and about the same as the Boulogne scheme. If, as seemed likely to disil-

[11] DBFP, First Series, vol. xv, p. 511.

lusioned observers within a year or two, Germany never had sufficient trade to pay more than 3 billion marks, "C" bonds could be issued only in 1957; the present value of the settlement fell to about 64 billion, and France's share shrunk to 35 billion or 8.3 billion dollars, a sad fragment of what many of her politicians and columnists had claimed would be forthcoming.[12]

Hence, the London schedule of payments meant a thinly disguised defeat for nationalist claims. It rankled even more because France had agreed to let Belgium have the first billion marks to be paid over the summer. Yet the result was not unfair: although Keynes did not believe the Germans could fulfill the London scheme, even this bitter and sometimes irresponsible critic of the Treaty urged the Germans to accept it as an improvement upon earlier demands. Nonetheless, the task of ratification was not easy, and when Lloyd George denounced the behavior of France's ally, Poland, in Upper Silesia, it became even more difficult. To appease the right Briand established a provisional embassy at the Vatican even though authorization of funds was still stalled in the Senate. Tardieu and Forgeot called for rejection of the London accords, but moderates felt that to reject them now would be to abandon the Treaty entirely. The majority voted with what one observer termed "saddened resignation." "The death in the soul . . ." sighed another, "ah, yes, as on the morrow of Spa. Thus we have undergone the latest—and let us hope it will really be the very last—disillusionment of victory."[13]

The vote reflected a year-long political realignment. The Radicals, who in the spring of 1920 had supported strict application of the Treaty, now approved Briand's more conciliatory trend, while Tardieu with his wearying lectures and Forgeot with his philippics spoke for the Chamber's discontented nationalists. The left responded positively to Briand's statement of confidence in Chancellor Wirth; the right was cool. After five days of debate Briand extracted a motion of confidence sponsored by diverse leaders from Herriot of the Radicals to Arago, Chairman of the Entente Républicaine. Arago's support, however,

[12] For the important discussions at London, see *ibid.*, pp. 488–507, 511–580. The key disagreement over interest on the "C" bonds can be followed, pp. 532–533, 537–539, 554–557, 567. Cf. the change between the version of May 2 (clauses 5 and 12) and May 3 (clauses 4 and 11), pp. 541–542, 567–569. See, too, Weill-Raynal, *Les réparations allemandes*, I, pp. 625–693; also Sally Marks, "Reparations Reconsidered: A Reminder," *Central European History*, II, 4 (1969), pp. 356–365, which is contested, but with only partial justice, by David Felix "Reparation Considered with a Vengeance," *Central European History*, IV, 2 (1971), pp. 171–179 [see Marks's "Rejoinder" v, 4 (1972), pp. 358–361].

[13] Keynes article of May 6, 1921, cited in Weill-Raynal, *Les réparations allemandes*, I, p. 659; also J. M. Keynes, *A Revision of the Treaty* (New York, 1922). "Saddened resignation," cited by Joseph Barthélemy, "Les décisions de Londres," *RPP* CVII, June 10, 1920, p. 460; "death in the soul": François Albert, *ibid.*, p. 459.

found little backing in the ranks of his own powerful conservative group. The vote was 390 to 162, and the opposition included 90 members of the right besides the Socialists.[14]

But if there were disappointments in the London schedule, did they not lie at the door of Tardieu and the other integral Treaty defenders as much as of Briand? Had they not insisted on a rigid policy to win an indefinite booty? The critics' fixation upon the total sums worked to obscure the fact that France would suffer most in any settlement that fell short of full damages. France had won no priority for repair of real war damages; whatever was received after the first billion gold marks was to go in fixed ratios to the various allies, not in order of urgency of reparation. Any deficiency in payments would be borne proportionally most heavily by those who had suffered most and had to rebuild whether or not compensation arrived. Briand had inherited this handicap. This did not mean that Briand was always forthright; he and Loucheur aroused distrust by trying to disguise their concessions. But the need for common action with the British compelled harsh compromises. Poincaré had urged repair of the English alliance even while he condemned Millerand's compromises, which were made for the sake of agreement with London. "It was in search of that impossible agreement," wrote a defender of Loucheur about 1921 policy, "that the efforts of the cabinet exhausted themselves."[15] Between London and the critics of the Bloc National there was precious little room for maneuver; Briand bent with the stronger pressure and for a year resolved his problems by oratory and vagueness. When his concessions could no longer be disguised at home, his position became untenable.

The German government signed the London agreement because it had no real choice. All political groups, including the SPD and Independents, felt that the demands were impossible to fulfill. Eventually, they believed, the Allies would have to recognize that if the German economy were crippled by insensate exactions, Europe as a whole must suffer. Still, there was bitter debate between the advocates of "fulfillment" and those nationalists who, as Georg Bernhard said, "thoroughly share the view, even if they state the contrary, that we can achieve the luxury of simply shoving the Versailles Treaty aside and not fulfilling it." Often the difference was one of means rather than ends. Advocates of fulfillment argued that only a year or so of compliance in good faith was needed to persuade the Allies to modify the reparation scheme; they talked of commencing fulfillment for a "transition period." This meant a new willingness to estimate Germany's capacity to pay and

[14] JOC, 1921, II, pp. 2440–2441 (May 26).
[15] Hoover Institution: Loucheur papers/5, f. 11.

abandonment of Fehrenbach and Simons' fruitless refusal to name any sums. Yet in French eyes the difference might not be important; by the fall of 1921 even the DDP's financial expert, Bernhard Dernburg, argued that Germany needed a ten-year interest-free moratorium to set her finances in order. The moderates would give Paris regretful excuses rather than sullen refusals. Neither helped balance France's budget.[16]

The debate over fulfillment made far more difference in terms of internal German politics. The Ruhr industrialist Paul Reusch—a relative moderate in fact—revealed some of the political stakes when he argued that Germany should reject the London ultimatum and take the risk of sanctions: "Let them march to Königsberg. . . . If the enemy occupies the Ruhr then part of the workers will turn away from the Social Democrats or left liberals and join the national current."[17] The reparations dispute thus became a fight over political and economic hegemony inside Germany.

The quarrel had become exceptionally bitter after the Allies settled on the Paris resolutions. Foreign Minister Simons delivered defiant nationalist speeches at Stuttgart and Karlsruhe in February. But even his misleading 30 billion mark offer at the first London meetings, which so infuriated Lloyd George, appeared too great a concession to some cabinet members and industrialist advisers. Hans von Raumer, the Minister of the Treasury, disliked the original 30 billion offer; Rudolf Havenstein, the President of the Reichsbank, and Stinnes never acquiesced in the provisional proposal on which Simons fell back. Until the last minute all agreed that 1 billion gold marks was the highest annual payment Germany could meet, and when Simons telegraphed his plans to the cabinet in Berlin several members supposedly threatened resignation. At a post-mortem session of the cabinet several days later, only President Ebert's personal intervention saved the Chancellor's action from being disavowed.[18]

---

[16] Bernhard in the Reparations Committee of the Reich Economic Council, November 9, 1921: DZA, Potsdam: RWR/613, p. 88; and cf. Bernhard on September 13 in the plenum: RWR/6, p. 962. Dernburg's view in "Der Markstürz," *BT*, November 6, 1921, a.m. Also Ernst Laubach, *Die Politik der Kabinette Wirth 1921–1922* (Hamburg and Lübeck, 1968), pp. 24, 75–76.

[17] BA, Koblenz: R 13 I (VdESI)/159, p. 30 (Vorstandssitzung, May 6, 1921). Cf. the May 13 report of the French Consul in Düsseldorf, Genoyer, on the industrialists' meeting at the Stahlhof, where it was allegedly argued that the occupation was inevitable and should be accepted. Min. Aff. Etr.: Europe, 1918–1929, Allemagne/464. Similar indications were given to British observers. See D'Abernon to Eyre Crowe, April 19, 1921, C8538/2740/18 in FO 371/6025.

[18] For cabinet discussions, GFM: ARK, 3483/1672/747035–747038, 747260–747291, 747329–747350; cf. Krämer to the Wirtschaftspolitischer Ausschuss of the Economic Council, March 9, 1921, in DZA, Potsdam: RWR/389, pp. 97–100 ff. Cf. also Bergmann, *Reparations*, pp. 62–67.

The failure of the London conference, and the subsequent occupation of Duisburg, Ruhrort, and Düsseldorf effectively destroyed the ministry. The cabinet's only *raison d'être* had been to avoid paying reparations, but this now seemed beyond Simons' capacity. Looking to the end of April, when the Reparations Commission had to set the overall schedule of payment, Fehrenbach and Simons gambled upon an appeal to President Harding and Secretary of State Hughes. German observers perceived the appeal as an act of desperation. The left was skeptical, the right angered at this gesture of weakness. Hessian DVP leader Eduard Dingeldey complained that Simons' cable was "a blow in the face of every honorable German."[19] The DVP's spokesman on public finance, Johann Becker, urged Stresemann to try forming a combination with the Center and with Nationalist support. Simons himself wanted to step down, but the Center Party ministers, Wirth, Brauns, and Hermes, pressed him to try one further offer to the Allies. Finally, after Washington declined a second plea for mediation, Simons refused to remain to face further DVP attacks or the Allied ultimatum that was expected momentarily from London. The Democratic Party ministers wanted the government to stay, but in the face of division inside the cabinet they too acquiesced on the evening of May 4.[20]

The People's Party believed that its chance to secure the chancellorship was at hand. But the Allied ultimatum that finally arrived on May 5 handicapped Stresemann. His own party was too closely identified as a center of resistance, even though Stresemann personally felt that Berlin had to give in. Submission seemed all the more necessary when the Polish-supported Korfanty rebellion in Upper Silesia broke out on May 3. Unless Berlin accepted the London demands, the French would not only occupy the Ruhr, but through the League of Nations commissioners in Upper Silesia would intervene on behalf of Korfanty's pro-Polish uprising. General Seeckt ruled out any direct German military suppression, presumably because the French warned that war in the West would follow.[21] As in 1919, the Germans apparently had to give

[19] For German "despondency" about the appeal to Washington see D'Abernon to Curzon, April 22, 1921: C8731/2740/18 in FO 371/6026; for Simons' calculations see his letter to the Mayor of Aachen: GFM: Büro des Reichsministers 5, Reparation, 3243/1642/716397–716398. Dingeldey's indignation in his letters to Stresemann April 22 and 27 in GFM: Stresemann Nachlass, 7002 = 236/3094/142375, 142411–142515. The German offer to Washington, April 25, cited willingness to accept a present value of 50 billion gold marks, but even so pro-German an adviser as D'Abernon thought the figure vague and uncertain: C 8672/2740/18 in FO 371/6026.

[20] Becker memorandum in GFM: Stresemann Nachlass, 7000 = 234/3094/141927–141929. Simons' desire to resign and the DDP attitude, BA, Koblenz: Koch-Weser Nachlass/12 (Diary, May 4, 1921).

[21] Stresemann was also locked in a behind-the-scenes rivalry with Eugen Shiffer for the DVP nomination. See Koch-Weser Nachlass/12 (May 5, 1921);

in—but who would take responsibility for signing the ultimatum? Stresemann sought to win concessions from Great Britain that would allow him to form a government that could sign, but the majority of the DVP parliamentary delegation remained stubbornly behind Stinnes and Vögler. As Koch-Weser of the Democrats noted wryly in the early hours of May 10, "Suddenly we [the old government] are very popular. We should stay."[22]

President Ebert, however, demanded a new government willing to seek not merely a general vote of confidence but authorization to accept the ultimatum. The SPD initially wished to stay outside, but Ebert prevailed upon his party colleagues to enter a new coalition. The President's choice of Joseph Wirth, Centrist Deputy and Finance Minister in the former government, came as a shock, especially on the right. "One can only say Donnerwetter! . . . The whole affair is without consolation," Westarp wrote his wife on the night of May 10.[23] Konrad Adenauer, the Center Party's Mayor of Cologne, came under brief consideration, but because Adenauer urged indirect taxes and a lengthening of the eight-hour day he was unacceptable to the Social Democrats. The new government placed the DVP in an embarrassing position: while Stresemann's party could have entered a government formed by the moderate Social Democrat and ex-Chancellor Gustav Bauer, participation under Wirth, with his pronounced leftist reputation as heir of Erzberger, was actually more difficult.[24]

The unresolved relationship with the People's Party was actually to become the barometric measure of Wirth's policy oscillations. DVP

---

also *Deutsche Allgemeine Zeitung*, May 5, 1921. For the views of Seeckt, Stresemann, and Simons on Upper Silesia see Koch-Weser, *ibid.*, and GFM: ARK, Kabinettsprotokolle, May 7 and May 9, 1921, 3483/1673/748019–748022 (May 7 and 9, 1921).

[22] Koch-Weser Nachlass/12 (Diary, May 9, 1921). For the old view that British delays prevented a Stresemann government, see Viscount Edgar D'Abernon, *The Diary of an Ambassador, Versailles to Rapallo, 1920–1922* (Garden City, N.Y., 1929), pp. 172–177 (May 9 and 12, 1921); but cf. the view of internal DVP division in Henry A. Turner, Jr., *Stresemann and the Politics of the Weimar Republic* (Princeton, N.J., 1963), pp. 86–87; also Laubach, *Kabinette Wirth*, pp. 13–19.

[23] For SPD preferences: Wilhelm Keil, *Erlebnis eines Sozialdemokraten*, 2 vols. (Stuttgart, 1948), II, pp. 232–234. The DDP, too, entered the coalition only in view of Ebert's threat to resign: cf. Koch-Weser/12 (Diary May 10); also Laubach, *Kabinette Wirth*, pp. 22–25. For Westarp's reaction: Gaertringen, Westarp Manuscript, Anhang Buch 2.

[24] Adenauer candidacy discussed in Rudolf Morsey, *Die deutsche Zentrumspartei 1917–1923* (Düsseldorf, 1966), pp. 381–384; DVP distrust of Wirth in Koch-Weser Nachlass/12 (Diary, May 10, 1921); also Dingeldey to Stresemann, September 10, 1920: GFM, Stresemann Nachlass, 6924 = 209/3088/138292. For Wirth's fiscal views, which alarmed the right, see VDR: SB, 345, pp. 790–795 (October 27, 1920).

cooperation seemed essential in view of the financial problems that now loomed with special urgency. Since the spring of 1920 the mark had begun to approach stability at approximately one-fifteenth its 1914 value, but over the summer of 1921, as transfers of foreign currency began, it slipped to one twenty-fifth. In September it broke sharply and by the end of the year depreciated to one-fiftieth.[25] The accelerating rate of depreciation was more disturbing than the absolute level. The delayed collection of taxes as prices rose rapidly would disastrously cut government revenues, create huge deficits, and thus just redouble inflation. Eroded on the one hand at home, the mark likewise slipped further on the international money market as the Berlin government sought to buy foreign currency for its first reparation payments under the London schedule. Even if fulfillment was to be only a transitory gesture, tax reform seemed urgent. But effective tax reform required support from labor and industry together: labor because the Socialists formed one pillar of Wirth's revived Weimar Coalition government, industry because it was generally believed that business resistance or evasion could cripple any tax measures. In the eyes of many industrialists, the People's Party represented their special delegation to the political system. A DVP cabinet role, or at least active DVP collaboration in drafting the new financial legislation, was a prerequisite for the cooperation of industry. The exhausting attempt to get Social Democrats and the People's Party together in a common program of reordering finances thus became the central domestic concern of the Wirth government until the Chancellor's final departure in November 1922.

Businessmen were not encouraging. Wilhelm Cuno of the Hamburg-Amerika line, Otto Wiedfeldt, and Max Warburg and Carl Melchior of the Warburg banking house all refused to join the government. To his employer, Krupp von Bohlen, Wiedfeldt scornfully reported Wirth's assortment of ministerial merchandise and the Chancellor's lack of promise.[26] Still, the Democratic Party members kept urging opening the cabinet to the right; Wirth reserved portfolios for the DVP; and Stresemann himself awaited an opportunity to enter the cabinet despite disclaimers to his right-wing party colleagues.[27]

The need that Wirth felt for industry's representatives was con-

[25] See tables in Costantino Bresciani-Turroni, *The Economics of Inflation*, M. E. Sayres, trans. (London, 1937, photo ed. 1968), p. 441.

[26] Wiedfeldt to Krupp von Bohlen und Halbach, May 20, 1921, in Fr. Krupp, A.G.: WA VII f. 1342; also Ernst Schröder, *Otto Wiedfeldt, eine Biographie* (Essen, 1964), p. 124; Lothar Albertin, "Die Verantwortung der liberalen Parteien für das Scheitern der Grossen Koalition im Herbst 1921," *Historische Zeitschrift*, 205 (1967), p. 577; Laubach, *Kabinette Wirth*, p. 34; BT, May 13, 1921, a.m., and May 20, a.m.

[27] Wirth speech, VDR: SB, 340, p. 3630; also Koch-Weser Nachlass/12 (Diary, May 10, 1921).

stantly to temper his personal ideological inclinations. Emotionally Wirth was virtually a populist, and perhaps one of the few true liberal democrats in his party. Even the labor leaders in the Center, such as Adam Stegerwald, were committed ideologically not to any notion of parliamentary democracy but only to a far more vague concept of *Volksstaat*, a populist, sometimes conservative notion of common-weal that might be satisfied by almost any particular regime. Joseph Joos, another Catholic labor leader, argued in 1922 that "the repub-lican state form is not the essence of the *Volksstaat* . . . the parliamen-tary means of government seem to us more a method than a principle."[28] Wirth's insistence on representative government in fact isolated him within the Center, and he never welded firm organizational ties. He was, moreover, mercurial and flighty, an indifferent administrator and bureaucrat, no more in control of the chancellery staff than of the Cen-ter Party press and apparatus. Indeed, the Center as a group never pressed Wirth's candidacy for the chancellorship, and by the autumn of 1921 would have been as happy to see him depart. According to Wilhelm Marx, the party wanted Wirth to remain in office only if the DVP entered the cabinet.[29]

The Chancellor, moreover, was as much a nationalist as a democrat. He shielded Seeckt's secret arrangements for Russo-German military cooperation, and while he urged "fulfillment," he really believed that long-term reparation was impossible no matter how large a tax bill was levied.[30] Ultimately, only the national commitment justified even temporary "fulfillment." Along with the Ruhr, the fate of Upper Silesia became the stake of the wager involved. Korfanty's rebellion posed the immediate threat, but there was also a longer-term issue. In Upper Silesia the 1921 plebiscite stipulated by the Versailles Treaty had pro-duced a pro-German majority. The Berlin government hoped that com-pliance on reparations would persuade the Allies and the League to assign the province to them entirely, even though the Treaty provided

[28] Joseph Joos, *Zentrumsprogramm und politische Zeitaufgaben* (Berlin, 1922), pp. 6, 8; Emil Ritter, *Die katholische Sozialbewegung Deutschlands im neunzehnten Jahrhundert und der Volksverein* (Cologne, 1954), p. 338. In contrast, Wirth argued that "the spirit of the Weimar Constitution is a good one and our constant concern must be that this spirit pervades the present regime," *Unsere politische Linie im deutschen Volksstaat* (Berlin, 1924), p. 42.

[29] Cf. interparty discussion October 18, 1921, in BA, Koblenz: R 43 I/1028; also Marx's view of Wirth's impulsiveness in Hugo Stehkämper, ed., *Der Nachlass des Reichskanzlers Wilhelm Marx, Mitteilungen aus dem Stadtarchiv von Köln*, 52–55, 4 vols. (Cologne, 1968), I, p. 256; cf. Arnold Brecht, *The Political Educa-tion of Arnold Brecht: An Autobiography 1884–1970* (Princeton, N.J., 1970), pp. 204 ff.

[30] Morsey, *Zentrumspartei*, pp. 490–496; Herbert Helbig, *Die Träger der Rapal-lo-Politik* (Göttingen, 1958), pp. 56–59, 85–86; Joseph Becker, "Eine Niederschrift Joseph Wirths über seinen Eintritt in das Reichskabinett 1920," *Zeitschrift für die Geschichte des Oberrheins*, 112, 1 (1964), pp. 243–254; Laubach, *Kabinette Wirth*, p. 24.

for partition according to local voting patterns. Only fulfillment, as Wirth and the Socialist Otto Wels told the Reichstag, would secure the contested territory.[31]

Such justifications set limits to cooperation as well as sanctioning it. Wirth—and Rathenau, too, who despite his intellectual gifts generally followed the policy leadership of the Chancellor—always saw that a nationalist reaction against fulfillment might destroy the cabinet's efforts at seeking Allied concessions by verbal compliance. The period of Wirth's chancellorship thus became a perpetual trimming, a constant exhausting search for political equilibria. Industry was balanced against the socialists, Russian possibilities against Western, a rhetoric of fulfillment against a constant effort to evade reparations, the search for fiscal reform against the wearied acceptance of inevitable inflation.

The financial question lay at the center of all these frustrations: only if Wirth solved the problem of government revenues was even temporary fulfillment possible. Alternatively, unless Wirth began to solve the tax question, the Allies would grant no further moratoria for future reparation payments. Effective closing of the budget gap was a necessity either to meet reparations or to win reprieves. But the financial question raised anew the basic social conflicts of the Reich, and Wirth proved unable to bridge them on any durable basis.

REPARATIONS, TAXES, AND THE DEMANDS OF GERMAN HEAVY INDUSTRY

The Wirth government promised an overhaul of German taxes in June 1921 to meet reparation needs. While existing taxes were based upon Erzberger's tough reforms of 1919, they were levied in paper marks and yielded only a fraction of what had originally been intended. Officials now estimated that, in current paper-mark values, obligations to the Allies would require levying 50 billion marks out of a total government expenditure of 100 billion. The new tax program was supposed to yield 80 billion. From the outset the proposals drew criticism from SPD and DDP ranks. Unless the deficit were completely eliminated, their representatives argued, the floating debt would continue to rise, the mark would continue to depreciate, and tax receipts would fall even further behind expenditures.[32] On its visit to Berlin in early fall, the

[31] VDR: SB, 349, p. 3630. Cf. F. Gregory Campell, "The Struggle for Upper Silesia, 1919–1922, *Journal of Modern History*, 42, 3 (1970), pp. 361–385.

[32] See Erich Dombrowski, "Das papiere Steuerbuckett," *BT*, August 7, 1921, a.m.; also Franz Silberstein's article the same day. In April, May, and June state expenses were averaging 120 billion paper marks annually even before the London schedule went into effect. For fiscal 1921, state income turned out to be only 40 percent of expenditure. Bresciani-Turroni, *The Economics of Inflation*, pp. 438, 441.

Allied Committee of Guarantees—a watchdog body established under the London agreement to supervise German finance and reparation provisions—also criticized the tax program and condemned the enormous budget deficits as the primary source of the mark's deterioration.[33]

Most Germans and even some foreign economists stressed instead the so-called transfer problem as the most immediate affliction of the currency. Even if Germany could raise the paper-mark equivalent of what she owed, the country did not have the balance-of-payments surplus to buy foreign currencies easily, but would have to throw ever greater quantities of marks on the money markets to scrape together dollars and francs or pounds. When the mark fell seriously over the summer, the transfer "pessimists" felt that their judgment was confirmed. To pay the first billion gold marks, Berlin had forwarded 150 million marks' worth of dollars and the rest in treasury notes within a few weeks after the London meetings. The treasury notes had to be covered in foreign currency by September 1, and to get the *Devisen* Berlin had to resort to expensive short-term loans from foreign bankers. While raising the first billion seemed exhausting in itself, Berlin faced further payments of half a billion or more every quarter-year thereafter. By late August, Keynes was arguing that Germany would never be able to meet her payments for 1922.[34]

The arguments made by Keynes and others who pointed to the balance-of-payments difficulties suited those Germans hostile to reparations only too well. Like Keynes, they could point to the cessions of territory and economic assets required by the Treaty and could argue that Germany was unable to achieve a sufficiently positive balance of payments to send money abroad. So long as an import surplus bedeviled the mark, the only way that Germany could pay reparations would be by purchasing for foreign currencies at increasingly adverse rates. Men such as Stinnes and Helfferich reflected convictions far more widespread than those of their own political and economic circles when they claimed that paying the reparations debt and stabilizing the currency were mutually exclusive.[35]

[33] For Committee of Guarantees in Berlin, September 23–October 14, 1921, and subsequent report see AN, Paris: AJ⁶/550, Folder 2, Annèxe No. 1026. Also FO 408/4, No. 37, Enclosure 1. Cf. Laubach, *Kabinette Wirth*, p. 44.

[34] Keynes cited by Bergmann, *The History of Reparations*, p. 99. For the difficulties with the first billion see Laubach, *Kabinette Wirth*, pp. 66–68; also German explanations in the protocol of the Berlin meetings with the Committee of Guarantees, September 27, in AN, Paris: AJ⁶/550, Folder 1.

[35] For this opinion see the executive meeting of the Iron and Steel Industrialists, October 21, 1921, BA, Koblenz: R 13 I (VdESI)/97. Summary of argument in Bresciani-Turroni, *The Economics of Inflation*, pp. 42–47; general line-up of monetary views in Howard S. Ellis, *German Monetary Theory 1905–1933* (Cam-

Nonetheless, the arguments were in good part misleading. Non-Germans who supported reparation pointed out that the Reich might demand of herself the same capital disinvestment she had inflicted upon others during the war. Within Germany, some socialists and an occasional bourgeois spokesman suggested that Germany could surrender part of her own capital to acquit her debt.[36] One proposal was, of course, the cession of industrial shares for reparation credit, a scheme the French repeatedly pressed but the British effectively vetoed. Both London and Paris realized that the underlying objective was less a matter of dividends and actual values than leverage over German industry and a chance to extract international industrial agreements.[37]

Even without the cession of capital, however, the transfer problem was not insoluble in theory. But if one wished to avoid transferring the German "substance,"—i.e., claims on her capital—it was at least necessary to tax enough to brake German consumption. Those who believed that reparation was impossible rigidly separated the "budgetary" problem of levying money at home from the "transfer" problem of sending it abroad by acquiring acceptable foreign currencies or gold. On the other hand, French advocates of reparation, and some German experts as well, understood that the internal "budgetary" problem and the "transfer" problem were not entirely distinct. The fall of the mark, they retorted to the German government's pleas of *non possumus*, was due to the failure to collect taxes effectively. This was correct over the long run. Keynes notwithstanding, the problem of internal collection and that of transferring the collected funds interacted. Even in 1921 the Socialist Rudolf Hilferding pointed out to the special sessions of the Socialization Commission convened to discuss reparations that it was the internal deficit that contributed to the adverse balance of trade: "In effect, the issues [of paper marks] increased internal prices, and that stimulated imports and impeded exports."[38] For two years

---

bridge, Mass., 1934), pp. 203–295. Even advocates of "fulfillment" such as Rathenau shared this assessment; see "Der Kern des Übels," *Vossische Zeitung*, January 1, 1921, in *Gesammelte Schriften* (3rd ed.): *Nachgelassene Schriften* (Berlin, 1928), pp. 219 ff. and his speeches, October 28, and November 12, 1921 in *Gesammelte Reden* (Berlin, 1924), pp. 314, 315, 349.

[36] See Eugen Leidig of the DVP to Stresemann, August 25, 1921, GFM, Stresemann Nachlass: 6997 = 231/3109/141379–141381—a proposal that Germany pay 2 billion gold marks per year from national income and 1.5 billion per year for thirty years from national capital.

[37] Weill-Raynal, *Les réparations allemandes*, I, pp. 630–632. Opposition registered by Jacob Reichert of the Verein deutscher Eisen- und Stahlindustrieller, February 21, 1921, R 13 I/158. British criticism and skepticism was expressed at several intervals: see Thelwall report from Berlin, December 11, 1922: C17162/331/18, in FO 371/7520.

[38] Cited in Bresciani-Turroni, *The Economics of Inflation*, p. 44.

more Hilferding had the privilege of repeating his diagnosis to unreceptive policy makers. Other economic experts, however, elaborated this focus upon the budgetary problem. If Germany created a budget surplus, they pointed out, it would produce a deflationary pressure that would contract the volume of imports and lower the price levels of German goods, making them more attractive to foreigners. Later in the decade the argument was extended to show that the recipients of German payments would undergo a price-inflationary tendency that would lead them to spend more on imports while it handicapped their exports. The effect upon both the relative *prices* of goods and upon money *incomes* in Germany and the Allied lands would together work to eliminate any balance-of-payments deficits that currency transfers would otherwise create. As was argued later in the decade against the Reichsbank policies of Hjalmar Schacht:

> As long as the Reichsmark equivalent of the reparations payment can be collected through severe taxation of the German economy and as long as the funds so raised are blocked and kept out of effective circulation the transfer will be possible. The motor force of the process, the cancellation of domestic purchasing power, brings about the ultimate result, the increase in exports; and the medium for the foreign payment, the foreign exchange, is thereby procured "automatically," as it were. In other words, the transfer problem is solved once the budgetary problem—the problem of raising the domestic funds without resort to credit creation—is solved.[39]

Such a confrontation of the budgetary problem required Berlin's acceptance of a relative austerity program so that the German citizen's consumption would remain below the per capita level of production and the government could transfer claims upon German goods abroad. It meant having Germans work an hour or two a week for the Allies. Substituting foreign consumers for Germans should not have led to a contraction of output or employment. But the difficulty lay in getting recipients to spend their reparation credits directly or indirectly for German goods and services. What made the reparation problem so

[39] Fritz Machlup, "Foreign Debts, Reparations and the Transfer Problem," in *International Payments, Debts and Gold* (New York, 1964), p. 412. (The essay dates from 1928.) In later essays Machlup reinforced his argument by demonstrating that a "multiplier" effect derived from international payments would increase a country's propensity to import. Likewise, in response to Keynes' gloomy claim that taxation and deflation could never lower domestic prices enough to induce foreign buyers to purchase the full amount of the reparation transfer, Swedish economist Bertil Ohlin showed that Keynes had failed to consider the effect of income increases on the recipient of reparation. See J. M. Keynes, "The German Transfer Problem," and Bertil Ohlin, "The Reparation Problem: A Discussion," both from *The Economic Journal*, xxxix (1929), and reprinted in *Readings in the Theory of International Trade* (London, 1961), pp. 161–178.

frustrating by late 1921 was that over the long run the arrangement was feasible, but in the short run it appeared impossible. Foreign tariffs and import quotas stood in the way of German exports; and even transfer "optimists" conceded that without free trade Germany's curtailment of domestic consumption would not automatically lead to equivalent foreign purchases. It might just bring a recessionary spiral into unemployment. Could German exports surge fast enough to meet the schedule of upcoming annuities set at London? British Treasury experts addressed the dilemma in mid-November 1921 as the system threatened to collapse. Contesting those who thought that world trade must remain at its given level and that German exports intended to pay reparations must hurt British industry, the Treasury argued that reparation payments could instead facilitate investment abroad and increase world "consuming power." Indeed Britain could well reinvest her payments in Germany to help develop German export capacity, and in the Third World to increase its purchasing power. Ultimately, competitive German and English goods could all find markets. The key was expanding purchasing power: in short, economic growth.[40]

The bind was the short run. The Treasury recommended reparation in kind as the answer. But Paris required cash relief as well. Yet even sober French observers admitted temporary German dilemmas. Mauclère, of the Committee of Guarantees, wrote Briand: "We must not be deceived; the fall of the mark creates great difficulties for applying the provisions of the state of payments."[41] At several intervals throughout 1921, Jean Parmentier, the chief permanent official at the Ministry of Finances, warned the premier about the problems of extracting cash from the Germans and urged more reparations in kind. On September 8, shortly after the Germans finished their first billion-mark transfer, Parmentier signaled that Berlin had had to resort to exceptional borrowing and gold sales. "This result sadly corroborates the prophecies of J. M. Keynes who foresees the impossibility of Germany acquitting her obligations this coming spring." Broadening the July 1921 Wiesbaden accords, negotiated by Loucheur and Rathenau to increase reparation in kind, appeared the only short-term practical answer. Reparation in kind, however, provoked bitter protests from French manufacturers, and there might be serious unemployment. "Doubtless, the utilization on a large scale of payments in kind and of foreign labor would require an education of public opinion, including making it clear that the restoration of the liberated regions by French industrialists at the cost of Germany and without damage to our national eco-

[40] "German Reparations: The Need for a Readjustment of the Present Schedule of Payments," and "Reparations in Kind," Treasury Memoranda of November 16, 1921, in PRO: CAB 27/72, F.C. 77 and 78.

[41] Mauclère to Briand, October 7, 1921, in Min. Fin. F[30]/1360.

nomic interests is a utopia." Nevertheless, Parmentier emphasized, the choice was between reconstruction by German industry and labor or by French industry at the expense of the French treasury. "The present state of our finances does not permit us to hesitate."[42]

Party alignments in the Chamber, however, set limits on how far Briand and Loucheur could follow Parmentier's counsel, even though by the fall of 1921 they largely shared his diagnosis. To his own frustration, Parmentier also found that his viewpoint, which reflected the preoccupations of the Rue de Rivoli, was contested by the Foreign Ministry, the Reparations Commission, and the Committee of Guarantees—agencies that had a greater bureaucratic stake in upholding the London schedule of payments. And while Parmentier declared that the London schedule was illusory for the near future, he, too, remained frustrated by German reluctance to face up to her correctable budgetary problem. A strong German government, he stressed, could raise the sums needed to meet reparations and even to amortize some of her debt.[43]

A German government, however, could be no stronger than the social groups it represented. Any successful tax program depended upon resolving the underlying conflict between social democratic and industrialist interests. This was all the more difficult when taxes were partially earmarked for unpopular reparations. Placing their hopes from the outset in an almost providential Treaty revision, the Wirth cabinet agreed that their fiscal program could not fully cover reparations burdens. This decision represented an initial compromise with the right.

The incidence of the new taxes also involved a political compromise. From the beginning the Socialists wanted some way of having the Reich share in business revenues. During the summer of 1921 they called increasingly for an appropriation of assets sheltered from inflation, a "seizure of real values" (*Erfassung der Sachwerte*). As early as May 17, Economics Minister Schmidt presented the project of his new State Secretary Julius Hirsch to the cabinet. This stipulated that industry turn over 20 percent of its stocks and bonds to the government. In addition, 5-percent bonds would be levied on landed property. The revenues would provide a minimal share of industrial and agricultural income for Berlin, while the capital could serve as collateral for foreign loans to meet reparation needs.[44]

But Schmidt and Hirsch's proposal met crippling opposition. The

---

[42] Note pour M. le Ministre, September 8, 1921, Min. Fin. F^{30}/1275.
[43] *Ibid.*
[44] GFM: ARK, Kabinettsprotokolle, Chefbesprechung, May 17, May 31 (for Wirth and Schmidt discussions), and June 24, 1921, 3483/1673/748030–748032, 748176–748177; 1674/748616.

State Secretaries of the Finance Ministry, Schroeder and Zapf, who were close to the DNVP and DVP, objected to the plan. The Democratic Party, which was represented in the cabinet, disliked Hirsch's "socialist influence."[45] Rathenau, Hirsch's adversary in the coal dispute a year earlier, condemned the tax program as a first step toward nationalization. The Social Democrats, who in a cabinet log-rolling maneuver had already accepted an unwelcome hike in indirect taxation, threatened to break up the coalition to push through their proposal.[46] But the Chancellor was not willing to support the Hirsch plan against growing criticism from the DDP and business spokesmen. The government delayed until August 6, while Schmidt and Hirsch sought to recast their ideas in the form of a corporation tax amendment that would have changed the corporation tax installments into a capital levy. Once again, Rathenau vetoed the scheme.[47]

The one concession to the Socialists Wirth permitted was a new property tax to replace the remainder of the Emergency Levy passed under Erzberger but vastly reduced by inflation. This new tax, with its emergency surcharges for fifteen years, was to take up to 4 percent of individual wealth annually. Coupled with the already existing income taxes, the bill might indeed force the wealthy to surrender some of their capital as well as income. Yet as the astute financial commentator for the *Berliner Tageblatt* noted, the proposed measure did not seem to frighten the wealthy. The level of shares on the Berlin bourse disclosed that investors were buying more heavily than ever the very capital

which presumably at this time is to be taxed especially heavily. Apparently they trust that owners of capital and assets which hold their value will once again succeed in extricating their neck from the noose; will once again calculate the taxes in their costs of production, pass them along in higher prices and finally, as during previous periods of price rises and tax reform, emerge richer and more triumphant than before.[48]

[45] Koch-Weser to his wife, May 26 and May 31, 1921, in BA, Koblenz: Koch-Weser Nachlass/27.
[46] See Anlage to June 24 Kabinettsprotokolle. GFM: ARK, 3438/1674/748617–748620. SPD threats on June 29.
[47] For the evolution of Wirth's views, see his speech of June 1, 1921: VDR: SB, 349, pp. 3711–3712 (as well as the opposition from conservatives, pp. 3733 ff. 3796 ff.). By June 24 Wirth spoke of *Besitzerfassung*, not *Goldwerte*, VDR: SB, 350, p. 4136. Cf. Laubach, *Kabinette Wirth*, pp. 61–66. For the Socialist corporation tax proposals which envisaged giving the government dividend rights (*Genussscheine*) rather than voting stock, see GFM: ARK, Kabinettsprotokolle, Anlage, July 29, 1921, 3438/1674/749052 ff., and discussion July 30, *ibid.*, 749095–749098. Cf. also David Felix's critical view of the tax schemes in *Walter Rathenau and the Weimar Republic* (Baltimore, 1971), pp. 31–32, 92.
[48] Felix Pinner, "Die Rache der Goldwerte," *BT*, August 20, 1921. For descriptions of the tax see this article plus the articles cited in note 32. In addition

The left thus felt more dissatisfaction with the government's compromise program than the right. Within the Reich Economic Council's new Reparations Commission, which the government had assembled for advice on how to meet the London obligations, Social Democrat Wissell reiterated his party's criticism of the ministry's tax plans for their failure to pull in real assets. In the general assembly of the Economic Council three days later, Wissell demanded legislation that would essentially carry out the original proposals of Hirsch and Schmidt by giving the government one-quarter of the shares in German corporations.[49] Wissell, the most conservative of Socialists in 1919, had become the most reformist of financiers by 1921—a good measure of how far to the right German politics had shifted.

Representatives of the business communities reacted with cautious defensive tactics against both the Wissell proposals and the government's watered-down plans for a property tax. In general, business representatives sought to make light of the socialist slogan, "seizure of real values," arguing that real values were far smaller in the postwar period than generally believed. Carl Siemens—like Rathenau a representative of the electrical industry, a political moderate, and affiliated with the Democratic Party—pointed out to the plenary session of the Economic Council that even if the state took 20 percent of industrial equity, the measure would yield far less than needed to pay reparations annuities. "In government circles," he charged, "there reigns an entirely false idea of business capacity." The Chairman of the RWR Reparations Commission, Hans Kraemer, who had brought in the innocuous final draft of socialization the previous spring, claimed that although the Economic Council might really prefer to accept Wirth's compromise property tax—the closest the government had come toward any "seizure of real values"—it could not come into effect soon enough to be worth the financial exertions it imposed.[50]

---

to the property tax, a tax on increase in property, a rise in the corporate income tax of 10 to 30 percent, and hikes in the coal tax, turn-over tax, and excise tax were also planned.

[49] DZA, Potsdam: RWR/6, pp. 935, 941–945.

[50] *Ibid.*, p. 99. Siemens' argument was based on the fact that gold-mark equivalents of share prices had declined since 1914. But the Socialists thought that values and assessments should be based on the market value of assets in the enterprise, not on stock prices reflecting current earnings, which despite serving as some hedge against inflation, were generally low in real terms. The question of equity prices was especially thorny. The reports of the Committee of Guarantees (AN, Paris: AJ⁶/526, Berlin Documents 241A and 241B) stressed the undistributed profits earned and stashed away during 1920 and 1921. But the intelligence division of the Reparations Commission argued a year later that concealed losses accompanied the advantages that inflation provided. To compete, German industry sold goods at a level that did not allow for depreciation. To restore their capital they issued new stock, lowering the value of outstanding issues. See re-

As Wirth had probably intended, a comedy of inaction now began, much as had marked the debate on coal socialization a year earlier. After Wissell presented his proposal for 20 percent stock cessions on September 13, it was sent back to the RWR's Reparations Committee. Here it found general support from Georg Bernhard and ill-concealed opposition from industry's representatives. Nonetheless, in the fall of 1921 most industrial spokesmen realized that blind resistance to either Wissell's scheme or Wirth's property tax was unwise. Stinnes and Silverberg spoke out for compromise within the Reichsverband der deutschen Industrie, while Wiedfeldt endorsed provisional reparation payments and was willing to accept temporary extraordinary taxes. In July Wirth invited fifteen business leaders—including Stinnes, Thyssen, Wiedfeldt, Hugenberg, Borsig, Siemens, Duisberg and Cuno—to discuss the problem of raising foreign currency for the Reich. Except for Hugenberg, most seemed sympathetic and realized that Wirth was not rushing to accept socialist financial recommendations. In late August the Chancellor told industrial representatives that he would kill the SPD proposals in exchange for a hard-money loan from industry, and most industrial leaders were willing to accept the bargain. Despite the resistance of Hugenberg and some of the other Westphalian steel industrialists, the Reichsverband approved a so-called "credit action" at its assembly of September 27–28. The industrialists proposed the formation of a consortium on the part of German firms that would pledge its members' collective assets to secure a large private loan abroad. The proceeds would be turned over to the government in return for credit toward taxes. In effect, industry offered to pay its taxes in advance and in a stable currency in return for Wirth's rejection of SPD fiscal measures.[51]

As during the coal controversy a year earlier, industry's plans were intended to preclude more radical policies. Before the credit action was even formally presented to the Economic Council, Arthur Feiler, editor of the *Frankfurter Zeitung* and sympathetic to business, exploited industry's proposal to argue for a conservative approach to financial issues. Passing the Wissell proposal, Feiler warned, would endanger industry's initiative. Indeed, the Social Democratic plan was not a financial remedy, but "an attempt to achieve nationalization by roundabout routes." Despite Hilferding's denial, Hans Krämer also insisted

port from Paris, November 2, 1922, C15921/331/18 in FO 371/7519. Share prices, in any case, declined sharply in November 1921. See D'Abernon to Curzon December 27, 1921, in FO 408/6, Nr. 70.

[51] Wiedfeldt to Reichsverband, June 14, 1921, in Fr. Krupp, A.G., WA IV 2556; Lother Albertin, "Die Verantwortung der liberalen Parteien," pp. 550, 578–582; Schröder, *Otto Wiedfeldt* (Essen, 1966), p. 125; Laubach, *Kabinette Wirth*, p. 68. Cf. the article on the Reichsverband credit action in *BT*, September 29, 1921.

that Schmidt and Hirsch were just trying to win what the Ministry of Economics had failed to achieve when it had worked for nationalization of coal, and he warned that such a course would prevent any raising of foreign credits.[52]

As intended, the industrialists' proposal for a credit action drove the Wissell plan to the background. In October the special RWR subcommittee convoked to discuss Wissell's idea substituted instead a formula by the Mannheim attorney Max Hachenberg. This stipulated that the government endow the private credit action with official status by creating a German Credit Community. The Credit Community would have a management elected by its own member corporations and would determine how much credit each member firm must underwrite. It would receive and allocate the tax receipts for the *Devisen* it passed on to the Reich.[53] Hilferding moved that Wissell's proposals be instituted by April 1, 1922, if the necessary credits were not raised, but Hachenberg successfully argued that such a provision would undermine the whole proposal. How could German industry expect to raise credit abroad, he asked, if foreigners feared that the capital base used to guarantee the loan might be eroded by state action?[54]

By October the government, too, intervened vigorously for the credit action. As industrialists such as Hermann Bücher realized, Wirth was pressed for a half-billion gold marks' worth of foreign exchange to meet his next reparation deadlines on January 15 and February 15, even though he hoped to discuss revision of the reparation schedule by the coming winter. Industry's assistance alone promised the foreign currency quickly enough, as the Chancellor told the RWR's Reparation Committee on October 11.[55] On the 20th he informed the Social Democrats that he did not want the threat of seizing capital brandished over the business community. The Chancellor, as Pinner accurately reported, was now resigned "that in this matter of 'seizing real values' one had to reckon with the mentality of the big industrialists."[56]

To gamble on industry's cooperation required pulling the DVP into

[52] See the Reparations-Ausschuss of September 15, DZA, Potsdam: RWR/612, pp. 270 ff.
[53] Summary report of the Arbeitsausschuss für die Beratung des Problems der Devisenbeschaffung für die Reparation, DZA, Potsdam: RWR/895, pp. 79–89.
[54] Arbeitsausschuss . . . October 18, 1921, DZA, Potsdam: RWR/896, pp. 156–160.
[55] For Bücher's views see Albertin, "Die Verantwortlichkeit der liberalen Parteien," pp. 580–582, and Laubach, *Kabinette Wirth*, pp. 84–85, for discussions with the Reichsverband on reparation revision, September 7. Wirth's presentation to the Allied Reparation Commission reported in U.S. Department of State Decimal File: 462.00 R29/1172.
[56] Wirth discussion with SPD in interparty committee, BA, Koblenz: R 43 I/1028. Pinner report in "Hinter den Kulissen des Staates," *BT*, November 5, 1921, p.m.

closer collaboration with the ministry. Stresemann as well as Wirth had been working toward this end with the support of the moderates in the People's Party, who were generally found among the representatives of banking, small business, and light industry. Stresemann's colleague Eugen Leidig, for example, stressed the need for a responsible approach to Germany's financial predicament. He harshly condemned both his own DVP and the Nationalist press for virtually applauding tax evasion through inflation, and he warned accurately that tax defaults would aggravate the inflation and could only radicalize the middle class on which the People's Party drew.[57]

Rapprochement with the Wirth coalition encountered a new snag, however, with the August 24 assassination of Matthias Erzberger. The murder of the Centrist leader—who had been hounded by a two-year-long hate campaign of the Nationalists—reunited the old Weimar coalition behind an emotional defense of the Republic. It briefly pushed the tax issue into the background and revived distrust of the DVP as a right-wing party. The crisis moved Wirth to stress his own democratic commitment. Speaking at Erzberger's graveside and then at Berlin, Wirth warned that unless the Republic were reaffirmed against extremists, German politics would degenerate into a battle between proletariat—including the Catholic labor force—and bourgeoise. Nonetheless, Stresemann still felt, after a confidential conversation with the Chancellor on September 3, that although Wirth might indulge himself with an emotional turn to the left, he yet feared that his all-important fiscal program would fail if he had to rely on the united and radicalized socialist parties.[58] Indeed, the Erzberger murder did not fundamentally detour Wirth from his attempt to reach a compromise between Social Democrats and industry. And on the side of industry, moderates feared the consequences of recurrent polarization. When the DNVP denounced the government's emergency ordinances against antirepublican meetings and publications and reasserted a militant, reactionary line at their party convention in Munich, non-Nationalist members of the Reichsverband der deutschen Industrie made clear their disapproval. In light of the charged passions, industrialists were especially anxious to secure DVP entry into the government as security against any further swing to the left.[59]

[57] Leidig to Stresemann, August 25, 1921, and Stresemann to Leidig, September 8, 1921, in GFM: Stresemann Nachlass, 6997 = 231/3109/141378–141386, 141387–141388. Wirth's attitude toward cooperation in R 43 I/2215.

[58] *Ibid.*, 6997 = 231/3109/141444–141446. For Wirth's speeches see his *Reden während der Kanzlerschaft* (Berlin, 1925), esp. p. 179.

[59] For Reichsverband attitude see report in GFM: Stresemann Nachlass, 6997 = 231/3109/141454–141464; the divide between the DNVP and other groups emerged in the parliamentary debates of September 30: VDR: SB, 351, p. 4629 ff. For business attitudes see Sorge to the Reichsverband, September 21,

Hence Wirth and the industrialists of the People's Party felt that they had more to gain than to lose by cooperation by the end of September. Important differences still separated the Chancellor and Stresemann's party, as discussions revealed on September 28, but they did not seem unbridgeable.[60] Cooperation from the left also appeared possible once the SPD Congress at Gorlitz finally approved future cabinet collaboration with the People's Party. From the Social Democrats' viewpoint, the Democrats and People's Party presented few essential differences. Like the DVP, many DDP members feared a rigorous tax program. On the right of the Democratic Party, Georg Gothein was especially incensed by the League of Nation's October 12 decision to cede large areas of Upper Silesia to Poland and denounced "fulfillment"—"so foreigners know we don't swallow everything like dogs." The SPD felt that it might as well work with Stresemann as Gothein; indeed they indicated willingness to drop their demand for a capital levy if the credit action materialized.[61] The delicate question remaining was Wirth's leadership. This was couched in terms of a further debate over the procedure for reconstructing the cabinet: whether it should involve collective resignation and new interparty negotiations, which would allow replacement of the Chancellor, or merely the addition of delegates from the DVP.[62]

The League of Nations decision on Upper Silesia, however, interrupted the momentum toward agreement on tax reform, credit action, and an enlarged cabinet. The Ministry had already declared that it would resign should the Allies, through the League of Nations, force Germany to cede any significant part of the disputed region.[63] Rathenau

---

R 13 I/158, cited in Albertin, p. 587, and Raumer to Stresemann, September 18, 1921, in GFM; Stresemann Nachlass 6996 = 230/3109/141144–141148, also the report on the Reichsverband 6997 = 231/3109/141454–141464.

[60] Ibid., 6996 = 230/3109/141242–141243.

[61] The SPD, however, did not seem satisfied with the agreement between the DVP and the government merely to accelerate the collection of one-third of the old Emergency Levy—now a trivial tax burden because of inflation. See Albertin, "Die Verantwortlichkeit der liberalen Parteien," pp. 584, 595–596; Stresemann's report to the DVP leadership in BA, Koblenz: R 45 II/28, and the report in GFM: Stresemann Nachlass, 6996 = 230/3109/141258–141269. For Gothein's outburst see the DDP papers in NSDAP Hauptarchiv film/f. 727.

[62] See Marx's discussions with the DVP on replacing Wirth in Hugo Stehkämper, ed., Nachlass Marx, II, pp. 237, 256, 262. Also BA, Koblenz: R 43 I/1304, "Niederschrift über . . . die Erweiterung der Koalition am 28. September 1921"; Albertin, "Die Verantwortlichkeit der liberalen Parteien," pp. 588–600; GFM, Stresemann Nachlass, 6996 = 230/3109/141242–141243; Laubach, Kabinette Wirth, p. 88; Turner, Stresemann and the Politics of the Weimar Republic, pp. 92–93.

[63] In view of the indignation over the transfer of Upper Silesia, it is worth noting that from November 1920, German firms prepared for the partition and the dangers of Polish take-over with Foreign Minister Simons' cautious approval.

had calculated that such a threat might lead London to press for a favorable partition on the basis of the German majority in the previous spring's plebiscite. Despite the opposition of Ebert, Foreign Secretary Rosen, and General Groener, and against his own judgment, Wirth felt pledged to retire by October 22, ten days after the arbitration verdict. He realized, moreover, that the Democratic Party now preferred to abandon the cabinet while even his own Center *Fraktion* was canvassing alternative chancellors who might please the DVP.[64] Formation of a new ministry, however, proved especially wearying. Ebert asked the old cabinet partners and the People's Party to search for a Great Coalition government. Agreement seemed feasible, but the DVP had second thoughts about entering a cabinet that was committed in theory to tax reform and reparation payments. It protested that the SPD had accepted the Upper Silesian decision without sufficient patriotic indignation. On October 22, Stresemann demanded time to consult his party once again. The Democratic Party, too, refused to cooperate in a new government, citing Social Democratic submission to the enemy, but clearly unhappy about the tax program. As was the case when the Democrats had quit the government in the spring of 1919, uneasiness about economic reform underlay the supposed divergence on foreign policy. Wirth's offer to step down for another Chancellor did not remove their objections. The Democrats permitted their member Gessler to remain as Defense Minister in a new cabinet in his own name, but not Rathenau whom Wirth badly desired to keep. The

---

Upper Silesian coal companies were prepared to offer half-price shares to French firms in return for the French pressuring the Poles into a secret convention, March 22, 1921. The convention freed any corporation with 25 percent of its stock in French hands from the threat of Polish nationalization. In return the French promised the Poles one-quarter of the shares they received from the Germans at acquisition cost plus 15 percent. The French hoped for acquisitions worth 400 million paper marks (c. 30 million gold marks); in fact, these prices were lower than prewar valuations. See GFM: Geheimakten, "Polen-Oberschlesien, Industrie 6," 8868/3414/E618486–618556 passim; also GFM, Büro des Reichsministers, "Oberschlesien 13," 3057/1455/D601539–601545. Stinnes, too, acquired control of major Upper Silesian coal mines, which he attached to the massive Austrian Alpine-Montan Gesellschaft, free from the dangers of Polish take-over that German firms faced. The Alpine-Montan Gesellschaft involved a notorious story in its own right. Stinnes had purchased his interests from the Italian financier Castiglione, who had acquired them just before the Austrian government was prepared to nationalize the concern. The quick sale was laid at the door of Joseph Schumpeter, then Austrian Finance Minister, who was enticed by needed Italian lire. See Charles A. Gulick, *Austria from Habsburg to Hitler*, 2 vols. (Berkeley, Calif., 1948), pp. 139–140; also Vorstand des Deutschen Metallarbeiter-Verbandes, *Konzerne der Metallindustrie* (Stuttgart, 1924), pp. 141–144.

[64] Intracabinet debates in GFM; ARK; Kabinettsprotokolle, October 10 and 12, October 21 and 22, 1921, 3438/1675/749668 ff. Cf. Interfraktionelle Besprechungen, October 17–18, in BA, Koblenz: R 43 I/1028; Laubach, *Kabinette Wirth*, pp. 97–103; Morsey, *Die deutsche Zentrumspartei*, p. 414.

Chancellor had to rest content with recruiting members of the former coalition partners in a "cabinet of personalities," which allowed the parties freedom of action in parliament.[65]

The loss of Upper Silesia, therefore, seriously undermined the Chancellor; yet as Rathenau bitterly commented to Carl Melchior after his own party had vetoed his continuing in office, "The effect of such castration on the enemy is precisely nil."[66] Most significantly, the partition of Upper Silesia undercut the rationale of fulfillment. Since May the government had continually justified fulfillment as a tactic designed to preserve the territorial integrity of the Reich. This argument was far less credible now. No one was yet willing to replace Wirth, but the conditions under which he held office became far more difficult.

At the same time, the Chancellor suffered a further rebuff on the credit question. Negotiations to work the People's Party into the government had been an implicit condition for industrial cooperation in the credit action. With the collapse of the cabinet and the setback for a wider-based ministry, the pivotal Coal Committee (Fachgruppe Bergbau) within the Reichsverband turned against the Hachenberg plan.

Representatives of heavy industry in the Nationalist Party, such as Hugenberg, Reichert, and Jakob Hasslacher of Rheinstahl, were still angry over the Wiesbaden Accords that Rathenau and Loucheur had brought to conclusion in early October. These complex agreements called for German producers to ship up to 7 billion gold marks of goods to French businessmen by May 1926 in lieu of money reparations. Hostile industrialists, however, condemned the terms. France was allowed a maximum of 52 percent of the total reparations due from Germany in any year. If she received excess payment in kind she would have to settle for a lower cash annuity. In negotiating the agreements with Rathenau, therefore, Loucheur had stipulated that only a maximum of 35 percent of German goods, or at most a billion marks' worth, would be counted toward reparation account in any year. The remaining 65 percent would be credited against the reparations due between 1925 and 1934. German critics felt that this amounted to extending credit to French purchasers. They also resented the low prices that could be imposed; for German suppliers could be forced to settle for French inland prices less the 1914 French tariff and transport charges.

[65] Stresemann to Ebert October 25, 1921, in GFM Stresemann Nachlass: 6992 = 225/3093/140620–140621; Albertin, "Die Verantwortlichkeit der liberalen Parteien," pp. 596–601; DDP debates in NSDAP, Hauptarchiv film/f. 726; Erich Dombrowski, "Die Erlösung der Kabinettskrise," BT, October 26, 1921, a.m.

[66] Rathenau to Melchior, October 31, and November 3, 1921, in Max Warburg papers/165a.

On the other hand, until mid-1922 the French importer had to pay his government a new and even higher tariff, which was bound to impede imports. Wiesbaden, in sum, was designed to ease government burdens arising out of reparations: Berlin saved cash payments, Paris was to be spared some reconstruction expenses. But the agreement did not effectively encourage the private transactions designed as a substitute.[67]

At the beginning of November Hugenberg and other right-wing industrialists as well as the Stinnes adherents in the Mining Group agreed to oppose the Reichsverband's credit action. At the association's meetings of November 4 and 5, Paul Silverberg, Hasslacher, and finally Stinnes himself attacked the pledge of credit that the Reichsverband had extended at its Munich convention in September. "The affair," noted Wiedfeldt with bitterness, "was essentially a German Nationalist thrust against the Munich Resolution and against the present composition of the Reichsverband leadership." Reichsverband Chairman Kurt Sorge, who was little more than on loan from Krupp, found himself embarrassed and powerless; indeed, Wiedfeldt advised him to resign his office although not to withdraw from the Presidium. Stinnes, Wiedfeldt thought, was less treacherous than Hugenberg, Reichert, and Hasslacher. While Wiedfeldt, Borsig, and Carl Duisberg of the chemical industry prevented a complete disavowal of the Munich resolution, they could not avoid new conditions being set for the credit action.[68] On November 10, the industrialist association formally hiked its price for helping the government, and asked for rigorous government economies, including denationalization of the German railroad system. The Executive Secretary, Bücher, explained to the press that in a democratic and parliamentary regime, state-owned enterprises could never get out of the red because of political pressure. What the industrialists wanted was an independent corporation in which the state, industry, agrarians, and unions might all have a voice—but one run on business principles.[69]

The railroads, it is true, were probably a wasteful enterprise; Allied reparations experts in 1924 would estimate that one-third of the labor

[67] See Felix, *Walther Rathenau*, pp. 73–78; Weill-Raynal, *Les réparations allemandes*, II, pp. 29–67; discussion in the Reparations Committee of the RWR, November 9, 1921, in DZA, Potsdam: RWR/613, pp. 52 ff. Reichert's hostile critique made at the Reichsverband meeting in Munich in late September was recapitulated in his *Rathenaus Reparationspolitik* (Berlin, 1922). Rathenau's defenses to RWR Reparations Committee on July 27; cf. *Gesammelte Reden*, pp. 211 ff., 230 ff.
[68] Wiedfeldt to Sorge, November 7, 1921, Fr. Krupp, A.G., WA IV 2556 (including extract of Wiedfeldt's own angry speech at Munich). See also Schröder, *Otto Wiedfeldt*, pp. 128–129; Laubach, *Kabinette Wirth*, pp. 120–121; Albertin, "Die Verantwortlichkeit der liberalen Parteien," pp. 607–609.
[69] "Die Bedingungen der Industrie für die Kredithilfe," *BT*, November 11, 1921, p.m.; also article in *BT*, November 6.

force was redundant. Employees had risen 25 percent between 1913 and 1920. Still, there were other causes for the railroad deficit, especially failure to adjust rates to the galloping inflation. By 1920 expenses were almost double income, making the railroad deficit of 16 billion marks about one-fifth the total German budget. The Socialists blamed the deficit on the war, depreciation of the mark, and, ironically, on the eight-hour day. Industrialists claimed that they could both cut freight rates and put the roads in the black. While the real rates were very low in gold-mark terms, the increases that had been decreed in 1920 and 1921 still annoyed business. As Transport Minister, General Groener also reduced the preferential concessions to heavy industry that the railroads had traditionally granted; moreover, the General had already clashed once with businessmen over reasonable rates and profits during the war.[70]

In special sessions of the Socialization Commission called to debate the railroad question in November 1921, it fell to Paul Silverberg once again to orchestrate the industrialists' demands with suitable public-welfare harmonies. Silverberg claimed that modernization and flexibility required private enterprise. Industry would pay the state for denationalization, but only by assuming the present deficit. In planning railroad service, the state administration, Silverberg charged, overlooked variations in intensity of traffic—a hint that business owners would keep the heavily traveled, well-paying lines and shut down the others. Private owners would also differentiate pay more radically according to education and service, perhaps even by eliminating collective contracts. In sum, Silverberg depicted a railroad run on behalf of heavy industry as a step toward "freedom and flexibility" and profitability.[71]

But this was all window dressing. The railroad demand was just the price of compromise between industry's reactionaries and moderates. Most businessmen must have realized that denationalization of the railroads was politically impossible, since it required a two-thirds vote of the Reichstag. Reaction outside the industry was thus bound to be bitter. Georg Bernhard had already criticized industry's niggardly offers and predicted renewed radicalization. Industrialist pettifogging in the Economic Council, he complained, made it impossible for middle-of-the-road members such as himself to oppose "irrational" economic demands of the left any longer. "The issue of seizing real assets

---

[70] On the railroads and SPD criticism: *Gutachten der Sozialisierungskommission über die deutschen Eisenbahnen* (Berlin, 1921); complaints about Groener's price policy, in the Union of Iron and Steel Industrialists, May 6, 1921, BA, Koblenz: R 13 I (VdESI)/165.

[71] *Verhandlungen der Sozialisierungskommission über die Organisation der Reichseisenbahn* (Berlin, 1921), pp. 162–168, 224–230.

will enter a very acute and radical stage at the moment the credit action of German industry can no longer be counted on."[72] The Socialists viewed the railroad demand only as a way of backing out of the credit union. Hilferding accused the businessmen of stabbing the Economic Council in the back:

> I must confess that if I have ever felt deceived it is at this time when I believed in the earnestness of the credit action. . . . What sense is there in the Economic Council if we negotiate for months—the great representatives of industry on one side, the workers on the other . . . —and seek agreement on an economic basis, when, at the very moment agreement seems achieved, part of industry declares "We are not going along," and the rest of industry simply submits?
>
> At the very moment . . . when negotiations are supposed to begin abroad, suddenly come these conditions . . . as if out of fear that one might really get the money from abroad. . . . Instead of imposing any burden on their own assets they want to seize and mortgage the most important possession of the Reich.[73]

For Wirth the industrialists' demands were embarrassing, not because he believed in the loan, but because their brusqueness endangered his improvised diplomacy *vis-à-vis* the Reparations Commission and London. The Chancellor was pursuing a dual policy: preparing to ask the Allies for a reparation reprieve even while he ostensibly sought to raise foreign currency for his next payment. As early as October the francophobe Governor of the Bank of England, Montagu Norman, said that no foreign loans would be forthcoming on the basis of a German industrial pledge. The credit action would thus be fruitless—an argument Stinnes also used. When Norman's own plan for exchanging British, French, and German bonds was rejected by the head of the Federal Reserve Bank in New York, he was just as happy, for it made him "more hopeful for a moratorium."[74] British treasury officials also believed that Germany was in no condition to carry out the London schedule of payments, but deeply resented her fiscal irresponsibility. On November 7, the British delegate to the Reparations Commission, John Bradbury, wrote that he still believed Germany should be able to create an export surplus of 2 billion marks, rising to 3 and even 4

[72] DZA, Potsdam: RWR/6, p. 1262 (November 4, 1921). The unions did renew their request for a 25 percent take-over of stock shares. See the ADGB and Afa-Bund to Wirth, November 21, 1921, in BA, Koblenz: R 43 I/2356.

[73] DZA, Potsdam: RWR/613, pp. 262–272 (Reparations-Ausschuss, November 25).

[74] Norman to Benjamin Strong, quoted in Sir Henry Clay, *Lord Norman* (London, 1957), pp. 198–201; for Stinnes' skepticism see Max Hachenberg, *Lebenserinnerungen eines Rechtsanwalts* (Düsseldorf, 1929), p. 335, cited in Felix, *Walther Rathenau*, p. 96.

billion marks within a decade. But in view of the catastrophic monetary situation, Germany had to be given a moratorium if she agreed to stop the printing presses, balance her budget, and consolidate her debt.[75] Given the ambiguities of British policy, Wirth needed the credit action proposals, if only to diddle London and demonstrate helpless good faith. Industry's arrogant new conditions threatened to alienate moderates abroad—yet they might also emphasize the desperation of Germany's financial situation. At the cabinet meeting of November 14, the Social Democrats expressed anger at the Reichsverband's demands and urged that the government renew its earlier projects for seizing "real values" in order to gain some leverage over industry. Yet all the ministers agreed that even if Berlin scraped together its three-quarter-billion-mark January and February reparations installments, it would face bankruptcy in the spring. The government had to win assurances that all subsequent 1922 cash payments would be excused. By the next day, Wirth had inferred from Bradbury that Germany would indeed win the spring reprieve, but must pay the installments due earlier. For this immediate payment, industry's short-term aid was crucial. The Chancellor had expressed willingness to approach the Reichsverband with a second, more limited credit action scheme. Despite disappointment with industry, "we can conduct no polemic," he insisted. Ebert agreed; moreover, if industry offered credit voluntarily or even under duress, he was prepared to ask coal miners for an extra hour of labor per day. Even when warned that the socialist trade-union federation was restive, Wirth still refused to threaten industry. Reparation demands thus offered the entrepreneurs new political leverage, so that the viability of the coalition depended upon the whim of big business.[76]

But Wirth's new deference toward industry offered slim consolation to the Reparations Commission when it visited Berlin in mid-November. Despite the Reichsverband's original rebuff, Berlin's negotiators talked on November 15 and 16 as if industry were still on the verge of raising 500 million gold marks abroad. On the other hand, they admitted that even a favorable vote of the Reichsverband executive could not bind individual firms; hence the German government could give no assurance that the credit action would materialize.[77] Bradbury was angered. "I do not want to have to grant a moratorium without making

[75] Bradbury to Horne: "What Can Germany Pay during the Next Five Years?" November 7, 1921 in PRO: CAB 27/72, F.C. 75; also CAB 24/131, C.P. 3554.
[76] Cabinet meetings November 14 and 15, 1921, in GFM: ARK, Kabinettsprotokolle, 3438/1675/749901–749914. On union attitude see the discussion of November 21 in the Chancellery, GFM: ARK, Ausführung des Friedensvertrags, 9523H/3679/285824–285827; also ADGB letter, cited above, n. 72.
[77] BA, Koblenz: R 2(Finanzministerium)/3056.

the industrials bleed," he wrote Basil Blackett at the Treasury as he reported on the disappointing sessions.[78]

But moratorium the British felt it must be—even without the winter payments. Rathenau, now serving the government in an unofficial capacity, visited London in early November and by the end of the month returned along with Rudolf Havenstein, the President of the Reichsbank. Their ostensible mission was to discuss raising credits for the Reich; in reality they were soon suing for bankruptcy. During the Cabinet's Finance Committee meeting on December 1, Robert Horne, the Chancellor of the Exchequer, insisted that if Germany were pressed for payment, default would be "inevitable" with "disastrous consequences to all concerned," including London banks that had 5 to 6 million pounds tied up in credits to German importers. In his accompanying memo Horne argued that Germany must be voted a reprieve, even if Britain had to threaten to withdraw from the Reparations Commission to force the support of Belgium and Italy. Five days later, Horne announced that he had urged Rathenau to have his government apply for a moratorium and had requested that Loucheur come to London for preparatory negotiations. Lord Norman, too, encouraged Rathenau to pursue the moratorium and advised Havenstein that he could expect no credits from the Bank of England.[79]

Wirth was not laggard in pursuing the moratorium, and on the cheapest terms possible. Rathenau estimated for Horne that Germany could actually pay 80 million gold marks every month during the course of a two-year moratorium; Wirth cabled that this was far too optimistic. Indeed, even Horne had envisaged two annual cash payments of only 240 million marks to cover occupation expenses. By December 12, Rathenau reported to the cabinet on his London meetings; as he summarized results, "gradually the idea of the moratorium won a foothold." Wirth formally asked the Reparations Commission for a moratorium the very next day.[80] Just as the statement of German finan-

---

[78] Bradbury to Blackett, November 21, 1921, in PRO: CAB 27/72, FC. 76; also FO 371/6038, C22282/2740/18. Cf. the materials in AN, Paris: AJ⁶/522, Gar./513/107A.

[79] Finance Committee meetings of December 1 and 6, 1921: CAB 27/71; cf. Horne memo in CAB 24/131, Nr. 3552. British request for Loucheur in FO 371/6039, C22953/2740/18. See also Walther Rathenau, *Tagebuch 1907–1922*, Hartmut Pogge-von Strandmann, ed. (Düsseldorf, 1967), pp. 263–275; Felix, *Walther Rathenau*, pp. 111 ff.; David Lloyd George, *The Truth about Reparations and War Debts* (New York, 1932), p. 405. For Norman to Havenstein, December 3, see GFM: ARK, 9523H/3679/285834–285835; for the pro-moratorium view that the Germans inferred, see Wirth to the Reichstag on January 26, 1922, VDR: SB, 352, p. 5558. For the moratorium request see AN, Paris: AJ⁶/522, Gar. 513/107/B.

[80] For Rathenau's discussions with Horne and Blackett on German capacity, see Sthamer to Wirth, December 6, 1921, and Wirth to Rathenau, December 8,

cial exhaustion was being won from the Bank of England, the Chancellor came before the Reparations Committee of the Economic Council and pleaded for an end to the bitter debate on the credit proposal. He asked that the Hachenberg motion—or a more recent compromise resolution suggesting both credit action and railway economies—be buried or passed without debate. Wirth hinted that England stood ready to intervene on behalf of Germany if the political scene looked tranquil. A few months earlier the credit action might have been helpful; now it was conspicuously tardy. The new motion was passed, then buried.[81]

More important was prompt action on the tax compromise to impress the Allies with German good will. Wirth asked members of the Economic Council to push their respective political parties toward agreement. A breakdown of the compromise over the inflammatory issue of "seizure of real values" would be disastrous; if, on the other hand, the tax program could be passed, the Chancellor claimed, then "a solution of the whole German question within the obligations of the Versailles Treaty" was possible. Originally acceptance of fulfillment had required a new tax program; now, seven wearying months later, it was clear that a quiet tax compromise was necessary to find the solution outside Germany—in short, to secure revision of reparations whether temporarily or permanently.

The possibility of revision became more enticing when Briand and Lloyd George met at London in December and then at Cannes in early January. Nonetheless, the Germans failed to secure as much from aligning the British with them as Rathenau had hoped. France and England did agree to some temporary revisions at London: the 500 million marks due on January 15, 1922, could be paid in quarterly installments stretched out to mid-April and would be the only cash required for reparations during 1922. As a prerequisite for the postponement, the Reparations Commission questioned Berlin about her plans for fiscal reform. A satisfactory German answer would have meant accepting a tax commitment more rigorous than provided by Wirth's program. Hence, Rathenau and Wirth waited for Lloyd George and Briand to meet again at Cannes to pressure the Reparations Commission into granting its moratorium without preconditions. By the date of Cannes, however, Briand faced more opposition in Paris. To appear tough, the Allies performed a sleight-of-hand that raised their 1922 cash requirement for reparation from 500 to 720 million gold

---

GFM: ARK, 9523H/3679/285878–285882; Rathenau's report to the ministers on December 12, *ibid.*, 285999–286003.

[81] DZA, Potsdam: RWR/613, pp. 400–408 (Reparations-Ausschuss, December 13). See, too, Wirth's speech to the Berlin press corps on December 4 in *Reden*, pp. 225 ff.

marks.[82] By conciliatory speeches Rathenau sought to restore the 500 million figure, but with Briand's resignation on January 14 the whole question had to be postponed until the great parley planned for Genoa in April. Meanwhile, under English pressure, the Reparations Commission adopted the Allies' agreement and provisionally suspended the initial January 15 deadline in return for a German stabilization plan and the payment of 31 million marks in foreign currency every ten days until the fixing of a new deadline. In short, Germany squeezed past January 15, but still needed to complete a tax and stabilization program to win a definitive moratorium for 1922.

Under this pressure the difficult interparty negotiations resumed in Berlin, no longer to enlarge the coalition but to secure simultaneous Social Democratic and DVP support for the tax legislation. The necessary compromises were hammered out between January 18 and 26. The Socialists had to drop the projected tax on postwar increases of wealth; they further had to accept a 3 percent rather than 4 percent maximum rate on the new property tax, and had to consent to a method of assessing landed capital that yielded lower values than they had sought. Collection of the Reich Emergency Levy, the cornerstone of the Erzberger reform, was accelerated, but not by as much as the SPD wanted. Originally scheduled to allow payment over thirty years, the Levy was now to be drawn in more quickly to compensate for the fall of the mark. One-third of each taxpayer's total obligation had been asked by legislation in 1920; the Socialists now sought two-thirds but had to settle for two-fifths. What the SPD felt it was extracting from the compromise was the promise of a forced loan that would supposedly raise about a billion gold marks and not just a pile of paper marks. The concept of a forced loan, in fact, was the political surrogate for the preceding summer's demand of "seizure of capital values." Like earlier SPD schemes, it too proved illusory.[83]

[82] For the London negotiation see DBFP, first series, vol. xv, pp. 760–805; the moratorium agreements are in Weill-Raynal, *Les réparations allemandes*, ii, pp. 95 ff., 114. For the German government's reaction to London—that it was a victory but still impossible—see the December 26 discussion in GFM: ARK, 9523H/3679/286008–286015. The Allies at London had in fact asked for 720 billion marks, but of this sum 220 billion were for army costs. At Cannes, army costs were included in an overall bill; moreover, it was stipulated that they could be covered by deliveries in kind, of which the total for 1922 were now lowered to 1450 million gold marks. Hence, Germany won a further reduction, although it was once again disguised by brandishing figures that were not truly comparable.

[83] On the stipulations see Felix Pinner, "Das Kompromiss," *BT*, January 26, 1922, p.m. The assessment victory was important for conservatives: because of inflation, the price of land and real estate was higher than normal yields would have determined. The SPD wanted assessment according to the high market prices; the DVP held out for decision by the Reichstag, where assessment on the basis of yield or twenty times annual revenue would prevail. Cf. Laubach, *Kabinette Wirth*, pp. 145–148.

Wirth's position seemed to be strengthened by the provisional agreement, and he was helped further by the return of the Democrats as full participants in the important Interparty Committee that coordinated the coalition. What, however, would be the final attitude of the DVP? Stresemann was ill during the major parliamentary debate over the compromise proposals. Becker defended the DVP's participation in the compromise, and a Communist motion against the cabinet was defeated by the four parties to the compromise along with the Bavarian Catholics. Independent Socialists abstained, and the DNVP left the Chamber rather than make the unpleasant choice between approving the government or seconding a Communist motion.[84]

But the danger of a new crisis did not dissipate. Shortly after the Reichstag debate a strike of state railroad officials and Wirth's appointment of Rathenau as his Foreign Minister threatened the crucial cooperation of the People's Party. The strike of public employees angered conservatives, who vented their rage against the supposed weakness of republican government. The inflammatory issue made it hard for the moderate Volkspartei leaders to keep their group in line. Within the cabinet, too, Andreas Hermes, the moderate Centrist Minister of Finance, and even Bauer, the conservative Social Democratic Vice Chancellor, objected to Wirth's efforts to negotiate with the railroad officials union via SPD intermediaries. Wirth finally won his ministers' approval for discussions, not with the striking unions themselves, but with their individual officials, who sat in the more general representative delegations of railroad employees. This legalistic compromise allowed a settlement after a week, but appeared as craven appeasement in conservative eyes.[85]

Critical of the policy of handling the strike, the DVP was also offended by Wirth's elevation of Rathenau to the Wilhelmsstrasse and threatened to abandon the tax compromise. The People's Party would have accepted Rathenau's appointment willingly only as part of a general cabinet shuffle that brought themselves in as well and preferably removed General Groener.[86] Despite the quarrel, the DVP did agree to cooperate further on the tax program, but negotiations for a Great Coalition were adjourned. As the next months revealed, the upshot was continuing parliamentary equivocation. In the bitter Reichstag discussion of the railroad strike, the DVP condemned Wirth's settlement.

[84] VDR: SB, 352, pp. 5577–5622 (January 26–27, 1922); BT, January 28, 1922.
[85] GFM: ARK, Kabinettsprotokolle, February 5, 1922, 3491/1742/750610–750617, 750622–750623.
[86] Albertin, "Die Verantwortlichkeit der liberalen Parteien," pp. 618–623; BA, Koblenz: R 43 I/1028 (Interfraktioneller Ausschuss, February 10, 1922) for DVP attitude; cf., too, Becker's speech: VDR: SB, 352, pp. 5593 ff.; and press reactions in Laubach, Kabinette Wirth, pp. 151–152.

Wirth, on the other hand, demanded a positive vote of confidence to reconsolidate his position. During the days before the vote the issue remained in genuine suspense. The three coalition parties had only 220 deputies, the potential opposition 222; but there turned out to be sufficient abstentions from Independent Socialists and Bavarians to give the government a 220–185 victory. Moreover, the Volkspartei did lend its critical support again to the government when the tax bills were finally worked out between March 8 and 10 and in further Reichstag debate on March 16. Nonetheless, Wirth had achieved a durable collaboration neither with industry nor with the party accepted as industry's representation in the Reichstag.[87]

What was the overall record of these nine months for the Centrist Chancellor? It was a mixed achievement. Wirth had set out to rule with the Weimar coalition but simultaneously win over the industrialist community and their DVP delegates. The Democratic Party, above all, sought this compromise alignment. From the outset, therefore, government policy acknowledged that without the cooperation of business and industry the German state could harness no economic resources for public purposes. The inclination of moderate business leaders such as Raumer, and moderate politicians such as Stresemann, was to cooperate with Wirth and to transform a left bloc into one they termed a bloc of the middle. But their cooperation was always hedged for two reasons: first because heavy industry found its interests moving it toward the far-right German Nationalists and acceptance of continuing inflation; second because unforeseen crises inflamed nationalist reactions even among rank-and-file adherents of the "liberal" parties. The emergency legislation of republican defense instituted in the wake of the assassination of Erzberger almost shattered DVP collaboration. The partition of Upper Silesia reopened the divisions that Wirth and Stresemann had hoped to keep closed. The railroad strike once again precluded a bloc of the center and polarized left and right. The murder of Rathenau in June 1922 finally helped make the gap unbridgeable for Wirth.

Because he stood firmly for combating the far right when Erzberger and later Rathenau were slain, Wirth earned a reputation as an exemplary and democratic Chancellor. Yet this was unfortunately a democratic stance that bore little fruit in shaping German social or political institutions. The major problem before the Reich was the financial one, and Wirth always felt he had to take account of the given economic forces—namely the industrialists. Labor was appeased

[87] VDR: SB, 352, pp. 5738 ff. (February 9, 1922); pp. 5749–5788 (February 10); pp. 5789–5824 (February 11); pp. 5867–5877 (vote of February 16, 1922); 353, pp. 6297 ff. (March 16–18, 1922). Also BT, February 16, 1922.

by the government's allowing certain nominal tax burdens to be imposed on capital; but it was industry that won the real concessions, that frustrated any tapping of corporate wealth, that mounted its own offensive for transforming the railroads and thus evaded even the voluntary pledge of credit it had earlier offered. There was a basic conflict between Wirth's heroic public defense of democratic institutions and his weary acquiescence before the sources of economic power and conservatism. "A promise made by Wirth does not amount to anything," the British member of the Reparations Commission's Committee of Guarantees summed up in November 1921. "True, he has an abundance of *bonne volonté*, but he has no backing and is utterly powerless."[88]

Despite the fact that the Wirth ministry included Social Democrats, the forces of economic conservatism were stronger than under Fehrenbach. Then, industry had had to conduct a defense against renewed socialization attempts—attempts precipitated (as they realized) by the stupidity of the extreme right and the Kapp Putsch, which had infuriated the labor unions. By late 1921, however, Paul Silverberg was employing his gifts of advocacy, not to defend the coal *status quo*, but to dismantle the only "socialist" institution Germany did possess. No matter how seriously the railroad denationalization attempt was intended, it pressed home·that industry had to be appeased. The reparation dilemma, in short, gave big business greater influence than it already possessed. Could the cooperation of industry be won on tolerable terms for the democratic state? Even if Wirth's government was willing to make concessions in economic affairs, incidents of political violence or a new show of French firmness could easily undo the precarious domestic compromises and drive industry's political delegates into opposition. The government, including its Social Democratic members, was indeed willing to sacrifice economic radicalism for economic compromise; yet finally the compromises entailed a begging out of reparation obligations that the Allies had to reject.

The Bankruptcy of Moderation (1922)

Unfortunately for themselves, Briand and Wirth were hostage to each other's moderation on reparations. At the same time each man's domestic position required firmness enough to keep the votes of the political center. This condemned both leaders to an exhausting oscillation between nationalist gestures and piecemeal negotiations. Ulti-

[88] Finlayson to Kemball Cook, included by John Bradbury to Robert Horne in Cabinet Finance Committee memoranda CAB 27/72, FC. 75.

mately it doomed both ministries to paralysis and collapse. Briand fell in January 1922; Wirth limped along until November, but stalemated and ineffective after the death of Rathenau, if not earlier. From December 1921, when the Germans requested a reparations moratorium, to the slaying of Rathenau little more than half a year later, both countries had to face up to the painful frustration of fulfillment.

Although Berlin had at last made an initial reparation payment by September 1921, according to interallied agreement France enjoyed none of the first billion marks, which were allocated for Belgium and then flowed to London to settle war debts. French conservatives and moderates were naturally uneasy about the future of reparations; and by the autumn of 1921 they were also upset about the Briand ministry's apparent rapprochement with a reemerging left. Radicals and Socialists generally approved Briand's policy of "trust in Wirth," and *bien pensants* worried that the two parties might cooperate in domestic politics such as the Paris by-elections scheduled for October. The government was weakened, too, by the whispers of scandal that surrounded the subsidies to the Banque Industrielle de Chine—a back-room affair in which Philippe Berthelot at the Quai d'Orsay had apparently used his official influence to save the overextended establishment with which his brother was connected. The political discontent of the right came into the open with the October parliamentary debates. On the eve of the autumn legislative session, Briand had delivered a major address at Saint-Nazaire. With his usual rhetoric he called for extending *"apaisement"* from the old religious issue to the international arena. The speech upset the adherents of the Bloc National, and Clémenciste deputy Georges Mandel complained of "this atmosphere of confusion, equivocation into which we are plunged, thickened by the words of Saint-Nazaire." When Alexandre Varenne of the SFIO moved to justify Briand, Mandel asked who had been defeated in the elections of November 16, 1919: "The majority, M. President of the Council, where is it? What do you mean by the majority? Where does it begin? Where does it end? . . . Is it among the victors or the vanquished of November 16 that you will seek the majority?"[89]

Briand dodged the question. His interpretation of November 16, he said, was that it meant a vote for peace, internally and externally. Peace could not be won by mere gestures of firmness, it required patience. And if the right was to call for "definition," then the largest group that had issued from the elections, the conservative Entente Républicaine, must define its own politics and renounce "reaction." The attack alienated the right, and in the subsequent balloting the 180-

[89] JOC, 1921, pp. 3585, 3590–3591 (October 19); Suarez, *Briand*, v, pp. 211 ff.

strong Entente Républicaine as well as the Independents of the far right voted against the government, while the Socialists abstained rather than vote with the opposition.[90]

The break with the Entente Républicaine appropriately reflected the underlying financial dilemma—the harsh choice between reparation or growing inflation. Keynes had written that Germany would default in 1922. Parmentier tended to agree, and political circles were worried too. "Will the payments really take place?" asked a commentator in the well-informed *Revue Politique et Parlementaire*. "In this regard—one cannot dissimulate—troubling skepticism has reigned for some time, both in France and abroad."[91] Although the 1922 "ordinary" budget would theoretically be in balance, the government was spending 7 billion francs in "recoverable expenses" for reconstruction—loans allegedly to be covered by future German payments. In the face of the sustained deficits, a regrouping on financial policy was also occurring. The financially sophisticated men of the center were discounting reparations and beginning to think about the unthinkable, living with inflation. Maurice Bokanowski, Rapporteur of the Chamber's Finance Commission and a middle-of-the-road member of the Bloc National, along with banker Robert Wolff, advocated a monetary policy to prevent the franc from rising above its present level of thirteen to the dollar. Revaluation to the prewar value of five to the dollar, they argued, would make debt charges and pensions a crushing deflationary burden. To be sure, the conventional wisdom still dominated political sloganeering. Raphael Georges-Lévy of the Senate insisted that full revaluation need not constrict credit and business: even if the number of banknotes diminished, their "velocity" or turnover would supposedly rise, and so would tax receipts to cover the heavier debt burden. Devaluation, whether legal or *de facto*, was "the solution of weak nations," revaluation, "that of courageous peoples, jealous of hard-won rights. Between the two France cannot hesitate. The franc of tomorrow will be that of the year XI."[92]

Those who still adhered to this orthodoxy feared that Briand himself might come dangerously under the sway of inflationist thinking. At Saint-Nazaire he had noted that the countries with high exchange rates suffered under an export handicap, while those like Germany with a slipping currency enjoyed an advantage on the world market. Indeed Briand was being pushed toward inflationist ideas. The French

[90] JOC, 1921, p. 3625 (October 31).

[91] Frédéric Jenny, "La situation financière et le budget de 1922," *RPP*, CIX, October 1921, p. 18.

[92] Raphael Georges-Lévy, "La stabilisation du franc," *RPP*, CIX, November 1921, p. 167; summary of Bokanowski-Wolff argument, *ibid.*, pp. 155 ff.

debt seemed bound to grow unless Germany paid her annuities, but Parmentier, at the Ministry of Finances, repeatedly warned that this was unrealistic.[93] Moreover, as the French delegate on the Committee of Guarantees indicated, France might be embarrassingly isolated in that international agency if Germany requested a moratorium and France refused.[94] Faced with the intractability of the reparation problem, Loucheur and Briand suggested the acquisition of German industrial shares and the cancellation of interallied war debts as ways out of their dilemma. But German industry was no more willing to give stock to the French government than to Berlin, and England steadfastly opposed any idea of France's pressuring the Reich into stock cessions. Loucheur renewed his earlier proposals on November 9 and December 8, asking first for 30 percent, then 20 percent of German industrial shares. By this time London authorities were primarily interested in helping Berlin lay the groundwork for a moratorium. Finally, of course, Washington's reluctance to consider an open write-off of the European debt made the prospects for French finances even gloomier.[95]

But facing up to the consequences of financial realities—whether this meant relying on reparation in kind, curtailment of government-financed reconstruction, or more extensive taxation—was still excluded politically. Why should France, the Bloc National would ask, impose on herself the austerity that defeated Germany refused to adopt? The solution for most *bien pensant* commentators was simply more pressure. "In a little while once again we are going to find ourselves at the crossing of the ways," Poincaré wrote in mid-November. "We will have to choose between a path which by renewing concessions would lead to the ruin of France and one, which by measures of firmness, leads to the necessary guarantees." Poincaré was bitter about Briand's policy of gestures. "We bestowed on Wirth," he wrote in reference to Briand's "confidence-in-Wirth" speech, "dithyrambic eulogies . . . and we re-

[93] Parmentier Notes for the Minister of Finance, February 18, September 8, and December 3, 1921 in Min. Fin. F^{30}/2275.

[94] Mauclère report of October 30, 1921, in Min. Fin. F^{30}/1360. The Committee of Guarantees convened in Berlin from September 23 to October 14, 1921, to hear German explanations of how difficult it had proved to transfer the first billion marks in reparation. The Committee's report to the Reparations Commission reflected their belief that German monetary woes were largely self-inflicted, yet still necessitated some modification of the upcoming payments. See AN, Paris: AJ^6 (Comité International des Réparations)/550 for hearings and report. Also FO 408/6, nr. 37, Enclosure 1.

[95] Hoover Institution: Loucheur Papers/5 f. 11: "La politique de réparations du gouvernement français au cours de l'année 1921," also f. 6: Note of November 30, 1921, and the memorandum, "Conversation avec M. Basil Blackett aux Chequers le 8 decembre 1921." Cf. Weill-Raynal, *Les réparations allemandes*, II, pp. 105–106.

served our severity and irony for those Frenchmen who were not blinded by official illusions."[96]

Faced with the breakdown of reparations, Briand sought to couple the question of annuities with the more general problem of French security. But here, too, he had little success. At the opening of the Washington disarmament conference in November, Briand faced Anglo-American criticism of French military pretensions. He defended the army from limitation, fought to exempt submarines from restrictions, but had to accept a third-rate status for the French surface fleet. Returning from Washington, Briand told the Senate on December 6 that he sensed "a certain malaise" in the country. "It has been said that the French government is being pulled in tow."[97] The Chequers meeting of December 8, the London Conference of December 18–22, and the Cannes conference in early January 1922 all mobilized this malaise against the ministry. Critics felt that the British connection was only hobbling French policy. At London on December 21, Briand followed up earlier approaches and presented Lloyd George the outlines for a Franco-British alliance. The Prime Minister was willing to offer Briand a guarantee pact against a direct attack upon France, but would specify no support if France needed to assist her own allies in Eastern Europe, where the populations were "unstable and excitable" and "might start fighting at any time."[98] Briand required a treaty that would enable France to oppose any major violation of the Versailles territorial settlement and not merely protect her against a less likely direct and unprovoked attack. Lloyd George also urged upon Briand his plan for a European economic conference to which Russia would be invited. Opening up the Soviets to Western trade, the Prime Minister explained, would help Germany establish a positive balance of trade, and up to half her proceeds from Soviet investments could be allocated to reparations. Seydoux was sympathetic: unless the Allies acted, he told Millerand, Stinnes seemed prepared to organize a great con-

[96] "Chronique de la Quinzaine," *RDM*, December 15, 1921, p. 473, and *RDM*, December 1, 1921, p. 712.
[97] JOS, 1920, p. 2041.
[98] Briand-Lloyd George conversation, December 21, 1921, in DBFP, first series, vol. xv, p. 786. The French Ambassador had broached the pact on December 5 and 14; see Min. Aff. Etr.: Europe 1918–1929, Grande Bretagne/69 (Pacte de Sécurité), Saint-Aulaire to Briand, December 14, 1921, and the French notes of the December 21 conference, pp. 28–43. On January 12, however, Premier-Designate Poincaré told the Prime Minister that the value of any pact without a military convention was "illusory" (PRO: CAB 24/132, C.P. 3612) and by the January 18 cabinet meeting the British were shelving the project (PRO: CAB 23/27, 2). Material also in Bibliothèque Nationale: Fonds Millerand, Carton: 1921–1922, Conférence de Cannes; Conversations de Londres; f. Conférence de Cannes, sf. 19; Comte de Saint-Aulaire, *Confessions d'un vieux diplomate* (Paris, 1953), pp. 584–592.

sortium that would give German industry an exclusive foothold, especially over Soviet railroads.[99]

Lloyd George pressed the French hardest on reparations. In the wake of his London and Chequers conversations from December 8 to 10, Loucheur returned to England on the eighteenth with a new reparations scheme, which would diminish German obligations up to 1928, but would entitle France to the major share among the allies on the grounds of her actual devastation. Payments would be made from the proceeds of a large international loan on which Germany would pay interest and amortization. In return for the lighter burden up to 1928, Germany would offer such guarantees as customs duties collected on a gold basis, the end of paper-money issues, better control of foreign-currency transactions and—a long-term demand of Loucheur—the pawning of a quarter of German industry's equity.[100] All in all, this so-called Chequers Plan reversed the advantages that Britain had wrested at Versailles and Spa. The British would get their reparations and collect their debt from France only from the preponderant share of a second series of loans to be consigned to the vague future. What inducement was there for London to agree—short of avoiding a complete European economic breakdown? Lloyd George argued successfully that the Chequers Plan would be feasible only if the United States were prepared to remit Britain's war debts, so that London in turn might lower her demands on Europe. With a great trade-off of debts and reparations excluded, the Prime Minister urged instead an immediate moratorium. In return Great Britain would accept the validity of the Wiesbaden accords and, to appease Brussels, would postpone demands for the large Belgian war debt installment to London. The Germans must promise budgetary retrenchment, undertake financial reforms, and draw upon the Reichsbank's gold reserves to help pay the 500 million gold marks in cash that would be demanded for reparations. Loucheur accepted the British proposals with alacrity, but found Lloyd George and his advisers reluctant to dictate effective control measures for Berlin's fiscal reforms. Briand and Lloyd George, how-

[99] See Lloyd George-Briand conversations, December 19 and 21, p.m., in Bibliothèque Nationale: Fonds Millerand, *ibid.*, and DBFP, first series, vol. xv, pp. 764–765, 782–785. Cf. "Note Seydoux: Reconstitution Économique de l'Europe," undated but presumably January 1922, in Fonds Millerand, *ibid.*, sf. "Soviets." For the negotiations over the new consortium see DBFP, first series, vol. xv, pp. 806–835 and PRO: CAB 31/11: Genoa Conference: Preliminary Negotiations, pp. 100 ff. The concept remained vaporous. Seydoux, who repeated his warnings about Stinnes' Russian plans at Genoa (CAB 31/5, S.G. 15), may have been alarmist.

[100] For the "Chequers Plan," drafted by Avenol, see Hoover Institution: Louis Loucheur papers/5, f. 6a; earlier conversations of December 8–10, *ibid.*, and in Louis Loucheur, *Carnets Secrets 1908–1932* (Brussels, 1962), pp. 185–188. Details of plan in Weill-Raynal, *Les réparations allemandes*, II, pp. 87–95.

ever, agreed to postpone the disputed issues until the Reparations Commission had talked with Germany's delegates and the Allied prime ministers reassembled at Cannes after the New Year. Experts prepared a draft of the moratorium agreement for ratification at Cannes: it was to be the last major interallied agreement until the Dawes plan.[101]

While pleading for effective Allied supervision of German finances, Briand had told Lloyd George that London could not understand the "state of public opinion" in France. From Paris's viewpoint, Germany was profiting from a wanton ruining of her finances. British observers indeed confirmed the diagnosis, but despaired of imposing the necessary remedies. Briand went to the January negotiations with conservative observers harshly critical of his diplomacy. Millerand feared that recognition of the Soviets would follow from Lloyd George's demand for a European economic conference; he also worried that Briand was about to settle for a booby-trapped security pact. Poincaré predicted disaster once again, and there were even reports that Briand was annoyed at Loucheur for having settled for too great a reparation concession at London.[102] Behind the scenes Seydoux suggested working Germany into a reciprocal security pact—as the Locarno treaties would provide—in return for Berlin's acceptance of the monetary and budget reforms stipulated at London. These arrangements would have to be carried out in cautious stages so that French nationalist opinion would not be alarmed. But the result would be to make French security demands less menacing to the Germans and less open-ended for the British.[103] At the same time, linking the security with the economic issue would impel the Germans to put their finances in order as a prerequisite for an international reparation settlement. Seydoux's effort to resolve the two Franco-German dilemmas jointly proved too far-ranging. Instead, Briand fought at Cannes to recover some of the concessions provisionally consented to at London, while Lloyd George pressed him on the general economic conference with the Soviets, Millerand badgered him with wires of alarm, and Rathenau, who was present unofficially, pleaded bankruptcy. Repeatedly Millerand insisted that the Soviets could be invited to the planned European economic conference only if they accepted the prior commitments of the Tsarist government, including its foreign debts. (Briand argued that Millerand himself had

[101] Conversation of December 19, 1921, a.m., DBFP, first series, vol. xv, pp. 761–762, and December 20, noon, pp. 768–772. For the final London proposals see pp. 800–802.
[102] See Millerand to Briand, December 21, 1921, in Bibliothèque Nationale: Fonds Millerand: Conférence de Cannes . . . , sf. "Soviets." For rumor of Briand-Loucheur dissension, see article by Quenne, January 7, 1922, citing Dernière heure. Brussels, Fonds Millerand, ibid.
[103] Penciled Seydoux note: "Alliance," December 26, 1921, in ibid., f.: Conférence de Cannes, sf., "Conversations de Londres."

formerly agreed that such demands would become operative only if Soviet leaders asked for prior diplomatic recognition as a condition for their participation.)[104]

Concerning the reparation issue, Briand wired Millerand on January 9 that "we are doing here everything in our power and have done everything humanly possible to safeguard French interests in the present situation."[105] Belgian, Italian, and British experts, however, viewed a moratorium as necessary; and a majority vote in the Reparations Commission was sufficient to grant one. If France consented, London would cede Paris 140 million marks of her 1922 payments and a more advantageous calculation of reparations in coal—otherwise, nothing. Briand asked Millerand to seek the opinion of the Council of Ministers in Paris and warned that he could not take responsibility for a rupture with the Allies. But Millerand, with the blessing of Briand's own Finance Minister, Doumer, dominated the Council meetings of January 10. The Ministry, reported Millerand, was dismayed that Briand seemed ready to accept a delay in payments without justification or guarantees.[106] Briand requested another council session for the eleventh and asked simply whether or not he was to break with the Allies. He telephoned on the morning of the eleventh to report that the Allies would ask Berlin to pay a billion gold marks in 1922. Millerand still insisted that the Council would reject a moratorium without guarantees, including deadlines for sanctions.[107]

It was evident that Briand had no room for negotiation without directly challenging Millerand before the Chamber. But this seemed excluded: Léon Daudet's threatening motion to summon a parliamentary session to discuss the conference already underway was rejected by only a small margin. Poincaré convoked his Senate Commission on Foreign Affairs, which added its own admonitory wires to those of the President. Briand asked for a further meeting of the Council and returned to Paris. There he found that the President's wires had been leaked to *Le Matin*—presumably by Barthou. With Briand present to argue his own case and inhibit intriguing, the cabinet united behind his

[104] Peretti de la Rocca (cabling Millerand draft) to Briand, January 7, 1922 (nrs. 8 and 9). Briand's response of January 8, and Millerand's telegram of the same day, via Peretti (nrs. 21–22–23–24), *ibid.*, f.: Conférence de Cannes, sf. "Soviets." The file is published by Suarez, *Briand*, v, pp. 362 ff. For the dispute cf. Alexandre Millerand, "Mes Mémoires Politiques," MS, and Raoul Persil, *Alexandre Millerand* (Paris, 1949), pp. 141–145.

[105] Briand to Millerand, January 9, 1922 (nr. 25), Fonds Millerand, *ibid.*; Suarez, *Briand*, v, pp. 382–383.

[106] Millerand to Briand, January 10, 1922 (nrs. 37–41), *ibid.*

[107] Briand to Millerand, January 10, 1922, 6:00 and 10:35 p.m. (nrs. 28 and 30), also report of telephone call, *ibid.* Millerand summary of Conseil des Ministres, January 11, 1922, to Briand at 12:20 p.m.

conduct of negotiations. But before submitting to a parliamentary vote, Briand denounced Presidential sniping and the failure to support his efforts, then announced his resignation to the Chamber.[108]

Briand's policy did have dangers. If the Germans continued to be more stubborn than the French, Lloyd George would persist in pressuring Paris for concessions rather than Berlin. Rathenau himself told Wirth's major officials that with one further moratorium (after 1922) the London schedule of payments would be effectively abandoned.[109] But was there a real alternative to the unavowed revisionism that Briand and Loucheur accepted? Briand's critics were not to have a better record: Millerand had already begun the process of reparations revision at Boulogne and Spa, while Poincaré himself would have to accept a new schedule of annuities. Unless French policy makers were prepared to break with England, face interallied debt demands, and watch their own franc depreciate, there was little effective choice but concession. Loucheur gambled on interindustry exchanges and reparations in kind: capitalist entente would supersede international coercion. This gamble, though, had its own illusory aspects: German heavy industry did not yet see advantages to the collaboration, while French industry's protectionist impulse precluded its full exploitation at home. Still, Loucheur and Briand (and Lloyd George) were groping toward a policy of trade expansion that might eventually have put reparations into a less poisoned atmosphere. As of early 1922, however, a policy of capitalist détente still appeared too insubstantial for French conservatives.

Although he might have been able to rescue a narrow vote of confidence in January 1922—the SFIO and the Communists would have abstained, most Radicals would have supported him, the center would have fragmented—Briand had no stable majority on which to elaborate his further policy. For the sake of a future comeback he might wish "to fall to the left,"[110] but given the electoral returns of 1919 he still could not durably govern on the basis of a left-center coalition. The growing tensions between the momentum of cabinet policies and the sentiments of the majority meant that the government had to go to someone who could win back the right and hold the center. Poincaré was the logical candidate, for he apparently promised firmness on reparation. Nevertheless, Poincaré too would vacillate almost a year before deciding to enforce sanctions unilaterally. It had been suggested in the British

[108] Daudet's motion of January 10, in JOC, 1922, I, pp. 2–3; Briand's speech to the Chamber, January 12, 1922, *ibid.*, pp. 18–22; see Suarez, *Briand*, v, pp. 390–406, for a pro-Briand version of events culminating in his resignation.

[109] Reichskanzlei discussion of December 26, 1921: GFM: ARK, Ausführung des Friedensvertrags, 9523H/3679/286008–286015.

[110] L. Marcellin, *Politique et politiciens d'après guerre* (Paris, 1923), p. 318.

cabinet that if Poincaré displaced Briand, he might actually negotiate a more satisfactory reparations arrangement. This was a false calculation, however. Poincaré was more demanding and less supple than his predecessor, as Lloyd George discovered in their first painful interview concerning the security pact on January 12.[111] The Prime Minister and the new French Premier were skilled at mutual provocation. At Boulogne on February 25, Poincaré even suggested that Great Britain had not assisted France efficiently in the summer of 1914. He refused to guarantee his personal attendance at the conclave of prime ministers in Genoa; he would not permit French participation if reparations were scheduled for discussion; and he resented English imputations that France was becoming chauvinistic and militaristic when she wanted no more than enforcement of the peace treaty. Lloyd George at least won Poincaré's grudging assent that if the question of reparations arose in connection with discussions of European economic conditions, it need not be ruled out of order. This was less than he and the Germans hoped, but still gave some scope for negotiating the definitive moratorium and preparing a small loan. Meanwhile, the Prime Minister warned, France and England stood on the verge of the greatest rupture since Fashoda. The two nations were indeed entering a period of *entente déplorable*, founded on a real conflict of interest. Britain wanted relations with Russia resumed and Germany appeased, which meant in effect that Germany's industrialists be appeased and the DVP enter the government coalition. No French minister had the parliamentary leeway for this program—certainly not Poincaré, who had finally come to power by constantly criticizing this slow postwar trend. But deciding to act independently did not necessarily assure the success of independent action. Poincaré was to discover that the possibilities for firmness were as limited as those of appeasement.[112]

At the same time that Briand capitulated to nationalist moods in Paris, Wirth had to confront similar pressures. The next chapter in the tax laws revealed the stress. Even as the Reichstag was finishing debate upon the legislation during latter March, the Reparations Commission responded to Berlin's December demand for a moratorium with the condition that for final approval of 1922's reparation relief by May 31, the Germans must impose 60 billion paper marks in additional taxes.[113]

[111] Predictions on Poincaré in Cabinet conclusions, December 16, 1921: PRO: CAB 23/27, 2; for Poincaré-Lloyd George discussion in Paris, January 12, 1922, see CAB 24/132, C.P. 3612.

[112] For the Boulogne meeting see CAB 31/11: Genoa Conference: Preliminary Negotiations, pp. 172–179.

[113] The status of the 1922 moratorium remained complicated. As noted above, on January 13 the Reparations Commission had asked Germany to pay 31 million

To rebuild the tax compromise in its last stages was politically impossible; but the legislation now seemed insufficient to extract the moratorium that had been its primary if unavowed objective since December. In the eyes of the German cabinet, the note threatened not only to torpedo the tax compromise, but to trigger a nationalist backlash that would preclude even limited fulfillment. At the cabinet discussion of March 24, Wirth observed that no democratic government could evade the national demand for a firm reply. Rejection of the new conditions would strengthen support for the cabinet among the DVP, Center, and Democrats, and it would not alienate the Socialists either. Rathenau hoped that a firm German response would make London more heedful of the Reich's financial peril. (In fact, over the past months British experts had become increasingly offended by Berlin's frivolous budgetary approach.) While Wirth still wanted to stress his commitment to fulfillment, Rathenau explained that fulfillment had never been an end in itself; it did not mean continuous and unconditional "Yes." It had saved the Ruhr, but now Germany had to take the risk of a "No." Ebert did not dissent. He pointed out that the Democrats in the cabinet were strongly under the influence of Stresemann's party, and both Democratic and People's Party cooperation had to be preserved by a speech with strong nationalist undertones.[114]

By its firmness the government secured initial unanimity within its own ranks and among the bourgeois parties. The DVP and Bavarian Catholics (Bavarian People's Party—BVP) joined with the coalition to approve the "No" to the allied tax demands on March 28. The Reparations Commission was offended, and Wirth's basic dilemma of being ransomed to the Allies as well as domestic opinion made the move a risky one. The opening of the Genoa Conference, however, precluded any immediate Allied reprisal. Throughout the spring the government would alternate dosages of nationalist rhetoric with promises of ful-

---

gold marks every ten days while working out fiscal reforms. With its note of March 21, the Commission set 1922 payments at 720 million marks—as envisaged by Lloyd George and Briand in December—but said the moratorium would be confirmed only at the end of May. If Germany had not undertaken fiscal reforms— including 60 billion paper marks in taxes above and beyond the tax compromise— she could lose her moratorium, be found in default, and liable to sanctions. On questioning from Berlin, the Commission admitted that an internal loan was a satisfactory way in theory to raise the 60 billion marks, but reaffirmed the need for taxation. See GFM: ARK, Ausführung des Friedensvertrags, 9523H/3682/ 286232–286246 for the note of March 21; *ibid.*, 286203–286209, for the Chefbesprechung of March 23; and *ibid.*, 286535–286538 for the further Repco note of April 13. Also Bergmann, *The History of Reparations*, pp. 113–121; Laubach, *Kabinette Wirth*, pp. 157–164; Weill-Raynal, *Les réparations allemandes*, II, pp. 149 ff.

[114] GFM: ARK, Kabinettsprotokolle, 3491/1741/751309–751312; cf. Wirth's speech VDR: SB, 353, p. 6613 (March 28); 354, pp. 6651–6657.

fillment, letting Bergmann and Andreas Hermes—the Center Party Finance Minister who maintained good relations with German industry and agriculture—speak to the Allies in tones of earnest cooperation while Wirth and even Rathenau addressed a domestic audience in the rhetoric of independence.[115]

Berlin still had some chance for a respite before the end of May, when the Reparations Commission would survey German fiscal progress and recommend final action on a moratorium. There were two emerging opportunities for German reparation diplomacy: one was the upcoming Genoa Conference; the other involved the financial experts whom the Reparations Commission announced it would summon to consider the conditions for an international loan to Germany. The two arenas were linked: by early 1922 it was clear, as Robert Horne proposed, that if Germany were to make any international payments it must be by channeling the proceeds of an international loan from Anglo-American and French banks to the French and British governments. Yet it was unlikely that bankers and financial experts would recommend such a loan unless they felt that reparation payments would be scaled down to less demanding levels. For the English and the Belgians, the Reparations Commission's April 4 decision to invoke a committee of bankers might lead to a reduction of annuities. Poincaré was not likely to welcome the experts, but he wanted to keep the loan question, with its corollary of reducing reparations, out of the Genoa Conference.[116]

Given the French veto on reparations discussions, sober German spokesmen, such as Rathenau and Carl Melchior, realized that Genoa offered no great possibility for a breakthrough: the Reich, Melchior told Horne, would have to make more impossible promises for the sake of "political window dressing."[117] Rathenau's first task at Genoa was to try and supersede the Reparations Commission's March 21 demand for 60 billion more marks in taxes as the price of a full-year moratorium. A second objective was to undermine the French thesis that depreciation of the German mark was internally caused, hence correctable by Berlin despite its reparation commitments. This last issue—important for the

[115] For Hermes' unhappiness with a "pronounced No," in view of Genoa and the precarious exchange rate, see GFM: ARK, Ausführung des Friedensvertrags, 9523H/3682/286317–286323, Chefbesprechung, April 4, 1922. Cf. Laubach, *Kabinette Wirth*, pp. 165–172; also Felix, *Walther Rathenau*, pp. 132–133, 149–150; Bergmann, *Reparations*, pp. 121–122.

[116] Proposal at the Allied Finance Ministers Conference March 11, 1922; cf. Weill-Raynal, *Les réparations allemandes*, II, pp. 133–134, 169–170; Laubach, *Kabinette Wirth*, p. 173; Karl Dietrich Erdmann, "Deutschland, Rapallo, und der Westen," *Vierteljahreshefte für Zeitgeschichte*, XI, 2 (1963), pp. 144–148.

[117] Max Warburg papers, 3a, "Melchior Notiz"; also GFM: Büro des Reichsministers, Genua, 3398/1734/738120–738121; Felix, *Rathenau*, p. 130.

question of future moratoriums—became a contest of formulas within the Conference's finance committee, which Germany eventually did carry. Simultaneously, German reparation expert Bergmann resumed his own Penelope's web of negotiations with Jacques Seydoux. They discussed a plan that would prolong for four years the 1922 level of reduced cash payments and would raise the money for them by a "small loan." Rathenau supported Bergmann's proposal at Genoa as the only available realistic basis for negotiations and cooling off the reparation problem. But as a provisional scheme it pleased neither the British, nor Rathenau at heart, nor German industry. For different reasons they all preferred final determination of a new, presumably lower reparation total coupled with a "big loan" to get payments underway.[118]

As it turned out, the Rapallo Treaty, concluded midway through the conference, was to interrupt the tempo of negotiations on either approach. The surprise pact between the Germans and Soviets angered the Allies. Lloyd George, however, could not afford to let Rapallo destroy the Genoa Conference, which he had billed as a major initiative to enhance his political position, bring Russia back into economic intercourse with the West, and reinvigorate Britain's lagging commerce. The Prime Minister needed a gesture of success to buttress a shaky coalition government that was being eroded by continuing Irish troubles, doubts about his disastrous pro-Greek Near Eastern policy, and Conservative Party restlessness with his centralization of power in the cabinet. Soviet negotiations with the West had to be kept open, therefore, so that some progress could be reported back to London and the promise of Soviet markets would inspirit British trade. On the other side, Wirth still needed to keep the Reparations Commission from finding Germany in default at the end of May. This required persuading the Allied leaders to direct the Commission to approve the halting German gestures toward stabilization of the mark. Only France had nothing to gain from Genoa. Indeed, Poincaré's angry speech at Bar le Duc a week after Rapallo threatened both the future of the Genoa Conference and unilateral enforcement of sanctions if the Reparations Commission found Germany in default. Mutual interest thus brought Wirth and Lloyd George together. After an initial plea that Wirth and Rathenau withdraw the pact, or formally subsume it under more general international agreements, Lloyd George finally came to terms. In return for the Chancellor's persuading the Soviets to continue economic talks at the Hague, the Prime Minister was prepared to denounce unilateral sanctions. Both national leaders thus served their

[118] Erdmann, "Deutschland, Rapallo, und der Westen," pp. 148–153; see Rathenau's attitude in the cabinet session of April 6, 1922, in GFM: ARK, Kabinettsprotokolle, 3491/1742/751420–751421; cf. Laubach, *Kabinette Wirth*, pp. 193–198.

interests by trading good will gestures that delayed painful confrontation.[119]

Genoa thus became an Alice-through-the-Looking-Glass exercise, where everyone ran frantically to keep in place. It outlined the dilemmas confronting each power until France finally lurched into the Ruhr. Germany, it revealed, had no policy except that of trying—as a member of the Economic Council aptly summarized it later—to tack through without paying reparations until new French elections replaced the Bloc National.[120] This was acceptable to Lloyd George, who seemed increasingly unwilling to challenge this attitude: although Bradbury grew frustrated at Germany's fiscal recklessness, the Prime Minister echoed German business views that an end to inflation and balancing the budget would lead to "a terrific collapse."[121] Still, Lloyd George had to avoid alarming the conservatives in his coalition who were friendly to France; he could not indulge in a drastic and public break of the old Entente. Moreover, his successor in late 1922, Bonar Law, was a more cautious diplomat and less willing to gamble on the serendipity involved in opening up Eastern Europe. Only France could be hurt outright by any agreement at Genoa; on the other hand, Paris could not solve her reparation and budget needs just by preventing agreements. Genoa thus confirmed the frustrations and costliness of the postwar reparation system. It made indecision the easiest alternative for statesmen, until indecision itself became too costly to maintain in terms of domestic support.

Although Rapallo interrupted the patient labors of Seydoux and Bergmann, by mid-May Berlin received another chance to win foreign assistance. Preparations began for the convocation of financiers summoned by the Reparations Commission. Finance Minister Hermes traveled to Paris and, seconded by Bergmann, fought to bring the Reparations Commission and his own government into accord so that 1922's provisional moratorium could be made definitive and the bankers would be able to discuss the conditions for an international loan. The heart of Hermes' painfully negotiated agreement stipulated that Germany would accept its March 31 level of floating debt from the Reichs-

---

[119] See Lloyd-George interview with Wirth and Rathenau, April 19, May 4, and May 7, in PRO: CAB 31/11, pp. 376–382; also CAB 31/5, S.G. nrs. 18, 25, 30; Wirth's reports of May 4 and 7 to Ebert are in GFM: Büro des Reichsministers, Genua, 3398/1734/738701–738704, 738712–738714. For Lloyd George's angry reaction to the Bar le Duc Speech see CAB 31/5, S.G. 18, April 26 conversation with Louis Barthou, who was representing France. On Lloyd George's political situation see Frank Owen, *Tempestuous Journey: Lloyd George, His Life and Times* (London, 1954), pp. 591–628.

[120] August Müller in the Wirtschaftspolitischer Ausschuss, August 29, 1922, DZA, Potsdam: RWR/393, p. 185.

[121] PRO: CAB 23/30, Cabinet conclusions of May 23, 1922.

bank as a maximum and would cover any increase by new taxation. It would not compel the Reichsbank to issue more marks, unless—and this was a major victory for the German delegation—receipts from foreign loans fell short of what was needed to pay the reparation payments due after April 1. This meant that Germany needed only to cover her own internal expenses; allied creditors would pay reparations. Yet even this seemed unacceptable at first to the Chancellor, who had warned Allied leaders at Genoa that no new taxes whatsoever were feasible. Personal ill-feeling separated Wirth and Hermes, especially since Rapallo. Moreover, the parties were opposed, Wirth claimed, and a new bout of currency depreciation might force a recourse to the printing press. In fact, turning to the Reichsbank's printing presses was now the only effective public finance program the government possessed; and ever since December, when Wirth had cautioned Rathenau in London, the government had feared tying fiscal reform to the conditions for a moratorium. Rathenau, however, felt that Hermes' agreement was still preferable to an acute crisis and a judgment of default. Finally Wirth did yield to Hermes' pleas from Paris, although for several days he claimed that acceptance would precipitate a ministerial crisis.[122]

Hermes' diplomacy helped secure the moratorium but could not win the loan. The financiers who convened in June predicated an international loan upon a partial write-off of reparations. The key American participant, J. P. Morgan, Jr., apparently felt that Poincaré was ready to scale down the total, but the Premier felt that France alone was being pressured into renunciations. The bankers, he responded, had no mandate to discuss the debt that America claimed from Europe and whose reduction alone might justify lowering the reparations total.[123] The upshot of the spring negotiations was thus an apparently intractable balance-of-payments and financial tangle. The British would not support a foreign loan without German financial reform. The French refused to support a moratorium unless—as Poincaré defined his policy—the Al-

[122] See Hermes' report of May 20, 1922 in GFM: Wirtschaft-Reparation, 9233H/3493/253210–253220; Oertzen report, May 24, in *ibid.*, 253280–253284 and Hermes' report in Büro des Reichsministers 5, Reparation, 3243D/1644/717771–717780; also *ibid.*, 717793 for the Finance Minister's May 25 warning from Berlin to Bergmann at Paris that a cabinet crisis was not to be excluded. Explanation of the final agreement on May 29 from Oertzen, 717804–717806, from Bergmann and Staatssekretär Fischer, 717843–717847 cf. 9233H/3493/253325–253330 for a May 29 defense of the agreement. For the discussion in the cabinet on May 22–23: GFM: ARK, Kabinettsprotokolle, 3491/1742/751892–751897. Cf. Bergmann, *Reparations*, pp. 130–133; Laubach, *Kabinette Wirth*, pp. 228–236; Erdmann, "Deutschland, Rapallo und der Westen," pp. 155–165; Felix, *Rathenau*, pp. 151–153.

[123] Poincaré's position stated in response to Herriot, JOC, 1922, II, pp. 1667 ff. (June 2).

lies received pledges or "guarantees" of payments such as customs receipts. But the Germans refused to undertake fiscal retrenchment without either a foreign loan or a moratorium.

Only the United States might unravel the deadlock: if it would cancel Europe's debts, Britain and France would consider lowering reparation. But for various reasons Washington would not simply accept cancellation. In January and February, Congress reclaimed negotiations over the debt by establishing a World War Foreign Debt Commission under its own control and likely to make remission more difficult. Secretary of Commerce Herbert Hoover felt that the London reparation system was doomed to collapse, but rejected any forgiveness of European debts. Hoover and Morgan were willing to lend more money to Europe, but they remained convinced that first the political bitterness and financial instability engendered by reparation had to be largely eliminated. New York banking leaders, moreover, were unwilling to act independently of the British, and the British were increasingly in disagreement with Paris. In effect, American conditions helped to reinforce the resistance of a Stinnes against the piecemeal revisionism of a Rathenau. Condemning the reparations system but refusing to annul their own demands, they encouraged the more hawkish advocates on both sides.[124]

The conflicting tendencies of German policy were poignantly summarized by the Stinnes-Rathenau dialogue that took place at the home of the American Ambassador the night before Rathenau was slain by nationalist right-radical terrorists on June 24. The debate took place in the wake of a government effort to pressure the Reichsbank to support the mark, an intervention opposed by Stinnes and his industrialist colleagues. At Ambassador Houghton's, Stinnes denied that he wanted any catastrophic inflation, but said he saw no use in stabilization of the mark until the reparation bill was fixed at a significantly lower level. Once this was done, he would cooperate with the internal measures required. Rathenau argued with Stinnes until after midnight: he could not base German foreign policy on a collision course with France. It was fine for Stinnes to look for a collapse of reparations to show the need for a sensible reduction of debts, but he had to avoid a demon-

---

[124] For the Bankers' conference, see Bergmann's report to Wirth, June 2: GFM: ARK, 9523H/3682/286566–286567 and the extensive presentation to the Cabinet on June 13, *ibid.*, 286586–286615. Cf. Denise Artaud, "À propos de l'occupation de la Ruhr," *Revue d'Histoire Moderne et Contemporaine*, 17 (January-March, 1970), pp. 8–11; also Werner Link, *Die amerikanische Stabilisierungspolitik in Deutschland 1921–32* (Düsseldorf, 1970), pp. 129–131; Melvyn Leffler, "The Origins of Republican War Debt Policy, 1921–1923: A Case Study in the Applicability of the Open Door Interpretation," *Journal of American History*, LIX, 4 (1972), pp. 585–601; Weill-Raynal, *Les réparations allemandes*, II, pp. 166–182.

stration of this catastrophic nature.[125] Torn between fulfillment and defiance, Rathenau died an advocate of fulfillment. Yet for over a year the government had set itself the task of reconciling the views of Stinnes with those of Paris, and the task was as frustrating as the unresolved argument at Houghton's. The Wirth government would finally fall in November 1922, but its real effectiveness and purpose ended earlier. The failure of its political mission dated at least from the Reparations Commission note of March 21, if not from the industrialists' disavowal of the credit action in November 1921. These events showed that business collaboration was available only at too high a price, or if attained at all yielded compromises that could not quell inflation or secure moratoriums.

Neither Wirth nor Briand could win the international gains that would appease nationalist or even moderate opinion at home. Throughout 1922, challengers on both sides of the Rhine would call for more hawkish policies and an end to trimming. Their impatience no longer stemmed from fear of radicalism or middle-class weakness. "In truth," wrote Lucien Romier in early May, "I believe that the upper, middle, and petite bourgeoisies of Europe have never been stronger or more consolidated."[126] Now conservatives felt vexed that they were not getting the decisive political results their power merited. If the call for confrontation proved as fruitless in its turn as the abandoned path of compromise, then rightist solutions as well as moderate ones would emerge discredited.

Without American assistance the balance of payments problems involved in reparation and war debts seemed politically insoluble. Statesmen wishing to avoid conflict proved unable to cut through the dilemmas on terms that satisfied their respective middle-class constituencies. The French coalition was unwilling to write off the savings that scaling down reparations would have entailed, the German coalition was unwilling to forego the income that paying them required, and the British were unwilling to help the French force them. The result of this stalemate was the occupation of the Ruhr.

Poincaré and Cuno, who followed Briand and Wirth, gave promise of responding to the impatience of their nationalistic supporters. They attacked the ambivalence and delays of earlier policy. In fact they remained bound by the same constraints. Although Poincaré enjoyed good will among conservative and nationalist circles, he still faced the financial and political difficulties that had vexed Briand. These were

[125] See Houghton's report in U.S. Department of State, Decimal Series: U.S. 462.00 R 29/1853; Stinnes' recollection in Gert von Klass, *Hugo Stinnes* (Tübingen, 1958), pp. 285 ff.
[126] R. [Lucien Romier], "Les faits," *JI*, May 4, 1922.

summarized by two memoranda he received within several weeks after taking office on January 14. On January 30, Jean Parmentier at the Ministry of Finances submitted a grim thirty-page report, which repeated earlier warnings that France had to prepare "definitive solutions within political reach which will bring us some real gains in place of perpetuating illusion."[127] Capital transfers from one nation to another were hard to work out, Parmentier argued; transfers in kind were easier, but limited by the reluctance of French manufacturers to see their own markets undercut. The totals that France might expect over fifteen years were about 30 billion gold marks in cash, 12 to 14 billion in goods. Given her allies' hostility, however, it was questionable whether France could exert enough pressure to collect for fifteen years. In any case, the country had to reconstruct her own devastated area in the shortest possible time, and the bonds floated for this purpose were already imposing an "intolerable" debt burden and could be resorted to no longer. The thrust of the long report was to emphasize the unworkability of the London schedule of reparation. The need for massive payments within a few years suggested an international loan to fund reparation; another major hope was interallied debt annulment. But three weeks after this warning, Morgan bankers Thomas Lamont, Dwight Morrow, and others wired that while they wished to help France, Paris had created a painful impression of imperialist pretensions at the Washington Conference. Now if she wanted assistance she must make an honest statement of what debts she could meet and stand ready to accept revision of reparation. The United States might scale down the French debt, but if French leaders were to wait for this before their own revision of reparation, "they shall wait in vain."[128]

When Poincaré briefed the Foreign Affairs Commission of the Senate at the moment that the financiers called by the Reparations Commission were assembling in Paris, he recognized that Germany could make no cash payments. He warned that he would compel French industry to go along with reparations in kind, such as those provided by the Wiesbaden accords, and he was ready to approve an international loan to fund German payments. He was not prepared, however, to accept unilateral reduction of reparations as a precondition for the loan; hence the bankers found themselves stymied. Given the deadlock, Poincaré would demand income-yielding collateral—"productive guarantees"—while Germany restored her finances.[129]

[127] Note pour le Ministre, 30 janvier 1922, "Le problème des réparations au debut de 1922," Min. Fin. F^{30}/1277.
[128] Wire from Thomas W. Lamont, Dwight Morrow et al., February 23, 1922, in Bibliothèque Nationale, Fonds Millerand. Carton: Président de la République, f. Documents remis au Président.
[129] Artaud, "À propos de l'occupation de la Ruhr."

Political considerations reinforced Poincaré's firmness. Since the end of 1921 a more partisan confrontation was emerging in France. Among the Radical Socialists a new Ligue de la République urged a left-wing program upon their party. Supported by Herriot, its spokesmen called for a National Economic Council, public control of "trusts" and banks, workers' control measures in industry, and a prohibition on clerical education. Meanwhile business representatives assailed the income tax and the eight-hour day, while in parliament the members of the conservative groups formed an Action Nationale Républicaine for more effective cooperation. Conservatives complained that Poincaré's prefects were reluctant to intervene on behalf of Bloc National candidates, as they met setbacks in the May 1922 regional elections.[130] Finally, at the end of the month and the beginning of June a major Chamber debate on foreign policy emphasized the growing divergence. Herriot claimed that his party sought the economic solidarity of Europe, while Poincaré pursued an outworn nationalism. To demonstrate the realignment on the left, the Socialists joined in support of a Radical Socialist resolution expressing a studied neutrality toward the ministry. Nineteen Radicals voted against the pro-government resolution alongside Socialists and Communists; only 26 voted on behalf of the Cabinet while 29 abstained. Even without the Radical Socialists, who also turned to the left on some bellwether amnesty votes, the government could retain a majority—but one more rightist and nationalist.[131]

Poincaré thus had less domestic room for maneuver. His position became even more unenviable when on July 12, the Germans, citing the new fall of the mark after Rathenau's death, asked for an end to all further cash payments through 1924. At the same time the new United States Foreign Debt Commission announced that France's obligations could not simply be postponed indefinitely. Poincaré now pressed more specifically for "productive guarantees" or "pledges" to demonstrate that Germany could not simply evade payment. For the duration of any moratorium, Paris wanted control of German state forests and mines transferred to the control of the Reparations Commission as well as a majority of shares in the chemical firms of the occupied zone. Taxes in the occupied area and a customs line on the Rhine would yield further receipts. The Committee of Guarantees, moreover, would exercise tighter control over foreign currencies from customs and ex-

---

[130] On the political scene: François Albert in *RPP*, cxi, June 1922, pp. 486–497; also Bonnefous, *Histoire politique*, iii, pp. 300–309; on the new groups see Georges Bourgin and Jean Carrère, *Manuel des partis politiques en France* (Paris, 1924), pp. 58 ff., 200–205. For business complaints about the eight-hour day, see *JI*, February 17, 23, 25, 26/27; March 1, 12/13, 19/20, 1922.

[131] JOC, 1922, pp. 1538–1547 (May 23), 1566–1582 (May 24), 1591–1603 (May 26), 1608–1625 (May 30), 1637–1653 (June 1), 1662–1675 (June 2).

ports as well as closer supervision over the Reichsbank. At the strained London Conference of August 7 to 14, Lloyd George refused to accept such a program: it would only yield tons of worthless paper marks and precipitate a catastrophe in Germany. Seizure of state mines and forests, he charged, could only follow a judgment of default; otherwise it would represent a breach of the Treaty of Versailles. Despite courtesies at the end, the disagreement was fundamental. Again the Reparations Commission struck a compromise that undermined Germany's obligation. Berlin was refused a definite moratorium without "radical reform" of her public finances, but the payments she owed until December could be covered by six-month German treasury notes.[132]

Poincaré became more stubborn as the autumn progressed. He wanted the reparation issue fearfully clear: France was not interested in offering general plans for monetizing German resources, he told the French delegate on the Committee of Guarantees. Instead she would wait for German proposals and seek productive guarantees. When he met with the Belgian premier and Foreign Minister on November 23, he was obviously set on entering the Ruhr: "At bottom," he said, "there is only one guarantee and that is coal."[133] The Allies met again at London from December 9 to 11. Lloyd George had been replaced by Bonar Law, who negotiated with far greater gentleness and apparent concern for France's genuine dilemmas. But the two powers were no closer on policy. Since the Balfour Note of August, which had sought to draw in the United States by promising forgiveness to Britain's debtors to the degree that Washington remitted British debts, the reparation and debt issue, as Bonar Law noted, had become "inextricably entangled."[134] Now each country looked for schemes to trade reparations against interallied debts; but all depended upon American generosity, which they knew was politically excluded in the short run. At London

[132] Weill-Raynal, *Les réparations allemandes*, II, pp. 192 ff., 203–204, for the policy of productive guarantees or pledges (*gages*). See PRO: CAB 29/97 (Interallied Conferences), I.C.P. 250, 251c, 251e, 251f, 251g, for the sessions of the London Conference, August 7–14. Cf. Lloyd George's report to the cabinet on August 14, in which the Anglo-French breach was presented calmly. The Prime Minister predicted that France would be unable to "smash up Germany before November." PRO: CAB 23/30.

[133] For rejection of any idea of offering a French plan for German payments, see: "Réunion du 18 octobre 1922 sous la présidence du M. le Président du Conseil," and for discussion with Belgians: "Réunion chez le Président du Conseil 23 novembre, 1922," both in Min. Aff. Etr., Europe 1918–1929, Allemagne/476.

[134] Bonar Law's phrase at cabinet meeting of December 11, 1922, PRO: CAB 23/32. For the Balfour note of August 1 see Weill-Raynal, *Les réparations allemandes*, II, p. 197. It was issued in the context of the World War Foreign Debt Commission's pressure for a war-debt settlement. See the controversy over the response in the cabinet on July 25, CAB 23/30. Political mood in France in Bonnefous, *Histoire politique*, III, pp. 332 ff. Cf. Garapon, *L'Echo de Paris*, November 18, 1922.

Poincaré suggested that the Treaty framers had meant to make settlement of interallied debts dependent upon recovery of claims from Germany and offered to earmark the remote C bonds for settlement of London's claims on Paris. Meanwhile the Germans petitioned for a moratorium through 1924 that might even suspend deliveries in kind as well as cash payments. Poincaré now raised occupation of the Ruhr as a sanction, but the British still refused to allow France greater control of German economic life as the counterpart for a moratorium.[135] Over Bradbury's objection, however, the Reparations Commission proceeded to find Germany in default on shipments of coal and lumber. This provided a legal prerequisite for imposing sanctions according to the Treaty; and although Poincaré and Millerand were apparently quarreling over how quickly to march, the French seemed increasingly set on moving into the Ruhr.[136]

As had been apparent since the Genoa Conference, British policy might show great vision in its approach to long-range problems, but it remained stymied in the face of the immediate dilemmas involving reparations. The Foreign Office recognized that even now Germany was offering France no guarantees of payment, and that it would be "unjust" to press Berlin's shadowy proposals on Paris.[137] On the other hand, London judged the French plans fruitless and harmful. When the Allies continued their discussions at Paris from January 2 to 4, the Bonar Law cabinet offered a new last-ditch proposal. The Bonar Law plan envisioned complex transfers of new reparation bonds among the Allies. Because of provisions that would allow for Germany's early redemption of her bonds at sizeable discounts, the French and other allies could settle their debts to Britain at great discounts as well. On the other hand, Belgium, Italy, and France were alarmed by the overall reduction of the reparations debt that the Bonar Law plan involved. The British argument that in fact the existing schedule of payments,

[135] For the December London Conference see PRO: CAB 29/97, I.C.P. 254–257, including the German reparation proposal as an appendix to I.C.P. 256. Poincaré had unofficially raised the proposal of cancelling interallied debts with C bonds at the August London conference, but withdrew the plan before discussion.

[136] For default vote, see AN, Paris: AJ⁶/519 (Procès-Verbal of the Reparations Commission, December 5, 1922). For Millerand's claim to have pushed Poincaré to a decision on November 13 see Millerand, "Mes souvenirs (1859–1941)," MS, p. 114; Jacques Chastenet, *Raymond Poincaré* (Paris, 1948), p. 245. *Le Temps*, November 29, 1922, dated the decision to enter the Ruhr as November 27, but cf. note 133.

[137] See the "Memorandum on British Policy in Germany" from the Central Department of the Foreign Office, November 23, 1922, in FO 408/8 (Confidential Prints: Germany), No. 437. Cf. *ibid.*, No. 519: "Memorandum on the Reparations Problem," December 5, 1922, which reaffirmed the need for German reforms but urged also a moratorium and scale-down of annuities.

with its C bonds of negligible value, was worth no more did not convince the Allies; it appeared instead as if Belgian and Italian reparation shares were being sacrificed to buy off Paris.[138] Poincaré asked pointedly how Germany could be made to pay after the four-year suggested moratorium if sanctions were constantly ruled out. Bonar Law insisted that the only way to collect was to make the German economy creditworthy, whereas sanctions would only preempt her collateral. Once again the German delegate, Bergmann, had arrived at the Quai d'Orsay with new proposals, but he had to remain so vague about the amount and guarantees that the Conference agreed with Poincaré they were not worth even a formal hearing. Neither Berlin nor London had acceptable alternatives; on the other hand, the British would not accept the French "guarantees" for a moratorium, which now included a control mission in Essen and take-over of the coal tax in the Ruhr and occupied areas. With Germany in default, however, Poincaré could urge sanctions if guarantees were precluded. He proposed occupation of Essen and Bochum and the establishment of a customs line between occupied and unoccupied Germany. Within two or three days, he warned, military action would be "of immediate necessity." In view of the unsatisfactory British alternative, the Belgian premier Theunis made it clear that his country would march with France. With the adjournment of the Paris conference, occupation of the Ruhr was a foregone conclusion.[139] Millerand continued to press for decisive action while parliamentary opinion also demanded an end to temporizing. "No way to retreat with this terrible Chamber," as Harry Kessler overheard among the fashionable Parisian left-wing circles he frequented.[140]

From the assassination of Rathenau in late June 1922 until the end of 1923, the pulsebeat of German civic life beat weaker and weaker. Right-wing terrorists, sheltered by a complaisant Bavarian conservative government, made war on the spokesmen for constitutional democracy. The booming industrial activity and high employment concealed the progressive expropriation of broad classes of the populace, as favored speculators or entrepreneurs pressed capital out of middle-class savings or labor's declining real wages. Flashy spending and deep poverty increased cheek by jowl in Berlin and other big cities. Our focus here, however, is less the general degeneration of public community than the

---

[138] For the intricacies of the Bonar Law plan: Weill-Raynal, *Les réparations allemandes*, ii, pp. 334–360. The proposal is printed with the proceedings of the Paris Conference, January 2–4, 1923: PRO: CAB 29/97, I.C.P. 259, Appendix A.

[139] *Ibid.*, I.C.P. 257–260. The pledges Poincaré wanted were also explained by Saint-Aulaire on December 24. See FO 408/8, No. 619.

[140] Harry Graf Kessler, *Aus den Tagebüchern 1918–1937* (Munich, 1965), p. 171.

organized groups whose transactions comprised what remained of political life. Even as civic commitment eroded, working class and business delegates continued to pursue coherent if contradictory objectives.

From the summer of 1922 Wirth found it increasingly difficult to hold together the social democratic and bourgeois elements of his coalition. The murder of Rathenau seemed initially to strengthen the forces determined to support the Republic as the parties from Independent Socialists to DVP rallied to support new emergency legislation against right-radical activity. While the People's Party was unhappy about Wirth's emotional calls to the left and his admission that the legislation would be applied exclusively against right-wing extremists, it resisted the temptation to go into opposition. Since the "protective" laws required a two-thirds majority as constitutional amendments, the DVP feared forcing the government into new elections, which might well crush the party in a bitter and polarizing campaign. Reproached by the conservatives within his party, Stresemann sensed that Germany was on the verge of cleavage, "even civil war," over the Rathenau murder and the inflation, which leapt forward again after the slaying. As he wrote to the German Crown Prince, new elections might well produce a socialist majority if the left campaigned "against the murder organizations and for cheaper bread."[141]

Because Wirth was able to group a broad front for the emergency legislation, an issue that might have become a crisis of regime did not significantly alter political alignments. How strange that the death of the aloof, often arrogant minister, who had fought for the prerogatives of the German entrepreneur, should touch such a chord in the working class! But it pressed home that the Republic rested upon German social democracy; it sent solemn working-class corteges through bourgeois Charlottenburg, and provoked some rioting in southern cities such as Darmstadt. Yet working-class anger remained directed primarily against the German Nationalists, who had never accepted the Weimar Republic and whose spokesman Helfferich had denounced Rathenau the day before his death. The given lines of party division were deepened but not moved.[142]

Party alignments closer to the center of the spectrum did change, but not because of the assassination. Independent of that tragedy, there was a legacy of working-class strength to contest. Earlier in 1922 the left wing of the Independent Socialists had finally seceded to the Communists. The Social Democrats wanted closer cooperation with the

[141] GFM: Stresemann Nachlass, 7014 = 248/3096/143999–144000. For Wirth's summons to the left see his discussion with the party leaders, June 28, 1922: BA, Koblenz: R 43 I/1020; also his Reichstag speech, VDR: SB, 356, pp. 8054 ff.

[142] Felix, *Rathenau*, pp. 171-174; Kessler, *Tagebücher*, pp. 155–156.

moderate wing of the party that remained; and after the remaining Independent Socialists joined the majority behind the emergency legislation, the SPD asked that they be brought into the cabinet. In mid-July the two socialist parties almost merged, but failed to reach a final agreement. This relieved the bourgeois groups who were unhappy at the idea of a united socialist parliamentary *Fraktion* 180 strong: "Everyone breathes again; the crisis has been averted," noted Marx in his diary.[143] Still, the two socialist groups did form a working union between their Reichstag delegations, and by September managed to fuse in a United Social Democratic Party (VSPD). The bourgeois factions noted the rapprochement with anxiety; five days after the socialists' Reichstag agreement in July, the Democratic and Catholic Center Parties inside the cabinet formed a working "Association of Moderates" with the DVP (the so-called Arbeitsgemeinschaft der Mitte). By October the new Association asked DVP entry into the government as a counterweight to the new strength of the United Social Democrats.

Would the Association of the Moderates advance or deter the goal of a Great Coalition? On the left of the Democratic Party, Anton Erkelenz feared that the new Association would lead the DDP to abandon its original role of serving as a bridge to the working classes. He predicted an acute Austrian-model polarization, which would eventually drive all bourgeois groups from his own Democrats to the German Nationalists into one reactionary camp. On the other hand, Carl Petersen, the Democrats' parliamentary leader, argued that the DVP was needed in the coalition to persuade the Allies to extend a reparation loan to Germany and to reduce party fragmentation. Stresemann's willingness to participate in a government with individual Socialists—including the former Independents, Hilferding and Breitscheid—suggested that Erkelenz's view was alarmist.[144]

Nevertheless, when it came to the major economic issues, the new Association did work against the Great Coalition and helped tilt the balance of power in the cabinet to the right. The Socialists already had to accept the conversion of the tax compromise's forced loan back into paper marks at a ratio that reduced its yield to one-twentieth of the originally intended 1 billion gold marks. In June 1922 the Socialists had still been able to defeat efforts to abolish state marketing of the wheat harvest. By October, however, they failed in an effort to pay for the first

[143] Marx diary extracts in Stehkämper, ed., *Nachlass Marx*, I, p. 277. For SPD developments, Laubach, *Kabinette Wirth*, p. 245; Friedrich Stampfer, *Die ersten vierzehn Jahre der deutschen Republik* (Offenbach, 1947), pp. 298–301.

[144] DDP Vorstand meeting July 19, 1922 in NSDAP Hauptarchiv/f. 728. Stresemann's view in GFM: Stresemann Nachlass, 7015 = 249/3096/144084, 144108–144111. See Stinnes' willingness to bring in USP leaders in his letter of July 29, *ibid.*, 144084–144086.

third of the requisitioned portion of the harvest at the prices promised three months earlier. Given the fall of the mark, the Socialist motion would have meant a bread subsidy for the towns at the expense of agriculture, justified they felt, since the mortgage burdens of the agrarian sector were disappearing in the inflation. Nevertheless, the party lost both the support of the Chancellor and a vote in the Reichstag that set them against all the bourgeois parties.[145]

The underlying question remained stabilization of the mark. The divergence of views here became acute as Bergmann and Hermes were concluding their negotiations for confirmation of the 1922 moratorium. On May 28, 1922, Stinnes told the Foreign Affairs Committee of the Reichstag that a rise of the mark would lead to unemployment, and Borsig, too, predicted possible catastrophe. In the cabinet session of June 13, Hirsch noted that a regrettably broad sector of business and even agrarian opinion agreed with Stinnes that currency stabilization would be a national catastrophe. Hirsch himself wanted intervention to redress the currency, and Bergmann, too, warned about the pessimism and resignation he was encountering.[146]

Throughout the summer and fall of 1922, the central issue in this debate centered on whether the Reichsbank could be forced to support any stabilization action. The Allies had wanted to strengthen the autonomy of the Reichsbank to restrict the issuing of banknotes. Now they saw that Havenstein's freedom of action contributed powerfully to the hopeless passivity with which Germany faced inflation. Even before Rathenau's death, the government looked forward only to the moment when it could ask for a total cash moratorium for several years. In the wake of the assassination, it moved quickly to petition again. Bergmann hoped that the British would effectively second Berlin's demand; still, as he recognized by the end of July, and as the London conference of August 7 to 14 revealed, the British could not override the French. Belgium, however, offered to accept treasury notes endorsed by the Reichsbank in lieu of remaining 1922 payments; but Havenstein successfully resisted anything that committed Reichsbank reserves. The stubbornness may have actually been welcome to Wirth, but the Reichsbank Director likewise vetoed any use of his gold reserves for money-market interventions. If the Reichsbank were compelled to undertake purchases of marks, Havenstein feared, its reserves would be quickly

[145] Laubach, *Kabinette Wirth*, pp. 244, 296; Chefbesprechung of September 20 and 21, 1922, in GFM: ARK, Ausführung des Friedensvertrags, 9523H/3683/286874–286878.

[146] For Stinnes and Borsig, see the report of the Committee of Guarantees, May 31, 1922: "La situation générale de l'industrie allemande," Doc. 744, in AN, Paris: AJ⁶/526, F. Ger. 513/114. For the June 13 discussion, see GFM: ARK, 9523H/3682/286586–286615.

swept away. More promising was the plan to float treasury bills as a sort of parallel monetary paper secured by the Bank's gold stock and sold to the public for foreign currency. But here, too, the Reichsbank was fearful. So long as the Central Bank remained independent and industry was unwilling, stabilization was indeed doomed to fail.[147]

In the apparently technical debates over how far to pledge the Reichsbank gold actually lay embodied the major social conflicts of 1922 Germany. In the Reich Economic Council, conservative and business representatives condemned imposing any obligation on the Reichsbank. Trade-union spokesmen were angered. If the gold reserve was deemed a *noli me tangere*, argued one, then a Soviet might one day be disposing of the gold "without the same delicate regard for the needs of the Reichsbank that the good sailors of November 1918 thankfully demonstrated."[148] Despite the rhetoric, labor's demands for stabilization efforts were not radical. They asked to draw on the credit capacities of the Reichsbank if, and only if, Germany were granted a further moratorium. But even after amendment, which weakened their key demand that would call upon the Reichsbank's credit into one that would merely secure its cooperation, the left's resolution still failed. It did not really matter, since France was not willing to grant a further moratorium, but the argument highlighted the impotence in the face of inflation.[149]

Without pinning down the Reichsbank, there was obviously to be no serious attempt to confront the inflation, only a renewed search for further reprieves. In October Wirth invited independent financial experts to come to Berlin, among them Keynes, and Gustav Cassel of Sweden, and report to the Reparations Committee on measures needed to restore German finances (measures that would, presumably, include a moratorium). The Belgian and British delegates were receptive to assistance, but wanted Germany to provide commitments for her own internal fiscal reform measures. The government, to the consternation of the usually friendly *Berliner Tageblatt*, stayed quiet. The Socialist Economics Minister Schmidt did move to prohibit using foreign currency in internal transactions and recommended a new gold-backed treasury note issue of 400 million gold marks. Havenstein objected again to pledging his gold—it was like cutting Samson's hair, he explained—and consented at most to an issue of 100 million marks. Mean-

[147] Laubach, *Kabinette Wirth*, pp. 246–257, 269–280, 290 ff. For Bergmann's disillusion with British support see his letter to Wirth of July 29, 1922, in GFM: ARK, 9523H/3682/286660–286668; the negotiations concerning the Belgian reparations can be followed in the same series.
[148] DZA, Potsdam: RWR/393, p. 226 (Wirtschaftspolitischer Ausschuss, August 29, 1922).
[149] *Ibid.*, pp. 201 ff., 257–258.

while, even moderate business leaders such as Siemens explained that their enterprises were forced to resort to gold-mark or dollar accounting: "A carpenter who prepares a door with an elastic yardstick would be called an idiot, but anyone dealing with the economy with a rubber-mark standard is called patriotic!"[150]

Once again Wirth had to square the circle: he had to persuade the Allies to grant a moratorium and perhaps a loan; therefore, he had to offer a plan for stabilization of the mark, thus to bring in industry behind the government. But industrial leaders would agree to no stabilization plan unless reparations were reduced and, as they now stridently emphasized, unless the eight-hour day was eliminated. Simultaneously, Wirth wished to keep the support of the Social Democrats, who insisted that stabilization efforts be instituted concurrently with negotiations abroad and defended the eight-hour day with tenacity. Pulled between the Allies, industry, and labor, Wirth seemed to drift to the right, despite his emotional surge leftward after the death of Rathenau. On October 16, Wirth called for a coalition from Crispien on the left of the United Social Democrats to Stresemann; but by October 23, the Chancellor was depressed and disheartened before the cabinet, saying, "Things can no longer be dragged on as before." He announced that he wished to bring in representatives of "the economy," that is, the industrialists linked to the DVP, and he hinted that he might have to accept their remedy of doing away with the eight-hour day. To the dismay of Minister Schmidt, he also envisaged that not only money reparations, but coal shipments as well, might have to be suspended over the coming winter. The important thing, he told his own Center Party and the press, was to get the People's Party into the government, and if not by a Great Coalition then at least through a cabinet of party-affiliated "personalities." On the renewed issue of increasing the harvest price to grain producers, the Weimar coalition split: the Socialists on one side, the Center and Democrats on the other.[151]

The Socialists, however, were still willing to delegate Hilferding to negotiate with Wirth and the DVP's delegate, Hans von Raumer, about a possible Great Coalition; and final crisis was delayed while the Reparations Commission visited Berlin to hear what stabilization measures Berlin might propose to qualify for a moratorium. Yet suggestions for stabilization of German finances were precisely what divided labor and industry and thus called into question Wirth's political future. Because

---

[150] Siemens, in *ibid.*, p. 246; Havenstein comment to the Cabinet on October 23, GFM: ARK, 3491/1744/753573–753575. See, too, his resistance in RWR/393 and his report to the Directors of the Reichsbank October 20, 1922, now found in DZA, Potsdam: Havenstein Nachlass.

[151] GFM: ARK, 3491/1744/753546–753570; Laubach, *Kabinette Wirth*, pp. 293–298; also the debate in VDR: SB, 357, pp. 8931 ff.

of the lowering political situation Wirth could only stall, hoping, too, that the economic consultants he had summoned would tell the Reparations Commission that Germany could take no effective action on her own. Within government circles, Moritz Bonn and Hilferding on the left urged the beginning of stabilization measures provided the Allies granted a moratorium and loan. Slightly more cautious, Bergmann and Carl Melchior wanted the Allies to change the annuities of the London reparations schedule, if not the theoretical total, as a condition of stabilization measures. On the other hand, industry's spokesmen would accept only a fixed but considerably lower reparation total.[152]

The dilemma became critical in the first fortnight of November. On November 5, Wirth presented ambiguous proposals as a delaying action to the Reparations Commission, angering Chairman Barthou but still avoiding any breakdown of the talks. Two days later the foreign economic "experts" did indeed declare that a new moratorium was the precondition for any successful stabilization action, but they also condemned the German refusal to exploit their own reserves: "No other currency has fallen into decay with so great a potential support still unused." On November 8, Wirth went a little further, and although he denied that he could force the autonomous Reichsbank into any action, he at least promised the Reparations Commission that he would continue payments in kind during any moratorium.[153]

Meanwhile, the Currency Committee of the Reich Economic Council presented its own resolution demanding some effort from the Reichsbank. By now, several key bankers and even the Vice Chairman of the Reichsbank, Glasenapp, admitted that the institution might have to tap its own reserves. "Must we be more papal than the Pope?" asked Georg Bernhard, the major Economic Council advocate of using the central bank assets, and he castigated as "absolutely false" the gloomy foreign-trade statistics that conservatives brandished to postpone stabilization. Bernhard won support for a resolution that, like the earlier version which had not passed, declared that "cooperation" from the Reichsbank was needed for stabilization.[154] The exact extent of "cooperation"

[152] Laubach, *Kabinette Wirth*, pp. 298–303; Bergmann, *Reparations*, pp. 150 ff.; Weill-Raynal, *Les réparations allemandes*, II, pp. 246–257.

[153] Laubach, *Kabinette Wirth*, pp. 303–306. See the "Majority and Minority Reports to the Reparation Commission by Technical Experts on the Stabilization of the German Mark," *International Conciliation*, 183 (January 1923), p. 24. The negotiations can be followed in GFM: Wirtschaft-Reparation, Ausführung des Londoner Ultimatums, 9231H/3491/252382 ff.

[154] DZA, Potsdam: RWR/911 for the currency committee and RWR/394, pp. 154–230 for the debate in the Wirtschaftspolitischer Ausschuss. Bernhard was right about the export statistics: German falsification had been spotted by the Committee of Guarantees in late 1921, and was cited by Briand at London. Rectification was made a condition of the final 1922 moratorium.

was purposely left vague, thus losing some would-be supporters of a stronger measure but gaining the votes of business representatives. Yet differences were bridged only precariously: Stinnes and Bernhard fought in the November 9 meeting of the Economic Council after Bernhard charged that key industrialists benefited from the inflation. The absent Stinnes, praised for his "glowing patriotism" by the other industrial spokesmen present, rushed to the meeting and said again that the only difference between him and Bernhard was "how, when, and under what conditions" Germany could stabilize. Stabilization really required, Stinnes asserted, a strong government that would restore Germany's most-favored-nation status, taken away by the Versailles Treaty until January 1925. It also demanded fifteen years of two hours more work per day, to be paid at regular salaries, not overtime rates. Long-term suspension of any wage disputes and of the right to strike represented further prerequisites for stabilization. Germany was a great enterprise that was not paying its way and had a huge debt; it must either become productive or fall apart as a nation.[155]

This attitude alarmed the Socialists. As one of the trade-union representatives asked, "Is the return to health to be carried out only on [the workers'] backs?" Their representatives pointed out that the tax system favored the well off because nonwage earners escaped withholding taxes—the only ones that were not depreciated by delay.[156]

Some guidelines for a reform effort, however, did seem in sight; Hilferding and Raumer approached an agreement that provided for a government stabilization plan—including a Reichsbank pledge of 500 million gold marks as collateral for the German share of an international reparations loan. This pledge represented, in effect, the financial precondition for formation of the Great Coalition. The thorny eight-hour issue was glossed over by the statement that the principle of eight hours would be upheld, but exceptions permitted.[157]

At this point, however, the intractability of the parliamentary situation shattered the progress toward the Great Coalition. The DVP insisted that it be invited to enter the new government as a party; Wirth consented, in part, suggested British observers, to remove Hermes—conservative at home but more conciliatory toward the Allies and critical of Wirth. Nonetheless, the old USPD members of the United

---

[155] DZA, Potsdam: RWR/394, pp. 307–396. For testimony to the impression Stinnes could make see the report of British industrial spokesman William Larke's conversation on November 1, 1922, in FO 371/7518: C 14791/333/18. Larke's companion Piggott predicted that Stinnes would be called on as "the saviour of his country."

[156] DZA: ZAG papers/30, November 10–11, 1922.

[157] See Raumer's statement in the Geschäftsführender Ausschuss of the ZAG, November 18, 1922, *ibid.*

Social Democrats were willing only to enter a coalition with individual DVP leaders, not to accept collaboration with the Party as such. Unable to bridge the gap between SPD unwillingness to go beyond a Great Coalition of party-affiliated personalities and DVP insistence on full party government, Wirth resigned on November 14—exhausted, under attack from within his own party, even fearful of assassination.[158]

Only the formalism of party or personal association in the cabinet separated the parties, charged Petersen to his DDP group, while he defended the Association of Moderates for preventing socialist hegemony.[159] But basic differences did persist between the opposite ends of a Great Coalition. As the ZAG session between industry and labor representatives on November 10 and 11 demonstrated, national business leaders did not really contemplate a meaningful German initiative toward stabilization. Bücher, of the Reichsverband der deutschen Industrie, warned that stabilization was possible only when the requirements of the Versailles Treaty were removed. Fritz Tanzler of the employer federations called for an end to the remaining demobilization ordinances, which legally embodied the labor gains of the revolution, including the eight-hour day. Labor spokesmen, naturally, attacked the inequitable tax system and could see that all the guarantees of labor's organized position in the Weimar state—the rights to factory consultation, the structure of labor courts and arbitration, the right to refuse overtime at regular wages—were under attack as supposed impediments to productivity.[160]

Formation of a Great Coalition might have forced the business elements in the People's Party to moderate their reactionary labor policies. Ironically, however, the Great Coalition seemed available in 1922 only if the Socialists were willing to sign away the eight-hour day in advance. This would have made it no gain at all. Rathenau's death, therefore, which had originally brought out Wirth's democratic commitment, ended by undermining the Weimar coalition since it inflamed all the issues that separated socialist and bourgeois Germany. Wirth's fall, however, did not resolve the situation one way or the other. The basic

[158] For details see "Die Kabinettfrage," *Frankfurter Zeitung*, November 14, 1922; Laubach, *Kabinette Wirth*, pp. 309–310; DVP letter to Wirth, November 13, in GFM: Stresemann Nachlass, 7019 = 253/3097/144570. Wirth's fears of assassination in Stehkämper, ed., *Nachlass Marx*, II, pp. 269–270, 279. Cf. the report of D'Abernon to Curzon, November 22, FO 408/8, No. 463, which stressed the rivalry between Wirth and Hermes, and the November 10 Kocherthaler report in the Max Warburg papers/196a, on the exhaustion of the government.

[159] NSDAP Hauptarchiv/f. 749.

[160] DZA, Potsdam: ZAG papers/30. See also August Thyssen's attack upon the eight-hour-day, October 14, 1922, GFM: ARK, L1501/5358/441225–441226. In fact, Ebert had indicated since the previous autumn that overtime work was negotiable if industry brought forth its own corresponding sacrifice.

political divisions of 1921 existed in 1922 and would continue to exist in 1923. The measures that the parties might agree upon were ineffectual in stabilizing the mark or sufficiently placating the Allies.

Nonetheless, if in 1922 the social gap appeared unbridgeable, it also appeared reduced by the time Wirth fell, and herein lay the irony of his failure. Wirth had just about achieved a common program on reparations and stabilization both with SPD representatives and business delegates, including the DVP negotiators and the businessman who was to follow him. When he resigned, his own policies were not rejected, nor were the French and German governments so far apart. Wirth had brought DVP and SPD delegates together by persuading the Reichsbank to pledge some of its gold for stabilization. Germany's foreign policy was to remain the same "fulfillment, but . . . ," which purchased some domestic agreement and might even satisfy the Belgians and British. Only an exhausted politician was discarded—but not the policy itself, nor the basic dilemmas it sought to solve.

There was an initial continuity, moreover, between Wirth and his successor. Wirth himself even invited Wilhelm Cuno to take the Foreign Ministry only weeks before Cuno succeeded him in the chancellorship. And although Cuno won the DNVP votes, he had been chosen by Ebert under the urging of his fellow Hamburg moderate, Petersen of the DDP. Wirth's effort to bring representatives of industry into a cabinet of personalities had not been far from Cuno's conception of organizing a ministry, and Cuno adopted his slogan for conditional fulfillment: "First bread, then reparations."[161]

Conditional fulfillment was, alas, built on illusions. It meant a fruitless effort to appease the French government and German business circles simultaneously. It depended upon a continuing faith in the efficacy of outside testimony and expertise—first, the confirmation of Germany's need for a moratorium provided by the experts summoned in November, especially in the report authored by Keynes, Cassel, and Brand; second, the belief that J. P. Morgan's new pressure for a scale-down might influence Poincaré; finally, Bergmann's continued reliance upon the good offices of Delacroix and Bradbury, the Belgian and British delegates to the Reparations Commission. Just before its resignation, Wirth's government suggested that Germany would pay reparations up to half the amount received in internal and foreign loans and

161 For the continuity of policy, Laubach, *Kabinette Wirth*, pp. 295, 313–314. For the nomination of Cuno and his background see Karl-Heinz Harbeck, ed., *Das Kabinett Cuno 22. November 1922 bis 12. August 1923* in *Akten der Reichskanzlei: Weimarer Republik* (Boppard am Rhein, 1968), pp. xix–xlvi; also Heinz-Hellmut Kohlhaus, "Die Hapag, Cuno und das deutsche Reich 1920–1923," Diss. (Kiel, 1952), pp. 115 ff. Also Johannes Fischart (pseud. Erich Dombrowski), *Neue Köpfe* (Berlin, 1925), pp. 116–117.

would use the other half to undertake stabilization measures. Once again the burden was on Germany's creditors, although the Reichsbank at least agreed to bring its gold into play after the rebuke from Keynes and his colleagues. By early December Berlin offered to begin stabilization of the mark without an external loan if she received a new moratorium. In a proposal originally worked up by Oskar Wassermann, Director of the Deutsche Bank, Germany promised to raise her own internal gold loan for stabilization in an amount proportional to the extent of any moratorium.[162]

Yet industry did not even approve of this sort of offer: Stinnes' *Deutsche Allgemeine Zeitung* attacked the proposal because it did not stipulate an upper limit; and Cuno instructed Bergmann that in view of industry's disapproval he should not be overeager about provisional solutions.[163] Stinnes' own plans, as he wrote to Melchior on December 26, was to offer 15 billion marks amortized at 5 percent and settle for a compromise of 20 billion marks amortized at 6 percent. Yet even the conservative Foreign Minister, Rosenberg, recognized that this proposal would only drive the French from the table without a counteroffer.[164] On the other hand, Wassermann and Bergmann's hopes to wrest a provisional moratorium and raise several billion gold marks outside Germany were probably themselves utopian. When presented unsuccessfully at London, they amounted to a demand that the Allies fund Germany's reparation payments because she was bankrupt, and grant her moratoria insofar as she could raise her own moneys at home.[165]

With the rejection of Germany's proposals at London, German bankers and industrialists met with government officials in Berlin between December 16 and 29 to hammer out proposals of desperation. In practical effect they would have meant little, for Poincaré had already been impelled to opt for sanctions both by the logic of his position and the insistence of Millerand. Nevertheless, urgent conferences took place in the German capital, where the industrial representatives—Bücher, Duisberg, Flechtheim, Reusch, Klöckner, Silverberg—decided that

[162] For the development of the Wassermann plan, see Bergmann's report to Hermes, who continued as Finance Minister, in *Akten: Cuno*, pp. 12–13; also Cuno to Bergmann and Melchior in London, December 7, *ibid.*, pp. 49–50; Melchior Notes, December 5 and 12, 1922, in Max Warburg papers/196a.

[163] For the *DAZ* attack, December 12, see *Akten: Cuno*, p. 65, n. 8; Cuno to Bergmann, December 10 in GFM: Büro des Reichsministers 5, Reparation, 3243/1645/718430.

[164] Max Warburg papers/156; Rosenberg to Embassy in Paris, December 22, 1922, in GFM: 3243/1645/718583. See, too, Mayer's pessimistic report of the same day concerning the alignments behind Poincaré in *ibid.*, 718584–718585.

[165] See PRO: CAB 29/98, I.C.P. 256 (December 10, 1922), for final German proposal and Poincaré's hostile reaction.

Germany could offer only a flat 15 billion marks. The delegates of the banking community, under Melchior and Franz Urbig, wanted a more extensive and realistic offer but lost, as one of their number, Louis Hagen of Cologne, voted with the industrialists.[166]

Cuno, however, seemed disposed to borrow the suggestion of his fellow Hamburg colleague, Melchior, which would commit Germany to pay off international reparations loans that would yield the Allies up to 20 billion marks immediately, with 5 billion to follow in 1927 and again in 1931. In fact, the final version of the proposal so whittled away the total by delaying payments and deducting interest charges that Bergmann, who was to present the plan in Paris, said later that he could not have proposed it with a clear conscience.[167]

As it turned out, the conference in Paris refused to hear the German proposals and shortly broke down because of British unwillingness to go along with the imminent enforcement of sanctions. The German plan in any case would have offered too little too late. Poincaré had been forced into sanctions by his long-term structuring of alternatives —as presented to London and Berlin and to the Bloc National. On January 11, 1923, French engineers and supporting troops moved to Essen. The Ruhr occupation, so long brandished as a deterrent, was employed as an actual weapon. The recourse was logical but unrewarding.

By its atmosphere of quasi-war, the Ruhr closed a brief but important political era. It sealed the failure of the old liberal center at political and economic reconstruction. Briand and Wirth had both sought to resolve their harsh financial and international problems on the basis of parliamentary strategies and compromises. The sharp divergences of interest in Germany and even the more modulated differences in French public opinion shattered their respective efforts. Both men also lacked the support of the United States that was needed to ease the underlying balance-of-payments difficulties. Ultimately, the political center would be reconstructed, once the Ruhr conflict demonstrated that nationalist approaches did not easily yield reparations or, in the German case, allow them to be cast off without penalty. But the new political equilibrium would be reconstructed along corporatist lines. Parliamentary coalitions would be less central to the process of reconciling social rivals and majorities of the center no longer the real basis of consensus.

[166] Melchior "Notiz," December 18, on conference of December 16; December 22 "Notiz," of December 20–21 conference; and December 30 "Notiz" of December 29 conference in Max Warburg papers/196a. Cf. *Akten: Cuno*, pp. 91–93.
[167] See *Akten: Cuno*, p. 443 (Ministerbesprechung of April 30, 1923).

· 5 ·

THE ATTRITION OF
THE LIBERAL REGIME
IN ITALY

THE POLITICAL ECOLOGY OF FASCISM

In Italy the inability to reestablish a stable centrist majority brought
not just a shift to the right, but destruction of the parliamentary regime.
In France and Germany great social conflicts were fought out indirectly, in controversies over foreign policy and taxation, which cush-
ioned the liberal state from the most corrosive effects of class antagonism. But in Italy struggles for hegemony were raw and unmediated,
and they overtaxed liberal institutions. Between 1922 and 1926 party
competition disappeared, as did guarantees of press and assembly and
the freedom needed for independent working-class organization. The
Fascists imposed first an unofficial terrorism, then a legal but coercive
regimentation upon the political arena, mass communications, and the
labor market.

These developments emerged from the inner decay of liberalism as
much as from any conquest from outside. Unprepared to acquiesce in
political democratization and to share power over their local government, factory, or fields, men of influence accepted or even patronized
Fascist violence. The failure of liberalism reflected the country's particular stresses: its ideological and social fragmentation, the inadequacy of clientele politics for control of a modern but harshly divided
polity, the vulnerable, creaky centralization of the administrative
system. Finally, the victory of fascism rested upon a further condition that merits emphasis here: a sociopolitical continuum between
town and countryside in the regions especially prone to Fascist incursion.

In France and Germany, reparation, tax, and labor conflicts reflected
class and party contests that were largely independent of local geographical determination. But in Italy the particular form of the liberal
response, the collapse of the social democratic left, and the rise of the
Fascist squads depended upon the unique political geography of the
Po Valley triangle and of Apulia. The prevalence of a "capitalist" agriculture with a proletarian labor force, the interpenetration of landlord
class and urban elite, the catalytic political role of urban youth upon
the countryside, even the very prefectural organization that divided

the police into encapsulated regions—all conditioned the particular form of counterrevolution.

Elsewhere in polarized agrarian Europe—for instance in the Danubian lands from Hungary to Austria to Bavaria or in East Elbia—reaction depended upon the "white" countryside neutralizing the "red" metropolis. Unrest was not a major problem on the land after the initial dislocation of defeat. The socialists had their bastions in major cities and found themselves surrounded by conservative hinterlands. In Italy, however, the counterrevolutionaries of the towns went to the aid of the beleaguered elites of the countryside. The revolt from the right arose in the relatively advanced, not the backward areas of the nation. The collapse of liberalism and the rise of fascism was the result of a unique interchange between town and country: in part it may have depended upon Mediterranean patterns of urban life, where towns remained the foyers of status and political activity even for rural entrepreneurs. This did not mean that swollen Turin or Milan were models of urban culture. As the major liberal spokesman, Luigi Einaudi, wrote, these large metropolises had a traditional civic core but were overwhelmed by commercial and industrial immigrants crowded round the old center: "all those who have abandoned their land and family to look for new. These are men who all deserve all the protection the State can give; but I find it hard to believe in their fitness to choose the governing class. *They are the new barbarians. . . .*"[1] But the provincial centers—a Verona or Forlì or Ferrara—were the nexuses of the civic spirit.

The web of affiliations and rivalries radiated outward from the middle-sized cities, towns, and *borghi* of the plains of the Po. Country folk, moreover, in the Po Valley and Apulia were concentrated in village and *corti*; they did not usually live on dispersed farms. It was easier to exert group pressure: first the organizational efforts of the Federterra, thereafter the devastating coercion of the *squadri* and the remolding into Fascist syndicates. The growth of fascism as a mass movement testified to the transformation of a delicate urban-rural balance of power: the upsetting of a political ecology among elites, middle classes, and peasant proletariat that liberal administration proved unable to rescue.[2]

What lay behind the explosion of antisocialist political violence in the late fall of 1920? By the closing months of the year exasperated

[1] Cited from *CdS*, June 15, 1923 by Adrian Lyttelton, *The Seizure of Power, Fascism in Italy 1919–1929* (London, 1973), p. 109.

[2] Cf. Dominique Schnapper, *L'Italie rouge et noire. Les modèles culturels de la vie quotidienne à Bologne* (Paris, 1971); also Schnapper, "Storia e sociologia: Uno studio su Bologna," *Studi Storici*, VIII, 3 (1967), esp. p. 569. Giotto Dainelli, *Atlante fisico-economico d'Italia* (Milan, 1940), plates 25, 26, 28 [based on R. Biasutti, "Ricerche sui tipi degli insediamenti rurali in Italia," *Memorie della Regia Società Geografica Italiana*, XVII (1932)].

bourgeois were ready to underwrite the use of coercion and reprisal against the left. By autumn, anxiety about impending civil strife and violence became self-reinforcing. Frantic rumors of conspiracy were one indication. At the end of September, for example, the prefect of Pisa warned that angered industrialists hoped to exploit a nationalist coup headed by D'Annunzio. By mid-October it was rumored that Generals Badoglio, Caviglia, and Giardino were organizing a *pronunciamento* with the backing of business leaders. On October 19, the *Idea Nazionale* virtually appealed for a military take-over from a political establishment that was "rotten, putrid and crumbling, morally and politically incompetent." Informers reported that Giardino, Luigi Federzoni of the Nationalists, Salandra, and Alberto Bergamini, the editor of the *Giornale d'Italia*, were conspiring daily at the newspaper's headquarters in downtown Rome. Government circles were jittery: in a state of exhaustion, Treasury Minister Meda phoned his wife in Milan: "You do not see how things are going . . . how do you want me to leave if certain events are in preparation . . . one can't move with security . . . anything can happen from one moment to the next . . . the tide is mounting, mounting."[3]

The ferment of conspiracy followed by only a few weeks the occupation of the factories in September 1920, which had convinced many bourgeois that they must look outside the government for guarantees of order. When Giovanni Amendola telephoned Luigi Albertini from Rome in early November, the Milan editor told him that it was too late to restrain many Milanese businessmen from supporting the Fascists.[4] In this respect, they were only following the quiet initiatives of the Giolitti government. During the October crisis, the Nationalist movement and not the Fascist organization appeared the nucleus of subversion. The Nationalists were outraged over the discussions that Giolitti was pursuing with the Yugoslavs in order to settle the outstanding Adriatic issues and remove D'Annunzio from Fiume. While some liberals, such as Amendola, sought to appease the Nationalists, the ministry worked to neutralize the Fascists. Giolitti's Foreign Minister, Carlo Sforza, and the Prefect of Milan, Alfredo Lusignoli, negotiated with Mussolini to keep him from encouraging D'Annunzio's marching on the mainland. While Nationalist spokesmen and press raged bitterly, the Fascist leader remained restrained and even gave guarded editorial

[3] *Idea Nazionale*, October 19, 1920: "Per l'ordine nazionale e sociale a qualunque costo!" ACS, Rome: Min. Int., Dir. gen. P.S., Div. Aff. gen. e ris., 1920, B. 45, f. "Movimento nazionalista," N. 25948 (Prefect of Pisa, September 26, 1920); *ibid.*, Notizio del 20 ottobre (report of meetings at *GdI*); *ibid.*, intercepted [Meda] conversation, October 21, 1920, N. 3169.

[4] *Ibid.* Intercepted conversation, November 7, 1920, N. 3270. Cf. Giampiero Carocci, *Giovanni Amendola nella crisi dello stato italiano (1911–1925)* (Milan, 1956), pp. 61, 72.

approval when Fiume was accorded autonomy by the Treaty of Rapallo in November (not to be confused with the German-Soviet pact
of a year and a half later). For Mussolini the tactic was part of an implicit new bargain with the Italian "establishment." It would lead both
to the alliance of Fascist squads with Po Valley agrarians and to Fascist inclusion in Giolitti's electoral coalition the following spring. On
the part of the government, the talks opened half a year of benevolent
toleration of Mussolini; if initially to forestall a combination with the
Nationalists, thereafter to exploit the growing disarray of the Socialist
opposition.[5]

These October developments thus prepared the way for a new phase
of Fascist activity: the political conquest of the Po basin, including
Emilia-Romagna and parts of Lombardy, then of the Venetian plain,
the Lombard uplands, Tuscany across the Appenines, and the tableland
of Apulia. The ministry was giving credentials to Mussolini at the
same moment that industrialists and bankers—to borrow Amendola's
alarmed diagnosis—were "rushing into the arms of fascism out of the
fear of socialism."[6] Yet even opinion leaders such as Amendola and
Albertini now conceded that the government had to sanction bourgeois
defense measures. The Socialists alone, Albertini wrote in late November, had created the ambiance of violence. No one had less right to
complain now if more blows were being received than given. The
Corriere's antisocialist commitment, he advised Amendola, allowed no
conciliatory response to reformists such as Turati, who called for pacification once right-wing violence was unleashed. Amendola worried that
the Fascist excesses covered "a desperate effort to defend economic
positions such as those of the Emilian landlords which really deserved
profound transformation." Nonetheless, he added, that did not detract
from "the complete adhesion of thought and heart with which I view
the anti-maximalist recovery." Likewise, the Neapolitan *Mezzogiorno*
admitted that "substitution for the deficient tutelage of the law by that
of individuals is among the most dangerous of methods . . . but it becomes a necessity when the public powers nap and violence increases
in boldness."[7]

[5] Renzo De Felice, *Mussolini il rivoluzionario, 1883–1920* (Turin, 1965), pp.
634–638; and the careful tracing of positions in Giorgio Rumi, *Alle origini della
politica estera fascista (1918–1923)* (Bari, 1968), pp. 92–110. Cf. *Idea Nazionale*,
November 7, 12, and 14, 1920, for denunciations of Giolitti's negotiations.

[6] ACS, Rome: Min. Int., Dir. gen. P.S., Div. Aff. gen. e ris., 1920, B. 45, f.
"Movimento nazionalista," intercepted conversation, November 7, 1920, N. 3270.
For the currents of opinion within landlord ranks, see Dino Donati, "Aspetti dell'
organizzazione agraria bolognese tra guerra e dopoguerra (1915–1919)," *Studi
Storici*, xiv, 2 (1973), pp. 404–429.

[7] Giovanni Amendola to Luigi Albertini, November 26, 1920, in Luigi Albertini,
Epistolario 1911–1926, 4 vols. (Verona, 1968), iii: *Il dopoguerra*, Ottavio Barié,

The spark for what became an all-out onslaught of fascist squads against local working-class organizations was provided by a bomb-throwing incident at the Bologna city hall, the Palazzo Accursio, as the new Socialist municipal council was to be inaugurated on November 21. The political situation in the North, however, had been growing explosive throughout the year. During the protracted agrarian labor disputes of 1919–1920, then as reaction to the strikes throughout the economy and public services, antibolshevik unions were formed and the Fascio di Combattimento established affiliated cells throughout the Po Valley towns (September 18 at Modena, September 20 at Ferrara, November 1 at Parma and Bologna, November 20 at Reggio-Emilia). By autumn antisocialist associations had filled the streets of most middle-sized towns with demonstrations against strikes or nationalist manifestations. Harbingers of systematic violence had already appeared: Milan's *Avanti!* had been sacked by a marauding nationalist mob as early as April 1919; in July 1920, local Fascists burned Trieste's Hotel Balkan—a center for Slavic labor groups in a region where ethnic and social clashes had become endemic. During September and October Fascists ravaged working-class centers in the towns of Venezia Giulia. A few weeks before the Palazzo Accursio incident, Bologna rightists had themselves taken to the streets in a systematic attack upon the left. Now, after the explosion, the scope of attacks widened.[8] Local clashes yielded to planned expeditions: Bologna Fascists led violent attacks in Mantua by December. Squads would obtain war-surplus trucks, speed along the Via Emilia from one locality to another under a different police jurisdiction, and converge to burn the local Chamber of Labor, the Socialist Party Headquarters, or the Federterra employment office.

---

ed., pp. 1438–1439. (This collection substantially reproduces the Albertini correspondence that has now been deposited in the Archivio Centrale dello Stato.) For Amendola's public position, see his article in *CdS*, November 18, also cited in Carocci, *Amendola*, p. 61. For Albertini's views, see "Il regime della violenza," *CdS*, November 23, 1920; also his letter to Amendola, November 25, in *Epistolario*, III, p. 1438. *Mezzogiorno* article cited in Raffaele Colapietra, *Napoli tra dopoguerra e fascismo* (Milan, 1962), pp. 142–143. Cf. "La questione capitale," *GdI*, January 28, 1921: "We cannot concede that the energetic action of the Fascists designed to defend the social order is comparable in any way with the subversive, revolutionary, and criminal maneuvers of the Bolsheviks, precisely whose intolerable violence has provoked the salutary and courageous reaction of the bourgeoisie."

[8] Ivanoe Bonomi, *La politica italiana dopo Vittorio Veneto* (Turin, 1953), p. 141. Cf. Mario Vaini, *Le origini del fascismo a Mantova* (Rome, 1961), pp. 133–134; Claudio Silvestri, *Dalla redenzione al fascismo, Trieste 1918–1922* (Udine, 1959), pp. 53 ff.; G. A. Chiurco, *Storia della rivoluzione fascista*, 5 vols. (Florence, 1929), II: *Anno 1920*, pp. 116, 128–129, 141–144, 167 ff. (the authoritative Fascist compilation); Partito Socialista, *Fascismo. Primi elementi di un'inchiesta socialista sulle gesta dei fascisti in Italia* (Milan, 1921, reissued 1963).

Noted labor leaders were ordered to leave their homes for residences in another region.

The very factors that had contributed to the power of the Socialist leadership now made it especially vulnerable to the Fascist assault. Federterra objectives responded primarily to the plight of the landless *braccianti*, envisaging ultimately the take-over of land by peasant collectives. Federterra spokesmen remained reticent about the aim of "land to the peasants," which they saw as sanctioning small individual holdings. They frankly sought instead to make labor contracts onerous enough that they would eventually compel landlords to cede their estates to their laborers. For small *coloni*, who already owned or leased small tracts worked by their family and perhaps a farmhand, this objective was uncongenial: they sought more land. Likewise, the Federterra program potentially conflicted with another major peasant class, the share-croppers, or *mezzadri* who remained numerous in Emilia and dominated Tuscany. During the conflicts of 1920, spurred by Giuseppe Massarenti of Molinella, the Federterra championed share-croppers' demands for a higher share of the farm product and heavier outlays on the part of the landlord. But again, the Federterra looked toward transformation of share-cropping into collective ownership, while the tenants themselves wanted to gain a greater degree of control over their own holdings. (Likewise, too, for the *obligati*: Romagna peasants on relatively fixed, virtually hereditary tenure.) *Coloni, obligati, mezzadri*: all retained sufficient control over the land so that the socialist vision of collective ownership had little appeal. From the viewpoint of the Federterra, however, they all had to be organized by championing their immediate claims or, if need be, by threats of vine-cutting and rick-burning. Unless the peasants cooperated, effective strikes and boycots were hard to sustain and the monopoly over hiring that was the key to Federterra power would be ineffective. But the tenant was often an unwilling ally; even more counterproductive, the owner of two or three family farms was depicted as being as great a class enemy as the proprietor of hundreds of hectares who hired *braccianti* by the seasonal job.[9]

[9] Luigi Arbizzani, "Lotte agrarie in provincia di Bologna nel primo dopoguerra," in Renato Zangheri, ed., *Le campagne emiliane nell'epoca moderna* (Milan, 1957), pp. 283–332; Luigi Preti, *Le lotte agrarie nella Valle Padana* (Turin, 1955), pp. 383–403; Arrigo Serpieri, *La guerra e le classi rurali italiane* (Bari and New Haven, 1930), pp. 260–279; Simona Colarizi, "Le leghe contadine in Puglia nel primo dopoguerra," *Storia Contemporanea*, I, 4 (1970), pp. 891–923; Angelo Tasca, *Nascita e avvento del fascismo*, 2 vols. (Bari, 1965), I, pp. 152–154, 206; Mario Missiroli, "Il fascismo e la crisi italiana," in Rodolfo Mondolfo, ed., *Il fascismo e i partiti politici* [1921], new ed., Renzo De Felice, ed. (Bologna, 1966), or in Missiroli, *Il fascismo e il colpo di stato dell'ottobre 1922* (Rocco San Casciano, 1966), pp. 95 ff., 135 ff. For the background of the labor situation where wage-

Many small landowners, moreover, were new proprietors and jealous of their recently acquired prerogatives. Land sales accelerated under the impetus of wartime inflation: borrowing was easier, crops brought more cash, leases were less valuable to landlords. The ambiance of radicalism, fear of land invasions, or just new salary burdens may have induced others to sell. The number of men working their own fields jumped from 1.1 million in 1911 to 2.3 million in 1921 (or from 18.3 percent to 32.4 percent of the males working in agriculture). Bonomi's testimony as well as statistical data points to a new stratum of small landowners; indeed, Bonomi's province of Mantua saw the greatest transfer of land during the war and postwar period. Similarly, the province of Ferrara, in which the Fascists organized early and in strength, was said to be virtually up for sale. Alongside the new owners, moreover, there were agricultural entrepreneurs who had parlayed humble rentals into leases on dozens of farms. The war, in short, had helped to create a new agrarian middle class unwilling to concede privileges to the delegates of landless labor.[10]

Labor's need for a hard-hitting tactic to force acceptance of year-round hiring, recognition of the monopoly of Federterra employment offices, and other gains thus imposed a tactic that was too rigid for the diversity of economic relationships in the countryside. The victories won by the Federterra during 1920 alienated landlords, but they also strained the inner cohesion of the peasant classes. Agrarian contracts prorogued during the war and after came up for renegotiation by the turn of the year 1919–1920. By February 1920 the Federterra had proposed its own tough new terms for *mezzadria* contracts, and then called work stoppages when landowners resisted. The proprietors resorted to strikebreakers brought in from outside or dissident peasants. Early sowing, spring cattle tending, summer wheat harvesting and threshing, rice or corn gathering or grape picking, depending upon specific regions, all provided occasions for violent clashes. By late July 1920 Giolitti's Minister of Agriculture, Marcello Soleri, appointed committees under the Brescia agronomist Antonio Bianchi to requisition the crops that were being left unharvested and to mediate an accord. The

---

labor dominated, see Friedrich Vöchting, *Die Romagna. Eine Studie über Halbpacht und Landarbeiter in Italien* (Karlsruhe, 1927); and on the ideological debate over the future of the peasantry, see Renato Zangheri, ed., *Lotte agrarie in Italia. La Federazione nazionale dei lavoratori della terra 1901–1926* (Milan, 1960), pp. lxxviii–lxxxii, lxxxviii–xcii.

[10] Arrigo Serpieri, *La struttura sociale della agricoltura italiana* (Rome, 1947), pp. 123–124; Bonomi, *La politica italiana dopo Vittorio Veneto*, p. 142; Istituto Nazionale di Economia Agraria, *Inchiesta sulla piccola proprietà coltivatrice formatasi nel dopoguerra*, vol. xv: *Relazione finale: L'ascesa del contadino italiano nel dopo-guerra* (Rome, 1938); Preti, *Le lotte agrarie*, pp. 408–409.

Federterra rejected the committee's first proposal, and only by October 25 was the so-called Paglia-Caldo contract agreed upon. It provided for 60 percent of the agricultural product to go to the share-cropper, recognition of the employment offices, year-round hiring quotas, and other new concessions.[11]

The victory, however, was ephemeral. As in the case of the industrialists who had just faced the occupation of the factories, landlords felt that their concessions were illegitimately extracted. Many were already receptive to authoritarian political formulas. By the fall of 1920 the agricultural association of Imola denounced the Paglia-Caldo accord, as similar agreements were being denounced elsewhere; and this time efforts by the peasants to resist were crushed by Fascist squads. While the landlords were to find aid among the interventionist youth of the towns, the working-class organizations in countryside and city did not coordinate their offensives. The Socialist town councils were often less "maximalist" than the agrarian organizers; two years after the great battle of 1920, Massarenti would complain that the Socialists, "closed in their municipal fiefs in the city, regarded our movement with fear."[12] Perhaps most important, neither the Socialists of the city nor those of the country coordinated their local battles with the struggle for leadership in Rome. When local Federterra organizations cracked under Fascist blows—and the inner disparity of peasant interests—the leaders were unable to fight either in parliament or in the Ministry of the Interior because party rigidity precluded bargaining for power. The Po Valley working-class leadership sought control of a satrapy, not corporatist leverage in the wider bargaining system. They were thus ultimately to sacrifice both: exiled by the Fascists from their local strongholds, self-exiled from the ministries at Rome.

On the other side, the bourgeois of the Emilian towns were sometimes landowners, or related to landowners; they resented Socialist town councils and the frequent strikes in the public services. Credit facilities, banks, and charitable foundations tied together the wealth of the towns and the countryside; organization of *fasci* would spread

[11] Arbizzani, "Lotte agrarie in provincia di Bologna," pp. 322–327; Nazario Galassi, "Fascismo e antifascismo nelle campagne imolesi," in *Le campagne emiliane nell'epoca moderna*, pp. 335–336; Preti, *Le lotte agrarie*, pp. 423–439; Franco Cavazza, *Le agitazioni agrarie in provincia di Bologna dal 1910 al 1920* (Bologna, 1940), pp. 171–187.

[12] Interview from *L'Ordine Nuovo*, June 8, 1922, cited in Arbizzani, "Lotte agrarie in provincia di Bologna," p. 317, n. For a discussion of the judicial treatment of the Leagues' offensive, see Guido Neppi Modona, *Sciopero, potere politico e magistratura 1870/1922* (Bari, 1969), pp. 245–250. On the organization of the landlords, see the coverage of the Confederazione Generale dell'Agricoltura in *GdI*, February 13, 1921 ("Gli agricoltori assenti?"), February 16, 1921, p. 3, February 17 ("Il parlamento della terra"), February 18, p. 3.

from provincial cities to smaller towns. Then once the squads cleansed the countryside at the behest of the agrarians the town elites would encourage their expeditions back to the larger cities to terrorize the local Socialists and sometimes force the Ministry of the Interior to suspend the local "red" administration.

In this osmosis of terrorism, landlords, lawyers, and business leaders found a new striking force among the middle class and lower middle class. Recent historians, comparing Italian fascism with nazism, have perhaps overstressed the relative distress of the lower middle class in Italy. Postwar pressures on the *ceti medi,* especially during the recession of late 1920 and 1921, were dislocating, but seem less agonizing a social problem in Italy than in Germany from 1919 to 1933. Nonetheless, most commentators of the period pointed out the ravages of wartime inflation and the infectiousness of nationalist rhetoric among the semicultured: the authoritarian potential of the baccalaureate. Just as transfers of income on the land were creating a new agrarian middle class, so wartime inflation undermined the security of the old middle classes in the towns:

> The classes who were defeated economically sought to make a comeback by means of the political struggle. Old conservatives, old officials who did not want to be retired, home owners, merchants, shopkeepers, small speculators, landowners: the old inadequate bourgeoisie who had merchandized everything so as not to upset their own privileges and comfort, limped into line in the *fasci* and shouted nasally, *Viva l'Italia,* in the same way they had shouted *Viva la republica* in the days of Red Week.[13]

Thus a decaying small-town bourgeoisie and a rising rural one reinforced each other. Both were defensive, either about newly acquired or newly threatened status and property. Veterans and university youth who had migrated politically from syndicalist or republican radicalism via interventionism to fascism were ready to lead them. Major landlords were prepared to defray the costs of meetings and transport and to contribute to their local newspapers; lawyers and bankers in the provincial centers intervened to prevent police response; and even Rome was willing to delay any effective repression of the new violence.

[13] Missiroli, "Il fascismo e la crisi italiana," *Il fascismo e il colpo di stato,* pp. 89–93, 155–156. The first such interpretation may have been that of A. Tilgher in articles of December 1919, reprinted in *La crisi mondiale e saggi critici di marxismo e socialismo* (Bologna, 1921), pp. 175 ff., and discussed in Enzo Santarelli, *Storia del movimento e del regime fascista,* 2 vols. (Rome, 1967), I, pp. 220 ff.; cf. also Renzo De Felice, *Le interpretazioni del fascismo* (Bari, 1972), pp. 177 ff.; and De Felice, *Mussolini il fascista,* I: *La conquista del potere 1921–1925* (Turin, 1966), pp. 112–122; and Luigi Salvatorelli, *Nazionalfascismo* (Turin, 1923), pp. 16 ff.

The urban-rural continuum shaped the process of Fascist take-over in Northern Italy up to the March on Rome. By the turn of the year 1920–1921, for example, fascism had spread north from the Modena region to the towns of lower Mantua, supported by local industrialists, wine producers, veterans, students, and an occasional lawyer. By late March, landlords and professional men were leading Squadrist expeditions, while former leaders of the old liberal and monarchical associations became directors of the Fascist organization in the city of Mantua. By the spring, too, *fasci* had emerged in the north, at Brescia and Verona, over the mountains in Tuscany, on the wheat-growing plains of Apulia, as well as throughout Emilia-Romagna. In Tuscany, where *mezzadria* remained the dominant form of tenancy, members of the older aristocratic families assumed leadership, preeminently the Marquis Dino Perrone Compagni, who enjoyed close connections with industrial as well as agricultural magnates. While tension existed between a pro-republican radical Fascist wing and the local elites, the escalation of antisocialist violence met the purposes of both. In some areas the tactics went beyond mere assault. Ferrara Fascists, under Italo Balbo and the former labor organizer and "Wobbly" Edmondo Rossoni, organized their own peasant syndicates as they destroyed the social democratic leagues, exploiting the resentments of *obligati* and small leaseholders as well as resorting to force to shatter the recently imposing Federterra. Landlords quickly grasped that Balbo's syndicates built upon the ruins of the old were preferable social "partners"; they signed new wage contracts and even conceded some land to the Fascist syndicates in order to woo *braccianti*. By the spring of 1921 local agricultural unions were passing as blocs into the Fascist syndical confederation. Meanwhile, punitive expeditions grew in frequency and scope, as Socialist cooperatives and party headquarters, railroad-worker centers, and radical newspapers were ravaged by squads paid and equipped by the landlords. In mid-September 1921 Balbo led 3000 Fascists to demonstrate in Ravenna; thereafter Fascists would descend by the thousand in military formation on other cities of the region.[14] By

---

[14] Tasca, *Nascita e avvento del fascismo*, I, pp. 169–187 (with table pp. 180–181); Chiurco, *Storia della rivoluzione fascista*, III: *Anno 1921, passim*, and especially the catalogue of squadrist activity, pp. 392–440; Vaini, *Le origini del fascismo a Mantova*, pp. 133–138; Carla Ronchi Bettarini, "Note sui rapporti tra fascismo 'cittadino' e fascismo 'agrario' in Toscana," in *La Toscana nell'Italia unita* (Florence, 1962), pp. 333–372. On the Fascist unions and agrarians' attitude, see Mario Racheli's preface to Giovanni Pesce, *Contadini d'Italia* (Rome, 1926), cited by Santarelli, *Movimento e regime fascista*, p. 282; also: Ferdinando Cordova, "Le origini dei sindicati fascisti," *Storia Contemporanea*, I, 4 (December 1970), pp. 973–980; Colarizi, "Le leghe contadine in Puglia," pp. 914 ff.; and cf. G. de Falco, "Il fascismo milizia di classe," in Mondolfo, ed., *Il fascismo e i partiti politici* (Bologna, 1966).

the following May Balbo marched 30 to 40 thousand unemployed on Ferrara and forced the authorities to promise to resume public works projects. The disciplined occupation signalled a series of massive temporary take-overs and exposed the feebleness of public authority in the North.[15]

Resistance was weak because of the divisions in the labor movement and the increasing toll of unemployment, but also because of official winking at lawlessness. The Ministry of the Interior proved incapable of resisting the new subversion. By the time of the election campaign of 1921, concerned prefects were informing Rome that they could no longer preserve order. The prefects' position was a weak one. For many months the Giolitti government chose not to view the Fascist threat seriously; the premier still hoped that pressure on the Socialists might be salutary and would make the reformists cooperative. Even where the prefect chose to act, his resources were limited. He possessed less authority than his French counterpart, because he could be short-circuited more easily by local elites. He shared administrative power with a Giunta of local notables, and should they determine to ostracize him, as would be the case for the antifascist prefect of Bologna in the spring of 1922, he could draw upon less authority from the capital. The Italian system copied the centralization of the French, but did not endow its civil service with the same jealous independence. Created by the Empire, the French administration of the Interior hoarded its prerogatives even when employed by the Republic. The Italian prefectural system of 1920 was really the creation of Giolitti, who had manipulated and formed it for the political goal of preserving his majority. Finally, as the ministries in Rome grew weaker during the course of 1921 and 1922, the prefects—most spectacularly Lusignoli in Milan—began to hedge their own bets and negotiated their own future under the fascists.[16]

Yet even where prefects were alert and hostile to fascism, they superintended a process of polarization that made counteraction difficult. Between March 21 and May 31, 1921, the number of local Fascist sections jumped, according to the figures of Giolitti's Undersecretary at

[15] Santarelli, *Movimento e regime fascista*, I, pp. 288 ff. Italo Balbo, *Diario 1922* (Milan, 1932), pp. 49–73. See also the materials on the strike of May 12–13, 1921, in ACS, Rome: Min. Int., Dir. gen. P.S., Div. Aff. gen. e ris., 1922, B. 45, f. "Ferrara," sf. "Disoccupazione."

[16] Robert Fried, *The Italian Prefects* (New Haven, 1963), pp. 116–162 ff.; Gaetano Natale, *Giolitti e gli Italiani* (Milan, 1949), pp. 45–54; for the prefects' role in the Fascist take-over, see Paolo Alatri, *Le origini del fascismo* (Rome, 1962), pp. 225–226, 244–246; Antonino Répaci, *La marcia su Rome, mito e realtà*, 2 vols. (Rome, 1963), I, pp. 185–191; Danilo Veneruso, *La vigilia del fascismo, Il primo ministero Facta nella crisi dello stato liberale in Italia* (Bologna, 1968), pp. 321–323; Lyttelton, *The Seizure of Power*, pp. 155–158.

the Interior, Camillo Corradini, from 317 with 80,000 members to 1000 with 187,000 adherents. Fascist sources claimed an even more rapid growth.[17] The statistic summarized a mass transfer of loyalties among citizens and civil servants alike. The situation was well revealed by a series of reports from Tuscany, where the government was weighing a crackdown on the Fascist squads. "The present conditions of the first district in regard to fascism," reported the district attorney's office (Regia Questura) at Florence, "can be summarized as follows: Existence in almost every commune of a section or of representatives of the fasci. 2. Sharp division of the populace into two parts: those against fascism—socialists, communists, anarchists, and popolari. Those in favor: all the diverse liberal gradations."[18] The results of the elections, reported the officer, only reinforced the division, because Fascists had been legitimized by inclusion in the ministerial coalition. Even more important, perhaps, was the silent approval that the *fasci* enjoyed among the public forces: this was evident in the very language of the report.

> The action of the *fasci di combattimento* in Florence and in other communes is starting to spread and spreading with vivacity, firmness, and at times with an audacity which the timid feel. Its adversaries have a real terror of it and their reaction is timid and cowardly since it always takes the form of ambushes. If discovered in time the authors flee cravenly.
>
> Sympathizers follow the fascist movement with satisfaction, and if they do not approve of it, they at least justify its violence, for they feel that in no other way would a scant minority of hardy souls have been able to wear down the preponderance of socialists, anarchists, and popolari who by virtue of government inaction would no doubt have driven Italy into a chaotic and bolshevik state as in Russia.
>
> The organs of the police are good in general, but one cannot deny that in the great majority, the officers (Carabinieri, Regia Guardia, and Questura) sympathize with the fascists, because they see in them the adversaries of the socialists and anarchists who insulted them and mistrusted them for so long.

Police complicity was a common diagnosis. Attempt at repression, the Florentine report continued, might produce a local civil war and

[17] Statistics from Corradini archive, cited in Gabriele De Rosa, *Giolitti e il fascismo in alcune sue lettere inedite* (Rome, 1957), p. 78. Cf. Chiurco, *Storia della rivoluzione fascista*, III, pp. 241–246, 318–321, 580; and Renzo De Felice, *Mussolini il fascista*, I: *La conquista del potere 1921–1925* (Turin, 1966), pp. 5–11, with résumé of Interior Ministry figures.

[18] ACS, Rome: Min. Int., Dir. gen. P.S., Div. Aff. gen. e ris., 1922, B. 62, "Fascio: Affari generali," f. 1° segue, report of June 19, 1921.

perhaps a police mutiny. The subprefect of San Miniato likewise pointed to the rapid spread of *fasci* and the public's "sense of rebellion and reaction to communist or bolshevik tyranny." Violence was charged to the left's original "intoxication with violence." Police repression, the subprefect agreed, would provoke the bourgeoisie to resistance, and would be difficult because of "the reluctance to oppose fascism decisively, especially in the lower ranks of the police. Such reluctance, it may be necessary to agree, is logical and human if not legitimate. Carabinieri, guards, and soldiers were accustomed to see themselves villified, spat upon, massacred by anarchists and socialists." Such diagnoses multiplied. From Volterra it was reported that several magistrates and even the district attorney were fascist sympathizers. In Arezzo the police viewed "the fascists as an ally in defeating subversive elements who have been the negation of the patriotic idea, and who until a few months ago, covered the public forces with insults . . . violence, and even atrocities."[19]

When officials or workers displayed firmness, as happened briefly during the summer of 1921, the Fascists might flee demoralized and discredited. This was the lesson of the clash at Sarzana near Genoa on July 21, 1921.[20] But such confrontation was rare. The police were reluctant to fire on squads, and often refused to aid the victims of their violence. If local raids were particularly brutal, they could be ascribed to outsiders; meanwhile, the provincial upper and middle classes also showed evident sympathy for the home-town *fascio*. In effect the government's effective authority stopped outside the prefecture door. In its stead a *de facto* Fascist control was imposed upon the Po Valley. By the summer of 1921, Fascists in some localities were levying a system of taxation—thinly disguised as appeals for contributions—upon proprietors and industrialists according to the size and value of their holdings.[21] Local elites and Fascist chieftains took in hand the extirpation of the last pockets of resistance. With the advent of spring planting in 1922, landlords and Fascists resumed simultaneous offensives in regions

[19] *Ibid.*, Subprefect of San Miniato, June 24, 1921; Subprefect of Rocco San Casciano, June 22, 1921; Regia Questura of Arezzo, June 16, 1921. On the question of bureaucratic complicity, see Neppi Modona, *Sciopero, potere politico e magistratura*, pp. 254–261, 303–306, who sustains a harsh indictment of partiality but finds no positive and official collusion between authorities at Rome and the fascists. Cf. the earlier accusations of collusion in Gaetano Salvemini, *The Origins of Fascism in Italy* (New York, 1973), pp. 307, 315; or Italian version: *Lezioni di Harvard: L'Italia dal 1919 al 1929*, in *Scritti sul fascismo* (Milan, 1961), pp. 531, 548, 553, 577; De Felice, *Mussolini il fascista*, I, 29 ff.

[20] Tasca, *Nascita e avvento del fascismo*, I, pp. 237–238; Chiurco, *Rivoluzione fascista*, III, pp. 459–460.

[21] ACS, Rome: Min. Int., Dir. gen. P.S., Div. Aff. gen. e ris., 1922, B. 63, f. "Finanziamento dei fasci di combattimento."

of Lombardy, Tuscany, and Emilia-Romagna to force the "revision" of agrarian labor contracts and to smash the hated Socialist cooperatives. Popolari and democratic liberals found themselves targets of Fascist intimidation alongside the Socialists.

The conflict in the Soresina plain of 42,000 acres and 300 estates north of Cremona during the first half of 1922 was perhaps the most significant. A redoubt for Guido Miglioli's radical "white" leagues, Soresina had remained resistant to Fascist penetration. Throughout 1920–1921, disputes had raged over the renewal of agrarian contracts, and the peasants won an advantageous arbitration decision in the summer of 1921 from the same professor Bianchi who had mediated the *mezzadria* dispute in Emilia the previous year. Hardly had Bianchi handed down his arbitration findings when the landowners denounced them and claimed that he had exceeded his authority. The agrarians passed to the offensive, dissolving their own agricultural association, which had acceded to the arbitration, and resuming their own liberty of action. By the end of 1921 they had refused to accept subsequent government compromises and instead enlisted the assistance of Cremona's Fascist leader, Roberto Farinacci. As in the neighboring province of Mantua, the agrarians virtually merged their forces with the local *fasci*. As the prefect, who sought to control the violence and arrange a new compact, reported: "The landlords of the province no longer intended to honor their signature. The idea penetrated that the Fascist cudgel would suffice to defend their interests and sweep away the labor headquarters and peasant leagues and bring back the old individual contract between proprietor and laborer."[22]

Why should the agrarians cede, when in the neighboring provinces order had already been restored? The agrarian-Fascist offensive quickly deepened into a wholesale attack on all constituted authority in the province of Cremona. Outside the Soresina region, which Miglioli dominated, the Socialist unions still remained strong. At first the old competition between red and white leagues led the Socialists to seek a separate agreement with the moderate landlords at the expense of the Catholics. Farinacci himself exposed this maneuvering in the Chamber of Deputies in December 1921. Nevertheless, the Fascist assault soon brought peasant unity, since it was clearly not restricted to the Soresinese. By the spring of 1922 the agrarians and Farinacci organized a tax

[22] ACS, Rome: Min. Int., Dir. gen. P.S., Div. Aff. gen. e ris., 1922, B. 45, f. "Cremona," sf. "Agitazione agraria," Prefect Guadagnini to the Ministry of the Interior, March 8, 1922. Cf. Preti, *Le lotte agrarie*, pp. 464–471; Veneruso, *La vigilia del fascismo*, pp. 206, 342–343, 353–365; Amos Zanibelli, *Le leghe "bianche" nel cremonese (dal 1900 al "Lodo Bianchi")* (Rome, 1961), pp. 141 ff. Antonio Fappani, *Guido Miglioli e il movimento contadino* (Rome, 1964), pp. 300–313.

strike to force the government in Rome to replace the Socialist and Popo-lari town councils. The proprietors claimed that the local governments had illegally increased their tax burdens; the prefect admitted that taxes were heavy, but charged that the legal objections were merely a way of conducting "a struggle without quarter . . . by a pedantic interpretation of the existing fiscal norms."[23] Fascist squads picketed the tax offices in the city hall and threatened reprisals against anyone making pay-ments. While the prefect sought to win time by suggesting inspection of municipal finances, the president of the Landlords' Association called upon Rome to dissolve the bolshevik town governments.[24] A fortnight after the tax strike was initiated, the prefect reported that Farinacci was being pressed onward by the "mad and above all in-transigent spirit of the commercial and industrial classes." After much effort the prefect got the Fascist leader together with Miglioli and by May 19 had extracted an agreement—only to have it denounced im-mediately by the Fascist-affiliated landlords. New violence and strikes gripped countryside and towns, and ultimately a labor agreement was signed only after the Fascists had seized power in Rome.[25]

Meanwhile, in early July Farinacci had demanded the removal of the Cremona town council and summoned his Fascists to occupy the town center. The prefect ceded, suspended the municipal government, and appointed a prefectural commission. The Cremonese Popolari in parlia-ment threatened to have the PPI reexamine its support of the Facta ministry in Rome, which prompted the government to cancel the pre-fect's action. But after Farinacci assembled 4000 Fascists in the city, sacked the *Camera del Lavoro*, the local Socialist paper, and marched on the prefecture—after, too, all the local "constitutional" parties de-manded the dissolution of the town council—Rome surrendered by July 17 and sanctioned the move.[26]

[23] ACS, Rome: Min. Int., Dir. gen. P.S., Div. Aff. gen. e ris., 1922, B. 45, f. "Cremona," sf. "Agitazione agraria," Guadagni to Undersecretary of the Interior, March 8, 1922. Veneruso, *La vigilia del fascismo*, pp. 386–392, discusses the gen-eral liberal hostility to socialist city governments and the liberals' exploitation of chronic financial difficulties.

[24] ACS, Rome: Min. Int., Dir. gen. P.S., Div. Aff. gen. e ris., 1922, B. 45, f. "Cremona," sf. "Agitazione contro tasse," telegram of Attorney Bellini, April 10, 1922; also letter from the Socialist Deputy Garibotta to the Undersecretary of the Interior describing the intimidations against taxpayers. Cf. Roberto Farinacci, *Squadrismo. Dal mio diario della vigilia 1919–1922* (Rome, 1933), pp. 106 ff., 114–119; Chiurco, *Storia della rivoluzione fascista*, IV/1, *L'anno 1922*, p. 100.

[25] ACS, Rome: Min. Int., Dir. gen. P.S., Div. Aff. gen. e ris., 1922, B. 45, f. "Cremona," sf. "Agitazione contro tasse," prefectural report of April 20, Nr. 9012, describing "intransigent spirit," and *ibid.*, sf. "Agitazione agraria," prefectural report of June 13, 1922, on the fate of the agreement.

[26] Veneruso, *La vigilia del fascismo*, pp. 354–360, 365; Farinacci, *Squadrismo*, pp. 125–138; "La partenza delle squadre fasciste di Cremona," *CdS*, July 17, 1922.

The Cremona conflict revealed how Fascists and liberals could converge in an assault on Socialist and Popolari strongholds, indeed on the very structure of democratic government at the local level. The tax-strike weapon proved attractive: it had been employed in Mantua; proprietors in Ferrara also demanded dissolution of the Socialist town governments before they resumed payments; and in Bologna a "Tax Payers League" headed by F. De Morsier, Sonnino's former secretary and a leader of the local liberal association, threatened a halt to their August installments in those Socialist communes whose governments were not removed.[27] The prefect of Bologna, Cesare Mori, was detested by the Fascists and isolated among the city's upper classes. In March 1922, he prohibited the landlords' importing outside farm labor during their renewed battle with the local leagues. He also sought to curtail Fascist violence and to protect the Socialist farm labor organizations. At the end of May Fascists from the entire Po Valley region descended on the city several thousand strong to demonstrate against him. The government sent troops, but their commander negotiated a truce with the Fascists and Mori was removed a month later. As the special inspector sent to the city reported:

> Mori is in a very difficult and painful situation. He is isolated, removed from any contact with the citizens, if one excepts a few conversations with Socialist or Popolari supporters; he cannot leave the prefectural palace and travel on the city streets since at the least he certainly would be insulted and booed. [The citizens] follow the will and initiatives of the Fascists entirely; hence among the class of businessmen, industrialists, and the bourgeoisie in general, including the "better society" of Bologna, no one intends to maintain any relations with Mori; no one ascends the steps of the prefecture.[28]

Events in Bologna and Cremona thus confirmed a joint liberal-Fascist assault on the whole postwar ascendancy of the mass parties. Insofar as any postwar revolution in Italy had threatened the bourgeois order, it had consisted of the transfer of provincial and municipal power in the North: proprietors had sacrificed a disciplined and controlled work force, liberals had lost their once undoubted local rule. Now, with the

[27] ACS, Rome: Min. Int., Dir. gen. P.S., Div. Aff. gen. e ris., 1922, B. 43, f. "Bologna," sf. "Agitazione contro fisco," prefectural report of July 20, 1922, and other reports in same file on tax strikes.

[28] *Ibid.*, B. 40, f. "Affari generali," Report of Inspector General of the P.S., Sgadari, to the President of the Council of Ministers, July 3, 1922. See also the report of June 30, 1922, in *ibid.*, B. 43, Cat. G. 1, f. "Bologna I° segue," describing the hostility of agrarians and merchants to Mori. Veneruso, *La vigilia del fascismo*, pp. 337–341, discusses the Bologna report and the weakness of the Undersecretary of the Interior, Casertano. (Facta, as President of the Council, was officially, if only nominally, Minister of the Interior as well.) Cf. Balbo, *Diario 1922*, pp. 76–82.

aid of the Fascist avant-garde, the reign of "disorder" seemed to be crumbling on the local level.

Such local take-overs climaxed with the Fascist assault on the industrial triangle (Genoa-Milan-Turin) and the reaction to the new Alliance of Labor's "legal strike" at the end of July 1922. In the last weeks of the month Balbo's Fascists moved down from Ferrara to Ravenna, leaving about ten dead and hundreds wounded. During the same days Fascist attacks in Novara and a Socialist general strike of protest led Mussolini to threaten a march of 30,000 Fascists on Milan and finally impelled Facta to suspend the Novara city government. By the end of the month exasperated Popolari had turned against the ministry, while the organizers of the "legal strike" sought to impose a last-ditch antifascist government. The Fascists met the strike by mobilizing throughout the North and threatening wholesale reprisals. In the wake of their counteroffensive in the large cities, they forced Rome to remove the Socialist city councils of Milan and Genoa. During the following month, Fascist demonstrators in Trent and Bolzano pressured Rome into abolishing the transitional administration of the annexed Austrian provinces, which had hitherto preserved a degree of cultural autonomy for the German-speaking subjects against nationalist pressures. As they had done in the Giulian borderlands against the Slovenes, the Fascists exploited ethnic antagonisms to consolidate their own local leadership. The government's agreement in mid-October to integrate Trent and Bolzano into the prefectural structure of the Kingdom signified a virtual end to Rome's capacity to impose any independent administrative measures against the will of the Fascists. With the North subverted, the Fascists were looking toward equivalent operations in the South when the parliamentary situation finally permitted their seizure of power.[29]

Despite the skillful Fascist orchestration of demonstrations and violence, the decay of liberal-democratic administration in the North was not necessarily irreversible. Difficult though it was to organize resistance, a strong and consistent administration at the Viminale could have mustered enough police or military power to discourage the Fascist rank and file and let the movement fall prey to its own inner tensions. But this was not what the "constitutional" forces of the North, who used and were used by the Fascists, desired. Even when left-liberals condemned Fascist violence, they tended to see a redeeming kernel of patriotic idealism, while conservatives frankly felt that the whole postwar curtailment of their authority was illegitimate and to be re-

---

[29] Balbo, *Diario 1922*, pp. 95–110; Chiurco, *Storia della rivoluzione fascista*, IV/1, pp. 189–191 on the seizure of Ravenna and pp. 399–414 on Trent and Bolzano; Veneruso, *La vigilia del fascismo*, pp. 361–373 on the industrial triangle and pp. 373 ff. on Trent and Bolzano. Also Répaci, *La marcia su Roma*, pp. 35–66; Tasca, *Nascita e avvento del fascismo*, II, pp. 337–356, 406, 485, n. 42.

dressed by almost any means. As much as violence, the key to Fascist success was the *de facto* merger with landlords' associations, local Liberal Party clubs, and groupings of commerce and industry. In the last analysis, this whole network of elites judged events at Rome in terms of whether an incumbent ministry would or would not permit the authoritarian reconstruction of the provinces. Only the parties besieged in the Po Valley—Socialists, then Communists and Popolari, plus a small group of consistent democrats—wanted Rome to reassert legality before the working-class and peasant "infrastructure" was decimated. But while Popolari and liberals disagreed on whether to crack down on the Fascists, both groups were still needed to provide a majority in parliament. This meant chronic ministerial feebleness and ultimately precluded real governance in the North. Rome and the provinces nurtured each other's helplessness: that was the final interaction between city and country that determined the collapse of the liberal regime.

FROM GIOLITTI TO MUSSOLINI: THE LIBERALS' SEARCH FOR ORDER

An effort by liberals to collaborate with the Fascists at Rome was bound to follow the growing alliance at the local level. From 1920 through 1925, the liberals' attempt to make use of fascism as a force for order, as they traditionally conceived it, formed a major theme of Italian politics. In this effort, moreover, they were largely successful, although the price in terms of liberal-democratic institutions became higher than many wished to pay. Still, until the Matteotti crisis of 1924, many influential liberals viewed fascism merely as a regrettably cruder but muscular wing of liberalism.

The continuity between Giolitti and Mussolini points up the convergence of liberalism and fascism. Giolitti's hope of integrating fascism into the liberal governing system was not entirely misplaced: Mussolini and many of the Fascist leaders remained tempted by the conventional rewards of ministerial power. The opportunities for traditional legal power provided by the parliamentary coalitions of 1921–1922 enticed the Duce, as did the subsequent possibilities for clientele politics based upon control of the South. While the role of revolutionary and rebel beckoned Mussolini—in his youth, then as a Socialist in 1912 and as an interventionist in 1914–1915, again in 1919 and 1925, and finally, of necessity in 1943—it was, precisely, a role. At each critical juncture Mussolini exploited his own revolutionary *persona* implicitly to blackmail the ruling groups of the country.[30] Giolitti and

[30] There is yet no adequate psychological or psychoanalytical study of Mussolini. De Felice's multivolume biography largely neglects this dimension; most revealing perhaps is Gaudens Megaro's study of the Duce's youth: *Mussolini in the Making*

Mussolini were appropriate adversaries: the old premier was guardedly respected by the Fascist leader, who was to borrow much of his manipulation of the system. As befitted their overlapping methods, they did not clash directly, but, between 1920 and 1927, in preemptive tactics and ironic barbs.

As a democratic liberal from 1901 through 1915, Giolitti's major contribution had been the recognition that industrialization was "raising" a new class to political participation, which he hoped to integrate into the distribution of patronage and power that wove together his majority.[31] He also sought to accommodate the nationalism that increasingly animated his bourgeois supporters, but in the bitter internal and international strife of 1911 to 1915 he could not reconcile Socialists and nationalists simultaneously. Once he could no longer absorb left and right together, Giolitti tended to tack, throwing concessions first to one side, then to the other in an effort to draw on alternative majorities if not one constant coalition. Thus he navigated in the fall of 1920, initially hoping to neutralize the Socialists and then seeking to compensate on the right.

Giolitti's method was in fact a suitable one for a complex society in which a functioning economy and peaceful administration depended upon appeasing antagonistic classes and interests. He exploited the political reserves of the backward South to take a relatively progressive stance in the conflicts of the more advanced half of the country—not unlike the Democratic Party in the United States between 1912 and 1948. But despite the cynical uses of patronage, Giolitti still believed that the rewarding of group interests had finally to be carried out through parliamentary mechanisms.

Mussolini was also tempted by the prestige that parliament, even when riddled by clientelism and patronage, paradoxically enjoyed in the Italian kingdom. More clearly than Giolitti, however, he under-

---

(London, 1927). Some inquiry into early psychological formation would be fruitful, however; for the periodic oscillations in Mussolini's career—his wistful attraction to political community, such as the Italian Socialist Party, and his violent rejection of gradualism—recapitulate the conflict present in early upbringing: the clash between combattive, radical Romagnol father and pious disciplined mother, Mussolini would smash through the constraints of the political milieu, as when he broke with the Reformists in 1912, embraced interventionism in 1914–1915, carried through the March on Rome, insisted upon a dictatorial solution to the Matteotti crisis, or defied the League of Nations a decade later. Yet there were often regretful glances at the bridges he had burnt, especially the breach with the major working-class movement. The behavior reflected successively the unresolved parental styles; but while for his parents' generation socialism had itself represented rebellion, throughout Mussolini's career the Socialist Party appeared as a conservative life option, as the Church had for his mother.

[31] See, above all, Giolitti's speech of 1901: *Discorsi parlamentari di Giovanni Giolitti*, 4 vols. (Rome, 1953–1956), II, pp. 626–633; also cited in Natale, *Giolitti e gli italiani*, pp. 418–423. Cf., too, the works cited above, Chapter One, n. 13.

stood that it was only one instrument among several for achieving a ruling consensus. When he came close to forgetting, his constituency reminded him and forced him to brandish anew the violent tactics that were the real currency of his movement. Yet Giolitti was right about Mussolini's willingness to enter the parliamentary bargaining system; and the liberals who supported Mussolini were correct about his willingness to preserve their social hegemony. Both knew that to use him successfully they must separate him from the squadrist side of fascism, and both in different ways attempted this. In this respect, however, they had only partial success. Mussolini resisted "agrarian fascism," which threatened to degenerate into a mere white guard at the behest of landlords who patronized it and also undercut his own central control. Nevertheless, he realized that without the squads and paramilitary apparatus in the Po Valley and later the National Militia, the liberal establishment would have little use for him.[32]

It was over whether to purchase Mussolini's aid despite the extralegal aspects of fascism that the liberals divided at each crisis from 1920 to 1925. Some rejected it at the outset; some remained with Mussolini all the way; most were willing to accept degrees of coercive methods—as they had in ruling the South or in entering the war. For a major segment of liberal opinion there was no epochal breaking point in October 1922: fascism meant a temporary suspension of parliamentarism as a way of organizing an orderly hierarchical society. Between 1920 and 1922 Giolitti's effort to show that parliamentary methods were still adequate for this goal failed to convince Italy's elites. They wanted a quicker and more decisive victory than he might well have provided them.

The calculations that extended first from Giolitti's plan to utilize Fascist support, then to the liberals' demand for coalition with Mussolini in 1922, and finally to reform of the electoral law in 1923 represented a logical political strategy. At each decisive point, important sectors of liberal opinion chose to work with Mussolini rather than cooperate with Popolari or reformist Socialists in restoring law and order in the provinces. Giolitti initiated this strategy in 1920–1921, and he sought to work it out again in the fall of 1922 although it fell to others to achieve a ministerial collaboration. In light of the PSI's failure at its January 1921 Congress of Livorno to expel a reformist Socialist faction that would then support his policies, the Fascists offered Giolitti a possible source of political strength. Without some infusion of new support, the premier possessed only a precarious majority. Business circles worried about the advent of recession and the collapse of major banks. They still resented the occupation of the factories, and resisted the mild

[32] Cf. Lyttelton, *Seizure of Power*, pp. 55, 62–65, 70–71.

moves toward workers' delegations in industry. Fiscal conservatives insisted that the "political price" of bread be eliminated: it stood for the fundamental unsoundness of postwar concessions to the left; so, too, for the financial "demagogy" motivating property taxes and the registration of bearer securities.[33] Despite extensive Socialist obstruction in parliament, by February 1921 Giolitti finally did pass the legislation needed to eliminate the bread subsidy. From the viewpoint of redressing the deficit, this was a major accomplishment; and along with the exemptions on the registration of securities that the Ministry of Finance now conceded, it indicated that the premier was heeding the demands of the financial and business community.

Elimination of the subsidy, however, provided few political dividends. A niggling malaise hung over Montecitorio that affected every faction. A group of predominantly Southern liberals, seeking to enhance their leverage, caucused as a new "Democrazia Sociale" and assumed a more independent stance vis-à-vis the government. Nitti and his followers still resented Giolitti's role in the collapse of the former's ministry the preceding June. The liberal right, grouped around Salandra, made parliamentary sessions painful by querulous complaints about the fate of Porto Barros, the secondary harbor of Fiume whose final disposition had been consigned by the Treaty of Rapallo to a mixed commission of Italians and Yugoslavs. The various strands of potential opposition united in attacks on foreign policy. The anti-French supporters of Nitti and the right joined in condemning Sforza for seconding Paris' reparation demands. Amendola and Einaudi demanded instead forgiveness of interallied debts and moderate reparations; they overlooked that Sforza was winning benevolent neutrality on the Adriatic questions while he pushed Yugoslavia toward concessions.[34]

Complaints about foreign policy were in any case a reflection and not a cause of parliament's discontent. The constant balancing of interests and concessions exasperated the liberals, and the quarrelsome debates threatened an ultimate fraying of the majority. In light of the Chamber's intractability, Giolitti determined to gamble on a new election "made" to the right despite the warning of advisers such as Meda and Alfredo Frassati, editor of La Stampa and recently appointed Ambassador at Berlin, who argued that proportional representation would

[33] For financial issues, Luigi Einaudi to Albertini, October 4, 1920, Albertini to Einaudi, October 7, 9, 20, 23, 28, in Albertini, Epistolario, III, pp. 1420–1431 (revealing also for the rising antisocialist temper of the two writers). For an embittered reactionary perspective see Maffeo Pantaleoni, "Il controllo sulle Industrie," GdI, March 2, 1921, now in: Pantaleoni, Bolscevismo italiano (Bari, 1922), pp. 87–96.
[34] See CdS, summaries, February 25, 26, and March 3, 1921, esp. Luigi Einaudi, "Riparazione e debiti," February 26, and Amendola's critique of March 20, now in Giovanni Amendola, La nuova democrazia (Naples, 1951), pp. 61–73.

produce the same disabling divisions in a new parliament besides adding a significant Fascist contingent.[35] Giolitti dissolved the Chamber anyway, and with the enthusiasm of right-wing liberals supervised the formation of "national blocs" that included the Fascists. *La Stampa* showed frank distress about a Turin list that paired Giolitti's follower Luigi Facta with the Fascist Cesare Rossi; even the *Corriere* could advise Milan's liberals merely that "The list is not commented upon. It is voted."[36]

Fascist squads also campaigned for it in a rather brutal fashion. While Giolitti and Corradini sought to check assaults on opposition campaigners, it proved difficult to curb excesses while the prefects were overseeing coalitions of liberals and Fascists under government sponsorship. The Popolari became the targets of a harsh new degree of violence, and in the South the pro-Nitti democrats who ran in opposition also faced reprisal. Nitti and Amendola complained bitterly that the prefects were winking at attacks upon their meetings and supporters: Albertini tried to clarify the situation on behalf of Amendola, but he had to throw up the task in resignation before government denials. Whatever the degree of violence, the 1921 campaign offered Mezzogiorno conservatives a new occasion to employ Fascist aid in the reconquest of "Bourbon" strongholds from the Nittian center-left. Conversely, it gave Fascists their first chance to throw down roots in the South by becoming a factor in the undergrowth of pressures and loyalties that marked the area.[37]

The fears of Meda and Frassati proved well grounded. Despite the official thrust of the campaign against Socialists and Catholics, the former lost only 17 seats out of 156 (123 Official Socialists and 16 new Communists), while the Popolari actually managed to gain 7. The "national blocs" returned 275 deputies in contrast to 239 in the 1919

[35] Alfredo Frassati, *Giolitti* (Florence, 1959), p. 32; also *Quarant'anni di politica italiana: dalle carte di Giovanni Giolitti*, III, *Dai prodromi della grande guerra al fascismo, 1910–1928*, Claudio Pavone, ed. (Milan, 1962), p. 329.

[36] *La Stampa*, April 20 and 21, 1921, cited in Gabriele De Rosa, *Storia del partito popolare* (Bari, 1958), pp. 180–181; and *CdS*, April 27, 1921, p. 4.

[37] Albertini to Amendola, April 17, 1921; Amendola to Albertini, April 20 and April 27; Nitti to Albertini, April 23 and April 26, all in Albertini, *Epistolario*, III, pp. 1463–1474. At this juncture Amendola's support of Nitti and his lesser degree of tolerance for the fascists, as well as his parliamentary duties, led to a separation from the *Corriere*. See Albertini's letter of January 8, 1921, Nr. 1214, pp. 1444–1445; Carocci, *Giovanni Amendola*, pp. 71–72. For the conduct of the campaign, see De Rosa, *Storia del partito popolare*, p. 174; Cesare Rossi, *Mussolini com'era* (Rome, 1947), pp. 98–99; De Felice, *Mussolini il fascista*, I, pp. 87 ff.; Santarelli, *Storia del movimento e regime fascista*, I, pp. 238–243. Superseded for some monographic detail and interpretation, the most penetrating synthesis for the whole era remains Luigi Salvatorelli and Giovanni Mira, *Storia d'Italia nel periodo fascista* (Turin, 1956).

legislature. But the difference corresponded to the 35 new Fascist representatives and was permitted, too, by the expansion of the Chamber to accommodate delegations from the former Austrian territories. There was, though, one important collapse of the Socialist vote in Romagna—from 67 to 32 percent in Ferrara and from 61.7 to 37.7 percent in the countryside—which revealed the devastating effect of Balbo's squads. Here had been the Leagues' and the Socialists' strongest redoubt; the results demonstrated how frail the base was. On the other hand, the results indicated that the polarization of the North was starting to afflict southern Italy as well. While the combined Communist and Socialist Party vote tapered off slightly in the cities of the North, it jumped sharply in the centers of Campagna and Apulia. In 1919 only 8.1 percent of Naples' voters had cast Socialist ballots, while now 27.9 percent voted Communist or Socialist. In Bari the combined working-class-party vote doubled, from an already imposing 26.6 percent to 52.6 percent. The results indicated a delayed yet significant involvement of the Mezzogiorno in postwar radicalism. Likewise, the massive invasions of Sicilian *latifondi* had recently begun in the wake of the occupation of the factories, over a year after the first land seizures in Lazio. Still, outside Apulia there was no strong labor organization, and the PSI controlled no communes.[38]

[38] Istituto Centrale di Statistica, *Compendio delle statistiche elettorali italiane dal 1848 al 1934*, 2 vols. (Rome, 1946), II, p. 42, and tables pp. 118–119. Also Ugo Giusti, *Le correnti politiche italiane attraverso due riforme elettorali dal 1919 al 1921* (Florence, 1922), pp. 96–98, 102–104, 109–110.

PERCENTAGES WON BY SOCIALISTS
(AND PCI IN 1921) BY REGION

	1919	1921		1919	1921
North	46.3	39.4	Campagna	4.8	9.13
Center	35.9	37.9	Puglie	18.0	20.0
South	10.0	13.3	Emilia	60.1	38.6
Islands	7.0	9.1	Lombardia	46.0	46.2

SOCIALIST VS. "CONSTITUTIONAL" VOTE FOR CITIES

	1919	1920*	1921		1919	1920*	1921
Milan	54–36	51–49	53–38	Rome	26–51	25–55	30–55
Turin	63–26	50–50	46–41	Naples	8–71	13–59	28–60
Genoa	23–58	29–51	21–63	Salerno	0.7–83	36–49	27–64
Venice	50–34	43–57	50–40	Caserta	1–91	0–78	2–89
Florence	50–38	46–49	46–47	Bari	27–55	29–56	52–42
Bologna	63–23	58–27	56–34	Palermo	6–83	11–81	16–76
Ferrara	67–15	67–33	32–60	Catania	7–85	0–100	12–82
Modena	60–28	53–47	45–38				
Reggio/E.	71–16	79– 0	10–55				

* Municipal Elections

As in 1913, the elections returned a Chamber more troublesome than its predecessor. Thirty-five Fascists, 11 Nationalists, supported by the funds of heavy industry, and 21 "Liberal Democrats" behind Salandra sought to work together as a parliamentary bloc of the right, allied closely with 23 deputies sitting as "agrarians." The 41 Democratici Sociali maintained their distance from the majority, and would become increasingly conservative. Ultimately more important, relations with the Popolari had become envenomed by the conduct of the campaign; an overworked and habitually nerve-wracked Meda had left the government in April; the next year would be marked by increased liberal hostility to the claims of political Catholicism and an effort to curtail PPI influence over the successive ministries. Southern liberals especially seemed increasingly subject to a revival of Masonic pressure. Within a fortnight of opening the new legislature, Sforza came under renewed attack by Nitti's followers and the right-wing opposition. While the government secured a narrow vote of confidence, the Democratici Sociali made a formal reservation about foreign policy. Rather than face an outright defeat and prejudice chances for a comeback, Giolitti resigned as he had in 1914.[39] Ironically enough, Albertini's paper expressed sincere regrets, praising elimination of the bread subsidy and the break with the Socialists. As it pointed out, despite the carping of the right no minister could have won more either in the Adriatic or at home—nor would the diverse strands of opposition permit a successor to enjoy more stability.[40] Thus Giolitti ended by earning the applause of the moderates—precisely those with the smallest national constituency.

The next year and a half demonstrated this continuing separation of the "real country" and the "legal country," the discrepancy between the groups in conflict and the powerless spokesmen for the constitutional order at Rome. The discrepancy revealed itself in the language of "legality" that all the disadvantaged groups, besieged Socialists and respectable liberals, increasingly and vainly invoked. "Legality," however, remained ambivalent. For the Socialists it meant an end to squadrism; for the liberals it meant stabilizing a coalition of the right and center. Most liberals were not prepared to pay the price of a truly legal order. In parliament this would have meant a more durable relation-

[39] For the "Demo-sociali" see *CdS*, June 28, 1921; Catholic resentments visible in Luigi Sturzo, *Popolarismo e fascismo* (Turin, 1924), p. 47; for Meda see *Carte Giolitti*, III, pp. 315–316; parliamentary debates, June 20–26 in AP: Camera, Legislatura XXVI, pp. 43–315; résumé in Domenico Novacco, *Storia del parlamento italiano*, vol. XII (Palermo, 1967), pp. 181–198.

[40] "L'opera di Giolitti," *CdS*, July 1, 1921; on the difficulties of an alternative policy: "La sola designazione," June 29, 1921.

ship with the Popolari. But liberals were becoming more impatient with Catholic political ambitions and peasant organization—not merely in the North, but in the Mezzogiorno where their own hitherto passive electorate was at stake and where, too, the networks of Masonry still played a significant political role. The consequence for parliament was feeble coalitions and a failure of ministerial decisiveness in confronting the Fascists.

In fact, many liberals were prepared to accept much of the Fascist movement, and this proved a further obstacle in the way of "legality." Giolitti's successor, Bonomi, repeatedly sought to draw a fine line between legitimate Fascist opposition—he had just campaigned alongside Farinacci in the National Bloc—and "brigandage" that had to be suppressed.[41] The new government took up the theme of "pacification" that Giolitti and Mussolini had both introduced before the resignation of the cabinet; but pacification, too, rested upon an equivocal view of what was taking place in the countryside, since it presupposed that left and right were both violating civil liberties and order to the same degree.

Pacification also meant that the government shed some of its pretensions to overarching the great civil struggle underway. Bonomi retained enough of his Socialist formation to distrust the transcendent concept of the state that many liberals advanced. But for the government to accept less exalted claims, for it to step into the melee of social and political struggle merely as a referee, implied that any level of conflict was normal and legitimate. Bonomi reduced the conservative pretensions of the government to transcendent state authority. But given the Fascist and landlord offensive of 1921, he did not reduce these claims in favor of the usual democratic rivalries of social groups acting under the ground rules of liberal competition. Instead he reduced them to purchase the renunciation of violence on the part of a movement that usually scorned democratic liberalism and would eagerly seize the authority discarded by Rome.

The encounter at Sarzana on July 21, where workmen and police shot at and scattered a Fascist force, killing sixteen, seemed to indicate that Bonomi was prepared to discipline the squads and not merely bargain with them. But Sarzana was really an inadvertent clash, and reflected no settled policy. Indeed, the emergence of the Arditi del Popolo—a self-defense formation among syndicalist and anarchist elements that

[41] Vaini, *Le origini del fascismo a Mantova*, pp. 143–145 on the Blocco nazionale in Mantua; for Bonomi's nuanced attitude toward fascism: "Appunti per la conversazione con i giornalisti," July 13, 1921, in ACS, Rome: Min. Int., Gabinetto di S. E. Bonomi, Ordine Pubblico, 1921–1922, f. 1; also the parliamentary debates, November 29 to December 6, in AP: Camera, Legislatura xxvi, pp. 1875–2131, esp. pp. 2101 ff.

offered the first working-class resistance to the squads—prompted more government circulars to prefects and police for "public order" than did the Fascists. The left's militia alarmed liberals and the ministry, even though the Socialists denounced the Arditi del Popolo and the Communists showed a certain embarrassment.[42] The possibility of a leftist revival made a pacification agreement more attractive. Such a truce would isolate any emerging worker or peasant militia. This appealed to the Socialist Party leadership as well as to the ministers. It would answer the misgivings and growing revulsion that many democratic liberals did feel about the Fascist thuggery in the Po Valley. At the same time, it avoided alienating the liberal right, which did not want premature dispersal of its white guard through direct police action.

There were also tactical advantages for Mussolini, who temporarily renounced the major asset of his movement by acceding to the Pact on August 2, but hoped to consolidate his own control. The vast increase of squadrist activity had allowed the fascist leaders in the Po Valley a virtual warlord status in the movement. They threatened his parliamentary strategy as well as effective leadership from Milan and Rome. Pacification promised to curtail fascist "polycentrism" and seemed prudent, too, in light of public uneasiness with squadrist depredations. But if the urban elites affiliated with fascism in Turin and Milan wanted discipline, the tempestuous leaders of the Po Valley were unwilling to accept it. Local violence still persisted. There were frequent newspaper reports of the crisis within fascism.[43] In mid-August the Emilian leaders convened their own conference at Bologna under Dino Grandi and disavowed the new direction of the movement; as a countermove Mussolini, supported by the Milan *fascio*, submitted his resignation from the Fascist Executive. Grandi organized his expedition into Ravenna in September in part to demonstrate his independence, and similarly

[42] On the Ministry's ambiguous directives against fascist violence and the more decisive response to the Arditi del Popolo: Neppi Modona, *Sciopero, potere politico e magistratura*, pp. 256–260, documents, pp. 428–435, and notes, pp. 303–309; see also materials in ACS, Rome: Min. Int., Gabinetto di S. E. Bonomi, Ordine Pubblico, 1921–1922, B. 1, f. 1 and f. 7: "Arditi del Popolo." For the latter group, see Paolo Spriano, *Storia del partito comunista italiano*, vol. I: *Da Bordiga a Gramsci* (Turin, 1967), pp. 139–151.

[43] The fascist crisis of 1921 can be followed best in Angelo Tasca, *Nascita e Avvento del fascismo*, I, pp. 223–281; and De Felice, *Mussolini il fascista*, I, pp. 124–193—rich and detailed accounts. Cf. Santarelli, *Movimento e regime fascista*, I, pp. 252–260, and the contemporary discussion by A. Gramsci, "I due fascismi," *L'Ordine Nuovo*, August 25, 1921, now in *Socialismo e fascismo. L'Ordine Nuovo 1921–1922* (Turin, 1970), pp. 297–299. For examples of tension see ACS, Rome: Mostra della Rivoluzione Fascista, Carteggi del Comitato Centrale dei Fasci: for instance B. 101, Ortore Orazio to Cesare Rossi, July 15, 1921, describing the dissensions inside the Fascio of Chioggia (Venezia) and complaining how the "fat bourgeois" had exploited the Fascists for personal ambitions.

other local *fasci*, such as Perrone Campagni's in Tuscany, denounced the Pact. Still, on both sides there were indications of uncertainty and unsettledness. Mussolini's parliamentary interventions, from the opening of the legislature on, advocated republicanism, pacification, and a common front with Popolari and Socialists all in turn—less a profound strategy than a flailing for an appropriate party role.[44] Squadrists, too, revealed bewilderment and demoralization when they met unexpected resistance, from the police and workers at Sarzana, then from the new Arditi del Popolo, and later at the "Massacre of Modena," where the Regia Guardia slew eight Fascists on September 26. Both sides realized their mutual dependence, and Grandi and Mussolini composed differences at the Rome Congress in November. Against the background of hostile Socialist demonstrations in the capital, Grandi reaffirmed his syndicalist program and the need for the squads; Mussolini emphasized an integral nationalism, authoritarianism, and *laissez-faire*. The structuring of a disciplined party confirmed his leadership and the legitimacy of parliamentary activity. The price was abandoning pacification over the pretext of a Socialist general strike in Rome, which was itself an answer to Fascist violence at the Party congress.

The liberal right was distressed with the internal Fascist crisis, and welcomed its resolution in November despite the abandonment of pacification. The *Giornale d'Italia* had condemned the Bonomi government for using force at Sarzana: theoretically, the premier might be correct to claim the imperatives of state authority against Fascist demonstrators, but practically he was wrong to equate fascist and communist violence. With Mussolini's provisional resignation from the Fascist Executive, editor Bergamini grew worried that the Fascist leader might be demobilizing the squads too precipitously. Fascism's function was essentially transitory, but the movement could be liquidated only when it became superfluous; premature demobilization "would weaken the national and conservative political forces and leave the ultrademocratic forces as arbiter of the country's destiny."[45]

These concerns deepened as the Bonomi government entered a prolonged crisis between December and February. The crisis in turn testified to a more profound realignment of political forces which, ultimately, would throw the liberals' political center of gravity further

[44] For Mussolini's adumbration of a possible coalition among fascism, the Popolari and the working-class movement (if not the Socialist Party), see his speech of July 23 in AP: Camera, Legislatura xxvi, pp. 561–562; also *Opera Omnia*, xvii, pp. 64–66; cf., too, Mussolini's maiden speech, which hinted at similar coalitions with the masses and called for disarmament on June 21: AP: Camera, Legislatura xxvi, pp. 89 ff. and *Opera Omnia*, xvi, pp. 440–446.

[45] "Da Sarzana a Montecitorio," *GdI*, July 23; "Il blocco ricostituito," *GdI*, July 26; "La crisi fascista," *GdI*, August 11, 1921, p. 3.

to the right and the Popolari further left. The collapse of pacification really removed Bonomi's only innovation in internal policy; now even in late December when he directed his prefects to confiscate weapons and dissolve extremist groups, the abstract order was impossible to execute.[46] Meanwhile, the Popolari's influence in the government, especially since Bonomi had granted them the Ministry of Justice which supervised church-state relations, appeared less and less tolerable to the liberals and especially the right. While the Popolari never were an ideologically consistent party, the political Secretariat under Sturzo and the PPI left wing converged in the fall of 1921 to condemn any rightist cabinet orientation and look toward an eventual coalition with the Socialists.[47]

The Salandran right was alarmed, and even democratic liberals resented the leverage that the Popolari exerted. To reassert their own influence, the diverse liberal democratic groups formed a new umbrella organization in November. Operating as a parliamentary caucus, it possessed little internal cohesion, including as it did Orlando, Giolitti, and Nitti, as well as the Southern Democrazia Sociale. But it allowed the Southern liberals, with their diffuse anti-Popolari resentments, to enhance their parliamentary role; and it shattered the precarious balance of power that had sustained the coalition. In mid-December, too, Giolitti and his followers moved to criticize the government's financial policies. As the Christmas recess came, Bonomi thus found himself under sharp attack from the Socialists for failure to quell Fascist violence and from the right and even democratic liberals on economic grounds. The ministry's unprecedented hommage at the death of Pope Benedict XV on January 22 seemed a gratuitous favoring of the Church, while the final bankruptcy of the Ansaldo-affiliated Banca Italiana di Sconto, which after having given long-drawn-out partial assistance Bonomi finally refused to avert, antagonized heavy industry circles and also creditors and account holders in the South. With the reopening of the Chamber set for February 2, a caucus of the new democratic group passed a resolution of no confidence, and Bonomi withdrew. The slow maturation of the crisis, and its equally agonizing resolution, meant that what was really at stake was the possibility of finding any coherent parliamentary majority.[48]

Enrico De Nicola, President of the Chamber, who had helped bring Socialists and Fascists together the previous summer, was called to form a ministry but could not unite the democratic group and the

[46] Circular notice to prefects, December 21, 1921, from ACS, Rome: Min. Int., Gabinetto di S. E. Bonomi, Ordine Pubblico, 1921–1922, B. 1, f. 1.

[47] De Rosa, Storia del partito popolare, pp. 205–207.

[48] Veneruso, La vigilia del fascismo, pp. 11–75; Novacco, Storia del parlamento italiano, XII, pp. 215–233.

Popolari. An attempt by Orlando also failed; on the other hand, it became clear that Popolari and Socialists were not yet ready for real cooperation. At the King's request, Bonomi went before the Chamber to request a formal vote of confidence that might at least indicate coherent alternatives. Nitti and the Popolari voted in favor of the ministry; other liberals either voted against or stayed away. The government tested a resolution that would have stressed its commitment to "legality." It was hoped that this might enable the reformist Socialists to join Popolari and Nitti Democrats. But the Socialists were not ready for this step; they accepted the motion calling for "legality" and then went on to vote alongside the right and many democratic liberals for an amendment that condemned the ministry for failing to achieve this and other basic goals.[49]

Giolitti was an obvious candidate now for the center and right; but the Popolari resented the Piedmontese leader. He had conducted the 1921 elections against them; his December criticisms of Bonomi had

[49] AP: Camera, Legislatura XXVI, pp. 2967–3020; also the account of events in *CdS*, February 15–17, 1922, and summary in Tasca, *Nascita e avvento del fascismo,* I, pp. 292–293, 358–362 (notes); Veneruso, *La vigilia del fascismo,* pp. 75–86; Novacco, *Storia del parlamento italiano,* XII, pp. 235–242.

The Chamber groups and possible alignments are shown below according to their registration in the summer of 1922, but reflect divisions since the 1921 elections. The Giolittian National Bloc consisted of 275 elected deputies, but some later aligned with Nitti and Amendola who had run independently.

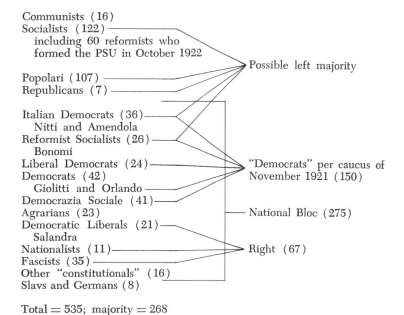

Communists (16)
Socialists (122)
    including 60 reformists who
    formed the PSU in October 1922

Popolari (107)
Republicans (7)

Italian Democrats (36)
    Nitti and Amendola
Reformist Socialists (26)
    Bonomi
Liberal Democrats (24)
Democrats (42)
    Giolitti and Orlando
Democrazia Sociale (41)
Agrarians (23)
Democratic Liberals (21)
    Salandra
Nationalists (11)
Fascists (35)
Other "constitutionals" (16)
Slavs and Germans (8)

Possible left majority

"Democrats" per caucus of
November 1921 (150)

National Bloc (275)

Right (67)

Total = 535; majority = 268

opened the self-serving crisis; and Sturzo was determined that parliament should not submit to his old *trasformismo* once again. Liberals resented the Catholics' "veto" of Giolitti, but as the *Corriere* pointed out, the Catholics were necessary components of a majority and were willing to accept other liberals. Giolitti contemplated a combination with De Nicola and Orlando in which he would play *éminence grise*, dissolve the Chamber, and decree a return to single-member constituencies—a virtual *coup d'état*—if the Popolari demurred. De Nicola and Orlando refused, and the crisis wound on until, after several other attempted combinations, Luigi Facta, a lieutenant of Giolitti from Turin, put together a ministry of Catholics and liberals, including two members of the Salandran right. In appearance little seemed altered, but actually parliamentary government had been seriously eroded. Outside Montecitorio there were new concentrations of forces on left and right; labor organizations had formed a new Alleanza del Lavoro around the armature of the CGL, while agrarians and industrialists had convened to map a common strategy. At Rome, the Giolittian democrats and the right had converged, both clearly hostile to any possible antifascist coalition of Turati Socialists, Nittian Democrats, and Popolari. Despite the refloating of a cabinet based upon PPI and liberal votes, initiative in the Chamber, as in the country at large, depended upon the right.[50]

In the wake of the crisis, liberals viewed the Popolari as illegitimate political extortionists. Fittingly, the bitter dispute in the Cremona region during the following months pitted the Catholic leagues against the fascist and agrarian right. In liberal eyes the situation became even more threatening when, in the wake of the anti-Mori demonstrations in Bologna, the Socialists finally moved toward a left-wing coalition. In June the parliamentary group decided that it would support any government determined to resist the Fascists. Although the national Socialist Party leadership disavowed the resolution, about sixty deputies maintained their stance and, with the CGL leadership, declared the independent responsibility of their own parliamentary group behind Turati, Treves, Modigliani, and Matteotti. Yet if the maximalists stubbornly waited for bourgeois crisis (even while their member-

[50] On the "veto": "Don Sturzo incombe," *GdI*, February 23, 1922; "La crisi e la responsabilità," *CdS*, February 23, and "Veti e siluri," *CdS*, February 25, 1922 (Less critical of the PPI than the *GdI*); also De Rosa, *Storia del partito popolare*, pp. 192–197; Sturzo, *Popolarismo e fascismo*, pp. 49–50. For Giolitti's plans, Marcello Soleri, *Memorie* (Turin, 1949), pp. 129–130; on the economic organizations, see I. Minunni, "L'accordo tra industriali e agrari . . ." *Idea Nazionale*, February 21, 1921; and on the Alleanza del Lavoro, see Spriano, *Storia del partito comunista*, pp. 192 ff. For the right's welcoming of the government as an antisocialist coalition, see "Dal ministero al governo," *Idea Nazionale*, February 28, 1922, and for an overall narrative, Veneruso, *La vigilia del fascismo*, pp. 95–126.

ship plummeted to one-third that of 1919), the reformists harbored their own facile illusion that bourgeois leaders would bid for their support. In fact Nitti was moving to the right even while Giolitti and Orlando had come to feel that Fascist inclusion in the government was more essential than Socialist. Bonomi now seemed most receptive to the reformists, but as the crisis in the summer was to reveal, he was unable to restore his support of a half-year earlier.

The parliamentary crisis that the liberals now feared was precipitated by Fascist violence in Cremona. When Farinacci summoned his squads to the city in July, they invaded the prefecture and ransacked the apartment of Guido Miglioli. Already uncertain about continuing its support for the cabinet, the PPI now withdrew its confidence to bring about the second major crisis in half a year. Liberals were caught between their fear of a leftist ministry and exasperation at the Fascists for upsetting the delicate parliamentary equilibrium. Facta's cabinet included two of Salandra's followers and seemed the most advantageous combination the right could win. Mussolini himself found the situation embarrassing. As the decisive parliamentary vote came up, he did not wish to desert the Salandran liberals with whom he had an informal party alliance; but if the Fascists joined them in supporting Facta, while Popolari, Socialists, and Nittians brought the government down, the vote of confidence might suggest a clear left-wing majority with an antifascist mandate. Mussolini thus ended by voting alongside the left and the PPI in defeating Facta on July 19.[51]

Despite the fears of the liberals and the right, neither Socialists nor Catholics were willing or able to work together. The maximalists and Communists rejected any collaboration with bourgeois ministers: better the victory of outright Fascist reaction, which would at least unmask the bourgeois state and unite the proletariat. The sixty Turati secessionists reaffirmed the necessity of collaboration, but declined to assure Bonomi that they would support a new government unconditionally. Similarly, Sturzo had been conferring with Turati and Treves, Matteotti and Modigliani, but the PPI as a whole was not prepared to enter a ministry with the reformist Socialists. To preserve its own internal unity, the Popolari called instead for a broad government of all but the extremes of left and right.

This left the outcome the upshot of clientelistic rivalries. Orlando, who was initially designated, proposed a grand cabinet of personalities

[51] The account of the crisis of July 1922 is drawn from Paolo Alatri, "Il secondo ministero Facta e la marcia su Roma," *Le origini del fascismo* (Rome, 1956), esp. pp. 118–144; De Rosa, *Storia del partito popolare*, pp. 218–273; Tasca, *Nascita del fascismo*, II, pp. 325–339, 376–384, n. 130; Veneruso, *La vigilia del fascismo*, pp. 452–522 (as well as pp. 278–299 on the split within the socialist ranks); Novacco, *Storia del parlamento italiano*, XII, pp. 255–264.

and pacification that would go from Mussolini as far left as possible. The Catholics, however, refused to support such a ministry, and Orlando ceded to Bonomi, who sought a center-left formula, the logical extrapolation of his situation in February. The Popolari were agreed, and Turati promised the votes, if not the participation of his group. Giolitti, however, remained hostile. He and his followers wanted Facta restored, presumably to serve as his "lieutenant" until he could arrange the great combination with the Fascists that he had no doubt contemplated since resigning the year before. The eighty-year-old minister considered that an antifascist policy was not feasible, and was flattered by his followers into believing that he alone could master the deteriorating situation. It was tactically imperative, therefore, to prevent Catholics and Socialists uniting under another's leadership. Corradini encouraged the torpedoing of Bonomi's ministry at Rome, while Giolitti's friend Olindo Malagodi published the ex-premier's decisive attack upon Bonomi's proposed antifascist ministry: "What good can come for the country from a *connubio* of Don Sturzo, Treves, and Turati?" A new government would either bring on civil war in combatting fascism or be quickly overthrown. In sum, Giolitti apparently condemned all alternatives but restoring the *status quo* in expectation of his own return. When the moment came—Corradini suggested November—Giolitti would step in for Facta, win Mussolini's participation with a few portfolios, have the squads disarmed, and accept the support of the exhausted and chastened Turati Socialists. Even the usually loyal *La Stampa* condemned Giolitti's veto of Bonomi: there was no guarantee that a center-left ministry could last, but the effort was worth making. Instead, after a succession of minor candidacies—including the inevitable refusal by Filippo Meda—the task returned to Facta as the militant forces of left and right in the country threatened direct action unless the crisis was resolved.[52]

The second Facta ministry had little control outside Rome. It was installed in alarm as the new Alleanza del Lavoro finally felt impelled

[52] Bonomi, *La politica italiana dopo Vittorio Veneto*, pp. 164–167, lays primary blame for his failure on Turati's refusal to promise definitive support. Cf. F. Manzotti, "Un momento della crisi della democrazia prefascista: l'incarico a Bonomi nel luglio 1922," *Il Risorgimento*, xvII (1965), pp. 119–124. For the calculations behind Giolitti's vetoes (directed against Orlando as well as Bonomi), see Corradini to Giolitti, July 19 and August 2, 1922, in Pavone, ed., *Carte Giolitti*, III, pp. 370–372, 377; Giolitti's letter to Malagodi discussed in De Rosa, *Storia del partito popolare*, pp. 258–260, n. 49. Fear of civil war cited by Giolitti to Facta, July 23, in Répaci, *La marcia su Roma*, II, pp. 28–29. For the overall evolution of the press toward the possible government coalitions, see Brunello Vigezzi, ed., *1919–1925. Dopoguerra e fascismo* (Bari, 1965), pp. 45–47 (on the *GdI*), 108–121 (on *La Tribuna*, Malagodi's organ), 221–230 (on the *CdS*), 333–338 (on *La Stampa*, which indicatively changed from a resolute antifascist stance to the hope for a coalition from Turati to Mussolini!).

to call its "legal strike" on behalf of a government of the left. Its first days were spent in surrendering the city halls of Milan and Genoa to the fascist counteroffensive against the legal strike, as between August 3 and 5 the Fascists embarked on an orgy of destruction throughout northern and central Italy. In the wake of the convulsion Facta appeared to hold power only on suffrance of the Fascists. There was no longer any notion that the premier's solution of excluding the political extremes was still viable. What the liberals, from Giolitti to Albertini and Salandra—even Nitti—now asked was how the Fascists could be brought into the government with the least cost to themselves. After the legal strike, as Salandra later wrote, fascism appeared "the salvation and the only valid garrison against subversion and anarchy. . . . It was necessary in my opinion to give a legal form to the inevitable advent of fascism without delay."[53]

Few liberals were so ideologically sympathetic as Salandra, but most now came to conceive the problem in the same spirit. The Duce must be persuaded not to resort to revolutionary means but to accept a peaceful collaboration. As in the fall of 1921, when liberals celebrated Mussolini's channeling of Fascist energy into a disciplined Party, now they pleaded for his restraint against the hotheads of his movement. After the Fascist take-over in Trent and Bolzano, Albertini virtually promised power to Mussolini if he would refrain from a *coup d'état*. A Fascist government, he argued, would perforce inaugurate a liberal program, since liberalism was tantamount to the assertion of state authority. Facta had to withdraw, he wrote his correspondent Emanuel on October 10, to forestall a *coup*; two days later he stated in the *Corriere*: "There is only one thing to do: quickly call the Fascists to share government responsibility . . . aid those of their men who most feel the gravity of the moment. . . . No one cannot wish that the situation be clarified with constitutional procedures."[54]

Liberal leaders by this time were racing to win Mussolini for their own coalition; even Nitti tentatively initiated probings, and in a political speech on October 19 called for new elections and integration of the Fascist ethos into the life of the country. New elections would clearly return a vastly increased Fascist delegation to Rome, but they

[53] Antonio Salandra, *Memorie politiche, 1916–1925* (Milan, 1951), p. 17. For the legal strike: Tasca, *Nascita e avvento del fascismo*, II, pp. 333–356; Spriano, *Storia del partito comunista italiano*, pp. 206–215, who emphasizes the reformists' initiative in the strike once their parliamentary negotiations failed. For Turati's own justification, see his conversation with Storti, July 31, 1922, in ACS, Rome: Min. Int., Dir. gen. P.S., Div. Aff. gen. e ris., 1922, B. 41, "Sciopero legalitario," f. "Affari generali."

[54] Albertini to Emanuel, October 10, 1922, in Albertini, *Epistolario*, III, pp. 1588–1589. Also *CdS*, October 6, 7 ("Lo stato liberale"), October 12, 1922 ("La via").

had become the apparent Fascist price for withholding from insurrection. Giolitti, too, opened negotiations with Mussolini through Lusignoli. This was a more serious affair for the Duce, for a combination with Giolitti offered a real route to power should he be unable to impose his own ministry. The ex-premier also sounded out the Popolari on joining a government; the Catholics were chastened and dispirited; their attack on Facta in July had yielded no results, and they felt isolated. What is more, Vatican authorities seemed more reserved toward the Party leadership, and the conservative elements within it were recovering influence. Still, Sturzo would enter a Giolitti government only if the Fascists were excluded, and the point of the ministry for the Piedmontese leader was precisely to bring Mussolini into the government as his ward. Isolated in Cuneo, Giolitti received his news from his followers—Porzio, Corradini, Sforza, and others—and they all nourished the illusion of his own indispensability.[55]

Even Facta may have been waiting for Giolitti to take the burden of government from his shoulders, although he entered into negotiations with the Fascists himself by the end of October at the King's behest. Giolittians feared a double game, with Facta seeking to keep himself in office by ceding a majority of portfolios in the cabinet. Facta was probably seeking to hold on, at least until his political mentor and captain had a stable alternative ready. But the government was feeble within as well as without: Salandra's follower Vincenzo Riccio, Minister of Public Works, wanted a rightist solution. Marcello Soleri, Carlo Taddei, the former Prefect of Turin and Minister of the Interior, and Giulio Alessio, Minister of Justice from the democratic left, were strongly opposed to the Fascists. Amendola, who was serving as Minister of Colonies, also rejected Fascist violence, but even he continued to rank fascism as a moral equivalent to the Socialist alternative.[56]

In sum, there could be no liberal antifascist stance, because with rare exceptions the liberals wanted fascism to share power. Mussolini, however, was unwilling to serve as a mere junior partner: he wanted elec-

---

[55] For the political activity in October, see Répaci, La marcia su Roma, I, pp. 387–427; De Rosa, Storia del partito popolare, pp. 278–298; Tasca, Nascita e avvento del fascismo, II, pp. 423 ff.; Alatri, Le origini del fascismo, pp. 213 ff.; for letters to Giolitti, see Pavone, ed., Carte Giolitti, III, pp. 385–392.

[56] Répaci, La marcia su Roma, pp. 415 ff., an account based on Facta's correspondence. For Alessio's effort to restore the impartial and effective administration of justice, see Neppi Modona, Sciopero, potere politico e magistratura, pp. 269–273, 314–316 (notes); also Giulio Alessio, La crisi dello stato parlamentare e l'avvento del fascismo (memorie inedite di un ex-ministro) (Padua, 1946), esp. pp. 27–42, who stresses Facta's resistance with bitterness. For Amendola's views—less important perhaps than his concrete support for Alessio's program—see his October 1 speech at Sala Consiliana, now in La nuova democrazia, pp. 143 ff.

tions that might give him a hundred seats or so in return for any coalition. Moreover, his Southern leadership, such as Aurelio Padovani of Naples, yearned for the glories of a squadrist campaign in the Mez-zogiorno. Mussolini habitually avoided foreclosing his alternatives; he appeased Balbo and Farinacci by planning the March on Rome from mid-October as well as readying an electoral campaign. When he him-self weakened momentarily in the final crisis before the promise of a few portfolios, his advisers, Michele Bianchi above all, pressed him to hold out for real control. Meanwhile, as the Fascists assembled at Naples on October 24 and the rightist ministers precipitated the final crisis by withdrawing from the cabinet a couple of days later, the lib-erals kept pleading for "legality." Legality now meant only avoiding a rupture of continuity at Rome or any gamble on antifascist resistance; it added up to the belief that the liberal state, as the *Giornale d'Italia* wrote, could assimilate even Mussolini. Mussolini, however, was de-termined to demonstrate that while he could compete in the liberals' arena, he would impose his own rules. The strategic planning for the March on Rome, which began its countdown on the morrow of the Congress of Naples, was not bereft of posing and bluff. But it confirmed the isolation of Rome: even if the capital could be defended success-fully, what sort of government and state could quell a military chal-lenge only at its own doorstep? It forced the military to weigh the costs of civil war upon their own inner cohesion; and it probably prompted the skeptical Victor Emmanuel to question the administrative com-petence of the premier—a professional politician seemingly insouciant about the dissolution of the state—who asked for a power of command beyond his visible capacities.[57]

The result was two years and more of liberal self-abasement. There was indeed continuity between liberalism and the fascism of 1920–1925, but the question was what balance would finally be struck between parliamentary and authoritarian government. One area in which the Fascists could easily bargain was economic. Before the Fascist take-over, Mussolini reaffirmed to the business community—in a major address at Udine on September 19 and in meetings with industrialists on Octo-ber 16—that fascism meant an end to the "statism" they detested.

[57] For the events: Efrem Ferraris, *La marcia su Roma veduta dal Viminale* (Rome, 1946), pp. 45–123 (a diary of the Chief of Cabinet at the Interior Minis-try, stressing Bianchi's influence in excluding a coalition outcome); also Répaci, *La marcia su Roma*, I, pp. 451–578; Alatri, "Il secondo ministero Facta e la marcia su Roma," in *Le origini del fascismo*, pp. 161–249; Lyttelton, *Seizure of Power*, pp. 83–93; from the fascist side, see Chiurco, *Storia de la rivoluzione fascista*, V, *Anno 1922 Parte II*. Also, *GdI*, September 23 ("La monarchia") and September 27 ("Liberalismo e fascismo").

It is possible to overestimate the degree of business support for Mussolini: writers have ascribed a concerted alliance between fascism and industrial capital; but in the political question as in all their organizational efforts, Italian industry revealed fragmented and *ad hoc* responses. The philo-fascism of Milanese business leaders, such as Antonio Benni or the banker De Capitani, was more enthusiastic than the cautious reserve of Ettore Conti (also a Milanese) or Fiat's Giovanni Agnelli. The "national bloc" created for the 1921 elections had brought together liberals and Fascists and provided an initial legitimization for the latter. If Turin's Fascist boss, De Vecchi, liked to prick at Agnelli, other Fascists such as Cesare Rossi, Ottavio Corgini, or Massimo Rocca craved the respectable partnership of industrialists. In May 1922 Rocca spurred the creation of a parliamentary caucus, the Economic Alliance, which united Fascist deputies with the presidents of Confindustria and the Confederation of Agriculture, men who, as liberals, were urging Facta to remove Socialist town councils. Industry spokesmen remained guarded: their dominant theme up to the actual March on Rome was the need to channel the Fascist movement into a national government under Giolitti or Salandra. Confindustria expressed the hope that the Fascists could help educate the working class to a more national consciousness. Likewise, industry's contributions were probably a function of local conditions before October 1922.[58] Nonetheless, fascism could promise what industry badly wanted: "strong" government, permanent limitations on labor, confirmation of the import duties recently accorded under Facta, final restoration of municipal government to liberal coalitions, higher indirect taxes, and an end to subsidies for the cooperatives that the agrarians especially hated.[59]

In return the liberal organizations moved toward closer collabora-

[58] For the attitudes of businessmen toward fascism during 1921–1922, see Piero Melograni, *Gli industriali e Mussolini. Rapporti tra Confindustria e fascismo dal 1919 al 1929* (Milan, 1972), pp. 9–30; Roland Sarti, *Fascism and the Industrial Leadership in Italy, 1919–1940* (Berkeley, 1971), pp. 29–40; Mario Abrate, *La lotta sindacale nella industrializzazione d'Italia, 1906–1926* (Turin, 1967), pp. 371–377; Valerio Castronovo, *Giovanni Agnelli* (Turin, 1971), pp. 302 ff., 360–371, who points out the stakes within the Fiat work force for Agnelli's politics; Renzo De Felice, *Mussolini il fascista*, I, pp. 121–122, 289–296; and his "Primi elementi sul finanziamento del fascismo dalle origini al 1924," *Rivista storica del socialismo*, nr. 22 (May–August 1964), pp. 223–251, suggesting the unimportance of industry support, as did Felice Guarneri, *Battaglie economiche tra le due grandi guerre*, 2 vols. (Milan, 1953), I, pp. 53 ff. For harsher views of industry's relationship, see Ernesto Rossi, *I padroni del vapore* (Bari, 1955), esp. pp. 33–37.

[59] For these economic issues: Catalano, *Potere economico e fascismo*, pp. 297 ff. on the business struggle for higher import duties; A. Cabiati, "Pagare le tasse," *La Stampa*, August 18, 1922, cited in Répaci, *La marcia su Roma*, I, p. 344; for the hostility to cooperatives, see Maffeo Pantaleoni's frequent denunciations in the *GdI*, including December 8, 1921, and January 15, 1922.

tion. Convening at Bologna from October 8 to 10, 1922, representatives of the diverse liberal associations worked to organize a new and united Partito Liberale Italiano. The initiative was dominated by the right, whose primary purpose was to impose a philo-fascist orientation upon their associates.[60] The chief issue of the convention quickly became that of the stance to be taken toward "democracy." Would the new party call itself liberal-democratic—as did the groups in the Chamber—or simply liberal? The controversy was more than semantic. The term "democracy" by now suggested an antifascist orientation that embarrassed the right. Moreover, the liberal conference followed in the wake of a last effort at reviving "democractic" unity in August and September. The old Sardinian deputy, Francesco Cocco Ortu, a loyal Giolittian, had supervised a last attempt to reinvigorate democratic forces by initiating a parliamentary caucus and organizing a schedule of meetings throughout Italy, to be addressed by Giolitti, Nitti, Orlando, De Nicola, Bonomi, and others. Giolitti, however, disavowed the campaign, and Cocco Ortu felt compelled to renounce it. It was clearly embarrassing for Giolitti while he was sounding out Mussolini's intentions. Once Cocco Ortu's abortive effort to reinvigorate an antifascist stance among the amorphous liberals proved abortive, the initiative passed to the right. Nonetheless, the liberal right could not guarantee the outcome of the Bologna conclave. Piedmont especially remained a stronghold of Giolittian democratic liberalism, and while the old leader was unwilling to take an antifascist stand, his supporters might not be ready to swallow a Salandran fellow-traveling with the Fascists. As De Capitani wrote Salandra, the occasion might provide a "not very creditable arena for the 'professionals' who see no other means outside parliamentarism. . . . What you say about 'democracy' is perfectly exact. If we want *to stand in good stead* with fascism, we can spare no tenderness for this *decrepit coquette* (not to say worse)."[61]

The Milan banker did not have to worry: the rightist liberals dominated the conference from the outset. In an effort to mime the Fascists and appear as a viable mass party, they even mustered their own "khaki shirts," who took an oath to king and liberalism. A few speakers sought to prevent internal divisions: Albertini warned of splitting

[60] Cf. ACS, Rome: Min. Int., Dir. gen. P.S., Div. Aff. gen. e ris., 1922, B. 90, f. "Partito monarchico," sf. "Siena," prefectural report of September 25, 1922. For accounts of the Congress, see *CdS*, October 10, 1922, p. 2, and October 11, p. 2; also reports from Nello Quilici's philo-fascist *Resto del Carlino* of Bologna, same dates.

[61] De Capitani to Salandra, September 19, 1922, in Lucera: Carte Salandra, 1922. For the effort by Cocco Ortu, see Répaci, *La marcia su Roma*, I, pp. 242–248. For the Bologna Congress and a harsh judgment on De Capitani, see the memoirs of another PLI participant, Alberto Giovannini, *Il rifiuto del Aventino* (Bologna, 1966), pp. 77–135, 164.

liberalism, and the conservative Belotti also asked for unity. The right set the tone of the conference, however, as elitist, antisocialist, and antidemocratic. "Democracy," charged one speaker, "has no other purpose than that of tying together liberalism and its natural enemy socialism." The Bologna liberal Alberto Giovannini, who presented a resolution for constituting a liberal party pure and simple, told the conference to "reject that democracy which had trafficked with social-ism, that democracy which has poisoned the country, prostituting it to socialism." Salandra's parliamentary colleague Sandrini thanked fascism and reaction for having saved liberal Italy. "In fascism I see the principle that unites us. Let there be an association, a collaboration between us and them."[62]

Despite these ideological provocations, the Piedmontese and other Giolittian liberals rarely spoke out in opposition. The *Corriere* reported that the democratic liberals could have mustered a vote hostile to the motion that rejected a "democratic" label and founded a Liberal Party without qualification, but that there was no effort to do so.[63] Instead groups representing 44,000 approved the antidemocratic stamp, 21,000 abstained, and 12,000 withdrew. Those in favor came most compactly from Tuscany and in part Lombardy, those against from Piedmont. Emilia and areas of Lombardy sent divided delegations. In general, the areas of Fascist strength coincided with those of the more reactionary liberal delegations. De Capitani was much relieved, and termed the congress "in a word: the triumph of good sense."[64]

In part, though, it was just a deluded effort to keep equal influence alongside the Fascists. Its major speakers invoked the name and doc-trines of Antonio Salandra and sought to claim his ideological heritage. Fittingly enough, Salandra, too, was to have his own moment of personal illusions in late October. Salandra was approached by Musso-lini on the twenty-third, because the Fascist leader calculated that Sa-landra's right-wing associate Vicenzo Riccio, inside the cabinet, could help precipitate the final crisis. The Fascists did not neglect to hint broadly that a Salandra ministry would be acceptable to them. With the collapse of Facta, the Nationalists would also have preferred a Salandra cabinet, as would have no doubt the monarch and court cir-

[62] *CdS*, October 10–12, 1922; also *Resto del Carlino*, October 10–12.
[63] A. G. Bianchi, "Dopo il congresso di Bologna," *CdS*, October 12, 1922, p. 2.
[64] De Capitani to Salandra, October 10, 1922, in Lucera: Carte Salandra, 1922. De Capitani added that "Contact with fascism is a necessity," and he was de-lighted to have received a picture from the Duce dedicated, he stressed, with "personal and *political* cordiality." On the right-wing stance of the conference, see Nino Valeri, *Da Giolitti a Mussolini. Momenti della crisi del liberalismo* (Florence, 1956), p. 108. For other meetings, see ACS, Rome: Min. Int., Dir. gen. P.S., Div. Aff. gen. e ris., 1922, B. 90, f. "Partito monarchico," sf. "Bergamo and Pisa: Convegno regionale liberale toscana."

cles. After the king had rejected Facta's demand to impose a state of siege and mobilize the army against the Fascists converging on Rome (October 28), he sought to secure a Salandra-Mussolini combination. But Mussolini had no reason to take second place once Victor Emmanuel had vetoed any resistance to the March on Rome. Salandra was happy enough to abandon his effort at a coalition once Mussolini refused to play a subordinate role. Instead, Mussolini created his own broad-based cabinet on October 30, including Nationalists, conservative Popolari, De Capitani, and delegates of the Democrazia Sociale.[65] Even a representative of the reformist Socialists—who had finally seceded from the PSI in early October—was invited, although his party vetoed collaboration.

The Salandra candidacy had been the most vaporous of all the liberal illusions of October 1922; once the situation degenerated enough to make a Salandra government appear possible, there was no impediment to a Fascist one. Salandra, moreover, was a spent force. As his correspondence at Lucera reveals, he was merely an ancestral god for the more self-serving philo-fascists such as De Capitani. They saluted him, praised his 1915 leadership and his *Risorgimento* liberalism, and informed him of workaday political events. But Salandra no longer exerted an active influence, and he was unprepared to assert leadership, leaving that to the new "elites" whose vitality he frequently celebrated. The brief belief in his ministerial candidacy suggested that the right-wing liberals overestimated their own political importance. Mussolini would exploit and be exploited by the liberal elites, but no longer through party mechanisms.

Through 1923 and 1924 the Partito Liberale Italiano remained divided between rightist and democratic liberals. But the formation did not bind the votes of any of the parliamentary deputies, as even Salandra made certain.[66] It was all the less significant because the Fascists carefully worked to subvert and atomize all rival party groupings: in part through decentralized but endemic violence—most notoriously the killing and exile of working-class representatives in Turin

[65] On the Salandra candidacy, see Répaci, *La marcia su Roma*, pp. 451–460, 546–558; Tasca, *Nascita del fascismo*, pp. 453–457, both of which condense the large memoir literature. For Salandra's own perception of the crisis, see G. B. Gifuni, ed., *Il diario di Salandra* (Milan, 1969), pp. 269–275 (MS in Lucera: Carte Salandra). Cf. De Rosa, *Il partito popolare*, pp. 285–302 for the negotiations for a Giolittian solution as mediated by Lusignoli.

[66] Draft letter to President of the PLI, December 2, 1923, in Lucera: Carte Salandra. For the continuing dispute between the Giolittian democratic liberals, led by Soleri within the PLI, and the right, see *GdI*, March 8, p. 2: "La sezione di Roma del PLI contro la infiltrazione democratica," also ACS, Rome: Min. Int., Dir. gen. P.S., Div. Aff. gen. e ris., 1923, B. 71, f. "Partiti politici," sf. "Partito liberale italiano," report of prefect of Bologna, July 5, on national council meeting.

in late December, 1922[67]—in part through a corrupting *trasformismo*. Socialists excepted, the Chamber remained generally compliant before Mussolini and quickly endorsed a grant of "full powers" for a year, supposedly on the informal assurance that the executive grant would be used only for trimming the bureaucracy or rationalizing tax laws. Only a few speakers complained; as one Socialist deputy pointed out, however, the system of bypassing parliament with decree legislation had been accepted since the war.[68]

While parliament became silent, Fascists were occupied in undermining rival parties on the local level. In the initial months of Fascist administration the government dissolved about twenty provincial administrations where the left was entrenched and, in its first year of power, 547 communal governments, 90 percent of which had been under Socialist or Popolari control. Left-wing newspapers were sequestered, and socialist cooperatives turned over to Fascist administration.[69] The first major political-party transformation was the Nationalists' merger with the Fascists. Ideologically akin to the Fascists, the Nationalists had worked for a government of the right and had mobilized their "blue shirts," the Sempre Pronti, against the Legal Strike. But the Nationalists claimed no revolutionary origin; instead they exalted a monarchical authoritarianism and might even have helped to defend Rome if Victor Emmanuel had ordered a state of siege. In the last months before the Fascist take-over and in the period subsequent, the Nationalists found themselves swollen, above all in the South and Center, by new recruits. Fugitives from all the old groupings, left as well as right, sought a viable party identification under the new government which might preserve their local position and influence against Fascist ambitions. While the Nationalist leadership cooperated with Mussolini at Rome, their Association was becoming a sanctuary for local elites or even leftist conventicles who needed a new label. To control this trend as well as to quell occasional demonstrations between rival "blue shirts" and "black shirts," the leaders of the two movements decided upon a party fusion in the winter of 1922–1923. Alfredo Rocco sought to guarantee status and funds for the Nationalists within the new formation, as well as one-third of the major posts in the future executive organs, but Mussolini vetoed any formal commitment of money or positions. Nonetheless, the Duce remained intellectually

[67] See Renzo De Felice, "I fatti di Torino del dicembre 1922," *Studi Storici*, iv, 1 (1963), pp. 51–122.

[68] AP, Camera: Legislatura xxvi, pp. 8390–8725 (November 23–25, 1922), and esp. pp. 8619–8620 for the Socialist Riboldi. Cf. Novacco, *Storia del parlamento*, xii, pp. 267–274.

[69] Santarelli, *Movimento e regime fascista*, p. 328.

dependent upon the Nationalists for whatever ideological coherence his future regime would possess.[70]

Absorbing the Nationalist Association into the Fascist Party did not, however, eliminate the influx of opportunistic recruits in the constituencies; instead it transferred the issue inside the PNF. Likewise, the proper relationship *vis-à-vis* the liberals and the Democrazia Sociale—a coalition partner—remained a dilemma. Fascist leaders resented the baronies that the old political class or social elites preserved, and sought jealously to undermine them wherever possible. At the Viminale, Bianchi's reports on the Southern political situation through 1923 allowed the government to keep track of the persistent effort to impose Fascist power. In Bari, for example, the old left-wing clientele that fascism had isolated was supposedly trying to take over the Fascist syndicates from within. In Messina, where the "Demo-sociale" leader di Cesarò dominated politics, the *fasci* found it hard to implant themselves; indeed, di Cesarò was exploiting his own cabinet position to delay Fascist penetration of his fief. In Sicily, Achille Starace reported, the Mafia was ready to pass "bag and baggage" into the Fascist camp in return for being left alone, but to accept them would alienate peasant sympathies. Sicily, in any case, needed Rome's attention; its political circles were upset at the suppression of the Ministry of Agriculture and would have to be soothed with a visit from Mussolini. Finally, in Naples Padovani's brand of Fascist radicalism and personalism presented a special problem, because it alienated the local elites that the Party hoped to woo. By late July the Grand Council painstakingly reviewed the progress that the Party and Fascist syndicates had made in capturing city councils, wresting control of unions, organizing and centralizing patronage, relief, and agrarian credit, eradicating *Nittismo*, and bringing Fascist dissidents to obedience. The methods were often old-fashioned, but the objective was clearly an authoritarian centralization of power.[71]

[70] For the relationship of Nationalists and Fascists, see Franco Gaeta, *Nazionalismo italiano* (Naples, 1965), pp. 217–230; Paolo Ungari, *Alfredo Rocco e l'ideologia giuridica del fascismo* (Brescia, 1963), is best on the ideological content; cf. Salvemini, *Lezioni di Harvard, Scritti* I, pp. 358–359; Salvatorelli, *Nazionalfascismo*, pp. 18–19 for the Nationalists' ideological hegemony; for the role of the Nationalists in the crisis of October, see Répaci, *La marcia su Roma*, I, pp. 273–276; also Raffaele Paolucci, *Il mio piccolo mondo perduto* (Bologna, 1952), pp. 287–297.

[71] The reports are found in ACS, Rome: Carte Michele Bianchi, B. 2, PNF, Direzione Segreteria Politica, "Relazioni sulla situazione delle Puglie e della Sicilia," July 7, 1923. For the Padovani situation, cf. Raffaele Colapietra, *Napoli tra dopoguerra e fascismo* (Milan, 1962), pp. 227–240. For the examination by the Grand Council, see the protocols of meetings 13 through 25, July 13–28, 1923, in Partito Nazionale Fascista, *Il Gran Consiglio nei primi sei anni dell'era fascista* (Rome, n.d. [1929?]), pp. 43–81.

Nineteen hundred and twenty-three was thus a year of decentralized repression and patient organizing, of trying to demoralize and isolate the traditional political forces, whether democratic or conservative, Masonic or Nationalist, and of working to entrench Fascists who were not just opportunistic converts.[72] In the North, too, fascism faced difficulties, for liberals often remained distant and reserved. Mussolini could explode violently against open liberal opposition, as when he ordered searches and confiscation of Piero Gobetti's Turin journal, *La Rivoluzione Liberale*.[73] Even the quiet independence and aloofness of the Turin industrial elite infuriated the Fascist boss, De Vecchi, and ultimately angered the prefect, Palmieri. Fiat's Agnelli was willing to accept the new government, whose promises of efficient management probably appealed to his concepts of industrial productivity. In return Mussolini elevated the Fiat leader to the Senate in March 1923. But this honor could not purchase Agnelli's renunciation of his claims to local political and social preeminence, nor overcome his guarded reserve toward Fascist unions. De Vecchi raged against "plutocracy" and tried to challenge the industrialist with an ill-timed strike by Fascist unions in October 1923, before being removed to the governorship of Somalia. The prefect was alarmed by De Vecchi's crude tactics, but at the same time he tried to undermine the Turin liberals, supported by *La Stampa*, by encouraging the pro-Fascist industrialists to unite in a new monarchical union in early 1924. Throughout the year, however, Mussolini remained circumspect. The Duce's stance toward industry as a corporate group was far more cautious than his contemptuous cat-and-mouse attitude toward the liberal political associations.[74]

While Mussolini's lieutenants contested the local nexuses of power, the premier himself undertook the major step toward national hegemony with a new electoral law. Within a few weeks after reaching Rome, the government revealed its intentions as Bianchi proposed an election bill that would enlarge the voting districts and reserve two-thirds of their seats to the slate receiving a plurality. The remaining one-third

[72] For the divisions in Masonry between pro-fascist, Scotch rite (Palazzo Gesù), and the sometimes antifascist (Palazzo Giustiniani) lodges, see Santarelli, *Movimento e regime fascista*, p. 334; also De Felice, *Mussolini il fascista*, I, pp. 349–353; and Cesare Rossi, *Mussolini com'era*, pp. 174–185.

[73] See Mussolini to Prefect Palmieri, February 8, 1923, and subsequent wires in ACS, Rome: Min. Int., Gabinetto di S.E. Sottosegretario [Aldo] Finzi: Ordine Pubblico, B. 9, f. 89, Torino, sf. "Giornale Rivoluzione Liberale." Parliamentary criticism of the government's moves in AP, Camera: Legislatura xxvi, pp. 9553–9557 (May 10, 1923).

[74] Castronovo, *Giovanni Agnelli*, pp. 371–391; Abrate, *La lotta sindacale*, pp. 378–390 [which incorporates the testimony of the "conservative" fascist: Raoul Ghezzi, *Comunisti, industriali e fascisti a Torino* (Turin, 1923)]; also Palmieri's report of June 26, 1923, in Segr. Part. del Duce, NA Microfilm, T586/1092/068502; and reports in ACS, Rome: Min. Int., Gabinetto di S.E. Sottosegretario Finzi: Ordine Pubblico, B. 13, f. 175, Torino, sf. 2, "Situazione politica."

would be divided proportionally among the minority contenders. Agreement existed far beyond the Fascist Party that some amendment of the 1919 electoral system was required, but differences persisted both within and outside Fascist ranks on the specifics. Liberals generally asked for a return to the single-member constituencies that had preserved their majorities before 1919. Yet Farinacci, too, defended the single-member constituency, in part because of his abiding hatred for the Popolari and the desire to undermine their position, in part because he may have feared that opposition or fellow-traveling lists could prevail in some of the enlarged districts. After the alternatives went to a committee of Nationalist and Fascist leaders, the Grand Council voted in late April to prepare a bill based upon Bianchi's proposal. Now, however, the final quota of seats awarded to the strongest list was left indeterminate for purposes of negotiation. On the other hand, for purposes of allocating the majority seats, the Kingdom as a whole was designated a single electoral college, which made nomination to the Fascist list a guarantee of election.[75]

The bill was a harsh one, yet most of the liberals in parliament acquiesced in the need for some "reform." In June Mussolini took pains to announce that he did not wish to undercut parliament, but to strengthen it and overcome the discredit into which it had fallen. Bianchi's original proposals for strengthened powers of dissolution were conspicuously dropped. The key, though, would be the attitude of the Popolari, who officially formed part of the government's coalition. Sturzo and other leaders solidly opposed abolishing the proportional representation system upon which their parliamentary strength depended. On the other hand, many Catholic deputies feared isolation, and to the dismay of the PPI left, Alcide De Gasperi, the Party's floor leader, suggested a compromise whereby a list achieving 40 percent of the vote could win three-fifths of the seats, but below 40 percent or above 60 percent pure proportional representation would be applied. Mussolini, however, was determined to impose his own law.[76]

The liberals' disarray and the internal party transformation that the issue provoked among Catholics made electoral reform an acid solvent of any further effective parliamentary resistance. In June Mussolini presented the bill to a Commission of Eighteen chosen from the Chamber and chaired by Giolitti. Its majority of ten—including Giolitti,

[75] De Felice, *Mussolini il fascista*, I, pp. 518–524; Partito Nazionale Fascista, *Il Gran Consiglio*, p. 30 (March 17, 1923), and pp. 35–37 (April 26).

[76] For examples of the conservative liberals' reasoning that the electoral law was a "political act" needed to bring the basically popular events of October 1922 within the normal orbit of constitutionality, see Salandra, *Memorie*, pp. 40–41; also Giovannini, *Il rifiuto dell'Aventino*, pp. 265–284. General narratives in De Felice, *Mussolini il fascista*, I, pp. 524–536; and Novacco, *Storia del Parlamento*, XII, pp. 280–292.

Orlando, and Salandra—accepted the principle of the new law. The minority of eight—including Bonomi, the Giolittian Falcioni, De Gasperi, and Turati—rejected the bill. If in parliament the PPI united in opposition alongside dissident liberals, the bill might well lose. Mussolini skillfully turned to conciliation, and abandoned the contemptuous rhetoric with which he had first greeted the Chamber in November. Although threatening dissolution, he discussed opposition concerns calmly and depicted a Fascist leadership that was disbanding the squads, hoping to win working-class representatives for a cabinet role, and trying only to heal the breach between parliament and the country at large. The address disconcerted the liberal opposition. While Amendola spoke in opposition and ringingly declared that parliament could not be an accomplice in its own suppression, he yet abstained on the initial votes. So, too, did Bonomi, while Falcioni now reversed himself to approve the principle of the law, which won a preliminary 235 to 139 with 77 abstentions.[77]

The implicit fulcrum of the debate was the PPI. As Turati reminded them on July 15, their sentence would be written by their own hands.[78] But the Popolari were in deep travail. Although, with the exception of some pronouncedly clerical conservative or philo-fascist Catholics, most had been hostile to Mussolini before October 30, they had still given the government a provisional vote of confidence, and their colleague, Stefano Cavazzoni, was serving as Minister of Labor and Social Welfare. Yet Sturzo resumed antifascist organizing at the end of 1922, and worked to pull the Party from its ambivalent posture. Despite resistance from Party conservatives, he summoned a PPI congress at Turin in April 1923 to confirm his leadership and policy for the Party. Justifying participation in the ministry as an effort to bring fascism into the orbit of liberal parliamentary government, the Congress still asserted the independence of the PPI. Nonetheless, the parliamentary party remained more "collaborationist" than the national delegates, and was shaken by right-wing secessions. Vatican support, furthermore, was less certain than earlier. While l'Osservatore Romano was reluctant to disavow Sturzo, the Vatican was sensitive to the de-

[77] AP, Camera: Legislatura xxvi, pp. 10415–10681, for the debates July 10–15 and the preliminary vote; Novacco, Storia del Parlamento, xii, pp. 287–350 has the text of Mussolini's report and the majority and minority reports of the Commission of Eighteen. Amendola's speech now in La nuova democrazia, pp. 155–177, and Mussolini's parliamentary address in Opera Omnia, xix, pp. 308–320. Indications that Mussolini's appeal to working-class representatives had some resonance came with D'Aragona's statement that his negative vote did not bind the CGL. See F. Turati and A. Kuliscioff, Carteggio, vi: Il delitto Matteotti e l'Aventino (1923–1925) (Turin, 1959), pp. 88–92.

[78] Turati's speech, July 15, AP, Camera: Legislatura xxvi, pp. 10654 ff.; cited in De Felice, Mussolini il fascista, i, p. 531, and De Rosa, Il partito popolare, p. 410.

fections among the Catholic business elites, concerned with squadrist pressure on its peasantry, and, finally, grateful to Mussolini for his assistance in keeping afloat the overextended Banco di Roma, the keystone of a national Catholic banking and credit network. With the electoral law now up for debate, Mussolini made it clear that Sturzo's leadership was intolerable for fascism: he allowed the Farinacci intransigents to rough up Catholic youth groups and resume their rhetoric of violence. On the other side, he introduced state educational reforms that Catholics had long advocated. This time the campaign worked. *L'Osservatore Romano* now indicated that electoral reform had "its advantageous side," while a spokesman for the clergy suggested in the Catholic *Corriere d'Italia* that Sturzo was heading the Vatican toward "embarrassment" with the ministry. The energetic PPI organizer was an obedient priest: he resigned as Political Secretary on July 10, the day legislative debate was introduced. With this loss, the disillusioned left and center of the Party agreed to abstain rather than vote against the electoral bill. The PPI right under Cavazzoni, however, broke ranks to approve the law. They were to be expelled, but they took with them their control of the Banca di Roma and the so-called Catholic newspaper "trust."[79]

Had there been decisive opposition, the Chamber might have wrested a better compromise on behalf of parliamentarism. An effort by the Popolari to amend the bill with De Gasperi's 40 percent requirement, then one by Bonomi to secure 33 percent, came closer to success; the latter was rejected by only 178 to 157, but with key liberals, including Giolitti, opposing it. The next day, July 21, the Chamber approved the entire law 223–123. In the Senate, which briefly discussed the bill in November, opposition was even more restricted, and approval was foreordained (165–41). Within a year after first addressing the Italian parliament as a contemptuous victor, Mussolini had a power to create a compliant majority that the most masterful practitioners of transformism had never possessed.[80]

Here was in fact the first major rupture in institutional life that the Fascist take-over had brought. Despite the March on Rome Mussolini's nomination was a legal and even logical one. While Mussolini had extracted "full powers," they had not been granted, or really requested, to remold institutions. Now the majority had altered the electoral law,

[79] De Rosa, "La legge Acerbo e le dimissioni di Sturzo," in *Il partito popolare*, pp. 375–417; Mussolini's threats in *Opera Omnia*, xix, p. 274; for the crisis within the Catholic ranks, see also *CdS*, June 27, 28, and July 11, 1923. For the Turin debates, Francesco Malgeri, ed., *Gli atti dei congressi del Partito Popolare Italiano* (Brescia, 1969), pp. 429–453.

[80] Novacco, *Storia del Parlamento*, xii, pp. 291–292; AP, Camera: Legislatura xxvi, pp. 10970 ff.; AP: Senato, Legislatura xxvi, pp. 5357–5421. Cf. Alberto Aquarone, *L'organizzazione dello stato totalitario* (Turin, 1965), pp. 37–39.

which amounted, after all, to a key provision of the monarchy's constitutional order. While the political leadership had gambled on the conservative ballast of the South and of the Catholic peasantry, the electoral law of 1912 and then proportional representation of 1919 had instead imparted a radical direction and had mobilized all the class antagonisms of the country in the political arena. The liberals had hardly been prepared for 1912, and they were even less equipped to work with the consequences of proportional representation. Not that the left had a majority, but the "constitutional" forces were unwilling to make the coalitions or even undergo the transformation from associations of notables to a mass party that they now required to exert control. The crisis of the Bonomi Ministry and its painful resolution in the winter of 1921–1922 demonstrated that the liberals would not govern with the Socialists and only reluctantly accepted the Popolari.[81] As a result of their unwillingness, they had now accepted an electoral law that made the government and its prefects and party apparatus the virtual arbiter of any new majority. During the debates, the Fascist Francesco Giunta had taunted the liberals that such a trusteeship was only logical after they had repeatedly voted confidence in the government.[82] But this was faulty reasoning: no legislative approval hitherto had so touched the fundament of the liberal regime which, despite all defects, had been the regime of the parliamentary majority.

The liberals, however, did not lose everything. The destruction of the Popolari as a coherent political force was one by-product of the extended debate, and that was a long-yearned-for goal. Another gain, albeit superficial, was the commitment now of the government to an electoral and coalition strategy: the liberals had paid a huge dowry, but Mussolini was at least pledged to marriage. And in that pledge was the greater probability that basic social arrangements would remain beyond danger, that any threat of Fascist "radicals" gaining the upper hand was averted, that Mussolini would really need the "flanking" support the liberals wished to provide. With passage of the electoral law, the last component of the parliamentary center collapsed—the Nittians and the Popolari. Parliamentarism promised to wither into a mere appendage of public life. On the other hand, economic and social representation within the extraparliamentary cadres of the emerging governing system seemed more secure. With the surrender of real electoral competition, the political center in Italy ended an ineffective search for stability and influence through parliamentary representation. But nothing was given up save liberty.

[81] Veneruso, *La vigilia del fascismo*, pp. 527–528.
[82] AP, Camera: Legislatura xxvi, p. 10613; also Novacco, *Storia del Parlamento*, xii, p. 284.

PART III
PATHS TOWARD CORPORATIST
STABILITY

The lesson of 1921–1922 was a wearying and disillusioning one. The parliamentary leaders who sought to govern on the basis of moderate liberal compromise could not retain durable majorities. Briand, Wirth, and Giolitti all resigned before outright defeat, but in frustration and stalemate. Their setbacks did not just mean ordinary reshufflings of ministries. In retrospect, they reveal a more basic failure of parliamentary capacity for decision making. When in the late 1920's political stability was reconstructed, albeit briefly, the procedures for balancing interests and resolving conflicts were transformed. Even in France and Germany, where parliamentary machinery continued to function, the sources of power began to shift elsewhere. Increasingly the legislative process tended only to register rather than to shape the results of bargaining between economic competitors or independent bureaucratic agencies.

Why this bleeding away of parliamentary authority? Parliamentary coalitions had been asked, in effect, to take over the hard choices involved in distributing the costs of war and reconstruction. During the war itself, civilian sacrifices had been apportioned by executive agencies, but now the wartime machinery lay dismantled. Moreover, each feasible parliamentary majority—whether a coalition of the left or right, or a union of the center—proved too internally divided to parcel out the contested social product. Issues of inflation and revaluation, or of wages and hours, which embodied the distributive contests, helped to disintegrate parliamentary majorities just as reparations had done earlier. What permitted stability after 1924 was a shift in the focal point of decision making. Fragmented parliamentary majorities yielded to ministerial bureaucracies, or sometimes directly to party councils, where interest-group representatives could more easily work out social burdens and rewards. This displacement permitted a new compromise: a corporatist equilibrium in which private interests assumed the tasks that parliamentary coalitions found difficult to confront.

The chapters that follow examine the decay of parliamentary bargaining and the trial-and-error evolution of the new system. There were sharp differences from country to country. Like the "classical" liberal parliamentarism and liberal market economy of the nineteenth century, corporatist stability represents an ideal type, not a literal description of the political process. Expressed differently, the corporatist stability discerned here was like the convergence point for political trends that had progressed different distances toward the horizon. Nearest to the observer, the Third Republic still seemed able to overcome many of its divisions by traditional parliamentary mediation. In France the late 1920's appeared as an Indian summer of liberal representation. But close examination suggests that the old party system could arrange compromises only with great difficulty. Coalitions splintered internally over vexing financial and monetary questions. The fumbling decisions of the mid-1920's increasingly depended upon *ad hoc* majorities of latent interests rather than upon formal parties.

In Germany and Italy corporatist trends had progressed further. Weimar's parties represented contending interest groups with starkest clarity, and Reichstag politics reflected their conflicting objectives. But in this very mirroring of the market place, the German parliament served more as collective notary than as legislator. Fire gutted the Reichstag physically in February 1933, but only after a decade during which the clash of interests hollowed it politically. Nonetheless, the German political system at least allowed for an open clash of interests. This differentiated Weimar from Italy in the 1920's. Rome, too, adopted a new corporatism, but at the behest of an interlocked fascist government and an older managerial and political elite. Fascism destroyed any socioeconomic rivalry among autonomous interest groups, while Weimar retained a pluralist competition. Measured by the yardstick of liberty and repression, the difference was crucial.

In the second half of the decade each country enjoyed an ephemeral era of stability, growth, and international détente even as the search for political consensus moved beyond the capacities of inherited liberal parliamentarism. The degree of parliamentary eclipse varied, from the French legislature's helpless floundering with financial issues, to Weimar's liberal corporatism, to fascist authoritarianism. In each case, though, the new departures and tendencies logically followed earlier political failures. The decade after World War I brought a series of attempted political solutions: the failure to impose radicalism in 1918–1919, the failure to reconstruct a viable parliamentary center between 1920 and 1922, and finally, as the following chapters will show, the failure of nationalist coalitions to bring about the dramatic results they promised. Only the new corporatist trends permitted the stability and resolution of conflict that neither the left, the old center, nor the traditionalist right could provide.

· 6 ·

BETWEEN NATIONALISM
AND CORPORATISM:
THE RUHR CONFLICT

During 1922 and 1923 the right achieved more political influence than at any point since 1918. Welcomed by conservatives, Poincaré and Cuno, not to mention Mussolini, indicated that they would end the temporizing of Briand, Wirth, and Giolitti. The new political trends, however, turned out to be more ambiguous. None of the three broke so sharply with the methods of his predecessors as the right desired. The Ruhr conflict, moreover, suggested that the German and French recourse to nationalist policies actually worked to undermine strong national authority. Instead it encouraged industry to negotiate its own agreements and to work toward a Europe of forges rather than fatherlands.

Even as nationalism revived, then, corporatist developments intensified. Business leadership especially encroached upon the functions of the nation-state: commentators began to suggest that sovereignty was dissolving in a new feudalism. In reaction there emerged what Luigi Salvatorelli described in *La Stampa* as a Europe-wide rancorous petit bourgeois nationalism, hostile not only to the organized working class but to "cosmopolitan" capitalism as well.[1] In 1923 right-radicalism surfaced in all countries as Fascist intransigents, German racists, and even the adherents of Action Française took to the streets.

It would be wrong, however, to attribute the reaction against interest-group domination only to radicals of the right. Centrist and liberal leaders also spoke out for upholding the national interest as they saw it against business encroachment. By the fall of 1923, Poincaré and Stresemann had invoked the nineteenth-century, continental liberal belief that the integrity of the public power must be preserved against regional or economic interests. Neither could entirely prevail. If they both resisted the new corporatism that parceled out political functions to the economically powerful, they still could not restore the traditional authority of the state. Although they faced each other as spokesmen for France and Germany, national conflict actually undermined their parallel efforts to preserve the integrity of public sovereignty.

Hence the Ruhr conflict produced contradictory developments. Tra-

[1] Luigi Salvatorelli, "Concordia discors," *La Stampa*, August 24/25, 1923.

ditional bourgeois nationalist values were initially reinforced by the Franco-German conflict. But the frame of bourgeois authority and values, the nation-state, was simultaneously weakened by the very interest groups who benefited from a nationalist political atmosphere. Whether traditional sovereignty would gain or lose was left undecided by the Ruhr conflict itself; only the new economic developments after 1924 could assure an outcome. Meanwhile, the Ruhr clash demonstrated only that right-wing policies often worked at cross purposes for their nationalist advocates.

INFLATION, SOCIAL DEMOCRACY, AND THE CHALLENGE TO SOVEREIGNTY IN GERMANY

Paradoxically, if any group stood to lose by the eclipse of state authority in Germany, it was the Social Democrats. Representatives of the non-Catholic working class, the Social Democrats were also the upholders of republican sovereignty. The erosion of national authority and of their own power proceeded together. German developments during the hyperinflation demonstrated the linkage only too well.

Under stress, Berlin's sovereignty evaporated. The futile, last-minute bargaining in the Reich Chancellery to formulate a reparations offer even before the French marched into the Ruhr pointed up the continued splintering of German society. The accelerating inflation and administrative bankruptcy thrust responsibility for a faltering foreign and financial policy into the hands of private interests, as when Paul Reusch suggested that the "occupational estates" of agriculture, industry, banking, and commerce secure the loans needed to stabilize the mark.[2] This mortgaging of economic groups—originally proposed for the abortive Credit Action of 1921—was finally to be adopted as a basis for the Dawes Plan; it confirmed that Weimar democracy under stress amounted to little more than compacts among the strongest German interest groups.

As it drew different classes together in resistance against the French, the Ruhr occupation seemed at first to reverse this trend. Nationalist indignation, spontaneous as well as orchestrated from Berlin, penetrated deeply enough to satisfy entrepreneurs that "workers, including left-wing Socialists and union leaders, would stand behind their employers."[3] The Social Democrats promised Cuno their support while the

[2] Reusch papers, GHH: 300193008/12; original GFM: ARK, Ausführung des Friedensvertrags, 9523H/3683/287114–287119; and reprinted in Karl Heinz Harbeck, ed., *Das Kabinett Cuno 22. November 1922 bis 12. August 1923* (Boppard am Rhein, 1968), pp. 101–103. Cited hereafter as *Akten: Cuno*.

[3] Report to Justizrat [Wilhelm] Meyer, BA, Koblenz: R 13 I (VdESI)/98. For the orchestration of resistance, see Chancellor to Press Chief, February 23, 1923, *Akten: Cuno*, pp. 271–276.

Nationalists, who had already backed him, urged that he place the country on a war footing.[4]

But unity was to be sorely tested by the policy of passive resistance that was adopted. The French and Belgian engineers and soldiers threw up an economic frontier around the Ruhr and required special authorization for all commercial shipments in or out. They hoped for a painless control of German factories and mines as "productive pledges," and planned to collect German coal taxes for reparation arrears. German producers refused to cooperate and resisted paying export taxes to the occupiers, which meant renouncing their sales abroad. As the French sequestered pithead coal, the Germans shut down their mines and banked their furnaces. Local officials were instructed not to carry out French orders, and railway workers also refused service. Berlin suspended the remaining reparations in kind, demanded that German producers pay their coal tax to the new offices of the Rhenish-Westphalian Coal Syndicate in Hamburg, and discontinued imports of French iron ore. All these measures proved inconvenient but not disabling to the French. The problem that at first appeared likely to cause most difficulty, the organization of rail service, was quickly mastered by the new Franco-Belgian railroad authority, the Régie. As the State Secretary in the Chancellery summed it up for Cuno, "Ultimately France can last longer than Germany."[5]

To keep inactive German workers from starving, Berlin adopted a massive welfare budget. In the weeks after January 11, 1923, the government worked out a system of Rhine-Ruhr aid for the previously occupied territory on the west bank of the Rhine, then for the newly occupied lands to the east. In the Rhineland to the west, the Düren agreement of February 10 provided that there would be no lay-offs. If a factory ceased production because of French interference, the workers would receive their normal wages; if it halted for other, indirect reasons, two-thirds of normal wages would be provided. The industrialists paid the wages; in return they were to be compensated through one of the various agencies being designed to funnel money to the Ruhr. By May 3 Berlin had assumed responsibility for the wages of all unpro-

[4] SPD support in VDR: SB, 357, pp. 9428–9429 (January 13, 1923); for DNVP attitude: Aktennotiz Hergt, February 3, 1923, DZA, Potsdam: DNVP Akten/2, p. 36.

[5] *Akten: Cuno*, pp. 260–261, n. 12. General description of the measures on both sides in Jean-Claude Favez, *Le Reich devant l'occupation franco-belge de la Ruhr en 1923* (Geneva, 1969), pp. 66–77, 100–114, 160–170. From a nationalist point of view, cf. Hans Spethmann, *Zwölf Jahre Ruhrbergbau 1923 bis 1925*, III, *Der Ruhrkampf 1923 bis 1925 in seinen Leitlinien* (Berlin, 1929), pp. 56 ff. and 113 ff., and IV, *Das Ringen um die Kohle* (Berlin, 1930); also Paul Wentzcke, *Ruhrkampf, Einbruch und Abwehr im rheinisch-westfälischen Industriegebiet*, 2 vols. (Berlin, 1930–1932). For the *Régie*: Paul Tirard, *La France sur le Rhin* (Paris, 1930), pp. 360–374.

ductive miners in the Ruhr (with retroactive payments to February); on June 5 it guaranteed iron and steel industrialists two-thirds the salaries of their furloughed workers and it moved the figure up to 100 percent in July.[6]

Only massive deficit financing, which further accelerated the already rampant inflation, could furnish this assistance. In effect the inflation itself became a method of taxation. It reduced the real earnings of households so that by means of newly printed money the government could claim a share of national income.[7] Under constant prices, conventional taxes would have been necessary; under skyrocketing prices they became insufficient, and currency depreciation alone allowed the state to keep a voice in allocating the national product—a condition, of course, that only made prices leap upward anew. In this respect, the experience of 1923 was only the culmination of the peculiar public finance developed since the war. The German budget had long since come to depend upon the hidden imposts of inflation levied upon those with paper claims to future consumption—whether public bonds, bank deposits, or pension payments to come. State expenditures, on the other hand, financed a large system of concealed subsidies, such as cheap railroad transport. More direct and efficient taxes proved politically impossible because of the resistance of powerful elements within the business community. When critics from the left protested, industrialists answered that direct taxation would lead to recession and working-class misery. It is important to reiterate that the inflation was not rooted in balance-of-payments or reparation difficulties, troublesome though these could be.[8] It represented a particular outcome of political struggles at home. The frantic resort to the printing press was a form of taxation imposed by the powerful industrial forces upon the weaker elements and lent a degree of public approval because of prevailing bewilderment about the causes of inflation and general acceptance of the right's thesis that ultimately the Allies were to blame.

The line between the fourfold price increase during wartime and

[6] Favez, *Le Reich devant l'occupation*, pp. 142–155.

[7] Cf. Phillip Cagan, "The Monetary Dynamics of Hyperinflation," in Milton Friedman, ed., *Studies in the Quantity Theory of Money* (Chicago, 1956), pp. 25–117. Cf. John Maynard Keynes, *A Tract on Monetary Reform* (London, 1924), pp. 41–62, for an early treatment of this concept.

[8] For a presentation of the balance-of-payments theories, see Howard S. Ellis, *German Monetary Theory, 1905–1933* (Cambridge, Mass., 1934), pp. 237–256. While this view served the arguments of the Nationalists, who blamed reparation, liberals such as Moritz Bonn also advanced it. For a decisive rejection, see Hilferding's report on the currency question in the summer of 1923 in DZA, Potsdam: RWR/398 (Wirtschaftspolitischer Ausschuss and Finanzpolitischer Ausschuss, July 11, 1923), pp. 117–199.

the millionfold increase between August and November 1923 was not clear cut. When the German government revalued old debts and bank accounts in 1925, the parties settled on June 15, 1922, as a watershed date in the erosion of the mark. Ten days later Rathenau's murder had led to a frantic effort to buy foreign currencies and a rapid depreciation of the mark. So, too, of course, had Berlin's first major reparation payments during the summer of 1921. During 1921 and 1922, at least, Germany enjoyed boom conditions, as the inflation fueled a heady aggregate demand at home. According to recent estimates, the inflation actually permitted German national income through 1922 to remain a higher percentage of 1913 gross national product than was the case for other European countries.[9]

Germans, who were sensitive to French charges that a thriving economy should be able to furnish reparations, argued, however, that the prosperity was spurious. "We are living today off our own fat," Rathenau had said in November 1921. "Our red cheeks are the cheeks of a fever victim who seems to be in glowing health and is consuming his own bodily strength." British observers confirmed this diagnosis: Germany's "industrial activity was taken as a sign of wealth, whereas in point of fact, it was a symptom of the redistribution and dissipation of her accumulated capital; the paradox was achieved of a nation beaming prosperity whilst its vitality was being sapped."[10] Whether the aggregate benefits compensated for the expropriation of the weaker elements of society cannot be answered. In any case, by 1923, even the rewards of this possibly destructive full employment were brought to a halt as production fell in the Ruhr. Henceforth inflation brought a more wrenching contest for a seriously diminished national product.

Who suffered? Since the history of the inflation has been written by its articulate victims, most accounts stress the anguish of the middle classes, the destruction of their savings, and their delivery to the appeals of Hitler. This traditional picture, however, is deficient on sev-

[9] Karsten Laursen and Jørgen Pedersen, *The German Inflation 1918–1923* (Amsterdam, 1964), p. 84. The author's figures are open to question. The contribution from abroad to national income overlooks the consistent underreporting of German exports and may also neglect the fact that the German price level in gold terms was low enough so that German exports involved a subsidy to foreign purchasers. Applying world-market prices reduces the foreign contribution. See Frank D. Graham, *Exchange, Prices, and Production in Hyper-Inflation: Germany, 1920–1923* (Princeton, 1930), pp. 209 ff., 260 ff. (Nonetheless, see pp. 320–324 for Graham's own optimistic assessment of the inflation's effect on the economy.)

[10] Walther Rathenau, *Gesammelte Reden* (Berlin, 1924), p. 349. Commercial Secretary Kavanaugh, "Report on Economic and Financial Conditions in Germany" (April 1924), p. 108, included in U.S. State Department Records relating to the Internal Affairs of Germany, 1910–1929, Decimal Series 862.51/1792.

eral counts. It oversimplifies a vastly complex trade-off of income and assets, and it overlooks the ravages of the mass unemployment that gripped Germany during the last quarter of 1923 and the first months of 1924. Even a brief survey reveals the difficulty of calculating family welfare, much less that of social groups.

Available data allows only inference as to the redistribution of income and assets. For no large organized groups were there real gains in the 1923 period of increasing misery. Those with access to foreign currency were personally well off: foreigners could enjoy bargain vacations in the Harz Mountains or on the North Sea or acquire real estate at bargain-basement prices. They could come for a modest vacation, stay at ever more luxurious hotels, and leave burdened with souvenirs far beyond their original budget. Speculative profits still remained to be made in special trading situations: Stinnes, for example, did well as Germany's wholesaler for British coal when Ruhr supplies were cut off. It is more difficult to calculate how groups fared collectively. In theory the inflation should have been income-progressive. Within occupational categories inflation tends to level wages and salaries, but it usually stimulates an increased demand for labor, with wage gains for the less skilled in each occupation—whether lower civil servants and office employees or manual workers. In 1923 Germany this effect tended to hurt the upper ranks more than it benefited those below. Top-level civil servants, for instance, saw salaries collapse to about one-third of prewar purchasing power; lower-level bureaucrats suffered perhaps an amputation to two-thirds.[11]

Much of the middle-class lament concerned assets and capital—claims to income extended over time rather than income in hand. Those deriving income from assets experienced divergent fates—from the notorious inflation profiteer at one end of the scale to the impoverished

[11] Karl Elster, *Von der Mark zur Reichsmark* (Jena, 1928), pp. 444–449; Costantino Bresciani-Turroni, *The Economics of Inflation*, Millicent Sayers, trans. (London, 1937), p. 313, also 286 ff., 328–330; for the general wage-equalization effects of inflationary periods, cf. Guy Routh, *Occupation and Pay in Great Britain, 1906–1960* (Cambridge, 1965), pp. 108 ff., 132–133; also William O. Ogburn and William Jaffé, *The Economic Development of Postwar France* (New York, 1927), p. 164. For the social effects in general see Moritz J. Bonn, *Wandering Scholar* (New York, 1948), pp. 276–278, 286–290; Peter-Christian Witt, "Finanzpolitik und sozialer Wandel in Krieg und Inflation 1914–1924," presented at the Internationales Symposium: Industrielles System und Politische Entwicklung in der Weimarer Republik, June 12–17, 1973, in Bochum. Still most valuable: Franz Eulenburg, "Die sozialen Wirkungen der Währungsverhältnisse," *Jahrbücher für Nationalökonomie und Statistik*, 122, 6 (1924), who points out the collapse of wage differentials, p. 784, emphasizes the survival of the actively employed middle class, p. 779, and notes that despite losses of earnings, civil service positions remained desirable and prestigious because of their relative security, p. 775, 789.

pensioner at the other. Major redistribution took place between different elements of the middle class without any necessary correlation with income levels. The effect may well have been regressive: the wealthier the citizen, the more inflation-sheltered a portfolio he was likely to possess.

Even a purposeful search for "gold values," assets whose worth would rise with the dollar rate, could not always yield success. An increase in the number of small businesses established early in the inflation testified to a transfer of money savings to less vulnerable real values. Between 1919 and 1922 these enterprises may have provided some shelter and prosperity. But by 1923 the small shopkeeper was in an unenviable position. Forced into cash payments by his wholesalers and asked for credit by his customers, he sought to hoard inventory. Land was a shelter for wealth in the country, where farmers saw their mortgage debts virtually nullified. Here, in fact, was the major cohesive class benefit from the inflation. But land ownership in the city turned out to be a financial millstone, because rent control was widely applied and eliminated returns on buildings. On the other hand, this helped alleviate some of the distress of those who leased accommodations.[12]

Besides farmers, those who gained most were entrepreneurs who could borrow to expand their firms or who could export. From 1919 and then after 1921 through the first half of 1923, a constant devaluation gave industry export premiums that became a vehicle for internal redistribution of income. In effect, the exporter effectively rented inexpensive German labor to foreigners and was paid in hard currency with which he could buy domestic goods and services ever more cheaply. Contrary to popular opinion, profits for industry did not arise from hoarding dollars or pounds abroad, but from bringing them home to exploit the tremendous differentials that *Devisen*, or foreign notes, possessed inside a Germany turning toward unofficial dollar transactions or a bookkeeping system.[13] From January 1923, however, the French occupation prevented export possibilities for Ruhr-based industries, and after July the gap between external depreciation and internal price rises narrowed, ending the export premium for the rest of Germany as well. By this time, however, Germans were preparing for monetary reform. Besides such omens of stabilization as the acceptance of gold-mark taxes and the airing of currency reform projects, the real

[12] Eulenburg, "Die sozialen Wirkungen," p. 773 on small businesses, and p. 774 on home ownership.

[13] Graham, *Exchanges, Prices, and Production*, pp. 187–188; Bresciani-Turroni, *Economics of Inflation*, pp. 300–302, for the advent of indexes and budgets. (The British consul in Munich used his chauffeur's budget to establish cost-of-living indices—see the reports in FO 371/7517.)

value of money balances stopped its descent and began to turn upward during the early fall—a phenomenon best explained by calculations that the constant printing of money must soon be halted.[14]

These discrepancies make it difficult to assess the middle-class burden in general. More to the point, the unequal destinies destroyed any traditional class interest; inflation wrenched apart the middle-class elements of Germany. It forced those who enjoyed relatively stable assets to participate in a fevered search for goods, while it plunged others into abject misery. Pensioners, retailers, and those who had patriotically held government bonds were the silent victims. Nonetheless, the notion that the middle classes were "destroyed" or that Germany was thereby made vulnerable to Nazism is simplistic in several respects. The percentage of national income earned by German assets was almost as large by 1929 as in 1914, although the holdings may have become far more concentrated.[15] The German father who had retained long-term corporate bonds or savings accounts found them revalued up to 25 percent by 1925; he might recover roughly the percentage that the French *père de famille* rescued after Poincaré's stabilization. The German lost the value of his public bonds—an amputation that struck trade-union friendly societies and savings banks as well as individual accounts. On the other hand, the service charge on the public debt was also absent from middle-class tax bills. Occasionally, too, the loss on any single asset was spread over several "generations" of mortgage or bond holders, each of whom had bought in the belief that the inflation was near its peak. Finally, it must be remembered that class lines were anchored deep despite the loss of assets. There is little indication that access to higher education—a crucial class parameter—varied much because of inflation. Enrollment in higher education rose slightly as fees became less expensive and the sons of minor officials, whose salaries remained relatively protected, sought their own credentials for

[14] Bresciani-Turroni, *The Economics of Inflation*, pp. 136–145 on prices, pp. 343–345 on October 1923 "loan"; Cagan, "The Monetary Dynamics of Hyperinflation," pp. 55–57.

[15] Simon Kuznets, *Modern Economic Growth: Rate, Structure, and Spread* (New Haven and London, 1966), pp. 168–170 (also "Quantitative Aspects of the Growth of Nations," IV, in *Economic Development and Cultural Change*, VII, 3, part II (1959), pp. 45, 86 ff. The value of public bonds still in the hands of their original purchasers was estimated at 15–20 billion paper marks in 1925. See Bresciani-Turroni, *The Economics of Inflation*, p. 325, note. For evidence of the rapid reconstruction of savings, see the surprising rapidity with which the capital of life insurance companies grew in 1924 and 1925: Hans Ulrich, "Der Währungszerfall, die Aufwertung und der Wiederaufbau bei den privaten deutschen Lebensversicherungsgesellschaften," *Jahrbücher für Nationalökonomie und Statistik*, 125, 2 (1926), p. 123.

public service.[16] Perhaps the incongruity between bourgeois status and economic distress helped to radicalize the middle class. But while electoral analysis shows that a buffeted middle class turned Nazi, so too did the farmers whose debts had been liquidated in 1923. In both cases economic developments subsequent to the inflation proved decisive.

In some important ways the working class lost more, even if its members did not suffer a greater deprivation of income. While well-to-do officials saw income more than halved, unionized workers probably suffered less drastic cuts. Their real wages would periodically lag behind rising prices and then catch up with new settlements. As the mark skidded faster and faster, the degree of loss becomes harder to calculate.[17] Moreover a drop in real wages, say, of 15 percent relative to 1913 meant harsh deprivation, whether of clothing, protein, or medical care.[18] Who can say which family suffered more? The unemployment that began to settle over Germany—rising, according to trade-union figures, from about 7 percent in mid-1923 to almost 30 percent by December—also hurt working-class family units. Women, young people, the aged who entered a vigorous labor market between 1919 and 1922 must have been among the first laid off. The second income that kept many households afloat or the modest earnings that supplemented pensions disappeared. Workers found it scarce comfort that entrepreneurial income did not gain as a whole at the cost of labor, especially since entrepreneurs did enjoy a larger share of national income than they would have under stable prices.[19] Labor resented the national banking policies that enhanced the entrepreneurs' ability to speculate at the expense of other groups. Finally, they resented the fact that they were subject to withholding and thus paid the only meaningful direct taxes.[20]

[16] See Roberto Michels, *Umschichtungen in den herrschenden Klassen nach dem Kriege* (Stuttgart–Berlin, 1934), pp. 104 ff.; Eulenburg, "Die Sozialen Wirkungen," pp. 776–779. For a more elitist perspective, stressing academic hardship see, Ringer, ed., *The German Inflation*, p. 108; also Ringer, *The Decline of the German Mandarins, The German Academic Community, 1890–1933* (Cambridge, Mass., 1969), pp. 62–66.

[17] For estimates of real wages, see Laursen and Pedersen, *The German Inflation*, p. 76. For the employed, real wages (1913 = 100) were 1919, 82; 1920, 78; 1921, 89; 1922, 67; 1923, 70. The average for all workers, given the unemployment of 1923, would be lower. Cf. Bresciani-Turroni, *The Economics of Inflation*, pp. 300–313.

[18] See the grim statistics on tuberculosis and disease, according to Prussian Minister of Health Franz Bumm, VDR: SB, 358, pp. 9779–9784 (February 20, 1923), translated in Fritz K. Ringer, ed., *The German Inflation of 1923* (New York, 1969), pp. 112–118.

[19] Laursen and Pedersen, *The German Inflation*, p. 116.

[20] See the DGB memo to the Chancellor, February 7, 1923, in *Akten: Cuno*, pp. 228–231.

In sum, the picture of welfare gains and losses is ambiguous. But workers suffered a dimension of loss that usually remains obscured in the conventional accounts. The contrast with the wartime experience is striking. Then, because of the need to win labor collaboration for full production, the unions extracted important new bargaining powers and corporate status. But the period of hyperinflation weakened labor's power. It eroded its collective wealth, the trade-union treasuries that allowed strikes that enforced political as well as wage bargains. When the stabilization crisis hit Germany in the winter of 1923–1924, organized labor's new weakness became evident. Industrial managers imposed massive wage cuts, which brought labor to a far worse relative position than in 1913. In addition, they reintroduced the ten-hour day and thus succeeded once again in passing much of their new taxation and reparation burden on to labor.[21] More generally, German democracy rested on a balance between working-class and traditionalist, largely authoritarian forces. Their power depended upon their political and economic clout as organized interests. The inflation and stabilization crisis gravely weakened the democratic forces of this equilibrium, thus undermining the social welfare state that the Weimar Republic incorporated.

In effect, Germany suffered a cruel but uneven catastrophe during the inflation, like the foundering of a great ship. In the crush to reach the boats, organized labor traveling tourist class might do better than the genteel rentiers in cabin class, many of whom ended up badly battered. As individuals, tourist passengers had few possessions to leave behind, while those in cabin class had to leave significant wealth below even if they elbowed their way to safety. Those in first class may also have lost shipboard riches, but these mattered little compared to their wealth on shore. Once the boats were launched, moreover, the crew and first-class passengers saw to it that those from tourist, numerous but now dispersed and disorganized, picked up the oars for the long row ahead.

The political issues of early 1923 testified to working-class disadvantages. Since the SPD remained at a distance from the Cuno cabinet, the major questions of economic policy reflected a socialist-bourgeois

[21]Eulenburg, "Die sozialen Wirkungen," pp. 782–783; Hans Hermann Hartwich, *Arbeitsmarkt, Verbände und Staat 1918–1933* (Berlin, 1967), pp. 67, 102. British observers noted how the working class was losing ground, although they sometimes differed as to whether wages were being reduced enough to restore German industry's export competitiveness. See William Larke report on German industry, November 26, 1923, FO 371/8750, C20556/313/18. (Larke was Chairman of the Federation of Iron and Steel Manufacturers.) See also the London *Times*, March 25, 1924.

division. Even if the *Mittelstand* suffered acutely, its distress was not mirrored in direct policy confrontations. No doubt the rise of right-radicalism in 1923 partially derived from middle-class discontents. But at the cabinet level the emergence of the Nazi movement expressed itself as a police problem and as one of federal-state relationships, not as a social or economic issue.[22] As of the spring of 1923, when the government considered its agonizing economic and reparation dilemmas, it did so in terms of the older bourgeois and socialist political antagonism.

Within a month of the French incursion, the Socialists sought to re-amend the government's tax bills, which had been weakened by the middle parties in the Finance Committee. In the parliamentary debate of March 8 and 9, SPD speakers condemned the legislation as amounting to tax forgiveness, a view endorsed by the State Secretary in the Chancellery, Eduard Hamm of the Democratic Party, who pleaded—in vain—for a more public-spirited policy to check inflation.[23]

Agricultural policy provoked the next Social Democratic dissent. To keep food prices under control during its tenure, the Wirth government had purchased the rye harvest in six installments between October 1921 and February 1922. The system had not worked well, and the forced delivery of grain at outdated mark values offered no incentive to farmers. In December 1922, the Social Democratic members of the Prussian state government proposed that as an alternative the Reich import badly needed fertilizer and trade it to farmers in exchange for quotas of their crop.[24] Federal Agriculture Minister Hans Luther rejected this solution, however. As Mayor of Essen, Luther recognized urban needs, especially the plight of the cities' poor, who would require a bread subsidy. Along with the Socialists, he recognized how greatly farmers benefited from the inflation, and he rejected the agrarians' suggestion for a government-sponsored grain corporation that would be effectively dominated by the very farmers from whom it would buy cereals. Luther suggested instead a return to the free market with a special state grain reserve for assisting the indigent. To cover costs, Luther claimed, farmers were prepared to deliver a quarter of their crop free of charge to the government in return for restoration of the free market.[25]

Luther's proposals hinged upon the brief stabilization of the mark achieved during February and March 1923. This momentarily brought

[22] Cf. memo of State Secretary Hamm, April 15, 1923, *Akten: Cuno*, pp. 377–383: also Gerhard Schulz, *Zwischen Demokratie und Diktatur, Verfassungspolitik und Reichsreform in der Weimarer Republik* (Berlin, 1963), i, pp. 404 ff.

[23] VDR: SB, 358, pp. 10003–10056, 10151–10192; *Akten: Cuno*, pp, 260–265 (memo of February 18, 1923).

[24] Discussion of Prussian proposal in cabinet session of December 8, 1922, *Akten: Cuno*, p. 54.

[25] Luther memo of February 12, 1923, in *Akten: Cuno*, pp. 243–250.

the price of cereals on the free market below what the government was paying. Although Socialists and Communists together called for a government grain reserve of 4.5 million tons to be collected in return for nitrates, they lost, first in the Budget Committee and then in the plenum, to the government's plan for a free market. The dispute opened up not only party divisions, but federal-state ones as well. It pitted the bourgeois Reich government once again against the Prussian Great Coalition, where the SPD had a dominant role, and revealed how class and regional division could interact.[26]

Finally, by the end of March tension arose between labor representatives and the government over how long to continue passive resistance without offering to negotiate. For about two months the German gamble seemed to succeed: besides frustrating French hopes for easy control of production, the government initiated a "stabilization action" that brought the mark from its January 30 low of over 40,000 per dollar to about 27,000 per dollar. For over eight weeks the currency held firm and even improved, as speculators who had sold marks short were forced to cover their original sales. But how was Germany to use its respite? Most political onlookers realized that passive resistance would become more difficult. Hermes told Center Party press representatives that negotiations must be initiated; Wirth agreed. The leader of the Social Democratic General Trade Union Federation, Leipart, warned that the French were getting more coal, that the high point of resistance had been reached if not passed, and that negotiations were needed "before our strength visibly declines." In the Foreign Affairs Committee of the Reichstag, the former Socialist Chancellor Hermann Mueller also called for talks: "Time works against us; every step exhausts our economy." While the Nationalist spokesman Helfferich sought to rigidify the cabinet's declared view that there could be no negotiations until the French had left the Ruhr, Stresemann himself tried to read a more liberal interpretation into government policy. In mid-April the head of the mine workers' union added that although his men were resolved to stand firm, resistance was now at its height and the government must at least publish the reparations offer it had never presented at Paris in January.[27]

[26] Cabinet session of March 19, *ibid.*, pp. 314–315 and nn. 1–4. By June, Luther presented revised proposals in light of the continuing inflation that would pay the needy two-fifths of the bread price directly, with the cost to be borne by a levy that farmers would pay according to the value of their rye. This was passed by the Reichstag on June 20. See *ibid.*, pp. 582–584.

[27] For Hermes' view, see his memo of September 21, 1923, included in Hugo Stehkämper, ed., *Der Nachlass des Reichskanzlers Wilhelm Marx. Mitteilungen aus dem Stadtarchiv von Köln*, 52–55, 4 vols. (Cologne, 1968), II, p. 101. Leipart warning, cited by Hamm in his note of March 28, 1923: cited with Helfferich, Müller, and Stresemann, *Akten: Cuno*, pp. 342–348; mineworkers' union chief,

Union fears were soon substantiated. The credibility of passive resistance depended upon stabilizing the mark, as cabinet adviser Kempner pointed out in a bleak mid-April memo; but it was impossible to support the mark at any fixed level and simultaneously finance the passive resistance. Open-market purchases of marks were not sufficient to support the currency if no domestic brake on consumption could be imposed. Few seemed willing to buy bonds, even when repayment in hard currency was promised. The effort to launch a gold note loan in the winter had proved, in Havenstein's words, a "lamentable failure." Max Warburg wrote Cuno of his difficulties in selling the 5 percent of the issue that his firm had underwritten—"I have never been refused and attacked so often; only a French officer would meet more resistance." And finally in mid-April the *Bank Archiv* confessed that only one-quarter of the 50 million dollar issue had been subscribed.[28] On April 18 the whole support action undertaken since late February collapsed, when the Stinnes interests initiated massive purchases of foreign currency. Official sources denied that Stinnes had deliberately sought to sabotage the support action: he had been commissioned by the government to purchase badly needed British coal, which apparently justified his search for *Devisen*. Nonetheless, Stinnes stood to lose by stabilization and had criticized the support action to Stresemann, while the newspaper he controlled, the *DAZ*, was merciless in its attacks upon any hint of reparation negotiations.[29]

Between April 18 and the end of June the mark depreciated another sevenfold (to 150,000 per dollar)—below the level, as bureaucrats ruefully noted, of even the pitiable Austrian crown. Even Bergmann admitted that Reichsbank action could no longer stabilize the situation and any attempt would merely result in the bank watching its own reduced gold reserves being washed away in the torrent.[30] Helplessness overtook the bankers: all awaited a providential turning point in foreign policy. The failure of the dollar-based loan in January seemed to foreclose effective raising of foreign currency at home. All the government

---

Hue, also cited *ibid.*, pp. 366–377 and n. 4. For Wirth warning, see Maltzan note in GFM, Handakten Schubert, L 1618/5683/490905. On February 24 Schubert reported that Bergmann was advising that banking circles and the right were asking "whither the purely negative resistance policy of the government would lead" 490908–490910. Cf. Max Warburg's admonition to Cuno on February 10, in Max M. Warburg, *Aus meinen Aufzeichnungen* (Glückstadt, 1952), p. 114.

[28] Kempner memo in *Akten: Cuno*, p. 390. Havenstein verdict on the loan: GFM: ARK, Kabinettsprotokolle, April 19, 1923, 3491/1746/754804–754806. Warburg letter and article in Max Warburg papers/157a.

[29] Cf. *Akten: Cuno*, pp. 399–403, 421, n. See the collected newspaper reports of Stinnes' foreign-currency dealings in BA, Koblenz: R 43 I/2445.

[30] *Ibid.*, p. 600. (Reserves had been about 250 million dollars in April and were about 180 million dollars in June.)

could do was to introduce a unified exchange rate in June based on the Berlin mark/dollar quotations and designed to curb excess speculation arising from intercity differences in the currency. Even this measure aroused opposition from industry and, above all, among Cologne and Hamburg bankers; for to conduct the foreign trade centered in those cities, banks and merchants had to discount marks even more drastically than in Berlin. As Economics Minister Becker pointed out a month later, the unified exchange rate was counterproductive: because the Berlin exchange rate overvalued the mark by the standards of the money markets abroad, no foreign currency was being offered at German bourses. Moreover, by July, according to the Foreign Minister, the floating debt had increased since January from 1.5 to 22 trillion marks.[31]

More generally, the collapse of the mark meant for the moment the virtual end of effective government in Germany. Not merely passive resistance, but public authority in general seemed doomed to prolonged and painful collapse. This was revealed by the effort to draft a new reparations offer in May. Desperately tuned to hints from London —when it probably should have sought more energetically to deal with Paris—the German government took its lead from Curzon's House of Lords speech of April 20 and submitted a new proposal including guarantees to bind German industry.[32]

Despite the opposition of the right, a new German offer was necessary for reasons of domestic politics. Passive resistance depended upon trade-union support, and without a German offer—as Ministers Albert and Gessler conceded—that support would be lost. At some point, Gessler admitted, Germany would have to raise the white flag, and it would then be ripe for disorder. Only a reparations offer now could help disarm later left-wing discontent at industry's seeming reluctance to make its own sacrifices for a settlement.[33]

At the ministers' discussion of April 30, with Hermes ill, Bergmann alone pushed for a meaningful advance in Germany's reparations proposals. The government leaders wished to stand by what was to have been presented at Paris in January; Rosenberg felt that to go further would be to reward the French for their occupation of the Ruhr. Berg-

[31] For the opposition to the *Einheitskurs*, see Melchior to Max Warburg, June 19, 1923, in Warburg papers/157a; the plea of the Reichsverband Vorstand to the Economics Ministry as described in the former's bulletin to its member groups on July 28: BA, Koblenz, Silverberg Nachlass/258, Tgb. Nr. 2303 III; Rhenish complaints in Louis Hagen's telegram of June 22, *Akten: Cuno*, p. 600, n. 7, also Kempner's note of June 25, *ibid.*, pp. 608–610; and the report on the floating debt, p. 623.

[32] For the German impressions of the speech, see *Akten: Cuno*, pp. 433–435; see also the advice of Melchior and Bergmann in the Max Warburg papers/157a, "Notiz für das Tagebuch," April 27, 1923.

[33] *Akten: Cuno*, pp. 437–438 (cabinet session of April 28).

mann condemned the earlier plan intended for Paris as derisory. Although it offered to service reparation loans to the Allies of 20 billion gold marks plus two later sums of 5 billion each, delayed payments and deduction of interest charges from the overall amount effectively reduced the present value of the offer to 12 to 15 billion. Bergmann stressed that the minimum ticket to further negotiations was a firm 30 billion without deductions. His warning, however, went unheeded, as what was essentially a redrafted Paris proposal was presented to the Allies on May 2. Hermes found the proposal so low that he thought of resigning, while Cuno and Rosenberg felt that it represented a major concession and were dejected by the Allies' harsh rejection.[34]

Still, Cuno realized that it was important to sustain a minimal dialogue. If no larger sums were to be offered, at least the German collateral securing a reparations loan must be spelled out. The Chancellor's discussions with business leaders, however, quickly revealed that they would impose unacceptable terms for any commitment of their own assets. Warburg warned his old Hamburg associate, Cuno, that he must go ahead and "incur the enmity of industry" by asking the Reichsverband to shoulder a collective gold-value mortgage or to surrender stock shares. Since the Versailles Treaty had not made private property subject to reparation liens, industry demanded a high price for the "voluntary" pledging of its capital. Although Stinnes wanted to refuse outright, the industrial federation finally offered to pawn resources that would yield 200 million gold marks yearly as part of a combined effort with German banking and agriculture to produce half a billion. In return, though, they demanded final abolition of the demobilization ordinances, with their protection of the eight-hour day, as well as emasculation of the crucial arbitration provisions of the Weimar Republic, which protected the labor unions.[35]

The cabinet was reluctant even to publish the Reichsverband stipulations for fear of provoking working-class anger. Union representatives led by Wissell denounced the offer as spurious and refused to bring the eight-hour day and restraints on dismissals under discussion: "Industry

[34] *Akten: Cuno*, pp. 440–444, for the cabinet debate of April 30; Rosenberg and Cuno's reactions, *ibid.*, p. 466, Viscount Edgar D'Abernon, *The Diary of an Ambassador; Rapallo to Dawes, 1922–1924* (Garden City, N.Y., 1930), pp. 222–223, 233 (diary entries of May 14 and 24, 1923). Hermes' attitude in his memorandum included in Stehkämper, ed., *Nachlass Marx*, II, pp. 106–107; also Hermes to Ersing, October 19, 1923, *ibid.*, pp. 112–114. For drafts and the note itself, see GFM: Wirtschaft Reparation, 9332H/3637/259193–259326.

[35] Warburg warning in the "Melchior Notiz" of May 11, 1923, Max Warburg Papers/157a; Reichsverband note, GFM: ARK, Ausführung des Friedensvertrags 9523H/3684/237638–237641; cf. *Akten: Cuno*, pp. 508–509; earlier industry resistance to any assistance emerges from the Hermes-Beuron memorandum of September 21, 1923, in Stehkämper, ed., *Nachlass Marx*, II, p. 103.

is seeking to deal with the state as an independent power," the labor leaders wrote, "and is making demands when it should be a question of carrying out civic obligations on behalf of the state." In their turn, agrarian representatives also set impossible terms for a new collective lien, including abolition of "expropriation" through the inheritance tax, the rejection of SPD proposals for partition of the big estates as well as an end to social democratic policies in Prussia, and finally a return to the free economy in agriculture.[36]

These consultations with industry and agriculture suggested that the Berlin government had fallen into little more than a brokerage role between antagonistic internal forces and foreign pressure. Only the Social Democrats, some DDP members such as the frustrated Chancellery Secretary Hamm, and the Center Party Minister of Labor, the Catholic trade union leader Brauns, tried to define a collective interest *vis-à-vis* the conditions set by Reichsverband and Reichslandbund. In a letter to Cuno, Brauns rejected the suspension of the demobilization ordinances protecting not only the eight-hour day, but unemployment benefits and security against lock-outs, unless they were replaced by new legislation. Nor could the arbitration guarantees—which the unions would need badly during the following winter—"be either done away with or dismantled." Hamm and the SPD likewise kept on pleading for effective taxation, for wages and pensions based upon recent price indices, and for meaningful reparations negotiations. But out of power, the SPD's only leverage was the government's need to keep the trade unions behind passive resistance.[37]

Cuno still lacked the strength to propose any comprehensive measures to halt inflation or settle reparations. While Brauns, Hermes, and Marx were prepared to put the Center Party behind an offer of more than 30 billion,[38] Cuno refused to go over that figure. The mark fell again sharply at the end of May, now to over 70,000 per dollar, and the rattled Chancellor credited the story that his Finance Minister Hermes was plotting to overthrow the cabinet and form a new government with the SPD. Hermes denied the charge, but did insist that negotiations were urgent and warned that the mark must collapse further. What he won was explorations in London, and a new note to the allies on June 7 which detailed the basis on which Germany would service a reparations loan. Industry was still assigned a share; some customs duties and in-

[36] Wissell letter of June 1, 1923; discussion with agrarian representatives, on May 29, and Reichslandbund letter of June 12, 1923, in *Akten: Cuno*, pp. 517–519, 537–539, 554–556.

[37] Brauns to Cuno, July 12, 1923: GFM: ARK, Ausführung des Friedensvertrags, 9523H/3684/287764–287766.

[38] See Stehkämper, ed., *Nachlass Marx*, I, p. 299. Cf. Hamm's report of May 27 that the unions wanted a 30 billion gold mark offer, *Akten: Cuno*, p. 515.

direct taxes were to be pawned, and now, too, the railroads would be reorganized and their revenues pledged.[39]

Despite this latest elaboration, Cuno and Rosenberg were effectively paralyzed, convinced they could make no higher reparations offer but spurned even by London until they did; still hoping that the Labour Party or British industry would force London to break with Paris; still demanding that passive resistance continue through the next winter, if need be, so as to enable Berlin to exploit the break in Allied ranks.[40] The Chancellor and Foreign Minister realized that the continuation of passive resistance depended upon the mark and that the mark could recover only as a consequence of a foreign policy success that seemed to elude them. They depended upon the trade unions to carry on resistance, but were too subservient to industry to make the reparations offer the unions demanded. Fearful that "chaos" would intervene if they fell, preoccupied with the ominous reported growth of communist paramilitary formations (the so-called proletarian hundreds), they found their best friends in a Bavarian state government that benevolently watched the growth of racist right-radicalism in its own territory. At the same time they quarreled increasingly with a Prussian state government that provided the only effective curb upon left- as well as right-wing subversive activity.[41]

In the last week in July, a rash of strikes and rioting swept the Ruhr and unoccupied Germany. Underlying the ferment among the working class was the inflation, which according to Wissell had created "a more serious mood than anytime since November 1918."[42] The Socialists now proposed weekly pay and pension supplements according to cost-of-living indices, and wanted government contracts awarded only to those firms that would cooperate. Labor Minister Brauns suggested related schemes—monthly contracts with automatic cost-of-living hikes in between. Several city governments were switching over to gold-equiva-

[39] Hermes to Cuno, May 31, Cuno to Hermes, June 2, 1923, in *Akten: Cuno*, pp. 532, 578; and Hermes to Ersing, October 19, 1923, in *Nachlass Marx*, II, p. 115. For the contents of the note, Étienne Weill-Raynal, *Les réparations allemandes et la France*, 3 vols. (Paris, 1947), II, pp. 415–416.

[40] See cabinet session of July 25, 1923, *Akten: Cuno*, pp. 660–661; also John Foster Dulles' report to Loucheur on Rosenberg's influence on Cuno, July 25, Hoover Institution: Loucheur Papers/12, f. 4.

[41] Cf. the discussion in the Foreign Policy Committee of the Reichsrat, May 30, 1923: *Akten: Cuno*, p. 524. For background on the right: Harold J. Gordon, Jr., *Hitler and the Beer Hall Putsch* (Princeton, N.J., 1972), pp. 49–119.

[42] DZA, Potsdam: ZAG Akten/31 (June 23, 1923); also cabinet session of July 3, 1923, *Akten: Cuno*, p. 617, discussions, pp. 619–622. See Wilhelm Ersil, *Aktionseinheit stürzt Cuno: Zur Geschichte des Massenkampfes gegen die Cuno Regierung 1923 in Mitteldeutschland* (Berlin, DDR, 1963), for communist activity; also Werner Angress, *Stillborn Revolution: The Communist Bid for Power in Germany, 1921–1923* (Princeton, N.J., 1963), pp. 350–377.

lent wages. Yet the cabinet still refused to sanction universal and legal "index wages," since they implied abandonment of the mark, and the ministers called only for more frequent adjustments than existed.[43] The only consolation in the situation was that unemployment, while vexing, was not yet catastrophic (7 percent). For the fall, however, loomed the specter of farmers withholding their harvest if offered only worthless paper, and thereafter civil war and disintegration. As the State secretaries warned grimly:

> What we have to fear is not so much a great political counter-movement of the badly supplied urban population. It is that the war of all against all for daily bread will begin in the city and that for the maintenance of order in their own regions the different parts of the Reich will proceed independently and the Reich will thus fall apart. That state no longer in the position to halt the collapse of its currency . . . necessarily loses its authority and ultimately its right to existence.[44]

At this point the government was deserted by its own bourgeois supporters. In a letter to Stresemann on July 23, Hans Raumer endorsed Socialist criticism of Cuno's economic policy as "completely devoid of plans or ideas" and urged the DVP leader to plan for a Great Coalition ministry. A harsh attack in the Catholic paper *Germania* on July 27 "burst like a bomb" and precipitated each party's reassessment. Within the DDP executive committee, Petersen spoke despairingly about the obligation to support the ministry but was warned by Schacht, "If you let this government continue to muddle about, parliament will bear the responsibility." On August 8 Stresemann implicitly posed his candidacy for the succession in a Reichstag address; three days later, under pressure from the spreading strikes, the Social Democrats announced that they would participate in a Great Coalition.[45]

Cuno withdrew, his team embittered. They felt the last British note to Poincaré was a significant step forward and believed that the gold note loan was showing some results. As Cuno saw it, his accomplishment had been to reconcile the DNVP with a Weimar government, and a Great Coalition would weaken passive resistance and unity at home. Economics Minister Becker predicted that new, rigorous measures

[43] Cabinet session of July 6, 1923, *Akten: Cuno*, pp. 625, 628; cf. the DDP proposal of a gold mark, Hermes-Beuron memo, Stehkämper, ed., *Nachlass Marx*, II, p. 104.

[44] Henric-Albert memo, July 27, 1923, in *Akten: Cuno*, p. 682.

[45] Raumer letter in GFM: Stresemann Nachlass, 7117 = 260/3098/145749–145752; cf. also Ernst Leidig to Stresemann on July 18, *ibid.*, 145699–145700. Description of the *Germania* editorial in Stresemann's letter to Kempkes, July 29, *ibid.*, 145781; Petersen-Schacht debate in DDP Vorstand, July 28, 1923: NSDAP Hauptarchiv/f. 729; Stresemann speech in VDR: SB, 361, pp. 11771–11778.

would no longer be accepted by the Reichstag, and the front against the French would collapse. In fact, just before Cuno's fall the Reichstag did accept new gold-based taxes, chief among them the so-called Rhine-Ruhr donation, which comprised the first solid step toward stabilization.[46]

The end of the Cuno government resembled the collapse of October 1918, when the discredited General Staff led to the installation of Max von Baden. Now, however, the measure of defeat was no longer the progress of Allied armies but the rout of the mark from 200,000 to 2 million per dollar within a fortnight. As in 1918, the right condemned the sell-out—something stronger must replace passive resistance, Hergt of the DNVP told Stresemann.[47] Once again the Social Democrats were called in to contain the forces of radicalism, and as in 1918 they responded patriotically and as a party of order.

At first the bargain was worth it for them, as perhaps it had not been nine months earlier, in November 1922. Then the key elements of the Association of Moderates wanted an end to the eight-hour day as a price for a great coalition. Now, worried by the upsurge of protest, the middle parties set fewer conditions, while the Social Democrats needed effective anti-inflationary measures to relieve working-class distress. The Great Coalition, moreover, was already functioning in Prussia, but it was at constant loggerheads with the federal government over the inflation and maintaining order: installing a parallel party alignment at the center would ease the conflicts that allowed the forces of an unpredictable radicalism to brew in the different states—whether the left-wing coalition with the KPD in Saxony or Nazism in Bavaria. In short, as the Center Party Minister of Labor Brauns observed, the change of government hinged upon the SPD.[48] Now the SPD was ready. But how long would bourgeois and socialist priorities coincide?

The experience of the Great Coalition was marked by two phases. Two decisive strategic renunciations—that of passive resistance and then of the old currency, initiated the Socialist and middle-party collaboration. Once the mark and the Ruhr struggle had been abandoned, the Great Coalition was to settle into much the same tug-of-war between working-class and business interests that had enfeebled earlier

[46] Cuno and Becker, August 12, 1923, in *Akten: Cuno*, pp. 734–735; also comments to Melchior in "Aufgabe von Melchior," August 16 in Warburg Papers/ 157a. For the taxes: Beuron-Hermes memo, September 21, 1923, in Stehkämper, ed., *Nachlass Marx*, II, p. 85; Karl Bernhard Netzband and Hans Peter Widmaier, *Währungs- und Finanzpolitik der Ära Luther* (Basel and Tübingen, 1964), pp. 89 ff.

[47] Stehkämper, ed., *Nachlass Marx*, II, p. 7.

[48] See discussion of Ministers August 12, 1923, *Akten: Cuno*, p. 737.

governments. With the end of passive resistance and the adoption of the Rentenmark, the Socialists confronted the same implacable choice the stalemated Republic always presented them: either to withdraw from the cabinet and lose their voice in shaping policy, or to purchase portfolios at the cost of assenting to economic sacrifices by their working-class supporters and alienating the socialist electorate. After three months of collaboration the SPD was to decide it could not pay the price of power.

For Stresemann, the one-time monarchist and annexationist, the collaboration with the SPD can be understood only with reference to his National Liberal background and the earlier evolution of his ideas on social democracy. Despite its entanglements with industry, Stresemann saw his party as the heir to a historic national liberalism, which had been the ideology that expressed the unity of the Reich as a national community above the special pleadings of private interests and secessionist tendencies. Now, too, the Social Democrats were fit partners, as he had learned between 1918 and 1923, no longer *reichsfeindlich* but *staatserhaltend*, hostile to social revolution and centralist.[49] Along with Stresemann, the SPD resented the forces of particularism, whether embodied in the Center Party's concern for the desperate condition of its own Rhenish constituency, or in heavy industry's advocacy of private reparation arrangements that would bypass the Foreign Ministry.

Stresemann's own political rhetoric was less analytic than cloyingly sentimental. Ambition, bordering on vanity, remained an important element in his character, as his collisions with Kardorff and Wiedfeldt in the fall of 1923 disclosed.[50] But the 1923 emergency permitted him to sort out his choices according to the older, significant polarities between national and private interests that national liberalism had understood. As early as March and April 1923, Stresemann had criticized Cuno for ineffective diplomacy, which could only mean failure to negotiate. The Nationalists, whom he had learned to despise, accused him of a new stab in the back and hunger for power. He dismissed their criticism, but was angered at the financial support they received from

[49] See Stresemann to D. Pauli, February 14, on the need to work with the SPD in GFM: Stresemann Nachlass, 7113 = 256/3097/145100–145102. For his National Liberal heritage, see his reading of Bennigsen cited in his letter of April 23, 1923, to Spangenberg: 7115 = 258/3098/145391.

[50] For revealing samples of Stresemann's personal reflections and political beliefs, see his letter to Bestchorn March 12, 1919, 6921 = 206/3088/137632–137634, also his 1921 diary fragments in *ibid.*, 7354 = 228/3171/116114 ff. For his collisions with Kardoff, see BA, Koblenz: Siegfried von Kardorff Nachlass/16; and GFM: Stresemann Nachlass, 7124 = 267/3011/146974–146982; Roland Thimme, *Stresemann und die deutsche Volkspartei 1923–1925* (Lübeck and Hamburg, 1961), pp. 34–40; Henry A. Turner, Jr., *Stresemann and the Politics of the Weimar Republic* (Princeton, N.J., 1963), p. 231.

heavy industry.[51] By the time he became Chancellor, Stresemann realized that the preservation of national unity required an end to the bleeding away of resources in the Rhineland and the Ruhr and a new remedy for the monetary crisis.[52] His first hope was to withdraw the decrees of passive resistance in return for French agreement to new reparations negotiations, an indication that they would abandon the *Régie* they had organized to run the Rhineland railroads, and permission for the German officials the French had expelled to return. Because Poincaré refused to concede anything until Germany abandoned passive resistance, Stresemann finally surrendered on September 26. As Severing pointed out, passive resistance had in effect already collapsed; the united front was finished and the workers were demoralized.[53]

Right-wing reaction to the announcement that Germany would cease resistance was fierce. To conservatives in Bavaria—who now imposed their own local quasi-dictatorship under Gustav von Kahr—and to nationalists in the North, the story of Socialist-inspired betrayal seemed to be repeating itself. "Here in Berlin there is general panic exactly as in October 1918," an informant told Westarp three weeks before the formal announcement. "The Social Democrats are hurrying to push the Chancellor into negotiations for capitulation." In the Reichstag a month later, Westarp repeated the charge that the predominant Social Democratic influence in the cabinet had led inexorably to the Ruhr surrender.[54] Even in Stresemann's own party, the businessmen Quaatz and Vögler sharply criticized the decision to end passive resistance as a failure of nerve, comparable, they felt, to the government's fear of abrogating the eight-hour day. What the right professed to desire, if

[51] Criticism of Cuno, March 19, in GFM: Stresemann Nachlass, 7114 = 257/3098/145243–145244; see, too, the comments in the Foreign Affairs Committee of the Reichstag, March 27, *Akten: Cuno*, p. 345; and the April call for negotiation in Gustav Stresemann, *Vermächtnis. Der Nachlass in drei Bänden*, Harry Bernhard, ed. (Berlin, 1932), I, pp. 55–57; criticism of the Nationalists in the letter to Miethke, May 1, 1923: 7115 = 258/3098/145429–145430.

[52] See August 23 cabinet statement in GFM: ARK, Kabinettsprotokolle, 3491/1748/756436–756438.

[53] Cabinet meeting of September 18, 1923, in *ibid.*, 3491/1748/756748–756751. Also his urging of mediation on London, September 13 and 18, in GFM: Büro des Reichsministers, Aufgabe des passiven Widerstandes, 3116/1529/640235–640236, 640270–640274. Severing comment in the cabinet on August 23: 3491/1748/756439. For French thoughts on the *Régie*, see AN, Paris: F[30]/1276, "Projet de société de gérance des Chemins de Fer Rhenans 1923."

[54] Westarp to Helfferich, September 1, Gaertringen: Westarp Nachlass; cf. October 8, 1923, in VDR: SB, 361, pp. 11968 ff. For the Bavarian opposition, see the cabinet session of September 27: GFM: ARK, Kabinettsprotokolle, 3491/1748/756851–756854; Schulz, *Zwischen Demokratie und Diktatur*, I, pp. 423 ff.; Gordon, *Hitler and the Beer Hall Putsch*, pp. 212 ff. See, too, the Reports of the Reich representative in Munich: GFM: ARK, 2138H/5569/591488–591489 (on Putsch rumors) and 591525–591526 on reaction to the end of passive resistance.

resistance must indeed be called off, was a provocative renunciation of the Versailles Treaty. Extremists indulged themselves in chimeric plans to provoke a state of war with France, in which England would switch sides and the results of 1918 would be redressed. Karl Jarres, conservative DVP member and Mayor of Duisburg, felt that an open break with France might risk a declaration of war and the temporary loss of the Rhineland, but would ultimately bring greater rewards.[55]

The same economic necessities that forced abandonment of passive resistance required abandonment of the old mark. By the summer of 1923 the inflation had outrun anyone's gains. The mark dropped from 1,000,000 per dollar on August 1, to 2 million by August 15, when Stresemann took office, to 6 million by the end of the month. The export premium created earlier by the quicker depreciation of the mark abroad finally narrowed and was reversed as internal prices paid by exporters—such as the cost of their once cheaper coal—now rose above the world-market level. Internal prices became pegged to the daily dollar quotations, but with supplements to allow for further depreciation. German firms, too, now confronted a credit and currency shortage that halted their business, as the real value of paper in circulation dwindled and the Reichsbank finally curtailed its loans to private industry. Unemployment, which had been contained at the 7 percent level, now began to grow rapidly as industries ceased operation, and industrial unrest and clashes also increased.[56]

Only because in the end the monetary catastrophe threatened industry and the most basic exchanges was it effectively confronted. Even then, the process lasted a further three months, in which the currency collapsed another millionfold. The delay was due to the rivalry of several stabilization schemes and interests, the inertia of Reichsbank President Havenstein, whose death alone cut short his resistance, and finally perhaps to the failings of the Socialist Finance Minister Hilferding as an effective administrator.[57]

[55] Thimme, *Stresemann und die deutsche Volkspartei*, pp. 34–40; Karl Dietrich Erdmann, *Adenauer in der Rheinlandpolitik nach dem ersten Weltkrieg* (Stuttgart, 1966), pp. 89 ff.

[56] Bresciani-Turroni, *The Economics of Inflation*, pp. 136–141, on price changes. For general economic developments cf., besides the German documents, the French reports in Min. Aff. Etr.: Europe, 1918–1929, Allemagne/426.

[57] Peter-Christian Witt contests this usual interpretation and claims that Hilferding was merely resisting Luther's regressive taxes. Communication of June 1973. For tax disputes in the cabinet see BA, Koblenz: R 43 I/2354. For the difficulties with Havenstein, R 43 I/962, Akten betr. Reichsbankpräsident (including exchange of letters between Havenstein and Ebert on the former's tenure); also cabinet protocols of August 20, 30, and November 5, 1923, in GFM: ARK, 3491/1748/756428–756431, 756492, and 3491/1749/757610. For Havenstein's own defense to the Central Committee of the Reichsbank on August 25, 1923, see DZA, Pots-

As currency reform projects matured, it became clear that the instituting of a new money demanded the same appeasement of special interests required of all other policies. The debate over currency replacement first emerged publicly on August 12, when Helfferich introduced legislation for a new bank of issue. Helfferich proposed that the professional "estates"—industry, trade, banking, and agriculture—be assigned obligatory mortgages to the extent of 5 (later amended to 4) percent of their 1913 fixed capital. These notes, to be called Rentenbriefe, would require interest payments at 6 percent and would be denominated not in terms of marks, but in quantities of rye or in percentage quotas of industry's coal and potash. Using them as backing, a new currency institute would issue marks for internal use likewise based on the value of rye. As a standard of value, however, rye was seriously defective: in the preceding decade it had fluctuated in real terms between 60 and 107 percent of its 1913 price. This meant that Helfferich offered rye—and its East Elbian producers—the advantage of a built-in price support: the Junkers could in effect sow and reap money, and their new mortgage burden would remain sheltered from any fall in the price of rye. The only persuasive argument for the rye mark was that it would at least win farm acceptance for the new money and avert the danger of urban starvation in the coming winter.[58]

Helfferich made a further effort to win industry's acceptance by stipulating that industry's share of the mortgage burden for the currency should be proportionally lighter than agriculture's. Industry's coal and potash assets would be assessed on a basis that lowered their lien value from about 2 to 1.4 billion marks. Industry realized, however, that Helfferich's project still favored agriculture, and if rye grown at home became more expensive than rye grown abroad, German labor costs would also climb and exports become less competitive.[59]

Industry, however, did slowly come to accept the necessity of bypassing both the old mark and the Reichsbank; and the concept of a mort-

---

dam: Rudolf Havenstein Nachlass/Zentralausschuss 1921–1923, and DZA: Büro des Reichspräsidenten: Präsidialkanzlei/300.

[58] See Helfferich's justification that one had to reckon with popular "imagination" in choosing a unit of value that had not been eroded: BA, Koblenz: R 13 I/278, "Stenographische Aufzeichnung über die Besprechung in der Reichskanzlei am 18.VIII.23." Helfferich's published explanation of his proposal in *NP(K)Z*, September 14, 1923. On June 23, the government had already legally authorized mortgages whose payments would be denominated in quantities of rye, wheat, or gold. For discussions of the projected reform, see Elster, *Von der Mark zur Reichsmark*, pp. 215–226.

[59] See Urbig's comment at the Erweiterte Ausschussitzung des Zentralverbands des deutschen Bank- und Bankiergewerbes, October 18, 1923, in Max Warburg papers/147a.

gage-based currency found increasing favor. Stinnes' collaborator, Friedrich Minoux, also suggested a new currency bank with bonds secured by a one-shot capital levy. More hesitantly, the Reichsverband called only for a new private bank to serve business, which would issue a parallel currency based on German *Devisen* holdings and foreign loans.[60] But with none of the new money projected for the public budget, the plan was ineffectual and self-serving. The banking community was perhaps even more conservative about launching a new money or bypassing the Reichsbank. Although it saw the political danger in too direct an opposition, the German banking association asked postponement of currency reform until the end of French economic control in the Rhineland and Ruhr. Until then, a switch to *de facto* gold accounting and the establishment of special credit institutes for each economic sector would serve instead. Finally, argued Warburg, the state might progressively issue a dollar-backed, small-denomination note that government offices would accept alongside the old mark.[61]

Under Hilferding's auspices the debate dragged on through August and September. Although no voice had been so insistent as Hilferding's that Germany must and could halt her own inflation, his own proposal of September 10 envisaged only an insufficiently capitalized note bank. In any case, the Reichsbank vetoed the share of backing the project required. Meanwhile the price of a loaf of bread soared from 30,000 marks on August 30 to 300,000 by mid-September and 15 million or more by mid-October. Food and Agriculture Minister Luther urged haste, but progress remained halting. Although the fundamental decision to adopt a new gold-valued bank note cleared the cabinet on September 13, disputes over taxation and deference toward agriculture held up final plans.[62] Luther's agriculture ministry officials began their own

[60] Discussions of stabilization plans, including the Reichsverband proposal for an industry bank, in the joint sessions of the Wirtschafts-politischer and Finanzpolitischer Ausschuss of the Economic Council, July 11, September 11–12, and September 28: DZA, Potsdam: RWR/398–399, 555. Also protocols of the Währungsausschuss, September 4, 6, 7, 1923, in RWR/911a. The Finance Ministry discussions on September 4 led to the preparation of two draft bills: one based on Helfferich's rye mark, one on a gold-denominated New Mark. The latter was adapted into plans for a *Bodenmark*, announced to business and agricultural representatives on September 19. After further discussion and settlement (1) on a lien of 4 percent of 1913 values, and (2) on denomination in gold, the project was submitted to the Reichstag on October 1 (Elster, *Von der Mark zur Reichsmark*, pp. 226–231).

[61] Spiegelberg minutes of October 6 session of Zentralverband des deutschen Bank- und Bankiergewerbes; Warburg note of October 9 meeting at the Discontogesellschaft; Presidium of Zentralverband to Finance Minister Luther, October 10, 1923; and Warburg's draft resolution: "Fragen der Währungs- und Devisenpolitik," Max Warburg papers/147a.

[62] See cabinet discussions of September 10, 13, 26, in GFM: ARK, Kabinettsprotokolle, 3491/1748/756619–756621, 756685–756691, 756841–756842.

project in mid-September, borrowing the mortgage basis of Helfferich's proposal but using a gold and not a rye standard. This was to be the form of the final proposal, but the fall of the first Stresemann cabinet over internal disagreement on October 13 brought further delay. In the reshuffle both Hilferding and von Raumer were brought down by their respective business and socialist adversaries. Hans Luther was moved to the Finance Ministry in the reconstructed cabinet, and within a few days completed the Rentenbank project, which under the new Enabling Act could be passed by decree. The bankers secured one concession when they persuaded Luther to avoid any fixed relation between the old mark and the new.[63] A permanent legal ratio, the bankers feared, would signify formal devaluation and a renunciation of debts that would destroy German credit abroad. (Whether credit actually existed was not considered.) Launched at the gold mark rate (which amounted to 4.2 per dollar), the Rentenmark would be exchangeable for the mortgage bonds, the Rentenbriefe, at the legal rate of 500 to 1. But while Rentenmark and Rentenbrief were assigned initial values in terms of the London gold price (and thus the dollar), they were not to be convertible into gold. Instead, alongside the old mark they would face the perils of the money markets. At their meeting on October 13 the cautious bankers also stipulated that the new paper need not be accepted by private parties as legal tender and won a change in name for the new institute from "Currency Bank" to "Rentenbank." At the final decisive cabinet session of October 15, two days before the decree authorizing the Rentenbank, Luther said he needed four weeks before launching the Rentenmark in order to terminate the Ruhr subsidies that might otherwise drag down the new money. Such a drastic cutoff, however, proved politically impossible.[64] And by early November the tempestuous flight from the old mark had raised the price of a loaf of bread to 165 billion marks, or 10,000 times its price of three weeks earlier.[65]

There was no guarantee that the old mark would not collapse further after November 20, dragging the new Rentenmark with it. But the new money held for two major reasons. It was settled that the government

[63] See the Bernstein report of the September 13 meeting, which included Luther and Koeth from the government; Havenstein and Glasenap of the Reichsbank; Rösicke for agriculture; Hilger, Hugenberg, Krämer, and Bücher from industry; Urbig, Frisch, Loeb, Warburg, and Helfferich representing finance and banking. Max Warburg papers/147a. See, too, Helfferich's letter to Hilferding from Stresa on September 18, in BA, Koblenz: R 13 I (VdESI)/278.

[64] GFM: ARK, Kabinettsprotokolle, 3491/1749/757146–757152.

[65] Netzband and Widmaier, *Finanz- und Währungspolitik der Ära Luther*, pp. 109 ff. Elster, *Von der Mark zur Reichsmark*, pp. 231–242. Bread prices in the Urbig report of October 18, Max Warburg papers/147a (cf. note 59) and GFM: ARK, 3491/1749/757596.

would receive a limit of 1.2 billion Rentenmarks—300 millions of which would suffice to wipe out the whole huge paper mark floating debt—no matter how desperate its needs. Such a tight purse signaled that the state was at last serious about stabilization. More generally, industry and the economy as a whole were desperate for some stable means of exchange. That the Rentenmark would survive was indicated by the favorable public reception to a stopgap gold loan in October, which was denominated in dollars and exchangeable after January 1924 into Rentenmarks.[66] No matter how astronomically prices and paper circulation had risen, gold equivalents of the money available had shrunk to a small percentage of 1914's volume. Havenstein, in fact, had misguidedly viewed his major task as hastening the supply of paper to prevent a total drying up of currency, credit, and thus of economic activity. To this end, he had acquired new printing presses, fretted over the communist presence on the treasury printer's factory councils, and acquiesced when municipalities and other agencies were granted permission to issue their own *Notgeld* or emergency currencies in August and September. When criticized for his give-away credit to industry, he could point out that the floating debt to the state so dwarfed private industry loans as to make the latter a small component of the inflationary supply of paper.[67] In any case, none of his measures had sufficed to keep up the quantity of real money, while of course they only helped the paper mark to plummet faster. Finally, in the last weeks of the old mark, Berlin sought to slow the collapse of the mark against foreign currencies by decreeing an artificially high exchange rate for the mark. A year earlier this might have signaled an earnest effort at stabilization: now, as Melchior reported to Luther on November 12, the result was to deprive the recent dollar-keyed gold notes of their rightful purchasing power, to disillusion the public about gold-mark notes, and to shed the "last bit of trust in Germany's ability to introduce any stable currency whatsoever."[68]

In fact, in the very week after Melchior's protest, policy changed, as the new Currency Commissioner Schacht prepared for the launching of the Rentenmark by letting the dollar rate surge upward from 650 billion to 4.2 trillion paper marks. The result was to shrink the real value of paper money in circulation, to bring the mark into line with public expectations, and thus to lower any adverse pressure that further depreciation might exert on the new currency. In Cologne and abroad,

[66] October gold loan in Bresciani-Turroni, *The Economics of Inflation*, pp. 343–344; Netzband and Widmaier, *Finanz- und Währungspolitik der Ära Luther*, pp. 31–32.

[67] See Havenstein's reports to the Zentralausschuss of the Reichsbank, September 20, 1922, February 2, 1923, August 25, and September 15, 1923, in DZA, Potsdam: Havenstein Nachlass.

[68] See Melchior to Luther, November 12, 1923, in Max Warburg papers/147a.

where the Rentenmark was unavailable, the old mark began to sink even further. But, if only from desperation, the Rentenmark held and helped stabilize the old marks, which the government continued to exchange at a trillion to one.[69] The recovery was a relief to most. Yet it, too, was achieved only by rewarding the powerful and penalizing the weak: Hilferding's primary emphasis on tax reform yielded to a technical measure that thrust the write-off of the public debt onto middle-class savers, pared the public payrolls, and was to nullify the Social Democratic voice over the government and the trade-union influence over the economy.

Until the outcome of the monetary reform became clearer at the turn of the year, parliamentary government came close to collapse. It was saved only at the cost of appeasing right-wing forces with the end of SPD's participation in the government and with the suspension, finally, of its symbolic conquest of 1918—the eight-hour day. While the strike wave of August 1923 had given the Socialists new leverage, they lost this power when the termination of passive resistance made trade-union cooperation less crucial. Pleading that it was heading for "certain ruin," heavy industry now prepared to pose its own ultimatums—including a special settlement with the French and Belgians in the Rhineland.[70] Nor was industry the only antisocialist force that mobilized. In Bavaria a conservative cabinet, radical-right paramilitary groups, and Nazis all bid against each other with inflammatory rhetoric and demonstrations of defiance, including Munich's declaration of a state of siege designed to nullify Berlin's authority. Relations with the left-wing Saxon Social Democrats, whom both Seeckt and Defense Minister Gessler hated for their opposition to clandestine rearmament, also heated up, and radical-right squads based in Coburg seemed ready to invade Marxist Saxony or even march to Red Berlin.[71]

The focus of anger on the part of the right—a source, too, of uneasi-

[69] See the then Currency Commissioner: Hjalmar Schacht, *The Stabilization of the Mark* (London, 1927), pp. 97–115. Given success, credit was disputed. For Helfferich's claims, see the DNVP pamphlet: "Die Wahrheit über die Rentenmark" (Berlin, 1924). Cf. Helfferich's disturbance at the credit given to Schacht in his letters from Stresa to Reichert on December 23, 1923, and on January 1, 1924, in BA, Koblenz: R 13 I (VdESI)/279.

[70] See BA, Koblenz: R 13 I/98, Protocol of October 5, 1923, meeting.

[71] Harold J. Gordon, "Die Reichswehr und Sachsen 1923," *Wehrwissenschaftliche Rundschau*, XI (1961), pp. 677–692; Hans Meier-Welcker, *Seeckt* (Frankfurt am Main, 1967), pp. 376–389; Francis L. Carsten, *Reichswehr und Politik (1918–1933)* (Cologne and Berlin, 1965), pp. 193 ff.; Otto Gessler, *Reichswehrpolitik in der Weimarer Republik*, Kurt Sendtner, ed. (Stuttgart, 1958), pp. 270–271; also the rich material from Gessler on Saxony in DZA, Potsdam: Präsidialkanzlei/762; and the complaints from business circles in BA, Koblenz: R 43 I/2309; and Walter Fabian, *Klassenkampf um Sachsen. Ein Stück Geschichte 1918–1930* (Löbau, 1930), pp. 139–141, 149–184, who stresses the local reforms that provoked the right.

ness even for conservatives within the coalition—remained the SPD's participation in the federal cabinet. At the very moment the Great Coalition nominally restored Social Democratic power, the balance of political forces was moving to the right. The shift was due in part to the new and more central role of the Nationalist Party. Earlier written off as irreconcilable, throughout 1923 the Nationalists won new influence because of their support for Cuno and then Helfferich's leadership in the currency reform. They might also serve to appease the agrarians and secure food supplies despite the currency deterioration. As they became a more important power factor, the fundamental theme Nationalists stressed was the impossibility of governing with the Socialists. "Since Bethmann we have amassed experience upon experience," as Oswald Spengler wrote Stresemann in late October, "that it is possible to govern only against the Social Democrats if one is to govern at all."[72] This, however, could only mean an authoritarian regime. Increasingly the right talked of imposing a so-called directorate, which would cooperate with the Bavarian opposition and govern without the Reichstag. "Parliament has failed," the Iron and Steel Industrialists concluded; only "strong willed and purposeful men" could rescue Germany.[73] The right-wing projects, however, were only the most drastic symptoms of an overall despair with parliamentary methods and party constraints. As early as August 5, Warburg noted with partial approval that Stinnes wanted a Finance Minister with dictatorial power. In the new Stresemann cabinet, the Interior Minister Sollmann and Vice Chancellor Schmidt, both of the SPD, saw the need for "a piece of dictatorship." Ebert and Stresemann agreed on the need for an enabling act that would require two-thirds of the votes of the Reichstag and that would sanction legislation by decree.[74]

What distinguished the authoritarian yearnings of the right was the desire, as Westarp wrote, not to give the present government decree power, but to replace it "by a dictatorial authority free from the pressure of the streets, the parties, and the party coalitions."[75] Where government plans envisaged the abandonment of any decree power upon a change in cabinet, the right wished to free the executive completely

---

[72] GFM: Stresemann Nachlass, 7163 = 3/3105/154358–154359, letter of October 20.

[73] BA, Koblenz: R 13 I/98, Minutes of October 5 meeting. When Stresemann asked the major economic organizations to condemn Bavarian separatist trends in late October, they refused the gesture of implicit support. See the VdESI circular, October 25, 1923, Nr. 5095, in BA, Koblenz: R 13 I/202.

[74] See Warburg to Arndt von Höltzendorff, August 5, 1923, in Max Warburg papers/147a; Sollmann and Schmidt in GFM: ARK, Kabinettsprotokolle of August 18 and 23, 3491/1748/756410, and 756440–756442; Ebert and Stresemann in session of October 1: 3491/1748/756908–756912.

[75] Action Program of the DNVP, cited in Westarp MS, "Ruhrkampf," p. 102.

from dependence upon a Reichstag majority. They certainly did not wish to provide the current Social Democratic coalition with an enabling act.

Plans for a directorate climaxed with the fall of the Great Coalition cabinet at the end of October. Seeckt was at the center of much of the plotting, encouraged by his own entourage and by right-wing politicians. He also tried—unsuccessfully—to invite Otto Wiedfeldt—former Krupp director, now Ambassador in Washington and the right's candidate for technocratic savior—to stand ready to enter a directorate cabinet. Stinnes, too, played with his own dictatorial projects, expecting, according to U.S. Ambassador Houghton, a communist uprising by mid-October that would prod Ebert to appoint a dictatorial triumvirate including Wiedfeldt, Seeckt, and his own lieutenant Minoux, and eliminate the eight-hour day.[76]

In Stinnes' projects dictatorship emerged as the only way to force labor into the longer working day he had long called for. Once again the issue of working time emerged as crucial to the entire role of social democracy in the Weimar state. As at the time of the collapse of the Wirth government, the eight-hour question prevented the durable cooperation of DVP and SPD, thus helping to destroy the Great Coalition, without recourse to any directorate. The first Stresemann cabinet resigned in early October, largely because the Socialists would not permit the eight-hour day to be annulled under the proposed enabling act. The SPD argued that if the People's Party wanted to abolish the eight-hour day, it should do so by means of separate legislation carried with the help of the DNVP—a suggestion the Socialists knew to be politically impossible at that time.[77] The dispute between the two wings of the coalition was further complicated by the issue of whether to treat the refractory Bavarian government harshly or by delay. DVP and Catholic Center sought to find a *modus vivendi* with von Kahr in Munich. SPD members understood that DVP conservatives hoped that the Socialists would leave the government, so that they could include

---

[76] The best evaluation of Seeckt (and Ebert) is now in Meier-Welcker, *Seeckt*, pp. 389 ff., 403, 411–415; but see also the tendentious Friedrich von Rabenau, *Seeckt—Aus seinem Leben, 1918–1936* (Leipzig, 1940), II, pp. 365–389; Carsten, *Reichswehr und Politik*, pp. 190–191; Schröder, *Wiedfeldt*, pp. 158–161. Reports of Houghton to State Department: Decimal Series 462.00 R 29/3074 and 862.00/1330; cited also by G.F.W. Hallgarten, *Hitler, Reichswehr und Industrie* (Frankfurt, 1955), pp. 65–71. Seeckt's letters to Wiedfeldt, November 4 and 10, and Wiedfeldt to Seeckt are found in the filmed Seeckt Nachlass, Reel 15, piece 72. Why, if Seeckt were serious, they were dispatched by ordinary sea mail, with its time lags, remains curious.

[77] For the debate on the Enabling Law, see the cabinet sessions of October 1, 2, and 3; and for the hope expressed by the DVP right wing that the Socialists would withdraw, see the Party leader discussion on October 2: GFM: ARK, Kabinettsprotokolle, 3491/1749/756908 ff., 756964.

the Nationalists instead. Nonetheless, party negotiators reached a compromise that left the eight-hour question outside the purview of the enabling act and permitted resurrection of the Great Coalition. The Socialists finally withdrew at the beginning of November, not over the eight-hour question, but to protest the procedure by which Gessler removed the Socialist-Communist coalition in Saxony.[78]

The week between the intervention in Saxony and the Hitler Putsch represented the most critical days for German parliamentarism since 1918. With the SPD in opposition, the cabinet rested on a minority coalition; Seeckt was conspiring for a directorate and even Ebert was thinking of a nonparliamentary cabinet, if only for a transitional emergency period. But parliamentary government survived by delay. While the fiasco of the November 7 Putsch helped to dislocate any further dictatorial initiatives and led Seeckt back to a more apolitical stance, the critical Reichstag session that threatened a vote of no confidence was postponed.

But the regime was rescued only at the cost of the Great Coalition. In the critical meetings of the cabinet and the "bourgeois party" ministers on November 2, it was agreed that the price of a Great Coalition was just too high for each side. Stresemann understood that the Social Democrats feared they would lose touch with their radicalized working-class constituency should they consent to emergency austerity measures. Luther claimed that the Bavarian question could not be settled with the Socialists in the Berlin government, while Gessler warned that troops from Bavaria were ready to march north and that the Reichswehr might refuse to stop them on behalf of the Great Coalition. In short, the far right was more dangerous and powerful than the socialist left, and the army could not be trusted. "Cleaning up Saxony," Stresemann told party leaders on October 29, "is the prerequisite of a victory over Bavaria." To preserve the unity of the Reich and escape from what Stresemann termed "the Scylla of fascism and the Charybdis of communism," the government had to bend to the prevailing wind.[79]

---

[78] For Gessler's adamant stand, see the cabinet session of October 27: GFM: ARK, 3491/1749/757443–757451; SPD complaints on October 29: 757504 ff. (The Socialists complained primarily that they were not consulted after the final warning to the Saxon government and before the intervention.) For the Bavarian situation, besides the ongoing reports of the Reich representative, GFM: ARK, K2138/5569–5570, see GFM: ARK, "Bayern," K2134/5565/588855 on secret armaments.

[79] See Schubert's report on Stresemann's considerations as presented to D'Abernon on November 2: GFM: Stresemann Nachlass, 7120 = 263/3099/146163–146164; and cf. the letter of the DDP leader to Stresemann saying that the latter agreed with him that SPD "neutrality" would still be sought: 7164 = 4/3105/154545; for the discussions of November 2: *ibid.*, 7120 = 263/3099/146165–146168, also GFM: ARK: Kabinettsprotokolle, November 1 and 2: 3491/1749/757559–757586. For the October 29 meeting with the party leaders: BA, Koblenz:

This did not make the far right happy with the reconstructed Strese-
mann cabinet of November 1923. The DNVP thought that a rightist
coalition was in their grasp, but made it impossible for the DVP to
agree when they insisted that Stresemann himself be removed. When
Stresemann fell before DNVP and Socialist votes in late November, the
Nationalists believed again that they stood at the threshold of power.
But their leader Hergt demanded from Ebert the dissolution of the
Reichstag whenever he called for it, and the inclusion of his party in the
Prussian state government—a price that proved too high for the other
bourgeois parties.[80] After several days of fruitless negotiations, including an attempt to win DNVP participation in a cabinet led by the conservative Catholic labor leader Adam Stegerwald, Ebert turned to Wilhelm Marx of the Center. Marx initially recommended Kardorff of the
DVP, but this nomination foundered on Stresemann's barely veiled
reluctance to accept the primacy of an ambitious party colleague.
Finally Marx himself formed a government, and the Social Democrats
granted him the votes needed for an enabling act, now freed from the
former restrictions on the eight-hour day. What they had not granted
their own government they felt compelled to yield to a more conservative one. The eight-hour day was one of their casualties; but the new
enabling act, which permitted its *de facto* suspension, also allowed a
respite from party feuding and rapid institution of needed financial
measures.[81]

In retrospect, the crisis of 1923 appears an especially painful example
of the basic dilemmas that faced Weimar democracy throughout its
brief history. Once again—as under Wirth, and as earlier in 1919—the
Social Democrats' misfortune was that the government must choose to
contain social tension on conservative terms or not contain it at all.
Stresemann could not oppose the anti-Marxist and antilabor forces—
Bavarians, Army, industry, DNVP, racists—and simultaneously master
the economic and political disruption. To overcome the inflation, to

R 43 I/2309; and for the Scylla–Charybdis reference, draft article for *Die Zeit*,
undated, GFM: Stresemann Nachlass, 7119 = 262/3099/146080.

[80] Elements of the DVP, as Dingeldey informed Stresemann on November 9,
were willing to "sell your head" to get the Nationalists in the government; Stresemann himself rejected Hergt's overtures of a DNVP-DVP coalition on November
19. See GFM: Stresemann Nachlass, 7124 = 267/3011/146950–146954; and November 19: GFM: ARK, Kabinettsprotokolle, 3491/1750/757823–757824; loss
of vote of confidence, November 23 in VDR: SB, 361, pp. 12241 ff. Cf. Werner,
Freiherr v. Rheinhaben, *Kaiser, Kanzler, Präsidenten. Erinnerungen* (Mainz, 1968),
pp. 212, 223–227, on Stresemann's relation with the DNVP and the events of
November.

[81] DZA, Potsdam: DNVP Akten/9, pp. 60–63: "Darstellung der . . . Verhandlungen zur Neubildung der Reichsregierung in der Woche vom 23–30 November
1923"; also Stehkämper, ed., *Nachlass Marx*, I, pp. 296, 303–304, 323 (Aufzeichnung vom 28.XI.23); for Kardorff rivalry, see above, note 50.

head off economic collapse and territorial fragmentation, and to restore control by a parliamentary ministry, he had to break with precisely those pro-labor forces that sought the same ends he did.

Since Germany was near armed rebellion, the terms of political settlement favored the parties potentially strongest in the streets. Weimar democracy continued to limp from social clash to social clash, patching together institutional compromises that favored either left-center or right-center. When a radicalized working class manifested its strength, as in November 1918, March 1920, June 1922, and finally July and August 1923, the Social Democrats could benefit: they could win a voice in the cabinet or extract legislative compromises that enabled them to recapture working-class support, which they had been in danger of losing to the Independent Socialists or Communists who had led the demonstrations in the streets. But more often it was the conservative and business interests that had to be bought off, as during the continuing financial crisis of 1921 to 1923, or as in the fall of 1923 when the right threatened extralegal action. By that point merely preserving the parliamentary system required the sacrifice of the Social Democrats. The SPD could refuse to participate in a government that suspended the social gains of 1918; but eventually—as in December 1923 and later under Brüning in 1930—they had to endorse conservative solutions in any case for fear of a total collapse of the parliamentary regime. As a result, much of what the right had sought through a directorate they won by parliamentary means.

Despite the fact that the political conflict centered on the SPD's political role, the alternative before Germany was not merely that of social democracy or bourgeois supremacy. What the antisocialist forces really represented were economic or territorial interests that undermined any defender of a traditionally conceived public interest in Berlin. With increasing insistence during the inflation and autumn crisis, non-working-class interests proposed political solutions that involved a new corporatism for Germany. Although the right was nostalgic for a traditional society, this new corporatism was not intended merely as a reversion to pre-industrial guilds and communities. As represented by the plans for a directorate, it aimed at the hegemony of the interests that wartime production needs had strengthened—with the proviso that the rightist groups powerful in 1923 wished to exclude labor. This new corporatism was not simply anachronistic; in many ways it presaged developments that would occur in all the industrialized countries; indeed, it indicated the line along which the Germans would reach a settlement once the right became willing to work with organized labor.

As of 1923, however, it was the SPD that joined Stresemann in the old longing to identify and defend a transcendent public interest—the Reich above all parties. While the SPD also spoke for a corporate group

386

in 1923, in its very weakness it required the state to preserve parliamentary ground rules and to prevent a relapse to authoritarianism; it also required the state to keep equilibrium in the market place through its Ministry of Labor. Outside Germany, Poincaré, too, joined Stresemann in equivalent aspirations. Like the SPD, both men identified with a national interest because they defended groups that were vulnerable in the Hobbesian competition of the market place. Both men were closest in background and loyalties to the middle-class individuals who occupied social positions between big labor and heavy industry, who had been most hurt by the long-term inflation since 1914. In this respect, Stresemann and Poincaré were complementary enemies, just as the corporatist forces in each country shared interests. Hence the analogous stands of Stresemann and Poincaré against their respective industrial leadership became as important for the last phase of the Ruhr struggle as the more obvious Franco-German conflict.

CORPORATIST FORCES VERSUS POINCARÉ AND STRESEMANN

If Germany's "estates" were to take responsibility for public fiscal policy, why should they not claim a major role in international negotiations? German business leaders, according to Bücher, the executive director of the Reichsverband der deutschen Industrie, must negotiate with their foreign counterparts to eliminate government interference in reparation issues.[82] Economic pressures suggested the same approach to French industrialists, and the German abandonment of passive resistance provided perhaps the final opportunity to wrest more tangible advantages than those provided by the London Schedule of Payments of 1921. "It cannot be repeated too often," commented the editor of the *Journée Industrielle*, "the Ruhr operation makes sense only if it tends to create new facts . . . and on these new facts, new solutions."[83]

Since 1920, French coal and steel interests had urged official support for their efforts to negotiate industrial ententes with German coal producers. Writing to Millerand before Spa, Robert Pinot called upon the Quai d'Orsay to demand German cessions of controlling stock shares in coal firms that had been major suppliers of Lorraine ore producers. As Minister of Reconstruction, Louis Loucheur initially welcomed similar plans, and as late as December 1921, Loucheur and Briand sought to win British approval for stock transfers as part of a general reparations settlement.[84]

---

[82] Bücher to Cuno, June 4, 1923, in GFM: ARK, Ausführung des Friedensvertrags, 9523H/3684/287695–287696; also *Akten: Cuno*, p. 538, note. The suggestion was resisted by the Foreign Ministry, however.

[83] *JI*, April 7, 1923.

[84] See above: Chapter Three, pp. 198–202 and Chapter Four, pp. 240, 275.

German industrialists were hostile to these efforts. In February 1922, Reichert of the Iron and Steel Industrialists told his colleagues that he had warned the Foreign Ministry to avoid any agreements leading to an international iron cartel.[85] French demands discouraged Germans from asking for international agreements. When some industrialists probed French willingness in March 1922 to reconstruct the prewar rail cartel, Pinot and Humbert de Wendel asked for stock shares as a guarantee of German deliveries of coke and progress toward a reparation settlement.[86] From the German side, Arnold Rechberg's schemes also provoked bitter reaction. Rechberg, who was the heir to Baden chemical interests and a bitter antibolshevist, saw a Franco-German economic entente as key to an anti-Soviet policy. In numerous trips to France and in letters to the Berlin government, he proposed that Germany give French and English firms new stock shares in German firms up to 30 percent of the old equity. For the Union of Iron and Steel Industrialists, however, this meant "the economic and financial enslavement of our German industry."[87] Similar plans by Gaston Japy and Jules Bernard, French iron industrialists whose projects were aired in the conservative press, were also condemned. Reviewing the proliferation of proposals at the end of 1922, Reichert insisted that Germany maintain as much independence from foreign ore producers as possible. If there were negotiations, German objectives must include conversion of reparation coal deliveries into private contractual sales, the suspension of duty-free import quotas for Lorraine, Luxemburg, and Upper Silesia, the end of French tariff discrimination, liberation of the Rhineland and the Saar from occupation and sanctions, and the downward revision of reparations: in short, the overthrow of the major economic clauses in the Versailles Treaty.[88]

Hugo Stinnes, on the other hand, was more willing to consider joint solutions, and was allegedly prepared in spring 1923 to defy govern-

[85] Reichert to Mayer, February 9, 1922, in BA, Koblenz: R 13 I (VdESI)/261. Cf. also Röchling to Reichert on June 21, 1922, recollecting events in the Saar: "Whoever delivers himself into French hands will be finished. Proof: the Stumm family in the Saar, the Mannesmann pipe works in the Saar, and many another."

[86] See "Entretien de MM. Humbert de Wendel et Robert Pinot avec le Dr. Georg Goetz, le 20 mars 1922, PAM/19062, f. "Questions diverses."

[87] See Rechberg's letters to Stresemann, especially April 20 and 26, 1923, GFM: Stresemann Nachlass, 7115 = 258/3088/145370–145373; also Eberhard von Vietsch, *Arnold Rechberg und das Problem der politischen West-Orientierung Deutschlands nach dem 1. Weltkrieg* (Koblenz, 1958), which overestimates the significance of the man's contacts. Reichert's memo opposing the plan, May 2, 1923, is in BA, Koblenz: R 13 I (VdESI)/255. January 1924 trips warily monitored by the British: FO 371/9729.

[88] See *JI*, August 5, 27, 28, and October 10, 1922; also Gaston Japy in the *Echo de Paris*, March 18, 1923. Reichert's report of December 1922: "Verhandlungsmöglichkeiten zwischen der deutschen und der französischen Eisenindustrie," is in BA, Koblenz: R 13 I (VdESI)/255.

ment prohibitions against delivering coal to France if private contracts could be arranged.[89] Early in 1922, Stinnes' ambitions had already led him to explore a German consortium to invest in Russia under the NEP; thereafter, he turned back to the West and negotiations with the Luxemburg steel magnate Emil Mayrisch, who enjoyed good relations in Paris. Finally, in the fall of 1922 he signed the Stinnes-Lubersac accords with the French head of the cooperatives for reconstruction of the devastated regions. A foe of Rathenau's Wiesbaden agreements, which extended reparations in kind, Stinnes sought parallel arrangements between private business. These would eliminate government control, raise the prices for German goods from the world-market level stipulated for reparation deliveries, and—as in the case of his agreement with Lubersac—provide his own firms with handsome commissions.[90]

Stinnes remained more flexible than other coal and steel men precisely because he was indifferent to political conditions. When Paul Reusch, however, was approached in April and August 1922, he told French emissaries that agreement hinged on the end of the Rhineland and Saar occupation[91]—an unrealistic condition even though Reusch felt that he had received initial reassurances. German industry may well have wished to pose insuperable obstacles, but the government hoped to win time in 1922 by making its Ruhr firms more receptive to French soundings. Probably outrunning what industry would have sanctioned, Wirth quizzed Lubersac on October 18, 1922, as to Paris' attitude toward industrial ententes. Poincaré, however, merely repeated that France would do no more than entertain German proposals for fulfillment of the Versailles Treaty.[92] Even if French iron interests remained unhappy with Poincaré's attitude, they simply did not possess the political influence that their German counterparts enjoyed. Still, the Quai d'Orsay did not entirely foreclose interindustry negotiations. When German sources asked that Stinnes, Klöckner, and Silverberg be permitted to converse with French industrialists on December 22–23, Poincaré's principal advisor, Seydoux, indicated that he was not fundamentally hostile to agreements between industrialists but did fear that the Germans were now merely trying to forestall Ruhr sanctions.[93]

[89] Margérie to the President of the Council, March 23, 1923, in Min. Fin., F^{30}/1277. For Stinnes' willingness to sell coal to the French, see Hermes to Ersing, October 19, 1923, in Stehkämper, ed., Nachlass Marx, II, p. 111.

[90] For the Russian plans, see Chapter Four, note 99. For the Stinnes-Lubersac accords, see Weill-Raynal, Les réparations allemandes, II, pp. 291–296.

[91] Reusch report to the Executive of the Verein deutscher Eisen- und Stahlindustrieller, March 15, 1923, in BA, Koblenz: R 13 I/255.

[92] See Lubersac to Wirth and Wirth to Lubersac, October 18, 1922; also Poincaré to Lubersac, October 21, 1922, in Min. Fin., F^{30}/1277.

[93] For these events, see Seydoux to Barthou, December 23, 1922, and to the German Ambassador in ibid., F^{30}/1277. Cf. also Melchior's note that as of Decem-

With the occupation of the Ruhr, the prospects for interindustry negotiations were initially shattered. Forced to halt their own production, German steel men demanded not only the cessation of reparations payments, but also suspension of the Treaty-stipulated import quotas that allowed Lorraine and Saar iron products into South German markets. At the same time, they asked French industrial leaders to remember that they had led the common struggle against working-class radicalism for five years and pleaded not to be undermined.[94] Once passive resistance collapsed, the Ruhr industrialists sought French help in abolishing the eight-hour day. Their Committee of Six pleaded with General Degoutte, leader of the Franco-Belgian force, for understanding of their high costs and export difficulties. "Industry," Peter Kloeckner confided, "was convinced that it had been a serious error to give in to socialist influence and to introduce a shortened working day after a lost war." While the industrialists planned to reintroduce unilaterally the old ten-hour day for the mines (or eight and one-half hours for underground work), they could not enforce the move against the labor unions and Berlin unless the occupying power was prepared to maintain order. This was the reward German labor was to reap for sustaining passive resistance. Degoutte, however, refused to intervene, and Kloeckner backed down. Poincaré emphasized to his ambassadors that Paris would not help German industrialists overturn the eight-hour day, while the French authorities leafleted Bochum to publicize industry's request and their refusal. In the face of worker anger, the plans for the longer day had to be temporarily abandoned.[95]

Why the industrialists' change from superheated patriotism to a search for collaboration? By September 1923 the impossibility of ex-

---

ber 18, 1922, the bankers and industrialists planning a final reparation offer in Berlin thought industry must make the French a proposal that mobilized their own resources.

[94] BA, Koblenz: R 13 I (VdESI)/98 Hauptvorstand, January 19, 1923.

[95] GFM: Stresemann Nachlass, $7118 = 261/3099/145990-146001$, "Aktenvermerk über die Besprechung der [6er] Kommission mit Gen. Degoutte am 5. Oktober 1923." Cf. Paul Reusch Nachlass, GHH:400101222/2, protocol of the meeting of the Zechen-Verband in Unna, October 6, 1923, where Kirdorff claimed that Degoutte was sympathetic to the overtime request. See, too, GHH:3001-93008/16, protocol of the meeting of the Nordwest Gruppe in Unna, October 11, for discussion of Degoutte's publicizing of the industrialists' request for overtime: "German industry has not experienced a greater fiasco for many years," said one participant. Poincaré knew how to exploit the eight-hour issue: he insisted that the eight-hour day be applied in all establishments that French authorities took over and be written into all contracts. On the other hand, he told his Ambassador in Berlin that France could not prohibit workers from accepting overtime from German employers—as indeed they were being forced to do. See Min. Aff. Etr., Europe, 1918-1929, Ruhr/32, Poincaré to Bourgin, November 13, and Peretti memo of November 20, also Ruhr/33, Poincaré to Margerie, December 4, 1923.

porting, the collapse of economic activity, and the curtailment of credit had badly hurt an industry that had earlier contemplated inflation with equanimity. Conscientious industrialists still made heavy payments to employees: GHH spent 460,000 gulden for food between July and mid-September.[96] Berlin's financial assistance to the unemployed and to industry was slated to terminate in October. Meanwhile, the Reichsbank was finally tightening its credit lines to private firms.[97] Berlin was rapidly losing control of most of the instruments of economic constraint or patronage, and in their new distress German industrialists had turned to those with economic power.

When General Degoutte called in Stinnes, Otto Wolff, and other industrialists, he thus found no refusal in principle to negotiations with the occupying authority. Stinnes told an unhappy Stresemann that the negotiations were industry's only alternative, unless Berlin provided industry with a transitional loan, granted exemptions from the coal tax, and extended the working day.[98] Finance Minister Luther, who planned to halt payments to the Ruhr by the end of October, agreed that industry was forced to negotiate with the French, but the Chancellor still publicly rebuked Wolff, who signed his own agreement on October 12, for undermining the authority of the Reich. For their part, the Ruhr industrialists regarded Stresemann's disavowal as a "betrayal," and feared that the cabinet's effort to start negotiations with the French might thwart their own.[99] They overlooked Stresemann's bitter alternatives: winter was approaching and unemployment mounting—105,000 workers in Essen alone and nearly 350,000 in the Ruhr basin were out of work; and the French were prepared to exploit the unemployment

[96] See the complaints of Vögler and Stinnes about the lack of credits to the cabinet on October 9 and discussions of credits on October 10, 20, and November 1, in GFM: Stresemann Nachlass, 7118 = 261/3099/146008–146014, and Kabinettsprotokolle, 3491/1749/757038–757042, 757259–757271, 757559 ff. For GHH, payments see Paul Reusch to Reichert, September 13, 1923, in GHH: 400101222/7.

[97] For Reichsbank policy, see Graham, *Exchanges, Prices, and Production in Hyper-Inflation*, pp. 65–66; Schacht, *The Stabilization of the Mark*, pp. 72–75; Favez, *Le Reich devant l'occupation*, pp. 344–345.

[98] For the reports on the Stinnes negotiations, see GFM: Stresemann Nachlass, 7161 = 1/3105/154192–154194, 154226–154228; Stresemann, *Vermächtnis*, I, pp. 160–164.

[99] Luther–Stresemann interchange at October cabinet meeting in GFM: ARK, Kabinettsprotokolle, 3491/1749/757043–757050. Wolff's motives for capitulation were complex: his major firms, "Rheinstahl" and Phönix, A.G., had corporate connections and affiliates in Holland; much of his capital was tied up in inventory that the French began to confiscate before he gave in; and the Dutch financiers who had taken new stock issues in July 1923 pushed him toward a settlement. See the memo by the British Commercial Secretary at Cologne, Kavanaugh, forwarded by D'Abernon, November 17, 1923, in FO 371/8749: C20153/313/18; also Vorstand des Deutschen Metallarbeiter-Verbandes, *Konzerne der Metallindustrie* (Stuttgart, 1924), pp. 222–227.

as a means of pressure.[100] Stresemann could not rescue the currency and support the Ruhr unemployed simultaneously. Restoring the monetary system seemed to be the first necessity. But this meant letting the mineowners negotiate with the French authorities, who would demand political concessions tending to separate the Ruhr and the Rhineland from the rest of Germany.

Paris' policy was veiled, if not confused. In the spring of 1923 high-level French officials had studied the possible establishment of a Rhenish state; and Serrigny, secretary to the premier, had questioned various ministries as to the guidelines that should be adopted for its finances and organization. In April, however, Poincaré apparently canceled the study abruptly.[101] In the absence of clear orders, the French proconsuls in the Rhineland—General Degoutte, who headed the MICUM (Mission Interalliée de Contrôle des Usines et des Mines), General de Metz, Commander of the French occupation zone west of the Rhine, and Paul Tirard, head of the Interallied Rhineland High Commission—sought to secure as extensive a degree of French control as possible. The coal-tax issue and the currency problem offered political and economic crowbars that could set Ruhr industry against Berlin, pry apart the Reich, and create a satellite Rhenish republic, even if it was one that remained nominally within the German federal system.

Stresemann's opposition to industry's negotiations with the French could not be sustained. Stinnes and the Ruhr mineowners offered to advance coal reparations on their own account up to 18 percent of their production in return for later remissions of taxes by Berlin. The arrangement that industry sought was onerous, but it had crucial advantages. It would allow the resumption of production free from the threat of French confiscation and would permit export of the output of the Ruhr. In a period of liquidity shortage, with new, heavy taxes levied upon a gold basis, industry's reparation offer promised the mineowners, in effect, a "coal mark," the monetization of their most plentiful resource.[102]

By October 23, Berlin felt that it had to acquiesce in industry's reparations offer but felt imperiled by the French claim to the German coal tax, including arrears since January. Poincaré was certain that the

[100] Unemployment figures for Essen from GFM: 9407/3654/269649–269652, "Niederschrift über die 1. Sitzung für Arbeitsfragen," and for the Ruhr basin (and the description of the pressure this caused), Min. Aff. Etr., Europe, 1918–1929, Ruhr/32, Bourgin report of November 10, 1923.

[101] Min. Fin. F^{30}/1276: Finance Minister to Serrigny in response to questionnaire of March 26, 1923; also Serrigny letter of April 5.

[102] See the cabinet meeting of October 20 in GFM: ARK, Kabinettsprotokolle, 3491/1749/757259–757262; also French delegate to the MICUM, October 20: GFM, Stresemann Nachlass, 7118 = 261/3099/146057–146059.

German coal barons, especially Stinnes, whom he described as the major obstacle to any accord since Spa, could well afford the tax.[103] Stresemann resisted again, but the industrialists' Commission of Six (Stinnes, Klöckner, Vögler, Reusch, Janus, and later Thyssen to keep him from negotiating on his own) decided that unless a collective agreement was quickly reached with MICUM, there would be a flood of individual arrangements. Under the pressure of Dutch creditors, as noted above, Otto Wolff's firms, Phönix and Rheinische Stahlwerke, had signed early in October. By the end of the month about a dozen other works, including Krupp, had capitulated and agreed that 82 million dollars worth of coal would be surrendered to cover the arrears in the coal tax.[104] By November 1, the Chancellor himself felt compelled to accept that coal taxes required by MICUM were to be compensated as taxes legitimately paid.[105] There was one further hurdle. Poincaré wanted to preserve the legalistic distinction between the pledges for reparations and the reparations themselves; hence, Degoutte stipulated that coal payments go into a guarantee fund against which occupation costs would first be drawn. Stresemann again refused compensation, and this time forced a compromise settlement. Coal advances, it was decided, should be credited by MICUM to the reparations account; the coal tax, arrears as well as future payments, would go temporarily to the new guarantee fund, for the moment to defray occupation costs but ultimately to be credited toward reparations.[106]

The final MICUM agreements of November 23 were costly for German industry, which had to pay 21 percent of its output until mid-December and 27 percent thereafter until April, when the agreement was slated to expire. Nonetheless, they were bearable if corporate indebtedness was not already excessive. In view of MICUM requirements,

[103] Poincaré's instructions to Bourgin, November 13: Min. Aff. Etr., Europe, 1918–1929, Ruhr/32, pp. 74–78.

[104] Paul Reusch Nachlass, GHH: 300193008/16, "Aufzeichnung über eine Sitzung der Nordwest Gruppe in Unna am 11. Oktober 1923" has the discussion of Thyssen; cf. reports on the negotiations with the MICUM, October 23 and 24, and the October 30 list of firms that had already come to terms. Also GHH: 400101222/2, daily reports on negotiations, especially Nr. 9 (October 23), Nr. 12 (October 31), and the "Aktenvermerk" of October 31.

[105] Cabinet session of November 1 in GFM: ARK, Kabinettsprotokolle, 3194/1749/757559–757563. Letter from Stresemann to the industrialists cited in Etienne Weill-Raynal, Les réparations allemandes, II, p. 478.

[106] Paul Reusch Nachlass, GHH: 400101222/2, reports Nrs. 14 (November 3), 15 (November 14), 16 (November 17), 17 (November 22). Also Stresemann to 6er Kommission, November 13, 1923; the November 16 discussion among Stresemann, Stinnes, and Vögler; and the Vögler report on the final negotiations with the French, in GFM: Wirtschaft Reparation, Allg. 4b., 9410H/3655/270157, 270010–270013; cf. Erdmann, Adenauer, pp. 79–80, 84, 103, 146. A clear British summary is provided by the retrospective Foreign Office memorandum of June 13, 1924, in FO 371/9766: C9407/79/18.

Paul Reusch, for example, reorganized the GHH holdings into a tighter corporate network and directed the affiliated firms outside the occupied region to funnel orders to the hard-pressed units in the Ruhr.[107] But for those firms built on rickety conglomerate lines during inflation, the MICUM obligations, along with the new, rigorous curtailment of credit, proved harder to weather, as the collapse of the Stinnes enterprises was to illustrate. In either case, step by step, a reluctant Stresemann had to turn over negotiations with the French and the paying of reparations to the spokesmen of heavy industry.

It was not German industry alone that pushed Berlin into these successive compromises of its own authority. As the mass of the Ruhr population confronted distress and impoverishment, Rhenish political leaders—especially the Center Party's Konrad Adenauer, who was then Mayor of Cologne—also pressed either for funds from Berlin or for the right to negotiate with the French. At Hagen on October 25, just outside the occupied territory, Rhineland delegates presented a series of bleak options to Stresemann. Duisburg's Mayor, Karl Jarres, wanted a defiant declaration to the French that survival of the Rhineland was their problem and that henceforth Germany viewed the Versailles Treaty as null and void. Such *Versackungspolitik* might well provoke a wider occupation, even a joint French and Czechoslovak-Polish invasion; but somehow from the rubble of a new war would emerge a liberated Rhineland. Adenauer was prepared to negotiate an indefinite separation of the Rhineland from Prussia, perhaps even from the Reich, claiming that this would thrust upon the French the burden of reviving the Rhenish economy and probably liberate Germany from other liabilities under Versailles. Stresemann opposed these drastic alternatives as fruitless. For the moment he and Luther were forced to prolong the Rhineland's unemployment assistance beyond October 30 and agree that the Rhinelanders under Adenauer could set up a Committee of Fifteen for political negotiations with Tirard. Faced with the Saxon and Bavarian issues a week later, forced to piece together a cabinet without the Social Democrats, Stresemann could only turn over the area's problems to its own political leaders.[108]

The new cabinet heatedly debated further assistance to the Ruhr populace. Speaking for Finance, Luther insisted that aid payments must cease by November 24, lest they drag down the new Renten-

[107] GHH: 300193008/18, Paul Reusch to Karl Haniel (one of the major family shareholders in the GHH and chairman of its overseeing board), November 4, 1923.
[108] Positions sorted out in Erdmann, *Adenauer*, pp. 98 ff.; also Hans Luther, *Politiker ohne Partei*, p. 178; GFM: ARK, Kabinettsprotokolle, October 24, 1923, 3491/1749/757360; Min. Aff. Etr., Europe, 1918–1929, Rive Gauche du Rhin/38, note of December 22, describing Rhenish political trends.

mark.[109] Stresemann vetoed any announcement of abandonment, but the government reluctantly authorized the Rhinelanders to take their own measures and envisioned the development of an autonomous Rhenish authority that might have the power to levy taxes.[110]

In the fortnight from November 14 to 27, Adenauer and his Committee of Fifteen broached to Tirard a succession of schemes for a Rhineland linked confederally to Germany.[111] The Committee's major success was its recognition by the French and Paris' abandonment of support for the out-and-out German separatists. From the end of October the French government was learning that the obscure separatist spokesmen had no influence with the economic leaders who controlled the coal and no popular roots among the workers.[112] Although total independence for the Rhineland might be impossible, Poincaré did envisage a semi-detached state with its own parliament, civil service, diplomatic representation, and railroad. Tirard agreed that such a development might be feasible, but he warned that the outright separatists could not be trusted. Degoutte, moreover, resisted their operations in the Ruhr. The wisest course was to encourage the established Rhenish leaders in their negotiations with Berlin.[113] Just as Poincaré was to remain intensely suspicious about private arrangements among industrialists, so he was cautious about going beyond the juridical framework of negotiations between states or their sanctioned representatives. The British, too, were now protesting against possible French encouragement of separatist plans, and even the Belgians were uneasy about their ally's objectives. With a keen sense of international constraints, aware that British neutrality had facilitated his victory in the Ruhr, and cautious by temperament, the French premier was not prepared to speculate on windfall gains.[114]

[109] Erdmann, *Adenauer*, pp. 98–135. GFM: ARK, Kabinettsprotokolle, 3491/1750/757789.

[110] GFM: ARK, Kabinettsprotokolle, November 17, 3491/1750/757996–758003; also Stehkämper, ed., *Nachlass Marx*, II, pp. 92–98.

[111] Reports on the meetings of the Verhandlungsausschuss with Tirard on November 14: GFM: Politische Abteilung IIa, Besetztes Rheinland, 9406H/3654/269517–269518, 269519–269520 and ff. Report on negotiations of November 23, *ibid.*, 269551–269552.

[112] Min. Aff. Etr., Europe, 1918–1929, Rive Gauche du Rhin/34, October 26 note for Poincaré from the Mission François Poncet; also Col. Gelin to Tirard, October 26, on the separatists' "total lack of aptitude to direct anything."

[113] Min. Aff. Etr., Europe, 1918–1929, Rive Gauche du Rhin/34, "Audience de M. Tirard par le Président du Conseil en présence de M. de Peretti le 30 oct. à 10h30." See also Poincaré's statement in JOC, 1923, pp. 3690–3691 (November 23), predicting a move for Rhenish autonomy.

[114] See the report of the British journalist Poliakoff's interview with Seydoux sent by Charles Mendl, Paris, to Lord Crewe, November 6, 1923, in FO 371/8748: C19316/313/18. Cf. Min. Aff. Etr., Europe, 1918–1929, Rive Gauche du Rhin/35, November 8 report of Saint-Aulaire's talk with Eyre Crowe; *ibid.*/36 for

The negotiations, however, between Tirard and the Committee of Fifteen achieved little. While the Committee submitted a scheme for an autonomous Rhineland that left foreign policy to Berlin, Tirard wanted a state that could exchange ambassadors and conduct its own (or rather the Quai d'Orsay's) foreign policy. Encouraged by various intermediaries, Adenauer drafted his own plans for Poincaré's scrutiny, but aroused little response. While dismissing the separatists, the President of the Council saw little advantage in the creation of simply another federal state within the German Reich. As a result the political negotiations became dormant. As a fellow Center Party member and Cologne lawyer, the new Chancellor, Wilhelm Marx, followed Adenauer's discussions more sympathetically than the old. But speaking out now as Foreign Minister, and supported by the able Wilhelmstrasse professionals, Karl Schubert and Ago von Maltzan, Stresemann resisted the arguments of the Rhineland negotiators more tenaciously than before and sought a resumption of direct Franco-German parleys. He also opposed, and forced some modification of, Luther's severe cut-off of financial aid to the Rhineland. Playing for time, in mid-December Stresemann proposed to the French a *modus vivendi* that would allow restoration of economic activity while the French kept their troops in the Ruhr.[115]

As this proposal and Poincaré's negative response both revealed, the crucial aspect of the Rhenish negotiations concerned not constitutional projects, but economic arrangements: the industrialists' agreements with the MICUM on the one hand and the currency question on the other. For the French a *de facto* erosion of Berlin's control appeared most promising where Berlin authorities had least to offer, in the area of economic support. As early as October 15, General de Metz bluntly told Palatinate industrialists that if they wished to resume production the question was "Do you accept my money or not?"[116] The Germans

---

Poincaré's reply to Crowe. For Belgian hesitations, see Ambassador Maurice Herbette's report to Poincaré, *ibid.*/35.

[115] Tirard rejection of Moldenhauer plea, November 26, in GFM: 9406H/3654/ 269548–269552; Erdmann, *Adenauer*, pp. 136–155; and note from a M. "X" [Adenauer] in Min. Aff. Etr., Europe, 1918–1929, Rive Gauche du Rhin/37; Stresemann resistance in GFM: Politische Abteilung IIa, Besetztes Rheinland, 9406H/3654/269548–269552.

[116] GFM: Politische Abteilung IIa, 9406H/3654/269501–269504. Tirard actually had played with the idea of Rhenish currency as early as January, and had conferred with French and Belgian bankers. Poincaré had objected that the government could not agree to a currency supported by the franc and guaranteed by Paris; he had suggested instead a new mark to be backed by German state property in the Rhineland. See Tirard to Poincaré, January 26, 1923, Nr. 45, and Poincaré to Tirard, January 28, also the revived suggestion by Tirard on April 13, Min. Aff. Etr., Europe, 1918–1929, Rive Gauche du Rhin/107.

hesitated to introduce the Rentenmark in the Rhineland and claimed that there was a danger of confiscation by the French. While the paper mark held at its 4.2 trillion-per-dollar ratio in Berlin after the new currency appeared on November 20, three days later in Cologne it hit its record low: 12 trillion. Urban emergency moneys—*Notgeld*—authorized by the cabinet, were refused by the Reichsbank branches in the occupied zone—to the anger both of Stresemann and Luther. In short, there was no money in the occupied area, and without money a collapse of all economic activity threatened.[117]

Naturally the French were preparing to fill the vacuum in collaboration with Rhenish bankers. On October 30 Tirard outlined his currency project to Poincaré, and by early November all sorts of rumors about banks for the region were afloat.[118] Most notably, Georg Solmssen, manager of the Diskonto-Gesellschaft, reported that Adenauer, the Cologne banker Louis Hagen, and industrialists Vögler and Silverberg would provide a capital of 100 to 150 million gold marks for a new Rhineland bank if the German government approved. It would be preferable, however, Solmssen argued, to force the French to show their true objectives and issue their own currency in the region.[119] Tirard, though, encouraged Rhenish bank plans rather than the adoption of the franc. Perhaps he had been cautioned by the French Finance Minister, de Lasteyrie, who feared the overextension of his own vulnerable currency. In any case, Tirard informed Poincaré, he was insisting on French control of the share capital.[120]

The key question would be control of the Rhenish bank. On November 3, Cologne banking circles led by Hagen's firm, I. H. Stein, report-

[117] GFM: Politische Abteilung IIa, 9408H/3654/269668–269674; Erdmann, *Adenauer*, pp. 119–120; Tirard, *La France sur le Rhin*, p. 391; Weill-Raynal, *Les réparations allemandes et la France*, II, p. 476.

[118] For résumé of Tirard discussion with Willy Dreyfus October 28, and his report of October 30, see Min. Fin. F^{30}/1276.

[119] Solmssen report in GFM: Politische Abteilung IIa, 9409H/3654/269840–269843 ff., 269826.

[120] See Tirard report on Lasteyrie, October 20, and bank plans of November 3, 1923, Nr. 574, Min. Aff. Etr., Europe, 1918–1929, Rive Gauche du Rhin/107. While Tirard negotiated with Hagen, Dorten and the separatists tried to interest an alternative group of French bankers in an analogous scheme. They apparently received some encouragement from the nationalist darling, General Mangin; they also claimed the support of François-Marsal of the Banque de l'Union Parisienne. François-Marsal, who was to serve as Finance Minister under Poincaré in the spring of 1924 and was also personally close to Millerand, disavowed the separatists. Meanwhile the Banque de Paris et des Pays Bas became the major French institution behind the abortive Rhineland scheme. See Tirard reports of October 30, November 4 and 5, and the reports by Tirard's intermediary Schweisguth, on October 30 and November 6, 1923, in *ibid.*, Rive Gauche du Rhin/107, pp. 215–225. Cf. Tirard reports Nrs. 609 (November 20), 616 (November 23), and 621 (November 26), *ibid.*, pp. 7, 28–29, 36, for further denigration of Adam Dorten, the separatist leader, in favor of working with Hagen.

edly decided that they would go ahead with the bank. France and Germany would each hold 40 percent of the stock, Belgium and Holland 10 percent each, according to one version; the ratio would be 60–40, German to French capital, according to another.[121] On November 6, the Rhenish provincial Landtag, of which Adenauer was an important member, convened and endorsed a project that allowed French capital up to 30 percent. Stresemann was naturally reluctant to endorse any such plan; the Hagen initiative was the most dangerous aspect of the Rhenish autonomy schemes precisely because it was the most feasible. As Schubert warned, it meant the end of any unified German economic policy and was a Trojan horse for outright separation of the Rhineland.[122]

Stresemann and Schubert sought help from the British, who, they calculated, wished to avoid French economic hegemony on the Rhine. Still, British policy was not entirely supportive. D'Abernon was unmoved by the argument that the Rentenmark would be undermined by a Rhenish currency, because London had little faith anyway in the success of the Rentenmark. Lord Kilmarnock, on the Interallied High Commission, felt that the Rhineland Bank would come into being and that British participation would allow London to exert leverage and stymie French preeminence. Ultimately, the Foreign Office officially stood aside and let the banking community determine participation. English commercial circles did fear that German firms would tend to import goods priced in the currencies that formed the reserve of the projected Bank. Exchange from a Rhine-mark into francs would be automatic, and the francs would be spent in Paris or Lille.[123] The French attempted to allay British preoccupations by claiming that a new Rhineland currency would restore enough economic activity to benefit England as well as France. Apparently hoping for agreement, Poincaré told his Ambassador in London that the British must get on board quickly. The Quai dangled shares in Ruhr mines and the Rhenish

[121] Report from the Hague in GFM: Politische Abteilung IIa, Besetztes Rheinland, 9409H/3654/269826; Solmssen to Schubert, November 7, *ibid.*, 269828–269829; also reports in *L'Echo de Paris*, November 7/8, 1923. British reports included in FO 371/8748–8749.

[122] Stresemann to Hagen, November 3, 1923, and Schubert to Sthamer, November 10, GFM: Politische Abteilung IIa, 9407H/3654/269717–269718; cf. Erdmann, *Adenauer*, pp. 119–120.

[123] See Schubert note of his discussions with D'Abernon, November 8 and 22, GFM: Politische Abteilung IIa, 9408H/3654/269726–269729; 9409H/3654/269844; also Hoesch report, December 7, *ibid.*, 269845. For British attitudes, see the exchange of views over Wigram's Foreign Office memorandum of November 24, in FO 371/8750: C21981/3/3/18; also the Interdepartmental meeting at the Foreign Office on November 27, officially leaving any decision to participate to the banks themselves; also the dissenting view of the British High Commissioner Kilmarnock, December 18: FO 371/8690: C22354 and C21687/129/18.

rail network as bonuses for joining the Rhineland Bank. As *Le Temps* argued, nothing was more urgent than that the English also capitalize the Rhineland Bank.[124] Still, London bankers did not agree; the Foreign Office made no positive intervention; and the Bank of England—directing the Committee of Clearing Banks—encouraged Berlin to resist.[125] The Belgians also had misgivings; High Commissioner Rolin-Jacquemyns had instructions to prevent the French from securing a majority control. If there were a Bank, Belgium wanted a tie-breaking power on the Board; otherwise she feared becoming more of a satellite and worried lest the French plans for the Rhine favor Rotterdam at the expense of Antwerp. Consequently, the French had to rest content with the Belgians' insistence that the total Allied share in any Rhineland Bank be limited to 50 percent and their pledge to coordinate voting on the Board of Directors. With Poincaré's Minister of Finance unwilling to sanction the franc as a backing for the Rhineland currency, Paris found it impossible to wrest greater leverage. In addition, Poincaré had to purchase the acquiescence and participation of the Luxemburg steel magnate, Emil Mayrisch.[126] Already Paris was learning that domination of the Ruhr was hard to exploit if London and Brussels remained unenthusiastic and the weakness of the franc limited unilateral financing of Rhenish autonomy.

By December, the German government had decided that the Bank could be sanctioned only if it were clearly dependent upon Berlin. In light of the apparent impediments to introducing the Rentenmark in the Rhineland, it was difficult to argue against the project outright. Inside the cabinet, Brauns, the Center Party Labor Minister, and Jarres defended the Hagen plan. The Prussian state representative and Hjalmar Schacht—Currency Commissioner and new President of the Reichsbank after Havenstein's death in November—opposed the scheme. Only

[124] Poincaré to the French Ambassador in London, December 8, 1923, Min. Aff. Etr., Europe, 1918–1929, Rive Gauche du Rhin/108, p. 71. Also the Quai's desire to win British participation and offering shares in the *Régie* and "even in the exploitation of certain Ruhr mines," in Cables 2412–2414, November 30, *ibid.*, pp. 42–44. Cf. *Le Temps*, December 6–7, 1923; Pertinax in *L'Echo de Paris*, December 9; and Hoesch report of December 7, in GFM: Politische Abteilung IIa, 9409H/3654/269846–269847.

[125] See the letter of Montagu Norman, Governor of the Bank of England, to the Treasury, December 14, 1923 (then forwarded to the Foreign Office), with the notice that the Committee of London Clearing Banks could not participate in the Rhineland venture: FO 371/8690: C21687/129/18. Norman, in fact, had already been encouraging the Germans to resist the proposal: see Sthamer to the Foreign Ministry, December 8, 1923: GFM: Politische Abteilung IIa, 9409H/3654/269823.

[126] Note on Belgian policy, December 4, 1923, in Min. Aff. Etr., Europe, 1918–1929, Rive Gauche du Rhin/108, pp. 53–57; also Tirard report, December 1, Nr. 635, *ibid.*, pp. 46–47. For Poincaré's approval of Mayrisch's participation, see Poincaré to Tirard, December 12, *ibid.*, p. 83.

if the new Rhenish bank of issue could later merge smoothly into the future German Central Bank would it be acceptable to Schacht.[127] In his mid-December proposal for a *modus vivendi* on the Ruhr, Stresemann indicated that a Rhineland Bank of Issue could be chartered only if the French recognized that it represented a sovereign concession on the part of Berlin. This angered Poincaré, who retorted that the bank was the Rhinelanders' own affair.[128] Given the clash of views and the pressure from the Rhenish economic leaders, Stresemann and Schacht resorted to the strategy of raising technical objections to the scheme. In a December 21 letter to Hagen, Chancellor Marx listed the conditions set by the cabinet and the Reichsbank: German shareholders in the new bank would have to reach unanimity on major policy decisions; the Reichsbank must preserve its own access to the occupied areas; the monetary units of the new bank must be based on German currency denominations and no coins were to be minted; interest rates had to be coordinated with the Reichsbank—a necessary precaution for any coherent German monetary policy. Finally, the new gold-note bank had to be willing to merge into any future German central bank, and the central bank must retain an option to buy a controlling share of the Rhenish institute at any time.[129]

By the end of 1923 the Rhineland bank had become the chief stake in a many-sided contest. Stresemann and the Foreign Ministry, supported by the Bank of England, opposed the new creation, as did the directors of the Reichsbank, who saw "illegal interference"[130] with their own right to issue currency. On the other hand, some industrialists, preeminently Stinnes, supported the proposal and were willing to put up a sizable quota of the German capital behind the venture. It promised them a badly needed source of credit at a time when the MICUM agreements, the conversion to the Rentenmark, and new gold-based taxes all severely strained their liquidity. The bank also fitted in with Stinnes' new plans for wide-ranging agreements with French industry.[131]

Hagen was angered at Berlin's impediments, but, as he warned, the French could still apply counterpressure. If Berlin did not approve the new bank, French authorities under the Interallied High Commission would confiscate any Rentenmarks introduced into the occupied terri-

[127] See Maltzan summary of the December 11 meeting to Schubert and Sthamer, GFM: Politische Abteilung IIa, 9409H/3654/269854–269855.
[128] Erdmann, *Adenauer*, pp. 169–170; Stehkämper, ed., *Nachlass Marx*, II, p. 17.
[129] Draft letters of December 21–22, GFM: Politische Abteilung IIa, 9409H/3654/269861–269867; Letter of Reichsbank Kuratorium December 19, *ibid.*, 269869–269876; cf. Stehkämper, ed., *Nachlass Marx*, II, pp. 106–111.
[130] *Ibid.*, GFM: 9409H/3654/269880–269883.
[131] See Friedberg memo of December 29, 1923: GFM: 9409H/3654/269877–269879.

tory.[132] Responding to Marx's conditions, Hagen argued that Tirard insisted upon a name that signified a bank of issue (i.e., Notenbank). He would not accept a Rhenish currency denominated in marks, refused coordination of interest rates with the Reichsbank, and demanded that the option rights of the German Central Bank be postponed for five years and even thereafter hedged with conditions. On January 7, Hagen reported that he could give up only the claim to coinage. Unless Berlin allowed him to meet the conditions, he warned, the French would establish the bank as part of the overall political arrangement they were to conclude with the Committee of Fifteen. At the turn of the year this still represented a serious threat, but the cabinet did not give in. Marx answered Hagen that the bank could be guaranteed a five-year minimum charter with yearly renewals after 1929, and he was ready to permit the name "Mark-Bank" if not Bank of Issue, but the other disputed points remained unresolved.[133]

Despite Poincaré's personal interest, the Rhenish gold-note bank remained abortive. Montagu Norman, refusing another invitation from the head of the Banque de Paris et des Pays Bas to join in capitalizing the project, boasted that he had killed it.[134] Norman further arranged 5 million pounds backing for Schacht's counterproject, the Gold Discount Bank; and throughout January he lobbied for it in the course of visits to Brussels and Paris. The Gold Discount Bank provided up to 20 million pounds of German and English funds in London to enable German industry to finance its foreign transactions. It gave Schacht an alternative to the Rhineland Bank that offered stable assets outside Reparation Commission jurisdiction. For Norman it helped reestablish the pound

[132] See Hagen to Chancellor Marx December 31, 1923, summarizing his meeting with Tirard, banking representatives from France, and the Belgian High Commissioner, Rolin-Jacquemyns, on December 27. Cf., too, Tirard's letter to Hagen, December 29, which claimed that Berlin's conditions were unacceptable for non-German banks and threatened that the validity of the Rentenmark must remain in question in the occupied areas. GFM: 9409H/3654/269888–269893. In fact, the French had decided within a week that they would allow the Rentenmark to circulate on a *de facto* basis: although Degoutte resisted initially, Tirard instructed him to give in, and by January the General told the Germans that he would "close his eyes" to its use. See Degoutte to Tirard, November 17, Tirard to Degoutte, November 20, and to Poincaré, November 21, in Min. Aff. Etr., Europe, 1918–1929, Rive Gauche du Rhin/108, pp. 12, 16–22.

[133] GFM: 9409H/3654/269900–269902, and Marx answer to Hagen, January 14, 269906; Stehkämper, ed., *Nachlass Marx*, II, pp. 111, 114–115; also memo of Schacht-Loucheur talk, January 9, 1924, Louis Loucheur papers/12, f. 22.

[134] See Atthalin and Finaly of the Banque de Paris et des Pays Bas to Norman, asking participation December 22, 1923; Norman's negative response to Finaly, January 2, 1924; Sthamer's summary of December 30; all in GFM: Handakten Schubert, L1420/5683/491601–491604; Sthamer report of January 2, in 9409H/3654/269897. The original of the Norman letter is in Min. Aff. Etr., Europe, 1918–1929, Rive Gauche du Rhin/108, p. 107. See also Sir Henry Clay, *Lord Norman* (London, 1957), pp. 138–150.

as a reserve currency in Central Europe against both franc and dollar, because Germany also recognized preeminent British interests in Danzig, Austrian, Czechoslovak, and Greek banks.[135]

By the end of January the French, too, had to renounce the project. The first run on the franc in mid-month suggested that their own finances were overextended and vulnerable to depreciation. On January 24, Seydoux and Parmentier, from the Quai d'Orsay and Rue de Rivoli, respectively, and Allix and Atthalin, the negotiators for the Rhineland bank project in Germany, met together to note that Tirard and Hagen felt they could no longer push ahead: "everyone is hostile including the Belgians." The Germans, moreover, were pressing for formal clearance of the Rentenmark's circulation in the occupied territory with its theoretical mortgaging of assets. (The *de facto* admission of the currency conceded earlier by the occupying forces did not satisfy Berlin.) France had no valid reason to resist formal clearance; in fact, the French could hope that in return for their clearance, Berlin might recognize the *Régie*. In any case the Rhineland Bank was dead.[136]

For Stinnes, too, January was a month of reversals. Less Franco-German reconciliation than the need for liquid assets—the francs that could be pumped in via a new Rhineland note bank or by stock trades with French interests—impelled him to become a supporter of Adenauer and an opponent of Stresemann. By mid-February Stinnes' associate Vögler, who had formerly advocated resistance to the bitter end, pleaded with the Chancellor for help with the costs of MICUM, and "the exhaustion of credit, the great losses." Political agreement with the French, if need be by the loosening of Rhenish ties to Berlin as advocated by Adenauer, had to be found by March 15, or heavy industry could not extend the MICUM accords.[137]

The change from a half-year earlier was remarkable. Industrial leaders who had then recklessly accepted the inflation and exploited the opportunities of national resistance to discipline labor now urged major

[135] See Schacht's testimony on the Gold Discount Bank to the newly convened Dawes Committee in January, included in GFM: Schubert Handakten, L1420/5683/491474 ff.; also 491457–491458 for his description of the bank as "the fulcrum for everything further." (Testimony also in Büro des Reichsministers, 5. 3243/1651/722527.) Cf. Hjalmar Schacht, *The Stabilization of the Mark* (London, 1927), pp. 128–150; Clay, *Lord Norman*, pp. 211–212; Werner Link, *Die amerikanische Stabilisierungspolitik in Deutschland 1921–1932* (Düsseldorf, 1970), pp. 231 ff. Further material on the Gold Discount Bank in AN, Paris: Commission Internationale des Réparations, AJ⁶/571, f. 1. See also below, Conclusion, note 12.

[136] Note of January 24, 1924, Sous-Direction des Relations Commerciales [Seydoux] and "Note sur le Rentenmark" of February 12, 1924, discussing admission of Rentenmark in Min. Aff. Etr., Europe, 1918–1929, Rive Gauche du Rhin/109, pp. 138 ff.

[137] Ritter [?] memo to Schubert on January 17 visit from Vögler; and Vögler to Marx, February 15, 1924: GFM: Büro des Staatssekretärs, MICUM Verträge, 4521H/2279/135069–135071, 135052.

concessions of German national authority because of their economic difficulties. No longer did they need labor's assistance; in fact, the contraction of economic activity and massive lay-offs provided the chance to inflict serious blows on the unions. Was business really seriously strapped? Mineowners claimed that MICUM forced them to sell their coal at 20 marks per ton when it cost 28 marks to produce; the French authorities asserted that actual costs were only 18 marks.[138] No doubt those entrepreneurs—Stinnes in the lead—who had used inflation to construct vast conglomerates now faced a harsh reckoning in the liquidity crisis of early 1924. Collectively, however, their distress was to be brief, and once again it was largely shifted onto the shoulders of their trade-union partners.

Negotiations for a Franco-German industrial agreement or a political settlement for the Rhineland were not to materialize in early 1924. Stresemann, who had shared Adenauer's pessimism in November, moved beyond it by January and worked to undercut the Rhenish initiatives. On January 9 in Berlin, government and Rhenish representatives decided that only the economic parleys would be pursued further, and Stresemann refused to endorse even this compromise agreement. On the same day he discredited Stinnes' claim to authority in speaking to the French financier Ernest Weyl. A week later he wrote Marx a harsh condemnation of Adenauer and Stinnes, claiming that the latter had little standing with such important business leaders as Krupp or the chemical industry. In view of the Foreign Minister's hostility, Hagen, Adenauer, and Stinnes had to curtail their negotiations. While Tirard wanted to deal only with a commission delegated by the Rhenish populations, Adenauer now had authority only to refer him to official Berlin spokesmen. In the industrial discussions the stalemate was reversed. While Paris demanded that Stinnes' soundings be pursued as official German policy through the embassy, Berlin refused to take up the issue at the governmental level. On economic matters Paris needed to commit the German authorities, on political ones to shunt them aside. Neither goal was accomplished in early 1924.[139]

Why, when most German politicians saw the Rhineland as slipping into French hands, had Paris won so little? Some of the answer lay with Poincaré's acute sense of political constraint. His entry into the Ruhr

---

[138] On costs, see memo of talks with Bergrat Herbig, February 28, 1924, *ibid.*, 134990–134994; also Sonderreferat Wirtschaft 9426H/3657/270822–270826. For industry's situation, see also the MICUM survey: Mission Interalliée de Contrôle des Usines et des Mines, *Enquêtes générales faites dans la Ruhr en 1923 et 1924*, 10 vols. (Brussels, 1924), II, *La question des combustibles en Allemagne*, pp. 53–60.

[139] Erdmann, *Adenauer*, pp. 173–175 ff. Cf. Stresemann's assessment of the changing balance of forces in his and Schacht's talk with Loucheur on January 9, 1924, in the Loucheur papers/12, f. 22.

was cautious to begin with—undertaken only after prodding by the President of the Republic, attacks from the right, and continuing German demands for ever longer moratoriums. Going into the Ruhr, however, did not remove the constraints upon the President of the Council. In the spring of 1923 the government had to renounce its plan for a 20 percent tax increase in response to a hostile Chamber, which was unable to comprehend why, if the Ruhr action was designed to win reparations, France's tax load must also be raised. Food prices were also rising ominously in the spring of 1923, and the agricultural sector, which paid few taxes, seemed to be enjoying disproportionally high commodity prices.[140] Despite the large parliamentary majorities approving Poincaré's action or at least answering his calls for unity, the government's situation was not really stable. The Socialists remained in opposition, while the Radical Socialists offered only a conditional adherence and asked for discussions with England. The preservation of ties with London thus became not merely a foreign-policy priority for Poincaré, but also a requirement for keeping Herriot's party from going into outright opposition. Finally, the Clémenciste nationalists kept up their querulous crossfire after January 11, demoralizing the MICUM offices in Essen as well as angering Poincaré. More force in the Ruhr, demanded Tardieu in his *Echo National*, provoking an acrimonious response in the Chamber debate of May 29 from Poincaré, who accused Tardieu of stabbing the government in the back.[141]

By May the government seemed at a turning—but it did not turn. The spring of 1923 brought the first stirrings of fascist admirers who hoped to emulate Mussolini's methods. After one of their own leaders was assassinated by an anarchist, the Camelots du Roi turned increasingly to agitation and thuggery, which culminated in an attack on the Christian Democrat Marc Sangnier and two other ex-deputies. This provoked charges from the left that Poincaré's Minister of Justice, Manoury, was not forceful enough, and also vexed the Republican *moderés*, who did not wish to be discredited by extremist hotheads.[142] In fact, despite the involvement of intellectuals around the Action Française, most of the country dismissed the far right. Paris newspapers played up their disquieting demonstrations, but reports from

[140] See the hostile reaction to the tax hike proposal in *L'Echo de Paris*, January 11–13, 16, 18, and 24, 1923; for complaints about agriculture, *JI*, June 17–18, 1923.

[141] Parliamentary situation in Edouard Bonnefous, *Histoire politique de la Troisième République, L'après-guerre 1919–1924* (Paris, 1961), pp. 325–355; also JOC, 1923, pp. 2195–2198 (May 29).

[142] Eugen Weber, *Action Française* (Stanford, 1962), pp. 137 ff.; evaluations of the Action Française in the provinces from AN, Paris: F IC III/1125–1134, "Rapports sur l'esprit public et les élections," especially the Prefect of the Manche in June 1923, Morbihan, March 1923, and the Vendée, June 1923.

the provinces indicated a marked lack of response. As usual, parliamentary circles enjoyed fanning the rumors of impending ministerial crises; and party questions—the obvious issue of the coalitions that would contest the 1924 elections—provided welcome relief from the dreary consideration of reparations and taxes. Observers of parliament awaited clarification of the great equivocation behind the 1919 majority: where would the Radicals go? Would Poincaré fall between Tardieu and Herriot, to be succeeded by the old manipulator Briand or the economic wizard Loucheur?

In the murky political atmosphere, despite the surface unity imposed by the Ruhr, there was restiveness with Poincaré and much political intrigue. Although still officially committed to Poincaré, nationalist circles as well as leftist ones contemplated Loucheur as a replacement. Loucheur traveled to London in April to discuss with Bonar Law his schemes for linking reparations to war-debt write-offs and separating the Rhineland from Prussia. The British were apparently uncertain about the purposes of the trip, as well as skeptical about Loucheur's personal abilities. But Loucheur wrote enthusiastically to the premier that Bonar Law and Baldwin were ready to intervene on behalf of France. Poincaré distrusted the initiative even while accepting Loucheur's reports, and he allowed the press to attack Loucheur while he absented himself from Paris. The premier understood that Loucheur's reports overestimated British commitment and seemed designed to enhance his own role.[143] For a month Loucheur's diary recorded discussions of possible government reshufflings—rearrangements that growing Belgian unhappiness at being dragged along into an open-ended occupation as well as English uneasiness also made more plausible. Still, the discontents with Poincaré were not effectively mobilized, because each potential leader of a successor cabinet—Barthou, Maginot, Loucheur—also carried on diplomatic functions on behalf of the President of the Council. Each distrustful of Poincaré—"That man will always stab you in the back," said Jouvenel at a dinner—they distrusted each other more.[144] Nonetheless, Poincaré was not totally averse to Loucheur's ideas, and during the course of 1923 was to move toward his more flexible notions of a settlement.

The tantalizing political questions of the day were partially clarified by the major Chamber debate of June 15. In his speech to the Chamber, Poincaré began to define his majority—"republican and nation-

[143] Loucheur's report to Poincaré April 10, 1923, on London discussions in Bibliothèque Nationale, Poincaré papers; also Loucheur papers/7, f. 7; for press criticism, see Pertinax in *L'Echo de Paris*, April 8 and 14, 1923. Also Louis Loucheur, *Carnets Secrets 1914–1932* (Brussels, 1962), pp. 119–126.
[144] Loucheur diary entries in Loucheur papers/12, f. 15.

al": rejecting a handful on the right and emphasizing the secularism that kept classical reactionaries at arm's length, but also rejecting collectivism and Blum's unfortunate phrase, "creative hatred"—rejecting finally those who would ally with the Socialists. This sort of formula was really no less ambivalent than Briand's old rhetoric, but the last condition meant that the Radicals had to show their cards. Herriot responded that the 1919 dream of union had broken down and that his party could no longer accept the sterile motto of "neither revolution nor reaction": of 82 Radicals, 58 voted against the government, while 8 abstained, and 12 broke with the Rue Valois headquarters to stick with Poincaré. The cabinet still carried the Chamber 356 to 162 with 40 abstentions, which meant that it had found a majority without the Radical Socialists.[145] Poincaré, however, was not yet willing to burn his bridges to the moderate left. The prefects seemed to receive no clear anti-Radical directives from the Ministry of the Interior, and the right continued to chafe at Poincaré's temporizing and wondered how he would reward his faithful majority.

Politicking continued to intensify in the summer and early fall. The Radicals organized in the country and sought a platform for an electoral cartel with the SFIO on the basis of support for the League of Nations, "diffusion of property," secularism, and "agreement between all who are not associates of Bloc National policies and hostile to violent and dictatorial methods whatever their origin." On the other side, Millerand stepped down from the nonpartisan figurehead role of the Presidency of the Republic. Apparently he hoped to dissolve the Chamber upon the end of German passive resistance in September, and to elect a parliament in the glow of the national triumph. This was impossible, but in a sensational departure from political neutrality at Evreux on October 14, Millerand again demanded a more powerful executive, defended religious reconciliation, and called for reelection of the Bloc National. In short, Millerand gave the right that gesture of support for which they had waited since spring from a premier who, they felt, depended upon their votes but refused to help their electoral chances.[146]

Political neutrality aside, Poincaré also antagonized important industrial interests who wanted his help in pressuring the German coal and steel interests into economic collaboration. The Ruhr occupation began by hurting French industry; the flow of coal to France was reduced and, according to Humbert de Wendel, three-quarters of the

[145] JOC, 1923, pp. 2563–2568, 2598; RPP, July 10, 1923, pp. 105 ff.; and Hoesch to the Foreign Office, June 15, 1923, in GFM: Büro des Reichsministers 7, 2406/1329/501375–501376.

[146] Bonnefous, Histoire politique, p. 338, for the Radical Socialist congress; Alexandre Millerand, "Mes souvenirs (1859–1941)," MS, p. 114; L'Echo de Paris, October 15, 16, p. 3.

blast furnaces of the Meurthe-et-Moselle were stilled by May. Why not use French force to extract tangible concessions for a hard-pressed French steel industry starved of coke supplies and threatened by loss of markets? Throughout April, Lucien Romier of the *Journée Indus-trielle* wrote that France must abandon the old texts to reach a new Franco-German agreement that would insure French coal needs for a generation.[147] Actually, the French iron and steel firms had already raced for Essen along with MICUM. Rather than let the French coal producers' association allocate the precious coke, the smelters' common coal-purchasing agency, SCOF, sent their own energetic representatives to hurry pithead coal from the Ruhr to France. Wary individual firms also sent in their own engineers to supervise transport and deliveries. Coke supplies continued to be monitored constantly as the spring went on.[148]

The business forces who advocated forcing German industry into international agreement were strengthened when Jean Schneider retired from the Directorate of the Comité des Forges at its April 19 meeting, leaving Wendel in unchallenged control. Schneider claimed disagreement over "general policy." His immediate grievance, however, was that the Comité des Forges was giving an unfair advantage to the Wendel firms in the distribution of scarce coke—a dispute that pointed up the divergent interests between steel interests on the frontier and those in the interior.[149] Momentum for Franco-German industrial agreements gathered when Paul Reynaud, one of their most enthusiastic advocates in the Chamber, was invited by Stinnes to Wiesbaden in June. The young deputy, however, gave up plans for the visit, claiming that Poincaré had exerted pressure against it.[150] His experience, the discontent of the steel interests, the criticisms of nationalist circles, even the questions from the left about policy objectives, all contributed to the feeling that Poincaré did not know how to exploit France's advantage, especially after the Germans gave up passive resistance. While the public at large welcomed the German collapse in September

[147] Wendel cited in Bonnefous, *Histoire politique*, p. 353; Romier in *JI*, April 7 and 8/9, 1923.

[148] For the SCOF (Societé des Cokes de Hauts-Fourneaux), see the reports on the Ruhr situation sent to Cavallier in PAM/18768, f. "Coke allemand jusqu'à 1925," including the discussion at the SCOF General Assembly of July 25, 1924.

[149] For the Schneider resignation, see Camille Cavallier's *compte-rendu* of the Comité des Forges' Comité de Direction, April 19, 1923. For complaints on coal distribution, see also Cavallier to Pinot, April 9, and Pinot's rebuttal, April 12, 1923: PAM/7246, f. Comité des Forges, Comptes-rendus et Correspondances 1917–1923. Cf. *JI*, May 1, 1923.

[150] Paul Reynaud, *La France a sauvé l'Europe*, 2 vols. (Paris, 1947), I, p. 42. Cf. Reynaud's presentations to the Chamber; JOC, 1922, III, pp. 2756–2765 (October 20, 1922), and pp. 4555–4568 (December 28, 1923). Also Reynaud, *Venu de ma montagne, Mémoires* (Paris, 1960), pp. 162 ff.

and the popularity of the government rose again in October, industry and its friends wondered what rewards Poincaré proposed to secure. Millerand, it seemed, was for wresting new economic advantages; he had long been friendly with Pinot of the Comité des Forges, and he disliked Poincaré's subtle calculations, which he saw only as indecisiveness. Certainly the proconsuls on the Rhine, Tirard and Degoutte, were pressing for an active policy. Only the premier seemed to cling to an outworn insistence on returning the reparations question to the constricting framework of the Treaty and the related reparations agreements.[151]

The Comité des Forges had its own extensive plans. On October 29 its directors held a special meeting to discuss what might now be demanded from Germany. Theodore Laurent and Léon-Lévy, Wendel reported, wanted extensive German stock cessions: 25 percent, as mentioned in 1920, was no longer "interesting"; now why not the majority of shares, "why not the totality?" Wendel proposed erecting a permanent customs barrier between the Ruhr and the rest of Germany and thereby prohibiting the export of coal eastward. The large excess Ruhr production would then have to be available for French purchase at sacrificial prices. Both groups agreed that the French government must take over the German state-owned mines and transfer them, not, of course, to the French coal producers (the Comité des Houillères), but to an agency of coal consumers, that is, the steel producers. The Versailles Treaty privileges for Lorraine and Saar exports would also have to be extended for twenty years.[152] The upshot of the discussion was a memo drafted by Pinot on November 13, approved by the directors two days later, and thereupon submitted to the President of the Council. Pinot repeated the traditional arguments about the imbalance of coal production since the war and the need to find exports, and set out the proposals that had been discussed. Solution A embodied Wendel's plan for a customs bridgehead of 30 kilometers around Duisburg, which would leave 6.5 million tons of coke available for France after consumption within the Ruhr. Solution B involved the take-over of German coal mines and their leasing to French steel firms. Solution A, according to the memo, was "liberal" because it stopped short of expropriation, but it would involve long-term military surveillance of the

[151] For public opinion in September and October 1923, see the prefects' monthly reports in AN, Paris: F IC III/1125–1134, "Rapports sur l'esprit public et les élections." Millerand's attitude in his "Souvenirs (1859–1941)," pp. 114–115 and annex 10. For his contacts with Pinot, see Cavallier to Pinot, February 7, 1922, in PAM/19010, f. Comité des Forges. For other criticism of Poincaré's "legalism" at this juncture, see Jacques Chastenet, *Raymond Poincaré* (Paris, 1948), pp. 248–254; Weill-Raynal, *Les réparations allemandes*, II, p. 492.

[152] PAM/7246: Comité des Forges; Commission de Direction, Compte-rendu par Camille Cavallier, November 1, 1923.

customs line and thus might antagonize Britain. Nor could it prevent Germany from so intensifying future Ruhr steel production that she might absorb most of the coal within the restricted customs zone. Solution B had the disadvantage that Germany could still hit the coal mines France acquired with special taxes designed to raise coal costs. Hence the take-over price that France would credit to Germany's reparations account, as well as the leasing charges to French steel producers, had to be low enough to keep French steel competitive abroad.[153]

Did the *maîtres des forges* expect the government to buy either scheme? In 1916 the Comité des Forges had asked for the annexation of the Saar and a 5 franc per ton export tax on raw iron and semiproducts that might be fabricated in Germany to the detriment of French steel firms. In 1920 Pinot had asked Millerand to bring home extensive stock cessions from Spa.[154] But neither at Versailles nor at Spa had the government seriously fought for these recommendations. French steel was in a far weaker position as a pressure group than German steel. Much of this was due to internal disagreements: repeatedly the French steel industrialists quarreled among themselves over coal allocation, tariffs, and markets. The Comité des Forges also remained at odds with the French coal producers. While in Germany coal and steel were corporately entwined, in France they usually confronted each other as countervailing forces. Indeed, the Comité des Forges plan of 1923 was as much a scheme designed to subdue the Comité de Houillères de France as the Germans.[155]

The differing governance of the two republics also contributed to the divergent roles of industry. The French parliamentary system still represented a congeries of local and smaller interests; the Reichstag was an arena for well-organized parties representing major economic federations. The Comité des Forges advocated self-serving policies, such as high tariffs, stock take-overs, and permanent customs frontiers in the Ruhr, that took little account of the other forces with which its government had to deal. The French Ministry of Commerce, however, had to

[153] See Cavallier's notes of the Commission de Direction's discussion of Ruhr plans on October 29, 1923, in PAM/7246, f. "Comité des Forges. Comptes-rendus de réunions. Correspondance," sf. "1923." The memorandum addressed to the government with a covering letter from Pinot to Cavallier, November 13, is included in PAM/7245.

[154] Spa proposals in PAM/19061; also AN, Paris: Millerand Papers; and AN, Paris: F¹²/8860. See above, pp. 198–202 for discussion.

[155] See Cavallier's comment to Pinot, April 22, 1923, in PAM/7246, f. "Comité des Forges . . ." sf. "1923." For insights into the conflict of interests between French cokeries and the steel industry, see PAM/7250 and 7251, with its comptes-rendus of meetings with the government coal authorities. See especially Pinot's report on discussions at the Ministry of Public Works, December 31, 1921, as reported at the Commission du régime des Cokes of the Comité des Forges, January 3, 1922, in PAM/7251, f. "Coke 1922."

remain responsive to secondary industry and agriculture, while Germany's Economic Ministry did not answer to a similar constituency. Moreover, France had no powerful labor ministry, and her trade unions played a more marginal role whether in power or in opposition. Although this pleased French business leaders, it also precluded a collaboration of industrial and union leaders that could influence public policy. The attitudes of the Foreign Ministries further contributed to different relationships with industry. The Quai d'Orsay valued its elegant independence from pressure groups: Pinot's proposals were regarded with a certain suspicion and rarely prompted sustained consultation.[156] The Wilhelmstrasse certainly did not want to surrender any prerogatives, bit it did wish to capitalize on German industrial strength in its drive to recapture great-power status. Throughout the negotiations of mid-decade, no matter how opposed Stresemann remained to the industrialists' usurpation of diplomatic functions, there was still valuable coordination between private and public interests through two or three key men: Trendelenburg at the Economics Ministry, Ritter and Schubert at the Foreign Office.

But even if Poincaré was likely to reject the extensive projects of the Comité des Forges, his reluctance to give French steel any significant support in pushing for German concessions remains remarkable. In fact, to the consternation of the British, MICUM did extract some stock shares as collateral for coal-tax arrears.[157] Further pressure might well have won advantageous interindustry agreements based on more extensive stock cessions and coal-ore exchanges. By early December French steel men felt that "the present state of the Ruhr . . . could not be more favorable to stock acquisitions."[158] Alternatively, Paris could have pressed for extension of the tariff and import privileges that the Versailles Treaty compelled Germany to concede France until 1925. Neither course was pursued. Poincaré was willing to contemplate these

[156] See the industrialists' complaints at the time of the London Conference in the summer of 1924, cited below, Chapter Eight, notes 103–104, from PAM/7230. In contrast to the Quai d'Orsay, the British Foreign Office valued the advice of reliable industrialists and kept the economic situation, with its lowering unemployment, in mind as a constant background factor to negotiations. On the other hand, it defended its autonomy in policy making from what it viewed as the more excitable officials at the Treasury.

[157] See the Board of Trade's inquiry to the Foreign Office, February 13, 1924, forwarded to Paris and Berlin: FO 371/9763: C2445/79/18; Addison reports of February 28, C3419 and C3651/79/18; also, Poincaré's assurance on February 27 that the shares would be returned—indeed, 25 percent had been given back—with payment of coal-tax arrears: C3471/79/18. Cf. Schubert's report of Addison's visit, February 28, in GFM: Büro des Staatssekretärs, 4521H/2279/134995–135000.

[158] René Grandpierre to Camille Cavallier, December 5, 1923, PAM/7630, f. "Ruhr."

approaches, but not at the cost of a reparations settlement; Paris remained content with the MICUM agreements, which, advantageous as they were, still did not force German industrialists to cede any degree of corporate control or to provide long-term coke supplies, or to extend the guaranteed import quotas for Lorraine ore. All heavy industry won —as in 1919—was control over the stocks of iron and steel confiscated by the government. An interministerial committee created in July attributed 50 percent of the metal to the Comité des Forges, 25 percent to other steel interests, and 25 percent to Belgium at reduced prices and with reduced tariffs. But this was a relatively trifling concession.[159]

Rather than exploiting his hold of the Ruhr beyond the MICUM accords, Poincaré moved instead toward limited acceptance of the Anglo-American plan for a committee of experts to review Germany's capacity to pay. This represented a remarkable concession in light of his recent triumph. He also vetoed a Ministry of Commerce proposal that would have had France announce through the League of Nations that it was unilaterally prolonging the tariff privileges granted by the Treaty of Versailles. Since early 1923, Serruys, the Undersecretary of Commerce in charge of foreign trade, had repeatedly urged prorogation of the German tariff-free quotas of Lorraine and Saar iron products. There was no response from the Quai d'Orsay, in part at least because of the rivalry between Seydoux and Serruys, which was to surface again at the London conference a year later. Whether or not the League could be exploited for Serruys' maneuver, Poincaré's decision to consult first with Britain was calculated to dash the scheme, since it was obvious that London would oppose any extension of France's commercial advantages. On the other hand, when Millerand also urged extension of the treaty privileges, Poincaré suggested that the Ministry of Commerce was really the reluctant agency. On December 6 he told the cabinet that the government could not press for extension of the trade privileges and that normal commercial relations must be resumed. Special economic agreements between French and German industry, he warned, would have to await the settlement of the reparations question. As Hoesch wired to Berlin at Christmas, if Poincaré had not braked French industry a series of private agreements would probably be under negotiation.[160]

Ultimately Poincaré relied on making the official texts work for

---

[159] Weill-Raynal, *Les réparations allemandes*, II, pp. 466–467.

[160] For the plan to extend the Versailles-Treaty privileges unilaterally and the premier's veto, see the undated "Note pour M. le Ministre," on extension of the five-year commercial privileges conferred by the Treaty of Versailles, in AN, Paris: F¹²/8864, Serruys folder. The Hoesch cable is cited in Stehkämper, ed., *Nachlass Marx*, II, p. 18.

France. France, he told the Chamber in late November, required only execution of the Treaty to restore good relations with Germany; she was not megalomaniacal. It was not clear that helping the French steel industry would aid the French treasury: reparations payments were required for that, and Germany itself illustrated the perils that arose when industry prospered at the expense of the state. The Lorraine lawyer had his own reservations about big business; he spoke not for the large concerns but of the trust that the independent middle classes had given French bonds and French credit. Preoccupation with the security question in the fall of 1923 and early 1924 further contributed to Poincaré's coolness toward separatist schemes or special Franco-German economic agreements that would offend London. From the summer of 1923, relations with Curzon were bad, and even Brussels' aid was precarious.[161] Poincaré was not prepared to court isolation; and he attracted the applause of the left and the votes of the Radicals when he observed to the Chamber on November 23 that collective action was preferable to unilateral measures. By the last months of the year Poincaré had made it clear that he wished to avoid extremes in both international and domestic politics. He claimed success in the Ruhr; the coal that France was receiving by the autumn adequately rebuked "the defeatists of the peace," who were as detestable as those of the war. Speaking for those defeatists, Léon Blum devoted three and a half hours to criticizing the Ruhr occupation as harmful both to French alliances and German democracy, then moved on to attack the Bloc National, "freshly redecorated, replastered and repainted in tricolor" for the upcoming elections.[162] But Poincaré himself had no love for the Bloc National, although Mandel once again sought to taunt him into siding with the faithful rightist nucleus of the 1919 majority. In short, Poincaré wanted to tack between Mandel and Blum, between relinquishing the Ruhr and isolating France. In effect, every unilateral step had constrained the Premier more than it had liberated him. Led into the Ruhr in part because of the pressures of his coalition, he found that the Bloc National conservatives and Clémenciste snipers had become ever more imperious as the President of the Republic acted

---

[161] See Curzon's proposal for a panel of "impartial experts" to review reparations, July 20, 1923, the French and Belgian rejections, July 30, the Foreign Secretary's reply in Parliament, August 2, and his notes to Brussels and Paris, August 11, in FO 408/11 and 12. Cf. Weill-Raynal, *Les réparations allemandes*, II, pp. 444–457. For indications of Belgian uneasiness, see the conversations with Delacroix, Brussels' delegate on the Reparations Commission and the Belgian Ambassador in Paris, Gaiffier d'Hestroy, July 10 and 19, in the Loucheur papers/12, f. 4.

[162] JOC, 1923, p. 3693 (November 16) for the rebuke to the "defeatists," and pp. 3699, 3703 (November 23) on collaboration with the Allies. Blum statement, *ibid.*, p. 3701 (November 23).

ever more independently. The more unilateral his actions, the more Poincaré seemed boxed into defense of a zealous but narrower majority. The political formulas of June 15, the departure from a union above parties and the temporary farewell to the Radicals ran against his conception of this own political mission. Tighter screws on Germany, whether economic or political, would only confirm these political trends, isolate him as a nationalist rather than a national spokesman, make him hostage to the Elysée and to the Rue de Madrid. Staying within the legal framework of the Treaty, accepting American reparations mediation, now that he had some trumps, meant recovering the options of the center.

Or so he calculated. Throughout the next months Poincaré would seek to limit the functions of the new Dawes Committee by confining its review powers to what Germany owed before 1930 and by insisting that it do more than merely reduce the reparations bill.[163] But it was not easy to limit the scope of the Committee's recommendations, and when France boxed herself into her own inflationary crisis she had to give much more away. Poincaré's opponents had a point: without seizing advantages for which the Treaty did not provide, the Premier might end up with nothing. A little coal did not compensate for reparations concessions and diminished freedom of action under the Dawes Plan. The legalistic mentality produced only empty hands. The Ruhr occupation ended with the same desultory objectives as it began.

Poincaré's policy must be judged as ineffective; France gained little she could not have had without the occupation of the Ruhr. That does not mean that Paris was acting perversely in embarking upon the venture; it was essentially thrust upon her by the logic of deterrence, not by beckoning future rewards. But as a strict adherent to texts, Poincaré did not effectively plan for what happened after the deterrent was invoked and gave French public finance and foreign policy an empty achievement.

The behavior of late 1923 ultimately reflected the contradictions in the man. Intensely complex and moody, dreading policies that allowed only one outcome, angering the right and Millerand by his apparent timorousness, Poincaré still pursued a simple vision, that of restoration. Restoration of the bourgeois France of 1913, honorable in its resistance to Germany, "republican" but "sound" in its politics, blissfully possessing a money (hence a set of expectations about the future) uneroded by inflation. The personality itself was often unattractive, for inner

163 Weill-Raynal, *Les réparations allemandes*, II, pp. 502–519 for Poincaré and the experts. For an assessment of the Ruhr policy in general see the exchange between Jacques Bariéty and Jacques Néré in *Bulletin de la Societé d'Histoire Moderne*, série 15 (1973), pp. 21–29.

ambivalence was masked by carping and self-righteous argumentation —a "phobia of responsibility" as Millerand saw it, a lack of loyalty to associates if retention of their policies became embarrassing, a fixation with texts and an absence of poetry and generosity. But complex men can follow simple goals, and Poincaré's vision was that of a nation that worked hard, saved much, defended its honor abroad, and lived in harmony at home.[164]

What for instance the young Reynaud suggested, what the interests pursued, were their own ends, not that mythical union for which Poincaré spoke. Like Stresemann, Poincaré incarnated an older state ideal; he did not wish to let his victory—nor Stresemann, his defeat— go to strengthen a new feudalism. German industry, with its influence over Berlin, its wanton augmentation of inflation, proved to Poincaré the perils of surrendering policy to business. But for both Stresemann and Poincaré the task of preserving an untrespassed realm for public policy was harder than it would have been a decade earlier, in 1913. Then, the activist nationalism that both represented strengthened domestically all the nonproletarian elements composing the bourgeois nation. In 1923 nationalism worked to enhance only the power of business and industry—in short, to fragment the bourgeoisie and reward organized capital. Nationalist confrontations no longer rewarded the middle strata that had been the original constituencies for Stresemann and Poincaré and whose well-being they identified with the general cause of liberalism and the nation. Both leaders sought to prevent the alienation of the fragmented middle classes, the buffeted reserves of an ailing liberalism—but, ironically, found each other painful obstacles in their joint task.

Still, they achieved considerable victories. Stresemann's was the greater. With the Rentenmark and Enabling Act, Berlin's authority was to recover, while Paris' was to decline with the financial crisis of early 1924. Nevertheless, both Poincaré and Stresemann managed to limit the international convergence of the corporate forces they distrusted at home. Stresemann, Luther, and Schacht frustrated the Rhenish note bank by their Fabian tactics; Poincaré won German coal through MICUM, not the Rue de Madrid. The upshot was a balance of power reached between national governments and major business

---

[164] Cf. the portrait in Pierre Miquel, *Poincaré* (Paris, 1961), pp. 450 ff., 470–476. For the "phobia of responsibilities," see Alexandre Millerand, "Mes mémoires politiques," p. 74; cf. Charles Benoist, diary entry of June 1, 1924 in *Souvenirs*, 3 vols. (Paris, 1934), III, p. 457 for Poincaré's irascibility under the strains of the Ruhr occupation and for the description of him as a *nouveau-pauvre*. For the most acid portrait of all, see the depiction of Rebendart in Jean Giraudoux's *Bella* (Paris, 1926). Giraudoux was one of the young literati cultivated by Philippe Berthelot, Under-Secretary at the Quai whom Poincaré removed in 1922.

forces by early 1924. It was best reflected in two parallel series of negotiations, one between German industrial representatives and the Comité des Forges, the other for renewal of the MICUM agreements scheduled to expire in mid-April.

The achievements and the limits of the industrialists' influence emerged in their talks on February 12, March 4–5, and May 13, 1924, when—after preliminary soundings in Berlin by Ernest Weyl and Pinot's delegate Piérard—Stinnes' representatives, Oberheid and Osius, conferred with Pinot, Léon-Lévy, and Seydoux in Paris. In introducing the initial exchange in February, Pinot and Léon-Lévy no longer insisted on the natural complementarity of Ruhr coke and Lorraine ore, but admitted that France needed coke more than Germany needed ore. They emphasized, however, that France still enjoyed the political advantage of its military presence on the Rhine and Ruhr. The French steel men then took Oberheid to talk with Seydoux at the Quai d'Orsay, where the official allegedly pressed for some form of French stock participation in German firms, whether partial holdings in many mines or total cession of a selected few.[165] After the initial exchange of views, Stinnes requested Berlin's recognition of further discussions; but by cabinet resolution on February 26, Stresemann and Jarres insisted upon French acceptance of the Dawes report as a condition for proceeding further. Even the rest of German heavy industry did not really desire the arrangements Stinnes was discussing, given the possibility envisaged by the Dawes committee for foreign credits and a new reparations settlement. By March 1924 Stinnes seemed primarily involved in a desperate effort to steer his own bloated enterprises through the deflation crisis; he refused to agree to the February 26 cabinet resolution, and lamely warned Stresemann that ultimately he was fighting for the German nationality of the occupied territories.[166]

Oberheid returned to Paris on March 5 to seek more definite proposals, but without official authorization to pursue them. Pinot now suggested that, as part of her reparations debt, Germany should cede

[165] The French account of the Oberheid-Léon Lévy conversations is in Min. Fin. F³⁰/1277, with a copy in the Loucheur papers/5, f. 13. The German version—which stresses the French admission of their own need for coke—is in GFM: Büro des Staatssekretärs, MICUM Verträge, 4521H/2279/135026–135032. Cf. Erdmann, *Adenauer*, pp. 175–184.

[166] See the Woltmann report, March 14, 1924, and Bücher's warning at the Essen meeting of industrialists, March 17, both in Paul Reusch papers, GHH: 4001012008/0. For the cabinet's essential disavowal of Stinnes, see the instructions to Hoesch, February 27, in GFM: Büro des Staatssekretärs, 4521H/2279/135021–135022, and Jarres to Schubert, *ibid.*, 135033. Also Stinnes' complaint to Jarres, March 12, 1924, in GFM: Wirtschaft Reparation, Allg. 6c, 9486/3575/278244–278246.

shares in mines that would provide the same amount of coke (4.5 million tons) as Lorraine had gotten from the Ruhr before 1914. German mineowners were also to sell to the Meurthe-et-Moselle forges 2.5 million tons of coke per year on a private basis, in return for French sales of iron ore to the Germans. Long-term contracts would "assure" German factories that they could import metal semiproducts from Lorraine duty-free after the commercial privileges of the Versailles Treaty expired in early 1925. Finally, new international steel cartels—especially one for rail manufacture—would be established as before the war.[167] No matter whether Stinnes was personally willing to enter such arrangements, France could not have them on such one-sided terms. Stinnes' corporate empire was tottering; he himself lay dying. If Stinnes could no longer overawe Berlin, or even his colleagues in Essen, neither could Paris, for both the expected provisions of the Dawes report and the run on the franc limited French independence of action.

The uneasy stalemate was also demonstrated in the concurrent MICUM talks, in which France enjoyed more leverage. By the winter of 1923–1924, the MICUM accords of November 23 provided France's only reparations income and represented the tangible return of the Ruhr policy. To the German government they were not only expensive, but an infraction of German sovereignty and independence; to the Ruhr firms they were a costly advance to the state at a moment when the companies concerned desperately needed credits.

In its search for "real values" during the inflation, industry had immobilized capital in new buildings and other fixed assets. The stock of investment funds available represented 10 percent of 1914's values. To discount commercial paper, the Reichsbank required a "gold clause" guaranteeing repayment in constant-value marks, and it charged interest of 10 percent. After April 7 the Reichsbank switched to simple rationing of funds, while private banks charged 12 percent plus commissions of up to 1 percent per month—an effective interest rate of 20 to 25 percent. Reflecting the credit stoppage was a fall in share prices from an index of 31.5 at the end of March to 20.2 at the end of May. Meanwhile, bankruptcies climbed: 8 in November, 17 in December, 31 in January, 41 in February, 66 in March, 133 in April, and 326 in May. The price of successful stabilization was a half-year liquidity crisis that enfeebled labor *vis-à-vis* industry, but at least partially constrained industry *vis-à-vis* Berlin and Paris.[168]

[167] Pinot report in Min. Fin. F^{30}/1277; also Stinnes to Jarres, March 12, with Osius reports on the talks of March 4–5 in GFM: Wirtschaft Reparation, 9486/3575/278244–278252.

[168] For credit needs in the spring of 1924, see the report of Maurice Frère's Intelligence Service of the Reparations Commission, Annex 2119c, July 3, 1924: FO 371/5793: C11317/371/18. The estimates of liquid capital from Elster,

For all parties—Berlin, Paris, and Essen—the renewal of the accords became a game of diplomatic bluff played against fellow countrymen as well as the enemy. The Foreign Ministry disliked Paris' dealing directly with the Committee of Six in Essen, but the alternative was the economic chaos of 1923, with possible loss of the Rhineland. The Foreign Ministry claimed that it could no longer compensate the coal owners for further advances to MICUM, lest its newly won monetary and budgetary stability be sacrificed—but in fact Berlin would have to come through if a settlement hung upon it. In contrast, the mineowners wanted to exert pressure on both Paris and Berlin so as to minimize MICUM's exactions while still making sure that the Ministry of Finance would continue to cover whatever was demanded. Although industry claimed up to the April 15 deadline that it could make no further coal deliveries, by mid-March the Ruhr leaders had privately accepted the need to acquiesce under duress so as not to endanger chances for the Dawes plan with its accompanying credits.[169] Finally, Poincaré wanted to avoid any official connection between the upcoming reparation settlement and the current sums he was drawing from Ruhr industry. His interest lay in extending the MICUM arrangements as long as possible, thereby rebutting any German claim that the new Dawes recommendation should immediately supersede the Ruhr accords.[170]

The result was that by April 10 the industry's Commission of Six had declared that it could not renew the MICUM agreements; the Franco-Belgian occupation authorities had threatened to resort to force as they had during passive resistance; and Berlin put itself on record as being unable to finance further deliveries. In the light of the Dawes report, released on April 8, Berlin argued that it was wrong for Paris to insist on agreement with private industrialists.[171] But even after Louis Barthou, the French delegate on the Reparations Commissions, indicated preliminary acceptance of the Dawes report on April 11, Poincaré refused to give up the MICUM arrangements. For a few days

Von der Mark zur Reichsmark, p. 389. German entrepreneurs' complaints about the lack of capital were many: see, among others Hans Fürstenberg, *Ein Land ohne Betriebsmittel* (Berlin, 1925).

[169] See the discussion in Essen on March 17, 1924, especially of Bücher's report on his Paris discussions and the assurances of forthcoming American credits. GHH: 4001012008/0. But for industry's official negotiating posture against renewal, see Vögler's statements as reported by Schubert to D'Abernon: GFM: Sonderreferat Wirtschaft, 9426H/3657/270962–270963. Also the instructions to Hoesch on April 10, summarizing the negotiations between MICUM and the 6er Kommission of April 8, *ibid.*, 270981.

[170] See Maltzan to the London Embassy, April 5, 1924, *ibid.*, 270964–270966. Also Hoesch's report of conversation with Peretti on April 13, 271034.

[171] Foreign Ministry to Hoesch, April 10, 1924: *ibid.*, 270981–270987.

more, Berlin sought to avoid renewal of the accords. Stresemann suggested that the foreign loan of 800 million marks, which the Dawes report envisaged as covering Berlin's first-year reparation expenses, should help defray MICUM deliveries in the meantime. This was a proposal the British quickly vetoed: why should London creditors foot the bill for the private rewards Paris was taking from Essen?[172]

Poincaré was not to yield, nor could he have retained conservative votes for the *double décime* tax increases had he weakened. But he no longer had his old freedom of action: France could not revert to a policy of confiscation and coercion in the Ruhr when her own delegate on the Reparations Commission had already welcomed the experts' report and her franc was hostage to J. P. Morgan. Even the MICUM negotiator in Essen, Frantzen, acted as if the ground had been shot from beneath him at the critical talks with Vögler on April 13.[173] The only upshot now could be a series of compromises. The Ruhr industrialists signed once again; this time Berlin covered the costs of the coal advances, but through the subterfuge of having the German railroads buy coal in advance from industry with bills of exchange. On the other side, the French lowered their coal tax and settled for a two-month extension of the accords rather than winning renewal until the start of payments under the Dawes plan.[174]

This to-the-wire drama repeated itself once again as the June 15 deadline approached. Berlin again insisted that MICUM deliveries be paid from the 800-million-mark foreign Dawes loan, or at least from the 200 million marks that the new German railway corporation was also required to provide to help finance the first-year reparation expenses. This still amounted to subtracting current MICUM deliveries from the first year's billion marks of reparations in kind, a maneuver the British still found absolutely unacceptable. Once again the upshot was a com-

---

[172] Schubert to Sthamer, April 12, 1924, GFM: 9426H/3657/271027–271029; Sthamer to Berlin, May 3, 271067 ff. Although the Foreign Office regarded the MICUM contracts as a possible infraction of the Versailles Treaty and an infringement of the powers of the Reparations Commission, they chose not to contest them seriously but to reserve their rights for the future. (See the minutes on prolongation of the agreements and accompanying comments: FO 371/9764: C5851/79/18.) On the other hand, Niemeyer at the Treasury and Montagu Norman both became worried about the German plan to defray the MICUM costs with the proceeds of a still hypothetical Dawes loan, and urged the Foreign Office to arrange a quiet extension of the agreements until acceptance of the Experts' Report by the Reparations Commission. The Foreign Office remained less perturbed, recognizing the bluffs being used on both sides. See *ibid.*: C6055/79/18.

[173] Negotiations of April 11 and 13, 1924, in *ibid.*, 271078–271090, 271091–271099, 271104–271119. Cf. also accounts in Reusch Nachlass, GHH: 400101-2008/0.

[174] GFM: 9426H/3657/271030–271031.

promise: MICUM further reduced its coal levy, while Berlin now offered 50 percent compensation to the coal firms. Although Stresemann
regretted not being able to throw over the MICUM system entirely in
June, he did not want to weaken the position of the new Cartel des
Gauches ministry. Two months later approval of the Dawes plan was
imminent enough for the German government to dispense with a further crisis and to accept the MICUM costs until the new reparations
system came into effect.[175]

By the compromises they incorporated, the MICUM accords exem-
plified the balance struck between France and Germany as well as
between public power and private assets. Poincaré was powerful
enough to make German industry pay, but too vulnerable internationally to attempt to sever the Ruhr economy from Germany. German
industry was weak enough to have to give in to the French, but retained enough leverage to force Berlin to pick up much of the bill. The
mixture of public and private solutions reflected the ambiguous state
of forces. As they merged into a general reparation settlement in the
spring of 1924, the Ruhr arrangements thus contributed to a new mix
of public and private power, a new balance between industry and the
state which marked the period of recovery.

Electoral consultations were awaited to clarify the situation, and it
was the turn of the United States to show a way out of the balance-of-
payments impasse that had brought France to the Ruhr and Germany
to the Rentenmark. But the electoral results were actually to prolong
the unresolved tensions, while the American funds that would eventually alleviate the international exchanges were still half a year from
being mobilized. In mood, Europeans seemed to want to leave behind
the rancor of reparations and to normalize international relations.
Loucheur told Poincaré that the Germans were ready to work and pay
reparations: "German good will exists. It was not born spontaneously;
it was created by our policy."[176] Poincaré no doubt was more skeptical,
yet he too shared the impulse for negotiation, realized the liabilities

---

[175] See discussion of Reichsbahn financing of MICUM agreements in *ibid.*,
271242–271244; MacDonald's rejection reported June 3, *ibid.*, 271247; the similar
plans by Seydoux and Montagu Norman to finance the agreements by increasing
the Dawes loan above $200 million: *ibid.*, reel 3658/271278–271280, and 271322–
271326; negotiations between the 6er Kommission and MICUM on June 12 and
15, *ibid.*, 271359–271370, 271371–271378; Stresemann's calculations to Sthamer,
June 27, and to Hoesch, June 29, 271431–271433, 271476 ff. For the government's
final assumption of the burden, see Ritter to Hoesch, July 24, and Maltzan's note,
August 1, 1924: *ibid.*, 271587–271589, 271595–271596. British view of negotiations
in FO 371/9766.

[176] Protocol of conversation with Schacht and Stresemann, January 9, 1924, Louis
Loucheur papers/12, f. 22.

of the nationalist advocates within his own country, and distanced himself from the Bloc National as from the Comité des Forges. Nevertheless, he was still closely enough identified with nationalist solutions to be eclipsed in the general reaction against hawkish diplomacy. In the face of the general sentiment for peace, European leaders would change course or be replaced. Still, that vague sentiment decided no institutional alternatives. The overriding issue of whether democratic, elitist, or corporatist procedure would determine public policy remained unresolved.

· 7 ·

MAJORITIES WITHOUT MANDATES:
ISSUES AND ELECTIONS
IN THE SPRING OF 1924

The recourse to policies congenial to the right intensified many conflicts but decided few. Confrontation politics did not establish the
clear-cut "order" its supporters desired. Even in Mussolini's Italy,
fascist authority stood poised undecidedly between coercion and consensus. Elsewhere, underlying economic choices remained unresolved;
antagonisms persisted in a trench warfare of politics that yielded
neither clear victory nor compromise peace. Germany had limped to
a parliamentary truce by virtue of the Enabling Act, but this promised
only a temporary respite from the stalemates in the Reichstag. Poincaré had taken the Ruhr action sought by the nationalists, but stubbornly refused to meet their demand for conservative electoral leadership. Political alignments in France remained ambiguous: while the
Radical Socialists decided to campaign alongside the Socialists, their
electoral partnership expressed no agreement on underlying financial
dilemmas. Nowhere was it clear what final economic and social allocations could secure political détente.

Could elections resolve the persistent political ambiguities? Within
little more than a month's span, voters in all three countries went to
the polls: in Italy on April 6, in Germany on May 4, and in France a
week thereafter. But the presence of important political alternatives
could not guarantee that the voting would yield clear decisions. Even
where significant majorities or shifts of opinion occurred, the results
were equivocal in terms of the issues at stake. Choices on the ballot,
it turned out, did not parallel real policy alternatives. Superficially decisive victories led merely to coalitions built around opportunity and
not policy.

The major institutional options thus remained unforeclosed. Besides
endorsing personalities, voters marked their ballots to indicate preferences about tax burdens, the power of labor, or the influence of old
and new elites. They left the polls, however, having done little to assure the outcome they wanted. Why were the elections so indecisive?
For reasons that differed in each country, the contending parties did
not present cohesive and consistent answers for the issues actually at
stake. Results thus suggested that even major parliamentary realign-

ment might prove insufficient to bring about a stable resolution of conflict. The reasons for that failure of resolution comprise the real story behind the elections and enable us to understand why corporatist alternatives to effective parliamentary representation developed.

THE LIMITS OF MUSSOLINI'S MAJORITY

Observers have read the Italian elections as a massive plebiscite in favor of fascism. As a vote of confidence, the percentage of the popular vote won by the government was impressive indeed. But the result left key questions in suspense: was the regime to continue as a quasiliberal or as an authoritarian government? Would fascism seek to displace old political leaders, subordinate them, or coexist with them? Why did a massive majority leave so many future developments unsettled?

The raw electoral results had been foreordained. The 1923 Acerbo law stipulated that the leading slate which received one-quarter of the popular vote would take two-thirds of the seats. Precisely because the Fascists had 356 assured places to divide, the composition of the Fascist list became the critical electoral variable. Not the voting, but the allocation of places became the crucial determinant of parliament's future role and introduced the ambiguity of the outcome.

The 356 places gave the government the opportunity to engineer a huge pro-ministerial combination out of all but the die-hard opposition, Socialist, Catholic, and liberal. Reinforcing the traditionalist aspects of the bargaining was the fact that the most reliable area for "making elections" remained the South. Fascism, however, had sprung up in the North: its original dynamic arose from the confrontation with labor in the Po Valley. Now its hold on power was to be determined by the electoral manipulation of that half of the country it had only begun to penetrate—and there by patronage and local pressures rather than through ideological conquest. Thus the elections brought a would-be revolutionary administration face to face with the most tradition-encrusted political habits of the Italian kingdom, and forced fascism to adapt its style to "that guerrilla warfare of men and clienteles" that constituted Mezzogiorno politics.[1] No matter how favorable the over-all results for Mussolini's list, the process of allocating its precious, safe places and coping with the entrenched political leadership of the South meant that the elections might give power to would-be radicals but yet not result in a radically different style of rule.

Elections, in fact, seemed almost superfluous. The government, it was expected as of late 1923, would request and easily win from parlia-

[1] Giacomo Lumbroso, *La crisi del fascismo* (Florence, 1925), p. 113; cf. Raffaele Colapietra, *Napoli tra dopoguerra e fascismo* (Milan, 1962), pp. 220–221.

ment renewal of its "full powers" for another year.[2] Despite its vaunted parliamentarism, the Partito Liberale Italiano (PLI) asked its members to endorse renewal of the decree powers.[3] In view of such compliance, the government's decision against renewal—to judge by Turati's reaction—came as "a stroke of lightning."[4] It was immediately clear that dissolution of the legislature and the creation of a new, solidly pro-fascist majority were to be consequences of the new course. Rightist liberals might swallow the decision, but they had good reason to fear the campaign under the Acerbo law. The leader of the hitherto compliant Democratici Sociali told the cabinet that even if he went along with the decision within the cabinet, his party might not back him up.[5] Competition as a party would be suicidal, since only one-third of the seats would be allocated to all nonfascist parties together. Personal places might be rescued if a berth in the government's slate could be found, but party structures were gravely threatened.

The desire to undermine contending and even cooperative party groupings, while coopting their popular personalities into the ranks of his own supporters, was one reason Mussolini decided to dissolve parliament two years before its mandate expired. But new elections were also needed to resolve tensions within the Fascist Party itself. Like so many of Mussolini's tactical shifts, the new elections represented an effort to master the Fascist movement as well as keep secure control over the state. The new President of the Council straddled uneasily two major warring tendencies in the Party. The militants, who demanded a thorough-going fascistization of the bureaucracy and political class, found their major spokesman in Roberto Farinacci of Cremona. On the other side, critics went so far as to ask, as did the "collaborationist" Massimo Rocca, "if the Fascist Party represents the necessary political support for Benito Mussolini, or if instead it is now living parasitically on his shoulders."[6] Similar splits had emerged dur-

[2] "I pieni poteri alla Camera," *GdI*, December 9, 1923.

[3] Ordine del giorno, Direzione nazionale PLI, December 1, 1923; included in Lucera: Carte Salandra; see Salandra response of December 2, opposing the "collective demonstration in the Chamber" that had been called for, as well as the PLI attempt to direct voting behavior: "I admit no interference from the Party executive in my line of conduct as a deputy."

[4] Turati to Kuliscioff, Rome, December 10, 1923, in Filippo Turati-Anna Kuliscioff, *Carteggio*, vol. vi. *Il delitto Matteotti e l'Aventino, 1923–1925* (Turin, 1959), p. 143.

[5] For liberal response, see "Nuova Era," *GdI*, December 11, 1923, which justified the decision in terms of the government's desire to have a popular mandate for foreign-policy reasons. For the Demosociali, see the statement by G. A. Colonna di Cesarò, Minister of Post and Telegraph, October 30, 1922–February 5, 1924, in ACS, Rome: Verbali del Consiglio dei Ministri, vol. xvi, November 27, 1923.

[6] Massimo Rocca, "Il fascismo e l'Italia," originally in *Critica Fascista*, September 15, 1924; reprinted in the same author's *Idee sul fascismo* (Florence, 1924), esp. p. 64, and *Il primo fascismo* (Rome, 1964), esp. pp. 87–88.

ing the 1921 crisis over the Pact of Pacification, briefly during the discussions about the seizure of power, and thereafter over the issues of squadrist violence and the role of the Militia in the months after the March on Rome. The ambitions of the *ras*, the fascist war lords such as Farinacci in Cremona or Baroncini in Bologna, lay at the bottom of the divisions. Since October 1922, tensions within the PNF had been further accentuated by the influx of new members—so-called fascists of the thirteenth hour, or the seventh day. This proved the case especially in the South, where nominally "democratic" groups as well as liberal cells affiliated themselves wholesale. In the South, too, the Nationalist Party had served as an alternative to fascism and absorbed a disparate membership. Landlords, professionals, industrialists, including antifascists, had sought an acceptable nonopposition label— only to be merged with the PNF in 1923. The overall result was the enrollment of political opportunists who sought no more than the enhancement of old status with new connections, and dismayed the older, more militant, and more purist members. On the other hand, the sporadic but ugly beatings and killings occasionally disgusted the more legalist adherents. Both developments worked to produce varieties of "dissidence": whether on the part of "revisionists" seeking a return to legality and collaboration with other conservative or nationalist groupings, or on the part of intransigents, such as Aurelio Padovani in Naples, who wanted a purification of fascism to eliminate the reactionary, privileged, and self-serving new adherents.[7]

While in the South Padovani protested the degeneration of pristine revolutionary ideals, in the North Farinacci detested the trends toward parliamentarization and normalcy, against which he repeatedly demanded a "second wave" of fascist dictatorship.[8] By late summer of 1923, however, "revisionism" seemed in the ascendant, as its major advocates—Massimo Rocca and the later Minister of Corporations, Gi-

---

[7] Lumbroso, *La crisi del fascismo*, pp. 61–65, on the post-1922 changes in the PNF, especially in the South; Colapietra, *Napoli*, pp. 227–240, and Guido Dorso, *La rivoluzione meridionale* (Turin, 1945), pp. 124–139, 148, for Padovani. On the tendencies toward dissidence, cf. also the report of Vice-Secretary Bastianini, "Il disagio del partito," in Mussolini to Bastianini, April 20, 1923: Segreteria particolare del Duce 242/R, cited in Giuseppe Rossini, *Il delitto Matteotti tra il Viminale e l'Aventino* (Bologna, 1966), pp. 69–70. Cf. also the scornful summary of intrafascist rivalries by the Communist Šaš (Guido Aquila), "Il fascismo italiano," in *Il fascismo e i partiti politici italiani*, originally a collection of studies issued by Rudolfo Mondolfo in 1923–1924, now reprinted by Renzo De Felice, ed. (Bologna, 1966), pp. 489–491. For the outcry against fascist illegality by party members, cf. Lumbroso, *Crisi*, pp. 114–118, concerning Alfredo Misuri and Ottavio Corgini.

[8] Roberto Farinacci, "La seconda ondata," *Cremona Nuova*, May 29, 1923, in Renzo De Felice, *Mussolini il fascista, i. La conquista del potere 1921–1925* (Turin, 1966), pp. 413–415.

useppe Bottai—downgraded the independent role of the Fascist Party and called for disciplined subordination to Mussolini's efforts at normalization. Rocca, a pugnacious and immodest but well-read publicist, had migrated from a prewar anarchism and nationalism via support for intervention to fascism, yet he continued to seek theoretical syntheses that would bridge fascism and traditional liberalism. Protesting "the veiled threats of a second wave," Rocca advocated a "technocratic" fascism. For Rocca and like-minded intellectuals, fascism should de-emphasize ideological allegiance in order to recruit cadres of experts (*gruppi di competenza*) under Party auspices to restructure education, industry, and public administration.[9] This proposal to impart an apolitical managerial thrust to fascism was in line with Mussolini's earlier ideas about *produttivismo*, but it angered the intransigents. They received it as an effort to shunt aside the veterans of party struggles when true fascists had "dreamed not of portfolios nor honors, but faced only prison or death."[10]

Throughout September the Party was rocked by a press polemic between intransigents and revisionists, who were probably discreetly encouraged by Mussolini himself.[11] While the revisionists appealed to Mussolini *vis-à-vis* the Party, the pro-Farinacci forces had to stress the autonomous role of the PNF, even against the Duce, as they earlier had exalted the *squadri* and the Militia. The revisionists went so far as to hint in public at the dissolution of the Fascist Party; and certain adherents, disillusioned by outbreaks of violence and reprisals, certainly urged it in private. Mussolini's long-term objective may have involved the formation of a far wider movement, which would absorb liberals and cooperative working-class and Catholic elements. But the revisionist campaign of September 1923 provoked a furious response from the pro-Farinacci press; and in the absence of Mussolini, a majority of the Executive Giunta of the PNF, including Michele Bianchi and

[9] Massimo Rocca, "Per una nuova Destra," *Popolo d'Italia*, October 1923, and "Diciotto Brumaio," *Critica Fascista*, September 24, 1923, reprinted in *Il primo fascismo*, pp. 55–61, 99. For Rocca's memoirs on this period, see his *Come il fascismo divenne una dittatura* (Milan, 1952), esp. pp. 145 ff.; for Bottai's ideas, see Giuseppe Bottai, *Vent'Anni e un giorno* (Milan, 1949); and *Pagine di Critica Fascista 1915–1926* (Florence, 1941), F. M. Pacces, ed. On technocratic flirtations in early fascism, see Alberto Aquarone, "Aspirazioni technocratiche del primo fascismo," *Nord e Sud*, April 1965, pp. 109–128. Cf. also Camillo Pellizzi, *Una rivoluzione mancata* (Milan, 1949), and Rocca, *Come il fascismo divenne una dittatura*, pp. 132 ff.

[10] Farinacci to Mussolini, August 4, 1923: Seg. part. del Duce, National Archives film, T 586/448/026223–026224.

[11] See the later letter of Filippo Filipelli to Mussolini, Seg. part. del Duce 242/R, cited in De Felice, *Mussolini il fascista*, p. 456. Filipelli was then an editor of the *Corriere italiano*, a Roman newspaper established as an "official" fascist organ and championing the revisionist cause.

Gino Baroncini as well as the Cremona *ras*, voted Rocca's expulsion from the Party. This excommunication threatened to make fascism appear far too intransigent and sectarian, and to threaten Mussolini's effort to win the collaboration of nonfascists. Going to the Grand Council, the President of the Council had Rocca's discipline commuted to a three-month suspension of political activity and won a resolution demanding the Party's support of the government "without clamor and public polemics." Fascism would not take second place to other parties, nor would it plead for their support, but neither would it "reject the technical collaboration of other elements provided it is loyal and disinterested." Local organizational activity, stipulated the Grand Council, was an ample enough task for the Party; on the national level, the government and its prefects were to remain entrusted with supreme authority. Mussolini thus prevailed over the militants, but if he was to keep them compliant his strategy of normalization and absorption of the other political forces had to bring early success. Elections under the Acerbo law offered the opportunity to make *trasformismo* work, to solidify his own rule and liberate him from the strident pressure of the *ras*.[12] Beyond tactical considerations, Mussolini may have responded to the impulses that intermittently continued to move him— the hope of achieving some common ground with working-class representatives, the grudging admiration for Giolitti, and the desire to win over his opponents to a massive, voluntary consensus.[13]

The immediate target of his electoral strategy, however, had to be the diverse liberal groupings. Mussolini wooed the liberals consistently throughout 1923. At an anniversary commemoration of the March on Rome on October 30, he told their delegates that Italy owed much to

[12] On the conflict, Lumbroso, *Crisi fascista*, p. 119; Rocca, *Come il fascismo divenne una dittatura*, pp. 152 ff.; cf. Rossini, *Il delitto Matteotti*, pp. 76 ff. For the suggestion of dissolving the PNF, see the Tuscan squad leader, Dino Perrone Compagni, to Mussolini, September 15 and 24, in Seg. part del Duce 94/R, National Archives film T 586/1093/068900 ff.; also "Governo e fascismo nella realtà politica," in the *Corriere Italiano*, September 16; cited in De Felice, *Mussolini il fascista*, p. 548. For condemnations of excessive Mussoliniism, see the citations from Farinacci in Rossini, *Il delitto Matteotti*, p. 75, n. 3. For the resolution of the Grand Council on October 13, 1923: Benito Mussolini, *Opera Omnia*, Edoardo e Duilio Susmel, eds. xx (Florence, 1956), pp. 39–40. On the supremacy of the prefects, demanded by Mussolini as early as June 1923, cf. also Alberto Aquarone, *L'organizzazione dello stato totalitario* (Turin, 1965), pp. 30–31, 340–341.

[13] On Mussolini's general political approach, see Piero Gobetti, *La rivoluzione liberale* (Turin, 1964), p. 191, about the "reprise" of Giolittian *trasformismo* on the part of the fascist leader: "The political struggle in the Mussolinian regime is not easy: it is not easy to resist him because he does not remain fixed with any coherence upon any position, nor upon any precise distinction, but is always ready for every transformation. Cf. De Felice, *Mussolini il fascista*, pp. 536–538, and Rossini, *Delitto Matteotti*, p. 59; also Gaetano Salvemini, *The Fascist Dictatorship in Italy* (London, 1928), esp. pp. 297 ff., and Cesare Rossi's works: *Mussolini com'era* (Rome, 1947), and *Trentatre vicende mussoliniane* (Milan, 1958).

liberalism, and that so long as they did not place their party above the nation he would accept their collaboration.[14] Common hostility to socialism had offered a first common ground; the elections would provide another.

Meanwhile, the government's economic policies also pleased Italy's bourgeois leaders. The *laissez-faire* policies that Mussolini had outlined at the noted Udine address of September 1922 were vigorously prosecuted by the new Minister of Finance, the recently fascistized Manchesterite, Alberto De Stefani.[15] In a well-timed address at La Scala a week before the April elections, De Stefani reviewed his economy measures with satisfaction: "the glorious announcement of the conquest of the balanced budget," as Einaudi sarcastically viewed it. Few noted that the trend had begun under Giolitti with the liquidation of wartime expenses and the grain subsidy. Instead, the Fascists were credited with bringing finances into order and fostering a good year for the economy.[16] Specific corporate salvage operations also created a grateful dependency, especially the refloating of the Vatican-affiliated Banco Di Roma, which helped to undercut the position of the Popolari.[17] Even more gratifying to the well off were De Stefani's tax concessions. The minister finally repealed the pending proposal for registration of bearer securities and allowed progressive wartime taxes to lapse. He further eliminated all inheritance taxes for closely related heirs, arguing that death duties hurt the South unfairly because its wealth lay in land, more visible and more effectively taxed than the portfolios of Northerners. Although he instituted a progressive income tax, maxi-

[14] Mussolini, *Opera Omnia*, xx, pp. 69–70.

[15] Ernesto Rossi, *I padroni del vapore* (Bari, 1955), pp. 42 ff.; cf. Ettore Conti, *Dal Taccuino di un borghese* (Milan, 1946), pp. 298–299; entry of October 31, 1922, expressing satisfaction with Mussolini's advocacy of ideas he had urged upon the fascist leader.

[16] Luigi Einaudi, "Il pareggio raggiunto," *CdS*, April 1, 1924; now in his *Chronache economiche e politiche di un trentennio, 1893–1925*, vii (Turin, 1965), p. 652. Einaudi was generally favorable, although he pointed out the prefascist accomplishment. For the speech: Alberto De Stefani, "Il bilancio finanziario dell'Italia," included in his *La ristaurazione finanziaria 1922–1925* (Bologna, 1926), esp. pp. 104–106. Laudatory coverage in *GdI*, March 30 and April 1, 1924. For estimates of revenues, expenses, and overall deficits according to different criteria, see F. A. Répaci, *La finanza italiana nel ventennio 1913–1932* (Turin, 1934), pp. 60–67. On these problems, too, see Ernesto Rossi, *Le entrate e le spese effettive dello Stato dal 1922–1923 al 1927–1928*, extract from *La Riforma Sociale* (Turin, 1929), pp. 16 ff. For the economic situation in general, see the cautious optimism of Giorgio Mortara, *Prospettive Economiche 1924* (Città di Castello, 1924), pp. xiii–xvi.

[17] On the question of subsidies, see Ernesto Rossi, *I padroni del vapore*, pp. 112–117; Alberto De Stefani, *Baraonda bancaria* (Milan, 1960); and in rebuttal— defending the Banco Di Roma against subverting the PPI, and attributing fascist subsidies to the desire to control the network of smaller Catholic banks and land credit societies—Gabriele De Rosa, *I conservatori nazionali. Biografia di Carlo Santucci* (Brescia, 1962), pp. 103–126.

mum rates remained only 12 percent, far below the French and German levels. Once Nitti's and Giolitti's special surtaxes lapsed, the incidence of the tax burden was hardly changed from before 1915, "no trace remaining of the great upheaval."[18]

Only labor relations remained to preoccupy the business community. The threat no longer came from the CGL, but from the Fascist labor "corporations." Although the strike movement had collapsed "to insignificant proportions,"[19] industrial leaders distrusted the Fascist syndicalists, especially Edmondo Rossoni, who wanted to establish joint "corporations" for industry and labor as well as secure monopoly bargaining power for his unions. The agriculturalists of the Po Valley were willing to merge with Fascist peasant unions and work for control from within, but Confindustria feared the loss of its independence. Industry had friends inside the government among those pressing for normalization. At a major Grand Council debate on the syndicates on March 15, 1923, the Under Secretary of State for Agriculture, Corgini— soon to break with the PNF on the issue of violence and illegal tactics —condemned the Fascist unions for having degenerated into instruments of class struggle. Speaking as invited delegates of industry, Antonio Benni and Gino Olivetti similarly complained that Rossoni was too sympathethic toward labor. While the Grand Council condemned union monopoly, Mussolini still praised the development of a single union as an important social and political development. His approaches to the trade-union leaders, which culminated in a conspicuous interview with former CGL leader Ludovico D'Aragona in late July, upset industrial spokesmen. On July 27, Benni and Olivetti again protested against the idea of a Fascist trade-union monopoly. The brewing national dispute was aggravated when Fascist syndicalists sharply attacked the industrial leaders of Turin on the eve of Mussolini's first official visit to the city. For the moment, conflict was avoided by a compromise formula. The November 16 meeting of the Grand Council explicitly recognized that Confindustria was the representative of the majority of entrepreneurs; three days later, in the Palazzo Chigi agreement, Confindustria representatives promised to recognize the Fascist unions. The compromise meant that Rossoni had to postpone plans for creating the single corporation that would align delegates of industry alongside those of labor, presumably under his authority as head of the Confederation of Fascist Corporations. Instead, except in agriculture, the Fascist "corporations" remained only labor delegations dependent on the state for real power, while organized industry re-

[18] Luigi Einaudi, *La guerra e il sistema tributario italiano* (Bari, 1930), pp. 99–100 ff., 231 ff., 249 ff., 291 ff., 399–403, 410–423, 483–484. Cf. De Stefani's speech of December 8, 1923, to the Senate in *Ristaurazione finanziaria*, pp. 98–99.
[19] Mortara, *Prospettive economiche 1924*, p. 418.

tained its own powerful, independent organization. It was still too early for industry to claim a final victory; Rossoni renounced no theoretical claims. But all the more reason for industrialists to see Mussolini's leadership and their own cooperation with him as the best guarantee against radicalization of the Fascist movement.[20]

From the viewpoint of general politics, the Palazzo Chigi agreement comprised just one aspect of preparation for the upcoming campaign. Arbitration among interest groups and efforts to patch over social conflict was all part of the steps toward the electoral contest. "Fascist electoral activity is phenomenal," Kuliscioff noted from Milan on December 20, describing the maneuvering for parliamentary nominations.[21]

Mussolini, however, made it clear that he wanted cooperation from individuals "above, outside and against" the old bankrupt parties. In a major address on January 28, 1924—the first to be staged theatrically in the Piazza Venezia—he claimed that to run for office would make the next months "among the most humiliating" of his life. But in a warning to the intransigents, he made it clear that fascism would play out the legalist tactic. If the old parties stood condemned, so too did Fascist sectarianism: "the mania for purity and for the spirit of 1919 on the basis of old guards, of the fascism of the first hour or the twenty-fourth, is simply ridiculous."[22]

The elections thus promised a chance to undermine the independence of the PNF as well as the old parties. Construction of the electoral slate—the so-called *listone* (Big List)—was entrusted to a Commission of Five, the Pentarchy, under Mussolini's direction.[23] The Duce was willing to brook the resentment of those Fascist members he had to sacrifice from the 356 sure places in order to win over prominent liberals.[24] As a result, the liberals posed little resolute opposition; only

[20] Felice Guarneri, *Battaglie economiche tra le due grandi guerre*, 2 vols. (Milan, 1953), I, p. 66; Mario Abrate, *La lotta sindacale nella industrializzazione d'Italia 1906–1926* (Turin, 1967), pp. 375–390; Piero Melograni, *Gli industriali e Mussolini. Rapporti tra Confindustria e fascismo dal 1919 al 1929* (Milan, 1972), pp. 52–67; Aquarone, *L'organizzazione dello stato totalitario*, pp. 113–118; Partito Nazionale Fascista, *Il gran consiglio nei primi sei anni dell'era fascista* (Rome, 1929?), pp. 19–25 (meeting of March 15, 1923), pp. 71–73 (July 27), pp. 96–97 (November 16). On the agrarians, Giovanni Pesce, *La marcia dei rurali. Storia dell'organizzazione sindacale fascista degli agricoltori* (Rome, 1929); and on Fascist syndicalism at this time, Eduardo Malusardi, *Elementi di storia del sindacalismo fascista* (Genoa, 1932), pp. 101–110.

[21] Turati-Kuliscioff, *Carteggio*, VI, p. 154.

[22] Text in *Opera Omnia*, XX, pp. 161–171; cf. *CdS*, January 29, 1924.

[23] See the report of the January 29 meeting of the Consiglio Nazionale del Fascismo and discussion of electoral procedure in "I particolari del programma elettorale fascista," *CdS*, January 31, 1924.

[24] Cf. "Intervista con uno che sa," *GdI*, December 11, 1923, for the expectation of Fascist discontent.

the so-called Constitutional Opposition, led by Bonomi and Amendola, ran as an ideological alternative. Other liberals hesitated between seeking places for themselves on the *listone* or running separately on alternative but nonopposition "flanking" or "parallel" slates. The national PLI leadership split over the issue of putting up separate liberal lists. It finally left the local organizations to decide whether to support the National List or put up their own.[25]

The decision often depended upon whether liberals stood more chance of winning seats by getting an assured quota of the *listone* or by competing for a share of the minority places.[26] The case of Gino Sarrocchi, Tuscan right-wing liberal and follower of Salandra, is illustrative. Sarrocchi felt that liberals of the right were not getting enough places on the national list, but he did not wish to join the "flanking" list that was suggested to him for Arezzo and Siena, since it seemed destined to have little success. On February 4, Salandra saw Mussolini to ask that thirty right-wing liberal deputies of the outgoing legislature be assigned *listone* seats. Despite winning Mussolini's "most solid and flattering assurances" that Sarrocchi could have a place, he had little success on behalf of the others, and Sarrocchi declined to run on the National List without his colleagues. The Salandrans reproached their leader for not bargaining hard enough; indeed, Salandra haggled over places only with diffidence, and despite feeling that Sarrocchi's final exclusion was "politically inexplicable," he still consented to give a major campaign address on behalf of the government at La Scala on March 19.[27] The hard fact was that in Tuscany there were only twenty-five seats available for the National List and three to four times as many would-be nominees. At least sixteen men with some claims for recognition wanted one of Florence's nine places. Only when Tuscan liberals threatened to run a "parallel" list, that is, a slate indicating an independent stance toward the government, was a compromise found.

[25] "La situazione politica dopo il discorso di Mussolini," *La Stampa*, January 30/31, 1924; "Orientamenti d'uomini e di partiti nella laboriosa vigilia elettorale," *CdS*, February 1, 1924. Cf., too, Cesare Sobrero, "I liberali e le elezioni," *La Stampa*, December 20/21, 1923.

[26] "La lotta pei 179 posti di minoranza," *GdI*, February 20, 1924; also "La campagna elettorale," *CdS*, February 22, 1924, p. 2.

[27] Salandra's version in his letter of February 18, 1924, to Costanzo Ciano, the new Minister of Posts: Lucera: Carte Salandra. Also, *Memorie politiche, 1916–1925* (Milan, 1951), pp. 42–44. In his speech of March 19, Salandra said he could accept Mussolini's dictatorship if the fascist movement were disciplined. See *GdI*, March 20, 1924, for the speech and Mussolini's letter of thanks of March 22, 1924, in Lucera: Carte Salandra. Cf. Giovanni Amendola, "Dittatura e liberalismo" (address of March 21, 1924), reprinted in *La democrazia italiana contro il fascismo, 1922–1924* (Naples, 1960), pp. 270–273, for a democratic-liberal rebuttal of the authoritarian Salandran position. On liberal annoyance with Salandra, see "Le liste per il Piemonte, la Liguria, e la Toscana," *CdS*, February 20, 1924.

A so-called *bis* list was created for Sarrocchi and two party colleagues along with three Fascists. The *bis* device was a slate approved by the government as an acceptable fascist choice, but seeking its seats among the 179 allocated to the minority.[28]

The major "parallel" lists were put up by the Giolittians, whose independent but nonoppositional stance was outlined at the Piedmont liberals' congress at Cuneo on February 20. Giolitti's decision disappointed Mussolini, who had hoped to add the prestigious name of the ex-premier to his own forces, or at least keep him from acting independently. Giolitti's lieutenant, Marcello Soleri, was offered five or six places on the Piedmont *listone* as well as a Senate seat for Giolitti; and in fact the temptation of the promised secure places did lead two intended Giolittian candidates to back out of the slate.[29] Nevertheless, Giolitti was not ready to back down, and in Piedmont he enjoyed strong local support, including that of Frassati of *La Stampa*. To the anger of the Prefect, Palmieri, Giovanni Agnelli also remained cool toward the Fascists and supported independent liberals through the "Associazione Democratica." (In turn, Palmieri brought Benni from Milan to urge industry's support for fascism and sponsored a pro-government "Unione Monarchica liberale.")[30] With regional support Giolitti could count on capturing a few seats, but the "parallel" lists established in Liguria and in the Abruzzi under Giolitti's old Under Secretary, Camillo Corradini, were less fortunate. These slates particularly provoked fascist anger, especially in the Abruzzi, where the Fascists turned to violence and decided to run a *bis* list specifically against Corradini. Since Corradini and Giolitti refused to label themselves as "opposition," the special hostility surprised some adherents. As Senator Garroni naively protested about the Genoa slate, "It is really strange that the Fascist leaders focus special opposition against this liberal list, which, leaving aside factors of personal sympathy, must necessarily approve the present state of affairs." He asked that Giolitti make it clear that no precautions were needed against a slate

[28] "La laboriosa preparazione delle liste di minoranza," and "Nel ultimo giorno per la presentazione delle liste," *CdS*, February 26, 1924. Cf. the letter of Ciano to Salandra, February 19, 1924, in Lucera: Carte Salandra, explaining that Mussolini "had" to impose an all-fascist list in Tuscany since the Pentarchy could not agree on nonfascist members. On the number of candidates, see Mario Malan, "La posizione dei partiti nazionali," *GdI*, February 6, 1924.

[29] Marcello Soleri, *Memorie* (Turin, 1949), pp. 178–181.

[30] See Palmieri to the Minister of the Interior, January 9, 1924, in ACS, Rome: Min. Interno, Gabinetto della S. E. Sottosegretario dell'Interno Aldo Finzi, Ordine Pubblico, B.9, f. 89: Torino. (Like De Vecchi, Palmieri showed a special aversion for Agnelli.) On *La Stampa*'s support, see Massimo Legnani, "'La Stampa,' 1919–1925," in Brunello Vigezzi, ed., *1919–1925. Dopoguerra e fascismo. Politica e stampa in Italia* (Bari, 1965), pp. 351–352. See also Valerio Castronovo, *Giovanni Agnelli* (Milan, 1971), pp. 377–384.

that was really just "an auxiliary of the National List."[31] Ultimately, what angered the Duce was not the ideological position that "parallel" or other slates might adopt, but the mere fact that rival party organizations persisted: their very existence precluded normalization and collaboration.

In the South, the capture of key personalities became the heart of the government's electoral strategy. Fascism did not dispose of the forces below Rome that it had to the North. "A vast movement on the part of public opinion," explained the *Giornale d'Italia*, "would not emerge without the adherence of the most representative figures of that district."[32] This meant that the government had to play the game of clientele politics even with self-styled democratic leaders. The wooing of Enrico De Nicola, amiable, moderate, and respected President of the Chamber, was symptomatic. Capturing De Nicola seemed especially important given the simmering fascist dissidence that still existed in Naples after the Padovani episode. In 1923, the militant syndicalist *ras* Padovani clashed repeatedly with the old oligarchies of the Nationalist Party, which after the nationwide fusion of the PNF and the Nationalists then flowed into Neapolitan fascism. Only the demotion and forced resignation of Padovani quieted the conflict. For Mussolini this outcome meant an alliance with the traditional elites of the Campagna rather than an attempt to contest their hegemony.[33] The consequences were even more pronounced in the Mezzogiorno—where the old oligarchies had never faced powerful challenges from the left—than in the North. The government was intent not on ideological conquest but on control secured by conventional means, which meant winning over entrenched local politicians even when they designated themselves "democratic." Ideology, for example, was downplayed when Francesco Giunta, a Secretary of the PNF and a member of the Pentarchy, opened the electoral campaign in Naples on January 27, two days after the official dissolution of the legislature. In his address at the San Carlo Theater, Giunta ostentatiously extended De Nicola "a deferential sa-

---

[31] Senator Camillo Garroni to Giolitti, March 27, 1924, in *Quarant'Anni di politica italiana: dalle carte di Giovanni Giolitti*, 3 vols., Claudio Pavone, ed. (Milan, 1962), III, pp. 404–405. For Giolitti's own insistence that "our list . . . will not be in opposition," see his letter to Alfredo Frassati in Frassati, *Giolitti* (Florence, 1959), p. 52; also the letter of February 28 to his son Giuseppe in Gaetano Natale, *Giolitti e gli italiani* (Milan, 1949), pp. 352–353. On the fortunes of Corradini's Abruzzi slate, see the exchanges in *Carte Giolitti*, pp. 399 and 405 ff. and in Gabriele De Rosa, *Giolitti e il fascismo in alcune sue lettere inedite* (Rome, 1957), pp. 90 ff.

[32] "Si opera per una vasta concentrazione di forze nazionali," *GdI*, February 9, 1924.

[33] Colapietra, *Napoli*, pp. 220–240; Dorso, *Rivoluzione meridionale*, p. 132: "It must be recognized that Padovaniism, weak at the time of the March on Rome, was absolutely without an elite that could struggle on the field of *trasformismo* with the old political men."

lute" from the Duce, outlined a pro-monarchy fascism tailored for Neapolitan conservatives, criticized his own party's militants, and finally announced that Mussolini had approved large appropriations for the port of Naples and the road to Salerno. In sum, he offered political flattery, pork barrel, and protection of the *status quo*, which moved Amendola to ask sarcastically: was it really worth the trouble to remake Italy, past, present, and future, just to discover Enrico De Nicola in Naples?[34]

The Southern politicians were the key to the electoral strategy. However, De Nicola's decision whether or not to run on the *listone* depended upon that of Orlando, who dominated the Sicilian political scene. In turn, Orlando's decision depended upon the strategy of the Democratici Sociali, the ideologically amorphous but regionally entrenched Southern faction that had emerged in 1921. Masters of the Masonic lodges and the Post Offices, the "Demosociali" had supplied three ministers in Mussolini's cabinet, one of whom joined the PNF. Still, Mussolini resented their party leverage and scornfully attacked their claims to independence in his speech of January 28. "Who are the real Demo-Sociali? Those for, or against us," he asked, and added that fascism negated "the whole sectarian democratoid-socialistoid ideology."[35] In response to this affront Demosociale minister di Cesarò left the cabinet, and the party executive insisted that if its men were to enter the national electoral list they must still run as party representatives. But if the Demosociali were to form a rival "parallel" list as Giolitti had done, Orlando would refuse to campaign with the fascist *listone* rather than go through a divisive electoral battle in Sicily. Without Orlando, the Fascists would lose De Nicola, and the Calabrian leader Guiseppe De Nava.[36]

This Southern imbroglio dragged on through several weeks in February. Orlando, Luigi Fera, and others were prepared to endorse and seemed about to win Mussolini's approval for a compromise that would allow a Demosociale "flanking" list to run with government approval, and let themselves return to the official slate, when the Demosociale executive insisted that any agreement be officially between parties, not individuals.[37] This seemed to doom the compromise, but

[34] Report in *GdI*, January 27, 1924. Amendola, "Vigilia elettorale," January 23, 1924, in *La democrazia contro il fascismo*, p. 228.

[35] Mussolini, *Opera Omnia*, xx, pp. 169–170. Cf. Dorso, *Rivoluzione meridionale*, p. 162, on the petit bourgeois, "transformistic essence" of the Democratici Sociali.

[36] "La situazione elettorale nel Sud e l'azione del governo," *CdS*, February 3, 1924; "Come i partiti prendono posizioni," *CdS*, February 5; "La laboriosa preparazione delle liste elettorali," *CdS*, February 7.

[37] Cited in "L'azione fascista verso gli esponenti del Mezzogiorno," *CdS*, February 9, 1924; the same sort of suggestion appears in the *GdI* of the same day ("Si opera per una vasta concentrazione di forze nazionali").

the Southern politicians badly wanted to join the *listone*. De Nicola in fact had already agreed to enter the *listone*, in expectation of a compromise agreement and of Orlando's candidacy. Once De Nicola was in the race, Orlando at last accepted a place with the supposed proviso that a Demosociale slate enjoy government neutrality. The wartime premier insisted to the City Council of Palermo that he had been sought for the National List not merely on personal grounds, "but also for the liberal and democratic ideas I have always professed."[38] Opponents of his collaboration continued to warn him that he would sacrifice all his traditional support in Palermo, but the real losers were the Demosociali.[39] Their party managers, who had sought to trade on the indispensability of their prestigious candidates, faced a revolt from those local leaders who were now forced into the arid terrain contested by the minority parties.[40] The Fascists, in sum, captured the major political names and thus the assurance of a strong Southern majority. Below Rome the would-be revolutionary regime had to bargain and cajole and to disavow its intransigents; but like the Piedmontese who had come before, from Cavour to Giolitti, the new Northern rulers managed to exploit the "personalist" loyalties of the South for their own ends. Amendola claimed that the South taught democracy,[41] but in fact it reinforced authority—not, however, without blurring confrontations of ideology and blunting radicalism.

By the February 26 deadline for the submission of candidacies, the outline of the contest was clear. Besides the National List, the Popolari and the reformist PSU (Turati, Treves, Matteotti) contested each electoral district, although these parties nominated candidates only for the minority places at stake. "Maximalist" slates in all districts but Sardinia, and Communists in all but the Abruzzi, also competed for

[38] "Orlando, Fera e De Nava s'accorderebbero col Governo," *CdS*, February 10, 1924; "L'accordo fascista con gli uomini del Mezzogiorno," *CdS*, February 12; "Le alterne vicende delle trattative . . ." *CdS*, February 13; "Orlando e De Nicola nella lista ministeriale," *CdS*, February 15. For the De Nicola-Mussolini correspondence, see Seg. part. del Duce, 318/R, National Archives Film T 586/459/029800 ff. esp. intercepted conversation 5007.

[39] See ACS, Rome: Min. Int., Dir. gen. P.S., Div. Aff. gen. e ris., 1924. B. 80, sf. "Sicilia: Elezioni." "Informazioni" of February 18, and February 29 and March 4, 1924.

[40] "La selezione dei candidati popolari, demosociali e delle opposizioni," *CdS*, February 17, 1924.

[41] Giovanni Amendola, "Il Mezzogiorno e la crisi politica," address of October 1, 1922, now in *La nuova democrazia* (Naples, 1951), esp. pp. 146–148. Cf., too, the comments on the "social, political and moral value of the so-called personal positions through which public life in the South is organized." They "have contributed effectively throughout the postwar period, and will continue to contribute tomorrow, to preserve a large part of Italy from dangerous political upheavals." For incisive comment on this elitist antifascism, see Dorso, *Rivoluzione meridionale*, pp. 165–72.

434

working-class votes. While the Catholics were less obviously split, they still suffered from profound divisions. Under Sturzo's leadership, the PPI had abandoned its early equivocal stance of "neither opposition nor collaboration" to run as a decided foe of the regime. But Filippo Meda, who advised a PPI "revisionism" to encourage Mussolini's own revisionist leanings, declined to run under the Popolari label. Catholic pro-Fascists and "national conservatives" also defected, as Mussolini began courting the Vatican with a conciliatory interview on the Roman Question, subsidies to the Banco Di Roma, and the restoration of crucifixes in schoolrooms. Midway through the campaign the Party had to face an open letter from 150 "major Catholic personalities" disavowing the PPI and calling for Catholics to support the National List.[42]

In addition to the National List, the Popolari, and the three Marxist groups, each district usually had at least four or five other slates. The dissident "revisionist" fascists of the North, adherents of Misuri or Forni, formed "Patria e Libertà" lists in Piedmont, Lombardy, and Emilia, while a pro-Padovani slate appeared in Naples and another dissident grouping in Apulia. The liberal forces ended up shattered. Aside from the individuals absorbed in the *listone*, liberals appeared on the *bis* lists organized to accommodate Sarrocchi in Tuscany and to oppose Corradini in the Abruzzi, and finally, for local reasons, in Rome and Apulia. The *bis* lists especially angered the opposition. They violated the understanding that the 179 minority seats would be reserved for the real opposition, and not contested by front-men for the government. Moreover, besides the *bis* lists, pro-Fascist "flanking" slates were also organized to accommodate those pro-government liberals for whom, especially in the South, there was no room on the National List. Giolittian "parallel" candidates, who avoided the term "opposition," fought for a quota of the vote in Lazio, Campagna, the Abruzzi, and Liguria, as well as in Piedmont, while the Demosociali sought to keep some foothold throughout the South and in Tuscany. Among the liberals, only Bonomi and Amendola's "Constitutional Opposition" in Lombardy and other areas of the North, in Campagna, Calabria, and Sardinia in the South, ran in outright opposition. Completing the tattered ranks of opposition were the Republicans in twelve constituencies, the small groupings of peasants, the ethnic minorities in the borderlands, and the Sardinian Action Party, a Garibaldian remnant surviving on local feelings for autonomy. The average urgan constituency thus had a choice of about ten lists, and over the whole country

[42] Gabriele De Rosa, *Storia del movimento cattolico in Italia*, II, *Il partito popolare italiano* (Bari, 1966), pp. 419–466; De Rosa, *Filippo Meda e l'età liberale* (Florence, 1959), pp. 225 ff.; De Rosa, *I conservatori nazionali*, pp. 87–89; Rossoni, *Il delitto Matteotti*, pp. 9–40.

approximately 1000 candidates vied for the 179 minority positions available.[43]

Of the candidates, Turati's Socialists, the Popolari, and the Constitutional Opposition were officially singled out as major foes of the government, although violence tended to erupt as a result of local rather than national hatreds. The dissident fascists in the North, the Popolari throughout, and Corradini's slate in Abruzzi became the special targets for beatings and an intimidation "unworthy of a civilized country," as Giolitti wrote his ex-Under Secretary, although all he could counsel as a response was Tolstoyan patience.[44] Toward the end of the campaign Mussolini sought to brake the violence because it might discredit the electoral results. He specifically ordered that the opposition press be allowed to function unimpeded, especially in Milan, where the *Corriere*'s studied refusal to comment on the slates enraged local Fascists.[45]

Mussolini was right: he did not need violence. Even if reinforced by electoral pressure and intimidation, there was a decisive pro-government consensus. The National List and the *bis* lists scored impressively with 4,653,488 out of 7,165,502 votes or 65 percent. The *listone* alone received 4,305,936 or 60 percent. The opposition's popular vote declined sharply. The combined socialist alternatives fell from 4,524,204 in 1921 to 1,051,842 (PSU 422,957; Maximalists 360,694; PCI 268,191).[46] In view of these results, the two-thirds provision of the Acerbo law corresponded very well with the popular verdict. Where the Acerbo law had significantly aided the regime was by demoralizing the liberals beforehand and leading them to seek places on the National List.

What was also striking was the extent of the socialist collapse, if compared, for example, with the socialist-communist vote in the German elections of March 1933, shortly after Hitler came to power. In that later test, held under similar conditions of partial intimidation and pressure, the Marxist parties still retained 30.5 percent of the vote. Of course, the Fascist elections followed the seizure of power by a year and a half, the National Socialist victory by only a month and a half.

[43] "La presentazione delle liste elettorali alle Corti d'Apello," *CdS*, February 28, 1924; "Elasticità necessaria," *GdI*, February 29, 1924.

[44] Corradini to Giolitti, March 21 and March 30, in Pavone, ed., *Carte Giolitti*, III, pp. 402–403, 405–414, and Giolitti to Corradini, March 24 and April 1, 1924, in De Rosa, *Giolitti e il fascismo*, pp. 21–23. On violence, cf. De Felice, *Mussolini il fascista*, pp. 582–584.

[45] Piero Melograni, ed., *Corriere della Sera, 1919–1943* (Bologna, 1965), p. xlix; "Le violenze contro il 'Corriere,'" *CdS*, April 10, 1924. Mussolini's orders in ACS, Rome: Dir. gen. P.S., Div. Aff. gen. e ris., 1924, B. 80, f. "Elezioni politiche," Telegram 13157, April 4, 1924, Mussolini to De Bono.

[46] Election results here and in tables from: Repubblica Italiana, Istituto Centrale di Statistica, *Compendio delle statistiche elettorali italiane dal 1848 al 1934*, 2 vols. (Rome, 1947), II, Table 44.

But just as significant, the Italian socialist strength had rested on rural as well as urban workers, while the German socialist vote was a city one. As the 1921 returns in Bologna and Ferrara had already indicated (see Chapter Five), the rural proletariat was vulnerable to Fascist take-over, both in terms of labor organization and voting allegiance. The Emilian countryside, which had once voted even more solidly "red" than the cities, now voted even more overwhelmingly Fascist: Bologna City piled up 61 percent for the National List, the province 79 percent.

Unfortunately, no statistical breakdown of urban and rural votes was published by any central source in 1924. Judging from the frag-mentary data in the press, the urban-rural difference was of less moment in the North. The Bologna results were unusually good for the National List in *both* city and country; the city of Genoa gave 45 percent to the National List, the province as a whole 38 percent; the city of Florence gave the National List 40 percent, and the province in its entirety 48 percent. In Milan the *listone* fared even worse than the conservative bloc organized for the communal elections of 1920. In the South the countryside rewarded Mussolini more distinctly. Urban Naples voted 43 percent for the National List, the countryside 77 percent, and the Fascist voters in Naples provided only 7 percent of the Campagna total.[47]

As a national tactic, Mussolini's "southern strategy" evidently paid off. The working-class parties to some degree, and the Popolari more decisively, fell off more in the South than the North.[48] What is more, outside the fascist heartland of Emilia and outside Tuscany—where the liberals had become predominantly Fascist fellow-travelers—it was the more southern regions that provided the heaviest majorities for the

[47] See the results reported in *CdS*, April 8 and 9, 1924; also Colapietra, *Napoli*, p. 282.

[48] GEOGRAPHIC CONTRIBUTIONS TO EACH PARTY'S VOTE (Percent)

	North	Center	South	Islands
Socialist Party, 1919	70.7	19.6	7.3	2.4
Marxist parties, 1921	67.8	19.3	9.8	3.2
(Socialist)	(68.0)	(18.2)	(10.4)	(3.4)
(Communist)	(66.1)	(25.4)	(6.5)	(2.0)
Marxist parties, 1924	73.4	14.7	8.2	3.7
(PSU)	(75.4)	(11.8)	(7.9)	(4.9)
(Maximalist)	(56.5)	(36.9)	(4.8)	(1.8)
(PCI)	(70.1)	(17.0)	(8.8)	(4.1)
Partito Popolare, 1919	61.1	17.4	14.8	6.7
Partito Popolare, 1921	63.7	16.9	13.0	6.4
Partito Popolare, 1924	76.4	11.5	6.2	5.9

North includes Piedmont, Liguria, Lombardy, Venetia, and Venezia Giulia. Cen-ter includes Tuscany, Marches, Umbria, Emilia, and Lazio. South includes Abruzzi, Campagna, Apulia, Basilicata, and Calabria.

National List.[49] This, however, was not a vote for fascism *per se*, but for the entrenched leadership of the South whom Mussolini had so sedulously coopted.

Despite the size of the victory, which exceeded even government expectations,[50] the vote hid ambivalences. There were uncertainties in terms of ideology and of resoluteness. The composition of the new Chamber appeared to reduce opposition to insignificance.[51] Nevertheless, the terms of election had been national consensus and "normal-

[49]

PERCENTAGES FOR THE NATIONAL AND BIS LISTS BY ELECTORAL REGION
(Rounded Off to Nearest 0.5 Percent)

1. Apulia	84.0	9. Marches	64.5
2. Abruzzi	83.5	10. Sardinia	62.0
3. Lucania	76.5	11. Venezia Giulia	60.0
4. Lazio/Umbria	76.0	12. Liguria	52.5
5. Tuscany	75.5	13. Lombardy	49.0
6. Campagna	75.5	14. Veneto	45.5
7. Emilia	71.5	15. Piedmont	44.5
8. Sicily	70.0		

North: 53.0 percent of 3,420,634 voters. Center: 74.5 percent of 1,182,848 voters. South: 80.0 percent of 1,742,575 voters. Islands: 68.5 percent of 819,445 voters. (The North includes Emilia, the South includes Abruzzi.)

[50] Cf. Acerbo's estimates of April 3, in ACS, Rome: Min. Int. Dir. gen. P.S. Div. Aff. gen. e ris., 1924, B. 80, "Elezioni politiche." The Fascists expected 52 percent for the *listone*, 4 percent for the *bis lists*, while actually both together netted 66.3 percent.

[51]

Presumptive firm majority:

National List:	355	(originally 356, but the vacancy after the death of De Nava during the campaign was attributed to the minority quota).
Bis lists:	19	
Total		374

Voting with the government at least initially:

"Flanking" liberals	10	
Giolittians	5–6	
Peasants	2–3	
Dissident Fascists	1	
Independent(s)	1–2	
Democratic Socialists	10	
Total		29–30

Presumptive opposition:

PPI	40	
Socialists	65	(25 PSU, 22 Maximalists, 18 Communists)
Constitutional opposition	14	
Republicans	7	
Germans/Slavs	4	
Independent(s)	1–2	
Total		131–132
	Grand total	535

ization"—collaboration with old political elements and a stress on the new legal phase of fascism.[52] The cost of the victory included acceptance of the power structure of the South. But had not the whole legalist tendency until recently been sharply contested within the party? If campaigning against Popolari and Socialists had kept militants temporarily occupied, were they still prepared to adopt the type of fascism sanctioned by the voting?

What is more, the majority might prove less overwhelming than it appeared. Not all of the 374 *listone* and *bis* delegates were Fascists. On the morrow of the election the *Corriere* estimated that there were 275 party members among them, but some of these were recent and opportunist recruits. In late February the *Corriere* had counted only 230, while the *Giornale d'Italia*—happy to recommend the List as a fusion of liberal with Fascist forces—claimed that there were 100 liberals in the bloc, which would have meant 250 Fascists. Cesare Rossi later provided a list of 150 names that he described as liberal rather than Fascist candidates. This meant that the Fascists comprised somewhere between 200 and 270 members of parliament.[53] Nor was the party any longer the cadre of authoritarian and radical militants. For a year and a half the intransigents had complained of the conversions that had swelled party ranks, forcing Mussolini to take a stance against "purism" and "veteranism" in his inclusive, even syncretic movement, and the election reinforced this trend. Thus the new Chamber impressively supported the government so long as "broadchurch" fascism prevailed, but it would not necessarily be a docile instrument if Mussolini should seek to return to more authoritarian government. Were king to be set against premier, then the cardboard structure of the *listone* might fall apart. Were the government to revert to the violence that had marked earlier days and reappeared in the campaign, then the liberals, despite all their yearnings for a safe collaboration and the *status quo*, might be forced into opposition. Many recent PNF members might also grow nervous and regret their opportunist affiliation. This indeed was the threat that the Matteotti crisis uncovered two months later.

Although an ostensible victory for fascism, the April elections linked Mussolini's regime to the constraints of parliamentary tradition and history. Preeminent among these was the latest aspect of the perennial Southern Question: the confrontation of an exploitative government in

[52] Cf. the New Year's editorial of the *Popolo d'Italia* stressing that fascism no longer required illegality. Cited in Giorgio Rumi, " 'Il Popolo d'Italia' 1918–1925," in Vigezzi, ed., *Dopoguerra e fascismo*, p. 507.

[53] "I seggi alle minoranze," *CdS*, April 9, 1924; "Come sarà composta la futura maggioranza," *CdS*, February 22, 1924; "Elasticità necessaria," *GdI*, February 29, 1924; Cesare Rossi, *Il Delitto Matteotti* (Milan, 1965), pp. 581–587.

Rome with the intractable and unremedied backwardness of the South. Ironically, the South imposed its own conditions in return for electoral help. It transformed the national-syndical impulse from a potentially revolutionary force into one that blunted its energies in winning over old clienteles, promising new favors, reassuring long-standing elites. The product was not particularly attractive; for if in the North fascism at least aligned with productive and dynamic entrepreneurs, in the South it too often shored up the heirs of the Bourbons. The elections indeed were an invitation to *trasformismo*, but the process worked two ways, both upon the old elites and upon fascism. Out of the vote emerged a style of rule still undefined and ambiguous: possibly a fascism that was a compromise with liberal usages and traditional elites, but if defections from the majority came to pass, perhaps a fascism that would have to abandon the vestiges of parliamentarism. The elections stipulated only that for the moment fascism excluded drastic social upheaval, that even while winning a massive endorsement it preserved many of Italy's existing social divisions.

The Limits of Social Democratic Eclipse

The SPD entered the German electoral campaign as the clear political target of the right. Indeed the Party was badly hurt in the May elections. Nevertheless, its special leverage in the Weimar political system persisted even as it went into opposition. Out of power for the next four years, its wishes could not simply be disregarded. Examining the reasons why reveals much about the workings of the Weimar Republic. Until the Depression, the major political alternatives before Germany shaped party configurations almost without reference to normal changes in popular opinion: the logic of issues and of the underlying social cleavages, not the passing will of the electorate, was the major determinant of political alignments. The 1924 elections, with their significant alteration of party strength but inability to change basic constraints upon coalition, reveals the geometry of the party system and tells us to look beyond the voting percentages for its axioms.

New elections seemed the only way out of the parliamentary impasse that had developed again since the fall of the Great Coalition. The enabling act, which delegated legislative power to the cabinet, was due to expire February 15, and thereafter the Reichstag would review the government's legislative decrees, especially the emergency tax ordinances. The first two tax ordinances of December 1923, issued by Finance Minister Hans Luther, were harsh but acceptable monetary

440

reform measures; they stanched the bleeding away of governmental revenue by levying additional taxes to make up for earlier depreciation and continuing the conversion to gold-mark tax obligations.[54] But the planned Third Emergency Ordinance presented far more political difficulty, as it broached the thorny issue of revaluation of all old debts. A decision by one of the Leipzig Supreme Court tribunals at the end of November had opened up the way for revalorizing debts that had evaporated in real terms. The judges avoided setting guidelines for how to carry out revaluation, but the widespread agitation on behalf of revaluation made Luther fear a morass of litigation and crippling business uncertainty unless the government set some standard procedures and rates. After some debate a Third Emergency Ordinance was prepared with a stipulation that all private mortgages and mortgage-backed corporate bonds would be revalued at 15 percent of their original worth.[55]

At this point, however, party interests came into conflict. Although the Reichstag was not in session, a "Committee of Fifteen" to consult on decree measures had been established as the price of Social Democratic support for Chancellor Marx in December. The disagreements encountered inside the Committee of Fifteen and the growing bitterness of the SPD toward the deflationary austerity measures indicated that they would oppose the revaluation measure when it came under Reichstag review. The Third Emergency Ordinance was finally decreed on February 14, only a day before the Enabling Act expired. Discussion with both Nationalist and Socialist delegates on February 19 showed that neither party could be reconciled: the Socialists, whose constituency included no great creditor interests, wanted a legislative prohibition on all revaluation, while the DNVP, who represented a great many *rentiers*, pressed for a higher percentage than the government was willing to allow. Nor were the hard-headed Luther, Jarres, Gessler, and the conservative Count von Kanitz personally willing to allow parliamentary amendment of measures they deemed essential. In re-

[54] Michael Stürmer, *Koalition und Opposition in der Weimarer Republik, 1924–1928* (Düsseldorf, 1967), pp. 33–34. Karl-Bernhard Netzband and Hans Peter Widmaier, *Währungs- und Finanzpolitik der Ära Luther 1923–1925* (Basel-Tübingen), 1964, pp. 137 ff.; and tables, pp. 209–214.

[55] Hans Luther, *Politiker Ohne Partei* (Stuttgart, 1960), p. 233, refers to "the fanatics of reevaluation." On the decision of the Leipzig tribunal, cf. Erich Eyck, *A History of the Weimar Republic*, 2 vols. (Cambridge, Mass., 1962–1963), I, pp. 286–288; John P. Dawson, *The Oracles of the Law* (Ann Arbor, Mich., 1968), pp. 465–475. For the Third Ordinance, Netzband-Widmaier, *Währungs- und Finanzpolitik*, pp. 183 ff.; also GFM: ARK, Kabinettsprotokolle, December 15, 17, 1923: January 22, 1924, 3491/1750/758186–758192, 758217–758220; 3491/1751/758692–758697.

peated cabinet meetings they stressed the impossibility of working with the existing Reichstag, and on March 13, before it had occasion to review the Third Emergency Ordinance, parliament was dissolved.[56]

The German Nationalists looked forward to the elections to give them the leading cabinet role that had been denied them in November. This made the SPD their preeminent opponent, in part because of ideological antagonism, in part because the Nationalists had not participated in the Great Coalition and could thus run as an uncompromised anti-Marxist party. The immediate aim was to reduce the Socialist percentage of the vote enough to discourage the middle parties from renewing the Great Coalition. Thus the interest of the right lay in an electoral polarization that would send working-class voters to the Communists and middle-class voters to the DNVP.[57]

Polarization was the worst possible electoral outcome from Stresemann's point of view, even though within the People's Party the spokesmen of industry effectively endorsed the DNVP strategy and sought guarantees against any new collaboration with the SPD. Alfred Gildemeister pressed Stresemann to choose either the Great Coalition or alliance with the DNVP. As of mid-December, Stresemann hedged by advocating a so-called *Volksgemeinschaft* that might include the Nationalists if they proved willing to cooperate with the other parties. Gildemeister attacked this as an effort to evade the real alternative. The conservative Darmstadt lawyer, Eduard Dingeldey, also demanded that in the upcoming campaign the DVP "intervene in forthright language to lay the foundation for a strong bourgeois government."[58]

DVP conservatives attempted to undermine Stresemann's middle-of-the-road formulation at a special session of the parliamentary executive on January 12. There they won a resolution arguing that while the *Volksgemeinschaft* might be formed in theory with Nationalists and/or Socialists, the fusion of SPD and USP prevented long-term cooperation with the left, leaving the DVP "to form the nucleus for . . . all nonsocialist popular forces." The tension inside the Party continued to mount as Stresemann moved to block Stinnes' Rhineland plans and

[56] BA, Koblenz: R 43 I/1020, "Besprechungen mit den Parlamentarien und Fraktionsführern des Reichstags," February 19, 1924; Netzband and Widmaier, *Währungs- und Finanzpolitik*, pp. 206–208; Stürmer, *Koalition und Opposition*, pp. 35–38; cf. Luther, *Politiker ohne Partei*, pp. 236 ff.; GFM: ARK, Kabinettsprotokolle, February 6, 29, March 7, 11, 1924, 3491/1751/759099–759102; 3491/1752/759771–759775, 759839–759840, 759861.

[57] Brauer report to Heydebrand, Berlin, April 28, 1924, in Gaertringen, Westarp Nachlass, pp. 397–398.

[58] See letter exchanges: Gildemeister to Stresemann, December 8 and 18; Stresemann to Gildemeister, December 10, 1923, in GFM: Stresemann Nachlass, 7395 = 88/3159/171536–171542; 171572–171574; Dingeldey to Stresemann, January 11, 1924, 171606.

told him that, given the memories of the inflation, the party could run stronger without him.[59]

By March, the DVP right wing struck out with their own organization, the National-Liberale Vereinigung. This new group represented the party's industrialists, organized chiefly by Vögler and, at second remove, Stinnes. Initially, the NLV was conceived as a caucus within the DVP, justified, in Gildemeister's words, "by the concern of party colleagues throughout the country" for a "strict national and anti-Marxist policy." As Reinhold Quaatz wrote in *Der Tag* of Berlin, perhaps the left wing of the DVP should go its own separate way. If "bourgeois circles" in the West of Germany remained formally within the DVP, they still did not feel ideologically distinct from the Nationalists.[60]

The self-styled "National Liberals" convened on March 26, three days before the national DVP congress. Vögler assailed the DVP's reluctance to fight Marxism and demanded the reversal of labor's postwar social gains in the factories: "The large factory without authority is an absurdity."[61] At the Volkspartei's Central Executive meeting on March 28, and at the full Party Congress the next day, Stresemann countered this move with the argument that outright opposition to social democracy would radicalize the left. Hitting at the right's dictatorial yearnings of the previous autumn, he condemned "the cry for a dictator" as the worst "political dilettantism." In return the rightist delegate Oskar Maretzky condemned the party leadership for desiring a compromise with the SPD at a moment when "the political power factors in the country offer us the possibility of bringing down the social democrats. The people want to put an end to revolution now. (Rejoinder: It's already been ended!) They want no more mercy, but an open battle. No neutrality, but a bourgeois coalition for the final combat."[62]

---

[59] Scholz draft of resolution to Stresemann, January 19, 1924, *ibid.*, 7395 = 88/3159/171625–171627; discussed with further citation in Roland Thimme, *Stresemann und die deutsche Volkspartei* (Lübeck-Hamburg, 1961), pp. 49–50. For the controversy with Stinnes, see Stinnes to Stresemann, March 20, and Stresemann to Stinnes, March 26, 1924, in 7124 = 267/3011/146995–146999; also Gustav Stresemann, *Vermächtnis. Der Nachlass in drei Bänden*, Harry Bernhard, ed., 3 vols. (Berlin, 1932), I, pp. 354–356 ff.

[60] Gildemeister to Stresemann, March 14, 1924, and Quaatz article, March 15, in GFM: Stresemann Nachlass, 7395 = 88/3159/171414–171419; on the National-Liberale Vereinigung, Thimme, *Stresemann*, pp. 52 ff.; and Henry A. Turner, Jr., *Stresemann and the Politics of the Weimar Republic* (Princeton, N.J., 1963).

[61] Reported in the *Berliner Börsenzeitung*, March 26, 1924, included in GFM: Stresemann Nachlass, 7395 = 88/3159/171484 ff.; cf. Thimme, *Stresemann*, pp. 54–55.

[62] BA, Koblenz: R 45 II (DVP Akten)/28, 5. Parteitag am 29./30. März 1924 in Hanover (as reported in "Sonderausgabe der National-Liberalen Korrespondenz" with text from the *Hannover Kurier*, pp. 166, 169).

Despite the attack, Stresemann held his party to a middle course by stressing that an alliance with the DNVP might set back his foreign policy. Representatives of the *Mittelstand* associations also cautioned against undermining the arbitration rights and other social gains won since 1918. A few days later the Party Executive (Zentralvorstand) voted to prohibit DVP members from forming special intraparty associations. This led to the exclusion of the National-Liberale Vereinigung in early April and the migration of some of its members into the Nationalist Party. The secession was less significant in terms of numerical strength than in the shift of key industrialists such as Vögler. Even as the Republic was moving toward a new stability, important elements of heavy industry disavowed the political center.[63]

Vögler's call at Hanover for authority in the factories was certainly no cry of desperation. The industrial leaders in the National Liberal Union were closer to recovering their prewar power than at any point since 1914. On January 27, Erich Koch-Weser had told the Democratic Party executive that whereas after the Revolution their party's fight to preserve the viability of the center had required combatting the SPD, now it meant opposing the right.[64] But rightist resurgence was not only political. Labor's power in the market place as well as the SPD's political role was under attack. The earlier victories of the trade unions —the eight-hour day, the role of the factory councils—were being reversed by the consequences of inflation and the stabilization crisis. "What is the situation?" asked Hermann Bücher of the Presidium of the Reichsverband der deutschen Industrie, in the social-policy committee of the Reich Economic Council in mid-January:

> Up to now, you on the employees' side have been at the helm. Only now when that era is over do you deny it. For four years you had decisive influence over the government; for a republic—and as republicans you must realize it most clearly—can only be governed by a majority and you had it. You disposed of the absolute majority, or at least the decisive minority, in that you exercised a determining influence given the fissures of bourgeois society. Now after circumstances have changed so that in August of last year we faced a complete void, leading no one knew where, the tables have turned

[63] Thimme, *Stresemann*, pp. 58–59. On final exclusion, see the Vorstand resolution in *Vermächtnis*, I, p. 384. The National Liberal secessionists would run in the April elections as *Landesliste*; Maretzky and Lersner won seats through a vote-sharing agreement with the DNVP and joined that party in the new Reichstag. For agreements of the new group with the Reichslandbund for electoral support, see DZA, Potsdam: 61 Re 1(Reichslandbund papers)/116, pp. 15–16 ff.

[64] NSDAP Hauptarchiv, DDP papers/f. 720.

somewhat. And now the scales are tipping toward our side, the side we embody as employer representatives.[65]

The reason for the turnabout was the pressure exerted by what a liberal expert later described as "gigantic unemployment," which followed the introduction of the Rentenmark and the crisis in the Rhineland.[66] Perhaps a million and a half workers outside the occupied areas were completely unemployed; another million and a half required partial assistance, and 2 million in the Ruhr had not yet returned to work. As Bücher told the Main Committee of the Reichsverband twelve days after his remarks to the Economic Council, unemployment "such as we had never previously registered" was facilitating the "process of recuperation in our whole social policy and wages policy." Reintroduction of the eight-hour shift in the mines and the ten-hour working period above ground could now be carried out without resistance. December and January's unemployment, said Bücher, provided "the hope of successfully removing all the evils brought about by the four years of socialist and Marxist policy."[67] The inflation and distress of 1923 had already begun to weaken the unions when the stabilization crisis struck. The Berlin membership of the German Metalworkers' Association, for instance, fell from about 150,000 in 1920–1922 to 75,000 by September 1923 and hit bottom at 50,000 in June 1924. The final collapse came after the union had been forced in the winter of 1924 to suspend its own unemployment assistance. As a later commentator noted, the crisis of 1923–1924 produced a "real panic." Five million trade-union members were lost, and the once powerful federation was reduced to "complete lack of influence." Strike days fell by almost half, while lock-outs to enforce wage cuts or supplementary hours increased almost fivefold over those of 1922.[68]

The result was the temporary collapse of the pattern of industrial relations patiently built up since the war. The Social Democrats had felt compelled to grant Marx the right to amend the eight-hour day.

[65] DZA, Potsdam: RWR/525, Sozialpolitischer Ausschuss, January 18, 1924, p. 233. Reprinted in Hermann Bücher, *Finanz- und Wirtschaftsentwicklung Deutschlands in den Jahren 1921 bis 1925* (Berlin, 1925), p. 41. Cf. Ludwig Preller, *Sozialpolitik in der Weimarer Republik* (Stuttgart, 1949), p. 294.

[66] Julius Hirsch, "Rationalisierung und Arbeitslosigkeit," in *Die Bedeutung der Rationalisierung für das deutsche Wirtschaftsleben*, issued by the Industrie- und Handelskammer zu Berlin (Berlin, 1928), p. 68. For unemployment estimates, see Netzband und Widmaier, *Währungs- und Finanzpolitik*, pp. 224 ff.; Preller, *Sozialpolitik*, p. 164.

[67] Bücher, *Finanz- und Wirtschaftsentwicklung*, pp. 50–51.

[68] Hans-Hermann Hartwich, *Arbeitsmarkt, Verbände und Staat, 1918–1933* (Berlin, 1967), pp. 67, 102, 412, table 9; Gerhard Kessler, "Die Lage der deutschen Arbeiterschaft seit 1914," in *Strukturwandlungen der deutschen Volkswirtschaft*, Bernhard Harms, ed., 2 vols. (Berlin, 1929), I, pp. 474–475.

The Emergency Ordinances of December 18, 1923, kept the principle of the eight-hour day but allowed such blanket exceptions that longer hours became general. In the Economic Council, employers still claimed that the new ordinance preserved the "absurdity" of the old working day and prevented a "reasonable" settlement of the eight-hour issue. Trade-union spokesman Urban more accurately saw the retention "in principle" as a "downright fraud" that meant nothing in practice.[69]

The employers wished to exploit the new situation created by the lapse of the old Demobilization Order of November 23, 1918. This had legally anchored the Stinnes-Legien eight-hours agreement for five years. Now the entrepreneurs demanded the revision of collective contracts, as permitted by the new Arbitration Ordinances of October 30 and December 29, 1923, although subject to certain ground rules, including agreement on both sides. By the pressure of lay-offs and salary cuts, the employers largely overrode the limitations. The Ruhr firms of the Union of Iron and Steel Industrialists (Arbeit Nordwest) secured a new contract on December 13 that provided for twelve-hour shifts. Heavy industry in Westphalia and in Silesia led in reimposing longer hours and reinstituting a 54-hour work week. According to the union leader Umbreit, employers were forcing their workers to sign blank-check agreements to any future changes in working hours that management might impose.[70]

Where was labor to find the strength to resist? The workers sought shelter in the arbitration provisions of the Constitution and specifically the Ordinances of October 30 and December 29, 1923, which provided for compulsory arbitration if disputes persisted, that is, if the unions could hold out. The employers, realizing how exhausted the unions were, upheld the principle of collective bargaining between free agents. Ernst Borsig and Fritz Tanzler of the Union of German Employers' Associations pressed union leaders within the now-moribund Zentralarbeitsgemeinschaft to accept "free agreements."[71] The Union of Ger-

[69] DZA, Potsdam: RWR/525, Sozialpolitischer Ausschuss, January 18, 1924, pp. 177–180, 187–190.
[70] Umbreit in RWR, *ibid.* Details of contract revisions in Hartwich, *Arbeitsmarkt,* p. 318, Preller, *Sozialpolitik,* pp. 146, 296–297, 304–306, and Ausschuss zur Untersuchung der Erzeugungs- und Absatzbedingungen der deutschen Wirtschaft [Enquête-Ausschuss]: IV. Unterausschuss, Bd. 2, *Die Arbeitsverhältnisse im Steinkohlenbergbau in den Jahren 1912 bis 1926* (Berlin, 1928), pp. 72–74. An additional hour was added each day for underground work; two twelve-hour shifts above ground (with two hours for breaks) became the rule again. The additional hour compulsory overtime was paid at the regular hourly wage rates.
[71] DZA, Potsdam: Zentralarbeitsgemeinschaft documents, 70 Ze 1, vol. 31/1, "Niederschrift der Sitzung des geschäftsführenden Vorstandes vom 10.I.1924," pp. 60 ff.

man Employers' Associations told the government on New Year's Day that if a rapid return to full production were desired, wages must be decided only by the negotiating parties. It also directed its members to disregard arbitration judgments if they were not "tolerable." In Berlin, the metal manufacturers refused to attend arbitration negotiations, pressured the unions into private collective bargaining in early January, and won a wage reduction plus an hourly extension of daily working time. Even von Seeckt, still legally responsible for public order, felt that the employers had "overstretched the bow" and directed his generals to intervene with industry so that radicalization would not result.[72]

Both the ZAG session and the January meetings of the Social Policy Committee of the Reich Economic Council provided forums for discussion of the new labor situation. Labor representatives were bitter; management was concerned primarily that the mopping-up operation was so difficult. As one labor representative said in the ZAG, "the battle must be fought out. In questions such as the basic lengthening of working time there can be no compromise, only conflict. The same holds for the wage issue."[73] In the Economic Council, Franz Habersbrunner came quickly to the point on behalf of the employers: social policy had to be cut to the measure of Germany's difficult economic conditions. Bücher said that the discussions had little purpose and even questioned the feasibility of unemployment assistance. Labor representatives were angered: Urban warned that although the unions might at present be prostrate because of the employers' pro-inflation policies, they would still recover to retaliate more effectively than in 1918. Max Cohen, the 1919 advocate of an economic parliament, a government appointee to the RWR and among the most conservative SPD members, charged that the employers had not even negotiated in good faith before resorting to lock-outs, "but merely dictated your will to the workers." Franz Roehr, representing the railroad workers,

[72] Seeckt cited in Preller, *Sozialpolitik*, p. 312. Employers' measures described in *ibid.*, pp. 315–316; Hartwich, *Arbeitsmarkt*, pp. 28, 34, 102, 221, 329; and Johannes Ewerling, *Vom Einigungsamt zum Treuhänder der Arbeit. Eine Skizze der Entwicklung des deutschen Schlichtungswesens und der auf Grund der neuen Arbeitsverfassung an seine Stelle getretenen Einrichtungen* (Düsseldorf, 1935), pp. 16–17, 20–21. Cf. Vereinigung der deutschen Arbeitgeberverbände, "Übersicht über Vereinbarungen und Schiedssprüche betreffend Arbeitszeitverlängerung, 15. 4. 24." Bergbau Archiv, Bochum: 15 (Fachgruppe Bergbau)/67, which reported that only 20 percent of workers facing contract renegotiation had reached agreements without arbitration and noted, too, that manufacturers were less zealous in imposing longer hours than managers in mining and heavy industry.

[73] DZA, Potsdam: 70 Ze 1 (ZAG)/ vol. 31/1, Geschäftsführender Vorstand session, February 15, 1924, pp. 39 ff.; cf. Leipart's comments at November 27, 1923, meeting, pp. 65 ff.

pointed out that new wages were being calculated according to dollar equivalents of the old mark wage rates, although internal prices had recently leapt far more rapidly.[74] Labor members of the Reich Economic Council, however, could do no more than vent frustrations. Industry was preoccupied with its export performance in the wake of mark stabilization. A fortnight after the RWR meeting, Bücher told the Main Committee of the Reichsverband that employers were determined "that price cuts must be continued, that they could be carried out only if it were possible to pay officials, salaried employees, and wage earners such low salaries and wages that purchasing power would sink considerably." Unfortunately, the deflationary process had already slowed since December, but "in consideration of the community as a whole," everyone had to make further sacrifices according to his subsistence level.[75]

The major constraint upon industry was its own lack of credit and operating funds.[76] Ruhr concerns, especially needed Berlin's help to facilitate renewed production under the MICUM agreements; hence industry could not simply ignore government arbitration as some businessmen proposed. The employers reproached labor for relying on compulsory arbitration when they supposedly believed in free collective bargaining. Despite their complaints, however, the employers had to submit to the arbitration ordinance. This legal protection as well as Berlin's control of credits ensured that labor's organization was not totally dismantled in early 1924. Nonetheless, the short-term sacrifices were harsh. Between late 1923 and the spring of 1924 the unions felt too feeble even to defend the impartial nature of the ZAG machinery, which they now feared was becoming just another agency to push for harsh labor settlements. After disputes in February and March as to whether collapse of the joint industry-labor board would entail disavowing all the remaining provisions of the original Stinnes-Legien agreement, the unions walked out in April. The employers seized upon the occasion to declare that the Arbeitsgemeinschaft was henceforth

[74] DZA, Potsdam: RWR/525, Sozialpolitischer Ausschuss, January 18, 1924, pp. 177–180 (Habersbrunner), p. 233 (Bücher), p. 183 (Riedel), pp. 187–190 (Urban), pp. 194–195 (Max Cohen), pp. 245–246 (Roehr).

[75] Bücher, *Finanz- und Wirtschaftsentwicklung*, pp. 52–53. In economic terms, the results of the stabilization crisis proved harsh but not permanently disastrous. Wage levels were lower than in peacetime, and more strike days were lost in 1924 than ever before, generally in protest against wage cuts. But real wages had risen again by the end of the year. See Preller, *Sozialpolitik*, p. 317.

[76] See cabinet discussions of industry's lack of credits: GFM: ARK, Kabinettsprotokolle, January 21, 1924; 3491/1751/758672–758677; also Stresemann's prediction of "collapse," in the cabinet meeting of May 15, *ibid.*, 3491/1753/760751; and Reparations Commission Report, cited Chapter vi, n. 168. For union recovery: Preller, *Sozialpolitik*, p. 298.

defunct, thus virtually ending that five-year experiment in partial labor-management cooperation.[77]

Likewise, inside the factories, the Factory Councils (*Betriebsräte*) were also forced to capitulate to management's demands in the crisis. In the disillusion with Factory Council performance, nominations for renewing *Räte* offices were often allowed to lapse or were not voted upon. The elections that did take place testified to the general demoralization or radicalization of the working class. Given unemployment, all Factory Council elections were liable to show a drop in votes, but it was the differential fall-off that was revealing. In the Ruhr the Catholic unions' vote declined from 78,000 in 1922 to 60,000 in 1924 (down 23 percent). The socialist unions fell heavily from 125,000 up through 1922 to 75,000 (down 40 percent), while the Communist-syndicalist slates dropped only from 117,000 to 97,000 (down 17 percent). Among railroad workers the total vote also declined, as did employment, but the SPD-oriented unions dropped from 302,000 to 170,000 (down 44 percent), the Catholic unions from 45,000 to 30,000 (down 33 percent), while the Communist-affiliated organizations, which had not even taken part in the elections in 1922, captured 56,000 votes in 1924. The rate of abstention did not change greatly—perhaps because the large size of the rail network and the simultaneous voting kept interest high—but the radicalization of the membership was significant.[78]

Early 1924 thus undercut the bases of the German labor-state compromise that had emerged in 1919, setting back the trade unions and social democracy. Within the factory, too, labor relationships apparently reverted to the older patriarchal relationships of the pre-1914 era.[79] Observers tended to see only a new efficiency: the labor force per plant declined and stayed down, while productivity and labor

[77] See the protocols of the ZAG Geschäftsführender Ausschuss of November 27, 1923, February 15, 1924, and March 3, 1924, in DZA: Potsdam: ZAG/ 31/1, esp. pp. 21–25, 39 ff., 65 ff. Also Hartwich, *Arbeitsmarkt*, p. 345. For the bitter labor conflicts in the Ruhr during the spring of 1924, see Bergbau Archiv, Bochum: 13 (Zechen-Verband)/549, "Zusammenstellung von Material über die Entwicklung des Streiks im Ruhrbergbau im Mai 1924." From May 6 to 27, workers struck unsuccessfully against the longer work week that employers had imposed: 68 to 74 hours for cokework employees, a full 48 hours underground for miners. Workers did secure some wage hikes, however. Cf. Rundschreiben 28 to Fachgruppe Bergbau employers, May 28, 1924, in Bergbau Archiv 15/200.

[78] Adam Stuempfig, *Die Stellung der Arbeitnehmerschaft Bayerns zum Betriebsrätegesetz* (Munich, 1927), pp. 24–25, 36 ff.; Josef Gerlach, *Die Betriebsvertretungsgedanke in seiner Entwicklung und praktischer Verwirklichung* (Giessen, 1930), pp. 25–29, 69 ff. Also, on Communist strength in the Ruhr *Betriebsräte* elections; see Alfred Krueger, "Die Wahlbewegung im Rheine und Ruhrgebiet," *BT*, May 1, 1924, p.m. This radicalization, by the way, was reversed in the latter 1920's as SPD and Catholic union delegates regained strength.

[79] Otto Neuloh, *Die Betriebsverfassung*, pp. 106, 220.

hours went up. But efficiency was purchased at a price: "In the Ruhr, only after 1923 did discipline become more rigid, and indeed so harsh that at times the workers defended themselves against it."[80] The reaction could not remain so intense for long; even by March employers were becoming more conciliatory, as their own credit situation further deteriorated and union funds began a recovery. Nonetheless, the working class had made significant sacrifices: the eight-hour day, the self-confidence of 1919, the sense of Weimar as a labor state. The arbitration institutions remained, wages rose again, but the special position won by unions in the war and the revolution was revealed as highly vulnerable.

The factory-council balloting, with its revealing pattern of combined abstentionism and radicalization, forecast the overall changes on the left in the upcoming parliamentary elections. The Social Democrats suffered at the polls, much as their affiliated unions had been hit in the factories. Similarly, the People's Party, which Stresemann had generally held on course as a moderate political force, was badly hurt as many adherents apparently deserted it for the rightist DNVP. The major quantitative changes of the 1924 elections—the growth of the Communists and Nationalists—thus indicated an underlying social polarization. The Democratic Party, too, was hard hit, losing almost 30 percent of its 1920 vote, probably to the DVP, or perhaps to the Nationalists directly.[81] With the exception, however, of the Democrats'

[80] Enquête-Ausschuss, IV. Unterausschuss, Bd. 2, *Die Arbeitsverhältnisse im Steinkohlenbergbau*, p. 262. Part of the productivity increase also lay in the capital investment carried on during the inflation and thereafter in the so-called rationalization. See Enquête-Ausschuss, IV. Unterausschuss, Bd. 7, *Die Arbeitsleistung in Stahl-und Walzwerke und ihre Abhängigkeit von Arbeitszeit, Arbeitslohn und anderen Faktoren* (Berlin, 1930), pp. 72 ff., 160–161.

[81]

	Party	1919	1920	May 1924
"Marxist"	USPD and/or KPD:	2,317,300	5,636,267	3,928,174
	SPD/VSPD	11,509,100	6,104,398	6,008,900
		13,826,400	11,740,665	9,937,074
	DDP	5,641,800	2,333,700	1,655,049
	DVP	1,282,384	3,919,446	2,694,317
	DNVP	2,415,721	4,249,100	5,696,368
	Zentrum	5,980,200	3,845,001	3,914,379
	Deutsch-völkische Freiheitspartei	——	——	1,918,310
	Others	132,500	332,100	1,165,900 (333,423 Dt. Soz.)

Electoral statistics from *Statistik des deutschen Reiches*, Bd. 315 (Berlin, 1925) Unless otherwise noted, all figures are from this source.

450

collapse in Bavaria because of special circumstances, their loss was less catastrophic than it had been when their support was halved in the June 1920 elections. This may well have been because the Democrats had been less conspicuous as allies of the Social Democrats in 1923 than during the year after the revolution.

The assault on the SPD was reflected in other results, too—either in abstention or as a direct leftist migration to the new proto-Nazi Racial Freedom Party. The success of the Racists, with 6.5 percent of the popular vote and 32 Reichstag seats, is usually viewed as the first Nazi electoral breakthrough, even though Hitler himself disliked the idea of competing in the spring 1924 election. The 1924 vote cannot be explained by the now classical model of middle-class radicalization that is usually applied to the Nazi successes of 1930–1933. While in certain districts this phenomenon played a role, in others the Nazi successes could have been produced only by a strong wave of abstentions among the radical left coupled with a corresponding increase on the radical right, or else by the direct migration of voters from one extreme to the other.

The notion that radical voters may have migrated directly from the "Marxist" parties to the Racial Freedom coalitions is startling in light of theories of middle-class extremism, but cannot be excluded. In contrast to the 1930–1933 period, when the Nazis gained at the cost of the other bourgeois parties—the DNVP, DVP, and the successor to the German Democrats—in the 1924 elections Nationalists and Racists *both* increased their votes simultaneously. And whereas during the elections from 1928 through November 1932, the combined "Marxist" vote rose in absolute numbers (although it fell in percentage terms owing to growth of the electorate), in 1924 it dropped in both absolute and percentage terms. A third general point: in the last years of Weimar the size of the electorate increased, but the number of potential voters who actually participated rose even more. In 1924, however, the number of voters increased more slowly and fell in percentage terms in respect to those qualified.[82] In short, in contrast to the late Weimar Republic, the 1924 racist vote emerged without an abandon-

82

Year	1919	1920	1924 (1)	1924 (2)
Eligible voters	36,766,500	35,949,800	38,375,000	38,987,300
Voting (percent)	30,400,300	28,196,300	29,281,800	30,290,100
	= 82.7	= 78.4	= 76.3	= 77.69
Year	1928	1930	1932 (1)	1932 (2)
Eligible voters	41,224,700	42,957,700	44,373,700	44,373,706
Voting (percent)	30,753,300	34,970,900	36,882,400	38,471,800
	= 74.60	= 81.41	= 83.39	= 79.93

ment of the bourgeois parties (outside of Franconia) and without a massive increase in voting participation.

The inference of left-to-right migration naturally depends upon excluding consideration of some party shifts as highly improbable. Presumably, voters could wander among the Marxist parties, and in 1924, adherents of the former USPD, which had split to left and right, had to choose between the Communists and Social Democrats. (A few local USPD organizations continued in 1924, but they did very poorly.) Thus both KPD and VSPD emerged stronger than they had in 1920, although the aggregate total of all Marxist groups—both in percentage and absolute terms—fell below the previous vote for the three social-istic alternatives. Given German voting patterns, it seems doubtful that working-class voters chose any of the bourgeois parties to their right in any significant number; disgruntled proletarian electors prob-ably either stayed at home or flirted with pseudo-radical alternatives. The bourgeois parties seem to have formed a pool, much as the Marx-ists did. Where the DDP and/or the DVP lost, the DNVP or its affili-ates gained. In a few places, such as Berlin, the National Liberal secession group benefited; in other areas agrarian slates emerged. Most generally, the political conditions that produced a Marxist collapse led to a relative racist victory. In the Catholic Rhineland, to cite the nega-tive correlation, Marxists fell little and racists gained little; here, of course, many working-class voters adhered to Catholic labor unions and the Center Party and remained constant in their loyalties. In areas such as Potsdam II (including western Berlin and part of Branden-burg), Potsdam I (eastern Brandenburg), Frankfurt an der Oder, East Prussia, Breslau, Thuringia, and Chemnitz, significant socialist losses— drops of 10 percent of the electorate or more—were found alongside significant racist gains.

Closer examination of individual areas sometimes confirms the idea of a Marxist migration, sometimes prevents more than an indeterminate calculation about either Marxist abstentions or migration. In urban, residential Charlottenburg (Potsdam II), for example, racists won 28,000 votes while the Marxist parties lost 28,000. What lends extra plausibility to the idea of a switch from extreme left to radical right is that although the DVP and DDP together lost 17,000 votes, the DNVP picked up the same number. In the city of Breslau, the racists won 22,-000 and the ideologically affiliated Deutsch-Soziale, 19,000—a total of 41,000 new votes for anticapitalist, anti-Semitic alternatives. The Prot-estant bourgeois parties gained in aggregrate 9 percent over 1920. But despite the fact that the electorate increased by 18,000, there were 36,000 fewer votes for the two socialistic parties. If there was no direct switch among radical alternatives, then a highly selective abstention forms the only explanation of the results. Throughout Germany a massive generation of voters, born between 1901 and 1904, was now flowing into the voters' pool. Conceivably, those of a Marxist family background might have sat the election out in disgust, along with their parents, but it seems unlikely.[83]

In addition to these clear cases supporting the hypothesis of radical abstention or a direct shift from one electoral pole to the other, there are further suggestive but less determinative cases. In Merseburg, racists gained 9.4 percent, while the socialist groups dropped 13 percent. In the city district of Naumburg, the racists won 28 percent of 29,000 voters. But although the socialist parties lost 14 percent of the total, the aggregate bourgeois parties also lost 17 percent. Similarly, in Thuringia, the picture is clouded. Marxists dropped from 48 to 40 percent of the electorate, a loss of 56,000 votes. Conservative alternatives (DNVP, Bavarian Peasant League, and Landbund) rose 40,000, while the DDP and DVP fell by 56,000 votes. Voting participation overall rose 60,000 in this district of 1 million. The Nazi vote might have borrowed from former radical strength on the left, might have come from the new voters, might have derived from the bourgeois losses. (Analysis of rural and urban voting, which might indicate more closely the sources of racist votes, is difficult for 1924, since the breakdowns by size of voting district that were provided for 1920 were omitted in the later statistics. In any case, 1924's racists, outside Franconia and Mecklenburg, performed strongly in the urban centers, notably Breslau.)

Finally, one must note those areas where the racists, for local reasons, did benefit from a radicalized middle-class vote. In Mecklenburg the Deutsch-völkische Partei won 21 percent of the vote, which was clearly drawn from the bourgeois parties. Mecklenburg, however, was the home province of the new group's northern leader and secessionist from the Nationalists, Albrecht von Graefe. Presumably he carried the DNVP organization with him. In Franconia, with a fifth of the electorate voting racist, the bourgeois parties dropped far more drastically than the Marxists, but here the religious issue seems to have dominated politics. Voters in northern Bavaria were traditionally hostile to the political Catholicism that dominated Bavaria as a whole. With the

---

[83] For age profiles, see *Statistik des deutschen Reiches*, Bd. 315, part VI. Statistical models for inferring voter migration have been developed, and I have sought to test the above hypotheses with a one-in-ten sample of Germany's thousand-odd electoral districts. But while the inferential model yields results for two-party systems, the six-to-seven party situation resisted significant computational analysis.

notoriously anti-Catholic General Ludendorff at the head of the ticket, the Racial Freedom Party may have appeared as a new and more effective Protestant alternative for the Franconians. In southern Bavaria (Upper and Lower), similar circumstances played some role, but a wave of massive abstentions also marked the voting. In fact, the racist vote in Bavaria had already ebbed since the Landtag elections in February, thus portending some return to normalization.

Thus three major patterns marked the Socialist (and the racist) vote in 1924; first, the Rhineland, where Catholic working-class voters helped stabilize the electoral situation and racists made few inroads; second, the regions of central Germany, Brandenburg, the agrarian East, and northern Silesia, where racist success seems to have benefited from the votes or abstentions of a homeless left; finally, Mecklenburg and Bavaria, where the racists scored smashing victories as products of preeminently local resentments.

The vote also reflects the nature of the Racial Freedom Party as it appeared in 1924. If former left-wing voters could migrate to racism, the new party must have appeared as a radical alternative with its intemperate attacks upon capitalism as well as upon Jews and Marxism. To working-class radicals who had been offered the "Schlageter line" of revolutionary nationalism during the Ruhr crisis, the jump to the radical right was not difficult. Nor had anti-Semitism been lacking in the Communist Party's rhetoric. Not until the Berlin Transport Workers' strike in the fall of 1932 did the radicalism of left and right share so intense a degree of common outrage against the liberal, capitalist *status quo*.[84]

In 1924, the SPD suffered as much as a component of the liberal, capitalist order as an opponent of it. The 1924 elections hurt the party in two ways. The left-wing abstentions, the vote for the Communists and possibly the radical right indicated a working-class rejection of the SPD's own involvement with the Weimar system, especially of its 1923 participation alongside bourgeois groups in the management of the economic and political order. The elections mobilized the electorate for a radical, if crude critique of the *joint* prominence of industry and labor in the German Republic.

At the same time, however, the elections reduced the power of labor *vis-à-vis* industry and big agriculture. If left-wing opponents of the SPD wanted to protest against the organized capitalism that coopted even labor leadership, their vote worked at cross-purposes. For the

---

[84] Indeed, the Nationalists tried to lump together their racist competitors with the Marxists. See *BT*, April 24, p.m., p. 3, "Vom Kampfplatz der Parteien . . . Die feindlichen Brüder."

elections strengthened the agrarian and industrial components of the Weimar system one-sidedly. The SPD did, indeed, form part of a political economy based on interest-group power, but it simultaneously worked to keep that political economy nonauthoritarian and more humane. Both aspects of its role in the Weimar state were undercut by the May elections.

From a position of supremacy in 1919, the Social Democratic electorate and overlapping trade-union membership had settled into a position of parity between 1920 and 1923. Their economic influence was confined to the Factory Councils, the Arbeitsgemeinschaft, or the advisory Reich Economic Council. The SPD was either outside the government or included in it only when industry's representatives also shared power. Now the electoral results of 1924 and the attrition of labor strength in the factories threatened even the claim to parity. Weimar had shed its origins as a socialist and revolutionary regime, had emerged as a "laborist" welfare-state, and now seemed likely to come almost prevailingly under the control of the industrialists, working behind the facade of party institutions.

Yet there were limits both to the influence of the right and to the decline of the Social Democrats. The elections did not automatically open the way to the Nationalists any more than the fall of Stresemann as Chancellor had done six months earlier. The foreign policy concerns of the moderates as well as the DNVP's tactical failures led ultimately to reconstruction of the middle-party coalition. The Nationalists had rashly condemned the Experts' report during the campaign; the SPD hoped to exploit the issue to reestablish their connections with the Center.[85] Positions on the Dawes report were probably not decisive for the electoral results. Domestic issues seemed paramount both to Anton Erkellenz of the Democratic Party, who blamed his group's losses on poor organization and the firing of government functionaries during the recent period of austerity, and to a DNVP commentator who credited his party's success to middle-class anger at the stiff new tax policies and to hopes for higher revaluation.[86] On the other hand, the Nationalists' brusque condemnation of the Experts' plan made their postelectoral bargaining situation difficult. Although the tension between the Socialists and People's Party precluded rebuilding a Great Coalition, a bourgeois government that united the Democratic Party and the Nationalists also seemed unlikely. Nor were the Center and People's

[85] Cf. Stürmer, *Koalition und Opposition*, pp. 38–48.
[86] Erkellenz to DDP Zentralvorstand, May 21, 1924, in NSDAP, Hauptarchiv/ f. 721. Bruns to Westarp, May 8, 1924, in Westarp Nachlass, Gaertringen.

Party yet prepared to build a coalition with the DNVP alone.[87] The political commentator for the *Tageblatt* exaggerated when he called the electoral results a "Pyrrhic victory for the right," but he was correct about the setbacks for DNVP hopes, which even Nationalists recognized. "Only someone who is blind or dishonest," Bruns told Westarp, "can speak of a DNVP victory."[88]

Even though the right wing of the People's Party badly wanted a coalition with the Nationalists, the Dawes issue kept the would-be partners apart. Few felt that the DNVP could afford to remain intractable; the DVP Minister of the Interior, Karl Jarres, predicted in the cabinet that the Nationalists must "ultimately approve."[89] But first the DNVP provocatively demanded on May 21 that ex-Admiral Tirpitz be designated Chancellor. Then they indicated that while in return for the Chancellorship they would permit reparations negotiations to go forward, they would not agree to accept the Dawes plan in advance. This proved too much: the Center Party had decided not to enter a ministry headed by a Nationalist Chancellor, and the DNVP assurances on the Dawes report were far too conditional. As Koch-Weser reported to the DDP Executive, "a huge gulf" persisted over foreign policy; and after the middle-party negotiators failed to get any further DNVP assurances on the Dawes plan May 24, the negotiations lapsed.[90] Stresemann accepted this result happily enough, and declared that the Nationalists would be serious about joining a cabinet

---

[87]   POSSIBLE PARTY COMBINATIONS IN THE NEW REICHSTAG

Parties	Seats	Coalitions
Communists	62	1) "Great Coalition": a majority, but
Social Democrats	100	rejected by DVP.
Democrats	28	2) Minority "middle-party" cabinet:
People's Party	44	requires SPD or DNVP support for
Center (Z)	65	a majority, and support from both
Bavarian People's Party	16	for a two-thirds (Dawes plan) vote.
Nationalists	96 + 10 affiliated	
Others	19	3) Bourgeois party majority: DDP, DVP, Z, DNVP (plus BVP and "others"). Perhaps feasible without the DDP, but the Center and
Völkisch	32	
Total	472	DVP excluded this solution.

[88] Bruns report, Westarp Nachlass; Erich Dombrowski, "Der Sieg der Verlegenheit," *BT*, May 6, a.m.

[89] Meeting of DVP Reichstagsfraktion and Parteivorstand, May 14; Stresemann, *Vermächtnis*, I, p. 408; Thimme, *Stresemann*, p. 73; GFM: ARK, Kabinettsprotokolle, May 15 and May 16, 1924, 3491/1753/760749 ff. and 760766–760770.

[90] Stresemann, *Vermächtnis*, I, pp. 408–410; NSDAP Hauptarchiv/f. 721; Zentralvorstand meeting of May 21, 1924.

only after the Dawes plan had become a *fait accompli* in the autumn.[91] But within his own party Jarres and Ernst Scholz, leader of the parliamentary group, were not yet ready to abandon their efforts. Prodded by Jarres' unwillingness that the old ministry should go before the new Reichstag, the cabinet resigned, and Marx was officially asked by Ebert to ascertain what cabinet could be formed "on the broadest bourgeois base." While the DVP right wing and the Center seemed willing to sacrifice Stresemann to the Nationalists, the renewed parleys collapsed when the DNVP demanded an end to the Great Coalition within Prussia. Even Generals Seeckt and Schleicher, who sought to mediate, could not bridge the gap between the parties.[92]

Stresemann had no regrets, nor did Chancellor Marx, who was anxious to preserve the pivotal cabinet role of the Center. Neither did the Democrats, who faced political isolation if a right-wing cabinet emerged. The Democrats had agonized over their alternatives on May 21 and 24. Erkellenz, Koch-Weser, and others felt that the Nationalists must eventually accept the Dawes report and join a new ministry, but that the DDP would still have to remain outside lest it be drawn to the right. Erkellenz described the Party's task as "the breaking of the German Nationalist wave." Since 1919 the DDP had conceived its *raison d'être* as being the only force acting against polarization, the bridge between left and right. Alas, no one felt compelled to use the bridge any longer.[93]

The Socialists remained separated from the new cabinet because of persisting differences of social and economic policy, but they were just as happy to avoid the responsibilities of government which had lost them votes to the Communists.[94] It was clear that they would support the Dawes settlement; meanwhile their votes allowed revival of the minority middle-party coalition. Between 1924 and 1928, the support of the SPD was to remain essential for Stresemann's foreign policy. This fact made the electoral results only one input into the formation of cabinet coalitions. Parliamentary majorities remained less

[91] GFM: ARK, Kabinettsprotokolle, May 24, 1924, p.m., 3491/1753/760865.
[92] For DVP attitudes: Hergt to Scholz June 2, 1924, in DZA, Potsdam, DNVP papers, vol. 77; cited Thimme, *Stresemann*, p. 75, n. 288. For the issue of the Prussian Great Coalition, see Stresemann's July 6 report to the DVP executive in BA, Koblenz: R 45 II/39, p. 281; also Stresemann, *Vermächtnis*, I, p. 412; GFM: ARK, Kabinettsprotokolle, June 3, 1924, 3491/1753/760924 ff.; and Stürmer, *Koalition und Opposition*, pp. 44–46. For the generals' intervention, see Friedrich von Rabenau, *Seeckt. Aus seinem Leben, 1918–1936* (Leipzig, 1940), p. 403; Francis Carsten, *Die Reichswehr in der deutschen Politik (1918–1933)* (Cologne and Berlin, 1965), p. 224; Hans Meier-Welcker, *Seeckt* (Frankfurt, 1967), pp. 445–446.
[93] DDP Zentralvorstand meetings of May 21 and May 24, 1924, in NSDAP Hauptarchiv/f. 721.
[94] *Vorwärts*, June 1, 1924, cited Stürmer, *Koalition und Opposition*, p. 47.

a consequence of general elections than of the logical permutations imposed by cross-cutting issues and socioeconomic interests. The representatives of the working class were needed for Stresemann's foreign policy; despite Stresemann's earnest hopes, the DNVP could not bring itself to support détente with any consistency. On the other hand, the pro-business forces in Stresemann's own party refused to sanction governments that included the Social Democrats during a period when tariffs, working time, and social insurance were up for decision. Hence, the elections weakened labor, but it was still a necessary supporter of any coalition seeking easier relations with the West. The right had been strengthened electorally, but it remained internally divided over its interest-group priorities—thus a final political equilibrium was still elusive, and stable alignments had yet to be established.

THE LIMITS OF THE CARTEL DES GAUCHES

While German voters turned away from Social Democrats and bourgeois moderates, the French electorate ostensibly moved to the left on May 11. The elections registered a stunning defeat for the Bloc National, primarily because the Bloc had all but disintegrated. Its success in 1919 had depended upon neutralizing the Radical Socialists, either by absorbing them in broad centrist coalitions or isolating them between the Socialists and the right. By 1922 it was becoming clear that this configuration was not to be repeated: Radical Socialists and SFIO were working toward an electoral alliance, while the conservative forces also grew more militant. In Paris the Radicals felt that they were being excluded from important Chamber commissions and from the chance to lead the committee work on important legislation.[95] In traditionalist departments, the right resumed its earlier clericalism, thus encouraging, according to the prefects, "a rapprochement . . . among all the elements of the left on the basis of a defense of secular principles." In March 1923, the prefects reported that even the *modérés* "regard the Bloc National label as having had its day."[96] Although the Ruhr conflict initially imposed a party truce, the Radical Socialists slowly edged away from Poincaré's majority, and by voting against the Ministry's foreign policy on January 11, 1924, made their break final.[97]

[95] Bibliothèque de Documentation Internationale Contemporaine, Lucien Lamoureux, "Souvenirs politiques, 1919–1940," MS microfilm, p. 639.

[96] AN, Paris: F IC III, "Rapports sur l'esprit public et les élections," Box 1127, Prefect of Finistère, March 31, 1924; Box 1125, Prefect of the Ain, March 18, 1923.

[97] JOC, 1924, pp. 61–80, 87 (January 11); 152–175, 185 (January 18). Cf. Michel Soulié, *La vie politique d'Edouard Herriot* (Paris, 1962), p. 130.

The end of the German passive resistance in September 1923 enhanced government prestige but gave the Bloc National no lasting political rewards. Millerand hoped to capitalize on that success by calling new elections immediately—a step no President had dared to take since the ill-fated MacMahon—and at Évreux he endorsed the majority he had helped elect in November 1919. Throughout the fall Millerand badgered the premier with complaints about the passiveness of the Minister of the Interior, Manoury, in preparing for the election, and labeled his indifference a public peril. In mid-October, the editor of the *Journée Industrielle* also hinted that Poincaré should speak out for the Bloc National and guide the majority toward a common program: six weeks later *L'Echo de Paris* urged that internal politics be "conducted, directed, and secured" to support the foreign policy supposedly approved by the entire country.[98]

What really threatened the majority, however, was not the premier's hands-off attitude, but the new burst of inflation as winter came in. Early warnings from the prefects emphasized the discontent of the minor officials, whose recent pay raises of Fr.1800 per year (then about $100) fell far short of their demands.[99] The public was angry at supposed government indifference to the swift increase in prices: "Examination of the state of public opinion," reported the prefect of Marseilles, "reveals how sensitive it is to the incessant rise in the cost of living," a finding he accented a month later with the warning that lower-ranking public officials would vote for left-wing candidates.[100] As early as November 1923, the prefect in Bordeaux predicted serious political reverses unless the inflation was "dammed up": "The attitude of postal employees, construction workers, grade school teachers, and the personnel of the financial administration makes me really apprehensive about the elections of 1924."[101]

With the attack upon the franc that began in late December, political disaffection became graver. At first commentators termed the sudden depreciation "economically absurd,"[102] but by January it developed into a full-scale monetary crisis that threatened to "overturn" parliamentary life.[103] From 85.6 per pound sterling the day after the New

[98] Alexandre Millerand, "Mes souvenirs (1859–1941)" MS pp. 116–120; Raoul Persil, *Alexandre Millerand* (Paris, 1949), pp. 150–152. *JI*, October 13, 1923. Garapon, "L'action nécessaire," *L'Echo de Paris*, December 1, 1923; cf. the same author's article in *ibid.*, January 18, 1924.

[99] AN, Paris: F IC III, Box 1125, Allier, December 1923; also Hautes-Alpes, December 14, 1923.

[100] *Ibid.*, Box 1126, Bouches-du-Rhône, December 1923 and January 1924. Cf. Box 1130, the report from Maine-et-Loire, December 1923.

[101] *Ibid.*, Box 1128, Gironde, November 19, 1923.

[102] Lucien Romier, "De grace, redressez-vous!" *JI*, December 21, 1923.

[103] François-Albert, "Chronique politique," *RPP*, 118, February 10, 1924, p. 308.

Year, the franc fell after a sharp selling wave on January 14 to 95.5 by January 24. January's depreciation initiated a more massive flight from the currency, which swept it from 100 to 123 between late February and March 8. Speculators based in Vienna or Amsterdam saw the franc as vulnerable once the mark was stabilized. By massive offerings of French currency for future delivery, they provoked uneasy holders of francs to unload their balances.[104]

The crisis was aggravated by the extreme reluctance of the Bank of France to assist any counteraction. The Governor and Regents hesitated to mobilize any of their $800 million in reserves to secure foreign loans or to lend funds to the Treasury and thereby overrun the stipulated limits on advances to the state. Even less would the Bank buy francs itself. In part it was reluctant to legitimize the depreciation of the currency by buying it at a depleted value. It also felt that without fiscal retrenchment, reserves would merely be squandered in futile support actions.[105] Neither was Poincaré personally happy about the idea of the Bank's intervention. With an innate distrust of bankers and modern finance operations, he pointed out to Robineau, the Governor, that it was not the business of France's great central bank "to mess about on the exchanges."[106]

But as the franc fell precipitously in early March, the conventional hands-off attitude became untenable. Maurice Bokanowski, the *rappor-*

[104] On the background of the crisis, see Georges Lachapelle, *Le crédit public*, 2 vols. (Paris, 1932), ii, pp. 164 ff., and the same author's *Les batailles du franc* (Paris, 1928), pp. 115 ff.; Eleanor Lansing Dulles, *The French Franc, 1914–1928* (New York, 1929), pp. 170 ff. The mechanics of the speculation were described in a note by A. Salomon Cahen to Maurice Bokanowski, *Rapporteur* of the Chamber Finance Commission, February 29, 1924. Bokanowski was the brother-in-law of Cahen's banking partner, Robert Wolff; he reproduced portions of the note in his second report on the government's finance bill: JOC: Doc. Parl. Annèxe 7353, pp. 639–644. Cf. the picturesque details of Raymond Philippe, an associate of Lazard Frères, in *Le drame financier de 1924–28* (Paris, 1931), pp. 25 ff.; and on the forward exchange as it functioned in 1924, James Harvey Rogers, *The Process of Inflation in France, 1914–1927* (New York, 1929), pp. 126–127, 237–243. For an evaluation of the German role in the speculation, which was often alleged to be a contributing factor, see Stephen A. Schuker, "The French Financial Crisis and the Adoption of the Dawes Plan, 1924," Diss. (Cambridge, Mass., 1969), pp. 106 ff.

[105] Hostile to the Bank of France are Robert Wolff, *Économie et finances de la France, passé et avenir* (New York, 1943), p. 156; David B. Goldey, "The Disintegration of the Cartel des Gauches and the Politics of French Government Finance, 1924–1928," (Diss., Oxford, 1964); cf. also Millerand, "Mes souvenirs," MS, pp. 116–120. More favorable judgments are in Lachapelle, *Le crédit public*, ii, pp. 167–171, and *Les batailles du franc*, pp. 117–129.

[106] F. François-Marsal, "Souvenirs: La crise présidentielle et l'éviction de Millerand," MS memoir of 25 pages written retrospectively for his son Claude, who communicated it for consultation.

teur of the Chamber Finance Commission, representatives of the important private firm of Lazard Frères, and Octave Homburg of the Banque de l'Union Parisienne, a personal acquaintance of the premier, all urged intervention and insisted that the gold reserves of the Bank of France be pledged to secure a massive foreign-exchange loan from J. P. Morgan. By the weekend of March 8/9, the franc could no longer find purchasers in New York, and even *Le Temps,* proverbially cautious and conservative, came out for supporting action.[107] But when Morgan insisted on French budgetary retrenchment as a condition for its support,[108] Poincaré initially bridled. Millerand's pressure for quick, decisive action was also offensive. Nevertheless, the President parried a threat of resignation by Poincaré and won his agreement to a confrontation with the Bank officials. At a Sunday morning conference at the Elysée, Millerand and Lasteyrie warned that without the Bank's aid there would be financial ruin and governmental crisis. Poincaré promised that the ministry would pursue its measures against inflation. Grudgingly, the Bank of France authorities agreed to pledge their reserves to guarantee the loans necessary for support of the franc.[109]

The immediate crisis ebbed when speculators quickly scurried to cover their short sales and the franc shot upward.[110] But its effect upon

[107] "La crise des changes," *Le Temps,* March 9, 1924. See also Wolff, *Économie et finances,* p. 156; Philippe, *Drame financier,* pp. 34–36, critical of Lasteyrie's role, but cf. Lachapelle, *Les battailes du franc,* p. 125, and Louis Marcellin, *Voyage autour de la Chambre du 11 mai* (Paris, 1925), p. 36. For Homburg's intervention, see Octave Homburg, *Les coulisses de l'histoire, souvenirs 1898–1928* (Paris, 1938), pp. 258–260; Philippe, *Le drame financier,* pp. 33–34.

[108] For the Morgan role see Herman Harjes, Morgan representative in Paris, to "Jack" Morgan, March 13, 1924, in Baker Library: TWL/ 83–17. While the Morgan credit strengthened the hand of the interventionists, the firm also encouraged the Governor of the Bank of France to press Poincaré for action to balance the budget.

[109] Jacques Chastenet, *Raymond Poincaré* (Paris, 1948), p. 257; Millerand, "Mes Souvenirs," pp. 116–117; Lachapelle (best informed from the viewpoint of the Banque de France), *Battailes du franc,* pp. 127–129, and *Le crédit public,* pp. 160–173; Wolff, *Économie et finances de la France,* pp. 156–157; Philippe, *Le drame financier,* pp. 34–36; Schuker, "The French Financial Crisis," pp. 124 ff., the best synthesis to date. More than individual citations can suggest, Schuker's detailed narrative served as a guide to the crisis of the franc and the subsequent legislative debate on new taxes.

[110] The brusque rise of the franc produced new controversies. The Bank's initial instincts were to push the franc as high as possible. Lazard representatives, those of J. P. Morgan, and British advisers as well urged stabilizing at a lower rate so as not to hurt French exports and business activity. See, Philippe, *Drame financier,* pp. 47–51; Lachapelle, *Les batailles du franc,* p. 130; J. P. Morgan & Co. to Morgan, Harjes & Co. (and for Clémentel), March 29, 1924, in TWL 95–11. The left sought to term the new franc level as an artificially maintained "electoral franc," which would sacrifice prosperity for the prestige of the government and a temporary lowering of prices. Immediately after the election Boris, in the

voters was to be devastating. The currency emergency forced the government to take unpopular tax measures. It was no longer possible to postpone new revenue bills as the government had done a year before, when the Chamber balked at tax increases.[111]

In view of the upcoming elections, it was natural for the left to oppose the requested 20 percent across-the-board tax increase—the so-called *double décime*. Even to muster a majority of the center and right was an achievement. The Bloc National was unlikely to disavow Poincaré in the midst of a crisis, but to support heavier taxes meant accepting the unwelcome fiscal argument that the massive state deficit —long sanctioned under the guide of the "recoverable" or "German" budget—lay at the base of currency depreciation. In a virtuoso, if pretentious, presentation of the tax bills to the Chamber, Bokanowski explained that while reconstruction costs had been covered by non-inflationary, long-term loans, the interest payments had piled up until they amounted to one-quarter of the total government expenditure. These had been "charged" against future German payments rather than defrayed by taxes, and as a result acted as a powerful stimulus to inflation.[112]

This explanation might seem obvious enough, but it was unwelcome truth to those who might be called "monetarists" and was slow to find acceptance on the center and right.[113] The advances of the Bank of France to the state represented "the origin and fundamental cause of our monetary disorder," according to spokesmen for the traditional view. Before the war, went the monetarist argument, the central

---

Quotidien, accused Millerand of using the reserve funds for campaign purposes. See Soulié, *Vie politique d'Edouard Herriot,* p. 145; François-Marsal, "Crise présidentielle," pp. 10–11.

[111] "The vote of the [government] proposals was the formal and explicit condition for the opening of credits," Poincaré told Herriot in debate. JOC, 1924, p. 1483 (March 21).

[112] JOC: Doc. Parl., 1924, Annèxe 6080, p. 156; also Roger M. Haig, *The Public Finances of Post-war France* (New York, 1929), pp. 93–98. The regular budget, which had been brought into balance, amounted to about 23.6 billion francs for 1924. Noncapital items on the "recoverable" budget, including interest on reconstruction loans floated after 1921 (earlier interest charges had been integrated into the regular budget) and pensions totaled about 6 billion francs. The government bills envisaged a billion in "economies" and about 5 billion from the tax increases. The money spent on reconstruction by the end of 1919 totaled 28 billion in current francs; in 1920, 18 billion; in 1921, 22.3; in 1922, 17.4; in 1923, 15.0; in 1924, 10.5. Edmond Michel, *Les dommages de guerre de la France et leur réparation* (Paris, 1932), p. 555.

[113] On the change of opinion, see the favorable review of Charles Rist's book, *La déflation,* by Edgard Allix: *RPP,* cxviii, January 1924, pp. 111–115. Bokanowski evidently drew on Rist's examples to show the need for budgetary equilibrium *vis-à-vis* mere contraction of the note supply.

bank had never issued notes exceeding its gold reserves unless they were secured by "good, commercial values, representing wealth created and circulated *in advance*." But a bank note given to the state did not cover increments of real wealth: "It was a supplementary purchasing power that could be exerted only to the detriment of other notes emitted in the normal way . . . it is a paper money that borrows the appearance of a bank note to live . . . as a parasite on the healthy circulation."[114] Monetary recovery thus required a reduction of the note supply. "What must be done at any price," *Le Temps* wrote, "is to reimburse each year at least the 2 billion promised to the Bank of France."[115]

Monetarists ignored the possibility that repayment might have disastrous effects on employment. The provisions of the François-Marsal agreement, which stipulated the return of 2 billion francs per year, had been carried out only in 1921 and 1922. Repayment then had been possible because there was a recession, during which the demand for money and bank credit fell. But as good times returned, so did the demand for money, so that entrepreneurs and credit institutions declined to renew short-term government bonds, forcing the Treasury to draw instead upon advances from the central bank.[116] When opponents of the François-Marsal agreement warned that carrying out its provisions might provoke a renewed recession, the monetarists insisted that this was not the case. Treasury loans repaid to the Bank, they argued, could be put at the disposal of private industry.[117] This argument, however, overlooked the fact that the operations needed to reduce the quantity of money would have inhibited businesses from drawing on credit for expansion. Only if prices and wages could be reduced in proportion to the declining stock of money could the François-Marsal Convention have left the level of business activity undiminished.

It was the conventional wisdom in the 1920's that such wage and price cuts should be easy to make. In fact they were to prove difficult

[114] Jules Descamps, "La politique monétaire," in *Problèmes financiers d'après-guerre* (Paris, 1922), p. 73—a collection of lectures in early 1922 sponsored by the Anciens Élèves de l'École libre de Sciences politiques.

[115] *Le Temps*, January 14 and March 16, 1924, as cited in Marguerite Perrot, *La monnaie et l'opinion publique en France et Angleterre de 1924 à 1940* (Paris, 1955), pp. 126, 139.

[116] Edgard Allix, *RPP*, cxviii, January 10, 1924, pp. 111–115; Rogers, *Process of Inflation*, p. 220; Dulles, *The French Franc*, pp. 136 ff.; Lachapelle, *Le crédit public*, pp. 147 ff. For a favorable view of the Convention, see Descamps, "La politique monétaire," in *Problèmes financiers*, pp. 168 ff.

[117] *Idem*. Also Germain Martin, *Les finances publiques et la fortune privée de la France 1914–1925* (Paris, 1926), pp. 44, 45, 421–428.

without serious recession, as was demonstrated by those countries determined upon deflation, such as England and Italy after 1925. Moreover, to attempt monetary contraction at a time of inflationary fiscal policy and high demand, as in France between 1922 and 1924, would certainly prove ineffective if not harmful, futile if not recessionary. French monetarists tended to see contraction of the money supply as an alternative to higher taxation for the purpose of redressing the franc and the value of loans. But this represented a bourgeois utopia that even conservative governments could not achieve.

The permanent officials at the Ministry of Finance understood the contradiction of the monetarist position. Implicitly their periodic reports to the Minister rejected the monetarist thesis and urged that inflation be halted not by reducing circulation but by balancing the budget. As early as November 1922, Jean Parmentier, Directeur du Mouvement Général des Fonds, pointed out that the state had spent twice its tax receipts and had been spared a German-style inflation only because the French bond market had been so absorbent. But the public debt was held in short-term notes; and if it was inaccurate to label these bonds a "disguised inflation" (since the bonds represented savings), they still represented a "potential inflation." If not continually renewed, they could produce an actual inflation and panic whose first symptoms would consist of an exchange crisis. The government, however, could not reduce the note supply hastily, because that would provoke massive demands for cash from the holders of short-term bonds. Instead the government had to reverse the pattern of deficit financing. Parmentier even suggested a reduction of pensions and the suspension of indemnity payments for war damages until reparations had been recovered. No public official, however, would have endorsed such a position at the end of 1922 or early 1923. Indeed, the government withdrew its original plans for a *double décime* in April 1923, when the Chamber showed resistance.[118]

A year later French options had narrowed. The Ruhr occupation had produced only limited results. Poincaré now pointed to the new experts' plan and not the industrial riches of Germany as its reward;[119]

[118] Min. Fin. F^{30}/1275, Parmentier memos of November 1922 and February 17, 1923, reasserting need to cut reconstruction expenditures. Published *in extenso* in Lachapelle, *Le crédit public*, pp. 140–146, 151–153. Pierre de Moüy, Parmentier's successor, continued the same warnings into 1924; see the disclosures in JOC, 1925, pp. 2146–2147 (April 9); and Edouard Herriot, *Jadis. D'une guerre à l'autre 1914–1936* (Paris, 1952), pp. 201–205.

[119] See Poincaré's answer to Blum, JOC, 1924, p. 1015 (February 22, 1924, 2nd session). Cf. Pierre Miquel, *Poincaré* (Paris, 1961), pp. 475–476. The government could apparently show that the Ruhr occupation was at least yielding a

but it was clear that the plan would also diminish France's leverage over Germany. What is more, excessive dependence of Paris upon foreign credits to sustain the franc would undermine French freedom of action and negotiating strength. Fiscal retrenchment seemed unavoidable.

The cabinet's proposals of January 14, 1924, for dealing with the situation comprised four major measures. The most essential was the proposal for the *double décime*, the 20 percent increase in all taxes. Just as controversial, however, was the government's demand for "decree power" to institute cutbacks in administration recommended by a study commission of the Chamber. To please conservatives, denationalization of the match monopoly was recommended. In return, the right was asked to swallow new controls on the income from unregistered bearer securities that would strike primarily at the well-to-do— a proposal which, because it demanded that the Bloc National minister and railroad magnate from Lyon drop his personal objections, was termed by an SFIO wit *le sacrifice d'Isaac*.[120]

These bills aroused resistance from both sides of the Chamber. Radicals and Socialists attacked less the tax increases than the request for decree power to prune administrative costs by eliminating subprefectural offices and local courts. Not only did such cuts trespass on areas of Radical Socialist patronage, they also provoked from Herriot and Paul-Boncour a cascade of rhetoric about republican virtue. The vote on the decree laws, Herriot warned the Chamber, "will demarcate the boundaries of the republican party," and he persuaded the Radicals to purge Poincaré supporters from their ranks, among them Albert Sarraut, Minister of the Colonies, and brother of the editor of the powerful *Dépêche de Toulouse*. The attack on the match monopoly, too, excited prolonged debate—*l'allumette sauvera le franc* was Vincent Auriol's caustic summary—for the left professed to see in it a conservative drive against all government economic activities.[121]

---

net profit. As of January 10, 1924, this came to about 500 million paper francs, and totaled when completed about 386 million gold francs. See Michel, *Les dommages de guerre*, pp. 53–54; cf. also Lamoureux estimates of expenses concerning war damages in JOC: Doc. Parl., 1924, Annèxe n. 537, II, pp. 136–159, p. 2140.

[120] Bracke's comment, JOC, 1924, p. 317 (January 26, 1924, 2nd session). Government legislation, JOC: Doc. Parl., 1924, Nr. 6972. Introduced formally January 14, 1924; Poincaré presentation, January 17, JOC, 1924, pp. 122–140.

[121] Paul-Boncour speech, *ibid.*, February 4, pp. 486–492; Herriot speech, *ibid.*, February 5, pp. 500–503. Auriol speech, *ibid.*, February 26, 2nd session, p. 317. On Herriot's pressure within the Radical Socialist party to impose discipline on this issue, see Soulié, *Vie politique d'Edouard Herriot*, pp. 132–133. As one prefect

The most basic question remained the tax increase. What was actually at stake deserves analysis, because it casts light upon the incongruity of French political divisions and illuminates the parliamentary crisis of the mid-1920's. The left attacked the tax increases both on political and economic grounds: "Your new taxes are the ransom of the Ruhr policy," charged Blum, "of that policy which for more than two years has prevented any amicable and productive settlement of the reparations problem." Auriol claimed that the oscillations of the exchange rate were a product not of economic forces but of France's unilateral and aggressive foreign policy. New taxes, claimed the left, should not really have been needed; once necessary, they should be fairer. Instead of the general increase, Herriot called for a levy on capital. Other members of the opposition repeatedly demanded rigorous checking of tax returns in order to end evasion and the alleged "scandal of the liberated regions," a topic that occupied the Chamber at length. "By adding the *double décime* to existing taxes," Auriol pointed out, "you will multiply and consolidate the iniquity of the present taxes." The state's predominantly indirect sources of revenue, he argued, were already too regressive.[122]

These judgments, however, reflected only a partial awareness of how the tax system worked. In a society where evasion was rife, real tax burdens are hard to measure, but in the new world of the graduated income tax the conspicuously wealthy seemed relatively vulnerable. Ritual calls for an end to the progressive tax "on persons" could no longer be seriously entertained.[123] It was true that income taxes— the progressive surtax (*impôt général sur le revenu*), the 7.2 percent flat tax on wages and salaries, and the 12 percent tax on dividends and interests—together accounted for only about 20 percent of 1923's

---

noted, it was less an issue of doctrinal importance that agitated his region than concern over the local effects that the envisaged decrees might have. AN, Paris: F IC III, Box 1130, Prefect of La Manche, February 20, 1924.

[122] For Blum arguments, JOC, 1924, p. 1014 (February 22, 1924, 2nd session); also Gilbert Ziebura, *Léon Blum*, Bd. 1 (Berlin, 1963), pp. 259–260. Auriol speeches JOC, 1924, pp. 308 ff., p. 319 (January 26, 1924). For the idea of a capital levy: Soulié, *Vie politique d'Edouard Herriot*, p. 133, and JOC, 1924, pp. 697–700 (February 13). On the question of fraud, see Michel, *Les dommages de guerre*, p. 169, who admits that because of haste several billion of about 100 billion in property indemnities might have been saved.

[123] For tax nostalgia, see "Les 'Quatre Vieilles,'" *Le Temps*, January 15, 1924; and Germain Martin, *Les finances publiques de la France et la fortune privée*, pp. 72 ff. As late as 1923, de Lasteyrie talked of trying to recreate a system in which the fisc and the citizen required less direct confrontation. Cited in Haig, *Public Finances*, p. 81, n. 35. For the persistent French approval of evasion, see Jean Dubergé, *La psychologie sociale de l'impôt dans la France d'aujourd'hui* (Paris, 1961), pp. 91–103.

government revenues.[124] But inheritance and excess-profits taxes, plus other, less important charges, brought the direct tax receipts to about two-fifths of the total yield. Nor were all indirect taxes regressive: luxury and consumption taxes were targeted at upper-income citizens.

The income taxes, moreover, bore relatively heavily on a narrow base of well-to-do. According to the 1924 assessments for the income surtax, fewer than 90,000 taxpayers would pay 2 billion francs (a mean of about 2200 francs on minimal incomes of 50,000). One million odd others would pay a quarter-billion francs, and remaining citizens would escape.[125] At the time, it was estimated that this progressive income surtax had as its revenue base only one-sixth of the total national income. In fact, since the burdens of this tax fell so differentially even among the few subjected to it, virtually all of it rested upon a reported tax base of about one-eighth to one-tenth the national income.[126]

In theory the flat taxes should have hit lower incomes, but they did not broaden the base effectively. Of 5 million self-employed farmers, only 6 percent paid taxes because the minimal taxable farm income was so high. Businessmen, on the other hand, had to pay flat taxes on all net income. About 0.8 million employees paid the basic wages and salaries tax of 7.2 percent, but up to 9 million may have been exempted. It was not the left, but Poincaré's ministry in the spring of 1923 that sharply reduced the number of those subject to this tax from 2.8 to 0.75 million by raising the minimal taxable income. More tax

[124] Jean Dessirier, "La progression des impôts en France et en divers pays," *Bulletin de la statistique générale de la France*, xiv, 4 (July 1925), p. 424.

ABSTRACT FROM DESSIRIER: TAXES IN MILLIONS

	1913	*1919*	*1922*	*1923*	*1924*
Progressive income tax	—	571	1,270	1,924	not in
"Schedule" taxes: on wages, salaries, self-employed;	—	298	1,362	1,882	not in
on securities	138	290	1,018	1,166	1,684
Inheritance tax	328	670	916	989	1,399
	. . .	. . .	. . .	. . .	. . .
Total direct taxes	1,853	4,527	9,888	10,536	13,163
Total state revenues	5,141	10,068	22,537	24,941	30,366

The death duties are here counted as "direct" taxes, although in France they were officially regarded as a species of registration tax and thus indirect. The income tax for 1924 was not yet known, but would evidently raise the direct tax total.

[125] Edgard Allix and Marcel Lecercle, *L'impôt général sur le revenu*, 2 vols. (Paris, 1926), ii, p. 339.
[126] *Ibid.*, ii, pp. 345–347.

equity might have been achieved by widening the base of direct taxes and reducing indirect excises.[127]

The resulting tax structure thus bore heavily on the poorer groups through indirect taxes and spared the middle-income elements from direct taxes, which it reserved for the wealthy. This is not to argue that the wealthy faced real tax hardship; it is to point out that as government revenues rose from about 10 or 12 percent of GNP in 1913 to perhaps 15 or 18 percent in 1924,[128] the wealthy may have escaped contributing to this increment less than the middle classes. One expert, examining the patchwork of state revenues, decided that the system had become more progressive since the war:[129]

[127] For the tax burdens on occupational groups, see Anon. "La capacité de paiement de la France," RPP, 125, October 10, 1925, pp. 13–14. Effect of the 1923 changes in Allix and Lecercle, L'impôt sur le revenu, II, pp. 332–333.

[128] Dessirier estimated about 30 percent of national income went to the public sector vs. 25 percent in Britain and 18 percent in Germany, "La progression," p. 438. But this percentage was based upon woeful underestimates of French national income. Dessirier's work was updated by L. Dugé de Bernonville and E. Chevry, "Les charges fiscales en France et en divers pays," Bulletin de la statistique générale, XX, 4 (July–September, 1931), pp. 535–560, who estimated that from 1920 a 16 percent national tax burden on a national revenue of 110 billion had risen to a 20 percent burden upon a national revenue of 151 billion in 1924, p. 559. And even these percentages were too high according to later estimates of French national income. Dugé de Bernonville's work in the latter 1930's calculated only revenus privés—based upon tax return estimates he himself thought were too low—and came up with 155 billion for 1924 and 172 for 1925. For the most recent work, see the Institut de Science Économique Appliqué: Cahiers, série D, Le revenu national, Nr. 7: La croissance du revenu national depuis 1870, Série AF, 4, 163, July 1965, esp. Tihomir J. Markovitch, "L'industrie française de 1789 à 1964: Sources et méthodes," pp. 3 ff. for discussion of Dessirier indices, and pp. 38–39 for an estimate of about 78–80 billion current francs for 1920–1924 average industrial production. To this could be added 65 billion for average agricultural production. See J. S. Toutain, Le produit de l'agriculture française de 1700 à 1958, Cahiers de l'ISEA, Série AF, 2 (Paris, 1961), table 75, p. 5. The total physical production, averaging here about 140–145 billion francs between 1920–1924, formed perhaps two-thirds to three-quarters of the overall gross national product. Cf. the review and estimates by Albert Sauvy, Histoire économique de la France entre les deux guerres, vol. I, De l'Armistice à la dévaluation de la livre (1918–1931) (Paris, 1965), pp. 275–277; net national revenue in current francs:

1913	1920	1921	1922	1923	1924	1925
41.8	32.0	104.3	118.2	147.5	188.0	209.5

[129] Haig, Public Finances, pp. 402–403. Cf. the calculations in Allix and Lecercle, L'impôt sur le revenu, pp. 50–55, which count nonluxury consumption taxes as regressive, and composing 43 percent of state net revenues for 1925, while direct and luxury taxes formed 18 percent, and 18 percent were made up of taxes with an indeterminate incidence.

Percentage of revenue from:	1913	1919	1925 (inflation)	1926 (after stabilization)
Taxes weighted vs. rich	46.5	61.4	66.0	59.5
Taxes weighted vs. poor	38.4	31.2	17.3	17.1
Indeterminate weighting	15.2	7.4	16.7	23.4

As it stood, therefore, the system was not gratingly unfair. The major departure from equity perhaps lay in the large exemptions for farm income. But this may have compensated for the heavy tariff protection that benefited manufacturing and industry. A simple percentage increase, such as the *double décime*, increased the regressivity of the system, but not enough to become an important factor in its own right. Admittedly, it did nothing to modernize the ramshackle tax structure, but it was perhaps the only way to get quick action without opening up messy distributive questions.

In sum, while the Socialists had a real complaint in the prevalence of indirect excises, the Radicals attacked a tax system from which their constituents largely benefited. Effective reform would probably have required hitting more of the middle strata than the wealthy. The Radical Socialist alignment with the Socialists thus depended upon a certain degree of fiscal mystification.

In fact, most valid Radical Socialist complaints brought them closer to the right than to the Socialists or to some of the fiscal sophisticates of the center. Radicals attacked the *double décime* more as a higher tax *per se* than as a tax on the poor. The small businessmen and shopkeepers patronized by the Radicals detested the turn-over tax as intensely as big businessmen, because it required detailed bookkeeping. (Indeed, corporate integration of buyers and sellers to escape the tax was easier for large firms.) The Radicals rashly promised to do away with the turn-over tax, although after coming to power, they, too, had to rely on it.[130] As defenders of the humble bourgeois, the Radical Socialists in opposition were not so different from many of the right-wing deputies in the majority. Pierre Taittinger joined Herriot in a lament for the *classes moyennes* on fixed incomes during the debate of January 25.[131] It was easier for the moderates of the center, such as Bokanowski, to accept the implications of new taxes—the fact, above

[130] On the turn-over tax (levied on the so-called *chiffre d'affaires*), see Carl S. Shoup, *The Sales Tax in France* (New York, 1930), pp. 47–89, 315–317. Cf. Bertrand Nogaro's address to the Radical Party Congress in Nice in 1925, reprinted as "La politique financière du parti radical," *RPP*, cxxv, November 1925, pp. 281–288, on the difficulties of replacing the unpopular tax.
[131] JOC, 1924, p. 288 (January 25).

all, that reparations would supply no panacea for inflation—than for many representatives of the conservative Entente Républicaine.

Despite the big businessmen in their ranks, such as François de Wendel and Auguste Isaac, the Entente clung to financial orthodoxy and in some cases to an archaic paternalism. "Our policy," stated one spokesman, "seeks to divide and disperse the large factory into a group of small workshops, . . . removing forever the possibility of social upheaval through the wisdom that comes from property. . . . We are for the family workshop, the family house, where husband, wife, and children work together, preserved from the temptations of the street and powerfully woven to each other."[132] Psychologically, they were rentiers more than entrepreneurs. As one caustic observer wrote of the Entente Républicaine several years later, "They are the party of the *petite bourgeoisie* who hoped to be saved by the *grands bourgeois*."[133] How could the government defend the franc, asked the editor of *La Journée Industrielle* in exasperation, if the bourgeois living on fixed incomes refused to pay higher taxes? "These bourgeois are moving toward suicide—unwitting suicide but suicide nonetheless."[134]

The tacit partnership of the Radical Socialists and Entente Républicaine would become more evident during the inflation after 1924. But for the moment politics reunited the old left. The upcoming campaign led Radicals and Socialists to join in a demand to hit the wealthy and to argue that indirect taxes provided the real spur to French inflation and the exchange crisis. Sensing electoral victory ahead, Radicals and Socialists could forge a campaign around the vague concept of greater relief for the little man.

The legislative fight over the government's new proposals was dominated by the awareness of the upcoming elections. Pushing the bills through the Chamber was far from easy. The far right was unhappy, and so were the Clémencistes. Tardieu had continued to pour his scorn on the meager results of the Ruhr operation. He saw the vote for the ill-studied taxes only as a way for the government to restore its image after two years of inertia: "The franc saved? No. Only face is saved, at best."[135] In general, however, the right was willing to swallow the bitter legislation if only the premier would reward them by more active electoral support. Poincaré did promise that the government would "do its duty and will easily justify to the country a Chamber that once again is able to put the national interest above particular

[132] Maurice-Charles Bellet (Deputy of the Haute-Garonne and Vice-President of the Entente Républicaine Démocratique), *La politique générale de la Fédération Républicaine de France. Rapport présenté au congrès des 23–24 avril 1924* (Paris, 1924).

[133] Emmanuel Berl, *La politique et les partis* (Paris, 1932), p. 37.

[134] Lucien Romier, "Les bourgeois mineurs," *JI*, December 7, 1923.

[135] JOC, 1924, pp. 678–679 (February 12, 2nd session). Cf. Soulié, *Vie politique d'Edouard Herriot*, p. 131.

interests"; similarly, *Le Temps* kept seizing upon every indication in debate that "the government and the majority are united before the country," against an alliance of Radicals, Socialists, and Communists.[136] Still Poincaré's reassurances were very delphic. The right still felt that the Ministry of the Interior was observing a disastrous neutrality, and in fact, Poincaré did want to free himself from dependence upon the right.[137]

Poincaré finally pushed the *double décime* through the lower house —the key vote was 312 to 205[138]—only to encounter unexpectedly stiff resistance in the Senate. The Radical Senators skirmished for a month, more over the decree powers than the tax increase, in spite of an earlier prediction that Poincaré would have no trouble there: "The Senate— that's his ball park (C'est son billard)."[139] The government finally prevailed, but only because the Senate Radicals abstained rather than provoke a government crisis in which a successor to Poincaré might place a far more militant supporter of the Bloc National, such as Maginot, at the Ministry of the Interior.[140]

A political situation in which Poincaré could carry legislation only with the help of abstentions from the center-left was unstable. The premier might be shrewd in avoiding any concrete statement of support for the Bloc National, especially since he privately predicted at the least "a slight slide to the left."[141] As usual, Poincaré was cautious and a trimmer. *Le Temps* became increasingly alarmed. After a convention of government functionaries had attacked the Ministry, the paper pleaded for the government to react: "Is it still thought sufficient to continue eternally the deceptive policy of Pontius Pilate?"[142] Following a surprise rebuff on procedure, which a resentful Chamber administered to the Finance Minister on March 26, Poincaré dropped the most unpopular members of his team: Lasteyrie, Manoury, and the ridiculed Minister of Agriculture, Henri Chéron, dubbed Chéron-la-vie-chère. Executing a "quarter turn to the right," Poincaré retained

[136] JOC, 1924, p. 124 (January 17, 1924); "Gouvernement et majorité," *Le Temps*, January 28, 1924.
[137] François-Albert, "Chronique politique," *RPP*, cxviii, February 10, 1924.
[138] Voting results, JOC, 1924, p. 1033 (February 22). The opposition included the Radicals, the Socialists, and various right-wing deputies such as Daudet; furthermore, the Clémencistes—Mandel, Tardieu, Ignace—and Loucheur and Briand, who in his Carcassone speech two days later identified himself with the opposition.
[139] Marcel Hutin, *L'Echo de Paris*, February 13, 1924.
[140] François-Albert, "Chronique politique," *RPP*, cxix, April 1924, pp. 97–100; for a summary of the Senate's action see François Goguel-Nyegaard, *Le rôle financier du Sénat* (Paris, 1934), pp. 160–177. For the Senate's hostility to Lasteyrie, see François-Marsal, "La crise présidentielle," MS, pp. 7–8. Debates in the Senate on the bill in JOS, pp. 274–470 *passim* (March 13, 14, 15, 16, 17, 18, 22); Berenger report in JOS: Doc. Parl., 1924, annèxe, N° 160, pp. 126–163.
[141] François-Marsal, "La crise présidentielle."
[142] "Les fonctionnaires et les élections," *Le Temps*, March 5, 1924.

in office only Le Trocquer and Maginot, the favorites of the Bloc National. Nonetheless, the Bloc could not secure the vigorous prefectural intervention they wanted in the campaign.[143] The legislative session ended mournfully for the incumbent majority: "Between the joyous murmurs of December 8, 1919, and the bleak solitude of April 13, 1924, exists all the space that separates a youth rich with hope and the heavy agony of regret."[144]

The Union Nationale forces went to the country in a mood of resignation. The tax increases made many squirm, although, as they explained, they were "indispensable to balance our budget" and had been made necessary "by the persistent defaulting of Germany."[145] There was still no hesitation to identify with Poincaré, no matter how shy about affiliation the premier himself might be. "To vote for us is to vote for Poincaré," declared the candidates of the Haute Garonne.[146] "With Poincaré defeated, Berlin will celebrate. The sacrifices demanded of the taxpayers are heavy, but the nation has understood their necessity, for they alone rescued a financial situation that threatened to become fatal to the country's credit."[147] Of course, the conservatives attacked "the partisans of internationalism and those who compact with them," and reminded voters of Malvy and Caillaux, the "inquisitorial taxes," and the inevitable encroachments of collectivism and communism that a left-wing victory would mean.[148] Now the tone was less aggressive than in 1919, and more pathetic: "France of the Ruhr has the same face as France of Verdun. The motto of 1924 is the same as that of 1914 because circumstances are equally tragic."[149]

The incumbents faced a Cartel des Gauches that was patched together primarily by the desire to revenge 1919. The SFIO entered the electoral agreements with professed reluctance, and in certain departments Radicals and Socialists never did manage to join forces. The left indicted the Bloc National for clericalism, an aggressive foreign policy, and the tax system. Although Herriot and the Radicals had originally sought to keep Poincaré distinct from the right in their political attacks, they dropped this subtlety as the campaign pro-

[143] François-Albert [pseud. Pierre du Clain], "Le bonneteau politique," *Le Progrès Civique*, March 22, 1924, pp. 14 ff. (reference from Stephen Schuker); on Lasteyrie, and for complaints about the prefects' neutrality, see Mamelet's comments in A. de Tarde and Robert de Jouvenel, *La politique d'aujourd'hui* (Paris, n.d.), p. 95; also L. Marcellin, *Voyage autour de la Chambre*, pp. 28–30.

[144] "Fin de législature," *Le Temps*, April 15, 1924.

[145] Poincaré's justification in JOC, 1924, p. 1015 (February 22).

[146] *Programmes, professions de foi et engagements électoraux de 1924*, ["Barodet"] JOC: Doc. Parl., 1925, annèxe 1471, pp. 303–304.

[147] *Ibid.*, pp. 135–136, Calvados: Liste d'Union Nationale.

[148] *Ibid.*, p. 516, Union républicaine et nationale of the Meurthe-et-Moselle led by Marin and Wendel.

[149] *Ibid.*, pp. 18–19, Union républicaine nationale of the Aisne.

gressed. When the premier's cabinet fell on March 26, *Le Progrès Civique* rejoiced in the defeat of "reaction" and labeled the tax legislation as the most iniquitous since the July Monarchy. When Poincaré termed the Cartel an alliance of fire and water, Herriot countered that the premier was "expressly linking his own destiny with that of the incumbent majority."[150]

Given a left that still spoke of the dangers of Bonapartism and clericalism, and a right that flaunted the revolutionary peril, the campaign was neither probing nor educational. "In the absence of vigorous programs . . . ," wrote Romier, "vague tendencies or past events are placed on trial."[151] In reality, major issues were at stake: as *Le Temps* argued, the entire legislature had been dominated by the problem of how to enforce the new European order and how to make Germany pay without disrupting the Allies. But while the Cartel argued for a policy that placed international harmony above the potential gains France might wrest by unilateral action, the issue did not result in clear-cut party discussions. Poincaré had declared that he would work with the report the Dawes experts would present, and the left had presented no economic alternatives for financing reconstruction. Primarily, the elections remained a contest of "mood"—the impatient rejection, or regretful acceptance, of policies that had showed little profit.

Because the sudden inflation and *crise des changes* crystallized voter malaise, they remained the crucial electoral variables: "Whatever it derives from, whichever way one turns, one finds a general explosion of discontent," reported the prefect of the Tarn in mid-February. "No doubt people are ready to bow before an ineluctable necessity, but the sacrifice to which all shall finally accede will leave a profound irritation that will be exploited by the opposition. . . . The functionaries, the small pensioners, the small rentiers who are numerous and whose situation merits serious concern, accuse the public powers of abandoning them. . . . There is anger against the so-called war profiteers, the nouveaux riches." Between January and March the country was falling into a fit of discontent, a "veritable stupor." From Cherbourg came reports that the fall of the franc had produced a "very acute and pained reaction. . . . One cannot conceal the fact that especially in the cities and important centers a very lively feeling of discontent has been provoked against the present chamber." In central France the prefect of the Indre reported that the government's opponents were successfully attributing the current economic woes to the Ruhr policy. At Rouen, "a wave of discontent and defeatism" swept across the department, while the crisis of the franc and high cost of living threatened

---

[150] *Le Progrès Civique*, March 29, 1924, and Soulié, *Vie politique d'Edouard Herriot*, p. 137.

[151] *JI*, May 10, 1924; "Fin de législature," *Le Temps*, April 15, 1924.

to undermine public morale and turn it against the government. The Allier's pro-ministerial list would go down to defeat, the prefect predicted, without some dazzling new success in foreign policy. From La Rochelle at the end of January came the prediction that if elections were held within a month, "it is beyond doubt that the Cartel des Gauches list would have a good chance to win in entirety." And in the week before the voting, the prefect of the Côte-d'Or added his ominous warnings about inflation and the elections.[152]

Pyrénées-Orientales offered a quantitative indication of the sudden disaffection. In Perpignan-Ouest on December 2, there had been a by-election to replace a deputy who had resigned. Radicals and Socialists ran a common candidate, but the government supporters won a "brilliant" victory—and one, the prefect prematurely forecast, that would influence the elections of the following spring. In the same department in February, however, the Socialist candidate who had been defeated in December won against the list sponsored by Emmanuel Brousse, a leader of the centrist Parti Républicain, Démocratique et Sociale, and by the Bloc National.[153]

Given the hands-off attitude of the Ministry of the Interior and the evident disaffection of the electorate, the victory of the Cartel seemed assured. Even those prefects who wished to organize local elections received little encouragement. The prefect in Bordeaux was especially anxious to establish a Union list that would capture all the majority seats, less in order to triumph against the left than to defeat Mandel. Despite arranging political meetings for the moderate forces of the PRDS, the prefect had constantly to plead for government support to keep the local dissident nationalist newspaper, *La Petite Gironde*, in line.[154] Nor could the fund of the Union des Intérêts Économiques, liberally sprinkled by the railroads, insurance funds, and members of the Comité des Forges, materially reverse the result. The money was used to encourage right and center groups to unite, and also to support dissident Radicals, perhaps even occasionally Communists who

[152] Prefectual reports, AN, Paris: F IC III: Tarn (Box 1132); Cherbourg, Manche, February 29, 1924 (Box 1130); Châteauroux, Indre, February 15, 1924 (Box 1128); Rouen, Seine Inférieure, March 22, 1924 (Box 1132); and similar news from Lyon, Rhône, March 14, 1924 (Box 1132); and Cantal, January 1924 (Box 1126); Allier, March 1924 (Box 1125); La Rochelle, Charente Inférieure, January 30 (Box 1126)—but here the prefect was at least cheered by the departure of the unpopular Pierre Taittinger for a Paris constituency; Côte-d'Or, May 10, and reference to missing report of May 6 (Box 1127).

[153] *Ibid.*, Pyrénées-Orientales, reports of December 15, 1923 and February 15, 1924 (Box 1131).

[154] *Ibid.*, 1128. Reports of November 19, 1923, and January 23, 1924. Mandel's tactic was to put together a list that would net enough votes to capture one seat by the proportional system. Later reports are missing from the Gironde. Reports from Seine-et-Oise, where Tardieu was running, are unfortunately also missing, as are all those from the Seine.

might pull votes from the major Cartel slates.[155] Yet this was an effort from which the government held aloof. Moreover, the corps of discontented functionaries probably served as propaganda arm, not to be overcome by the money of the Bloc National. The Cartel press, spearheaded by the *Quotidien*, shattered the earlier preponderance of the *modéré* newspapers.[156]

The left's mobilization for the campaign contributed to the large vote brought out by May 11. Whereas abstentions in the 1910 and 1914 elections had been about 23 percent and in 1919, 29 percent, they now fell to 17 percent.[157] In 1919 the abstentions could be attributed to a disgruntled nonsocialist left, which had been caught without an attractive alternative, a problem that the Cartel now overcame. But if leftist sympathizers were drawn to the polls, there was no great migration of votes; indeed, to see the results as a victory of the left is partially misleading. The militant right was clearly defeated. Daudet, Arago—the leader of the Entente but a man unpopular in his own constituency—Isaac, Castelnau, Lasteyrie, Tardieu, Mandel, Reynaud all lost. Mandel's strategy of winning a place by proportional representation failed, because although his list earned one seat, it was a popular local priest who headed his list and took the place. Tardieu was apparently the victim of another manipulation permitted by the system. Enough voters who chose his slate crossed off his name so that by relatively few votes he fell to the bottom of his list and thus missed out when the seats were divided proportionally.[158] In raw

[155] On UIE support for the Communists, see the report of Lucien Romier to Emile Moreau, in Moreau's *Souvenirs d'un gouverneur de la Banque de France* (Paris, 1954), p. 524; Louis Marcellin, *Voyage autour de la Chambre*, pp. 28–30, reports subsidies in Pyrénées-Orientales. Cf. J. Barthélemy, *Essai sur le travail parlementaire et le système des Commissions* (Paris, 1934), p. 250, for Socialist willingness to expose the sources of PC funds. On the UIE activity in general, see the discussion above in Chapter Two, pp. 102–104. In the 1924 inquiry it was admitted that insurance companies provided 800,000 francs, the railroads 1 million, and the chemical industry 250,000. See *Enquête sur l'origine de tous les fonds électoraux, JO: Impressions*, Tome XXXII, 2098, pp. 83, 166–168, 193. On the support of dissident Radical lists in an effort at "cuisine électorale," see the testimony of L. Poulen, *ibid.*, p. 96. On the limits of the intervention by the economic associations, cf. Albert Thibaudet, *La république des professeurs* (Paris, 1927), p. 157.

[156] François-Albert [pseud. Pierre du Clain], "Bonneteau Politique," *Le Progrès Civique*, April 8, 1924, pp. 12–13, on government aloofness (reference from Stephen Schuker). For the Cartel's campaign, see Soulié, *Vie politique d'Edouard Herriot*, pp. 136–140. Newspaper venality was widely institutionalized. Poincaré discouraged François-Marsal's investigations into the sources of funds for left-wing papers and admitted that he had his own funds for influencing the press abroad. See François-Marsal, "La crise présidentielle," MS, pp. 11–12.

[157] Georges Lachapelle, *Élections législatives du 11 mai 1924* (Paris, 1924), pp. 35–36.

[158] See Maurice Privat, *Les heures d'André Tardieu et la crise des partis* (Paris, 1930), p. 116, for the allegation of Poincaré's role in this maneuver. Tardieu won 76,000 votes, while the lowest successful candidate netted only 24,000.

votes, moreover, the slates of the Cartel, or of the SFIO—where the Socialists ran against "National Radicals" not disposed to form a Cartel —won more than the Union or concentration lists. But they did not really receive more than the *combination* of union lists and National Radicals, who had generally remained faithful adherents of the Poincaré government.[159] Now, however, the impetus of the election was such that the National Radicals and Républicains de Gauche would provisionally back a left-wing ministry: as usual the votes served less to change ideologies than to influence the coalition behavior of the floating center. But how long the pivotal Gauche Radicale, which formed the right wing of the new majority, would consistently vote with the left on social and economic issues remained to be seen.[160]

[159]

Party Tendencies	Votes	
Conservatives and A.F.	328,003	
Union/Bloc National lists	3,190,831	$= 4,211,060$
Républicains de Gauche; National Radicals	1,020,229	
Cartel des Gauches	2,644,769	$= 3,394,416$
SFIO running separately	749,647	
Communists	875,812	
Diverse	89,235	
Total of mean votes per slate	8,898,526	

[160]

CHAMBER ALIGNMENTS

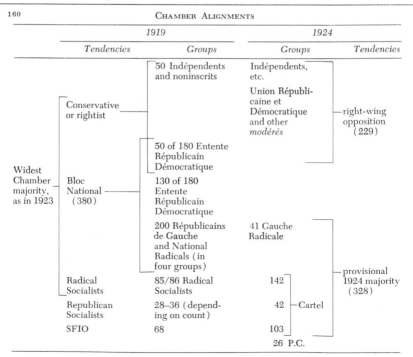

476

It was easy enough for the victors to remove the President, who had identified himself with the outgoing majority. Poincaré did not wish to remain around for this confrontation: "We must not give the appearance of clinging to power," he told an angered Millerand. The left decided on a "ministerial strike": Herriot and Steeg were successively discouraged from attempting to put together a cabinet, and it was left to the hapless François-Marsal to carry out a forlorn attempt to present a government before the new legislature.[161]

Millerand reproached Poincaré, but the two leaders conceived of their mission in different ways. Millerand had always valued an impetuous loyalty and conspicuous, decisive actions; he identified patriotic virtue with the majority that had sent him to the Elysée. Poincaré wished to hold himself in readiness for those moments when a divided country called to him. That meant always minimizing clashes; his duels with Herriot, for example, were marked by courtesy and reserve. Poincaré could not abide being identified as a man of any party narrower than that of the middle classes as a whole. "Union," that is, bourgeois union, was the principle that brought him to power in 1913 and 1922, and would do so again in 1926. But the call for union always meant a call for sacrifice, often for fiscal austerity, certainly for sacrifice of party in-fighting among the bourgeois parties. And the call for unity could hold together a majority only so long. With the welling up of partisan politics, Poincaré sensed that his own field of action had become impaired. A French bourgeois acceptance of sacrifice was the condition of Poincaré's viability, and such acceptance was ephemeral. As early as autumn 1923, prudence had warned him of the need to step out of the path of a reunited left in which Radicals and Socialists once again joined hands.

The dumping of Millerand was, however, one of the few successes of the Cartel. Their efforts to elect Painlevé as President failed, and their policies were to be further frustrated. The electoral results, in fact, only partially translated the electorate's preoccupations. The oft-depicted "little" voters who rallied from abstentions to the Cartel in 1924 voted in protest—not protest against the Ruhr policy itself, but against its unfruitfulness in easing France's economic and financial dilemma. Ever since the war, the outstanding leaders of National Union—Clemenceau, Millerand, Poincaré—had asked Frenchmen to choose perpetual vigilance and unremitting concern for the fruits of victory. Heroism and strenuousness had not appeared to pay, however; even Poincaré recognized that the country was too weary for his program.[162] If in 1919 many middle-class voters had been concerned

[161] François-Marsal, "La crise présidentielle," pp. 13–25; Millerand, "Souvenirs," pp. 121–123; Persil, *Alexandre Millerand* (Paris, 1949), 162–166.
[162] Chastenet, *Poincaré*, p. 260.

lest the Socialists sabotage the victory, that victory had been largely frittered away by 1924. Judging from the prefects' reports and the glowing resolutions of the departmental *Conseils Généraux*, had the elections taken place half a year earlier, Poincaré would have had a resounding centrist majority. Above all, it was the financial panic that hurt the old majority. Frenchmen had followed the *crise des changes* with pained bafflement. Not without cause, they reproached the government for inactivity until too late, when only unpopular taxes could be prescribed.

Yet the elections of May 11, 1924, were held under bad conditions, in that what many people desired to choose was not adequately reflected in the alternatives before them. This is often the case with protest votes, and much of the 1924 vote was a protest vote. France wanted tranquility and a vacation from heroism: fewer "Verduns," financial or otherwise. Ultimately the vote was misleading, because it threw together a coalition ambiguously poised between old and new issues and alignments. On the left, the old Radicals, who condemned decree power and the "clerical revival" while lamenting the plight of the bourgeoisie, teamed up with the Socialists under the umbrella of a fervent if vague internationalism, an ill-considered belief that the tax system was rampantly unjust, and a desire to avenge 1919. This *mariage de convenance* gave *Le Temps* brief hope that perhaps the old centrist majority might be resurrected with a slightly redder hue than before.[163] On the other hand, the Cartel angered other right-wing papers, which prepared for a Manichean confrontation with the forces of collectivism.[164] By predicting the collapse of the currency, they helped unchain a self-fulfilling prophecy compounded by Radical Socialist confusion on financial matters.

The stable franc was still the ligament of bourgeois society in France, the basis of all rational planning and expectations for the future. But no one wanted to pay the price. Conservatives and the center had not wished to renounce the mirage of reparations until very late; the left disliked the taxes that reconstruction necessitated. The political reflex action of forming a new left bloc distorted the decisions to be made, which were how to apportion the costs of war and reconstruction. The Radicals did not realize that essentially they shared the same answer to this question as much of the right—and this because of the widely diffused ownership of property in France. The basic inconsistency in the French political system continued to lie in the ambiguous role of the Radical Socialist Party. Politically its adherents wanted a victory of the left, socially they desired only the policies

163 *Le Temps*, June 3, 1924.
164 Cf. *L'Echo de Paris*, June 3, 1924.

of the center. Men voted left in protest against a financial development that the left parties were to accentuate. That is why the elections produced two years of agonizing ambivalence.

Germany and France, therefore, along with Italy, still faced major decisions—alternatives that despite the great shifting of electoral majorities could not be confronted by the new parliamentary balance of forces in any resolute and clear-cut manner. In Rome the Fascists could celebrate their victory of April, and a month later the French left could headily demand *"Toutes les places et tout de suite."* But ultimately the problems at stake lay not in party majorities but nation-wide conflicts that had been critically transformed in the past decade. In Italy, the advent of universal suffrage and international involvements had thrown the liberals' state into crisis. The Giolittian solution of fuzzing alternatives and coalitions had failed twice, but the persistence of a tissue of patriarchal relationships in the South had helped to postpone a radical coming to terms with mass suffrage and its consequences. Nor had Mussolini yet decided how to confront the overall issue: hating yet respecting the mass parties, collaborating with yet detesting the traditional elites, he wanted consensus, but without ransoming himself to the old cadres. The elections won him time, won him postponement of a final choice between a narrow party dictatorship or submission to the old elites. Apparently he had gained a majority, and one submissive to him. (This meant that he needed the Fascist revisionists less than in the previous year, and the luckless Massimo Rocca, renewing his polemic, was now expelled from the party.) But if the majority were to become less submissive, then Mussolini's dilemmas would return. Like Giolitti, Mussolini, too, had fuzzed alternatives, since his ultimate social and political choices were harsh. His electoral triumph however, allowed him to avoid the choices only so long.

In France and Germany other contingencies were to influence the choice of the basic socioeconomic alternatives. But the two nations had problems less self-contained, more conditional upon each other and ultimately upon the United States. Interest groups and class conflict still centered upon the financial issues bequeathed by the war, by the diminution of European resources, and by the disruption of international trade flows. America could help rebalance capital flows by feeding money into Germany so that the German business community might countenance payments to Paris that would help stanch French inflation.

As of the spring of 1924, however, parliamentary incompatibilities remained acute. The German political representatives who were willing to approve the conditions of American intervention remained those of the working class and the center, not those who had won the election. To put the Dawes recommendations into effect meant securing the support of a majority that included the SPD and some of the DNVP. Certainly the new French majority was prepared to welcome the American intervention and a reparations settlement; but its domestic policies antagonized the conservative elements, who also stood to gain from stability. Thus, in both France and Germany alignments on domestic and foreign questions ran at cross purposes; and so long as they did, any electoral result—whether to right or left—was likely to perpetuate unresolved problems and preclude the economic stability needed to soothe political conflict. Only when a new majority could embrace the left's foreign policy, while the left accepted, whether from weakness or conviction, the right's demand for economic immunity, could stability be achieved. As things developed, it proved easier to buy the conservatives' acquiescence in international détente by means of "soundness" at home: in the mid-1920's the pocketbook was to prevail. Ultimately, it was this sort of grand trade-off that led beyond the equivocations of early 1924 and into the period of stability that marked the next half-decade. But it was to be achieved less under the auspices of the 1924 majorities than by interests acting in new coalitions.

· 8 ·

ACHIEVING STABILITY

From the summer of 1924 to the end of 1926, Europeans passed through a period of painful bargaining that finally resolved the equivocations and inconclusiveness of the postwar settlements. The compromises struck, both within and across national boundaries, were sometimes acknowledged, sometimes tacit. In both cases they provided the scaffolding for the fugitive equilibrium between the Dawes plan and the depression. This equilibrium represented a significant sociopolitical achievement. It was not easily arrived at; it imposed selective and heavy costs as well as rewards, and although brief, it had the same architecture as the stability achieved again after World War II and extending into our own times. To analyze the process of attaining equilibrium, the burdens of maintaining it, and the vulnerability it concealed helps us get at the true measure of what was preserved in the wake of World War I.

The second half of 1924 opened the way to a whole series of settlements. After the collapse of the mark and the erosion of the franc, the imbalances of the European economy and of international exchange finally forced review of the reparation settlement. Reawakened U.S. participation in European affairs through the Dawes plan and subsequent American loans were to transform the internal politics of Germany, the relations between France and Germany, and ultimately the whole economic position of the continent. United States funds would help purchase German industry's cooperation with the Weimar regime, thus enabling new coalitions to form governments without Socialist participation as the balance of power in Berlin shifted to a more conservative basis. The end of the Versailles Treaty's restrictions on German commercial policy in 1925 opened up the possibility of working out new tariff agreements and drew East Elbian agricultural interests toward participation in the German regime. "Rye and iron"—the conservative economic elites of the Empire—reappeared between 1924 and 1926: republicans neither by commitment nor by reason, they consented briefly to become republicans from interest.

Within other countries, parallel tendencies led to conservative or rightist solutions. A British Conservative government began five years of office in late 1924. In France, although it required two years for the Cartel des Gauches majority to disintegrate, Poincaré was back as premier in July 1926. In the course of 1925 and 1926, Mussolini finally opted for thoroughgoing dictatorship and rejected the charade of liberal politics that had tempted him. In different ways, the failure of the British General Strike of 1926 and the passage of the Fascist exceptional laws in the same year confirmed the failure of the postwar left.

New relationships emerged between Germany and the Western powers. The London Accords of August 1924, which sealed the Dawes plan, the 1925 French withdrawal from the Ruhr and the protracted negotiation of what became the Locarno pacts, marked the visible progress of détente. At the same time a series of important commercial accords finally relinked the French and German iron industries. The new trade and steel accords paralleled the more celebrated political and military accommodations—in effect, paying off the right in cash while Briand and Stresemann's handshakes rewarded the left in spirit.

This outcome typified the mid-decade settlements, which had to provide some reward for each powerful constituency or interest group to purchase stability. In the democratic states, these settlements could not be absolute right-wing victories—and even in Italy traditional elites surrendered more power to the fascist regime than they desired. Nonetheless, the new equilibrium preponderantly rewarded the right; for the right had proved itself stronger in the streets and in the market place than a divided working class, while the verdicts of the ballotbox had been too ambiguous to provide a clear alternative mandate.

The new conservative stability also brought the end of a decade of inflation. No longer were trade unions bought off with inflationary contracts whereby industry passed its wages bill to the fragmented middle classes. There could be, however, no return to the currency relationships of 1914 without disastrous setbacks to production. The inflation that had ravaged savings during the previous decade had finally to be ratified as a historical fact. This was easier for industrial producers than rentiers. New and lower currency parities had to be accepted in the face of middle-class opposition. But despite the write-off of old paper assets, ending a decade of currency depreciation still imposed rigorous deflationary pressures upon domestic economies and heightened export competition. Both consequences intensified the consolidation of capitalism at home and across frontiers.

Stability, in sum, rested upon complex trade-offs. The clearest way to bring them to light is to view in turn the different conflicts that were pacified. The first insight into the settlement comes from analysis of the parliamentary instability that plagued both France and Germany. Both countries suffered from a failure to secure stable parliamentary majorities because political parties faced two cross-cutting sets of issues at once. They had to grapple with the traditional conflicts between working-class and bourgeois forces and more recent disputes centering on monetary revaluation that pitted homeowner, white collar, artisan, and small business representatives against more cohesive producer groups. Party systems that had developed around the first set of issues proved less able to settle the second. Coalitions appropriate for the monetary questions emerged only slowly, and at the cost of much political agony.

The second major aspect of the settlement became evident in the wearying economic negotiations between the heavy industry of France and Germany. Business organization in both countries was strengthened, as anxieties about excess capacity and fierce export competition encouraged new cartel arrangements. The preoccupations of prosperity, not its rewards, powerfully contributed to the new corporatist equilibrium.

The development, finally, of the Italian regime during the same critical years, 1924–1926, suggests that fascist corporatism opened up an authoritarian resolution of the same class tensions existing elsewhere. Stabilization in Italy shows fascism and the liberal corporatist order, as achieved in Weimar and forecast for France, not as equivalents, but still as alternative solutions to the divisions besetting all three countries.

Inflation, Revaluation, and the Decomposition of Parliamentary Politics

The equilibrium achieved in the latter 1920's was that of the tightrope walker, exerting and precarious. Parliamentary transactions helped construct this relative stability but only haltingly and awkwardly. The Reichstag and the French National Assembly had to confront major economic issues but lacked party coalitions that could offer coherent alternatives. Ultimately *ad hoc* majorities emerged to pass important legislation; nevertheless, stabilization and settlements between interests seemed to emerge despite parliament and not by virtue of it.

The politics of currency readjustment was especially preoccupying and corrosive for political parties. Ending a decade of inflation inflicted political anguish on both France and Germany. Between 1924 and 1926, French politics centered in effect upon the issue of how extensive a transfer of wealth through inflation would take place. The Germans had already struggled with this issue in a far more catastrophic form. Now they debated how much the holders of former paper assets might legally regain, specifically the scope and rates of revaluation for former bank accounts, mortgages, corporate bonds, and insurance policies. After *de facto* stabilization of the franc in 1926, revaluation arose as an issue in France, too, as bankers and political leaders discussed the appropriate legal exchange rate that should finally be set. In both countries, the working class, farmers, and industries that produced goods for export or just had high corporate debt stood to lose most from significant revaluation or a high exchange rate. Final legal stabilization of the franc at a high ratio to the pound and dollar would inhibit foreign demand, impose heavy internal debts and taxes and lead to unemployment and recession.[1] In Germany, revaluation of mortgages at high percentages of their pre-inflation value—or even turning over the claims to the courts, which were generally sympathetic to rentiers—would impose large, deflationary debt burdens on agriculture and industry. On the other hand the millions of middle-class families who had savings accounts liquidated in worthless marks or collected a life insurance policy sufficient to buy a postage stamp clamored for compensation. In Germany individuals bought shares in mortgages (*Hypotheken*) as a form of saving: when Oswald Spengler came into 50,000 marks in royalties in 1919, he searched around for a suitable mortgage for a conservative, albeit improvidential investment.[2] Even before stabilization of the mark, all such mortgage holders bitterly contested the legitimacy of being paid off with valueless legal tender.

In Germany these middle-class creditors finally were to see their dreams for extensive revaluation yield to the pressure exerted by corporations and landlords. Likewise in France, bankers and business spokesmen ultimately compelled Poincaré to relinquish his original hopes for pegging the franc at a high and prestigious value. The fact that centrist or right-center ministries had to sanction the destruction of savings indicated the evolution of conservative politics from a broadly conceived bourgeois defense to a painful balancing of corporate interests. Bourgeois commitment alone could not determine whether Poincaré and Hans Luther would restore the capital of the middle classes for whom they had earlier spoken or would opt for the mutual needs of business and labor. The issue of revaluation, in sum, confronted French and German bourgeois representatives with an uncomfortable choice between consumers and producers, citizens and interests.

In terms of parliamentary politics, the revaluation issue became acute as one of the dilemmas raised by German Nationalist participation in the national government. The reasons for that participation themselves reflected the new primacy of interest politics and the

[1] Cf. J. P. Morgan & Co. to Herman Harjes, Morgan, Harjes & Co., Paris, March 29, 1924, and thereafter submitted to the Cartel's Minister of Finance, Etienne Clémentel, on the consequences of excessive revaluation: Baker Library: TWL 95–11.

[2] Walter Struve, *Elites against Democracy* (Princeton, N.J., 1973), p. 235.

eclipse of ideology—reactionary as well as democratic. In light of the May 1924 elections with their strong Nationalist showing, it was expected that the party would enter a government coalition if it accepted the provisions of the Dawes plan. Nationalist votes were required for ratification of the legislation carrying out the Dawes recommendations since the key provisions for pledging the assets of the German state railroads apparently required constitutional amendment and therefore a majority of two-thirds. The cabinet planned to seek the necessary legislation before final signature of the agreements in London on August 30. It was prepared, however, to sign the treaties and then win subsequent ratification. If DNVP opposition were to preclude a two-thirds Reichstag majority, the cabinet considered a national referendum, although finally Ebert and Chancellor Marx threatened new parliamentary elections, which would have isolated the Nationalists in a difficult political campaign. Stresemann preferred to win over the party than to drive it into opposition. It represented too massive a constituency to keep unreconciled to his efforts at détente with the West. His own party colleagues, moreover, seemed ready to sacrifice him as Minister if that were the price of a right-wing coalition.[3]

The Nationalists, however, did not facilitate their own entry into the governing coalition. Their leadership under Oskar Hergt and Graf Westarp was erratic and their membership divided. Diehards, such as Westarp himself, resisted normal political participation; even entering a government must be only a means for more bitter opposition, if not against the Republican format, certainly against the parliamentary regime.[4] Yet since the fall of 1923, many of the powerful industrialists affiliated with the DNVP were urging acceptance of a reparation settlement.[5] Despite the bitter opposition of Alfred Hugenberg, the Reichs-

[3] For the government's discussion of the need for a two-thirds majority to carry the railroad legislation, see Schacht in the May 3 meeting of cabinet ministers and the testimony of State Secretary Joel, June 11 and August 16, 1924, in Günter Abramowski, ed., *Die Kabinette Marx I und II. 30. November 1923 bis 3. Juni 1924. 3. Juni 1924 bis 15. Januar 1925. Akten der Reichskanzlei: Weimarer Republik*, 2 vols. (Boppard am Rhein, 1973), I, p. 603, II, pp. 661, 994 ff. Consideration of legislative alternatives or dissolution in the case of defeat in the Reichstag, August 21 and 27, *ibid.*, II, pp. 992–995, 1002–1003.

[4] Westarp to Lindeiner Wildau, September 1924, DZA, Potsdam: DNVP Akten/ 86, p. 98 ff.

[5] Cf. Westarp's perception of growing industrialist pressure in Westarp Nachlass, Gaertringen, "Ruhr Kampf" fragment, chapter 4, p. 170. For an estimate of industry-affiliated deputies in the DVP (16 or 31 percent) and DNVP (10 or 9 percent) see Carl Duisberg to Paul Silverberg, March 13, 1925 in BA, Koblenz: Silverberg Nachlass/259 and summarized in Michael Stürmer, *Koalition und Opposition in der Weimarer Republik 1924–1928* (Düsseldorf, 1967), p. 286. For the relationships between ideology and interests see Lothar Döhn, *Politik und Interesse. Die Interessenstruktur der Deutschen Volkspartei* (Meisenheim am Glan, 1970), pp. 12–34, 108–129.

verband der deutschen Industrie endorsed the Dawes report.[6] Its provisions would reestablish German economic sovereignty in the Ruhr and Rhineland and would facilitate badly needed credits from abroad.[7] The plan stipulated an 800-million-mark foreign loan, promised to open the tap of far more extensive credits from America unofficially, and also remained compatible with Hjalmar Schacht's Gold Discount Bank that had mobilized English credits and German capital holdings abroad.[8] Although German industry would collectively have to guarantee and service a new series of bonds, the Ruhr entrepreneurs agreed that this obligation was preferable to prolonged export taxes.[9] Rejection of the Dawes plan, on the other hand, would mean at best long and painful negotiations while the French continued to extract MICUM payments. It might even lead to outright French confiscations, renewed inflation, withdrawal of American cooperation: in short, all the perils of 1923.

There was a further inducement to DNVP collaboration. Half the parliamentary party belonged to the Reichslandbund, and agriculture also wanted a government voice over tariff policy. The high prewar

[6] See the debate between Silverberg and Hugenberg on July 2, 1924, in the Main Committee of the Reichsverband and included in BA, Koblenz: Silverberg Nachlass/355.

[7] See Étienne Weill-Raynal, *Les réparations allemandes et la France*, 3 vols. (Paris, 1947), II, pp. 521–626; Harold G. Moulton, *The Reparations Plan* (New York, 1924). The Dawes plan established a more feasible schedule of payments rising from a billion marks in kind its first year to 2.5 billions from 1928–1929 onward and allowing for possible supplementary payments keyed to economic performance. Germany no longer had to scrape together foreign currency; instead the government paid Reichsmarks to the Reparations Agent in Berlin who arranged for the transfers as he thought feasible. To cover the yearly payments bonds were to be assigned to industry, a transport tax was enacted, and the German national railroads were reorganized into an autonomous public corporation that would issue 10 billion marks of its own bonds. As a counterpart to acceptance, the German government was to receive 800 million marks ($200 million) of foreign loans, along with 200 million marks from the Reichsbank to pay German producers for the initial reparations in kind, avoid a total moratorium, and inject badly needed credits into the post-stabilization economy. In effect, the $200 million meant that Americans, British, to a lesser degree the French and others, would finance reparations. What remained to be negotiated at the London Conference of July and August 1924 were important questions of timing and enforcement: when French troops must be withdrawn from the Ruhr, and whether creditor nations would retain the right to enforce sanctions unilaterally as France and Belgium had done in 1923. In large part because of financial pressure upon her, France had to relinquish such prerogatives. See Stephen A. Schuker, "The French Financial Crisis and the Adoption of the Dawes plan, 1924," Diss. (Cambridge, Mass., 1969).

[8] For the Gold Discount Bank, see Hjalmar Schacht, *The Stabilization of the Mark* (London, 1927), pp. 129–150; also Gustav Stresemann, *Vermächtnis. Der Nachlass in drei Bänden*, Harry Bernhard, ed., 3 vols. (Berlin, 1932), I, pp. 386–389.

[9] For industry's awareness of future American credits and its feelings about the required bonds, see Hermann Bücher to the "Northwest Group" of the Union of German Iron and Steel Industrialists, March 17, 1924: GHH: 4001012008/0; also in GFM: Ritter Handakten, L1491/5352/436750–436751.

duties on foodstuffs and raw materials had been suspended when Germany had gone to war in August 1914, and the Versailles Treaty had prohibited reimposing protection until January 1925. The constant inflation had provided *de facto* protection by raising the price of foreign commodities, but stabilization created a virtual free-trade situation for the first time in forty years. Agriculture was particularly distressed as French and Canadian grains competed in West German markets. 1924, moreover, only introduced longer-term structural difficulties. Despite the inflation's wiping out of mortgages, farmers were quickly to fall back into short-term and high-interest debt in the mid-1920's. Although the overall farm debt of Germany was lower than before the war, because of expenditure for "rationalization" and the tightness of credit the proportion of national farm revenue required to service the farm debt rose from about 7 percent in 1913 to 7.5 percent in 1925–1926 (to hit 14 percent during the depression). Large landowners, especially, undertook the most extensive "intensification" programs and became indebted most heavily. The Junkers could no longer sit on their estates and indulge in a principled reactionary refusal to play the political game in the Republic.[10]

The tariff issue emerged in the summer of 1924 concurrently with the Dawes plan. The landlords had a fervent spokesman within the cabinet, the Minister of Food and Agriculture, Count Kanitz, son of the Kanitz who had championed Junker claims in the 1890's. Immediately after the spring 1924 elections, Kanitz demanded restoration of the old protectionist Bülow tariff, claiming that a favorable tariff bill could win the necessary votes for the Dawes legislation. Antitariff forces, however, were also influential inside the cabinet: the trade-union wing of the Center, represented by Heinrich Brauns, the Minister of Labor, especially resented agrarian protection. Only by including the duties in a bill that simultaneously reduced the turnover tax on food, could the cabinet agree on a tariff proposal. Nonetheless, when the government did finally present the legislation to the Reichstag the day before the crucial Dawes vote, a Social Democratic and Communist walkout prevented a quorum. The proroguing of the legislature after ratification of the London agreements meant that the tariff was to remain unresolved until the next spring. Thus even if the DNVP did not win immediate restoration of the Bülow tariff, it had a major stake in the coalition "logrolling" to come.[11]

[10] Max Sering, *Deutsche Agrarpolitik auf geschichtlicher und landeskundlicher Grundlage* (Leipzig, 1934), pp. 109–116; Alexander Gerschenkron, *Bread and Democracy in Germany* (Berkeley and Los Angeles, 1943), pp. 108–110, 124–125.

[11] See Kanitz's interventions and discussions in the cabinet sessions of June 19, 26, and July 2, 1924, *Akten: Marx*, II, pp. 717–722, 743–746, 762–763. Cf. BA, Koblenz: Erich Koch-Weser Nachlass/30, entry of August 21, 1924, pp. 89 ff.; Stürmer, *Koalition und Opposition*, pp. 49–56.

The pressure of industrialists and landlords thus converged to press the Nationalists to accept the Dawes legislation and enter the ministry. Seeckt, who feared tighter military control, also urged ratification, and at the request of the Foreign Ministry the American Ambassador impressed upon Westarp, Hergt, and Otto Hoetzsch how vital acceptance was for American credits. Yet despite blandishment and threat, Hergt and Westarp still persisted in their opposition, apparently calculating that after inflicting a provisional defeat, they could dictate more advantageous cabinet participation as well as a less burdensome reparations agreement. Their adamant leadership did hold the DNVP delegation against the railroad legislation in the second reading of August 27; but on the final vote two days later, 48 Nationalist deputies deserted to furnish the government with its two-thirds majority.[12]

The vote signaled a new era in Weimar politics. Ratification of the London accords helped undercut the political extremes and ideological antagonism, focusing attention instead on the division of economic burdens that had to be worked out through coalition bargaining. In September, Foreign Ministry spokesmen correctly predicted that Nazis and Communists would lose half their strength in new elections.[13] Despite Hergt and Westarp's stubbornness, moreover, Stresemann still pressed for DNVP participation in the government. Negotiations to enlarge the cabinet dragged through the autumn but became stalemated over the Center Party's demand that either the new coalition should include the Social Democrats along with the Nationalists (a combination never to be achieved in Weimar), or the coalition of Center, Democrats, and People's Party should continue in office. Stresemann's colleagues, however, insisted on an opening to the right and finally the DVP withdrew from the coalition on the eve of the new parliamentary session. After the long and fruitless negotiations, Marx dissolved the Reichstag and called new elections. The December voting confirmed the relaxation of tension, as the Racist vote fell sharply and on the left the Social Democrats recovered strength from the Communists. The ebbing of extremism, however, did not diminish the harsh

[12] See Hergt to Marx, evidently in late August, in DZA, Potsdam: DNVP Akten/ 86, p. 124, and Westarp to Hergt, August 23, 1924, in Westarp Nachlass, Gaertringen. For the political considerations brought to bear see Maltzan to German missions abroad, September 9, 1924, in GFM: Geheimakten, Frankreich, Pol. 2, 5881/2756/E430219–430227; also Roland Thimme, *Stresemann und die deutsche Volkspartei, 1923–1925* (Lübeck and Hamburg, 1961), pp. 79 ff.; Werner Liebe, *Die Deutschnationale Volkspartei, 1918–1924* (Düsseldorf, 1956), pp. 76 ff. On Seeckt's role: Francis Carsten, *Reichswehr und Politik 1918–1933* (Cologne and Berlin, 1964), pp. 221–224; Hans Meier-Welcker, *Seeckt* (Frankfurt am Main, 1967), pp. 446–447.

[13] Maltzan memo, cited above, GFM: 5881/2756/E430219–430227.

conflicts between industry and working-class representatives, including those in the Center Party. It thus proved a painful task to construct a new government. Stresemann and Marx failed to unite the Center and the Nationalists in late December. Finally, in the new year a "government of personalities," which included Nationalist cabinet ministers and civil servants, was pieced together under Hans Luther, the former Mayor of Essen and Minister of Finance.[14]

The collaboration of the Nationalists, though, remained conditional at best. Stresemann hoped that portfolios would bring responsibility. There were, he argued, two major political forces contending in Germany: the Socialists and the conservative *Bürgertum*. To avoid violence there must be a synthesis between them.[15] But the Nationalists were hardly educated to the idea of political toleration, much less synthesis. As was the case when Hindenburg was elected as federal President in early 1925, DNVP support of the cabinet seemed to anchor and normalize the regime. Unfortunately, the Bürgerblok facilitated participation in the government without commitment to democracy. In fact, the new coalition did not even guarantee DNVP commitment to Stresemann's diplomatic initiatives. The Nationalists' growing misgivings over the security negotiations of 1925 were temporarily held in check by their desire to complete the tariff legislation and by the diligent mediation of the DNVP Minister of the Interior, Martin Schiele. Schiele and the party moderates, however, were overwhelmed by the hostile vote at the conference of DNVP delegates on October 23, 1925, which demanded that the Nationalist parliamentary party reject the Locarno draft treaties and that their ministers leave the government.[16] Yet, despite the Nationalist reversion to a cantankerous opposition, their ten-month participation contributed to the relative stability of the latter 1920's. This was not merely because the large right-wing party had agreed even halfheartedly to play by the rules of the Weimar system. The crucial contribution was the DNVP's brokerage in a new compromise among interest groups, even at the cost of alienating many of its voters. The Bürgerblok experience confirmed Weimar corporatism even if it could not enhance Weimar democracy.

The issue of currency revaluation was played out within the framework of Bürgerblok interest-group politics. Revaluation had actually

---

[14] For cabinet negotiations in the fall of 1924 and early 1925, see materials in BA, Koblenz: R 43 I/1020; Thimme, *Stresemann und die deutsche Volkspartei*, pp. 90–93; Stürmer, *Koalition und Opposition*, pp. 73–78; election results in *Statistik des deutschen Reiches*, vol. 315.

[15] Article for *L'Ère Nouvelle*, reprinted *Vermächtnis*, II, pp. 330–331.

[16] Manfred Dörr, "Die Deutschnationale Volkspartei 1925 bis 1928," Diss. (Marburg, 1964), pp. 167–201; Stürmer, *Koalition und Opposition*, pp. 107–127.

been introduced in November 1923 and January 1924, when Germany's constitutional judges had taken the unusual step of declaring that all monetary legislation and settlements had to be subjected to criteria of good faith and equity, which should compensate those who had mortgages, savings, or other claims liquidated during the inflation. The Government's Third Emergency Tax Ordinance of late 1923 had responded to this judicial directive by providing for an initial limited revaluation of 15 percent. The decree was valid only until mid-1925, but in the meanwhile savers and creditors mobilized angrily against its low ceiling on revaluation. The constitutional tribunals lectured the cabinet and even threatened the ministers with personal liability for losses sustained under the Emergency Decree.[17]

The revaluation issue was a poisoned chalice for all the government parties, and a fine partisan opportunity for those outside. In economic terms alone, business and agriculture shared similar objectives. They needed to minimize revaluation, or at least to standardize it by law so that future credit needs could be rationally calculated. Labor, too, could be hurt by the dislocations attending major revaluation, but the issue impinged less directly upon them than upon industry. In any case, politics did not strictly follow economic logic. Revaluing old debts was a popular election plank in 1924, for it beckoned millions of middle- and lower-middle-class voters. For the parties in the opposition it offered a chance to snipe at the government parties who provided indecisive leadership. National Socialists, Communists, and German Nationalists held out visions of 100 percent revaluation in their search for votes during the fall campaign. As a party, the Social Democrats remained relatively unmoved by this middle-class issue; however, they allowed their spokesman Wilhelm Keil to advocate individual revaluation settlements as high as economic conditions permitted. After the elections, once the Nationalists had joined the government and tempered their stand, Keil was to delight in baiting the DNVP with their own excessive promises, even though his personal enthusiasm for the

[17] See Chapter Seven, n. 56, and cabinet meetings of December 15 and 17, 1923, and January 22, 1924: GFM: ARK, 3491/1750/758186–758192, 758217, and 3491/1751/758692–758697. For the legal controversy: Arthur Nussbaum, *Die Bilanz der Aufwertungstheorie* (Tübingen, 1929); also Karl Bernhard Netzband and Hans Peter Widmaier, *Währungs- und Finanzpolitik der Ära Luther 1923–1925* (Basel-Tübingen, 1964), pp. 183 ff. For the continuing resistance of the Economics Ministry (even when in DNVP hands) to extensive revaluation see its proposals of February 1925, designed to defend the "economy" against extensive consumer wishes by limiting revaluation claims to 22 percent, restricting retroactivity until June 1, 1922, and forcing the claimant to concede a partial mortgage, or defer interest, to let the old debtor fulfill his revaluation obligations more gradually. See DZA, Potsdam: Reichswirtschaftsministerium/15415: "Stellungnahme zur Aufwertung," February 5, 1925; "Der Standpunkt des Reichswirtschaftsministeriums in der Aufwertungsgesetz," February 6, 1925.

revaluation cause prompted occasional reproaches of demagogy from his own ranks.[18]

With the opening of the Reichstag, the Nationalists and Center Party who formed the base of the coalition, faced uncomfortable and divisive choices. They harbored divergent interest groups, and key electoral supporters expected significant revaluation. As mortgage holders, Catholic cathedral chapters and monastic foundations exerted pressure on the Center leadership. "Even bishops turned to me with earnest words of admonition to let right and justice prevail," noted Marx later. "As if it was not primarily a question of preserving the life of the nation!" As the Catholic Labor Minister Brauns wrote to a member of the Fulda cathedral chapter, one had to come to terms with devaluation. A definite if limited recovery of savings was healthier than an excessive revaluation that would overburden the Reichsmark and provoke a new inflation. And as Marx had to remind one priest who rebuked him, ultimately it was not the policy of limiting revaluation that destroyed savings, but a lost war and the Ruhr conflict.[19] Beyond the churches there was a broad middle-class constituency that hoped for the restoration of savings accounts or mortgages and had organized its own pressure groups, including a Creditors and Savers Protective Association. The Nationalists had consistently wooed this middle-class vote throughout 1924, first by criticizing the Third Emergency Tax Ordinance, then by nominating one of the most prominent revaluation spokesmen, Judge Georg Best, to a secure seat on the DNVP's electoral list. Best prepared legislation that called for review of each debtor-creditor relationship and reestablishment of debts according to the respective property ratios of the two parties both before and after the war. From one point of view the attempt to respect earlier patterns of wealth in distributing the burden of the inflation was the fairest possible, but business foresaw a spate of lawsuits. The DNVP was particularly torn between its business and agrarian interests on the one side, and those of the middle-class creditors whose cause it had adopted in the campaign.[20]

For the new cabinet the situation became even more divisive when in early March Keil introduced the same motion to suspend the Third Emergency Tax Ordinance that the DNVP had itself presented the preceding June. Luther met this maneuver by threatening to resign if he did not get the entire cabinet's support in rejecting the SPD resolution. The campaign for the national Presidency that lay imminently

[18] Wilhelm Keil, *Erlebnisse eines Sozialdemokraten*, 2 vols. (Stuttgart, 1948), ii, pp. 305–308.

[19] Hugo Stehkämper, ed., *Der Nachlass des Reichskanzlers Wilhelm Marx. Mitteilungen aus dem Stadtarchiv von Köln*, 52–55, 4 vols. (Cologne, 1968), iii, pp. 82, 121, 124.

[20] Dörr, *Deutschnationale Volkspartei*, pp. 325–333.

ahead also endangered the coalition, since the Center and Nationalists supported different candidates. Before electioneering prompted new promises of revaluation, Luther calculated, the Nationalists had to be pledged to support a government bill. As an estate and factory owner with little patience for the creditor demands, Schiele, too, wanted the government to dictate a bill and demand DNVP support. Best, he claimed, had little support in the Nationalist parliamentary party; and indeed when Best called for extensive revaluation in the Reichstag he met only an embarrassed silence from his DNVP colleagues. While spokesmen for the creditor interests accused the Nationalists of perfidy, industrialists in the party complained that even the 25 percent revaluation of mortgages the government contemplated was intolerably high. It could be accepted only if the Dawes plan bonds that industry had to issue were counted as part of the revalued debt. On March 17 and 18, Luther again demanded support for the government's project from cabinet members and party leaders. Case-by-case revaluation would destroy German credit and mean "the suicide of the German people"— a judgment reinforced by the refusal of New York bankers to grant a loan to the Agricultural Rentenbank Credit Institute so long as the possibility of high revaluation settlements still existed. Provisionally, at least the coalition parties agreed to unite behind the government bill but they reserved the right to present further amendments to the cabinet.[21]

The opposition, however, continued to exploit the DNVP's internal divisions. When the Nationalist city counsellors in Berlin sought to withdraw their own measure that provided for the extension of revaluation rights to elderly savers who had held municipal bank accounts, the SPD passed the bill and enlarged its coverage.[22] The Democratic Party also sought to profit from the government's embarrassments. Koch-Weser told the DDP executive on February 2, that their party should let the Nationalists bring down Luther and meanwhile avoid any clear position on revaluation; as late as June he elaborated a strategy that enabled the Democrats to appeal to the right-wing voters who would emerge embittered by the DNVP's reneging on revaluation commitments.[23] The committee of the Reichstag reviewing the legislation threatened to bring in its own bill which would permit

[21] Cabinet discussions of March 7 and 17 and the conference with party leaders, March 18, 1925 in GFM: ARK, Kabinettsprotokolle, 3543/1833/763714–763718, 763877–763895. Cf. Keil, *Erlebnisse*, ii, p. 310; Hans Luther, *Politiker ohne Partei* (Stuttgart, 1960), pp. 229–233; *BT*, March 19, p. 3, "Die Entscheidung über die Aufwertungsfrage," Stürmer, *Koalition und Opposition*, pp. 92–97.

[22] *BT*, March 20, 1925, Beiblatt, p. 2.

[23] NSDAP Hauptarchiv, DDP papers/f. 729, Vorstand meetings of February 2 and June 11, 1925.

extensive settlements. By early May, Best himself joined the antigovernment members of the committee and when the DNVP sought to remove him, the SPD offered him one of their own committee seats. Hergt's feeble explanations in the Reichstag that the Nationalists wished to avoid controversial debate on the issue provoked derision from the SPD, the Democrats, and the Racists alike.[24]

Finally by mid-May Luther did succeed in winning interparty agreement on a definitive statute. The draft precluded extensive revaluation but did let the DNVP show its constituents some improvement over the Third Emergency Tax Ordinance and some heeding of Best's suggestions. Mortgages remained revalued at 25 percent of their real worth; but whereas the earlier government draft had limited revaluation only to debts liquidated after December 15, 1922, now the creditor could claim revaluation for debts settled another six months further back. Keil moved to raise the claims of "old owners"—those who possessed corporate bonds as early as July 1, 1920—from 10 to 25 percent of their earlier value. On the other hand the "new owners," who had presumably bought bonds for negligible real value, were to be limited to a claim of 2.5 percent. State and federal bonds were to be redeemed for bonds worth 5 percent of the original debt, with redemption dates determined by lottery. Municipal bonds offered slightly more chances for recovery. Hergt wearily said that the DNVP's decision to compromise required courage; in the last analysis, he felt, that one had to choose between a system of individual adjustments that would prolong uncertainty and unrest, and a compromise that would restore calm to the economy. In the commission the DDP Party delegate Dernburg essentially accepted the draft; the Socialists and Communists remained opposed. Outside the commission the Revaluation associations condemned the draft while Best left the Nationalists to join the National Socialist parliamentary group.[25] "The view is widely held among the people," Hamburg creditors wrote Marx—whose own clear stance against high revaluation had probably cost him dearly in the Presidential campaign, "that our present government is only a willing tool of heavy industry and big capital."[26]

Only a few more maneuvers were to delay this epitaph written to middle-class hopes for recovering claims on wealth that had long since been expropriated by other social groups or squandered in the war. In the Reichstag floor debates a final SPD motion, introduced by Keil,

[24] Keil, *Erlebnisse*, II, pp. 313–314; *BT*, May 13, 1925, p. 3.
[25] *BT*, May 14, 1925, p. 3; May 15, 1925, p. 4; May 15 p.m., p. 3; May 16, 1. Beiblatt, p. 2; May 17, p. 3. Résumé of final laws in U.S. Department of State 862.51/1987 (private loans) and 1988 (public loans).
[26] Letter of the Hamburg Association for the Protection of Creditors and Savers, cited in Stehkämper, ed., *Nachlass Marx*, III, p. 126.

to raise the basic revaluation rate for mortgages from 25 to 40 percent failed 151 to 244; the bill itself passed 230 to 197. Hindenburg alone had the opportunity to delay the law further by calling a plebiscite to test it among the electorate. But faced with the threat of the cabinet's resignation should he reopen the painful issue, the recently elected Reichspräsident signed the law.[27] Even this, however, did not eliminate bitterness and agitation. Revaluation pressure groups sought to reopen the issue and sought a plebiscite once again in 1926. The legislation, moreover, still allowed many tangled revaluation questions to go before the courts. It was estimated that Prussia alone had to employ 3000 more officials just to handle the cases, which amounted to 2.8 million by January 1928. Lower tribunals and the Supreme Court faced a thicket of legal dilemmas: the responsibility of home purchasers for mortgages that prior owners had paid off in depreciated marks, the effect of the dates of property transfer, the subsequent values of land, etc.[28] From the criterion of monetary stability, economic recovery, and full employment, Luther, Schiele and Marx were right: the devastating transfers of wealth that had taken place in the inflation had finally to be conceded. But the results contributed to middle-class resentment: just as Best himself left the Nationalists to join the proto-Nazi group, many disillusioned DNVP voters looked to the new Economic Party, a middle-class splinter group that drew on the resentments of civil servants, pensioners, and homeowners whose property had been eroded first by rent control during the inflation and thereafter by heavy tax increases. As Marx noted, with great charity toward his often immoderate critics, revaluation continued to be the major preoccupation "of the best part of the loyal and hard-working bourgeoisie."[29]

The politics of French public finance produced similar distress and political fragmentation. The parliamentary crisis under the Cartel des Gauches emerged in part from the incompatibility between socialists and moderates among the left coalition. But it also arose out of the conflicting interests within the middle-class parties themselves. Two related financial dilemmas confronted the government; first a budget deficit, second a limit upon money in circulation that was enforced by a rigid monetary orthodoxy. The deficit could be defrayed by either

[27] *BT*, July 11, 1925, p. 3; July 16 a.m. and p.m.; July 17. Also VDR: SB, 386, pp. 2934–3263 (July 10-16, 1925).

[28] Nussbaum, *Bilanz der Aufwertungstheorie*, pp. 15 ff.; John P. Dawson, *The Oracles of the Law* (Ann Arbor, Mich., 1968), pp. 465 ff.

[29] Marx to Cardinal Bertram, April 10, 1927, in Stehkämper, ed., *Nachlass Marx*, III, p. 128. For the infusion of organized homeowners and *Mittelstand* elements into the Economic Party, Martin Schumacher, *Mittelstandsfront und Republik. Wirtschaftspartei-Reichspartei des deutschen Mittelstandes* (Düsseldorf, 1972), pp. 80–86, 115–116.

leftwing or conservative policies. While Herriot and the SFIO urged taxes upon capital, the moderate Radicals and Gauche Radicale joined the opposition in a demand for "economies" and "confidence in capital."[30] In practice this meant abandoning any effective taxing of dividends and interest and relying more upon indirect excises and paring expenses. The split within the majority thus precluded any consistent financial policy.

The monetary dilemmas, on the other hand, originated in the legal ceilings that set limits to the notes in circulation and to the Treasury's borrowing from the Bank of France. The ceilings corsetted business and government alike, especially in a period of inflation. The result was a vicious circle of monetary embarrassment. Each time circulation or Bank advances approached the legal ceilings, fears of further inflation led the holders of short-term National Defense bonds to cash them in, while holders of franc balances scrambled for other currencies or gold. Consequently government bonds, including long-term *rentes* sagged in value and the franc fell on the exchanges. The government required new paper money to meet its own rising expenses and to redeem the bonds presented for payment; hence it had to borrow anew from the Bank of France and put more notes into circulation—ultimately to crash through the given legal limits, or as the French expressed it, *crever le plafond.*

There was no strict economic reason to undergo these crises, but the left generally held the same awe of the ceilings as the fiscally conservative and hesitated to change the rules of the game. Even when it demanded a capital levy that could only aggravate the flight from government bonds, the left failed to press for adequate circulation and debt limits once and for all. Advances would thus encroach upon and exceed the legal limits, and the Cartel government was forced to resort to twenty-four hour occult loans from private banks to pay back the Bank of France in time for its weekly statement. This expedient ransomed the cabinet to the bourgeois public for its short-term bonds and to the major banks for its weekly cover at the Bank of France. Only when the surge of advances and the depreciation of the franc led to the defeat of a ministry would the National Assembly reluctantly ratify a new ceiling.

Why did the Cartel chain itself to the fetishism of the ceilings? Only

[30] A typical call for "confidence" and the need to reassure holders of the 150-billion-franc short-term debt is in "Exposé sur les finances publiques," presented to the Senate Commission on Finances by its *rapporteur* Henry Bérenger, June 4, 1924, and included in Min. Aff. Etr., Fonds Président Herriot/4, f. 1. For the general dilemmas of financial policy: David B. Goldey, "The Disintegration of the Cartel des Gauches and the Politics of French Government Finance, 1924–1928," Diss. (Oxford, 1964).

a few days after Herriot and Finance Minister Clémentel took office, the new Directeur du Mouvement Général des Fonds, Pierre de Moüy, urged the government to press immediately for a higher ceiling and for another renegotiation of the 1920 François-Marsal convention that obligated the state to repay the Bank of France two billion francs per year. The Bank, on the other hand, insisted on orthodoxy: "The danger of inflation under whatever insidious form it might be presented is a death threat to be avoided at any price."[31] Clémentel initially accepted this judgment, and Herriot, too, adopted the rules of the game rather than tangle with the bankers or risk a defeat in parliament.

These divisions on fiscal policy and the acquiescence in the conventional banking wisdom effectively doomed the Cartel. From the outset little united the ministry but republican mystique. The forced resignation of President Millerand, the suppression of the embassy at the Vatican, the negotiation of the Dawes plan and a promise to evacuate the Ruhr, the amnesties for Caillaux and Malvy, finally in November the reinterment of Jaurès in the Panthéon, all created an emotional ambiance of left-wing fraternity. In turn, these symbolic gestures stimulated organization on the right and a harsh sense of confrontation as the Fédération Nationale Catholique, Millerand's Ligue Nationale Républicaine, and newer would-be fascists, assembled mass rallies and denounced the leftist threat. In fact, France suffered not from the depredations of the left but from its divisions and weakness. The SFIO refused to enter the government and granted it only conditional support. After forcing out Millerand, the Cartel failed to elect Paul Painlevé to the Elysée; the presidency of the Senate was captured by the moderate Selves, and the Senate itself remained a conservative breakwater to the anger of Socialists and militant Radicals.[32]

[31] Moüy memos of June 17 and 27, 1924, in Min. Aff. Etr., Fonds Herriot/6, f. "La crise de 1924." Also: Georges Lachapelle, *Le crédit public*, 2 vols. (Paris, 1932), ii, p. 196 for Moüy warning and pp. 203–204, for Robineau, Governor of the Bank of France, to Clémentel, July 17, 1924. (Cf. Lachapelle, *Les batailles du franc*, Paris, 1928, pp. 142 ff.) As Lachapelle reports, *Le crédit public*, ii, p. 207, the Bank had already called attention to infractions of the debt ceiling or circulation limit in late 1923; and recourse to private loans to cover the advances from the Bank of France had occupied under François-Marsal in 1920. But before the left came to power, these expedients seemed to cause little concern. Robineau's successor, Emile Moreau, recognized the political nature of the Governor's interventions and of his dominating Secretary General, Aupetit. See E. Moreau, *Souvenirs d'un gouverneur de la Banque de France. Histoire de la stabilisation du franc (1926–1928)*, (Paris, 1954), pp. 1–2.

[32] For the events of 1924, Jacques Chastenet, *Histoire de la Troisième République*, vol. v, *Les années d'illusions 1918–1931* (Paris, 1960), pp. 119–123, 128–134; Edouard Bonnefous, *Histoire politique de la Troisième République*, vol. iv, *Cartel des gauches et union nationale (1924–1929)* (Paris, 1960), pp. 25, 33–59; for the removal of Millerand, F. François-Marsal, "La crise présidentielle de 1924," MS; a gossipy rightwing perspective on the Cartel is Louis Marcellin,

Even under the Cartel, French politics remained a struggle for the loyalties of the Radical Socialist Party and the political center. On the pressing financial questions the Radicals could produce no coherent solution. When Clémentel renewed the Morgan loan of $100 million in the summer of 1924, the Morgan bankers warned him that Poincaré's taxes still had not covered the budgetary deficit. Most immediately the government might raise the bank rate, limit its own borrowing from the Bank of France, and thereby make its own bonds more creditworthy and diminish its need for further advances.[33] Despite misgivings Morgan renewed the loan. Nonetheless, the circulation of bank notes remained high; the government could not resolve to raise interest rates and thus increase its own carrying charges; finally it could not settle on a tax program. On the other hand, as of late 1924 no official was willing to discuss raising the level of circulation. Robineau, the Governor of the Bank of France, warned solemnly that "no measure would be more fatal" than such an increase, and Herriot reiterated his own determination not to sanction inflation.[34] By the following February, however, Robineau reversed himself to impose what he later admitted was a "veritable ultimatum" and demanded that the ministry seek parliamentary authority to raise the ceilings.[35] For Herriot to consent would alarm the Cartel's moderates and risk defeat; to refuse would lead the Bank to reveal its concealed advances to the state. After feverish conferences, Herriot won a month's delay in order to attempt various technical operations and launch a pay-in-advance tax scheme that offered contributors a five percent discount. But results proved disappointing, and the Bank refused to support any government intervention in the money market with its own reserves. The left, too, was impatient: Blum wrote Herriot on March 25 that no democratic gov-

---

Voyage autour de la Chambre du 11 mai (Paris, 1925). For newspaper reports and other material on the progress of the Ligue Nationale Républicaine: Bibliothèque Nationale, Fonds Millerand.

[33] See J. P. Morgan & Co. to Morgan, Harjes & Co., Paris (for Clémentel), August 1, 1924, Nr. 2476 in Baker Library, TWL 95–11; also Russell C. Leffingwell to Dean Jay of Morgan, Harjes, June 28, 1924, TWL 113–2.

[34] Robineau letter of December 29, 1924, in Lachapelle, *Le crédit public,* II, pp. 209–210. For reassurances against inflation see Herriot to the Chamber, January 17, 1925: JOC, 1925, I, pp. 102–107 and Herriot's interview with the Chairman and *rapporteur* of the Senate Finance Commission on February 27 as reported the next day to the Commission, included in Min. Aff. Etr., Fonds Herriot/6, f. "La crise de 1924." The Bank of France credited the Treasury with the Morgan loan ($89 million outstanding) against its advances, but only at the official rate of 5.18 francs per dollar, not the open market rate. Credit at the market rate (then 30 francs per dollar) for the then remaining $31 million was immediately granted Poincaré on his accession to power. See Moreau, *Souvenirs,* p. 41.

[35] Letter of February 26, 1925, in Lachapelle, *Le crédit public,* II, pp. 215–216.

ernment could continue to live "from due date to due date" at the sufferance of the Bank. He urged a levy of one-eighth to one-tenth of personal property and the mortgaging of business assets and suggested stabilizing the currency at about one-third its pre-war parity, twelve to fifteen per dollar.[36]

Publication of this program and alarmist articles in the conservative press accelerated the fall of the franc. On April 2, the ministry began to disintegrate, as Clémentel resigned, evidently unhappy about the projects under discussion for a capital levy, but also hurt because Herriot disavowed his suggestion that the ceiling, not on advances but on circulation might be raised.[37] Herriot floundered: he appealed to the right by abandoning the registry book that he had planned to require for recording dividend payments (a concept originally introduced by Poincaré and Lasteyrie and hardly radical!). At the same time his new Minister of Finance, Anatole de Monzie, brandished a forced loan of ten percent. Finally on April 9, Robineau published his damaging ledgers and exposed the government's evasion of the legal ceilings. Two days of bitter debate in the Chamber and Senate culminated in the ministry's defeat at the Luxembourg as François-Marsal accused the government of "shaking the sturdy constitution of the middle classes" and the centrist Senators broke from the Cartel.[38]

What followed was fifteen months of parliamentary agony as successive governments oscillated between trying to hold the votes of the Socialists on fiscal policy and the moderates on monetary issues. Paul Painlevé succeeded Herriot for six months with Briand at the Quai d'Orsay and Joseph Caillaux at the Rue de Rivoli. Caillaux's financial views were now impeccably orthodox; and this prewar champion of a progressive income tax canceled plans for a capital levy. Although he quarreled bitterly with the directors of the Bank of France for their refusal to support the franc on the money markets, Caillaux ended up succumbing to the left, not the right, for he divided the Cartel by his fiscal orthodoxy.[39] When the Socialists pressed for exempting small

[36] Blum to "Mon cher Herriot," March 25, 1925, in Min. Aff. Etr., Fonds Herriot/6. Reproduced from Le Populaire in Lachapelle, Le crédit public, II, pp. 229, n. 1.

[37] Clémentel's reproachful note to Herriot, penciled notes on the Conseils du Cabinet, April 2, 6, and 10, 1925, in Min. Aff. Etr., Fonds Herriot/6; also Lachapelle, Le crédit public, II, pp. 225–227. Cf. Clémentel's financial history of the ministry, Le Temps, March 16, 1929.

[38] JOC, 1925, pp. 2127–2167 (April 9); JOS, 1925, pp. 836–859 (April 10); François-Marsal citation, p. 839.

[39] See Raymond Philippe's critique: Le drame financier de 1924–1928 (Paris, 1931), pp. 76–82. For a journalistic, somewhat vicious, account of Caillaux's role in 1925–26, see Georges Suarez, De Poincaré à Poincaré (Paris, 1928), esp. p. 19, for the Journal article of June 18, 1925. Cf. Alfred Fabre-Luce, Caillaux (Paris,

firms from the unpopular turnover tax, the Senate, concerned by the deficit, insisted on across-the-board application. Caillaux seconded the Senate view and temporarily united a majority of "concentration"— center-right and center-left—against the Socialists in the Chamber.[40]

This new majority of July 12 threatened the end of the Cartel, but was still premature and depended upon the balance of forces within the Radical Party. At the party congress in Nice in mid-October, Caillaux clashed with Herriot, who again called for a capital levy and warned that he could no longer support a government drawing upon even one vote from the right. Bertrand Nogaro skillfully sought to define a Radical Socialist financial policy that represented a middle-ground. Although the "turnover" tax could not simply be abandoned, Nogaro conceded, it might be transformed into a less vexing production tax, closer to the modern value-added tax. The Radicals, Nogaro suggested, might look for further progressivity in the tax system by working for government refunds for large or poorer families as compensation for the indirect excises they paid. Finally, the inflammatory capital levy, he soothingly indicated, could be regarded as an added increment on income tax since it would have to be spread over many years.[41] Given the premises of Radical Socialism, which involved an emotional appeal to the left, some willingness to make the fiscal system more progressive, but a desire to avoid real sacrifice, Nogaro's report was sober but innovative. Nonetheless, it stood little chance of becoming effective party policy in view of the personal duel between Herriot and Caillaux—the burly professor with the common touch and populist appeal against the reputedly brilliant, if erratic, financial wizard, fastidious, arrogant, and impassioned in debate. The Party seemed caught between their starkly contrasted alternatives.

In light of Herriot's threats and subsequent clashes within the cabinet a few days after the party congress, Painlevé felt compelled to resign in order to remove Caillaux from his ministry. He returned with new left-wing financial remedies, including postponement of the December treasury bond redemptions and a 14 percent property tax that would be spaced over 14 years. Not surprisingly, the sensitive franc skidded again and the conservative wing of the Cartel deserted the

---

1933), pp. 213 ff.; Emile Moreau's generally admiring portrait, July 18, 1926 (but Caillaux appointed him Governor), *Souvenirs*, pp. 31–32; Rudolph Binion, *Defeated Leaders: The Political Fate of Joseph Caillaux, Henry de Jouvenel, and André Tardieu* (New York, 1960), pp. 86–107.

[40] JOC, 1925, pp. 3452–3471 (July 12).

[41] Suarez, *De Poincaré à Poincaré*, pp. 32–45, for the Radical Party Congress; Nogaro's report printed as "La politique financière du Parti Radical Socialiste," *RPP*, cxxv, November 1925, pp. 272–293.

government which met defeat at the conclusion of the parliamentary debates between November 17 and 22.[42]

As successive efforts to form a government by Briand, Paul Doumer, and Herriot all indicated, no consistent majority remained. The Radical Socialists seemed condemned to sacrifice the support of the moderates to their right or the Socialists to their left. The centrist majority of July 12 did not promise enough Radical votes. Any effort at right-center union would only reunite the Cartel in opposition.

Having demonstrated that the original Cartel was unable to form a cohesive government, President Doumergue redesignated Briand, the master of the *majorité de réchange*, or the winning of votes from one side to pass the policies of the other. The half-year Briand experience demonstrated that bourgeois consensus was sufficiently frayed that even successful budgetary retrenchment could not halt the depreciation of the franc. After initially choosing Loucheur, whose proposals to crack down on tax evasion and amortize the debt again intimidated the moderates, Briand decided on a centrist option and installed the venerable Paul Doumer at the Rue de Rivoli.[43] Doumer's orthodox proposals to raise the price of tobacco and impose a tax on payments—the unpopular turnover tax in a new guise—provoked the Cartel majority on the Chamber Commission of Finances to produce their own counter-budget built around a new, heavy inheritance tax. After exhausting weeks of debate, Briand barely managed to defeat the left's proposals as 44 Radical Socialists joined Communists and Socialists in voting against the ministry, while 56 of the party joined moderates and conservatives in support, and 26, including Herriot, abstained. It required a new Briand ministry finally to piece together a program that offered enough concessions to left and right to eke out precarious support. The registration of bearer securities and official records for dividends were designed to win back the left; a higher turnover tax and "civic" tax were palatable to the moderates, and Briand thus finally extracted a vote for a balanced 1926 budget by late April.[44]

Nonetheless, the budget could remain in balance only if the franc did not depreciate, and Briand's feeble consensus was not compelling enough to reassure bond and currency holders. The franc had stood at 60 to the pound when Poincaré had left office two years earlier; it had

[42] Cabinet clashes in Suarez, *De Poincaré à Poincaré*, pp. 45–58 (emphasizing the Monzie-Caillaux rivalry); debates in JOC: 1925, pp. 3722–3741 (November 17), 3752–3773 (November 18), 3780–3795 (November 19), 3801–3845 (November 20), 3857–3879 (November 21), 3890–3913 (November 22).

[43] For the formation of the new ministry and December legislation, Bonnefous, *Histoire politique*, IV, pp. 101–104.

[44] *Ibid.*, pp. 107–115, 123–124; Joseph Barthélemy, *Essai sur le travail parlementaire et le système des commissions* (Paris, 1934), pp. 278 ff., 334 ff.; and JOC, 1926, pp. 2137–2185 (April 28; final debate); JOS, 1926, pp. 1045–1069 (April 28).

lost 50 percent of its value by the time Herriot fell close to a year later; it had slid from 110 to 130 per pound in the weeks after Loucheur's tenure during December 1925. Now the franc declined even more alarmingly: from 145 on May 5, to 160 on May 15, and 172 on May 19. The new depreciation seemed to be triggered by recent adverse balance-of-trade figures and the new taxation aimed at dividend income. It suggested that even if moderates in the Chamber endorsed Briand's compromise proposals Frenchmen with savings did not. Moreover, the Bank of France remained glacially uncooperative. At an early May meeting at the Rue de Rivoli, Regent Edouard de Rothschild announced that no intervention on the money markets promised success until a conservative government had returned to power.[45]

American authorities effectively endorsed this bleak and self-fulfilling estimate. When on May 8, Parmentier approached Benjamin Strong, Governor of the New York Federal Reserve Bank who was then traveling in Europe, Strong refused to extend a $100 million loan even if it was secured by the gold reserves of the Bank of France. Conditions for such a loan, he emphasized, had to include agreement between the French government, "the Blum-Herriot group," and the banking community. Nonetheless, Briand's new Finance Minister, Raoul Péret, resolved the government had to attempt to halt the depreciation by buying francs with its own funds, including the $89 million remaining of the Morgan loan. After intensive debate between May 19 and 31, the Bank apparently assented. In fact, according to Parmentier, it treated Péret disgracefully by promising support in raising American credits, but then "stabbing the government in the back and paying the press to defend its actions."[46] After ten days of spending $56 million produced no significant appreciation of the franc, the support action was suspended. Montagu Norman in London and Strong, who now arrived in Paris, pointed out that circumstances were different from the spring of 1924. Then, foreigners had been speculating against the currency, and the American loan had forced them to cover their short sales, sending the franc up on a rebound. But now it was the confidence of French holders of capital that was lacking. The flight from the franc would cease with political reassurance—implicitly, a government of "union"—but not before. In Paris, Strong told Péret that further American loans were fruitless, and that as Director of the New York Federal Reserve he did not want to be put in the unenviable position of carting away the gold

[45] Philippe, *Le drame financier*, pp. 95–106.

[46] Lester V. Chandler, *Benjamin Strong, Central Banker* (Washington, 1958), pp. 361–367; Lachapelle, *Le crédit public*, II, pp. 264–267, and *Les batailles du franc*, pp. 162–172; Parmentier "gossip" reported by Herman Harjes to TWL, June 22, 1926, in Baker Library, TWL 113–5.

reserves of the Bank of France.[47] Péret understood the message: although he himself did not possess the stature to put together a government of union, he was to conclude that this was the necessary step for financial recovery.

The constraints on the ministry were all the more pressing because of the government's war debt to the United States. The issue did not divide Frenchmen politically. From Communists to nationalists, all parties asserted that Washington should relinquish its claims. Instead, the United States Treasury informally placed an embargo on private as well as public loans until repayment terms were settled. By the spring of 1926, a number of French financiers and political experts had decided prompt settlement was necessary to win American credits and relieve the pressure on the franc. Further postponement, they felt, could only mean worse terms for Paris. Although French negotiators originally sought a guarantee clause that would effectively release them from payment if German reparations failed, Washington resisted this connection. Finally, the French concentrated on winning the most favorable financial terms and by April 1926 concluded the so-called Mellon-Bérenger agreement.[48]

The political implications of the debt settlement turned out to favor the conservative forces in France. A weak government could not survive a ratification debate: even though Briand felt it necessary to submit the accords to the Chamber he did not press for discussion or a vote. Ratification, however, as Mellon himself indicated, was a prerequisite for American loans; and without loans stabilization was possible only under conservative auspices. The Mellon-Bérenger agreement thus curtailed the options of any government which did not inspire "confidence." It made the pressure for bourgeois "union" in defense of the franc all the more irresistible.

On the other hand, the debt issue did not provoke a simple division of left and right. Like the question of inflation it separated sophisticated entrepreneurial and middle-of-the-road political leaders from more old-fashioned representatives on the left and right. Left and right together felt aggrieved by international fiscal constraints just as they reacted most emotionally to the franc's loss of value. Those who were ready to accept inflation and those most prepared to accept the

[47] Note on conversation between Strong and Péret, May 19, 1926, in Min. Fin. F[30]/1361. Ellen W. Schrecker, "The French Debt to the United States, 1917–1929," Diss. (Cambridge, Mass. 1973), pp. 251–252, summarizes Péret-Robineau exchanges, May 5 to June 8, found in F[30]/2350. Pierre Freyssinet, *La politique monétaire de la France, 1924–1928* (Paris, 1928), pp. 46–54, 76 ff. criticizes plans to purchase francs without fiscal reform, as carried out in 1924.

[48] Schrecker, "The French Debt," pp. 219–245; and on Mellon's pressure, J. P. Morgan & Co. to TWL, May 7, 1926, Baker Library, TWL 172–29.

debt agreement came from the political center: for instance Bérenger himself, the former *rapporteur* of the Senate Finance Commission and currently Ambassador in Washington, and Maurice Bokanowski, the financial spokesman of the center right who had led the Chamber forces on behalf of the *double décime* two years earlier. The debt issue thus produced an alignment similar to the one on monetary stabilization. In France, as in Germany, the vexing redistributive questions that lay underneath the issues of inflation, revaluation, and international payments did not primarily separate left and right, but those who saw economic health and their own interests involved with production and employment from those concerned with savings.

Given the new franc depreciation in late May and early June, Briand and Péret sought to marshal that precious and elusive "confidence" from the holders of francs and bonds by abandoning the registration of dividends and reducing taxes on nonlanded capital. At the same time they tried to remove the financial question from the party arena by appointing a committee of experts to recommend a comprehensive monetary and fiscal program. This was a gesture to the Americans as well as French bondholders; however, neither the tax cuts nor the new committee could reconcile conservatives and reassure holders of capital. In the week after June 7, the franc fell from 160 to 174 while the *bien pensant* press attacked any plans for open-market action that might endanger the Bank's gold reserves. On June 15, Péret resigned, critical of the Bank of France, but conceding that only a government of union could arrest the fall of the currency.[49]

After managing to win a vote of confidence Briand himself resigned the same day to try and reconstitute a ministry of national union extending from the Socialists through Poincaré. This proved impossible— as did Herriot's effort to form a ministry with conservative collaborators, including Lucien Romier, the editor of *Le Figaro*.[50] Unable to accept Poincaré's clear conservative fiscal program, Briand now put together another ministry of concentration with Caillaux as his Finance Minister. Once again this represented a moderate solution that failed to command middle-class and bourgeois confidence. In the beautiful late spring weather with factories and businesses humming prosperously, Frenchmen were bewildered by the parliamentary disintegration and their collapsing currency. Briand's government proved unable to reverse public anxiety. Nursing his grudges of a year earlier, Caillaux began his new tenure by replacing Robineau as Governor of the Bank

[49] For the discussion of Péret's resignation: JOC, 1926, pp. 2527–2531 (June 15); also Péret letter in Lachapelle, *Le crédit public*, II, pp. 272–273.

[50] See Suarez on "la folle nuit," *De Poincaré à Poincaré*, pp. 59–89; also François Pietri, "Crises d'avant-guerre," RDM, March 15, 1959, pp. 258–260.

of France with Emile Moreau. This move alarmed conservatives, although Briand had enough political credit in the right-wing Fédération Républicaine to prevent an immediate parliamentary revolt. The report of the experts that was issued on July 4, implicitly justified a switch of Bank leadership by urging a more interventionist role. More fundamentally it stressed the need for "economies" that would balance the budget and encourage the repatriation of capital.[51] For the most part bankers, the experts shared the assumption, though, that foreign funds would ultimately be necessary to stabilize the franc. As both Léon Blum and Louis Marin pointed out on July 7, the government, too, was wagering on foreign credits as the experts recommended. But as they reminded Briand, credits required ratification of the debt refunding agreement.[52]

The bare majority of 22 that the ministry extracted after an extended debate which featured several days denunciation of the Mellon-Bérenger accord, indicated that such ratification was highly unlikely. Even the relatively favorable debt settlement that Caillaux brought back from London in mid-July could not improve chances for approval of the American agreement. Consequently, Caillaux decided to ask for wide-ranging decree power to institute measures appropriate for financial recovery and monetary stabilization, probably including ratification of the Washington settlement. In a dramatic session Herriot deserted the Chair of the Chamber to oppose the request from the floor, while Marin denounced the proposal from the republican right. Briand understood that he had lost from the outset.[53]

Doumergue called upon Herriot to face the consequences of his successful opposition by finding a new government. Outside the parliament the franc, which had already fallen from 173 to 202 between June 30 and July 16, now plummeted to 240. The Bank of France announced that the ceilings would cave again within twenty-four hours. Angry mobs surged against the gratings of the Palais Bourbon and booed the new cabinet. When Moreau, the new Governor of the Bank, demanded immediate parliamentary approval for higher ceilings, he offered conservatives the chance they needed to trounce the new ministry. The government was immediately defeated upon its first appearance before

---

[51] For the second Caillaux experience, Fabre-Luce, *Caillaux*, pp. 230–243; cf. Schrecker, "The French War Debt," pp. 254–258; on the experts' report, Philippe, *Le drame financier*, pp. 106–110, 122–123; Freyssinet, *La politique monétaire*, pp. 89–135; Moreau, *Souvenirs*, pp. 16–17. Cf. Suarez, *De Poincaré à Poincaré*, pp. 162–163, 182, for conservative disquiet with the removal of Robineau.

[52] For Marin and Blum interventions on July 7, see JOC, 1926, pp. 2767–2768, 2771–2782; also the July 9 vote, pp. 2860–2861.

[53] JOC, 1926, pp. 2962–2981 (July 17); memo on the objectives of the decree powers is found in Min. Aff. Etr., Fonds Herriot/12. For Blum's earlier attack on the plan, July 7, see JOC, 1926, pp. 2772–2773.

the Chamber, July 21, retaining only the votes of the Socialists, Radicals, and Painlevé's small group of Republican Socialists.[54]

The vote signified the final collapse of the 1924 majority. Poincaré now won the support from the Radicals that he could not claim until the financial and parliamentary situation seemed truly desperate. He quickly constructed a ministry that included all the discordant elements of the past years: Herriot, Briand, Barthou, Bokanowski, Marin, Painlevé, and his former irritating challenger, Tardieu. Herriot was the key hostage. Radical Socialist participation indicated the restoration of a bourgeois and middle-class consensus that savings were to be protected from taxes on capital or the disguised levies of inflation. Only the Communists remained in outright opposition; the SFIO abstained; and the new premier received massive majorities for an emergency tax program and then approval for the decree power denied to Caillaux. Most important perhaps he won authorization for the Bank of France to sell francs below the official rate of 1914. This finally authorized the Bank to engage in operations on the money markets and to reconstitute foreign reserves as the franc rose in value. As Moreau noted, the decision implied that the government and the Bank had abandoned any plan to recover the monetary unit of 1914. By August 10, Poincaré convoked the National Assembly to Versailles to establish the long-called-for amortization authority by constitutional amendment, thus placing its reserves beyond the reach of any future left-wing government. The left had buried Jaurès in the Panthéon; Poincaré took the parliament to Versailles to sanctify a sinking fund. The respective gestures illuminated much about the different values of the left and of bourgeois France. Yet both in their way represented "republican" triumphs and were the product of the same legislature.[55]

Judging by programs and legislation Poincaré did little more than Briand had done when he briefly balanced the 1926 budget in April. In possession of power, Poincaré proved delphic and vacillating—alternating between assurances that he would soon ratify the debt agreement as well as establish a fixed value for the franc and further postponement of action. But Poincaré's success did not ultimately depend upon technical measures. "Confidence" meant putting a sound bourgeois leader in control and securing the acquiescence of the Radical Social-

[54] Moreau to Herriot, July 21, 1926, in Min. Aff. Etr., Fonds Herriot/12; cf. Moreau, *Souvenirs*, pp. 36–38; JOC, 1926, pp. 3013–3027 (July 21).

[55] Pierre Miquel, *Poincaré* (Paris, 1961), pp. 542 ff. for political ambiance; measures summarized in Lachapelle, *Le crédit public*, pp. 291 ff.; Alfred Sauvy, *Histoire économique de la France entre les deux guerres*, vol. I, *De l'armistice à la dévaluation de la livre (1918–1931)* (Paris, 1965), pp. 85–88; Moreau, *Souvenirs*, August 9 entry, p. 69, on significance of the authorization to buy foreign exchange above the 1914 par.

ists. Despite occasional fears that the franc would emulate the mark, the French crisis was not of the same magnitude as the German one. The franc was stabilized at one-fifth its prewar value. If it had not been for political uncertainty it might well have been stabilized at a higher rate. Stabilization achieved earlier—say at 75 to the pound in 1924 or one-third the 1914 value—would have meant more of the national income going to bondholders at the sacrifice of nonrentiers, who might have lost real income through indirect taxes and unemployment. Stabilization later with a slightly undervalued franc meant vigorous demand, independence from American loans, and leverage on the Bank of England such that French financial influence remained potent in Eastern Europe.

The left, indeed, won what it had allegedly desired. Although it had to accept what was probably a slightly more regressive tax structure under Poincaré, it did win lower transfer payments to the holders of the public debt. But while the Socialists would have sought to bring this about by means of a forced consolidation or capital levy aimed at the wealthy, what they ended up with was an indiscriminate forced loan through inflation. The losses were spread over broader sectors of middle-class Frenchmen than the SFIO intended, for the Socialists, too, enjoyed significant middle-class support. It was precisely the broad swath of this shared sacrifice through inflation that provided the basis for Poincaré's "union" coalition of 1926.

Temporarily the Radical Socialists, whose clientele included many injured by the inflation, had to fall into line behind Poincaré. Ultimately, they, too, paid a political price for their inner inconsistencies; for the ministerial carousel and inflation of 1924–1926 contributed to the erosion of the party system in which they had played the pivotal role. By the ambiguities they encouraged—by their contribution to left-wing electoral victories and to conservative coalitions on monetary policy, by their inability to choose between the projects of Herriot and those of Caillaux, by their traditionalist concern with the quantity of money even as they threatened a tax on capital calculated to weaken the franc—the Radicals precluded effective leadership. Their own dilemmas, moreover, epitomized the uncertainties of parliament in general as it confronted the problem of allocating the internal costs of the war and reconstruction. Louis Marin's Union Républicaine Démocratique, a conservative grouping separated from the Radicals more by temperament or regional habits or fear of collectivism than by social composition, was equally baffled. The convergence of Marin and Herriot on behalf of parliamentary prerogatives and in opposition to the decree authority sought by Caillaux was representative of a more fundamental identity. Both parties together—Marin's dominant in the legislature of 1919, Herriot's in the Chamber of 1924—testified to the bewilderment of the *classes moyennes.*

Like Germany, France in 1926 entered upon a prolonged revaluation controversy. Until legal stabilization in June 1928, the decentralized, small-creditor interests backing the Fédération Républicaine (the name for Marin's group in the Chamber) kept pressing for upward revision for the franc.[56] Poincaré, too, was inwardly reluctant to confirm the write-off of 80 percent of the prewar franc's value. Among the regents of the Bank of France, Rothschild and François de Wendel stubbornly resisted legal stabilization until revaluation. But the pressure of business spokesmen against appreciation became more intense when the currency rose to 140 per pound in mid-November 1926. Moreau's assistant, Charles Rist, private bankers such as Raymond Philippe, and various Chambers of Commerce urged quick stabilization. Moreau understood their fears of an overvalued currency but remained cautious. Too clear a signal that the franc would not be allowed to rise further, he was warned by his expert on exchange operations, could provoke renewed speculation against it. More fundamental, Poincaré inwardly yearned for a franc at 100 to the pound and was reluctant to stabilize at 140. While he relied increasingly on Moreau, it still took time to dissipate the initial mistrust that the premier had felt for a Governor appointed by the despised Caillaux.[57] Nevertheless, on December 20, 1926, events forced the Bank to intervene as the pound slumped and the franc shot up toward 120. Buying pounds in London and New York, Moreau decided, and Poincaré tacitly accepted for the moment, that further appreciation would be catastrophic.[58]

While the Bank now was resolved to hold the franc at 120, the currency was still not convertible into gold and had no value fixed in law. By the spring of 1927 speculators were wagering on a franc of 80 or even 60 to the pound, and Rothschild and others pressed for allowing

[56] For the meetings of the Fédération Républicaine see Bonnefous, *Histoire politique*, IV, p. 112; on the revaluation controversy, Sauvy, *Histoire économique*, I, pp. 89–91.

[57] For Poincaré's vacillations on stabilization and revalorization see Moreau, *Souvenirs*, November 3, 15, and 22, 1926, pp. 153, 160, 165. For the premier's change in personal attitudes toward the Governor, see July 22 and 26, pp. 42, 44–45; and Doumergue's testimony, February 14, 1927, p. 236. Fear of new speculation November 18 and 19, pp. 162–163. It is important to note that Poincaré did not simplistically seek to push the franc higher but initiated his own purchasing-power-parity study in the fall of 1926. See Jacques Rueff, "Sur un point d'histoire: le niveau de la stabilisation Poincaré," *Revue d'économie politique*, 62, 2 (1959), pp. 169–178.

[58] *Ibid.*, December 20, 1926, p. 182.

the money to float upward. Poincaré resisted their arguments; nonetheless, holding the franc down and keeping the pound high had its own dangers. The Bank had to emit and sell so many francs that it threatened to unleash a new bout of inflation. The government and Bank had to choose either to establish a fixed value by law or let the currency appreciate and risk a recession. Until it opted for one course or the other, great, unsettling waves of currency threatened to swamp the frail craft of monetary management. Still, Poincaré and Doumergue were reluctant to stabilize. They felt that the required legislation would demand a more disciplined parliamentary majority than the old Cartel Chamber offered. On the other hand, they rejected the notion of dissolving the legislature before it completed its term in 1928.[59]

The traditionally charged political atmosphere that preceded the end of a legislature led to political coalitions around inherited alignments. Marin was a major leader in the "union" of center and right and the Radical Socialists unsuccessfully renewed the Cartel des Gauches. Yet even after an almost plebiscitary victory in May 1928, Poincaré seemed reluctant to confirm a new value of the franc. Marin was even more opposed, charging that the stabilizers wanted "to favor the big banks while he and his friends intended to safeguard the interest of the lowly and humble." Bankers, businessmen, and Léon Jouhaux of the CGT, however, all reiterated the case for legal stabilization. Moreau, too, became more resolute; he threatened to resign and warned the premier, "As respectable as is the past one must think of the future of France."[60] Poincaré now moved to enact legal stabilization; he imposed ministerial discipline on Marin and solemnly recited to the Chamber all the arguments that he had formerly resisted, citing Britain and Denmark as countries whose production and employment had languished from the single-minded pursuit of prewar exchange levels.[61] "I rejoice," wrote Blum with some irony, "that Poincaré has finally succeeded in persuading himself that any effort at new revaluation would be chimerical."[62] On June 24, 1928, the franc was legally defined at a value equal to about 124 per pound or 20 centimes of the "Germinal franc" that Poincaré wistfully remembered.

The differences that separated the French and German republics were reflected in their respective inflations and their revaluation compromises. German industry had been powerful enough to push inflation

[59] *Ibid.*, February 14–15, pp. 234–238; April 27–28, pp. 292–293; May 9–16, pp. 304–313; May 23, 1927, p. 321. Poincaré's postponement of legal stabilization announced JOC, 1928, pp. 438–442 (February 3).

[60] Moreau, *Souvenirs*, p. 573; also May 31, pp. 574–575; June 7 and 13, pp. 580, 584–585. For the Jouhaux intervention, see Rueff, "Sur un point d'histoire."

[61] JOC, 1928, pp. 2026–2028 (June 24, 1928).

[62] "Le nouvel emprunt," *Le Populaire*, May 3, 1928; cf. *Le Populaire*, June 16 and 19, 1928, for approval of stabilization.

to limits that France had never approached. French industrialists remained preeminently bourgeois, sharing the broad middle-class interest in savings and stable money. Not French industry, but bourgeois rentiers in general (and, until the advent of Moreau, the Regents of the Bank as well) contributed to inflation despite their preference for a stable currency. They did so less to profit consciously from speculation than as a traditional response to anxiety provoked by a threat from the left.

Even those French entrepreneurs who did profit from the export premiums created by the 1925–1926 inflation could never have imposed the same policy of fiscal paralysis as in Germany. François de Wendel would have benefited as an exporter from a cheap franc but pressed high revaluation—perhaps from dislike of Moreau, party affiliation with Marin, or, it was suggested, to avoid higher wage demands.[63] In any case, the French political system did not allow corporate groups the same leverage that the German did. The contradictory coalitions—the merry-go-round in which Herriot and then Painlevé were succeeded by Briand, in turn brought down by Herriot and Marin, after which all reappeared with Poincaré—testified to the curious role of the French parliament. While the German cabinets reflected the alignment of forces in the economic arena, the French Chamber and Senate never became so direct an extension of interest groups. The Chamber was not elected by centralized proportional representation with its secure national seats for party *Bonzen* and functionaries, which allowed German parties to exert a stronger and more centralized power than their French counterparts. The close connection of deputy and constituency in France, even under the modified proportional representation of 1919 and 1924, made the mediation of local interests a key function of the Chamber. Reversion to single-member districts reinforced the old clientelist trends in the incoherent electoral contests of 1928. The role of the prefect reinforced the influence of local notables and deputy for he brought the power of Paris to the province. Notables, deputy, and prefect together had a common interest in their fief and thus served as counterweight to the centralist tendencies of the regime. The indirect selection of notables for the Senate and its role as a buffer against either radical economic initiatives or right-wing political crusades further contributed to the ballast role of the parliament.

The price of this stabilizing role was immobility and preoccupation with out-of-date conflicts. Only in 1926 did the majority of Frenchmen get the solution that they were trying to vote for in 1924: normalization of relations with Germany by piecemeal appeasement and stabilization of their currency. The French parliament could still represent the gen-

63 Moreau, *Souvenirs*, May 16, 1927, p. 312; December 1, 1927, p. 439.

erality of citizens as individuals but only at the cost of delay and ritualism. The German Reichstag debated current issues more directly but represented corporate interests more faithfully than those of the middle strata.

The years between 1924 and 1928 also revealed a new development. If one considered each national party system as composed of a collectivist left, a liberal-democratic left, a liberal right, and a nationalist right, new and important cross-linkages now existed between collectivist left and liberal right on the one hand, and between nationalist right and liberal-democratic left on the other. Whereas elections—the parliamentary contests in France, the plebiscites and Reichstag polls in Germany—pitted the "lefts" against the "rights," inflation and revaluation produced new affinities. Even though Wilhelm Keil played politics with revaluation on behalf of the SPD, a collectivist left representing labor and a liberal right speaking for business interests could both accept the results of inflation. But it was far harder for the middle-class elements behind both the liberal-democratic left and the nationalist right to acquiesce.

The new cross linkages had implications, too, for the structure of parties. Although French parties were generally less cohesive than their German counterparts, in each country the inflation issue tended to place in the same camp those parties in which powerful producer interests tended to dominate internal decision making. In the other camp it put those parties more responsive to generalized consumer or middle-class grievances. This second group could prove volatile and unruly as the Radical Socialists, Union Républicaine Démocratique and German Nationalists all demonstrated. At the May 1926 congress of the conservative URD, Louis Marin had to defend the very concept of a united party against Georges Bonnevay's call for individual action.[64] And while the DNVP was bitterly antidemocratic in ideology, in terms of internal decision making the Party was as responsive to the grass roots as any other: witness the landslide resentment of the local Nationalist associations that compelled the leadership to quit the cabinet over Locarno. Westarp confided to Stresemann that as party leader, "he was conducting a struggle against a hydra; if he cut off one head, two new ones appeared."[65]

The result of party fragmentation was parliamentary confusion. The Reichstag and the French Chamber were thrown into prolonged indecisiveness because parties were uneasily perched between old coalitions built around antisocialist issues and new alignments reflecting broad producer interests or, on the other side, distressed middle-class

[64] Bonnefous, *Histoire politique*, IV, p. 138.
[65] Stresemann, *Vermächtnis*, II, p. 145.

savers and consumers. As the emergence of splinter parties in Germany, from the Economic Party to the Racists, and the stirrings of a radical right in France both suggested, the disparate middle-class elements felt aggrieved by the success of the broadly organized producer interests. The settlement of inflation and revaluation between 1923 and 1928 reflected the transition to a representational system that seemed increasingly harsh on the very social elements who had earlier formed the main reserves for parliamentary liberalism.

The growing division between producers and savers or consumers— the distinction that Weber sensed when he separated *Erwerbsklassen* from *Besitzklassen*[66]—does not mean that the old split between working-class and bourgeois parties faded away. By 1926 in Germany, at least, this opposition again became preeminent. Nonetheless, so long as the German economy expanded, the Socialist-bourgeois dichotomy did not paralyze the political system. For one thing, Stresemann continued to draw upon Social Democratic support for the foreign policy that led him from London in 1924 to Locarno, Thoiry, Geneva, and finally The Hague. An implicit Great Coalition continued to support the policy of détente with the West. Secondly, even the Bürgerblok found it impossible to ignore working-class aspirations; for until 1930 at least, the powerful Christian Trade Union representation in the Center Party precluded a reactionary policy. The Catholic trade-union leader Brauns held the pivotal Ministry of Labor with its power of compulsory arbitration from 1924 until 1928 and bargained consistently for restoring the eight-hour legislation that had been suspended in 1923.

Indeed a grant settlement of outstanding labor issues seemed within reach by the fall of 1926 when Chancellor Marx sought to overcome the parliamentary stalemate that had developed since the Nationalists left the government a year before. Marx sought to work out a compromise with Herman Müller of the SPD that would create an implicit Great Coalition to pass unemployment insurance legislation. Both the right wing of the People's Party and the left of the Social Democrats forestalled this latent cooperation, however. The DVP spokesman Ernst Scholz aggressively called for "bourgeois unity" against Socialist demands, while Philip Scheidemann blew open the question of secret rearmament on the floor of the Reichstag, attacking the military collaboration with Russia and manpower subterfuges, and burning the SPD's bridges to the Marx cabinet.[67] Marx now turned again to the Nationalists and constructed a new Bürgerblok ministry. His own Cen-

[66] See Chapter One, above, pp. 20–21.

[67] For the momentum toward a Great Coalition, see *BT*, October 17, November 1, 12, 13, 19, December 1, 1926. Stürmer, *Koalition und Opposition*, pp. 162–181; Dörr, "Deutschnationale Volkspartei," pp. 255–256; Carsten, *Reichswehr und Politik*, pp. 243 ff.; also Marx's evaluation of the crisis in Stehkämper, ed., *Nachlass Marx*, I, pp. 417–418.

ter Party was prepared to accept the coalition with the right only if it enacted a progressive labor policy. The DNVP, in fact, proved less rigid on the issue of working time than the DVP, although final regulation was a difficult matter still fraught with the emotional memories of 1918 and 1923. What emerged in the cabinet's interparty committee and then in a special subcommittee was a compromise that Brauns designed over the bitter objections of industrialists such as Kirdorf, Vögler, and Thyssen. The new law did not restore the legal prohibition on work longer than eight hours, which had been effectively suspended in December 1923, nor did it sanction liberty of contract as industry demanded—especially since serious recession gripped Germany during 1926. Instead overtime work remained legal but paid at a 25 percent premium. For light industry this provision roughly codified existing practice; but for mining and metals, which had reimposed a ten-hour day at regular pay, the financial penalty was heavy enough to cause a return to the eight hours. Thus by April 1927—eight and a half years after the demobilization ordinance of 1918 and three and a half years after its effective suspension—the most symbolic social controversy of the Weimar Republic was settled under Catholic and conservative auspices.[68]

Within a few months the Bürgerblok coalition also passed an unemployment insurance bill after two years of quarreling in the Reich Economic Council and earlier cabinets. It even passed a compromise law on the protection of the Republic—originally passed as an emergency measure against "the enemy on the right" after Rathenau's murder—but now accepted by the DNVP. Not all clashes of interest could be resolved. Collaboration with the Nationalists forced Marx to tack to the right and angered his own trade-union colleagues in the Center. The Catholic labor leaders remained restive under the Bürgerblok and focused their resentments upon a new civil service pay scale that strengthened the top ranks at the expense of the lower ones. The Catholic union chief Imbusch scathingly reproached Marx for lacking any sense of justice. On the other side of the coalition the DVP's industrialist spokesmen resisted putting into effect the eight-hour legislation that the Center labor leaders had laboriously constructed. A traditional area of controversy provided the final blow to the Bürgerblok when the DVP withdrew from the coalition because of Nationalist and Center Party plans to strengthen confessionally supervised education.[69]

[68] For compromises involved in passage see Stürmer, *Koalition und Opposition*, pp. 206–207, 304–307; also Ludwig Preller, *Sozialpolitik in der Weimarer Republik* (Stuttgart, 1949), pp. 363 ff. Friedrich Syrup, with Otto Neuloh, ed., *Hundert Jahre staatliche Sozialpolitik 1839–1939* (Stuttgart, 1957), pp. 278–282.

[69] Stürmer, *Koalition und Opposition*, pp. 213–225, 242–247; Stehkämper, *Nachlass Marx*, iii, pp. 339 ff.; Josef Becker, "Joseph Wirth und die Krise des Zentrums

Although the elections resulted in a Great Coalition once again, it remained a tenuous collaboration. The government remained hostage to the continuing tension between working-class and business interests. The great lock-out by the Westphalian iron industry in the fall of 1928 was the Ruhr's response to an arbitration edict it refused to accept: an attack on the social constitution of the state that prefigured the later rebellion against its political institutions.[70]

The stability of 1924 to 1929 thus remained fragile at best. But that the compromises were tenuous does not mean that they were doomed. Weimar had not solved the problems afflicting its farmers and middle classes, but had started to reconcile the major corporate interests. In the years from 1924 to 1929 domestic politics seemed dominated by several overlapping contests. Parliamentary resolutions varied in efficacy for each one. The first was between farmers and the urban economy and represented a rear-guard defense in a long war of attrition. Agriculture gained by the inflation, resisted high revaluation, but could not effectively protect itself in the sharp decline of farm prices that characterized the Western economies after World War I. In the per-family division of national income since 1913 farmers gained the least.[71]

The second contest was between the fragmented white-collar and middle-class interests and the broadly organized forces of labor and industry considered as a bloc together. With the inflation and then revaluation, this contest, so the middle-class groups felt, was settled to their detriment. Looking back over a decade, the storekeeper or craftsmen or middling civil servant felt that runaway prices and the failure of revaluation had sacrificed him to big business and big labor. In fact, it is not clear that these groups had lost so badly. Those on salaries shared in the general proportional gain that wages and salaries registered as a component of national income. The fate of craftsmen and merchants in monetary terms remains under debate. Nonetheless even higher incomes could not diminish the feeling that a fragmented middle class was assaulted from above and below. Craftsmen and mer-

---

während des IV. Kabinetts Marx (1927–1928). Darstellung und Dokumente," *Zeitschrift für die Geschichte des Oberrheins*, 109, 2 (1961), pp. 405–419; Eberhard Pies, "Sozialpolitik und Zentrum, 1924–1928," Bochum symposium paper.

[70] For political tensions, Helga Timm, *Die deutsche Sozialpolitik und der Bruch der grossen Koalition im März 1930* (Düsseldorf, 1952); labor disputes in Ernst Fränkel, "Der Ruhreisenstreit 1928–1929 in historischer-politischer Sicht," in *Staat, Wirtschaft und Politik in der Weimarer Republik. Festschrift für Heinrich Brüning* (Berlin, 1967), pp. 97–117; Ursula Hüllbusch, "Der Ruhreisenstreit und die Gewerkschaften," Bochum symposium paper.

[71] Dietmar Petzina, "Grundriss der deutschen Wirtschaftsgeschichte," in Institut für Zeitgeschichte: *Deutsche Geschichte seit dem Ersten Weltkrieg* (Stuttgart, 1973), pp. 696–697; Georges Castellan, "Die soziale Bilanz der Prosperität," Bochum symposium paper.

chants were unhappy participants in the long-term reduction of independent proprietors.[72] A great deal of their malaise centered on the slow attrition of their position as consumers and savers rather than earners. In the last analysis questions of dignity and status were at stake: German democracy seemed to reward only organization and collective action on one hand, or speculation and buccaneering on the other.

The third major contest took place between the major interests organized as producers, namely industry and labor. In a period of real economic growth there could be dividends for both sides. Yet under the conditions of currency stabilization and harsh international competition the prosperity of each seemed to require limiting the claims of the other. The outcome of the rivalry favored management in 1924, but by 1928–1929 labor drew abreast as the unions recovered from the feebleness of the stabilization crisis. Taking working time as an index, the situation had actually swung back in the workers' favor. Real wages had also risen sharply, although they had been abnormally low in 1923–1924.[73] And despite the persistent unemployment the collective per-worker share of wages in the national economy was significantly greater than in 1913. The Socialists understood that their "social power" as Hilferding said, was a function of their "political power," and vice versa.[74] Even under the Bürgerblok the Socialists retained

[72] Castellan, "Die soziale Bilanz," arrives at a surprisingly favorable estimate of per-family shares of income; cf. Petzina's estimates for wages and salaries, "Grundriss der deutschen Wirtschaftsgeschichte," pp. 763, 773; also Simon Kuznets, *Modern Economic Growth* (New Haven, 1967), pp. 208 ff.; for general malaise, Heinrich August Winkler, *Mittelstand, Demokratie und Nationalsozialismus. Die politische Entwicklung von Handwerk und Kleinhandel in der Weimarer Republik* (Cologne, 1972), esp. pp. 26–39, and tables 289 ff.

[73] For wage changes, Gerhard Bry, *Wages in Germany, 1871–1945* (Princeton, N.J., 1960), pp. 181–187. For working time see Preller, *Sozialpolitik in der Weimarer Republik*, pp. 147–148.

Percent of Labor Force in a Work Week of		Industries			
		Metals	Chemicals	Printing	Textiles
May 1924	under full time	11.1	–	0.3	2.2
	up to 48 hours	25.4	56.0	50.3	15.4
	48 to 54 hours	42.4	36.2	47.7	78.1
	over 54 hours	21.1	7.8	1.7	4.3
Oct. 1928	under full time	9.4	3.0	1.0	25.9
	up to 48 hours	56.3	69.6	88.0	41.5
	48 to 54 hours	29.3	20.0	9.0	31.7
	over 54 hours	5.0	7.4	2.0	0.9

[74] Rudolf Hilferding, "Die Aufgaben der Sozialdemokratie in der Republik," Sozialdemokratischer Parteitag 1927 in Kiel, *Protokoll*, p. 170.

political power: they dominated the Prussian Great Coalition and had an important voice in major municipal governments with expansive public works.[75] The power of the Minister of Labor to declare a binding arbitration when requested by one of the parties in a labor dispute was a further asset. Reliance on friendly Ministers of Labor, however, meant sacrificing autonomy in the market place and ransoming the labor movement to political developments beyond its control. When in 1932 Franz von Papen installed a former Krupp executive as Minister of Labor, fired Rudolf Wissell, the Social Democrat then serving as chief government arbiter, and removed the SPD ministers in Prussia, he perversely confirmed Hilferding's analysis: by 1932 working-class wages and working-class power had collapsed together.[76]

These three contests had different outcomes. Parliamentary politics could not remove the structural handicaps of German agriculture, and by the late 1920's farmers were abandoning even the DNVP. Of the other two, the contest between industry and labor proved most disabling to parliamentary consensus in the short-run. It was the recrudescence of traditional class conflict in the wake of the Depression that crippled parliamentary forms in Germany and endangered them in France. Nonetheless, before the Depression proto-welfare-state compromises seemed feasible and imminent. A wealthier Europe would achieve them more easily after World War II.

The struggle between those organized as producers and those buffetted as consumers or savers proved less dramatic, but perhaps more persistent. It remained an affliction of differential growth and prosperity and not merely of depression. Inflation only aggravated it. This new rivalry proved especially troublesome to control politically because it divided the older middle-class parties from within, thus operating as a powerful solvent on traditional coalitions and incapacitating party mediation. Hence, the limited but politically debilitating contests of mid-decade that arose over currency issues, above all, signaled future difficulties. Since the issues dividing producer groups and stranded middle classes sapped representational capacity from within the party structure, they forced a relocation of the agencies of consensus and mediation. Parliamentary decision making would become increasingly a shadow play for corporatist settlements. The conflicts of the mid-1920's did not destroy parliamentarism, but they did suggest an inner hemorrhaging of its former strength.

[75] See Carl Böhret, *Aktionen gegen die "kalte Sozialisierung" 1926–1930* (Berlin, 1966), pp. 172–186, for political stakes of municipal socialism; also Otto Büsch, *Geschichte der Berliner Kommunalwirtschaft in der Weimarer Republik* (Berlin, 1967), who sees non-partisan support.

[76] Hans-Hermann Hartwich, *Arbeitsmarkt, Verbände und Staat 1918–1933* (Berlin, 1967), pp. 241–243.

IRON, STEEL, AND THE INTERNATIONAL
ORGANIZATION OF CAPITALISM

The halting of inflation and currency fluctuations was of far-reaching
importance for the consolidation of industry across frontiers as well as
within each society. While the new gold-exchange standard erected in
the mid-1920's restored expectations of stability conducive to international commerce, it also made price competition far more rigorous for
commodities traded across frontiers. This development, too, strengthened the corporatist organization of Western Europe, as governments
and industries alike sought to secure their countries' share of a contested international market.

Deflationary pressure, moreover, only added to the harsh competition caused by overproduction of basic commodities, both agricultural
and industrial. World markets could not absorb the bumper crops of
wheat or the rising output of iron and steel without sharp price declines. Both American and Central European agriculture were afflicted
with long-term price woes. The iron and steel industries also suffered,
because consumption dropped after the war while ore supplies and
steel capacity grew. But the producers of the field and of the forge
could respond differently. Agriculture remained decentralized and resisted centralized efforts to limit output until the New Deal, the Third
Reich, and the Popular Front in the 1930's. Iron and steel manufacturers were far fewer in number, and could expect to secure a high
degree of control of the market on their own initiative. They were organized more effectively in Germany than in France, Belgium, or
England; but everywhere the size of the productive units as well as
government concern with national export performance encouraged the
organization of heavy industry. Foreign-trade figures provided a rough
measure of the national interest: cartelization in the cause of increasing exports was hard to resist. The world of restored international trade
of the late 1920's was thus particularly susceptible to the reorganization of capitalist efforts. Opportunity as well as necessity impelled big
business to seek control over challenging and volatile markets.

No issue better illustrated the quest for market control than that of
Franco-German steel production (see figure on page 518). The search
for international organization demonstrated first of all the limitations of
industrial collaboration. To edgy onlookers in Britain, for instance,
French seizure of the Ruhr seemed to have facilitated a powerful continental system for coal and iron. Sober English observers, however,
foresaw how difficult it would be to engineer such a combination: "The
Franco-German coal-iron combine is an old bogey which was originally
trotted out to make our flesh creep shortly after the armistice," wrote

516

John Bradbury to counter the alarms sounded by the Board of Trade and the Treasury, "and which we may rely on having set up again every time either a Frenchman or German think the moment opportune for trying to put the fear of God into us. It leaves me quite unperturbed."[77] Bradbury's perspective was valid: the Franco-German combination was not destined to be the nucleus of a monolithic industrial concentration on the Rhine. Laboriously worked out, it represented an effort to meet the difficulties caused by the excess iron-producing capacity in Lorraine: capacity that burdened French steel magnates and threatened the inland markets of German steel producers. Rather than examine the Franco-German negotiations as the path to industrial hegemony, the historian must describe them as responses to potential distress. Ultimately they reflected the failure to envisage a society of high mass production and sustained growth. Limited as the Franco-German negotiations were, they illuminate major themes of economic reorganization in the 1920's: the restriction of output in lieu of the expansion of markets, the need to cartelize industry at home or bind it into price associations or pools, and the corporatist response to insecurity, as powerful industries and the state sought to shield themselves from market uncertainties.

Throughout the spring of 1924, the question of how Germany would exploit her regained tariff sovereignty began to preoccupy officials and industrialists on both sides of the Rhine. Articles 261–265 of the Versailles Treaty had stipulated that Germany must refrain from raising her tariffs and must treat the Allies on a most-favored-nation basis for five years, until January 10, 1925. This restriction meant trade concessions made to any one country had to be extended to all; hence, Germany could not discriminate, for example, against French iron and steel imports. Germany was also precluded from using selective tariff hikes or quotas to negotiate reductions from Paris—to trade, say, French imports of German machines or Rhine wines for German imports of rails or sheet metal. A further important treaty provision had required Germany to extend duty-free entry for a "contingent" of Alsace-Lorraine products based on the output of 1911–1913, a provision

[77] John Bradbury to Otto Niemeyer, September 28, 1923, included in the British Delegation to the Reparations Commission's dispatch to Wigram, November 1, in FO 371/8747: C19094/313/18. For the Board of Trade's original concern, see Curzon to Crewe, October 29, 1923: C18388/313/18. William Larke, Chairman of the National Federation of Iron and Steel Manufacturers, also monitored the negotiations, noted their difficulty, the limited utility, and the limited threat: Larke to H. Fountain (Board of Trade), December 29, 1924, FO 371/9869: C19557/14053/18. Cf. the report by the Commercial Secretary in Cologne, Kavanagh, for similar views: C18829/14053/18. For Larke's assessment of late 1923, see his communication with Lampson at the Foreign Office, November 26, 1923, FO 371/8750: C20556/313/18.

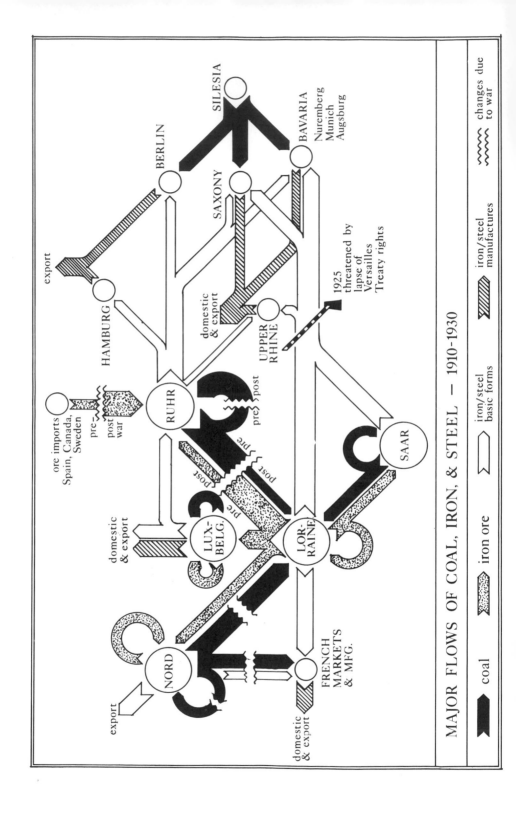

MAJOR FLOWS OF COAL, IRON, & STEEL — 1910-1930

Legend:
coal
iron ore
iron/steel basic forms
iron/steel manufactures
changes due to war

SILESIA
BERLIN
SAXONY
BAVARIA
Nuremberg
Munich
Augsburg
1925 threatened by lapse of Versailles Treaty rights
HAMBURG
export
domestic & export
UPPER RHINE
RUHR
ore imports Spain, Canada, Sweden
pre-war
post war
domestic & export
LUX-BELG.
LOR-RAINE
SAAR
pre post
pre post
pre post
NORD
export
FRENCH MARKETS & MFG.
domestic & export

intended to prevent "disannexed" Lorraine mines and foundries from being brutally cut off from their pre-1914 German consumers. Coal and steel products from the Saar—integrated into the French customs domain until 1935—were likewise to enjoy duty-free entry for five years, and so were those of Luxemburg, which left the German customs union after the war. These provisions were not merely theoretical guarantees. Although Ruhr steelmakers imported far less Lorraine ore, savings in transportation costs still made it worthwhile for the electrical manufacturers and the tool and machine makers of Southern Germany and the factories of Mannheim, Augsburg, Nuremburg, and Munich to import steel plates, sheets, rails, beams, wires, etc., from Lorraine and the Saar.[78] For this reason the Versailles Treaty rights had become a cornerstone of French commercial policy. Without them, French iron and steel would face a crisis of overproduction greater than that of 1922. It was, therefore, vital to the French to prolong access to German markets as long as possible beyond January 10, 1925.

So long as France could exploit her presence in the Ruhr and a new reparation settlement seemed distant, the dangers to French industry appeared remote. But once the French had accepted the experts' report, the possibility of using duress to win extension of privileges faded. Perhaps Paris could find allies among the South German manufacturers who badly wanted to keep their access to the Saar and Lorraine; perhaps the French government could hold up withdrawal of troops either from the Ruhr or from the Cologne Zone of Allied Occupation, also slated for evacuation on January 10, 1925. French strategy was still undetermined. By late 1923 Poincaré had rejected the idea of using the Ruhr occupation to force extension of the "contingent."[79] And just as there were conflicting interests in Germany between Ruhr steel and Southern manufacturers, so in France there were divergences. Some iron and steelmakers were willing to countenance the end of the "contingent" for Lorraine and the Saar if they could have a high tariff to keep prices up at home, while those enjoying extensive sales of iron and steel to German outlets had a vital interest either in lowering the

[78] On this question see the viewpoint of the Union of German Iron and Steel Industrialists: *Die Eisenversorgung Suddeutschlands* (Berlin, 1925), in BA, Koblenz: R 13 I (VdESI)/421. Connections of French and German industry up through 1922 also in Paul Berkenkopf, *Die Entstehung und die Lage der lothringisch-luxemburgischen Grosseisenindustrie seit dem Weltkriege* (Jena, 1925).

[79] See the report on the meeting of the French interministerial committee for commercial agreements, January 16, 1924, in the January 31 "Note pour la Sous-Direction Europe": Min. Aff. Etr., Europe, 1918–1929, Allemagne/523, pp. 7–17. The mechanism that might have been used to prolong the contingent was article 280 of the Versailles Treaty, which envisaged France's appeal to the Council of the League of Nations if Germany failed to live up to agreements. But France would have had to make such an appeal one year before the expiration date, that is, by January 10, 1924.

general level of Berlin's tariffs or prolonging their privileges of duty-free entry. Whether the French government would emphasize getting French products into Germany or keeping German products out of France still had to be fought out. Nor could the decision be made only in reference to the needs of the iron and steel industry: agriculture, wines, textiles—all had needs to take into account. The gardens of Provence served the groceries of the Palatinate, and French agrarian interests were well represented in the Chamber and the Senate.

No matter what the outcome, the stakes of the tariff controversy were high: whether the Europe of the mid- and late 1920's would plunge into trade wars and economic crises, whether it might master a transition to a liberal free-trade equilibrium, or whether it would achieve an international economic order based upon the sharing of a fragile market among large-scale economic groupings. The last became the system that emerged, thus complementing the results of monetary stabilization and helping to shape domestic political economies as well as the international one—helping to determine, in short, the nature of capitalist society in the years before the Depression.

Glancing at the complex 1924–1926 trade negotiations as a whole may help to make clear the major objectives. Quite simply, French iron and steel interests desired access to German markets for their potential excess of production over domestic demand of perhaps 3 to 8 million tons per year. German steel men increasingly felt a need to limit European production overall, for the postwar glut meant low and oscillating prices. But there were complications enough to make trade-off difficult. The French government preferred to rescue its iron industry as part of a general trade agreement that lowered German tariffs for all major French exports, including agriculture. Failing that, it would work to prolong the "contingent" for Lorraine and Saar steel. The German government wanted neither to lower tariffs nor arrange tariff-free contingents. It badly wanted most-favored-nation treatment (or the "minimal tariff," which served as the French equivalent), and needed to gain access to French markets for its machined manufactures. In return for the concessions and to help secure an overall limitation on iron and steel production, the Germans were willing to countenance private arrangements that would amount to tariff rebates for Saar iron and steel. But then arose the further question of whether such rebates should be extended to Lorraine as well. On both sides, finally, complications were multiplied by the fact that each heavy-industry group was normally more protectionist than its respective government, but the two had always to work in tandem. All these factors made the process of reaching the essential trade-off a long and painful one.

Negotiations developed in three phases: a period of French anxiety in 1924, one of German distress in 1925, and finally the working out of a compromise in 1926. As of the spring of 1924 the Germans felt they would enter the talks with France in a strong position. By acting tough against the Saar, predicted State Secretary Ritter, who handled commercial negotiations at the Foreign Ministry, Germany would force the French to concede most-favored-nation treatment. This would prevent Paris from applying discriminatory tariffs against German goods as she had during the inflation by means of antidumping legislation, and as she continued to do by virtue of the prewar treaties still in force with Britain and other countries.[80] On the other hand, the German government did not wish to write a blank check for big business, in part because it wished to preserve its independence (severely compromised by the MICUM negotiations), in part because heavy industry was staking out a high-tariff position the government did not necessarily share.[81]

The first critical interchange came at the London Conference of August 1924. Here was one of the last opportunities for the French to use their military leverage to extract a tariff agreement from the Germans. But the French were already divided. The Ministry of Commerce under Raynaldy and its permanent secretary for foreign trade, Serruys, urged caution in making overtures for a commercial treaty. New French tariffs needed as bargaining points were not yet ready, and Serruys wanted to extract a simple extension of the "contingent" for several months while a new tariff structure was prepared. He also warned against reintroducing the old French demand for share holdings in German cokeries. Clémentel and Herriot, presumably advised by Seydoux, decided, however, to press for more.[82] In a talk with Stresemann on August 11, Clémentel called for a new Franco-German trade treaty and noted that it would create a good effect on the bankers, whose cooperation in floating the $200 million Dawes loan was essential to the inauguration of the new reparations system. Stresemann countered that evacuation of the Ruhr would also produce a favorable

[80] Ritter memo, undated, presumably spring 1924, in GFM: Handakten Ritter, Frankreich, L177/4079/L051721–L051723. Also the memorandum concerning German-French economic negotiations, April 28, 1924, *ibid.*, L051724–L051726 provides background of earlier talks.

[81] For GFM reluctance to call in business, *ibid.* For industrialists' demands, see VdESI to Economics Minister Hamm, May 26, 1924, *ibid.*, L051714–L051718; also Reichsverband questionnaire on tariff needs, March 1, 1924, in GHH: 40010122/2.

[82] See Morin report to Camille Cavallier and Marcel Paul, August 13, 1924, PAM/7230, f. Accords franco-allemands. Clémentel and Herriot's initiative diverged from Seydoux's earlier position that the trade-treaty negotiations could not be tied to the question of the Dawes plan or evacuation of the Cologne Zone. See Seydoux draft July 10, 1924, and Herriot letter to Minister of Commerce July 18, 1924 in Min. Aff. Étr.: Europe, 1918–1929, Allemagne/523.

impression.[83] Two days later the French presented a treaty draft for German scrutiny: Germany was to concede most-favored-nation treatment; France would grant German goods the minimal tariff extended to trade-treaty partners instead of the prohibitive general tariff. Beyond that reciprocity ceased. The duty-free admission of Alsace-Lorraine products would continue for three years beyond January 10, and Germany would concede the French stock shares in Ruhr coal mines as well as long-term contracts exchanging Ruhr coke against Lorraine ore. If final agreement could not be secured by January 10, Germany was to prolong the present situation for six months in return for some unspecified concessions.[84]

What motive did Germany have for accepting such a one-sided compact? Clémentel claimed that France had not fully exploited the Versailles rights to which she had been entitled, but surely the Germans could not assent to that proposition. A date for evacuation of the Ruhr would have to be conceded by France in any case. Herriot told the Senate and Chamber on August 22 that the London Conference was dominated by the evacuation question and he must promise some withdrawal date.[85] The negotiations made it clear that the bankers who were to underwrite the $200 million loan to Germany were the effective fulcrum of negotiations. In light of the role that Morgan had played in stabilizing a weak franc in March, and in view of the precarious agreement among the Cartel on financial questions, Herriot was vulnerable. He raged against the bankers even to Stresemann: after the American financiers demanded twenty-five conditions, he had asked, in a sarcastic reference to Berlin's conditions for neutrality in 1914, whether he need not cede two provinces as security. Nor did MacDonald wish to rescue Herriot: the Socialist Prime Minister found the pressure of international finance a useful curb on French influence over Germany. Herriot, in short, had to cede a withdrawal date (plus other important concessions such as the Reparation Commission's right to determine default) without reference to the trade treaty.[86]

There were, however, important questions of timing that Herriot and Clémentel might exploit. Germany wanted France out of the Ruhr quickly; in addition, evacuation of the Cologne Zone on the West Bank of the Rhine, scheduled for January 10, was to take place only if

[83] GFM: Handakten Ritter, L177/4079/L051707–L051708.

[84] Ibid., L051709–L051710. Also the cables sent for cabinet scrutiny now in Abramowski, ed., Akten: Marx, II, pp. 1295, 1313–1317.

[85] Herriot to Chamber and Senate in JOC, 1924, I, pp. esp. 3006 ff. and JOS, 1924, pp. 1194–1199 (August 22).

[86] For the negotiations see Stresemann to Foreign Ministry, August 13, 1924. GFM: Büro des Reichsministers, 5n. Akten betr. Londoner Konferenz, 1924: 3398/1737/740380–740384: also Abramowski, ed., Akten: Marx, II, pp. 1295–1296 and ff.

the Allies were convinced that Berlin was faithfully carrying out its disarmament and other treaty obligations. First, Clémentel and Herriot sought to bargain for extension of the "contingent" by threatening delays in quitting Cologne. German industry, however, had foreseen this danger and intervened. On August 11, Hermann Bücher and Peter Klöckner told the cabinet ministers left in Berlin that in view of its corporate bond obligations, MICUM and tax burdens, and general losses, industry could not tolerate such a trade-off; extension of the "contingent" was simply inadmissible.[87] On the timing of the Ruhr issue, Herriot and Clémentel negotiated badly. While Herriot insisted that he would be overthrown if he promised to leave the Ruhr in under a year, Clémentel indicated that the date was negotiable in return for trade concessions—and thus probably encouraged Stresemann for a few days (August 11–16) to think that he could have an earlier evacuation without a trade treaty. Stresemann agreed with the industrialists that Germany should resist French pressure for extension of the "contingent." Because the British as well as the Germans pressed France to leave the Ruhr quickly, Herriot settled for German acceptance of a year's delay and actually agreed to date the year from the August signature of the London accords, not the scheduled entry into force of the agreement in October.[88] In short, France was sufficiently isolated and enough of a hostage to the financial pressure of her allies that Herriot could not really use political and military pressure to extract tariff concessions. Stresemann consented to trade negotiations, but they were to be held between political equals. The French would have to talk as economic negotiators, not victors.[89]

Two parallel series of discussions thus began in October: first, official delegations under Trendelenburg of the Reich Economic Ministry and Raynaldy of the French Ministry of Commerce met to draft a general trade treaty. The initial meetings concentrated on discussion of the French counterpart for most-favored-nation status; however, at

[87] For the concerns of the Ruhr industrialists, see Reichert to Reusch, July 30, 1924, in Paul Reusch Nachlass: GHH: 400101222/7. Meeting with the cabinet in Abramowski, ed., *Akten: Marx*, II, pp. 945–948; also Simons to the German delegation in London, August 11, 1924, Hamm and Simons to London delegation, GFM: Handakten Ritter L177/4079/L051705–L051706, L051703–L051704. Cf. Reichert to Luther, August 12: "The French feel themselves at a strong political advantage," *ibid.*, L051690–L051695.

[88] Stresemann to Foreign Ministry, August 13, 1924, in GFM: Büro des Reichsministers, 3398/1737/740380–740384; Maltzan to Cabinet, August 16, 1924, 3398/1737/740470–740472.

[89] See Stresemann to the Reichstag, August 23, 1924, in Stresemann, *Vermächtnis*, I, pp. 508–509. Cf. Herriot to his Minister of Commerce and Industry, July 10, 1924—on the illusory character of article 280—and July 18 on the need for direct conversations on trade: Min. Aff. Etr., Europe, 1918–1929, Allemagne/523.

the sixth session Raynaldy raised the issue of Lorraine iron exports as "the one to which France attached its primordial interest."[90] Neither the German government nor German industry had any interest in hastening discussion of this issue. Negotiations thus slowed and initiative passed to the theoretically private talks between French metallurgical experts headed by Léon-Lévy and a German team under Fritz Thyssen. Here private and ministerial interests diverged.

The French government—by and large seconded by Wendel—wanted first to seek German reduction of tariffs. Serruys was prepared to be rebuffed, but he expected that Germany would at least have to offer some sort of rebates for Saar and Lorraine products.[91] Although Wendel was willing to follow Serruys in seeking lower German tariffs, Léon-Lévy regarded the policy as dangerous. Reporting to the Comité des Forges on the unsuccessful talks of November 27, December 2, and December 16–18, Léon-Lévy explained that only a substantial German tariff cut (from 12 to 4.5 marks per ton) would allow Lorraine steel a chance to compete in the German market; and he feared the official negotiations might settle for smaller and futile general tariff reductions. Futile, that is, except for Wendel, who because of his own access to cheap German coke might still be able to remain competitive across the Rhine. In any case the German industrialists had refused to consider any tariff reductions whatever, and wanted a 50 percent increase instead. Nevertheless, German marketing syndicates might be willing to buy a quota of French metal products and absorb the tariff costs if the French would discuss overall agreements to limit production and end the world crisis of overproduction.[92]

When they returned to Paris, however, the Germans announced that their agreement to purchase the equivalent of the old "contingent" extended only to the Saar and must exclude products from Lorraine. But for the French producers, Lorraine's situation was more precarious and compelling; the Saar acquisitions they shared were newer, controlled through separate holding companies, and their fate was subject to the plebiscite of 1935. If Paris wanted the steel producers to agree to a trade treaty, then it must win them first an extension of the contingent. Now, however, the Germans even proposed that an international steel

[90] AN, Paris: F[12]/8862, "1924: Procès Verbaux des Séances."

[91] See the industrialists' discussion with Serruys, December 1, 1924, reported by E. Henry to Camille Cavallier and Marcel Paul, in PAM/7230, f. "Accords Commerciaux."

[92] See Cavallier's notes of the Comité des Forges meeting, December 11, 1924, in PAM/7230, f. "Accords Commerciaux." It was also encouraging that for the first time since the spring of 1924, the Germans were willing to discuss reviving IRMA (the International Rail Manufacturers' Association). From 1924 through 1926, the German attitude toward IRMA was to remain an index to their overall willingness to strike a wider bargain.

pact should apply only to production for export, not for the home market. This would have meant that French raw iron and basic steel would be shut out of Germany, while the Reich's machines and manufactures could still flow into France. In short, at the end of 1924 the French outlook was gloomy and uncertain. Whether the Germans would actually purchase Lorraine steel on a contingent basis and whether the French government would support its industry in the negotiations remained obscure.[93]

The resort to parallel talks between official and business delegations encouraged new forms of industry-wide organization and pressure. For Ruhr iron producers the quest for higher tariffs and the need to strengthen their own corporate power went hand in hand. As they maneuvered for a higher tariff in late 1923 and early 1924, the raw iron producers (heavy industry) sought to keep the large electrical firms and other manufacturers of steel products from waging an antitariff campaign. As early as December 8, 1923, the manufacturing interests agreed to an "armistice," whereby tariff discussions with heavy industry would be kept confidential and out of the press. This did not preclude the manufacturers from asking the Ministry of Economics to suspend the existing tariff on iron and steel in January 1924 as a supposed remedy for the industrial crisis that had followed the Ruhr occupation and currency reform. In meetings of March 27 and 28, 1924, representatives of the iron and steel producers and the manufacturers agreed to work for a tariff consensus within the framework of the Reichsverband der Deutschen Industrie, and they met again in June.[94]

The critical interchange, which took place between October 8 and 10 in Berlin's Hotel Esplanade, pointed up both the opposing and convergent interests. Heavy industry badly wanted a high tariff, if only as a bargaining counter with the French. Paul Reusch admitted to his fellow Silesian and Ruhr producers that he would be satisfied if the tariff in force could merely be renewed; but his colleagues insisted that they must demand a 50 percent increase to open discussions. As spokesman for German General Electric (AEG), Felix Deutsch responded that his industry required tariff reduction or faced bankruptcy.[95] Heavy industry could not simply disavow the wishes of the electrical and

[93] See Léon-Lévy to Minister of Commerce Raynaldy, December 30, 1924: PAM/7230, f. "Accords Commerciaux."
[94] BA, Koblenz: R 13 I (VdESI)/350 has the protocol of the Zollausschuss and Hauptvorstand meetings, March 27 and 28, 1924, with résumé of earlier developments. For the June 16 meetings, see R 13 I/352.
[95] "Niederschrift über die Verhandlungen der eisenschaffenden Industrie betreffend die Zollberatungen im Reichswirtschaftsministerium am 9. und 10. Oktober 1924 und der gemeinsamen Zollverhandlungen mit der eisenverarbeitenden Industrie am 8. Oktober 1924." R 13 I/355.

other manufacturers; otherwise Deutsch and Raumer would raise the whole tariff issue in the Reich Economic Council and mobilize a free-trade coalition among the Center and SPD. Joseph Reichert and Hans von Raumer had already clashed in the Economic Council a fortnight earlier, when the manager of the Union of Iron and Steel Industrialists had argued that only a well-protected iron industry could afford to pay high wages.[96] As chairman of the Esplanade conference, Bücher outlined a compromise procedure. Both in private and now in the negotiations, Bücher agreed that Ruhr industry must be protected "in the interest of the whole economy": tariffs were a "question of the common good." If the 4 million tons of iron and steel that the French produced in excess of their requirements were dumped in Germany, both raw iron producers and the manufacturers would "go kaputt" together. For the moment, he suggested, both groups should demand a maximum tariff to brandish in negotiations with Paris and a minimal tariff to concede to trading partners. The essential machinery for any tariff compromise, he suggested, was a reorganized association of steelworks that could start a common fund to compensate the manufacturers for the costs of a new tariff.[97]

Bücher's proposal was the logical next step. With the encouragement of the Economics Ministry, the representatives of heavy industry formed a new Raw Steel Community (Rohstahlgemeinschaft or RSG). Assigning individual firms quotas according to their production, the RSG was to serve as a central seller and purchaser of all basic steel.[98] It would confront the French concerns as a monopoly agency of great power, and could also exert significant leverage over the German engineering and manufacturing firms. As negotiations between the French and German teams grew serious at the end of 1924, the Ruhr industrialists feared especially that the French would encourage German exporters to fight protectionism at home in return for low French tariffs on manufactured goods. Vögler was told from Paris that while most German manufacturers were standing firm against French blandishments, Deutsch and Raumer were threatening to lead a low-tariff

[96] Cf. Reichert to Reusch, October 24, 1924, GHH: 400101222/7. Cf. Raumer's speech of June 20 to the Mitgliederversammlung des Zentralverbandes der deutschen elektrotechnischen Industrie: "Die weltwirtschaftliche Umstellung seit 1914 und die sich hieraus ergebenden Aufgaben der zukünftigen deutschen Handelspolitik . . . ," R 13 I/346.

[97] "Niederschrift über die Verhandlungen der Sachverständigen der eisenschaffenden Industrie . . . mit der eisenverarbeitenden Industrie am 8. Oktober 1924," BA, Koblenz: R 13 I/355; also Bücher to Reusch et al., October 4, 1924, GHH: 400101290/4.

[98] Niederschrift über die Bildung einer Rohstahlgemeinschaft," October 14, 1924; also Thyssen to Reusch, October 24, and "Niederschrift" of the same day reporting Trendelenburg's desire for an industrial association in view of the French negotiations: GHH: 400101222/0.

insurrection.[99] The Ruhr leaders moved to avert this peril by buying off the engineering industries and centralizing negotiations in their own hands. With Trendelenburg's support, Ruhr leaders reached agreement with the AVI—the association of manufacturing industries—by December 18. The South and Central German manufacturers agreed not to oppose a tariff hike on basic iron and steel in return for a special export fund. The fund would defray the higher costs of production imposed by any new tariffs and thus let finished goods compete abroad. The question of the Lorraine and Saar contingents, which South Germany wished to maintain but which were slated to expire four weeks later, was left provisionally unresolved. Meanwhile, the Ruhr leaders promised the exporters that they would try to win them access to French markets if they did not insist on renewing the contingents.[100]

The so-called AVI Agreement represented a further step in the growing corporate influence of the Ruhr firms. But the accord did not automatically secure a high tariff and adequate protection. The government warned the iron and steel producers that it could approve their private arrangements only if the needs of the manufacturing industries in terms of steel supplies and export markets were respected.[101] By the spring of 1925 industry learned that the cabinet planned only to renew the 1914 tariff in effect, not to introduce higher duties. And whatever tariff protection would be provided, the extent of the French inflation during 1925 made Lorraine iron and steel competitive in the German market. Indeed, while the German tariffs theoretically went into effect for Saar and Lorraine products on January 10, payment of the tariff was actually put on a credit account to await settlement in a final treaty. Although the French exporters might ultimately be billed retroactively, they had to pay no current duties; and in fact, the final trade treaties of 1926 annulled the interim tariff debts.

The 1924 trade negotiations also encouraged attempts to consolidate French industry. From the outset, the Comité des Forges tried to control the discussions with the Germans and give priority to the needs of the iron and steel industry. Pinot asked Serruys for a special restricted meeting as early as September 4: why should there be a large general conference to discuss negotiations? "What light, and what useful aid,

[99] Schröder to Vögler, December 6, 1924, GFM: Ritter Handakten, L 177/4079/L051959–L051961.
[100] Protocol of December 18, 1924, ibid., L052188–L052189.
[101] See Rieth memo in GFM: Büro des Staatssekretärs. Verhandlungen der Eisen- und Stahlindustrie, Eisen Pakt, 4480H/2219/E091433–E091434. For heavy industry's pressure on behalf of a higher tariff, cf. Mathies' report of January 7, 1925, conversation with Köngeter, who suggested that industry could carry on with its private talks only if the official negotiators advocated a tariff hike, ibid., E091428.

could our colleagues who do not make steel bring to this subject?"[102] But the Comité des Forges—in part because it was identified as a natural opponent of the Cartel des Gauches—never found a really receptive ear in ministerial chambers. Unlike the industrial delegates of Germany and Britain or their own banking colleagues, few French industrialists were present or influential at the London Conference. Serruys criticized French industry for treating Herriot like a "plague bearer, ignoring him, insulting him, leaving him to the mercy of an English Labour Party surrounded and guided by British industry and banks."[103]

Yet the distance between government and industry did not merely originate with a left coalition. While German officials in the Foreign and Economic Ministries had coordinated their efforts with Thyssen, Vögler, and others, Poincaré had kept industry at arm's length. Neither did Seydoux, who was more sympathetic and served as Poincaré's key adviser, bother to establish effective liaison. Serruys at Commerce clashed with Seydoux at the Quai, and in any case had other constituents besides the steel magnates, while in general each government office acted to preserve its own freedom from the importuning of private industry.[104]

Divergences enough, moreover, existed among the steel industrialists over the old question of coal supplies and the pressing new issue of tariff protection. These two problems intersected. The Wendel interests, who enjoyed secure and relatively inexpensive coke supplies, could accept a lower steel price structure, hence less protection, than those who purchased coal more dearly. Similarly, Wendel was more willing to renounce reparations coal—sold by the state at a price high enough to subsidize less favored producers—and happy to substitute private contracts instead. The Ministry of Commerce tended to favor

---

[102] Pinot to Serruys, September 4, 1924, AN, Paris: F[12]/8864, f. "Elbel."

[103] See Morin to Cavallier and Marcel Paul, August 13, 1924, PAM/7230, f. "Accords Commerciaux."

[104] The German and British foreign offices seemed more willing than the Quai d'Orsay to distinguish between individuals and firms seeking government intervention for their own interests and the objectives of industrial groups that might serve the ends of state policy. The Foreign Office dismissed businessmen who sought advice or protection for their ventures abroad, but it remained understanding and supportive of commercial policy in general. The Wilhelmstrasse, too, remained leery vis-à-vis Stinnes, but knew that the vigor of German heavy industry was one of its major trumps in the post-Versailles era. Stresemann himself argued for a higher tariff in late 1924, because he wanted greater leverage as he took up the interlocked negotiations over trade agreements and evacuation of the Cologne Zone of occupation. (See his memo of November 28, 1924, in GFM: Handakten Ritter, L177/4079/L051461–L051466.) The French, however, proved less capable of using economic trumps; indeed the iron capacity of Lorraine proved an embarrassment, and the Saar more a drain than an asset. A few years later they did exploit their banking role in Eastern Europe, but the initiative came more from the Bank of France than the Quai.

the low-tariff producers. But the need to preserve unity among the steel men in view of the German negotiations, as well as the fact that the Dawes plan placed a premium on France's continued acceptance of reparations coal, limited Serruys to a compromise that sanctioned private coal contracts with the Germans only for tonnages beyond the minimum reparations delivery.[105]

Serruys still displeased the protectionists among the French steel men, especially Camille Cavallier, the venerable and crotchety director of Pont-à-Mousson. When he briefed the directors of the Comité des Forges on October 21, after the opening Franco-German discussions, Serruys reported that the Germans were not asking for low French tariffs on raw iron and steel, but were seeking instead low duties on chemicals and machines and metal products. Nonetheless, France could not raise her steel tariff even if Germany were indifferent; a higher duty would raise the domestic price level of raw iron and steel to a point where the prices of French metal products would rise above German imports. This view worried some of Serruys' audience. A. Dreux, of the Societé des Aciéries de Longwy, argued that the granting of the minimal duty would open up the French market to Germany and Belgium: the Wendels, who were preoccupied with winning extension of the "contingent" for Lorraine's exports to South Germany, might become low-tariff advocates, but the steelmakers of the North could not. Why, asked Dreux, was the government interested solely in protecting the manufacturing industries? After hearing other, similar complaints, Serruys warned the steel industrialists against exaggerated demands. As he told Pinot, the Cartel parliament was unlikely to accept large tariff increases. The Chamber Commission on Tariffs had agreed to a 15 percent increase for the machine producers and consented not to lower the existing duty on iron and steel, but apparently that represented the extent of what could be promised. Dreux wrote Cavallier in deep disappointment: "I was almost the only one to speak and defend the cause of our industry but it was as if I had preached in the desert. . . . The fate of our industry is settled; it is being sacrificed completely, not to the Germans, but to the machine industry, without any concern for the possible consequences to us."[106] As Dreux later objected, everything was being sacrificed to a secondary objective, the

[105] See Serruys' Note for the Minister of Commerce, September 21, 1924, summarizing discussions held with industrialists at the Ministry of Public Works, September 19 and 20. AN, Paris: Min. Commerce, F^{12}/8864; also Cavallier's résumé of Comité des Forges discussion of selling reparation coal, September 25, 1924, in PAM/7230, f. "Accords franco-allemands."

[106] "Entrevue du Bureau du Comité des Forges avec M. Serruys et les experts de la Métallurgie, 21 octobre 1924; compte-rendu de M. Maurice," and Dreux to Cavallier, October 25, PAM/7230, f. "Accords franco-allemands."

Alsace-Lorraine and Saar "contingents." "We have not been able to unite in advance to form, as you say, a united front to oppose not only the Germans but our own government and M. Serruys in particular."[107]

The respective French and German situations thus had some points of similarity, but important differences as well. Neither German nor French producers were to get a massive tariff on raw iron and steel. Protectionists on both sides were to be disappointed. Each government was concerned about the whole range of its exports in the 1924–1925 negotiations, not just with iron and steel. Luther told heavy industry that wine and chemicals must also be considered; Serruys informed the Comité des Forges that the machine builders must get some benefits. In mid-December he disclosed that the French government had agreed to extend a minimal tariff (the one applied to trading partners) from the outset.[108] In each country the Ministries of Foreign Affairs and Commerce or Economics had to maximize a broad and conflicting set of commercial objectives.

Nevertheless, heavy industry could not unite in France as they did in Germany. For one thing, French coal firms were independent and had opposed interests on the price of coke and fuel. Furthermore, while the Ruhr producers consolidated their power through the Rohstahlgemeinschaft and the AVI Agreement, French iron and steel firms quarreled according to whether their primary markets were internal (Schneider, Pont-à-Mousson) or in South Germany. The protectionists emerged as increasingly uninfluential in the Comité des Forges. Cavallier was old, testy, and disappointed when he accused the Comité des Forges of defending itself badly. "You certainly understand that the difficulty lies in this," he wrote to one of his managers: "that the Wendels, having their coal, do not desire the protection of French metallurgy. Wendel's interest is evidently that the other French metallurgists hold the devil by the tail. In 20, 30, 40, or 50 years there will be only one steelmaker in France, the house of Wendel."[109] But Wendel was not the only one to dislike protectionism. Even though Cavallier commanded respect for his age and venerable position, Pralon accused him of losing perspective in his Nancy retreat.[110] As Théodor Laurent, Director of the Forges et Aciéries de la Marine et d'Homecourt—corporately linked to Pont-à-Mousson—wrote Cavallier, there were two groups among French steel producers: first, the pro-

[107] Dreux to Cavallier, January 25, 1925, PAM/7245, f. "Correspondance avec M. Pralon."
[108] See Emile Henry to Cavallier, December 15, 1924, *ibid.*
[109] Cavallier to E. Henry, March 25, 1925, *ibid.*
[110] Pralon to Cavallier, March 30, 1925, answering Cavallier's letter of March 25, in PAM/7245, f. "Correspondance avec M. Pralon"; and PAM/19061.

tectionists who wanted a closed internal market—such that even if they faced prohibitive tariffs elsewhere, *"tant pis*, the essential is to be protected at home." Second, those who thought it impossible to recover the prewar degree of protection and recognized that, in view of the excess French steel capacity since 1918, no tariff could prevent a ruinous price competition at home. French iron and steel, therefore, had to gamble on export and on trade treaties; specifically, it had to give the Germans low tariffs in return for extension of the "contingent." Dreux and Cavallier, noted Laurent, represented the first strand of thought; Wendel, Pinot, and Pralon defended the second; Léon-Lévy— chief of the negotiating team—allegedly wavered, thrown toward Cavallier by German stubbornness and wooed back by Wendel and Pinot's persuasion.[111]

This split was to remain within the French ranks throughout the 1925 and 1926 negotiations. By and large, the protectionists lost; the vision of the enclosed self-sufficient market gave way to that of a Darwinian export competition. Precisely to survive that competition, agreements had to be reached. The fundamental overcapacity of European steel forced a truce among capitalists that was to become the economic corollary of Locarno.

Why was agreement finally reached? In part, German and French needs were still complementary enough to allow for some degree of understanding. The French needed outlets for their excess output; the Germans could absorb more of their own product internally, but had to export the machines and electrical goods that their steel consumers manufactured. In short, Germany should absorb French steel in raw or semiproduct form; France should absorb German finished goods.

But what overcame the basic hammerlock that the German steel industry enjoyed because of French excess capacity? Certainly it was not the political power of the German manufacturing industries, since these had sold their policy voice for tariff rebates. Rather it was the French inflation of 1924–1926. With the steady depreciation of the franc, German steel consumers found it increasingly attractive to buy from across the Rhine. More Lorraine steel came into Germany after it was subject to duty in 1925 than when it was tariff-free for the same period in 1924. What is more, German producers lost their export markets as French iron crowded them off the steelyards of third countries.

By early 1925 German officials and industrialists found themselves at loggerheads. Officials needed the industrialists to extend the contingent in a private form by buying a quota of French iron and steel and re-

[111] Laurent to Cavallier, April 4, 1925; Léon-Lévy to Cavallier, March 30, 1925, *ibid.*

bating the duty. (Legislative extension of the contingent was undesirable because it would require equivalent concessions to be offered to all trade partners.) Without the contingent the French would negotiate no wider treaty. The industrialists complained that they were not getting sufficient tariff protection in view of the French depreciation. At the Chancellery on March 11, Klöckner claimed that the French could sell basic iron products for 137.50 marks per ton in South Germany. To meet this price, Ruhr producers allegedly would have to take a loss of at least 12.50 marks. If the German RSG had to agree to rebate a duty on Saar and Lorraine iron, their sacrifices would be even heavier. The government, therefore, would ultimately have to bear the costs of the contingent. Vögler warned that the evacuation of the Ruhr and the Cologne Zone had to be solved before the industrialists reached any contingent agreement, or the French would only set a new price for leaving Cologne. French iron, he complained, was even reaching the Berlin market despite the transport costs. "We are completely incapable of competition with France. The contingents are intolerable for German industry"—or tolerable, he conceded, only if reached as part of an overall agreement limiting steel output.[112]

Not all interests agreed, of course. South German finishing industries claimed that the price of 135 marks per ton, which they reported in the instance of wrought iron, was 20 marks higher than would have been the case without the duty. The machinery producers kept up their well-documented antitariff campaign throughout the spring. Hermann Röchling, the Saar iron magnate, who would suffer if Ruhr industry held up renewal of the contingent to press for a high tariff, argued that present duties sufficed.[113] There was, finally, considerable irony in the Ruhr's bemoaning the French inflation after German industrialists had exploited equivalent export bounties so ruthlessly for five years. The steel men now argued that they could live without the general trade treaty that the Ministry of Economics sought; they "could only gain by postponement and dragging out of the negotiations," as Vögler said. They did not need access to French markets. But as the Chancellor reminded them, other economic groups had "a significant interest

[112] Protocol of Reichskanzlei meeting concerning trade negotiations, March 11, 1925, GHH: 400101222/7.
[113] For the wrought-iron question, see the memorandum of the Handelskammer of Reutlingen, May 11, 1925, BA, Koblenz: R 13 I (VdESI)/347. For the submission of the Verein deutscher Maschinenbau-Anstalten—who emphasized that German motors and machine tools faced high foreign tariffs and thus required cheap steel—see R 13 I/346. For Reichert's controversy with the machine builders, see his early comments in the Hauptvorstand of the VdESI, October 20, 1924, R 13 I/346, and his statement of May 15, 1925, R 13 I/347. For a report of Röchling's views, see *ibid.*

in a speedy conclusion of negotiations with France." Moreover, tariff protection for industry was politically impossible at the moment. The Nationalists would not sanction an iron tariff without getting the agricultural duties they had sought the preceding summer. The Center Party, however, still resisted grain protection, and the issue had to be postponed for the duration of the Presidential campaign. Only thereafter did a compromise become feasible in which the Center agreed once again to an agricultural tariff in return for a reduction in the taxes on foodstuffs within Germany. Over the opposition of the Nationalists and the wine interests the government also pushed through the Spanish trade treaty, important in its own right but also intended to exert leverage on the French to come to a tariff agreement. Indeed while agriculture and the Ruhr pursued tariffs for simple protection, the Economics and Foreign Ministries saw them principally as tools for broader and more complex bargaining.[114]

Both government pressure and the depreciation of the franc thus pushed the Ruhr producers to come to terms on the "contingent." On March 18, after delaying for a year, the Germans finally began serious talks on the revival of IRMA.[115] By April 2, Fritz Thyssen, German leader of the private delegation, conceded that "if the period is not too long, the contingent seems bearable to me." The presupposition he added was that the question of evacuation of the Cologne Zone also be solved.[116]

The problem now was that the Germans wished to concede as small a "contingent" as possible. While willing to grant privileges for the Saar—where the Germans were anxious to preserve economic influence in any case—they did not want to make concessions to Lorraine. The French, by contrast, cared more about Lorraine than the Saar. Although the Saar lay within French customs territory, several of its major firms were still under German control, and the ultimate French hold over the region was problematic in view of the plebiscite. Even while the French negotiated for the contingents, their financial embarrassment forced withdrawal of the notes of the Bank of France as Saar currency. In 1923, Lasteyrie had vetoed use of the overex-

[114] Vögler and Reichskanzler Luther in March 11 meeting, GHH: 400101222/7. Tariff situation in Stürmer, *Koalition und Opposition*, pp. 99 ff.

[115] Gerwin to Reusch, February 7, 1925, and March 18 memo on talks in GHH: 400101222/2. This folder documents German delaying strategy throughout 1924: explanation to Marx, March 29, 1924; Pinot to Piérard, May 8, indicating real interest on the French side; Gerwin to Reusch, May 10; protocol of discussion with Piérard on June 26; Reusch to Gerwin, July 11 ("I am quite agreed that the negotiations should be drawn out as long as possible."); also inquiries from the French in October and December.

[116] Thyssen report to "Stahlwerksverband," April 2, 1925, GHH: 400101222/2.

tended franc in the Rhineland; by 1925, in its effort to stay below the currency ceiling, the Cartel had to restrict the franc even further. Serruys made it clear to the Paris representative of French-controlled Saar industry, Bommelaer, that there could be no Saar agreement unless the Germans gave satisfaction to Lorraine as well.[117]

The Germans were unhappy about concessions to Lorraine, but could not really resist further. "We can't go on producing the way we have been," admitted Jakob Hasslacher of Rheinstahl at the April 2 meeting of the Stahlwerksverband; "the German and foreign markets must finally be put in order, and by agreement with France so that we can use our entire strength to get a stronger inland organization." Vögler, too, pleaded for a settlement: if France did not secure a contingent for Lorraine, she would demand a far bigger slash in the overall German iron tariff.[118]

The way to a face-saving compromise emerged from the vulnerable German-controlled steel industry in the Saar. Müller, the director of the former Stumm works, proposed that the German Raw Steel Community purchase a contingent of Saar iron and steel based on the output of 1913 and at a price high enough to cover the industry's tariff costs. Since Saar industry no longer directed the 1913 level of output to Germany but sent much of it to France instead, her producers could retrocede some of the tariff compensation to Lorraine.[119]

The Müller proposal enabled provisional agreement to be reached in Luxemburg on June 16/17 after further intensive bargaining. Discussions in April and May were delayed by the fall of the Herriot government and the death of Léon-Lévy, the principal French industrial negotiator. Each side finally met at Paris on May 30 with its tariff proposals. The French demanded that one of several alternative packages of raw steel, semi- and finished products from the Saar and Lorraine pass tariff-free into Germany. The Germans tried to minimize concessions, pointing out that Luxemburg steel interests—predominantly the ARBED of Emile Mayrisch—were also demanding contingents. Mayrisch played an important role at this juncture. He owned important foundries within Germany at Eschweiler, Aachen, and Cologne (Felten & Guillaume), and threatened to expand his own steel output inside Germany if his manufacturing plants were short-changed in the steel allocations determined by the RSG. Presumably, he would ex-

[117] See memo of Cavallier-Bommelaer meeting, April 9, 1925, in PAM/19061, f. Comité des Forges de France. For the corporate structure of Lorraine industry, Berkenkopf, *Lothringisch-luxemburgische Grosseisenindustrie*, pp. 46–47.

[118] See Aktennotiz of April 2, 1925, GHH: 400101222/2.

[119] Aktennotiz, *ibid.*; also Müller plan as described by Bommelaer to Cavallier, April 9, 1925, PAM/19061.

ert the same leverage to secure a Luxemburg contingent for the German market.[120] What the Germans offered at Paris was an overall contingent of 1.5 million tons for all products from Lorraine, the Saar, and Luxemburg. But in return they demanded that the Saar works, which had largely passed under French corporate control except for Roechling and Neunkirchen, join the Raw Steel Community. If, moreover, the RSG had to cut back its total purchases because of slack market conditions, then the foreign contingents would also have to be lowered along with the quotas assigned to German firms. The Ruhr negotiators ultimately prevailed on these latter points. In return they agreed to a 1.75 million ton contingent that would effectively rebate half the German import duties through the purchase prices offered by the RSG. Finally, the German delegates successfully stipulated that entry into force of the Luxemburg agreement would have to await completion of a trade treaty between the two governments. The trade treaty, they felt, was a necessary basis for arriving at the private limitation of international steel output, which remained their underlying goal.[121]

Because of this last provision, the Luxemburg agreement proved stillborn. Conditional upon a trade treaty, it lapsed when negotiations broke down for several months in mid-1925. As a provisional measure, the government delegations signed an arrangement that envisaged a 700,000-ton contingent for Saar products alone. The Germans did not wish to leave the Saar firms in distress. But the French could not favor the Saar over Lorraine; Wendel, for one, resented the preference that Saar products would get in South Germany unless Lorraine shared in the tariff rebate and could lower her steel prices accordingly.[122] Reflecting this preoccupation, Serruys asked the Germans for a six-mark rebate to Lorraine for every ton of Saar metal the Germans subsidized—tantamount to the compensation the abortive Luxemburg agreement would have provided.

The German negotiators found Serruys' stipulation "a huge demand . . . completely out of the question."[123] On behalf of the German in-

[120] See the record of the meeting between Thyssen, Poensgen (Phönix), and Mayrisch, GHH: 400101222/2; on Mayrisch, see Jacques Bariéty, "Sidérurgie, littérature, politique et journalisme: une famille luxembourgeoise, les Mayrisch, entre l'Allemagne et la France après la première guerre mondiale," *Bulletin de la Société d'Histoire Moderne*, série 14 (1970), pp. 7–12.

[121] See Gerwin's memorandum on the Luxemburg discussions of June 16, 1925: GHH: 400101222/2.

[122] Wendel address at Chamber of Commerce in Metz, September 11, 1925, reported by Emile Henry to Cavallier, September 28, PAM/19061, f. Comité des Forges de France.

[123] See Trendelenburg memo, September 28, 1925, in GFM: Ritter Handakten, L177/4080/L053469–L053474; also Schubert to negotiators in Paris, August 11, 1925, L052501–L052502.

dustrialists, Ernst Poensgen initially warned the Saar firms at the end of July that he could offer no rebates intended for Lorraine. Lorraine's compensation had been designed as a counterpart for the French joining an international iron agreement to limit European steel production. As Poensgen wrote Pinot, international regulation of the market had to be achieved before a Lorraine contingent was negotiated. Pinot answered sharply that the Germans should stop foot-dragging on IRMA if they wanted the general agreement.[124] While the Germans seemed to ease their stance on the rebate by mid-August, they did insist that Saar firms who were to enjoy tariff privileges must join the RSG. They understood that this would antagonize the firms under French control, because it meant subjecting vital economic decisions to the Ruhr producers.[125]

At this point the Saar concerns split into two camps. Those under French control endorsed Serruys' conditions and refused to join the RSG, while Roechling and Neunkirchen agreed to join the RSG but disliked retroceding tariff payments to Lorraine. The result was a prolonged deadlock. At the end of August, leading German negotiators met with Humbert de Wendel and Théodor Laurent to review the unsatisfactory progress toward resurrecting IRMA and working out the contingent. The Germans complained that their finishing industries had yet to receive any tariff concessions and that the overall steel-limitation agreement was no closer. The French felt that their Ruhr counterparts were negotiating in bad faith. The mood at the following luncheon was glacial.[126]

The cold war between the steel industries accompanied a more general breakdown of the trade negotiations. Along with providing for the 700,000-ton Saar contingent, the official negotiators, Trendelenburg and Chaumet (the new French Minister of Commerce), had agreed on July 11 not to raise tariff rates against each other while talks were underway. But during the summer the Germans imposed higher wine tariffs, arguing that France was taxed only along with every other country. The French, however, were within their rights to read the tariff increase as a violation of the July 11 commitment, and they retaliated by invoking a law that let them double the duty on coal imported beyond the reparations account. In turn, the Germans refused to submit the provisional Saar contingent for Reichstag ratification until the French lifted the "prohibition" on German coal imports

---

[124] Poensgen to Saar industrialists, July 23, 1925; Poensgen to Pinot, July 30. See Pinot to Gerwin, August 17: all in GHH: 400101222/7.
[125] Memo of August 10 meeting, *ibid.*
[126] Memo of Cologne discussion, August 29, 1925, *ibid.*

and dropped their demand for a six-mark rebate from the Saar to Lorraine.[127]

Unfortunately, different groups wanted different agreements for different reasons. The steel producers of the Ruhr sought the limitation of steel production; they had no use for the contingent by itself. The Economics Ministry, however, wanted to wrest a favorable trade treaty from Paris with most-favored-nation status for German manufacturers. Over the summer the Ministry started imposing agricultural tariffs they knew would hurt French wine growers and vegetable suppliers in the harvest months ahead. It also wanted quick completion of the Italian and Spanish trade treaties, so that it could brandish the concessions made to Italian wine and produce and Spanish ore as a threat to the French. But the Foreign Ministry did not want to endanger the trade treaty, which it envisaged as a complement to its own negotiations for a security pact. Ritter told Trendelenburg that the Luxemburg agreement had been favorable for Germany and that it would be a great loss if economic reconciliation faltered. Stresemann, too, wanted progress. In January 1925 he had refused to break off the trade negotiations when the British and French delayed leaving the Cologne Zone; in the autumn he urged Briand to intervene with his Commerce Ministry.[128]

There still remained compelling economic reasons to overcome the crisis: the pressure of French agricultural interests in Paris and the distress of German iron in late 1925. An important step forward was taken in October, when the French agreed that most-favored-nation treatment (or the equivalent minimal tariff) would eventually be granted in any final trade treaty. For the provisional treaty, which would govern commercial relations for several months or more, as well as for the first eighteen months of the definitive treaty, the French still wanted to impose special handicaps on German goods. But they were ready to guarantee that their minimal tariff would not be raised for the duration of a treaty, and were prepared to adopt a coefficient system that would protect the Germans against changes in value of the franc.[129] In part, Paris was responding to agricultural protest voiced in the Chamber. In the November 12 debate, Cartel des Gauches

[127] See Ruppel in Paris to the Finance Ministry, July 28, Hoesch to the Foreign Ministry, July 31, and Trendelenburg summary of September 28, 1925, GFM: Handakten Ritter, L177/4080/052540–052541, 052534–052535, 052469–052474.

[128] Ritter to Trendelenburg, GFM: L177/4080/052486–052489; Stresemann, Vermächtnis, II, pp. 20, 291–294; also: Stresemann to delegation in Paris, GFM: L177/4081/052770.

[129] Trendelenburg to Pünder and Schubert, November 27, 1925, GFM: L177/4080/052698–052703.

deputies from the Bouches de Rhone and elsewhere attacked the government for the inconclusive character of the negotiations: Germany had raised agricultural duties so much that French grapes, flowers, and all harvest crops faced a "Chinese wall." Meanwhile, Italian and Dutch farm products, which enjoyed most-favored-nation status, were streaming into Germany. Unless the government wished to face rural rebellion, it must reach at least a short-term *modus vivendi*.[130]

Simultaneously, the economic situation of the German iron and steel industry grew more depressed. The Ruhr was happy to see the Luxemburg agreement dead, but by autumn it needed some economic breakthrough. As Reusch told the Langnamverein assembly and the Northwest Group of the Iron and Steel Association in mid-December, "The crisis in which we have now lived for months continues; it is growing more acute from day to day." Parliament allegedly heeded no complaints; the government refused to recognize the precarious state of the iron industry, which was caught between excessive burdens for social insurance, taxes, and interest while France continued dumping her metal in Germany.[131] The extent of distress was revealed by the particular difficulties of the Krupp firm throughout 1925. In the summer Krupp informed the government that it was finally willing to destroy 34 huge lathes that the Allies thought suitable for the manufacture of armaments. But the price had to be an infusion of British capital. "Destruction of the lathes and purchase of stock shares cannot be separated," wrote Wiedfeldt to the Foreign Ministry on August 1.[132] In the following months no great financial improvement occurred. "Can Friedrich Krupp, A.G., carry on as an independent enterprise with prospects for success?" asked Wiedfeldt in a gloomy review that weighed the possibility of loosening family control over the enterprise. The family's equity in Krupp in 1914 and in February 1922 had been 450 million marks; now at the beginning of 1926 it was down to 120 million. Wiedfeldt did not advocate whether the firm must go public or not, but he outlined stark alternatives.[133]

Under pressures such as these, the Germans moved toward agreement. Emil Mayrisch revived the industrialists' talks in January 1926 on the basis of a recent Thyssen proposal for limitation of steel production by Germany, France, Belgium, and Luxemburg. Although the figures were changed, Thyssen's plan became the basis for agreement.

[130] JOC, 1925, pp. 3678 ff. (November 12).

[131] "Sonderausdruck aus Nr. 1 der Wirtschaftlichen Nachrichten," January 6, 1926, GHH: 400101221/4. Cf. Reichert to Posse, L177/4080/052812–052815. The Langnamverein was a powerful Westphalian economic association dominated by Ruhr coal and steel entrepreneurs.

[132] Fr. Krupp, A.G., WA III 239.

[133] "Denkschrift über die Finanzlage," Fr. Krupp, A.G., WA IV 1417.

Each steel producer, he suggested, was to pay into a central fund roughly 5 marks per ton of steel produced. From the outset this would raise the market price. An international committee would set European steel production totals quarterly, and each nation would be assigned a quota. Those firms that produced less than their quota would be paid 5 marks per ton for the amount they underproduced; those exceeding their quota would be charged an extra 5 marks per ton for the amount they overproduced.[134] The French quickly accepted the principle of the plan, but protracted argument followed over the percentage quotas each national steel industry should receive. Recession had gripped the German producers in early 1926, so they did not wish to use current production as a base for calculating their national quotas; while the French claimed that many of their factories were still suffering from wartime damage.[135] Differences also arose over the Saar contingent, which, it was now agreed, must be solved as part of the larger settlement. Throughout 1926 the Germans sought tariff-free entry of their machines into the Saar; Serruys initially refused, since the Germans refused to compensate Lorraine, but admitted that he might relent if France secured a long-term contingent for the Saar alone.[136]

The basic Franco-German agreement on both the steel quotas and the Saar terms was reached at a July 8 conference in Düsseldorf.[137] Ironing out details, however, still proved vexing. Wendel and the Lorraine producers demanded that if they limited their iron exports to Germany, the Saar must impose a ceiling on the tonnage if sent into France. The French-controlled Saar firms, moreover, were still resisting the idea of entering the Raw Steel Community and pressing to have the tariffs that had been debited against them since January 1925 wiped from the books.[138] Finally, in mid-August, a further com-

---

[134] Thyssen to Gerwin, December 29, 1925. GFM: Ritter Handakten, Eisenverhandlungen, L1489/5352/436452–436453.

[135] Protocol on Luxemburg talks, January 30, 1926, *ibid.*, 436449–436451; also discussions of February 10, 436475–436480. Cf. Théodor Laurent to Poensgen, March 31, concerning French claims that "only coefficients separate us," *ibid.*, L436444–L436445; Poensgen to Ritter, April 26, summarizing Paris talk of April 22 and continued disagreement over quotas, L436436–L436438.

[136] Posse and Hoesch memorandum on talk with Serruys, March 15, 1926, *ibid.*, L436489–L436492.

[137] For this meeting, see Ritter's memo on Poensgen's telephone report from Düsseldorf, *ibid.*, L436412–L436413.

[138] See Laurent on behalf of the Comité des Forges to Poensgen, July 15, 1926; Poensgen to Reichswirtschaftsministerium, and Poensgen to Laurent, July 24, 1926, *ibid.*, L436367–L436381. The Germans wanted the Saar producers to have the right to export into France up to one-third their steel output—not merely the 500,000 tons per year that the French proposed on the basis of the low Saar production of 1925.

promise was struck: most of the French firms agreed to enter the RSG, but on conditions that allowed for easy withdrawal. Berlin annulled the tariff charges outstanding, while the French agreed to a flexible ceiling for the Saar tonnage that could be shipped to France. Final signature was put off until the overall steel-limitation pact was completed.[139] Now it was the Belgians' turn to hold up the general settlement; there was no general Belgian trade organization and each firm bid for its own steel quotas, so no agreement could be reached until late September.[140] At that time the iron limitation agreement could be signed pending detailed completion of the Lorraine and Luxemburg contingents,[141] including one last hurdle: the French-controlled Saar firm of Dillingen had paid its duties in cash since 1925 and wanted compensation equivalent to the annulment of tariff debts that had been granted to the other French-controlled concerns. The claim would have been insignificant, except that Dillingen was controlled by the chief French negotiator on the Saar issue, Laurent. The Germans demanded compensatory privileges for their machine exports to the Saar, but finally in early November granted the reluctant firm credits toward future duties as compensation.[142]

This completed the horse trading. By early November both major agreements could finally be signed. The Germans won their international steel agreement, the Entente Internationale de l'Acier, whereby production guidelines were set and a central treasury established. Each producer paid in $1.00 per ton, while those whose output fell below their quota could draw $2.00. Over-producers were penalized $4.00. The Germans were unhappy about the 1926 base for the percentages that were authorized for each country. But they won a variable quota system: when the authorized European output rose from 25 to 29 million tons, their percentage share would increase from about 40 to 43 percent, while the French would drop from about 32 to 31 percent. In accompanying agreements, the German Raw Steel Community agreed to give Lorraine steel producers 3.75 percent of its German sales. Rather than arrange for duty-free imports or tariff rebates, the sales price was set about 10 percent higher than the French market price, effectively canceling out the effect of the German duties. In

[139] See the "Niederschrift" of the discussions in Paris, August 2 to 14, *ibid.*, L436335–L436338.

[140] "Aktenvermerk" of discussions of September 17 and 20 concerning an international raw steel agreement, including Belgian complaints about low quotas, *ibid.*, L436266–L436268.

[141] Cf. Poensgen to the Reichswirtschaftsministerium, October 1, 1926; and text of Brussels protocol, *ibid.*, L436609–L436648; also GFM: Büro des Staatssekretärs, 4480/2219/E091264–E091266.

[142] Memo of October 4 and 5, GFM: Handakten Ritter, L177/4080/436643–436645; protocol of Luxemburg meeting, November 4, 1926, L436578–L436581.

return for French agreement not to ship steel into Germany beyond the RSG quota of 3.75 percent, Ruhr industry promised not to compete within France or her colonies. Luxemburg won similar arrangements, which gave her 2.75 percent of the German raw steel sales. Parallel agreements assigned about 8 and 3 percent of German pig iron consumption to Lorraine and Luxemburg, respectively. The Saar was given a duty-free contingent of 1.55 million tons for iron and steel products of all types in return for Paris' granting the minimal tariff on German machines sent the other way. This represented a temporary concession on the part of German industry, but in effect heralded the end of French economic control and reincorporation of the Saar into the German customs system.[143]

Finally, the ponderous negotiations for a general trade treaty moved toward completion. In February 1926 negotiators had concluded a "spring vegetable treaty," which granted French farmers three months' access to German markets for green peas and other seasonal products. In return the French granted certain German exports special interim tariff reductions.[144] The provisorium was amplified in April and renegotiated during the summer—but not without a bitter dispute over French wine, which the Germans refused to include as a privileged import. The political situation was too precarious for both the French and German coalitions to allow important concessions. Berthelot went so far as to promise a reduction of French troops in the occupied Rhineland if the Germans could admit a quota of French vintages. But even Stresemann insisted on economic concessions in return, and finally Paris let the demand drop. In return Germany agreed to a six-month provisional trade treaty on August 5. The stabilization of the franc made agreement more urgent for Paris and more acceptable for Berlin.[145] By November the French agreed to further concessions, intended to become part of a definitive compact once the French tariff had been worked out in the Chamber. Negotiations clouded again

[143] C. Nattan-Larrier, *La production sidérurgique de l'Europe continentale et l'Entente Internationale de l'Acier* (Paris, 1929), pp. 289–300.

[144] For a summary of the 1926 treaties, see the report of the Chamber Commission des Douanes: JOC: Doc Parl., Nr. 3965, Annèxe au procès-verbal de la séance du 15 fevrier 1927, and included in Min. Aff. Etr., Europe, 1918–1929, Allemagne/525. Cf. GFM: Büro des Staatssekretärs, 4482H/2221/E093347–E093348, for communiqué on February 12, 1926 agreement.

[145] Berthelot interview with Hoesch, June 26, 1926, reported in GFM: Büro des Staatssekretärs, 4482H/2221/E093399–E093404; also report on Stresemann-Margérie (French Ambassador in Berlin) conversation June 28, E093414–E093416; Stresemann to Hoesch, June 29, emphasizing the need for stabilization of the franc, E093417–E093420; Schmieden and Rieth to Berlin, July 6, indicating French willingness to postpone wine demands, E093440–E093441; also reports from Paris, July 26 and August 5, 1926, 4482H/2222/E093442–E093445, E093450–E093451.

during the winter of 1926–1927, as the French pressed again for concessions on wine. The battle over wine became spirited enough to involve the major officials of the Foreign Ministry, but the Germans refused to make further provisional concessions. With a new Bürgerblok government being negotiated in early 1927, it was an awkward moment to impose further demands upon German agricultural interests. Yet the fact that what had been a battle over steel was now a struggle over wines showed the progress achieved, and the treaties were finally signed during the course of 1927.[146]

What was the upshot of these hard-fought agreements? The French effectively protected their home and colonial markets in raw iron and steel; they won, in addition, a spillover into Germany for their excess capacity. The Germans won a return to predictability. What they regarded as their own status as the pitiful giant of the European steel industry—their vulnerability first to the provisions of Versailles, then to French inflation—effectively ended. As usual, their tales of woe had been sentimental and excessive. Germany, too, had long enjoyed the addictive advantages of inflation. And even after 1926, under the Entente Internationale d'Acier, while their production climbed, their penalties did not average more than from 1 to 2.5 marks per ton in 1927.[147] Meanwhile, the different interests groped toward more binding cartels for different branches of production: the celebrated IRMA reappeared as ERMA (European, not International); pipe manufacturers and others were also working toward a more managed capitalism—when the Depression intervened to destroy all these agreements like the fragile structures they were.

In light of the political stability and the great spurt of productivity and output that Europe achieved between 1924 and 1929, the international agreements can be seen to have formed part of a larger structure of capitalist settlement. The coal-steel community of the 1920's rested on a series of compromises, as did the internal equilibria of the French and German republics. The Steel Entente had been sought as the economic counterpart of Locarno; like Locarno, it was a limited settlement that calmed some areas of conflict (the quantity of output), but not others (price), and was destined to be swept away by unforeseen convulsions. Meanwhile, both settlements showed that, in the political and economic spheres, nationalist or unilateral solutions had

[146] On the renewed wine controversy see Hoesch report, December 23, 1926; Ritter's memorandum of February 1, 1927; Margérie-Schubert conversation, February 7, 1927, in GFM: Handakten Ritter, L177/4081/053342–053345, 053282–053283, 053252–053253, and *passim*.

[147] Nattan-Larrier, *La production sidérurgique*, p. 310.

come to appear too costly and even unnecessary. The momentary advantages that the Germans had enjoyed by virtue of their inflation ultimately led to the French use of force, which entailed the costly passive resistance and the subsequent MICUM accords. For Paris, the temporary returns from MICUM were quickly overshadowed by preoccupation with what the Germans could wrest after the deadline of January 10, 1925. Berlin's regaining of tariff sovereignty came to count little in view of the advantages that Lorraine smelters obtained from the French inflation. Ultimately these vicissitudes on both sides prevented predictability, impeded rational investment and market development; ultimately, as the Germans had said, the market had to be set in order.

But the order had both costs and advantages. Governments of the Bürgerblok did not give German steelmakers a tariff dreamworld. It was clear that the Cartel des Gauches would not fulfill the old protectionist longings of French industry, but neither would Poincaré. There were many reasons for this half-way tariff policy: the governments of the mid-1920's were themselves conservative compromises; they allowed the left to have local bastions of power and granted it a foreign policy of apparent reconciliation. The men in charge of the mid-decade ministries still regarded themselves, moreover, as spokesmen for a public weal: Luther, Stresemann, and Poincaré had all fought the pretensions of industry in 1923–1924, and would do so in 1925–1926. Heavy tariffs seemed a surrender to the clear-cut interest-group politics they wished to avoid. Likewise, the French Ministry of Commerce, the German Foreign Ministry and Economic Ministry were headed by permanent teams who saw their roles as impartial civil servants.

Yet the civil servants could no longer negotiate without the corporations. The two parallel series of talks, the one between ministries, the other between industrialists, epitomized the balance of forces that had been struck. This did not mean that the industrialists dictated to the civil servants; indeed, at many points during the protracted negotiations there was evidence of the state setting the framework and the conditions for business agreement. The state had to ensure that the needs of its other economic sectors would not be sacrificed to iron and steel. Nonetheless, that industry in which domestic concentration of enterprises was most intensive had become by far the dominant area of concern. Iron and steel production had moved from being one of many private industries to a new crucial activity, lying between private and public sectors.

The particular political thrust of the iron and steel negotiations— their contribution to a stabilized corporate pluralism—depended upon the basic factor of overcapacity. This overcapacity exerted pressures similar to the international deflationary tendencies of mid-decade brought out by currency stabilization. Both deflationary stabilization and the overproduction of the mid-1920's produced the same Malthusian preoccupations, the same fear of saturated markets, the same enthusiasm for rationalization. Rationalization meant enhancing productivity by a host of methods—scientific management imported from the United States, technological advances in plant design, the take-over of smaller units by larger ones. In steel, both rickety debt structures and economies of scale in blast-furnace size impelled consolidation and the abandonment of smaller and less profitable works. Vereinigte Stahlwerke, grouping the Phönix and old Stinnes interests under Vögler, was an excellent example of the results; the town of Jarrow was another. Rationalization, in fact, was a gimmicky concept: it suggested great technical advance while in fact it presupposed a limited and finite market and helped to undermine purchasing power even as it increased productivity.[148]

Rationalization at home, the iron entente internationally, testified to the anxiety underlying the capitalism of the 1920's. Even while the European economy enjoyed major growth, there persisted constant, nagging concern. The concern was not always focused correctly. When central bankers such as Strong or Schacht worried about the system's dependence upon short-term American loans, they pointed out a major dilemma. But when business circles saw the capacity for growth as largely behind them, when they viewed the economy as a mercantilist cockpit, the diagnosis was less well founded. European industrialists envied the American market, praised Ford, but felt that their underlying need to export precluded the high-wage–low-price capitalism the Detroit innovator represented.[149] For industrial as well as financial activity, the international economy seemed to businessmen more a burden than an opportunity, to be lived with only by means of cartels that limited production and kept up prices. There was a yearning for autarchy, but until the 1930's a bad conscience about yielding to it. Ironically, even as the Europeans looked longingly to

[148] See, above all, Robert Brady, *The Rationalization Movement in German Industry* (Berkeley and Los Angeles, 1933); contemporary German opinion in the essays put out by the Industrie- und Handelskammer zu Berlin, *Die Bedeutung der Rationalisierung für das deutsche Wirtschaftsleben* (Berlin, 1928).

[149] See, for example, Herbert von Beckerath, "Die Bedeutung des inneren Marktes in Amerika," *Mitteilungen des Vereins zur Wahrung der gemeinsamen wirtschaftlichen Interessen in Rheinland und Westfalen* (January 1927), Heft Nr. 1, esp. pp. 75–81; A. Deteouf, *La réorganisation industrielle* (Paris, 1927); cf. Charles S. Maier, "Between Taylorism and Technocracy: European Ideologies and the Vision of Industrial Productivity in the 1920's," *Journal of Contemporary History*, v, 2 (1970), pp. 54–59.

what some termed the "neocapitalism" of the United States,[150] the presuppositions of prosperity were not so different there. For through their trade-association fervor and their Hooverite concerns about efficiency, American businessmen were also expressing an implicit concern about the finiteness of growth and prosperity. This shadow side, the Malthusian anxiety, is often overlooked under the confetti of stock-ticker tape, but it constantly conditioned how business dealt with prosperity.

In Europe, it was the industries that were most preoccupied that were also the most powerful. If chemicals and electricity had enjoyed the political centrality of coal and iron, the institutional response might have been different. Instead, the internal and international dilemmas of iron and steel (and agriculture) forced the stabilization of capitalism less through market than through political mechanisms. Prosperity was briefly secured by the fusion of public and private power, by the strengthening of industrial associations, the maintenance of prices, and the effort to lower labor costs. This form of stabilization proved unable to guarantee prosperity; and in large part the very market anxieties that brought it forth contributed to its fragility. The preoccupation with saturation of the market prevented any emphasis on the motive role of consumption, whether on the part of the state or through mass purchasing power. It was thus difficult to forestall the cyclical downturn that the late 1920's dreaded. But if anxieties about overproduction helped consolidate the corporatist pluralism of the 1920's, the system could outgrow its early formative climate. As the years after World War II were to demonstrate, similar forms of economic organization could produce an equilibrium that operated under the assumptions of growth and expansion.

CORPORATIVE STATE IN CORPORATIST EUROPE

There were alternative paths to stability in the 1920's. They all involved new fusions of economics and political power: more consistent state interventions in the market, and a greater role in the formulation of public policy entrusted to industry. Italy adopted a harsher path

---

[150] See E. Giscard d'Estaing, "Le néocapitalisme," *RDM*, August 1, 1928; for economic stagnation: Ingvar Svennilson, *Growth and Stagnation in the European Economy* (Geneva, 1954), pp. 82 ff., 105 ff., 124 ff.; for efforts to discipline the United States, see Ellis Hawley's essays on Herbert Hoover, esp. his contribution to *Herbert Hoover and the Crisis of American Capitalism* (Cambridge, Mass., 1973). For the general theme, see Charles S. Maier, "Strukturen kapitalistischer Stabilität in den zwanziger Jahren; Errungenschaften und Defekte," in Heinrich August Winkler, ed., *Organisierter Kapitalismus. Voraussetzungen und Anfänge*, (Göttingen, 1974), pp. 195–213.

toward this new stability than did France or Germany, but with many of the same results. Under the conditions prevailing in republican Germany, powerful industrial and agrarian delegations could themselves secure the corporatist representation that protected their interests. In France, the safeguarding of particular producers' interests was less politically preoccupying than the monetary security of a broad bourgeois elite. Economic and political organization remained more fragmented but less necessary for stability: inherited institutions protected traditional hierarchies. In Italy, all the elements of the interlocked elites—industrial managers, civic leaders, political "notables"—also sought protection of privilege, but the old political mechanisms for assuring it had proved unreliable. The men who by day ran cotton mills, banks, estates, and engineering firms, and who by night dined with the prefects, had felt overwhelmed by the democratization of prewar institutions. They were thus prepared to acquiesce, or even assist, when an authoritarian party set out to create new political ground rules.

Many, however, remained equivocal toward fascism because the movement was still turbulent and potentially radical. Fascist syndicalists and ex-squadrists—subject at best to a precarious discipline within the new National Militia—yearned for an overturning of traditional hegemonies.[151] While their vision of a future syndical order might be murky, their contempt for the country's encrusted leadership was deep and bitter. Self-interested plutocrats, a fusty bureaucracy, a web of parasitic banks and Freemasons, and constantly carping liberal editors still suffocated the society that the Fascist intransigents perceived. The revolution had yet to be carried through.

For a brief period the old elites tolerated the continuing influence of the radicals within the movement. The alternative seemed to be a democratic regime with extensive Socialist if not Communist influence. Mussolini, moreover, had to be treated gingerly, since he could change quickly from a sober imposition of authority toward an inflammatory rabble rousing that would unleash further disorder. By sedulous collaboration, the "flankers" of fascism hoped to wean him away from the intransigents.[152] While the elections had reinforced the legal position of fascism, they had left the nature of Fascist rule unclear. Inside the Party the so-called revisionists and the ex-liberals who had donned

---

[151] For the unions, see Fernando Cordova, "Le origini dei sindacati fascisti," *Storia Contemporanea*, I, 4 (December 1970), pp. 925–1010; also Adrian Lyttelton, *The Seizure of Power. Fascism in Italy 1919–1929* (London, 1973), pp. 150 ff., 269–304 on the Party, pp. 244–250 on the Militia, and pp. 217 ff. on the unions.

[152] For the *fiancheggiatori*, see Renzo De Felice, *Mussolini il fascista*, II, *L'organizzazione dello Stato fascista 1925–1929* (Turin, 1968), pp. 7–10.

black shirts after the March on Rome could be counted on to work for a quiet collaboration. Outside the Party there were also liberals ready to collaborate, and who had accepted places on the electoral slate or run as "flankers." All these elements could calculate that the longer fascism remained in power as a parliamentary coalition, the more it would become ensnared by the temptations, usages, and politicking of the Italian system.

Ordinary circumstances might have produced a protracted jockeying for power between intransigents and moderates, but the events surrounding the murder of the Socialist parliamentary deputy Matteotti catalyzed the internal tensions of the movement. Ultimately Mussolini was to give the Fascist radicals a political victory by the creation of a rigorous dictatorship. But even while embarking upon authoritarianism in 1925 and 1926, the Italian prime minister was to secure to the old dominant groups much of their former social and economic preeminence. Especially in the economic realm, he was to reward business leadership by limiting and then suppressing working-class protest, disciplining Fascist unions, and encouraging industrial take-overs by large-scale firms.

Even before the 1924 crisis, a new structure of decision making in Rome had helped to strengthen the industrialists' policy voice. The government made the Fascist Party's Grand Council a new, important forum, where Fascist syndicalists and industrial spokesmen debated labor policy before Mussolini. No equivalent link between representatives of the PNF, major interest groups, and the state had previously existed. The result was to place a premium on the effective organization and representation of industry, to enhance the role of Confindustria, and to centralize social and economic conflict.

This was a development that might well have evolved from below given the strength of the labor movement after the war. Giolitti, in effect, had mediated social conflict after the Occupation of the Factories. But his intervention had been exceptional, and liberal Italy had not developed a means of arbitration such as the Weimar Republic possessed in its Ministry of Labor. Moreover, Giolitti had governed more through a combination of diverse sources of power than through central and well-defined agencies. While he alienated the conservative entrepreneurs of Milan, he retained a strong Piedmontese home base, including support from Agnelli of Fiat and Frassati of *La Stampa*. With the powerful assistance of his Undersecretary at the Interior Ministry, Corradini, Giolitti had effectively mastered the civil service and prefectural system—at least until the spring of 1921, when he miscalculated the degree of Fascist subversion in the countryside. He commanded extensive patronage, had once enjoyed the acquiescence of reformist labor leaders, and benefited from the veneration paid his age and experience. But the emergence of political Catholicism and the radicalization of the Socialists, not to say the Fascist surge, had caught him off base. With the advent of fascism he surrendered to a self-described "Tolstoyan" counsel of patience bearing on fatalism, coupling disdain for the crudeness of Mussolini's supporters and despair that the body politic could choose better.[153]

During the early years of fascism Mussolini drew on some of the same sources of strength as Giolitti, but he also adopted different approaches. At first the South yielded only slowly to political manipulation, although by 1924 the Fascist leader had successfully wooed many key deputies. Many prefects switched their loyalty with alacrity, among them Palmieri in Turin.[154] Labor remained hostile—but then, labor had not aided Giolitti when he needed support in 1920–1921. The Vatican deserted the Popolari to encourage the philofascist Conservatori Nazionali, which seceded from the PPI in the summer of 1924.[155] Until the Matteotti affair, the liberal conservatives gave Mussolini ample support. In short, Mussolini fell heir to many of the assets Giolitti had controlled. Furthermore, by moving the chief threat of social radicalism from the CGL and Socialist Party organizations to the syndicalist leaders within the Fascist Party, Mussolini made crucial his own arbitrating position over government and party.

The aftermath of the Matteotti murder required Mussolini to balance forces differently; it made each side, fascist and liberal, more insistent on a policy in conformity with its own interest. The major intransigent spokesman, Roberto Farinacci, now pressed for a "second wave" of fascist revolution. Stripped of its rhetoric, this tended to mean a ruthless spoils system for PNF stalwarts coupled with large-scale repression. The advocates of normalization inside and outside the Party wanted Mussolini to provide guarantees against Farinacci's adherents and the Fascist syndicalists, who were urging more government support for the Party's labor organizations. These conflicts were already built into the equivocal situation left by the April elections.

---

[153] Gabriele De Rosa, *Giolitti e il fascismo in alcune sue lettere inedite* (Rome, 1957), pp. 23–28; cf. Nino Valeri, *Da Giolitti a Mussolini: momenti della crisi del liberalismo italiano* (Florence, 1956), pp. 192–193; Gaetano Natale, *Giolitti e gli italiani* (Milan, 1949), pp. 42–44; Lyttelton, *Seizure of Power*, pp. 111–113.

[154] For Fascist inroads in the South and Turin, see above, pp. 346, 422–434, and reports of 1923 in ACS, Rome: Carte Micheli Bianchi, B. 2, PNF, "Direzione Segreteria Politica." Lusignoli in Milan helped to negotiate Mussolini's take-over but by 1924 joined the opposition in the Senate after being removed as prefect in May 1923; see Lyttelton, *Seizure of Power*, pp. 155 ff.; also Valeri, *Da Giolitti a Mussolini*, pp. 153–177.

[155] Gabriele De Rosa, *I conservatori nazionali. Biografia di Carlo Santucci* (Brescia, 1962), pp. 90 ff.

Even without the slaying they would have necessitated some decision, but the murder served as a catalyst, and by compromising the Fascists directly made Mussolini's intervention urgent.[156]

The Matteotti murder shook public opinion because it emanated from the coterie of the Prime Minister and struck with brutality at the parliamentary opposition itself. In December 1922 Fascist berserkers in Turin had killed eleven workmen; in 1923 and 1924, "lessons" were administered to Fascist dissidents, such as Misuri, and to the liberal spokesman Amendola.[157] Matteotti's disappearance and presumed death after an unexplained absence of over two days (June 10–13) followed his denunciation of fascist electoral thuggery in the Chamber, which was still regarded as a sanctuary for criticism. The murder belied the regime's 1924 pretense of operating according to legal and traditional procedures. Coupled with other acts of terror, it evoked deep uneasiness among marginal supporters who wanted fervently to be able to overlook repeated fascist violence.

Mussolini sought to depict the deed as the work of a small criminal element that would be severely punished. Nevertheless, the murder confirmed the resolve of some of the liberal opposition, the Popolari, Socialists, and Communists, that further participation in parliamentary work would be a shameful implicit collaboration. Not all agreed: Giolitti refused to join the so-called Aventine secession and chose to remain at Montecitorio, claiming that the duty of the opposition was to remain in the Chamber.[158] Had there been any decisive sign of opposition from the monarch or the army, the April majority might indeed have disintegrated and Mussolini been displaced, as he was nineteen years later. In the wake of the murder, all but the Fascist intransigents seemed prepared to accept a new cabinet that would call for new elections. Sforza and Frassati sent Giolitti a report that envisaged the ex-premier returning to champion the monarch against the Fascist

[156] For the most recent and best résumés of the Matteotti crisis, see Lyttelton, *Seizure of Power*, pp. 237–268; also Lyttelton, "Fascism in Italy: The Second Wave," in W. Laqueur and George L. Mosse, eds., *International Fascism 1920–1945* (New York, 1966 = *Journal of Contemporary History*, I, 1), pp. 75–100. Cf. De Felice, *Mussolini il fascista*, I, *La conquista del potere 1921–1925* (Turin, 1966), pp. 19 ff.; G. Rossini, *Il delitto Matteotti tra Viminale e Aventino* (Bologna, 1966), pp. 59 ff. on political implications. Cf. Gaetano Salvemini, *The Fascist Dictatorship in Italy* (London, 1928), pp. 317–432, for an early synthesis.

[157] Renzo De Felice, "I fatti di Torino del dicembre 1922," *Studi Storici*, IV, 1 (1963), pp. 51–122; Gaetano Salvemini, *The Fascist Dictatorship in Italy* (London, 1928), pp. 287 ff.

[158] For the formation of the Aventine, see De Felice, *Mussolini il fascista*, I, pp. 627–643; Alberto Giovannini, *Il rifiuto del Aventino* (Bologna, 1966); for doubts about the tactic, see Filipo Turati—Anna Kuliscioff, *Carteggio*, VI, *Il delitto Matteotti e l'Aventino* (1923–1925) (Turin, 1959), June 14, 1924, p. 200. Giolitti's attitude in Marcello Soleri, *Memorie* (Turin, 1949), pp. 182–183.

Party as head of a government with army participation and martial-law powers.[159] But the trouble for the liberals, as the report pointed out, was that new, antifascist elections would produce a left-wing surge that might well oust Giolitti in turn and lead to a dominant socialist influence. This was a price most liberals and "flankers" were unwilling to pay. A Salandra-Orlando combination appeared no more likely than a Giolittian one, unless as a facade for generals installed by the King. Victor Emmanuel, however, rejected this outcome; despite urgings and petitions, he refused to venture a move that might escape control and topple the monarchy.

The tactic of the non-Aventine liberals, distressed at the regime's crude illegality but fearful of any leftist resurgence, thus became one of repeated appeals to Mussolini to cleanse his party. If the President of the Council would only rebuke Farinacci and his cohorts, he could still make fascism a worthy contributor to Italy's restoration.[160] This reliance on Mussolini extended into the PNF and the government itself, where four uneasy ministers—including Federzoni and De Stefani, who were tokens of respectability—threatened to resign but finally resumed their posts in a rearranged cabinet. Despite declarations of opposition in the Senate by Albertini and Sforza, Mussolini was able to secure a tempered vote of confidence (225 to 26, with six abstentions) on a resolution, stiffened by Croce, that entrusted to the government the task of restoring conditions of legality. While the Senate vote was partly admonitory, it still allowed Mussolini to demonstrate to the Chamber that the independent upper house remained behind him.[161] It also provided further leverage with the King. In the cabinet reshuffle of July 1, two adherents of Salandra, Casati and Sarrocchi, entered the ministry, as did one right-wing Catholic Senator, Cesare Nava. In short, Mussolini won enough nonfascist support to stem any large-scale defections from his majority. The "flankers" believed that they were forcing the Prime Minister away from his party militants; instead, they helped him over the most difficult moment through which the government had passed.[162]

[159] See July report forwarded by Sforza in *Quarant'anni di politica italiana. Dalle carte di Giovanni Giolitti*, 3 vols. (Milan, 1962), III, Claudio Pavone ed., pp. 424–425.

[160] See *GdI*, July 15, 16, 20, 1924.

[161] Domenico Novacco, *Storia del parlamento italiano*, vol. XII (Palermo, 1967), pp. 387–391, for résumé of debate. Cf. Croce interview to *GdI* in July 1924, which justified the Senate vote as "prudent and patriotic." Fascism, explained Croce, had answered real needs but could create no institutions. It needed time to fulfill its function as "a bridge of passage for the restoration of a more severe liberal regime in the framework of a stronger state." Interview included in Benedetto Croce, *Pagine sparse*, 3 vols. (Naples, 1941–1943), II, pp. 376–379.

[162] See *GdI* satisfaction with cabinet shuffle in "Governo di collaborazione," July 2, 1924.

Even while Mussolini moved to reassure and hold liberal collaborators, he did not turn drastically against the squadrist and radical elements in the Fascist Party. On July 19, he told Fascist labor organizers from Turin that the industrialists were ungrateful and might have to be coerced into class cooperation. To the Grand Council on July 22, the Duce still declared himself "antinormalist." Normalization, he charged, amounted to antifascism pure and simple and a return to a discredited democratic regime.[163] In view of the workers' defections back to the CGL unions since Matteotti's death, Mussolini called for elaboration of corporative institutions. By September he appointed an exploratory Committee of Fifteen (then transformed in January into one of Eighteen, dubbed the Solons) that was to draft corporative initiatives for the next stage of the fascist revolution.[164] Meanwhile, at the critical National Council of the PNF at Assisi in early August, Mussolini continued to encourage the party radicals, attacking the Freemasonry they detested and saluting the "old historic provinces" whose political virtues the leaders of agrarian fascism liked to contrast with the decadent parliamentary usages at Rome. Nonetheless, Mussolini did not give full rein to the intransigents. He advised the enthusiasts of the "second wave" to remain tranquil. Fascism was passing through a moment of isolation, and silence was prudent. If need be, fascism would retain power by force, but for the moment the Party had to submit to a resolute discipline and spirit of sacrifice.[165]

How long could Mussolini successfully balance the countervailing claims of flankers or liberals and the party militants? In mid-August, when Matteotti's corpse was finally brought to light, Mussolini's political situation became precarious again. The organized *combattenti*, who claimed the moral legitimacy conferred by the trenches as validly as did the Fascists, condemned the government at their convention. The liberal press continued its demands for normalization, attacking above all the role of the Militia. But liberals remained hesitant and divided. Salandra considered a formal announcement of opposition after Mus-

[163] Benito Mussolini, *Opera Omnia*, Eduardo and Duilio Susmel, eds. (Florence, 1956), xxi, pp. 19, 22–23; Roland Sarti, *Fascism and the Industrial Leadership in Italy 1919–1940* (Berkeley, Calif., 1971), p. 67.

[164] For the working-class situation, see De Felice, *Mussolini il fascista*, i, pp. 639 (on inflation), 666–667. Cf. labor leader Tullio Cianetti's report, February 13, 1925, ACS, Rome: Carte Cianetti, b. 1, for Fascist "disintegration" at the Terni steel plant in the wake of local squabbles and the Matteotti affair. For the Council of Fifteen, see Alberto Aquarone, *L'organizzazione dello stato totalitario* (Turin, 1965), p. 53.

[165] The August 7 speech to the National Council, as delivered, is reproduced in De Felice, *Mussolini il fascista*, i, pp. 775–785. Liberal democrats who reproached fascism for its violence, noted Mussolini, might well be forced for punishment to read Taine on the French terror.

solini's address to the Fascist National Congress, but he was dissuaded by party colleagues. Following a further contemptuous threat by Mussolini at Monte Amiata on August 31, Casati and Sarrocchi threatened to resign from the cabinet but then relented.[166] After a Fascist deputy was slain by a left-wing fanatic on September 12 and Fascists retaliated with demonstrations and pillaging, the "flankers" threatened to withdraw all support. In the various local liberal associations, Mussolini supporters found it a touchier task to carry resolutions of support for the government as they prepared for the Liberal Party congress at Livorno in early October. The congress was anxiously monitored by the government, and special care was taken to avoid local disruptions.[167] Despite the earlier philo-fascist gains, the PLI showed serious division. The Congress listened to Giolitti's lieutenant Soleri with enthusiasm, and rejected a resolution that simply approved of government policy. Instead it called for restoration of legal conditions and claimed that the liberals, including those elected on the *listone*, retained full independence in parliament.[168]

Leading industrialists were also distressed and divided. Einaudi rebuked them for their silence in a major *Corriere* article on August 6 and provoked a public controversy that most major industrialists would have preferred to suppress. Although Einaudi failed to move Confindustria president Benni, who was determined on collaboration, he did prompt uncomfortable debate. On September 4, after the near ministerial crisis provoked by Sarrochi and Casati's temporary resignation, Olivetti intervened in a discussion of the National Federation of Engineering Industries to discuss Confindustria's relation to the regime. As Olivetti told his colleagues, Italian industrialists could not disinterest themselves in politics: the Fascist syndicates' black flag in their

[166] The provocative Monte Amiata remarks were balanced by a conciliatory interview published a day later in *GdI*; both in Mussolini, *Opera Omnia*, XXI, pp. 50–65; cf. Luigi Albertini, *Epistolario 1911–1926*, 4 vols., Ottavio Barié, ed. (Verona, 1968), IV, pp. 1552–1553.

[167] *Ibid.*, pp. 673–679; also, for the situation of the liberals: *La Stampa*, August 19/20, September 15/16, 25/26, 29/30 (on the PLI), October 3/4–7/8 on the Livorno congress and the *combattenti*; *GdI*, August 24, 26, 30, September 25, 27, October 2–8, 15, 1924. Cf. Brunello Vigezzi, ed., *1919–1925. Dopoguerra e fascismo. Politica e stampa in Italia* (Bari, 1965), pp. 56–59 (on the *GdI*), 245–251 (*CdS*), 353–364 (*La Stampa*). For the divisions within the local liberal parties, see reports in ACS, Rome: Min. Int., Dir. gen. P.S., Div. Aff. gen. e ris., 1924, B. 105, f. K7, "Partito liberale," sf: Bologna, Florence, Genoa, Perugia, Pisa, Siena, Venezia. For government concerns: Federzoni to prefects in the Tuscan region, September 9, 1924, N. 21465.

[168] "I liberali per la constituzione," *GdI*, October 7, 1924, also coverage of congress, October 2–8; *La Stampa*, October 3/4–7/8. Cf. Luigi Albertini, "I liberali al congresso di Livorno e i partiti politici in Italia," *CdS*, October 2, 1924, included in his collection of opposition statements: *In difesa della libertà* (Rome, 1947); responses to the speech in Albertini, *Epistolario*, IV, pp. 1814–1820.

offices would be as dangerous as the red. On behalf of Confindustria five days later, Ettore Conti, Pirelli, and Olivetti warned the government to restore order and trust, the liberty of syndical organizations and freedom of assembly, and to subdue the militia. Along with colleagues of the electrical industries, Conti continued to work for the perennial return of Giolitti and finally went so far as to urge Mussolini's resignation in the Chamber debates of December 3.[169]

The price for preserving industry's support would have to be Mussolini's control of his syndicalists. Yet the Fascist trade-union leaders were becoming more militant as workers reverted to the CGL-affiliated unions after the Matteotti murder. Fascist unions initiated successful labor negotiations at the end of September, but wanted to push industry even harder in light of rapid price increases. Impatient "corporation," i.e., union, leaders threatened to drop the term "Fascist" from their title if it proved a handicap. Under pressure from militant syndicalists, Rossoni asked Mussolini, "Did fascism intend to furnish to the corporations those means and aids (syndical legislation; collaboration between Party and corporations) needed to activate its own program of integral syndicalism?" By December Rossoni faced being outflanked by his activist union chiefs, who themselves felt that increased militance was needed to keep their factory footholds. While Rossoni disclaimed any desire to break with Mussolini, he did ask for the premier's "better understanding of union needs."[170]

Mussolini's compromise course was also endangered by bitter controversy over the Militia. As a legal party army and redoubt of squadrism, the Militia was a center of liberal criticism. The general officers of the regular army also viewed their paramilitary rivals with resentment, and several spoke out in the Senate against its acquisition of army weapons. In turn, Militia members chafed at the concessions made to the liberals, especially the removal of the charismatic Italo Balbo as commander. The more Mussolini sought to soothe the liberal elites, the more worrisome became the possibilities of demonstrations or even a coup.[171]

---

[169] Luigi Einaudi, "Il silenzio degli industriali," CdS, August 6, 1924, now in Chronache politiche ed economiche di un trentennio (Turin, 1961), VII, pp. 765–769, 780–783, 784–789; also Piero Melograni, Gli industriali e Mussolini. Rapporti tra Confindustria e fascismo dal 1919 al 1929 (Milan, 1972), pp. 74–95; Albertini's urging of the article, July 30, 1924, Epistolario, IV, pp. 1788–1789. For Olivetti intervention, see Mario Abrate, La lotta sindacale nella industrializzazione in Italia 1906–26 (Turin, 1967), pp. 422–423.

[170] Seg. Part. del Duce, NA Microcopy T586/453/028096–028099, 028114–028117.

[171] Giorgio Rochat, L'esercito italiano da Vittorio Veneto a Mussolini (Bari, 1967), pp. 441–448; Lyttelton, Seizure of Power, pp. 244–250, 258–260, "Second Wave," pp. 82–83; De Felice, Mussolini il fascista, I, pp. 681–685, 689–690.

The political tensions climaxed in November and December once the Chamber reconvened and Giolitti announced his formal opposition. As press criticism mounted, the government introduced a censorship bill that finally provoked Salandra into open criticism and dismayed even Fascist deputies. It suggested that the government itself felt menaced and near collapse. Rival caucuses formed within the majority. Fascist militants met with Michele Bianchi, while forty-four Fascist moderates gathered at the home of former Nationalist leader Raffaelo Paolucci, who had been informed that the King would look with favor upon an initiative for a government of national concentration.[172]

Mussolini responded to this disintegration with his usual dual thrusts. He introduced a new electoral law that promised a return to single-member constituencies. The bill was designed to slow the defections of the liberals and Fascist moderates, nostalgic for the predictable contests and coalitions of the old districts. But the project was soon overshadowed. On December 27, the final crisis opened with the publication of Cesare Rossi's "confession," which accused Mussolini of complicity in the Matteotti slaying. The *Corriere* and *Giornale d'Italia* called for the cabinet's resignation. Instead Mussolini suggested that he would ask for a quick vote on the 1925–1926 budget so that he could prorogue the Chamber for the entire year. Although Salandra finally resigned as chairman of the Budget Commission in protest, Mussolini wagered on liberal disarray. On December 28, 250 prominent Milanese liberal politicians and industrial leaders, including Benni, Conti, De Capitani, and Senator Greppi, gathered to vote overwhelmingly a resolution of support for the government.[173] Cabinet members Casati and Sarrocchi finally prepared to urge resignation upon the cabinet and thought they had the support of Federzoni. But in the critical cabinet session on the afternoon of December 30, they clumsily suggested Federzoni as a successor, prompting his disavowal as well as Mussolini's angry refusal to withdraw. Forced finally to a decision by his own members of the cabinet, Mussolini now threatened to take to the streets. While he could not win endorsement of full dictatorial powers, he did extract a vague declaration that justified authoritarian measures for the safeguarding of the country's "moral and material

[172] De Felice, *Mussolini il fascista*, I, pp. 691–694; Lyttelton, *Seizure of Power*, pp. 262–264. Giolitti statement in Novacco, *Storia del parlamento italiano*, XII, p. 392. For Salandra see G. B. Gifuni, ed., *Il diario di Salandra* (Milan, 1969), pp. 301–302.

[173] Prefect's report of December 28 meeting in ACS, Rome: Min. Int., Dir. gen. P.S. Div. Aff. gen. e ris., 1924, B. 105, f. Partito Liberale, sf. Milano. Cf. De Capitani to Salandra, December 29, 1924, and "Nicolino" d'Atri to Salandra, same date, in Lucera: Carte Salandra.

interests." Once again Casati and Sarrocchi withheld their own resignations for a few days: their irresolution was representative of the liberal elite as a whole.[174]

Now, too, the enthusiasts of the "second wave" intervened. Farinacci and Curzio Suckert (Malaparte) reminded Mussolini that the Fascists of the provinces had entrusted him with a revolutionary mission. On December 31, apparently under the guidance or approval of the Party Directory, Fascists in Florence sacked Liberal political headquarters, Masonic lodges, newspaper offices, and demanded that Rome impose dictatorial measures. Mussolini met with the Consuls of the Militia the same day and promised that he would silence the opposition when the Chamber reconvened on January 3. The choice appeared either a definitive break with the twilight liberalism or a Fascist Party insurrection. In a brief parliamentary address on January 3, 1925, Mussolini accepted historical responsibility for all that had happened since June, taunted the opposition to substantiate its charges of a Fascist Cheka, and announced that he would repress the Aventine's subversion by force if necessary. Federzoni ordered the prefects to shut down and dissolve suspect political organizations such as "Free Italy," the network of Aventine supporters in the provinces. Newspapers were reduced to bland commentary or forced to suspend publication; from squadrist intimidation the regime moved to legal suppression.[175]

Nonetheless, the events of January 3 still retained some ambiguity. Many liberals saw no epochal turning point. Before the session, but after Mussolini's intentions were clear, Salandra, Orlando, and Giolitti had finally met together—only to decide against any formal pronouncement. Even after the speech, only 9 of 24 Salandra supporters were prepared to vote against the government, and De Capitani moved to create a National Liberal Party for further collaboration.[176]

On the other hand, Mussolini worked to regain independence from the Fascist intransigents. Federzoni's major concern in the days after January 3 seemed to be the policing of the turbulent hotheads in the

[174] De Felice, *Mussolini il fascista*, I, pp. 694–703; accounts of December 30 in *Diario di Salandra*, pp. 311–312, and 321 on final Casati and Sarrocchi resignations (of these right-wing Rosencrantz and Guildenstern, Casati was more resolute on a final break; Sarrocchi feared political reprisals in Fascist Tuscany). Cf. Salandra's earlier account of the final crisis in *Memorie politiche* (Milan, 1951), pp. 66–68.

[175] De Felice, *Mussolini il fascista*, I, pp. 711–716; cf. Attilio Tamaro, *Venti anni di storia (1922–1943)*, 2 vols. (Rome 1953), II, pp. 56–57; Lyttelton, "Second Wave," pp. 90–97. Speech in Mussolini, *Opera Omnia*, XXI, pp. 235–240.

[176] Cf. *Diario di Salandra*, pp. 321–323, and *Memorie*, pp. 69–77; also De Capitani to Salandra, January 4, 1925, explaining how torn he was between his "loyalty" to his old leader and the need not to weaken the government, also Salandra to De Capitani, ironically acknowledging the new party, May 1925. Lucera: Carte Salandra.

movement. Two weeks later the gadfly Suckert could ask: "Was it a sincere act of revolutionary faith or rather a supremely skillful tactical maneuver . . . ?" If the elections of April 1924 had worked as a party solvent or *trasformismo* upon the liberal groupings, the 3rd of January was *trasformismo* at the expense of the Fascist Party. It mollified the radicals by granting their easiest demands—force and repression—so as to postpone their more vague and more troublesome desire for a wholesale displacement of the traditional elites. Naming the chief spokesman for the second wave, Farinacci, as Party Secretary in February was consistent with this approach. The strident spokesman for the Fascist revolution was to preside unwillingly over a year of party eclipse for the benefit of the state and the Duce—a trend that Mussolini had already foreshadowed in his brilliant address to the National Council the preceding August. By June 1925, what was to be the last National Congress of the PNF carried out its tasks, as Maurizio Maraviglia wrote, by saying little, listening a good deal, and taking its decisions unanimously. Not all party militants accepted a docile integration, however. The intransigents in the superheated Fascist milieu of Florence, who had already mobilized for the crisis of late 1924, launched a bitter "anti-Masonic" crusade that culminated in murderous demonstrations against critics and foes in October 1925. These proved the last major outbreak of decentralized terrorism. An irate Mussolini moved to purge the Florentine organization and finally dissolve the squads. In the months to come, Mussolini removed Farinacci as a half-hearted enforcer of discipline, took over the Ministry of the Interior from Federzoni, and allowed Alfredo Rocco to draft the exceptional legislation of late 1925 and, even more repressive, the police powers of November 1926.[177] The Party Secretaryship and major leadership positions remained important baronies but because of their leverage at Rome, not their reserves in the provinces. With his hegemony over the Party as well as the opposition confirmed, Mussolini now had to confront the continuing social divisions of the country. Dictatorship might suppress open conflict but could not magically eliminate Italy's deep social and moral fissures.

For Mussolini, economic policy choices could not be divorced from political choices. Power in the Fascist state depended upon controlling the state bureaucracy, especially the nerve center of the Interior Ministry, commanding the Party with its Militia and labor movement, ap-

---

[177] Lyttelton, *Seizure of Power*, pp. 277 ff.; De Felice, *Mussolini il fascista*, I, pp. 725–730, and II, pp. 55 ff., 134; Maurizio Maraviglia, "Il valore del congresso fascista," *Gerarchia*, IV, 7 (July 1925), p. 411. See Aquarone, *L'organizzazione dello stato totalitario*, pp. 66, 382–385, 386–392 for subsequent disciplining of the Party in 1925–1926.

peasing the regular army and the Court, and purchasing the toleration of the old *classe dirigente*. Thus Mussolini could not simply transform the PNF into a traditionalist right-wing cohort; he needed to preserve its disruptive potential, especially the elan of its syndicalists, to counterbalance both Confindustria and the residual socialist loyalties among the working class. Fascist labor policy was thus a matter of political calculation as well as of economic choice.

The legacy of the Matteotti crisis was a rekindled militance among Fascist labor leaders. The partial recognition that the Fascist unions had won in the Palazzo Chigi agreement of December 1923 did not guarantee their competitive position among workers who were buffeted by inflation in late 1924 and embittered by the renewed Fascist violence. When Fascist union leaders convened at the end of December 1924, Mario Rachele, the head of the Corporation of Agriculture, and Arnaldo Fioretti, chief of the doctors and nurses, attacked Rossoni's party loyalty and called for autonomy. Others wanted adherence only at the summit organs of the PNF and freedom of action at the base.[178] In the wake of January 3 Mussolini could show more sympathy for the militants' objectives, and the Grand Council endorsed a new union campaign late in the month. Mussolini warned the prefects in February that a resurgence of agitation could be expected in the spring.[179] In March, Rossoni and Augusto Turati—party and labor leader from Brescia—threatened to lead the Fascist unions in steel strikes throughout Piedmont and Lombardy in order to press for wage supplements. Mussolini was of two minds about the movement. While he wished to intimidate the old liberal elite whose newspapers condemned the labor unrest, he also feared reinspiriting the old Socialist unions. The latter organizations, such as Turin's FIOM, found themselves in a difficult situation, squeezed between hostile employers and Fascist competitors. While FIOM hoped to avoid a major strike that would provoke government repression, a Fascist work stoppage would impel the FIOM to lay down their tools as well. When the Fascist-led strike finally broke out in Brescia, Mussolini warned against its possible revival of the "old pernicious socialist habits. It is useless to make this a race to the reddest," he cautioned, "because in my opinion the urban masses are in a vast majority refractory to fascism."[180] Yet in view of Mussolini's

[178] Protocol of December 30–31 meeting of fascist syndical leaders, Seg. Part. del Duce, NA T586/453/028114–028117.

[179] Edoardo Malusardi, *Elementi di storia del sindacalismo fascista* (Genoa, 1932), pp. 114–116; Partito Nazionale Fascista, *Il Gran Consiglio nei primi sei anni dell'era fascista* (Rome, 1929), pp. 161–162; De Felice, *Mussolini il fascista*, II, p. 91.

[180] Bruno Uva, "Gli scioperi dei metallurgici italiani del marzo 1925," *Storia contemporanea*, I, 4 (1970), p. 1028; Lyttelton, *Seizure of Power*, pp. 315–317, emphasizes the unique strength of the Fascist unions in Turati's Brescian fief.

earlier encouragement of militancy, Rossoni pressed forward, arguing that industrialists had already profited too much from fascism. And since Mussolini accepted at least a brief Fascist strike, FIOM, too, had to move—taunted both by the Fascists on the right and the Communists on the left. The result was a unique Fascist-supervised labor offensive throughout the North—the most massive strike effort between 1922 and 1944.

As so often before, each party in the dispute had to fight more than one enemy. FIOM was combatting Fascist competitors as well as employers. The industrialists were angered, but uncertain how to resist Fascist labor claims. Reports of contacts between Augusto Turati and Bruno Buozzi, the CGL leader, disturbed them. While some of the Turin industrialists, especially Agnelli, seemed prepared to encourage even the Communist factory delegates in an effort to contain Fascist syndical inroads, most of the business community still feared the CGL more than the Fascist unions.[181] They were thus prepared to buy peace from Rossoni rather than reradicalize their workers. What Fascist labor organizers really wanted, however, could be granted only by Mussolini, not Confindustria: namely, the destruction of CGL competition and a role in national economic policy. But Mussolini himself was not prepared to bestow such exclusive social and economic power on the syndicates. The strike had to be cut off quickly, and despite Turati's resistance, Federzoni mediated the dispute from Rome on March 13 and 14. FIOM prolonged its own walk-out an extra day, in part to demonstrate that the workers were striking at their direction, not that of Rossoni and Turati; and indeed 80,000 of the 100,000 prolonged their brief stoppage under the FIOM.[182]

The strike represented the high point of Fascist syndical autonomy. While the Fascist labor movement was helpful against industrialists who remained lukewarm toward the regime, Mussolini insisted that it be under better control. He could favor corporative initiatives without having to accept Rossoni's methods of achieving them. The Committee of Eighteen was drafting plans for corporative reorganization that was safely centralized and conservative, perhaps excessively so, according to Mussolini.[183] On April 24–25, the Grand Council conducted hearings on the strike. Officially praising the effort, it declared, however, that the unions had not only to improve working-class conditions but to prepare the "gradual and harmonious insertion of the syndicates in the life of the state." The Grand Council also stipulated

[181] Abrate, *La lotta sindacale,* pp. 417–419; Uva, "Scioperi," pp. 1040–1043; Malusardi, *Elementi di storia,* p. 121.

[182] Uva, "Scioperi," pp. 1043–1050, 1067–1077.

[183] Aquarone, *L'organizzazione dello stato totalitario,* pp. 53–54.

that strikes be cleared with the Party leadership and that Party as well as union officials nominate the unions' provincial secretaries. There were to be no *ras* in the labor movement.[184]

Reconciliation with industry and further centralization of trade-union control followed in the summer and fall. Mussolini made a major gesture toward big business—especially the reserved leaders of the electrical industry such as Conti—by replacing De Stefani and Nava as Ministers of Finance and National Economy with Giuseppe Volpi and Giuseppe Belluzzo. De Stefani, a staunch exponent of the *liberista*, free-trade ideas of an Einaudi and Pantaleoni, had won praise for his tax relief in 1923 but incurred antagonism from protectionists such as the sugar interests. By early 1925 industry was critical of his measures designed to halt speculation on the slipping lira, and was unhappy over an economic situation that combined inflation with a depressed stock market and sluggish business conditions. Volpi, a Venetian industrialist and financier with important connections to the Commerciale network, and Belluzzo, a steel executive, engineer, and sponsor of a coming generation of technically trained middle managers, were viewed more favorably in business, if not Party circles.[185] The switch portended that Mussolini was preparing his own realignment of "rye and iron" in line with the consolidation of primary producers that was occurring throughout Europe.

As in Germany, the political consequence was a new impetus for corporatist representation. The April strike revealed that final distributions of power still remained to be defined; now in the months ahead both sides contended for decisive influence. Rossoni and the Fascist labor leaders wanted to secure a monopoly of labor representation for their unions, but also avoid sacrificing their own autonomy as the state elaborated its regulation of the labor market. The struggle for autonomy was to be a three-year retreat that Rossoni was doomed to lose, for it pitted him not only against wary representatives of industry but also against rivals in the Party. The Committee of Eighteen's majority report envisaged elective professional corporations to govern economic life, with employers, workers, and employees and technicians each electing one-third of their corporate college.[186] The recommendations

[184] PNF, *Il Gran Consiglio nei primi sei anni*, pp. 173–177; Malusardi, *Elementi di storia*, pp. 118–119.
[185] Felice Guarneri, *Battaglie economiche tra le due grandi guerre*, 2 vols. (Milan, 1953), I, pp. 162–164; Sarti, *Fascism and the Industrial Leadership of Italy*, pp. 53–54, Lyttelton, *Seizure of Power*, pp. 354–358; also François Perroux, *Contribution à l'étude de l'économie et des finances publiques en Italie depuis la guerre* (Paris, 1929), pp. 141–157.
[186] Texts in Seg. Part. del Duce, 242/R, Gran Consiglio, T586/1122/073986 ff.; cf. Louis Rosenstock-Franck, *L'économie corporative fasciste en doctrine et en fait* (Paris, 1934), pp. 40–43.

remained an academic corporative curio, which the government finally shelved in October. The industrialists disliked the dilution of their authority; Party spokesmen such as Farinacci, who had become important in mediating the April dispute, objected to the project's rejection of compulsory state arbitration. Rossoni distrusted the electoral provisions that would deprive his unions of a monopoly status in representing workers. What he sought was a system of corporate councils for each industry that would settle labor conditions and exercise a central economic planning. Within each corporation, the Fascist unions would acquire exclusive rights of collective bargaining and representation and ultimately would exercise an equal voice in entrepreneurial decisions.[187] The essential was to draw upon the authority of the state and Party to secure monopoly representation and to force industry to deal with the Confederation of Fascist unions as a powerful autonomous bloc. The danger to be avoided was a *Gleichschaltung* and reduction to a hollow bureaucratic shell. The Fascist syndicalist Angelo Olivetti pointed out this danger in his minority-of-one report for the Committee of Eighteen. The distinction between "juridically recognized syndicates and corporations" was particularly delicate, "with exquisitely political elements." The corporation was a public-law agency of the state; the syndicate was a supposedly autonomous association, but within the state's "zone of influence" if granted legal recognition. How, asked Olivetti, did one grant legal status to the syndicate without making the corporations a merely redundant bureaucratic shell? He did not answer his own query, but warned: "prevent politicization, which today is penetrating the corporations and poisoning all of union life, from penetrating the corporations and making them objects for political speculation."[188] The admonition was to the point but fruitless. The key to the emerging economic regime was its subjection to political control; the open question was where control was to reside.

For the Fascist union chiefs, assured representation of the workers within the factories was the precondition for effective bargaining as a component of the regime. Above all, this meant eliminating the internal factory commissions, the Italian equivalent of the German factory

[187] Lyttelton, *Seizure of Power*, pp. 317–318; also Rossoni's article, "Il sistema fascista dell'organizzazione," *La Stirpe*, February 1926, cited in De Felice, *Mussolini il fascista*, ii, pp. 274–275.

[188] Seg. Part. del Duce, 242/R, Gran Consiglio, T586/1122/074201 ff. Agostino Lanzillo, another former syndicalist who had migrated to fascism, also warned about possible bureaucratization even as he sought to stamp a "revolutionary" interpretation upon the law: AP: Camera, Legislatura xxvii, p. 4851 (December 5, 1925), cited partially in Aquarone, *L'organizzazione dello stato totalitario*, pp. 468–469.

councils and a continuing stronghold for Communist and Socialist workers' delegates. Most industrialists also sought to eliminate the commissions, but they feared Rossoni's plan to replace them with factory trustees representing the Fascist unions. Turin's industrialists, moreover, were astute enough to work with the internal commissions to forestall complete Fascist control over their plants. Fiat commission elections in the spring of 1925 had produced first Socialist and then Communist majorities, a situation Agnelli exploited to resist Fascist claims for recognition. On August 18 he quickly negotiated a special wage increase with his communist internal commissions that angered Fascists and the Socialist-affiliated FIOM alike.[189] The maneuver only postponed recognition of the Fascists, who intimidated the internal commissions into resignation. The real decisions were taking shape at Rome, where the Fascist metalworkers' corporation, Confindustria, and government and Party negotiators bargained for a new industry-wide contract, which Gino Olivetti told Turin's unhappy industrialists they must accept. The upshot was not merely a contract for the metals industries, but a fundamental pact between Confindustria and Fascist syndicalist representatives, the Palazzo Vidoni agreement of October 2. The compact stipulated that Confindustria recognize the exclusive bargaining rights of the Confederation of Fascist Corporations and negotiate with it as an equal. Olivetti remained skeptical that the Fascist leaders could really guarantee harmonious labor relations, and still disliked granting monopoly negotiating rights to any spokesmen for the working class. Still, Confindustria confirmed its own official role in the system of state-sponsored collective bargaining. It postponed establishment of the labor-management corporations that Rossoni was urging. Most important, perhaps, industry managed to resist the Fascist syndical demand for factory trustees, and thus recovered complete control of the work force in the plant. Representation of labor was entrusted to a union bureaucracy that needed party support to eliminate its old rivals, and that had failed to create equivalent ligaments of loyalty and good faith among industrial workers. When strikes were prohibited the following year, Rossoni's confederation was further deprived of an effective mass base: Confindustria and the Fascist regime both augmented their power at labor's expense.[190]

[189] Abrate, *La lotta sindacale*, pp. 438–446. Valerio Castronovo, *Giovanni Agnelli* (Turin, 1972) pp. 416–421, emphasizes tactical improvisation—in part ceding a small, special wage addition to avoid a general increase—rather than any deep antifascist strategy.

[190] *CdS*, October 2, 1925, p. 2, "I rapporti fra industriale e sindacati fascisti"; De Felice, *Mussolini il fascista*, II, p. 9; Aquarone, *L'organizzazione dello stato totalitario*, pp. 119–121, 439; Dino Giugni, "Esperienze corporative e post-corporative nei rapporti collettivi di lavoro in Italia," *Il Mulino*, v, 1–2 (January–February 1956), p. 5.

A comparison with Germany is instructive. In effect, Mussolini was carrying out the transformations of 1918 and 1933–1935 simultaneously. Under authoritarian auspices, Mussolini was instituting from above the same sort of corporatist organization that the German revolution of 1918 had consummated. Stinnes and Legien trusted each other; Olivetti and Rossoni could not, but fascist power compelled agreement. German officials between 1914 and 1918 had prepared the Arbeitsgemeinschaft by surrendering public-interest controls of wages, prices, and working conditions to industry and labor jointly. Theirs had been an effort to avoid economic conflict in wartime. For Mussolini the dialectical uses of power were more complex. Syndicalism, Mussolini insisted in a *Gerarchia* article and to the PNF congress in June, was an essential part of the Fascist transformation. Class collaboration had to involve more than merely disguised exploitation; in this respect Mussolini faulted the committee of Eighteen's majority report. Still, syndicalism had to be disciplined within the sphere of state authority, it had to enhance power and not undermine it.[191] Having to come to terms with industry, he did so as part of a bargain that consolidated his own authority. Industry's leadership achieved an official status; the regime moved to end autonomy of the labor market. But even as Mussolini imposed a corporatist organization upon Italy, he did so under authoritarian and not pluralist conditions. Like Hitler, he undercut Fascist as well as Socialist representation in the workplace and created a labor front that depended upon the authority of the regime. As Hitler would do again, Mussolini turned to the representatives of newer industries to create a partnership between fascism and the economic elites. Electricity and chemicals, including hydrocarbons, would become the most closely linked in the fascist economies. Turin's engineering industries and even Ruhr steel were not to resist fascism in any meaningful way, but they were to remain more elitist, less dependent upon state sponsorship, and less wholehearted in their collaboration.[192]

The subsequent development of Fascist corporativism reflected first the growing role of Alfredo Rocco, Minister of Justice, then later of Giuseppe Bottai, who was to control the Ministry of Corporations. Rocco was the architect of the repressive legislation of late 1925 and 1926, which culminated the clamp-down initiated in the wake of January 3. Replacement of elected local officials with appointed *podestà*,

[191] "Fascismo e sindacalismo," and address to PNF, June 22, 1925, in *Opera Omnia*, xxi, pp. 325–336, 359.
[192] Cf. Arnaldo Mussolini: "This is the century of chemicals and electricity. We can't stay forever in the epoch of iron and steel," cited in Lyttelton, *Seizure of Power*, p. 359. On chemical development, see Rosario Romeo, *Breve Storia della grande industria in Italia* (Rocca San Casciano, 1963), pp. 143 ff.; for German fascism, see Dietmar Petzina, *Autarkiepolitik im dritten Reich* (Stuttgart, 1968).

elevation of Mussolini into Prime Minister and Head of Government
with control over the parliamentary agenda, further controls over the
press and strengthening of the prefects, dissolution of opposition parties
and associations, new political penalties, and a special tribunal for the
defense of the state represented Rocco's innovations.[193] His fascism
increasingly set the tone for the claims of the regime. It contrasted
with the syndicalism of Rossoni, the intransigent freebooter militancy
of the Farinacciani—now controlled by being coopted into a glorified
but irrelevant party—and the "revisionist" effort at rapprochement
with liberalism. Instead, Rocco, who had been a founder of the prewar
Nationalist Association and had entered fascism with the fusion of the
two groups in 1923, advocated a stern conservative authoritarianism.
With Mussolini he invoked the idea of "totalitarianism"—not in the
later sense of a fascistic suffusion of all life and thought, but an absolute monopoly of authority by the state. The guarantor of this power
could be neither a legislature nor a party, but the executive, its bureaucracy, and the judicial system. Italian Nationalism had also drafted
the later Fascist appeal to producers and technicians, the demand that
class conflict be subordinated to the cause of national power and
wealth. At the same time, nationalism had never embraced the populistic themes of fascism. The ebullience of the Arditi and the crude
violence of the squadrists had not swept away its disciplined exaltation
of authority, hence its ideological acceptance among court circles and
other elites that resisted the Blackshirts. Rocco himself borrowed from
a tradition of efforts by legal authorities to elevate the law into the
emanation of central and superior authority. While Mussolini borrowed ideological themes from Sorel and Pareto, the *guardasigilli* (as
the chief of the justice ministry was called in antique terms) remained
closer to Taine and Maurras. In contrast to later German legal theorists,
who glorified the almost irrational will of the Führer as the source of
all law, Rocco's preoccupation remained that of transcendent law and
state norms: the Duce remained an instrument of some harsh Hegelian
legal rationality.[194]

[193] Aquarone, *L'organizzazione dello stato totalitario*, pp. 75–76, 84–86, 90–92,
94–100, 393–394, 412–415, 418–420, 427–428.
[194] Paolo Ungari, *Alfredo Rocco e l'ideologia giuridica del fascismo* (Bari, 1963),
esp. pp. 86 ff.; Franco Gaeta, *Nazionalismo italiano* (Naples, 1965). Rocco, *Scritti
e discorsi politici*, III, *La formazione dello stato fascista (1925–1934)* (Milan,
1938), esp. pp. 869–877 (report on legislation codifying decree-law provisions),
921–925 (legislation on the prerogative of the head of government–prime minister–secretary of state), 985–992 (law on the judicial discipline of collective
labor relations). For German legal theory, see Franz Neumann, *Behemoth: The
Structure and Practice of National Socialism* (New York, 1966), pp. 83ff., 452–
458; Michael Stolleis, "Gemeinschaft und Volksgemeinschaft. Zur juristischen
Terminologie im Nationalsozialismus," *Vierteljahreshefte für Zeitgeschichte*, 20, 1
(1972) pp. 16–38.

For Rocco, as for the Nationalists, syndical and corporative representation was not intended as a guarantee for labor, as it was for the ex-Wobbly Rossoni, and never as a path toward industrial self-administration as it was for German corporatists or for Professor Gino Arias, who drafted the discarded majority report of the Solons. Fascism rather would "reestablish the equilibrium among classes," which the French Revolution and liberalism had shattered; it would reconstruct and consolidate the state and let Italy "open this new cycle in the history of humanity."[195] Rocco's harsh antipluralist conception well fitted Mussolini's objectives in the wake of the turbulent labor and Party situation that marked the spring and summer of 1925. Militant syndicalists and Party intransigents reinforced each other in 1925, and Mussolini moved to contain both. With the general dissatisfaction with the Committee of Eighteen, Mussolini entrusted Rocco with drafting labor legislation that would transform the Palazzo Vidoni provisions from a compact between associations into a system of state control of the labor market. Official Fascist representatives, chosen from each sector of economic life by a minimal 10-percent vote in labor elections, would alone have the right to negotiate collective contracts. Special labor courts were to be attached to each appeals tribunal of the kingdom to arbitrate disputes. Strikes and lock-outs, no longer needed and pernicious for the national interest, were to be prohibited.[196]

Neither Fascist syndicalists nor leaders of heavy industry were initially happy with the new proposals. Deprived of the right to strike, Fascist union leaders saw little further chance to bid for the loyalty of the working classes. Industry remained wary about centralization. But at least, the Chamber committee under a pro-business Fascist, Ernesto Belloni, and with Benni as secretary, strengthened the barriers to Rossoni's desired "mixed" syndicates. Its draft also exempted private industry from the compulsory arbitration laid down for the public services and agriculture. This immunity provoked a major, open debate in the Chamber in early December 1925. As a condition for syndicalist support for the new legislation, Rossoni demanded that it apply to private industry. Speaking for Confindustria, Benni resisted adamantly, while Rocco intervened to explain the allegedly technical difficulties that had led him to limit the scope of the bill. Agricultural representatives, however, also asked why their enterprises should be singled out for compulsory arbitration. Since it was difficult for the government to preserve the appearance of economic impartiality if it excluded

---

[195] Rocco, *Scritti e discorsi*, III, pp. 981, 985.
[196] Arias report cited above, n. 186; cf. outlines of Rocco report to the October 6 Grand Council, in Partito Nazionale Fascista, *Il Gran Consiglio nei primi sei anni*, pp. 186–188.

industry, Mussolini himself intervened to declare that all industry would have to accept compulsory regulation. Confindustria representatives had little choice but to submit to the amended wider coverage of the new law.[197]

Nonetheless, the new system of arbitration was never really to constrain them. The economic associations retained the right to review all disputes before the labor courts did; indeed, the labor courts went virtually unused and by 1937 had reviewed only 41 controversies and found it necessary to issue binding judgments in only 16. The real power of overseeing collective contracts fell to the Ministry of Corporations, which became less concerned about the equity of agreements than the number of firms and workers it could bring into its jurisdiction. The new legislation, finally, did not prohibit nonrecognized unions outright, but it did relegate them to a shadow realm with the right neither to conclude collective contracts nor to strike. The disspirited CGL leaders finally dissolved their organization in the winter of 1926–1927.[198]

Industry's spokesmen now had to abandon their claim to autonomy and add the adjective "Fascist" to their confederation's official name. In return, their delegate, Benni, became legally empowered to sit as Confindustria's spokesman in the Grand Council and not merely participate as an *ad hoc* representative. Confindustria's internal structure remained inviolate and it could effectively resist challenges from small industry, who now found it impossible to organize their own alternative federation.[199] Industrialists still fretted over the power of their Fascist syndicalist social "partner." Rossoni was continuing his agitation for a corporative organization that would yoke labor and management into common industry-wide structures. Business spokesmen resisted, and asked the government instead to break up Rossoni's massive Confederation of Fascist Unions lest it challenge the state like the old CGL. As each further step was taken to elaborate a corporative structure that allegedly superseded liberal capitalism, Rossoni's own insti-

---

[197] Aquarone, *L'organizzazione dello stato totalitario*, p. 128; debate in AP: Camera, Legislatura, xxvii, pp. 4849–4855 (December 5), 4879–4888 (December 9), 4904–4922 (December 10), 4926–4970 (December 11). Rocco report in *Scritti e discorsi*, iii, pp. 959 ff. Cf. Rosenstock-Franck, *L'économie corporative*, pp. 54–65.

[198] Aquarone, *L'organizzazione dello stato totalitario*, pp. 135–136; critical commentary in Rosenstock-Franck and Gaetano Salvemini, *Under the Axe of Fascism* (New York, 1936), pp. 67 ff. For the work of the Ministry of Corporations, see Bottai's report to the Grand Council at the end of July 1927, Seg. Part. del Duce, 242/R, T586/1122/074555 ff.; also De Felice, *Mussolini il fascista*, ii, pp. 453–454.

[199] De Felice, *Mussolini il fascista*, ii, p. 266, cites Confindustria defeat of small-industry grouping; cf. Abrate, *La lotta sindacale*, pp. 446–447, 452, n. 40, for Turin industry's discomfort at Confindustria prominence; also Lyttelton, *Seizure of Power*, p. 326.

tutional power was to be whittled away—sacrificed to the authoritarian claims of the state as represented by Mussolini and Rocco, to the competing ambitions of the Fascist Party Secretary Turati and the Under Secretary at the Ministry of Corporations, Bottai, and finally to the entrenched influence of heavy industry.

According to the terms of the labor legislation of April 1926 and the stipulations of the subsequent administrative "norms" or *regolamento*, which received initial approval in mid-May but were then redebated until finally decreed in July, Rossoni's Confederation of Fascist Corporations was regrouped into six branches. These were to represent the employees of industry, commerce, banking, agriculture, land transport, maritime and air transport—to which a federation for free professionals (intellectuals) was also added. Such a division hardly handicapped the employer organizations: Confindustria remained the spokesman for industry, and while it lost the right to represent transportation firms, it was given supervision over artisan groups. The Landlords' Federation of Agricultural Syndicates likewise retained control over its sector of the economy.[200]

As early as March, Rossoni had sought to avert impending fragmentation of his Confederation. He initially proposed a unified employer federation for all economic sectors, so that his equivalent position over labor would not seem disproportional. He also pressed for a common corporative authority for overseeing labor as well as industry, and succeeded in prompting plans to establish a new Ministry of Corporations. Alarmed industrialists feared that Rossoni himself would inherit this new fief, which was to be set up as a sort of planning Ministry by the *regolamento* under discussion. But Mussolini reserved the portfolio for himself, and turned the Under Secretaryship briefly over to Edoardo Suardo, a well-disciplined Fascist in good standing with the older political and court establishment, and by November 1926 to Bottai, the former exponent of revisionism. Rossoni still forced reconsideration of the *regolamento* in the exhaustive Grand Council debates of June 25 to 28, and wrested the provision that some overarching directorate for the Fascist unions would be preserved.[201] He managed thereby to retain for the moment his own position at the head of a Confederation of Fascist Unions, much like his old group and one that embraced all

[200] Aquarone, *L'organizzazione dello stato totalitario*, pp. 136, 146, n. 1; De Felice, *Mussolini il fascista*, II, pp. 270–276; cabinet session of May 18 on *regolamento* cited in Mussolini, *Opera Omnia*, XXII, p. 129.

[201] Lyttelton, *Seizure of Power*, pp. 326–328, summarizes Rossoni's article in *La Stirpe* of March 1927 and changes in *regolamento*. For employers' concern about the Ministry, see Olivetti to Mussolini, May 1, 1926, in Abrate, *La lotta sindacale*, p. 459; Grand Council sessions of June 25–26 in PNF, *Il Gran Consiglio i nei primi sei anni*, pp. 210–213.

of the new employee groups with the exception of the air and maritime workers, who remained autonomous. Despite this accomplishment, much of Rossoni's power had already eroded. With the delineation of separate economic sectors, the role of any central union federation was weakened. Indeed, in agriculture, where a "mixed" syndicate existed and the federation of landlords had merged with the agricultural union, the employers exploited their joint corporation to try to oust or limit the participating union leaders. Finally, the new *regolamento* subjected all recognized unions to rigorous government control over officers and policy, which Confindustria could effectively evade. As Rocco admitted, his laws were intended to "discipline" the unions, not to create a state within the state.[202] On the other hand, the Justice Minister's own hopes for policing industry—including the Magistracy's power to subpoena books for adjudicating disputes—were thwarted. Employers retained the right to suspend salaries or make lay-offs while work disputes were under litigation, which obviously made pressing disputes risky and costly. Rossoni thus emerged with still extensive but weakened authority. Industry remained if not entirely free from control, in a powerful and independent bargaining position for concessions and favors.

The legislation of April 1926 was celebrated as a revolutionary accomplishment. Mussolini did conceive of his labor laws as a genuine way of overcoming the traditional class antagonisms of a capitalist economy. But industry had been too long an ally, the working classes too long an enemy or sullen onlooker, for the new norms to apply even handedly. In March 1926, Benni submitted a long proposal to the Grand Council, which asked for exemptions from eight-hour restrictions and attacked Rossoni's objectives: "Permit me to tell you that just as the parliamentary state has come to little, so the concept of the constitutional factory has also proved a failure. Interference in authority is not possible: the only possible hierarchy in the factory is the technical one required by the productive order. . . . Industry is not personified by the capitalist or the stockholder but by its directors, its chiefs, and by the organizers of the enterprise."[203] Benni sounded the technocratic accents of fascism as they had emerged in the "revisionist" debate of 1923 and 1924; increasingly, they became the rhetoric of the industrial leadership as it pushed for lower labor costs in the name of productivity and rationalization.

No matter how genuinely Rossoni championed labor interests, he faced too many opponents to defend them successfully. Alfredo Rocco's

---

[202] Rocco, *Scritti e discorsi*, III, p. 991; cf. De Felice, *Mussolini il fascista*, II, pp. 270–271.
[203] Benni statement in Seg. Part. del Duce, 242/R, Gran Consiglio, T586/1122/074296–074309.

authoritarianism obviously left no freedom for a militant representation of the working class. But during the in-fighting from 1926 to 1929, it was to be the more supple and opportunist Bottai who finally undercut Rossoni. Bottai had fought as a revisionist alongside Massimo Rocca in 1923 and 1924: he disdained the squadrists and would-be revolutionaries in favor of a collaboration with the economic elites. On the other hand, he rejected the rigid logic of Rocco's fascism for a more ductile ideology, which praised Fascist renovation and managerial revolution. The result was inspired "trimming." While Bottai rejected the crudities of agrarian fascism, he defended a disciplined party sufficiently to forge a working alliance with the new PNF secretary Augusto Turati. Respectful of the economic elites, he still advocated no neoliberal restoration of the market, but elaboration of the Ministry of Corporations, which he dominated as Undersecretary from November 1926, as a coordinating mechanism for the economy. These ambitions ultimately involved disputes with the Ministry of National Economy;[204] but the major opponent initially was Rossoni, who still hoped to make the Confederation of Fascist Unions the fulcrum of economic decision making. Rossoni's syndicalism, Bottai argued, perpetuated outdated appeals to class struggle. Syndicalism was appropriate for an earlier stage of political development, but was intended to serve only as a step toward a "corporativism" in which the prefascist conflicts would disappear entirely. The dispute was confusing in terminology, because the Fascist unions or syndicates called themselves corporations. But the new meaning of corporativism implied a facade of labor-management councils that would coordinate industrial planning under government control. Syndicalism, on the other hand, was an embarrassing adolescent remnant of an earlier fascism.[205]

Mussolini himself was too mercurial in his attitude toward syndicalism to help the union leader. He found industry harsh in its labor policy as of late 1926—a period of stabilization difficulties in Italy during which business leaders behaved as ruthlessly as German employers had in early 1924. Mussolini also resented the industrialists' resistance to his effort at revaluation of the lira. For about half a year Rossoni was allowed to embark upon a new campaign against cuts in real wages and the abrogation of the eight-hour day.[206] Responsive to Rossoni, Mussolini also encouraged formulation of a new "Charter of Labor" that would complete the Fascist labor legislation and guarantee

---

[204] Aquarone, *L'organizzazione dello stato totalitario*, pp. 137–138, nn. 1–2.

[205] Giuseppe Bottai, "Chiarificazione necessaria," *Critica fascista*, May 1, 1928; De Felice, *Mussolini il fascista*, II, pp. 331–332.

[206] Cf. Herbert W. Schneider, *Making the Fascist State* (New York, 1928), pp. 209–210, which overestimates Rossoni's success in resisting wage cuts; Lyttelton, *Seizure of Power*, p. 329.

workers' rights. But its fate was symptomatic of the unions' real in-security. Management delegates of the five new employer associations seized the intragovernmental discussions of the proposed charter to attack Rossoni for his choreographed "peregrinations" throughout Italy, in which he leveled "the most ferocious accusations and insinu-ations against the employers, their associations and their directors, resorting to images and expressions that easily impressed the minds and ingenuous souls of the workers." The employers harshly insisted that any charter must omit stipulations of a minimum wage, shorter hours, severance pay, holidays beyond six days, or further develop-ment of social insurance. They also demanded that employment offices be kept out of Fascist union hands: a blow against the structure of party patronage. Mussolini still went ahead and, through the Grand Council, charged Bottai with working out a charter that would bring up to date the protection of labor.[207] Bottai convened representatives of unions and employers at the Ministry of Corporations in February, and managed to reconcile the views of Rossoni with those of the em-ployers in agriculture and other associations. But Confidustria's rigid-ity required the Under Secretary finally to present two drafts to Musso-lini in April. In both drafts the concept of a minimum wage was rejected—"removed from any general rule and entrusted to the agree-ments of the parties in collective contracts," according to the consensus draft, "contrary to the dignity of labor," in Confindustria's view. The project that won Rossoni's approval stipulated that the employment offices would be dependent upon the Ministry of Corporations and that the offices would have priority in placing new workers; Confin-dustria insisted that the state would control employment of workers. The consensual draft emphasized the reciprocal contributions of work-ers and employers to economic life although reserving executive control to the employer; Confindustria reaffirmed the "full sovereignty of the state" and the role of "private initiative" as the "fertile source" of pro-duction. Corporative organs were "consultative" and charged with formulating "general norms"; employer associations were entrusted with "pursuing the technical objectives concerning economic develop-ment" and ensuring productive discipline among their members. Both drafts promised only vague gains for labor and hedged the duties of employers with immunities, but Confindustria resisted any effort of

[207] See Confederazioni Padronali to PNF Secretary Turati, December 27, 1926, in Aquarone, *L'organizzazione dello stato fascista*, pp. 482–484; also Confederazioni dei Datori del Lavoro in Seg. Part. del Duce, 242/R, Gran Consiglio, cited in Aquarone, p. 143, nn. 1–2; De Felice, *Mussolini il fascista*, II, pp. 287–289, reprints the December 27 letter including substantive objections. For the affirmation to go ahead with a charter, see the Grand Council meeting of January 7, 1927, in PNF, *Il Gran Consiglio nei primi sei anni*, pp. 244–245.

the Fascist unions to claim any new voice in management. Faced with the difficulty of reconciling the harsh counterclaims behind the veil of rhetoric, Mussolini turned to Rocco, more authoritarian and less cautious than Bottai, who was just beginning his tenure at a Ministry that had no clear-cut executive authority. Rocco's draft accepted Confindustria's emphasis on the social role of private initiative. He also sought to shield the employers' traditional rights of hiring and firing from Fascist pressure through employment offices. Still, Rocco's stern warning of punishment for strikes or lock-outs and his rigid authoritarian tone were modulated in a final draft that stressed the obligations of labor more than the iron control of law. After final approval of the Grand Council on April 21, the charter was published with great ballyhoo as the founding of the corporative state.[208]

The end result can be easily dismissed as meaningless. Even the government was careful to state that the charter was a statement of purpose to guide future contracts and legislation but that it had no force of law. The Fascist unions reserved the notion that employment preference be given to Party or union members—but this was effectively nullified later in 1927 when the Grand Council reaffirmed the principle of employer choice. Still, the charter provided bizarre testimony to the conflicts that the regime still faced, even if it managed to muffle the contending parties under layers of cotton-wadding rhetoric. Rocco's nation, "an organism having its own ends superior to those of individuals, its life surpassing those of individuals, and its means of action overarching those of individuals . . . a moral, political, and economic unity of which the Fascist state is the historic realization," was in truth void and abstract.[209] Not the transcendent substance he fancied, Rocco's state was a coercive potential up for grabs. The syndicalists wanted it to guarantee a hierarchy of labor; the industrialists sought its authorization of property and technocratic education. In the last analysis, Mussolini cared only that whichever principle was consecrated be consecrated only through his regime. Fascist labor had no independent force outside the regime once the workers and Party radicals were brought to heel. Industrialists still controlled alternative sources of real power, and thus to keep their adherence Mussolini had

---

[208] Bottai and Rocco drafts as well as final charter reproduced in De Felice, *Mussolini il fascista*, II, pp. 525–547; bargaining procedure discussed *ibid.*, pp. 284–286, drawing on the Bottai archive; consecration of the charter in Grand Council, April 21, 1927, PNF, *Il Gran Consiglio nei primi sei anni*, pp. 246–253 (although the resolution said new contracts based on the charter must recognize the new competitive difficulties for Italian industry). For a realistic evaluation of the charter and its illusory role, see Umberto Romagnoli, "Il diritto sindacale corporativo ed i suoi interpreti," *Storia Contemporanea*, I, 1 (1970), pp. 117–121.
[209] Charter of labor draft, De Felice, *Mussolini il fascista*, II, p. 537.

finally to flesh out the abstraction of the state with their priorities for authority. Hence the paradox of fascist sovereignty: the more grandiose the regime's claim to transcend the party arena and the marketplace, the more it became hostage to those few political forces it still tolerated—occasionally the Party, the army, and the court, industry, and its in-house labor movement, which offered no real and enduring counterbalance. Ironically, the Fascist state and the Weimar state were both vulnerable to domination by powerful social groupings: the former because it claimed vast but formalistic authority, the latter because it could hardly generate a credible image as public guarantor.

Whatever tonality favorable to labor that the charter retained depended, too, upon the temporary anticapitalist mood that accompanied the "battle of the lira" and the effort to roll back prices. The deflationary program of late 1926 and 1927 required real sacrifice, and only urban labor and the peasantry could provide it. Before publication but after approval in the Grand Council, the charter's stipulation that the costs of recession and monetary revaluation had to be borne equitably was excised. PNF Secretary Turati led the sacrifices by imposing a 10 percent wage cut on agrarian workers in his home town of Brescia on May 2. Rossoni had little choice but to consent. In October the Party sanctioned general cuts for all wage earners from 10 to 20 percent. Deflation imposed further costs: it increased the debt burdens of the new proprietors in the North and kept underemployed labor bottled up in the South. Later in 1927 a "ninth hour" was instituted. As Felice Guarneri, later Minister of the National Economy, wrote, the new corporative structures were of platonic value. What counted was the return to the "normal" output of labor and the end of the postwar "wave of laziness."[210]

Rossoni became a growing nuisance. If he could not block wage cuts, he still angered Mussolini by declaring that the effort to roll back prices had failed. "We must not lightly offer polemical themes to antifascists the world over," the prime minister rebuked on September 20, prohibiting Rossoni from public speeches until further clearance.[211] Meanwhile, Bottai moved to the offensive. In January 1928 he sought to disbar individuals, such as Rossoni, from holding office in individual

[210] Guarneri, *Battaglie economiche*, I, p. 145. For wage cuts, see Salvemini, *Under the Axe*, pp. 183–187; Lyttelton, *Seizure of Power*, pp. 344–345. For a recent study that sees *real* wages as rising, cf. Carlo Vanutelli, "Occupazioni e salari in Italia dal 1861 al 1961." *L'economia italiana dal 1861 al 1961* (Milan, 1961), pp. 570–571, but the statistics used may be unreliable. For the manipulation of statistics, see Salvemini, *Under the Axe*, pp. 231–237. Cf. also the careful evaluation in Melograni, *Gli industriali e Mussolini*, pp. 225–229, citing Bocchini report on short-time imposed.

[211] Seg. Part. del Duce, Edmondo Rossoni, T586/453/028104.

corporations or unions and in union federations at the same time. His Ministry expanded its jurisdiction over labor mediation, working out collective contracts and leaving only occasional disputes for the new labor courts. Likewise, Augusto Turati, who had replaced Farinacci as Party Secretary with the mission of disciplining the Fascist movement, also turned against the labor leader to maintain the superiority of his own Party barony. Finally, Mussolini grew concerned that in light of the provisions for the large syndical voice in nomination of the single list of candidates who would run for the Chamber in 1929, Rossoni's influence as head of the Fascist unions would be excessive. In late November 1928 Mussolini "unblocked" or broke up Rossoni's Confederation into seven autonomous divisions.[212] The rationale was to create a symmetrical bargaining situation with the delegates of industry. The real thrust was to undercut the troublesome labor leader. Rossoni summoned the provincial secretaries of his unions to Rome in protest. His Southern leaders were especially angered; they felt that only the unions had enabled fascism to organize a mass base in the Mezzogiorno. But the reaction quickly dissipated. "Bottai," the political professionals were reported to agree, "chose the right moment to put Rossoni on the shelf."[213]

For industry, the success over Rossoni represented an extension of the victories secured over the socialists in 1921 and 1922. But while industry's reaction in the early 1920's had involved a broad class appeal for the defense of order, the triumphs of the late 1920's were achieved as "corporatist" successes. Under Mussolini, social competition evolved from the traditional defense of the *classe dirigente*, which many members of the elite had despaired of winning on peaceful terms, to that of interest-group maneuvering. Fascist success enabled the Italian economic elites to reassert their mastery of the factory and the labor market. But it required them to surrender older claims to control political decisions. More precisely, it meant relinquishing the claims to a certain degree; for the informal influence that the major industrialists could exert through *podestà* and prefect on the local level, through the Grand Council at Rome, remained enormous. Up to the Great Depression, Fascist rule thus consolidated old and threatened hegemony by means of new authoritarian organizing principles—principles that, even if imposed by dictatorship, were still in line with transformations underway throughout Western Europe.

[212] Lyttelton, *Seizure of Power*, pp. 347–348; De Felice, *Mussolini il fascista*, II, pp. 329–337; Melograni, *Gli industriali e Mussolini*, pp. 240–242.

[213] Seg. Part. del Duce, Edmondo Rossoni, T586/453/028112–028113. "Voci di Montecitorio dal 21 al 27 novembre 1928 VII." For Rossoni's lieutenants, *ibid.*, 028149–028152.

The setback for the Fascist unions was partially a consequence of the deflation that attended the effort to stabilize and revalue the lira. Postwar Italy was afflicted with chronic inflationary pressures: the need for massive imports of raw materials, an interruption of tourism, curtailment of emigration, therefore, of funds remitted from abroad, and the overhanging interallied debts kept the lira steadily descending on the money markets. By 1925 the depreciation was seen as contributing to the sluggish performance of the economy and to a significant decline in stock-market values and savings.

No sustained inflationary interests drove the lira downward. As in France, there was widespread business sentiment that the stability of the currency was a necessary precondition for new expansion. The export premium that currency depreciation bestowed might benefit textile manufacturers, especially important in Lombardy, but not sufficiently to outweigh the malaise produced by inflation. And heavy industry predominantly required stabilization; for in Italy the giants of steel manufacturing, construction, and chemicals were preeminently importers of raw materials who produced for the home market. The greater the slippage of the lira, the worse their own ratio of costs to revenue. Just as decisive, much of the Fascist constituency was middle class, concerned with savings in bank accounts or real estate and building. These groups had adhered to fascism to protect a new prosperity, not from economic desperation, and there was no further gain to be derived from their anxiety or radicalization. Austria and Germany, no doubt, remained vivid in Mussolini's memory when, at Pesaro in August 1926, he promised that his people would never suffer "the moral shame and economic catastrophe of the bankruptcy of the lira."[214]

Action seemed especially appropriate once the war-debt issue had been settled advantageously for Rome. The Mellon-Volpi agreement effectively cancelled a major fraction of Washington's claims. With the pound restored to gold in 1925, and the French inflation finally contained by July 1926, Italian stabilization measures seemed to offer a fair chance of success.[215] Shortly after the return of Poincaré, Mussolini

[214] Mussolini, *Opera Omnia*, xxii, pp. 196–198; Lyttelton, *Seizure of Power*, p. 342, cites the arguments for saving the small saver and property holder advanced by B. Griziotti et al., *La politica finanziaria italiana* (Milan, 1926), as influencing Mussolini. See too Giovanni Carano Donvito, "L'inflazione e il Mezzogiorno," and "La deflazione nei riguardi del Mezzogiorno," in *Giornale degli Economisti e Rivista di Statistica*, xli (April 1926), pp. 216–227, and xlii (March 1927), pp. 120–137.

[215] See Thomas Lamont's July 20, 1926, memo for Mr. Podesta of the Banca d'Italia, which pointed out that until the French stabilized their franc it was difficult to halt depreciation of the lira, because the public psychologically associated the two currencies. Baker Library, TWL papers, 190-20. For plans concerning stabilization before Pesaro, see Gian Giaccomo Migoni, *Problemi di storia nei rapporti tra Italia e Stati Uniti* (Turin, 1971), pp. 43–93.

addressed a major policy recommendation to Volpi that combined fascist rhetoric and hard fiscal analysis. He warned that "the fate of the regime is bound to the fate of the lira." Unless "the battle of the lira" were won, the opposition would profit. It would be especially humiliating for a self-declared totalitarian government to succumb to the petty complaints and corridor coalitions of the nonfascist political remnants. Stabilization, emphasized Mussolini, must involve revaluation. "Do not defend the lira only to slow its fall, but defend the lira to raise it up again."[216] Between the autumn of 1926 and the spring of 1927 the government thus undertook a concerted open-market campaign for revaluation through a special Institute of Exchange. By November 1926 the lira no longer needed special support and had mounted from almost 150 per pound to about 90—the rate Mussolini had inherited in 1922 and that he wished to reestablish. While there was consensus on stabilization, the parity of 90—the so-called *quota novanta*—aroused the anxieties of industry and finance as well as the skepticism of financiers abroad. Even Volpi allegedly preferred a ratio of 120. On November 3, the major industrialists, including Crespi, Falck, Agnelli, Conti, Olivetti—even Benni—convened at Milan to voice their worries about the new impediments to exports, the squeeze on liquidity, and the onset of recession.[217] The *quota novanta*, though, became a test of prestige for Mussolini. When London bankers as well as the Morgan partners expressed concern, the Bank of Italy reacted: "Anglo-Saxons want to impose their will, and that is extremely humiliating."[218] Economic considerations became secondary: like the Charter of Labor currently under discussion, the strong lira would guarantee Fascist prestige and prove its claims to transcend special interests at home.

Fascism retained a latent hostility toward finance and big business

[216] ACS, Rome: Carte Volpi di Misurata, b. 6 (letter of August 8).

[217] Memorial of November 3 meeting in Carte Volpi, *ibid.*; cf. also the report of December 20, 1926, by Mylius, Varzi, and Crespi, detailing the difficulties of the cotton industry. For the Banca Commerciale's earlier hesitation about rigorous stabilization, see its Report in *Rassegna Italiana* (April 1925). Volpi's preferences cited by Guarneri, *Battaglie economiche*, I, p. 159; cf. De Felice, *Mussolini il fascista*, II, pp. 243–244.

[218] Stringher to Nathan in London, October 31, 1926; also Stringher to Volpi, October 31, 1926, both in Carte Volpi, b. 6. For the revaluation episode as a whole, see Roland Sarti, "Mussolini and the Industrial Leadership in the Battle of the Lira 1925–1927," *Past and Present*, 47 (May 1970), pp. 97–112; De Felice, *Mussolini il fascista*, II, pp. 224–263, recapitulating "I lineamenti politici della 'quota 90' attraverso i documenti di Mussolini e di Volpi," *Il Nuovo Osservatore* (May 1966), pp. 370–395; Pietro Grifone, *Il capitale finanziario in Italia* (Turin, 1971), pp. 56–77. More than the other writers, De Felice emphasizes the battle of the lira as being directed against the industrialists; Sarti stresses how linked the goals of industry and fascism remained. Cf. Valerio Castronovo's evaluation, "Potere economico e fascismo," *Rivista di Storia Contemporanea* (1972), p. 291.

that could be mobilized among the old squadrist elements, Farinacci at their head. The sophisticated industrialists and bankers linked to the Banca Commerciale, including Crespi, Conti, and even Volpi, aroused resentments that Mussolini could invoke to counterbalance the bourgeois establishments. The Commerciale with its prewar links to German banks had long been a target of Nationalist and Fascist hostility; it represented a veritable Freemasonry of finance with great but intangible influence that resisted crass political pressure. Rival industrialists were also ready to criticize the Commerciale. Pio and Mario Perrone of Ansaldo—the Ligurian shipbuilding and steel combine linked to the rival Banca di Sconto before its bankruptcy in 1923—had prodded Nitti during the war to restrict the Commerciale. In the spring of 1924 they proposed to the government the formation of a Grand Council of Economic Defense to supervise investment, plan industrial activity, and take over Italian banking activities abroad. The Perrones did not ask to be restored to their own directorships, which they had been forced to surrender for depreciated shares in the Banco di Roma when their firms had crashed, but they did offer their expertise as members of the suggested Council. They cited Stinnes as the type of industrialist imperialist, who in league with the Commerciale was limiting Italian economic expansion. Ironically, their own concepts were closely allied to those of Stinnes. The heart of the Perrone plan was nationalization of the Commerciale and compulsory cartelization. For both Stinnes and the Perrone brothers the grandiose combinations were designed to facilitate the expansion of huge, vertically integrated enterprises, and later to rescue the overextended giants from their creditors. Industrial megalomania wiped out the distinctions between private ambition and public planning.[219]

Mussolini did not salvage Ansaldo, although by the 1930's the role of the Istituto per la Ricostruzione Industriale (IRI) was not so different from what the Perrone brothers had outlined. Moreover, Mussolini did retain some distance from the Milanese and Turin industrialists the parvenu Perrone brothers so resented. The *quota novanta* prevented too close an identification with the business elites. Long disputes with the electrical industries over electricity prices during 1925 and 1926 revealed antagonistic interests, and a fortnight after Pesaro, Giacinto Motta of Italian Edison publicly defended contracts on a gold basis rather than trusting the Fascist future of the lira.[220]

[219] Perrone memo: "Per il riordinamento delle banche e delle industrie nazionali," ACS, Rome: Archivio della Presidenza del Consiglio, 1924, f. 6/I, n. 1295. Cf. Lyttelton, *Seizure of Power*, pp. 335–336.

[220] For price disputes with the electrical industry see the materials in ACS, Rome: Archivio della Presidenza del Consiglio, 1926, f. 3/8, nr. 1121, including *Secolo* article by Motta, August 23, 1926.

Conti's speech to the Senate of May 1927 must finally have convinced Mussolini that any concessions would only ransom him to the old elites who grudgingly accepted fascism for their private gains. While Volpi thus sought to stabilize at 120, Mussolini's supporters raised the specter of a *quota* 75. The Fascist leader himself suggested a dramatic level of 80 to 85 but finally acquiesced in the original parity. By July 1927, Volpi was pleased to have been able to avoid revaluation above 90.[221]

In the longer perspective the divergence with industry was secondary. Even while the business leadership quarreled with fascism it reaped important silent victories, just as large landowners had benefitted the year before from the new agrarian duties that accompanied the "battle for grain." Now Volpi raised industrial tariffs and encouraged shipbuilding. Mussolini was prepared to accept big business's price for a deflationary crisis: the reduction of wages and the concentration of corporate ownership. Lower profit margins hurt small producers more than large, and 1927 witnessed a take-over splurge such as marked the concurrent German rationalization movement. By legislation in June 1927, the government provided tax advantages for mergers, which jumped from an average of 16 per year until that point to 266 in 1928 and 313 in 1929. As the Perrone memo had declared in 1924: "it is necessary to bear in mind a crude truth: while the principle of free competition is the economic theory of the present moment, in reality the practice of the lives of those nations with a great industrial civilization is the trust or cartel." As in Germany again, widespread efforts were launched to increase the productivity of labor while imposing a ninth hour and wage cuts, including enthusiastic experimentation with scientific management, above all, the "Bedeaux system." More crassly than in the United States and France, if not Germany, rationalization and scientific management, however, amounted to veiled appeals for factory authoritarianism and technologically justified exploitation.[222]

Indeed, the *quota novanta* proved consistent with the general trends of 1925–1926 both inside Italy and in the international economy. At home, deflation served to establish the government's voice over

[221] Conti speech, May 21, 1927, cited, De Felice, *Mussolini il fascista*, II, 254–255; also Ettore Conti, *Dal taccuino di un borghese* (Milan, 1946), pp. 375 ff.; for the "dramatic" 80–85: "Appunti del Capo del Governo," April 26, 1927, Rome: Carte Volpi, b. 6; Volpi's relief reported by Giovanni Fummi (Morgan representative in Italy) to Lamont, July 14, 1927, TWL Papers, 190-23.

[222] Paola Fiorentini, "Ristrutturazione capitalistica e sfruttamento operaio in Italia negli anni '20," *Rivista storica del socialismo* (January–April 1967), pp. 134–151; for mergers, see F. Vito, *I sindacati industriali. Cartelli e gruppi* (Milan, 1930), pp. 288–293; Lyttelton, *Seizure of Power*, p. 360.

national economic policy even while it granted new control over the structure and organization of industry to the most powerful firms and associations. In the international context, the *quota novanta* formed Italy's contribution to the overall deflationary thrust of the late 1920's. As with Germany, Italy's return to a gold-exchange standard was encouraged by infusions of American capital. Loans increased in size and frequency once the debt question was settled and the currency stabilized. Considered superficially, the excessive stabilization represented a step toward autarky. But while it handicapped the exports of light industry, it still accentuated the growth of a heavy industry dependent upon foreign raw materials. The Italian tendency did not fundamentally run counter to the Anglo-American-sponsored international capitalism of the gold-exchange standard. It was actually a tragic caricature of that system: rewarding the powerful, disciplining the weak, imposing by political duress and economic consolidation what other societies worked toward by market forces alone.

Lest this argument be misread, let it be emphasized that so far as concerns the dimensions of liberty, whether for individual or association, fascism diverged basically from the practices of the German Republic and from the long-standing traditions of the French. But in his restructuring of social and economic relationships, Mussolini's solutions resembled those elsewhere. Fascism did not suppress the causes of capitalist strife and class rivalry; it encouraged the centralization and coordination of that conflict such as was developing in other societies. There was a crucial difference: in Italy the outcome was predetermined. Rocco's *Magistratura del Lavoro* was reminiscent on paper of the Weimar Labor Ministry, but until 1932 Weimar's arbitration authority remained a defender of labor; whereas Italy's was hardly invoked at all. Fascism did not particularly hasten the technological modernization of industry, but it did hasten its modernization in terms of corporate organization. As everywhere else, industry in Italy grumbled about the handicaps that state policies imposed. As elsewhere, it was learning to play a new game and confront a new continuum of political-economic decision making.

Mussolini's corporatist system varied from that of Weimar (and certainly from the still largely traditional social confrontations in France). The Italian system was designed to consolidate the power of a ruling group supposedly independent of the powerful forces contending in the marketplace. The Weimar government comprised the very representatives of the socioeconomic arena, and reflected their social power as well as parliamentary strength. In actuality, the Fascist regime remained in a reciprocal and symbiotic relationship with the old forces of order. Even as the state asserted new claims over the control of all policy, including economic decisions, it ceded to business leaders extensive control over industrial organization. But the emerging system was not a simple reaction. As Agnelli's biographer notes, those abroad hostile to fascism expected that the revaluation controversy would lead to a conservative business triumph over fascism. Instead, it increased industry's need of state protection by means of tariffs, labor regulation, and exclusion of foreign competition by subsidies at home or outright prohibition of investment from abroad. When the Depression struck and industry languished further, the government was to step in even more actively—through its state holding companies—and erect a parapublic economic sector. The emerging web of private and public dependencies amounted to a wartime economy in peace; but this, too, presaged developments not merely for authoritarian experiments but for all the capitalist economies of the West.[223]

[223] Castronovo, *Agnelli*, p. 463. For the Fascist economy in the depression, see Castronovo, "Potere economico e fascismo," pp. 301 ff.; Romeo, *Breve storia*, pp. 158–172.

CONCLUSION:
THE STRUCTURE AND LIMITS
OF STABILITY

Stability is a relative term. Even the briefest glance at politics, labor relations, and the international economy reveals that no bright sunlit years separated Dawes plan from Depression. How can one write of meaningful stabilization, some might object, in view of the Nazi take-over and the violence and war that lay ahead? I would disagree. A discernible equilibrium among economic interests, classes, and nations finally emerged after many false starts. A combination of coercion, pay-offs, and exhaustion produced a broad political settlement. The equilibrium was certainly hostage to continuing American prosperity and the control of German national resentments. But the collapse of the structure does not mean that we must abandon study of the plans and foundation. They could serve for less rickety edifices.

It would also be foolish to deny the conservative political achievement of the late 1920's. After mid-decade—with the return of Poincaré, the election of President Hindenburg, Britain's return to gold and easy weathering of the General Strike, the silence of suppression in Italy—the passions of domestic conflict abated. Conferences between nations began to yield agreements and not merely endless wrangling. Locarno, Geneva, and The Hague produced only transient results, yet the public read in them a spirit different from the constant disputes before 1924. Statesmen now argued over incremental issues of more or less: would occupied German territory be evacuated sooner or later? How quickly would reparations be scaled down? How much of Europe's debt would Washington write off? Exhaustion and frustration attended such bargaining, but cataclysm was not invoked. A Western economy linchpinned upon American participation was functioning again. Savings were reconstituted, even though the great squandering of 1914–1918 cost at least a decade of development. For those who wrote or performed, a new republic of letters seemed at hand. Harry Kessler chatted at cafes about Proust and Valéry, flitting among the celebrities of a culture that embraced Berlin and Paris. When in October 1929 he noted the death of Stresemann, he also recalled that Diaghilev and Hofmannsthal had been taken in that same year: 1929 . . . *"wahrhaftig eine année terrible."*[1]

[1] Harry Graf Kessler, *Aus den Tagebüchern 1918–1937* (Munich, 1965), p. 288.

Throughout this book our task has been to understand how the reconstruction of a conservative, "bourgeois" equilibrium was achieved across the unparalleled violence, costs, and passions occasioned by World War I. This has sometimes meant departing from the events that were most conspicuous to stress conflicts that were more prosaic but often more decisive. Elections, for instance, usually made less difference than contemporaries, or historians, thought they did; the Ruhr invasion may have changed little that would not have otherwise occurred; such brief explosions as the Kapp Putsch or the Occupation of the Factories altered even less. It would be grossly inaccurate to say that these events signified nothing, for they signified a great deal in the sense of making manifest underlying tension and conflict. But they altered little, demolished few arrangements that were not already undermined. Their institutional legacy was slight.

This is not to claim that nothing had changed or that life in the late 1920's recreated *la belle époque*. In fact, just restoring the facade of stability required significant institutional change. It is worth mustering them in summary review.

1. Whether under liberal or authoritarian auspices, group conflict was being resolved by what—with some reluctance—we have termed corporatist approaches. In other words, social priorities were increasingly decided not by traditional elites nor by the aggregation of voters' preferences. Elections resolved less than the day-to-day bargaining between industry and labor or among different business, agricultural, and party interests. If these groups failed to negotiate coherently or did not set clear priorities—the French situation in the mid-1920's—policy was becalmed in a Sargasso of ineffective parliamentarism.

The key to consensus or mere civic peace was either forcible suppression or constant brokerage. Any major organized interest could disrupt a modern economy or imperil social order, hence had to be silenced by duress or granted a minimum of demands. The need for brokerage switched the fulcrum of decision making from the legislature as such to ministries or new bureaucracies. During the war, ministries of munitions had developed into economic planning agencies. Under men of ambition and energy such as Rathenau, Loucheur, and Lloyd George, they extensively regulated the labor market and the allocation of scarce raw materials. The coopted private business in this task, sharing public powers to increase the scope of regulation.[2] Although war-

[2] See Chapter One, Part Three; also Paul A. C. Koistinen, "The 'Industrial-Military Complex' in Historical Perspective: World War I," *Business History*, 41 (1967), pp. 378–403; E. M. H. Lloyd, *Experiments in State Control at the War Office and the Ministry of Food* (London, 1924), pp. 18–26, 259 ff.; W. Oualid and Charles Picquenard, *Salaires et tarifes, conventions collectives et grèves: La politique du Ministère de l'Armament et du Ministère du travail* (Paris, 1928);

time controls were not retained, the 1920's did not simply revert to the degree of market freedom prevailing before 1914. The Weimar Interparty Committee and Ministry of Labor, the Fascist Grand Council and Ministry of Corporations, in a lesser way the French Coal Agency and Ministry of Commerce (and if Herbert Hoover had had his way, the U.S. Department of Commerce) took on new political tasks. Parliamentary decision making never recovered fully from the eclipse into which it had fallen during the war. By 1925 governments collected and spent perhaps 20 to 25 percent of national income, in contrast to about half that share before the war. Parliaments did not work well in deciding how to levy this new burden. They worked even less well in trying to adjust the internal burdens of currency depreciation and revaluation. Traditional parties had taken form around earlier issues, and they proved too divided internally for this invidious allocation.

2. From 1918 until about 1924 the chief *political* objective for most bourgeois forces, parties or interest groups, amounted to exclusion of the socialists from any decisive influence on the state. Bourgeois resistance outran opposition to specific social democratic programs, which were generally moderate and reformist. Rather, the working-class parties represented a threat to what was seen as good order just by their new prominence and potential power. Later in the 1920's coalitions with social democrats did become acceptable, but only when social democracy acquiesced in the economic conceptions of its bourgeois partners. If the socialist left seriously presented its own economic objectives on the national level, alarmed conservatives fought back. They resorted either to decentralized but simultaneous boycotts of government bonds and money (as in France), or to concerted political opposition to taxation within the terms of coalition politics (as in Germany), or to extralegal coercion (as in Italy). In the face of such opposition, social democratic forces could not maintain positions of leadership or even parity at the national level. As Engels had foreseen shortly before his death in the 1890's, the socialists had wagered on legality while their opponents were prepared to indulge in violence. Turati recalled the prediction when his party majority foreswore reformism.[3] What more touching tribute to the nineteenth-century liberal

---

Gerd Hardach, "Französische Rüstungspolitik 1914–1918," in Heinrich August Winkler, ed., *Organisierter Kapitalismus. Voraussetzungen und Anfänge* (Göttingen, 1974), pp. 101–116; Alberto Caracciolo, "La crescita e la trasformazione della grande industria durante la prima guerra mondiale," in Giorgio Fuà, ed., *Lo sviluppo economico in Italia* (Milan, 1969), pp. 197–212; Luigi Einaudi, *La condotta economica e gli effetti sociali della guerra italiana* (Bari, 1933), pp. 99–178.

[3] Friedrich Engels, "Introduction" [1895], to Karl Marx, *The Class Struggles in France, 1846 to 1850*, Karl Marx and Friedrich Engels, *Selected Works*, 2 vols.

belief in the *Rectsstaat* than that European social democrats should have been its most tenacious defenders!

3. A defining characteristic of the corporatist system that we have sought to analyze was the blurring of the distinction between political and economic power. Clout in the marketplace—especially the potential to paralyze an industrial economy—made for political influence. Consequently, economic bargaining became too crucial to be left to the private market, and state agencies stepped in as active mediators. Not surprisingly, labor questions became some of the most crucial tests of political stability. The economic issues were grave in their own right, but they also represented political disputes. The trade-union movements, more precisely the non-Catholic federations, represented the arm of social democracy in the marketplace and were combated as such. If the union federations contributed to the political influence of social democracy, however, they also increased its liabilities during a period of economic recession and unemployment. Working-class forces that were defeated in the marketplace were usually administered blows in the political arena as well.

a. The first major setback after the war was the limitation of factory representation, such as was embodied in works councils. The council movement had promised a restructuring of capitalism from the workplace outward. Even after its messianic transformation failed to materialize in 1918–1919, factory representation still beckoned the working class. Factory representation was elective; it was responsive to immediate grievances; it offered a foothold on issues of management. But the 1920's brought one defeat after another for plant representation. In France the movement hardly got started; in Germany the councils were legally restricted in scope; in Italy they were conceded by Giolitti as a diversionary measure and were eliminated by Fascist union leaders—who could not capture their majorities—in concert with industrialists. Fascist union leaders in Italy and later in Germany did not abandon the idea of entrenching their own agents in the factory. But Mussolini (and later Hitler) had no more reason to sanction powerful plant delegates than had earlier leaders.

The last major phase of the Italian controversy developed during the spring of 1929 as Fascist union leaders, who had been set back by the "unblocking" of their confederation the previous fall, initiated a new campaign to install factory trustees. Only the trustees, claimed the labor leaders, could prevent industrial managers from abusing the legislation that protected workers. Their campaign culminated in a

---

(Moscow, 1958), I, p. 136; Turati's quote to the Socialist Congress of Bologna in October 1919, cited in Angelo Tasca, *Nascita e avvento del fascismo*, 2 vols. (Bari, 1965), I, p. 274, n. 81.

syndicalist congress at Milan's Lyric Theatre at the end of June and early July, after which Mussolini intervened to restore discipline. In a series of extensive "Intersyndical" conferences from July 6 to 12, the union leaders accused the industrialists of hostility to fascism and evading collective contracts. Mussolini recognized the validity of the charges, but refused to install the factory trustees. Instead he talked about the need for rationalization and technical improvements. Over a summer of debate the union leaders were forced to retreat, abandoning the claims to plant representation and becoming more receptive to schemes for rationalization that they had earlier characterized as exploitative. By its September meeting the Intersyndical Committee unanimously rejected the principle of factory delegates.[4]

b. The upshot was characteristic of the capitalist economies in general and not just the fascist system. If the 1920's began with the left pressing for democratization of the factory, it ended with the right calling for rationalization, Americanism, Fordism, the Bedeaux plan, or equivalent nostrums. All these systems claimed that labor could be utilized as another form of capital, subject to efficient analysis and organization. The trade conditions of the late 1920's, which impelled export competitions and cost cutting, made these schemes attractive. But the right also seized upon scientific management as a political weapon. Invocations of "the organization of labor" really became appeals to factory autocracy in the name of industrial efficiency. Europeans of the left and right gave excess credit to scientific management as the motor of American prosperity and social harmony, because it fitted their respective ideological premises. The left decried a more subtle means of exploitation; businessmen on the right celebrated its efficiency. European industrialists in particular sought a system of labor control that did not entail just an outdated reassertion of factory paternalism. They could not resurrect the *Herr im Hause*, but the impartial engineer and technician of management could provide the same authority.[5]

[4] Sessions of the Comitato Centrale Intersindacale in ACS, Rome: Carte Cianetti, B. 4; controversy followed in Piero Melograni, *Gli industriali e Mussolini. Rapporti tra Confindustria e fascismo dal 1919 al 1929* (Milan, 1972), pp. 276–311.

[5] For the European industrialists' exploitation of scientific management, see Charles Maier, "Between Taylorism and Technocracy: European Ideologies and the Vision of Industrial Productivity in the 1920's," *Journal of Contemporary History*, v, 2 (1970), pp. 54–59, including further citations; also André Philip, *Le problème ouvrier aux états unis* (Paris, 1927), pp. 39–87, for a social democratic evaluation; cf. Dzherman M. Gvishiani, *Organization and Management: A Sociological Analysis of Western Theories* (Moscow, 1972), pp. 174 ff., for the latest specimen of a Russian interest beginning with Lenin. On the roots of Nazi labor policy in Weimar's entrepreneurial attitudes, see T. W. Mason, "Zur Entstehung des Gesetzes zur Ordnung der nationalen Arbeit, vom 20. Januar 1934," Bochum Symposium paper, June 1973.

c. While the right defeated worker delegation in the factory, it had to accept certain transformations as irreversible. Entrepreneurs in fascist Italy and Weimar Germany had to come to terms with some continuing trade-union organization and accept collective bargaining. No matter how hollow the forms of labor representation might become under fascism, businessmen could not simply eliminate them entirely. Of the three countries considered here, France alone lagged in the obligation to recognize collective bargaining, as did the United States outside Europe. Both nations, though, would enforce union contracts by the mid-1930's. The Matignon agreements and the Wagner Act imposed requirements on French and American entrepreneurs similar to those of the Stinnes-Legien and Palazzo Vidoni agreements. The reader will rightly object that only the external forms were alike, but that the thrust of democratic and fascist regulation was antithetical. Still, the form was important, for it signified that fascist as well as democratic regimes had to negotiate collective settlements and group bargains. Fascist labor delegates might be spurious representatives for Turin's metalworkers or the *braccianti* of Emilia, but they still retained some influence as a bureaucratic interest group in a political system that claimed to subsume and resolve all social conflict.

Nonfascist societies had to purchase the cooperation of the working class as well as compel it. The left won peripheral rewards in the re-arrangement of power in the 1920's. Social democrats retained important political control at the municipal and state level. They won important extensions of social insurance from conservative governments in Britain, France, and Germany. These countries also accepted foreign policies aimed at softening the outcome of 1918: a goal that the left had sought since the Armistice. The achievement was largely symbolic—the spirit of Geneva—but important nonetheless.

4. In the long run the major possibility for social consensus derived from a slow transformation of the principles of class division. Class consciousness was undergoing a double evolution. In the world of work, identification as proletarian or bourgeois was becoming less compelling than interest-group affiliation, less a principle of common action in the economic arena. Yet the world of production was only one reference point for social stratification and political loyalties, and one of diminishing importance throughout the twentieth century. While European socialism appealed to man as worker from its origins, the European right sought to make social roles outside the sphere of production the major determinants of political allegiance. Insofar as party competition followed divisions in industry and commerce, the right could not outbid the traditional left. On the other hand, the right could appeal to man insofar as he was concerned as consumer or as

saver about the value of money, as a newspaper reader about the prestige of his nation-state, or even as a commuter about his rights to uninterrupted tram service. Work experiences did not become more unified; a few still commanded, many still followed orders. But mass transit, the cinema, radio, vacations, less formal dress made workplace identity less encompassing and facilitated new collective consciousness.

It was ironic that fascism should encourage this development. For fascism boasted that it had superseded the empty liberal abstractions of citizenship to regroup men as producers. Syndicalism and corporatism supposedly followed from the priority of *homo faber*. In fact, fascism and the right in general increasingly appealed to men outside the workplace. Fascist culture, political rallies, collective gymnastics, and Blackshirts were calculated to build a new unity. Whereas the left celebrated man's liberation and rationality in the world of work, the right appealed to audience-man. As the concept of the "proletariat" had once replaced "mob" or "rabble," so now, for social theorists, "masses" replaced proletariat. By the latter 1920's, former socialists who had become discouraged at the attrition of their support discovered the same appeal to "instinctual" rather than rational loyalties in a neosocialism that verged toward fascism.[6]

In retrospect, the left's stress on plant representation and works councils can be interpreted as a last effort to reinstall a producer's consciousness among the old working class. It was rebuffed, and the centrality of work experience as a political rallying point failed with it. It was fitting that observers pointed to Mussolini's *dopolavoro* and Hitler's *Kraft durch Freude* as characteristic contributions of fascist labor policy. Both were regimentations of leisure. Bureaucratically, the *dopolavoro* served as one more organization to pit against the fascist labor unions. But it also amounted to a major attempt to alter class perceptions and experiences.

By the end of World War II democratic parties, too, would sense the recasting of class identification and appeal to men in their roles

[6] For a major statement, Hendrik De Man, *Zur Psychologie des Sozialismus* (Jena, 1926), pp. 137–157. Cf. Robert Michels, "Der Aufstieg des Faschismus in Italien," *Archiv für Sozialwissenschaft und Sozialpolitik*, 52, 1 (1924), p. 71: "For the psychologists of the masses the history of fascism offers a field of observation of huge dimensions." Michels' major essay, "Psychologie der antikapitalistischen Massenbewegungen," *Grundriss der Sozialökonomik*, ix/i (Tübingen, 1926), pp. 241–359, amplifies the theme, mostly with reference to socialist movements, however, and provides major bibliography. Recent approaches to the problem in: Edward R. Tannenbaum, *The Fascist Experience: Italian Society and Culture* (New York, 1972); Gino Germani, "Fascism and Class," in Stuart J. Woolf, ed., *The Nature of Fascism* (New York, 1969), pp. 65–96; Renzo De Felice, *Le interpretazioni del fascismo* (Bari, 1972), pp. 113–144, who summarizes the work of Fromm, Adorno, et al.

outside the workplace. But committed to work as the defining human experience, social democrats resisted coming to terms with the new principles of group identification in the 1920's, while the right exploited the change. The factory hierarchy defended by Antonio Benni or Albert Vögler could remain intact if outside the plant gates new common experiences eroded old class identities.[7] Bourgeois society was preserved by creating new stakes in continuity, providing access to a community of consumption or sentiment if not of production. The left denigrated these common experiences as spurious, but for better or worse they proved integrating and persuasive.

Two major sorts of tension arose to imperil and then undermine the equilibrium of the 1920's. The very corporatism that facilitated political stability simultaneously imposed fundamental dilemmas. One was the difficulty of reconciling the conflicting priorities of the international economy and domestic needs. The other involved the fate of those who were battered by the very corporate restructuring around them.

1. While the issues of inflation and revaluation encouraged corporatist organization, they also imposed limits to the degree of stability that might ultimately be achieved. Equilibrium remained hostage to the discrepancy between the demands of an international economy and the pressures for compromise between groups at home.

a. The politics of revaluation was an international phenomenon. Each country's debates took place in an overarching context of deflationary pressure that accompanied establishment of the gold-exchange standard. Only in Britain and in Italy did the forces desiring high revaluation triumph: in Italy because a fascist policy of prestige, self-sufficiency, and political hegemony over industry dictated elevating the lira; in Britain because the country had accepted sufficient taxation and deflation to make restoration of the gold standard appear feasible at $4.86 per pound as the City advocated. In both countries the price of high stabilization was unemployment and recession.[8] And while Germany was no longer saddled with major internal debt, Berlin had to meet Dawes annuities. Although foreign loans more than covered this burden, they also made independent monetary policy difficult, and Reichsbank President Schacht sought to recover control and insulate

---

[7] See above, pp. 443, 567.

[8] For monetary stabilization, see Stephen V. O. Clarke, *Central Bank Cooperation, 1924–1931* (New York, 1967), pp. 45–107; Hjalmar Schacht, *The Stabilization of the Mark* (London, 1927); Karl Elster, *Von der Mark zur Reichsmark* (Jena, 1928), pp. 215 ff.; W. A. Brown, Jr., *England and the New Gold Standard 1919–1926* (New Haven, Conn., 1929), pp. 181–233; D. E. Moggridge, *The Return to Gold, 1925: The Formulation of Economic Policy and Its Critics* (Cambridge, 1969).

Germany from the vicissitudes of capital flows by restrictive credit measures. The quest for autonomy thus led to deflationary policies in Germany as well.[9]

The overriding thrust toward monetary stabilization came in part from across the Atlantic. The economic trends of the second half of the 1920's reflected American conditions for alleviating the balance-of-payments difficulties that impeded capitalist stability. Since Woodrow Wilson's intervention of 1917, the United States had sought to secure a liberal democratic and capitalist comity of nations. Former Wilsonians, New York bankers, and members of the Republican administrations of the 1920's now defined an international dimension to American and European economic health. As they saw it, the interests of both continents converged in the need for stability, the absence of political rancor, and a favorable climate for entrepreneurial initiative. It was apparent that the United States had become the guarantor of such a political economy.[10]

Before 1914, growing international trade had depended upon shared rules of exchange summarized by the international gold standard. Minor jiggling of internal prices and employment levels permitted international equilibrium. Domestic adjustments were facilitated because investment abroad returned income flows that eliminated any need for radical austerity measures to balance international accounts. Mismanagement and failure occurred, but not really in any pursuit of a positive balance of payments. The war, however, forced massive liquidation of European assets abroad, made the United States Europe's creditor, and dislocated trade flows within Europe and between Europe and her markets elsewhere. By 1922—to take the date when American financiers and leaders sought to step in again—it was clear that some restoration of prewar trade and capital flows was needed, to rebuild not merely currency balances but the old equilibrium of social classes. The alternative was envisioned as economic chaos: the immiseration of the middle classes, the bolshevization of labor, a threat not merely of revolution but of gratuitous waste and suffering.

In theory there were several options for America's role in restoring financial and with it social equilibrium: cancellation of war debts, in-

[9] R. Stücken, *Deutsche Geld- und Kreditpolitik 1914–1963* (Tübingen, 1953), pp. 69–76; Rolf E. Lüke, *Von der Stabilisierung zur Krise* (Zurich, 1958), pp. 232–239; Gerd Hardach, "Die beiden Reichsbanken: Internationales Währungssystem und nationale Währungspolitik 1924–1931," Bochum Symposium paper, June 1973.

[10] Joan Hoff Wilson, *American Business and Foreign Policy 1920–1933* (Boston, 1973); Carl P. Parrini, *Heir to Empire: United States Economic Diplomacy, 1916–1923* (Pittsburgh, 1969); N. Gordon Levin, Jr., *Woodrow Wilson and World Politics: America's Response to War and Revolution* (New York, 1968).

creased purchases abroad, investment in Europe. Politics at home mili-
tated against the simple cancellation of debts. Southern Democrats
and Western Republicans, including old Progressives, resented the
Versailles settlement, suspected "Eastern" bankers, and feared that
their depressed farm constituents would face higher taxation. State
and Treasury Department leaders remained cautious after the Senate's
rejection of Versailles and the establishment of the Congressionally
dominated World War Foreign Debt Commission. Americans who had
interests in international trade and remained sensitive to European
business needs did work to minimize the Old World's debts through
interest reductions and extension of payment. The write-off amounted
to perhaps 43 percent of the total burden, but it still left an unsettling
obligation in existence. Massive imports were also precluded, in part
because of the protectionist policy pursued through the 1920's, but
also because Europeans manufactured or grew little that Americans
could not provide more cheaply for themselves. This left investment
abroad—especially in Germany, where capital scarcity and high productivity promised special rewards. The only prerequisite to this capital flood was regulation of the reparations issue, which Americans
helped to supervise from 1924 on.[11]

In the range of alternatives for the Atlantic economy, the American
relationship with England was critical. London had been the world
financial center and remained a major force for international stabilization. This relationship included elements of cooperation and rivalry.
The central bankers in New York and London, Benjamin Strong and
Montagu Norman, shared a deep commitment to restoration of the
gold standard or gold-exchange standard in which pound and dollar
would together serve as reserve currencies. Some conflicts of interest
existed: London could gain from interallied debt forgiveness, the
United States could not. Strong also feared that Norman's proposals
of 1922 might commit the United States to inflationary policies and
easy money in order to ease Britain's and other countries' revaluation.
Americans resisted again when Norman's financing of Schacht's Gold
Discount Bank threatened to cut the dollar out of Eastern and Central Europe. But U.S. representatives on the Committee of Experts

[11] Wilson, *American Business and Foreign Policy*, pp. 124–136; Benjamin D. Rhodes, "Reassessing 'Uncle Shylock': The United States and the French War Debt, 1917–1929," *Journal of American History*, LV, 4 (1969), pp. 787–803; Ellen W. Schrecker, "The French Debt to the United States, 1917–1929," Diss. (Cambridge, Mass., 1973); Melvyn Leffler, "The Origins of Republican Debt Policy, 1921–1923," *Journal of American History*, LIX, 4 (1972), pp. 585–601; Harold G. Moulton and Leo Pasvolsky, *War Debts and World Prosperity* (Washington, D.C., 1932), pp. 396–415. For an emphasis on structural European difficulties in producing for the American market, see M. E. Falkus, "United States Economic Policy and the 'Dollar Gap' of the 1920's," *Economic History Review*, 2nd series, XXIV, 4 (1971), pp. 599–623.

won a compromise with the German promise of an early return to a gold currency and full convertibility. American and British aspirations came back into alignment, especially because of London's need for continued support from New York upon the return to gold in 1925. Hewing to the high rate of $4.86 required the Federal Reserve Bank's continuing cooperation in preventing the draining of gold across the Atlantic. For about three years the priorities of the two monetary systems coincided, and this masked the true extent of British weakness and dependence. Strong and Norman overlooked until 1927 that the gold-exchange standard made greater demands on domestic economic policies than its prewar counterpart. It required more austerity in Britain and militated for a low-interest policy in New York, which contributed to superheated stock speculation. In short, the effort of convertibility really required a joint Anglo-American monetary policy when the two countries had different domestic requirements. Yet until the end of the 1920's, both partners felt that the banking leadership, commercial advantages, and the general facility of international exchange justified the adverse effects at home. Prosperity masked the inner stresses of the system, and indeed appeared to follow from it.[12]

No monetary system, however, can be free of the social-class relationships within which it is designed. Naturally enough, this one enhanced the influence and prestige of the central bankers and the representatives of the great private houses such as J. P. Morgan or Lazard Frères. As Strong repeatedly lectured, it depended upon bankers keeping their independence from national treasuries that might be tempted into inflation or exchange controls. Central bank sovereignty indicated that a country was a safe haven for stabilization loans and long-term foreign investment. But the gold-exchange standard had broader social repercussions as well. It remained America's price for remitting capital back to Europe. While it endured it required Europeans to maintain a permanent deflationary pressure at home. Such vigilance entailed clear social and political consequences: a downward

[12] Clarke, *Central Bank Cooperation*, pp. 34–40, 124 ff.; Milton Friedman and Anna J. Schwartz, *A Monetary History of the United States, 1867–1960* (Princeton, N.J., 1971), pp. 283–292; Lester V. Chandler, *Benjamin Strong, Central Banker* (Washington, D.C., 1958), pp. 316–331, 438–459; D. Williams, "London and the 1931 Financial Crisis," *Economic History Review*, 2nd series, xv, 3 (1962–1963), pp. 513–528; W. A. Brown, Jr., *The International Gold Standard Reinterpreted, 1914–1934*, 2 vols. (New York, 1940), ii, pp. 779–806. For the 1924 German issue, see Chapter Six, pp. 396–402, and Werner Link, *Die amerikanische Stabilisierungspolitik in Deutschland 1921–32* (Düsseldorf, 1970), pp. 223–240. For the 1924 controversy over Reichsmark convertibility see the extensive letter from Princeton economist and Dawes plan expert, Edward Kemmerer to Charles Evans Hughes, June 24, 1924 in U.S. Department of State Decimal Series 462.00R296/386. From Kemmerer's viewpoint the U.S. had championed an impartial and efficient gold exchange standard, while the British sought to work Germany into a sterling trade area.

pressure on employment, hence a restraint upon working-class bargaining power; an impulse to cartelization, "rationalization," and the subjection of small producers to large ones throughout Europe. American concepts of a stable international financial order—"the old fashioned religion which our firm has been sending to successive governments for the last three years," to use Thomas Lamont's phrase[13]—thus tended to reinforce a corporatist and bourgeois social settlement.

b. Yet if the international economic system exerted deflationary pressure, the requirements of *domestic* equilibrium would work the other way in the long run. Within each country the growing corporatist organization of interests made a recourse to long-term creeping inflation ever more likely. The avoidance of conflict demanded that no significant pressure group felt so aggrieved in the "allocation of burdens" that it might try to disrupt the economic or political system. So long as real national income kept approximate pace with the aggregate claims of different interests, the allocation of costs and benefits presented relatively little difficulty. But as had been demonstrated during World War I, inflation was available as a tempting if spurious way to purchase social peace. The easiest way for harried ministries or divided coalitions to arbitrate struggles between powerful interests was to pay off each one's claims in paper values without resistance. The real worth of the income shares would then work itself out subsequently. So long as aggregate income claims increased faster than real growth, the corporatist bargaining system entailed creeping inflation.[14]

Happily, the later 1920's enjoyed enough real expansion to offset inflationary pressures. The pressure that currency stabilization also exerted on domestic economies also counteracted the new institutional causes of inflation. The underlying bargaining mechanisms that made for inflation between 1914 and 1924 did not disappear, however. They were revealed no longer by the ravages of currency depreciation but by the limits that labor and industry jointly set upon appreciation or evaluation. Even while international performance demanded rigorous scrutiny of domestic price levels, long-term inflation lurked as a natural peril of corporatist bargaining in times of prosperity.

True, if any of the social partners accepted restraint, or if substan-

[13] Lamont to Russell C. Leffingwell, April 28, 1925, Baker Library, TWL, 103–111.
[14] The concept of cost-push inflation is relevant but tends to emphasize labor aspirations one-sidedly. See Fritz Machlup, "Another View of Cost-Push and Demand-Pull Inflation," *Review of Economics and Statistics*, vol. 42 (1960); P. Streeten, "Wages, Prices, and Productivity," *Kyklos*, xv (1962); F. W. Paish, "The Limits of Incomes Policies," in Paish and J. Hennessy, *Policy for Incomes* (1968), all reprinted in R. J. Ball and Peter Doyle, eds., *Inflation* (Harmondsworth, England and Baltimore, Md., 1969), pp. 149–185, 219–254.

tial unemployment weakened labor's bargaining power, the premises were altered. When the Depression struck, European governments tried ever more desperately to follow the deflationary priorities of the international system, then had to abandon this catastrophic competition to rescue employment and stability at home. After World War II the corporatist impulse to inflation reappeared as an affliction of prosperity. Yet the tensions that exist today between corporatist inflation and the priorities of international competition were first signaled as acute in the 1920's. Business rhetoric in that interval of expansion testified to the new antagonisms and anxieties that have remained inherent in corporatist prosperity.

2. The inflationary decade from 1914 to 1924 had brought together strong unions and big business in a price-wage spiral at the expense of the middle strata of society. Unfortunately, the deflationary *Konjunktur* thereafter did not reassure the middle strata. Income streams might be reconstituted, but the 80 percent write-off in currency values on the Continent was confirmed and not recovered. The movement toward the concentration of enterprises and the growth of large firms also struck at middle-class independence. The number of independent proprietors declined. Even if income for these beleaguered middle-class groups remained steady, their sense of independence and patrimony must have been eroded.

Ultimately, the unorganized losers—whether old middle-class artisans, shopkeepers, small producers, marginal farmers burdened with debts, or the new middle class of clerical workers and office employees —felt the need for defense. Losers both in inflation and revaluation, their reaction was to attack the corporatist collaboration of labor and industry. Unable to organize in a cohesive economic phalanx, for they faced diverse markets, they could still organize politically. The results would combine hostility to liberalism and organized labor with a vague rhetorical anticapitalism. Weimar Germany could not survive this new strain; France could—among other reasons, because the less developed corporatist organization of her society evoked a less intense right-radical response. The Radical Socialist constituency avoided fascism in the 1930's for the same reason that it had endured economic confusion in the 1920's: the continuing viability of economically archaic modes of livelihood. French democracy was to remain buffered by the society's proverbial reluctance to organize.[15]

[15] Heinrich August Winkler, *Mittelstand, Demokratie und Nationalsozialismus* (Cologne, 1972), and Winkler, "Extremismus der Mitte? Sozialgeschichtliche Aspekte der nazionalsozialistischen Machtergreifung," *Vierteljahreshefte für Zeitgeschichte*, xx, 2 (1972), pp. 175–191, for the best recent syntheses of the huge literature on Nazism and middle-class resentment. For a prediction that the French middle classes in the 1930's must provide a reservoir for fascism, see Leon Trotsky's *Whither France?* [1936] (New York, 1968), pp. 12–24.

If National Socialism is viewed in the perspective of Weimar's corporatism, it becomes evident how different it remained from Italian fascism. The difference takes us to the heart of the developments underway in the 1920's. At the beginning of the decade Italian fascism emerged as a new, coercive way of reestablishing a scaffolding for elites once the old one had corroded with mass suffrage and the war. It involved a coalition between traditional leadership groups and new middle-class allies as well as a young, urban bourgeois cadre mobilized since Intervention. Nazism grouped some of the same elements, but the mix was different, as were the reasons for its success. Before the seizure of power the role of traditional elites may well have been smaller in Nazism, the middle-class objectives more predominant. In the absence of more than a few local studies, estimates of social composition must remain risky. But statements about function are possible. In Italy fascism remedied a defective organization of middle-class and elite elements. If Italy had earlier developed a liberal corporatism to replace her antique parliamentary and party structure, fascism might well have appeared unnecessary for bourgeois defense. On the other hand, if Germany had not passed through the crucible of capitalist corporatism, Nazism might have seemed unnecessary for middle-class viability. Italian fascism substituted for prior organization in the political arena or marketplace; German Nazism arose in resentment against the organization that seemed to dominate.[16]

Nazism thus testified to the success of restoration in the 1920's. The elites of industry and land succeeded too well in the Weimar Republic: by engineering their restoration within a corporatist framework, they provoked a grass-roots rebellion against the capitalist marketplace—against all its liberal rules of the game as well as its economic outcomes. While Italian fascism testified to the preindustrial formation of the Italian elite, Nazism reflected what was simultaneously most retrograde and most modern: retrograde, because in Germany the guild usages of the pre-Napoleonic era—the stress on municipal independence,

---

[16] Cf. De Felice, *Le interpretazioni del fascismo*, pp. 256–266, for an emphasis on German-Italian parallels in mobilizing the resentments of the *ceti medi*. For a résumé of what studies exist on social composition of the Italian Fascist Party (which became more "respectable" and upper-echelon between 1925 and 1928), see Renzo De Felice, *Mussolini il fascista*, vol. II, *L'organizzazione dello stato fascista, 1925–1929* (Turin, 1968), pp. 188–192; and Adrian Lyttelton, *The Seizure of Power: Fascism in Italy 1919–1929* (London, 1973), pp. 54–71, 303–305; the most recent study on Germany is Jeremy Noakes, *The Nazi Party in Lower Saxony 1921–1933* (London, 1971). Cf. William S. Allen, *The Nazi Seizure of Power: The Experience of a Small German Town* (Chicago, 1965) and the review of earlier literature in Seymour Martin Lipset, *Political Man* (New York, 1963), pp. 127–151. Cf. Charles S. Maier, "Strukturen kapitalistischer Stabilität in den zwanziger Jahren: Errungenschaften und Defekte," in Winkler, ed., *Organisierter Kapitalismus*, pp. 206–208.

estatist divisions, elaborate self-enclosed associations—were carried forward to clutter up the twentieth-century sociopolitical landscape; modern, because corporate capitalism and corporatist pluralism have increasingly prevailed as forms of social organization since the 1920's in all Western societies. Nazism tried to build off pre-industrial corporatism and annul the more recent. It ended by destroying the first and leaving the second largely unscathed.

At the end, the history of the 1920's besets us with its contradictions: Nazism as the revolt against the corporatist state; French democracy tenable because of its relative backwardness in terms of corporatist organization; the utility of international deflation to consolidate a social order that would tend ultimately to purchase stability by continuous doses of inflation.

These paradoxes testify to the discrepancy between change and its perception. The history of the 1920's is marked by the inadequacy of its contemporary ideologies to analyze true social transformation. The categories implicit in political activity—the explanatory approximations embedded in left vs. right, bourgeois vs. socialist—overlapped with the realities of conflict but obscured some of the true stakes. The slogans of the 1920's—the electoral efforts to form bourgeois blocks or "unions" against a factious left, to unite the tenacious holders of small property with socialists against "reaction"—encouraged conceptions of a polarized society that were increasingly irrelevant. Only when basic ideological outcomes became the central stake of struggle again in the 1930's did the model of polarization temporarily reconverge with the real struggle underway. Meanwhile, party labels and contests revealed little of social tensions and transformation.

Each side offered its own distortions. Conservatives were successful in restoring to the 1920's the appearance of happier days, but they insisted on a concept of bourgeois society as their supposed goal. Their model was archaic: it implied that conservatives wanted a sharp separation of state and society, public and private sectors, and furthermore that stability was to be rescued from a militant proletariat. These images of society were not adequate to comprehend reality as the 1920's continued the restless push toward corporate organization that World War I had generated. Organization was sensed to be the prerequisite of group survival, the basis for holding on to a secure percentage of national income or a stable share of votes, power, and prestige. Devolution of authority on interest groups had advanced between 1914 and 1918 and now continued in the 1920's. Either by dialectical tricks or cudgeling opponents into submission, supporters tried to claim that this development was actually enhancing public authority. Undoubtedly feudalism had also been presented as a prop to kingship. Bourgeois victory was briefly secured, but only by resorting to the corporatist settlements that undermined the basic anchoring conceptions of the bourgeoisie. Rescuing bourgeois Europe meant recasting bourgeois Europe: dealing with unions (or creating pseudo-unions as in Italy), giving state agencies control over the market, building interest-group spokesmen into the structure of the state.

An analogous structure of stability arose and endured after World War II, based on agreement between chastened social democrats and moderates either to share or to alternate power and to exclude more extreme alternatives of right and left; upon a Western internationalism hinged on coal and steel exchanges and exclusion of Russia; upon U.S. resolution of a balance-of-payments crisis and similar demands for convertibility; upon the interpenetration of state and economy within each national unit. The system after World War II thus retained the old liabilities—the prolongation of Cold War rigidity, confinement of much of the working class to a political ghetto, and an end to criticism of the authority relations in an industrial economy in return for increased welfare. To what degree alternatives were practical cannot be discussed here.

Presumably the system bought sufficient acquiescence to continue through the 1960's. Institutions no longer trembled under the blows of the old challengers or the issues of income distribution that vexed the 1920's. Instead, decolonization agonies or old ethnic antagonisms proved debilitating at times; while the very success of corporatist equilibrium brought its own brief rebellion at the end of the 1960's against the bureaucratic, rationalist terms of stability. Finally, the pressures toward corporatist inflation immanent within the system seem to have emerged as a basic affliction—aggravated today by a rise in primary product prices that the 1920's never faced. This does not mean that internal contradictions must overwhelm the stability attained. Some of the tensions today are reminiscent of those of the late 1920's, but the popular base of prosperity is broader; the reorientation of men as consumers and audience has proceeded further. But neither are all crises to be surmounted without deep change. Distributions of power and privilege can alter swiftly; at the very least they evolve inexorably. In the wake of the catastrophes that followed, historians perceived the 1920's as the often congenial, yet darkening twilight of the liberal era. But if a twilight decade, the 1920's was one of morning as well as dusk, slowly bringing into focus the transformations that carried capitalist societies through a half-century transit. The upheavals that have intervened, or those still to come, should not obscure that conservative achievement.

BIBLIOGRAPHY

Preparation of this inventory has painfully emphasized the limitations of my research. For any broad consideration of political and economic stabilization almost all documentation is of potential value, and for a period as close as the 1920's one can merely attempt to take intelligent samples. Orientation of research around different issues and conflicts rather than parties or groups has required reading that is certainly eclectic and perhaps diffuse and deficient. I have sought to exploit a wide variety of archival material, but there remain gaps, which I signal below. Naturally I remain indebted as well to the scholarly monographs and syntheses contributed by others.

I have not broken down archival collections into consistently fine subgroups, nor have I listed particular cartons or folders. The footnotes provide a closer identification of relevant documents. Moreover, anyone who has dredged through archival holdings understands how unevenly material is dispersed: how many folders must be skimmed to come finally to a collection that is dense and rewarding.

A preliminary word about the different categories of documentation:

1. Foreign Ministry archives are too rich to be left to students of international relations alone. Any negotiations that concerned economic issues entailed studies and discussions of business conditions at home and abroad and often consultation with industry leaders. The different foreign ministries vary in the value of their records. The German Foreign Ministry records are meticulously organized by functional as well as some geographic divisions. Carbons of papers were sent upward through the bureaucracy or to other agencies according to their general importance. Reading the files at the level of the Reichsminister or the permanent State Secretary provides insight into significant issues, but for many important questions with economic repercussions, the files of the lower desks or the personal files of second-echelon officials are even more important. The necessary research tool is George O. Kent, *A Catalog of Files and Microfilms of the German Foreign Ministry Archives*, 4 vols. (Stanford, 1962–1972).

The French records are sparser, in part because of losses sustained in 1940 and 1944, but also because the inner organization of the Quai d'Orsay was less elaborate and systematic. Its diplomacy relied on brilliant division chiefs—Seydoux, Laroche, Peretti—more than thorough staff procedures. It also maintained a distance from industry spokesmen that diminishes the value of its records for students of internal affairs.

The British Foreign Office rivaled German efficiency although it worked differently. Fewer permanent departments kept files; instead documents were "jacketed," then to rise for scrutiny, comment, and disposition. Important reports and position papers were printed and circulated as "confidential prints," but selection was limited. Since I wished to check British policy and observations only as it impinged on the political issues of the Continent, I explored only a tiny outcropping of this archival massif. I am indebted to my colleague Stephen A. Schuker who helped guide Widener Library's acquisitions of the filmed Public Records Office holdings of the 1920's. For the pre-1921 years I relied on the printed *Documents on British Foreign Policy*, First Series.

In view of the differing causes of Italian domestic divisions I did not use foreign ministry documentation in Rome. I took soundings in the Records of the Department of State Relating to the Internal Affairs of France, of Germany, and of Italy (U.S. National Archives record groups M560, M336, and M527, incorporating State Department Decimal Series 851.50, 851.51, 862.00, 862.19, 862.51, 865.00, 865.51) and also in the decimal series concerning reparations (462.00R296). But I did not utilize these sources consistently and have omitted them from the list below.

2. Records relating to internal affairs differ in value from country to country. Cabinet protocols are important for Germany (and often Great Britain), more rudimentary in Italy, and to my knowledge unavailable for France. German cabinet papers form part of a large Reich Chancellery collection with many issue-oriented files now held at the Bundesarchiv and being published selectively (see below). Selections are also available as part of the filmed German Foreign Ministry holdings (Alte Reichskanzlei). Limited time at Potsdam precluded an equally thorough use of the Presidential Chancellery files although some files were used. The Italian cabinet protocols (*verbali*) are generally perfunctory, and the cabinet documents (*atti del gabinetto*) preserved as part of the archive of the President of the Council are uneven in value. They include petitions from economic groupings which are of greater significance in the late 1920's; but I have relied primarily on Adrian Lyttelton's excellent discussion and evaluation for this period: *The Seizure of Power. Fascism in Italy 1919–1929* (London, 1973). The Rome central state archives store the massive Ministry of the Interior files with their prefectural reports broken down by year, region, and subject—a major source for political and economic trends. No equally broad collection seems available in France for the twenties. I was allowed to consult a special file of prefectural reports on "Esprit Public" submitted during 1923–1924 in view of the elections.

For questions of public finance, the French Ministry of Finance holdings include valuable memoranda from the permanent Directeur du Mouvement Général des Fonds which starkly posed policy alternatives. German Finance Ministry records were more technical and less revealing on broad issues, but can be supplemented by Max Warburg's important records. And while Italian Finance Ministry files are unavailable, the Volpi papers contain lengthy correspondence with Mussolini concerning the revaluation of the lira.

The dilemmas of heavy industry are illuminated by the French Ministry of Commerce archives as well as the holdings of the national coal authority (Bureau National de Charbon). German Foreign Ministry monitoring of coal and iron negotiations as well as the Ruhr situation allowed for some archival equivalence across the Rhine. One major source had to remain underutilized because of limits of time and cumbersome procedures. Although early visits to the Deutsches Zentralarchiv in Potsdam allowed scrutiny of the record of the German Nationalist Party and of the Provisional Economic Council—the latter revealing for the extensive policy discussions among labor and management delegates—an effort to arrange a later consultation of the holdings of the Economic Ministry was unsuccessful. I was, however, provided with certain selected microfilmed documents on revaluation as this book was being proofread. There remains rich material pertaining to tariff and labor issues of the latter 1920's. Dirk Stegmann, who has worked extensively in these papers, will be able to provide a full picture of interest-group logrolling in the period of stabilization.

The archives of corporations and industrial federations proved immensely valuable. The holdings of the former Pont-à-Mousson foundries offer only a partial view of the French steel community yet an important one, especially since Wendel's records remained closed to me. German firm archives are more accessible: the Gutehoffnungshütte files are especially rich; Krupp also made available important documentation. At the Bundesarchiv the scholar can consult the informative records of the former Union of German Iron and Steel Industrialists with transcripts of important business meetings and the papers of Rhenish industrialist Paul Silverberg. At the Bergbau-Archiv in Bochum there are several files important for the history of Ruhr mining and labor relations. I know of no Italian equivalents presently open to scholars; however, Mario Abrate has had the opportunity to exploit the archive of the Turin Industrial League, and although his interpretations can be questioned, he has presented rich material. See *La lotta sindacale nell'industrializzazione in Italia 1906–26* (Turin, 1967).

3. For political organization the personal papers listed below become essential. The Stresemann and Westarp collections are important

597

for the DVP and DNVP; Koch-Weser for the Democratic Party. The Segreteria Personale del Duce is really an "official" collection, but along with its important Grand Council file it extensively documents the cross-currents of fascism as do the Farinacci and Bianchi papers. The Salandra correspondence in Lucera illuminates the elitist politics of right-wing liberalism. Newspapers are not sufficiently reliable for following critical economic or international negotiations, but are crucial for understanding party rivalries and electoral contests. Political pamphlets, printed speeches, and résumés of party conventions are available in several collections at the Bundesarchiv, the holdings of the Volksverein für das katholische Deutschland at the Mönchen-Gladbach municipal library, and the Bibliothèque de Documentation Internationale Contemporaine at Nanterre.

4. I have not listed printed memoirs, writings, and letters save for a few essential editions. Along with articles, monographs and other secondary sources they are cited fully at first reference in each chapter, where the reader can find them grouped topically. For historical background, works of sociology and specific sociological analyses, the reader should refer to the citations in the Introduction and Chapter 1, Sections 1 and 2. For discussions of entrepreneurial organization and business policy see Chapter 3, Section 3; Chapter 4, Section 2; Chapter 6, Section 2; Chapter 8, Section 2. For labor relations see Chapter 1, Section 3; Chapter 3, Sections 1 and 2; Chapter 6, Section 1; Chapter 7, Section 2 (German conditions); and Chapter 8, Section 3 (Italian developments). Labor conflicts in the Italian countryside are discussed in Chapter 1, Section 2; Chapter 3, Section 2; and Chapter 5, Section 1. For works concerning monetary difficulties see the notes to Chapter 4, Section 1 (reparations and public finance); Chapter 6, Section 1 (inflation); Chapter 7, Section 2 (French public finance); and Chapter 8, Sections 1 and 3 (revaluation). Sources relating to foreign policy will be cited in Chapter 3, Section 3; Chapter 4, Section 1; and Chapter 6, Section 2. Writing on political parties and elections is noted preeminently in Chapters 2 and 7.

A final note: the essays referred to in the footnotes under the general category of Bochum Symposium papers have now been published: Hans Mommsen, Dietmar Petzina, and Bernd Weisbrod, eds., *Industrielles System und politische Entwicklung in der Weimarer Republik* (Düsseldorf, 1974).

I. Manuscript Sources

1. *Official Archives*

France
Ministère des Affaires Etrangères, Quai d'Orsay, Paris.
Série: A Paix (Carton 1374)
Série: Europe, 1918–1929
Allemagne
Rive Gauche du Rhin
Ruhr
Fonds Président Herriot
Ministère du Commerce, Archives Nationales, Paris (F^{12}).
Ministère des Finances, Archives Nationales (F^{30}) and consultable at the Ministry.
Bureau National de Charbon, Archives Nationales (AJ^{26}).
Commission Interalliée des Réparations, Archives Nationales (AJ^6).
Rapports sur l'esprit public et les élections, Archives Nationales (F 1C III).

Germany
National Archives microfilms of the German Foreign Ministry (T 120).
Major divisions include:
Büro des Reichsministers
Büro des Staatssekretärs
Politische Abteilung II (Western Europe)
Besetztes Rheinland
Abteilung II: Wirtschaft
Sonderreferat Wirtschaft
Wirtschaft Reparation
Alte Reichskanzlei
Kabinettsprotokolle
Kabinettsbildung
Collections by subject now available at the Bundesarchiv, Reichskanzlei (R 43 I)
Collections arranged by person
Gustav Stresemann Nachlass (See under Personal Papers)
Ago von Maltzan Nachlass
Handakten des Ministerialdirektors Karl Ritter
Handakten des Staatssekretärs Carl von Schubert
Reichsfinanzministerium, Bundesarchiv, Koblenz (R2)
Reichskanzlei, Bundesarchiv (R 43 I)

Büro des Reichspräsidenten (post-1933: Präsidialkanzlei), Deutsches Zentralarchiv, Potsdam (06.01)

Vorläufiger Reichswirtschaftsrat, Deutsches Zentralarchiv (04.01) Includes transcripts of plenary sessions and Finanzpolitischer, Sozialpolitischer, Wirtschaftspolitischer, and Reparations-Ausschüsse.

Zentralarbeitsgemeinschaft, Deutsches Zentralarchiv (70 Zel) films of central committee, 1918–1924, provided by Gerald Feldman.

Great Britain
Cabinet Office: Public Records Office microfilms held by Widener Library, Harvard University.
Cabinet Conclusions (CAB 23)
Cabinet Memoranda (CAB 24)
Cabinet Committees (CAB 27:71, Finance Committee)
Interallied Conferences (CAB 29)
Foreign Office: Public Records Office microfilms at Widener Library.
Political Correspondence (FO 371)
Confidential Print: Germany (FO 408)

Italy
Archivio della Presidenza del Consiglio, Archivio Centrale dello Stato (ACS), Rome:
Archivio del Gabinetto
Consiglio dei Ministri: Verbali
Serie Speciale: Prima Guerra Mondiale, 1915–1918 (1920)
Ministero dell'Interno, Direzione Generale della Pubblica Sicurezza, (ACS), Rome:
Divisione Affari Generali e Riservati (1914–1926)
Divisione Affari Generali e Riservati (1903–1949)
Divisione Affari Generali e Riservati, Prima Guerra Mondiale
Ministero dell'Interno:
Gabinetto di S.E. Bonomi: Ordine Pubblico
Gabinetto di S.E. Finzi: Ordine Pubblico
Ufficio Cifra, Telegrammi in arrivo, Telegrammi in partenza.
Mostra della Rivoluzione Fascista, ACS.
Segreteria particolare del Duce, ACS; available also as National Archives Microcopy T586.
Among the massive Ministry of the Interior Files the Direzione Generale della Pubblica Sicurezza, Divisione Affari Generali e Riservati (1914–1926) comprises the major record with continuing prefectural reports on parties and associations. The large Segreteria particolare ex-

tends until 1945 and is arranged by correspondent but includes many records pertaining to the Grand Council as well. The first roll of the National Archives Microcopy provides a detailed inventory of its holdings. The "Mostra" contains the material assembled for the Fascist Party exposition of 1932. The portions of relevance include descriptions of controversies between local elites and fascist militants before the March on Rome.

2. *Parties, Pressure Groups, Corporations*

Deutsche Demokratische Partei papers, available at the Bundesarchiv but read here as part of the NSDAP Hauptarchiv, Stanford University microfilm of the original Berlin Document Center holdings, rolls 36–38.

Deutsche Volkspartei papers, Bundesarchiv (R 45 II)

Deutschnationale Volkspartei papers, Deutsches Zentralarchiv (53 Vo 2)

Wirtschaftsgruppe Eisenschaffende Industrie (Verein deutscher Eisen- und Stahlindustrieller) Bundesarchiv (R 13 I)

Wirtschaftsvereinigung Bergbau; earlier: Fachgruppe Bergbau, Bergbau-Archiv, Bochum (15)

Compagnie de Saint-Gobain-Pont-à-Mousson, archives at La Châtre (Indre):
  Direction Générale: Camille Cavallier
  Direction Générale: Marcel Paul
  Service Commercial; Service des Mines; Service Central des Usines, etc.

Friedrich Krupp A.G., Villa Hügel, Essen:
  Werksarchiv, including Otto Wiedfeldt papers
  Familienarchiv

Gutehoffnungshütte A.G. Firmenarchiv (including Paul Reusch papers), Oberhausen.

Klöckner Berghau Victor-Ickern A.G., Castorp Rauxel, Bergbau-Archiv (25).

Zechenverband papers, Bergbau-Archiv (13).

3. *Personal Papers, Including Unpublished Memoirs*

France
  F. François-Marsal, "La crise présidentielle et l'éviction de Millerand," MS communicated by his son Claude François-Marsal.
  Louis Loucheur papers, Hoover Institution, Stanford University.
  Lucien Lamoureux, "Souvenirs politiques 1919–1940," MS at the Bibliothèque de Documentation Internationale Contemporaine, Nanterre.

France (*cont.*)

Alexandre Millerand papers, Bibliothèque Nationale, Paris.

Alexandre Millerand, "Mes Souvenirs (1859–1941): Contribution à l'histoire de la Troisième République," MS communicated by his son Jacques Millerand.

Raymond Poincaré papers, Bibliothèque Nationale (of little value).

Germany

Gustav Stresemann Nachlass (filmed as part of the National Archives, German Foreign Ministry collection):

Allgemeine Akten (1924 and after)

Deutsche Volkspartei Akten

Industrie Organisation

Politische Akten

Kuno Graf von Westarp Nachlass (in possession of Friedrich Freiherr Hiller von Gaertringen, Gaertringen):

"Konservative Politik in der Republik 1918–1932. Neue Aufgaben und Ziele bis zum 6.6.1920," MS.

"Ruhrkampf Fragment," MS.

Correspondence

Max Warburg papers, formerly at the Warburg Institute, London, now at M. M. Warburg-Brinckmann, Wirtz & Co., Hamburg.

Nachlässe at the Bundesarchiv, Koblenz:

Moritz Julius Bonn

Eduard Dingeldey

Otto Gessler

Georg Gothein

Siegfried von Kardorff

Katherina von Kardorff-Oheimb

Erich Koch-Weser

Wichard von Moellendorff

Gustav Rösicke

Paul Silverberg

Gustav Traub

Rudolf Wissell

Nachlässe at the Deutsches Zentralarchiv, Potsdam:

Rudolf Havenstein

Conrad Freiherr von Wangenheim

In addition the filmed *Nachlässe* of Generals Hans Seeckt, Wilhelm Gröner, and the papers of Kurt von Schleicher and Colonel Haeften, formerly at the Bundesarchiv, were also consulted although they proved peripheral.

Italy
Mussolini papers: see under Segreteria particolare del Duce.
Antonio Salandra papers, Biblioteca Comunale "Ruggero Bonghi,"
Lucera.
Carteggi at the Archivio Centrale dello Stato, Rome:
Michele Bianchi
Tullio Cianetti
Roberto Farinacci
Giovanni Giolitti (all important items have been printed. See,
below: *Quarant'anni di politica italiana: dalle carte di G.G.*).
Francesco Nitti
Vittorio E. Orlando
Carlo Schanzer
Andrea Torre
Giuseppe Volpi di Misurata

United States
Thomas W. Lamont papers, Baker Library, Harvard University
School of Business Administration

II. Published Primary Sources

1. *Parliamentary Papers, Government Publications, and Related Records*

A. parliamentary sessions

Atti del Parlamento Italiano, *Discussioni della Camera dei Deputati*, Legislatura xxiv-Legislatura xxvii, vols. 918 ff. (1917 on).
Atti Parlamentari della Camera dei Senatori. *Discussioni*, vols. 929 ff. (1917 on).
Journal Officiel de la République Française. Chambre des Députés. *Débats Parlementaires* (1917 on).
Journal Officiel de la République Française. Sénat. *Débats Parlementaires* (1917 on).
Verhandlungen der verfassungsgebenden Deutschen Nationalversammlung. *Stenographische Berichte*, vols. 326 ff. (1919–1920).
Verhandlungen des Deutschen Reichstages. *Stenographische Berichte*, vols. 344 ff. (1920 on).

B. material relating to elections

Istituto Centrale di Statistica and Ministero per la Costituente, *Compendio delle statistiche elettorali italiane dal 1848 al 1934*, 2 vols. (Rome, 1946).

Procès-Verbaux de la Commission d'Enquête sur les conditions dans lesquelles le Comité de l'Union des Interêts Économiques est intervenu dans la dernière campagne électorale, ainsi sur l'origine des fonds ayant servi à tous les partis en 1924. Journal Officiel, *Impressions*, xxxii, No. 2098 (Paris, 1925).

Programmes, professions de foi et engagements électoraux de 1919 (Paris, 1920).

Programmes, professions de foi et engagements électoraux de 1924 (Paris, 1925).

(These volumes were informally known as "Barodet.")

"Die Wahlen zur verfassungsgebenden Deutschen Nationalversammlung am 19. January 1919." *Vierteljahreshefte zur Statistik des Deutschen Reiches*, 28.Jg. 1919, 1. *Ergänzungsheft* (Berlin 1919).

"Die Wahlen zum Reichstag am 6. Juni 1920." *Statistik des Deutschen Reiches*, Bd. 291.

"Die Wahlen zum Reichstag am 4. Mai und am 7. Dezember 1924," *Statistik des Deutschen Reiches*, Bd. 315.

French electoral results are available in the "Barodet" volumes or Georges Lachapelle, ed., *Élections législatives du 16 novembre 1919* (Paris, 1919) and *Élections législatives du 11 mai 1924* (Paris, 1925).

C. PUBLISHED MINISTERIAL RECORDS

Germany

Akten der Reichskanzlei: Weimarer Republik, Karl Dietrich Erdmann and Wolfgang Mommsen, eds.:

Das Kabinett Scheidemann. 13. Februar bis 20. Juni 1919, Hagen Schulze, ed., (Boppard am Rhein, 1971).

Das Kabinett Cuno. 22. November 1922 bis 12. August 1923, Karl Heinz Harbeck, ed., (Boppard am Rhein, 1968).

Die Kabinette Marx I und II. 30. November 1923 bis 3. Juni 1924. 3. Juni. 1924 bis 15. Januar 1925. Günter Abramowski, ed., (Boppard am Rhein, 1973).

Quellen zur Geschichte des Parlamentarismus und der politischen Parteien, 1. Reihe:

Die Regierung des Prinzen Marx von Baden, Erich Matthias and Rudolf Morsey, eds., (Düsseldorf, 1962).

Die Regierung der Volksbeauftragten, Erich Matthias and Suzanne Miller, eds., 2 vols. (Düsseldorf, 1966).

Great Britain

Documents on British Foreign Policy, 1919–1939, First Series, E. L. Woodward and Rohan Butler, eds. (London, 1947 on).

Italy

Gli atti dei congressi del Partito Popolare Italiano, Francesco Malgeri, ed., (Brescia, 1969).

Partito Nazionale Fascista, *Il Gran Consiglio nei primi sei anni dell'era fascista* (Rome, n.d.).

D. MATERIAL RELATING TO ECONOMIC ISSUES

Bureau International du Travail, *Enquête sur la production. Rapport général*, 5 vols. (Paris, 1923–1925).

Ausschuss zur Untersuchung der Erzeugungs- und Absatzbedingungen der deutschen Wirtschaft (Enquête-Ausschuss):
  III. Unterausschuss, *Die deutsche eisenerzeugende Industrie* (Berlin, 1930);
  III. Unterausschuss, *Die Rohstoffversorgung der deutschen eisenerzeugenden Industrie* (Berlin, 1928);
  IV. Unterausschuss, *Die Arbeitsverhältnisse im Steinkohlenbergbau in den Jahren 1912 bis 1926* (Berlin, 1928).

Istituto Nazionale di Economia Agraria, *Inchiesta sulla piccola proprietà formatasi nel dopoguerra*, vol. xv, Giovanni Lorenzoni, *Relazione finale, L'ascesa del contadino italiano nel dopoguerra* (Rome, 1938).

Mission Interalliée de Contrôle des Usines et des Mines (MICUM), *Enquetes générales faites dans la Ruhr en 1923 et 1924*, 10 subvols. (Brussels, 1924).

Verhandlungen der Sozialisierungskommission über den Kohlenbergbau im Jahre 1920, 2 vols. (Berlin, 1920).

Verhandlungen der Sozialisierungskommission über die Organisation der Reichseisenbahnen (Berlin, 1922).

2. *Press and Periodical Literature*

A. NEWSPAPERS AND JOURNALS

France

L'Action Française: Ultra-nationalist daily; except for Jacques Bainville the "paranoid style" in French politics (Charles Maurras and Léon Daudet).

L'Echo de Paris: Bourgeois right-wing nationalist; clerical and military influences (Pertinax and Marcel Hutin).

La Journée Industrielle: Coverage of business and industry; friendly to manufacturers yet often independent vis-à-vis heavy industry (Lucien Romier through 1924).

Revue des Deux Mondes: Fusty, *bien pensant* biweekly, featuring Académie Française style, but a well-informed "Chronique de la Quinzaine" written by Raymond Poincaré, 1920–1921.

France (*cont.*)

Revue Politique et Parlementaire: monthly coverage of legislation and politics; open to political statements, commentary, and fiscal analyses of the left center and *moderés*; a revealing "Chronique politique," written by François Albert and after 1924 the less informative Edouard Julia.

Le Temps: "Official," gray, fiscally orthodox.

Germany

Berliner Tageblatt: DDP-affiliated Berlin daily; good political and economic coverage (Theodor Wolff, ed.; Felix Pinner, financial columnist).

Berliner Lokal-Anzeiger: Lively, rightwing daily; Hugenberg affiliated.

Deutsche Allgemeine Zeitung: Former "official" *Nord-deutsche Allgemeine* sold to Stinnes in 1920 and largely reflecting his views.

Neue Preussische (Kreuz-)Zeitung: Prussian conservative and Nationalist (Westarp and Otto Hoetzsch).

Italy

Il Corriere della Sera: Milan's major daily, reflecting Albertini's elitist liberalism until his removal in 1925 (Albertini, Luigi Einaudi, Giovanni Amendola).

Il Giornale d'Italia: Conservative Rome daily reflecting a Sonnino-Salandra viewpoint and somewhat to the right of the *Corriere*.

L'Idea Nazionale: Close to being the *Action Française* of Italy: Nationalist and intemperate, financed by heavy industry.

La Stampa: Alberto Frassati's Turin daily; generally liberal-democratic and friendly to Giolitti.

Coverage of the press was facilitated for the 1918–1919 period by the General Staff of the British War Office: *Daily Review of the Foreign Press: Allied Press Supplement, Enemy Press Supplement*, and *Economic Supplement*. Clipping files in many of the German archival collections consulted allowed broad coverage of special topics. Newspapers thus sampled included the weekly *Deutsche Arbeitgeber-Zeitung* (organ of the employers' association), the *Deutsche Tageszeitung* (agrarian conservative), the *Kölnische Zeitung* (DVP and pro-industry), *Vorwärts* (Social Democratic). The Emeroteca at the Biblioteca Nazionale in Rome also allowed reading in additional newspapers for periods of special interest: *Il Resto del Carlino* (the liberal, increasingly philo-fascist daily of Bologna) and *Il Sole* (Milan's business daily). I did not follow the Fascist *Popolo d'Italia*, but utilized Mussolini's *Opera Omnia* (see below).

B. PUBLICATIONS OF SOCIAL AND ECONOMIC INTEREST

Archiv für Sozialwissenschaft und Sozialpolitik (A journal for brilliant sociology, and valuable analysis of social-reform legislation especially after the revolution).

Archives de la Chambre de Commerce de Lille, vols. LIV and ff.

Bulletin de la Statistique Générale (Studies of income and wealth).

Compte rendu des Travaux de la Chambre de Commerce de Lyon, 1919 and after (these yearly publications offer some insights into regional economic concerns in France).

Riccardo Bacchi, *L'Italia ecònomica nel 1919*, and following years.

Giuseppe Mortara, *Prospettive economiche*, 1921 and following (Major annual reviews of the Italian economy including banking and finance).

L'Organizzazione Industriale (Confindustria biweekly).

Le Reveil Economique (Union des Interèts Economiques biweekly— but more frequently near elections; of interest for 1919).

La Riforma Sociale (Einaudi's journal with interesting studies of taxation and wages).

Veröffentlichungen des Reichsverbandes der deutschen Industrie (Special studies and protocols of some discussions among industrialists).

3. *Selected Published Papers and Correspondence*

Luigi Albertini, *Epistolario 1911–1926*, Ottavio Barié, ed., 4 vols. (Verona, 1968).

Benito Mussolini, *Opera Omnia*, Duilio and Edoardo Susmel, eds., 35 vols. (Florence, 1951–1963), esp. vols. XIX–XXIII.

Der Nachlass des Reichskanzlers Wilhelm Marx, Hugo Stehkämper, ed., 4 vols. (*Mitteilungen aus dem Stadtarchiv von Köln*, 52–55, 1968).

Quarant'anni di politica italiana: dalle carte di Giovanni Giolitti, vol. III, *Dai prodromi della grande guerra al fascismo 1910–1928*, Claudio Pavone, ed. (Milan, 1962).

Gustav Stresemann, *Vermächtnis. Der Nachlass in drei Bänden*, Harry Bernhard, ed., 3 vols. (Berlin, 1932).

Filippo Turati-Anna Kuliscioff, *Carteggio*, 6 vols. (Turin, 1949–1953).

This index provides brief identification of persons, organizations, and specialized terms. Place names occurring in lists of electoral percentages or strikes have not generally been indexed. Neither have names in footnotes unless substantive discussion is involved. I have relied on subject entries with national subdivisions rather than upon omnibus listing under "France," "Germany," and "Italy." In conformity with their respective usages, French and German names including "de" or "von" have been alphabetized under the major part of the name, while Italian names beginning with "De" or "Di" have been indexed under those prefixes. German umlauts count as an "e" following their respective vowels and have been alphabetized accordingly.

Camelots du Roi (Action Française "youth group"), 404

Camera del Lavoro (local Socialist labor foyers), and Fascist attacks, 309, 319

Cannes Conference (1922), 268, 276, 278–279

capital levy, discussed in France, 466, 495, 498–499, 505–506

capitalism: and corporatism, 565, 567, 577; developments in, 10n, 15, 594; and planning, 143, 146; resilience and vulnerability, 136, 150–151, 544–545

Caporetto (Italian defeat, 1917), 120

Caprivi, Leo (Chancellor, 1890–1894), 34

carbonari, 24

caroviveri (high cost of living), 117. See also inflation, prices

Cartel des Gauches (1924 electoral coalition of Radicals and Socialists), 103, 478, 496, 508, 522, 528; and elections, 472–474; and finances, 494–496, 500, 534; political divisions within, 481, 494–496, 498–500, 505, 508; and trade negotiations, 534, 537–538

cartelization and cartels, 12, 416, 483, 516–517, 576, 590

Casati, Alessandro (rightwing liberal deputy), and cabinet crises of 1924, 550, 552, 554–555 and 555n

Cassagnac, Paul de (rightwing deputy), and labor, 193

Cassel, Gustav (Swedish economist), and report on German finances, 297, 302

Castelnau, General Curières de, 475

Castiglione, Camillo (Italo-Austrian financier), 261 n

Catholic Center Party, see Center Party

Catholics, organization of, 7;
in France: 31, 95, 99–100
in Germany: 35, 158, 452–454; and Factory Councils, 449; and social issues, 223, 491, 512. See also Center Party, German
in Italy: and elections, 116, 123–124, 128–129, 435; and Giolitti, 123, 183, 336, 548; and labor conflict, 174–175, 335–336; and Mussolini, 348–349; and politics, 89, 123–124, 133, 179–180, 336. See also Partito Popolare Italiano

Cavallier, Camille (director of the

Pont-à-Mousson foundries), 71, 199, 529–531

Cavazzoni, Stefano (Popolare Minister of Labor and Social Welfare under Mussolini), and electoral law, 348

Caviglia, General Enrico, 307

Cavour, Camillo Benso di, and Italian South, 434

"ceilings" on monetary circulation and Bank advances, in France, 495, 498, 504

center, in politics: coalitions, 229–231; failure of, 304

Center Party, German (Deutsche Zentrumspartei: Catholic political formation): and elections of 1924, 452; ideological currents within, 248; and parliamentary politics (1919–1920), 161, 165, 170, 172; (1921–1922 and Wirth), 234, 245, 248, 261, 298; (1924 and after), 455–457, 488–489, 491, 512; and Rhineland, 372; and socioeconomic issues, 158, 223, 491, 526, 533

central bankers, role of, 588–590

Centralverband deutscher Industrieller (prewar heavy-industry pressure group), 67

ceti medi (lower middle classes), and fascism, 313

CGL, See Confederazione Generale del Lavoro

CGT, See Confédération Générale du de la Production Française

CGT, see Confédération Générale du Travail

Chamber of Commerce: in Lille, 71, 79, 195; Paris, 78; Lyon, 80; urge franc stabilization, 507

Chamber of Deputies:
French: 95; and political groups, 107–108, 333n; representation of interests (compared with German system), 509; and taxes, 404, 462, 466, 470; and trade negotiations, 537
Italian: 51, 134

Charter of Labor (Carta del Lavoro; Fascist labor guidelines), 569–571, 574

Chaumet, Charles (French Minister of Commerce, 1925), 536

chemical industry, 545

cheminots (French railway workers), 155–157

Chequers meeting and plan (1921), and reparations, 276–277

Gauche Radicale (pivotal party in Cartel des Gauches legislature), 476, 495
Gelsenkirchen mining firm, and Stinnes, 210
Gemeinwirtschaft, see "common economy"
General Électric Company, German (AEG), 141–142
General Strike of 1926, in Britain, 482, 579
general strikes; in France, 159; Germany, 63–64, 169, 213; Italy, 80, 113, 134, 175. *See also* strikes
general tariff, French (protectionist duties levied as bargaining counter), 522
Geneva, as site of League of Nations, 511, 579
Genoa: elites in, 42; and legal strike, 337
Genoa Conference, on European economic reconstruction (1922), 269, 282–285, 292
geographical factors, and Italian fascism, 305–306
Georges-Lévy, Raphael (conservative finance spokesman), quoted, 274
Gerarchia (Fascist review), 562
German Credit Community (structure for proposed lien on industry, 1921), 258
German-Luxemburg Mining and Smelting Company (keystone of Stinnes empire), 61, 210
German Raw Steel Community (Rohstahlgemeinschaft), *see* Raw Steel Community
Germania (Center-Party newspaper), attacks Cuno, 372
Germany, Southern, its industry, 61
Gessler, Otto (DDP member; Minister of Defense), 172, 261, 368, 441; and intervention in Saxony, 381, 384n
GHH, *see* Gutehoffnungshütte
Giardino, General Gaetano, 116, 307
Gildemeister, Alfred (rightwing DVP secessionist), 442–443
Giolitti, Giovanni (liberal democratic political leader; repeated premier): background and ideas, 25, 28, 128, 231, 323; and crisis of liberalism, 230; criticizes Bonomi, 332; difficulties and failures, 27, 187, 189–191, 328, 353; and elections,

127 (1919), 325–328 (1921), 431, 432n, 436 (1924); factory council proposals, 190, 582; finances and taxes, 127–128, 190–191, 325, 427–428; and Fiume and Treaty of London, 119–120, 182, 325; and industry, 185–188, 547; and labor and socialism, 35, 189, 193, 324, 548; methods of rule, 26, 35, 183, 323–324, 479, 547–548; as ministerial possibility, 113, 180–182, 333–334, 336, 340–341; and Mussolini and fascists, 307–308, 315, 322–324, 337–338, 340–341, 355, 426, 479, 547–548, 554–555; and Nitti, 119, 127, 182; during occupation of the factories, 185–187, 189; parliamentary majorities and tactics, 110, 128, 182–183, 323, 332; Piedmontese base, 125, 547; and the Popolari, 334, 338; reformist program, 127, 183–184; registration of securities, 180; rejects the Aventine, 548; and the right, 52, 111, 191, 323; and the South, 323, 434; strengths and weakness, 125, 182–183, 187, 189–191, 231; supports Fascist electoral law, 347, 349; and tariffs, 86
Giolittians, 50–51, 112
Giovannini, Alberto (liberal leader; active in PLI), 342
Giornale d'Italia (rightwing liberal Roman newspaper), cited, on classes, 28; on 1919 elections, 124, 127–128; on fascism and legality, 331, 338, 432, 440, 554; on Nitti, 117, 122
Giunta, Francesco (Fascist leader), 350, 432–433
Glasenapp, Otto von (Vice-President of the Reichsbank), 299
Gobetti, Piero (antifascist publicist): on classes, 19, 28–29; and Fascist persecution, 346
Goblot, Edmond (French social critic), on bourgeoisie, 31–32
Gold Discount Bank (instituted by Schacht for foreign credit, 1924), 401–402 and 402n, 486, 588
gold-exchange standard, and the economy of the 1920's, 516, 577, 588–590
gold standard, 587–588
Gothein, Georg (conservative DDP Reichstag delegate), 159, 161, 165, 172, 219n, 260

Hilferding, Rudolf (*cont.*)
145–146; on Social Democratic
power, 515; and socialization of
coal, 140, 217–218; stabilization and
currency reform plans, 299–300,
376–379
Hilger, Ewald (Silesian coal mining
executive), quoted on unions, 60–
61; at Spa, 206
Hindenburg, Marshall Paul von (Reich
President, 1925–1934), 135, 164,
166, 168, 489, 494, 579
Hirsch, Julius (State Secretary at
the Ministry of Economics), and
capital tax plans, 254–356, 358; and
coal pricing policy, 214–215;
urges stabilization, 296
Hirsch, Paul (Minister-President of
Prussia), on nationalism, 165
Hitler, Adolf (National Socialist
leader in Munich), 359, 384, 436,
451, 562, 582
Hoesch, Leopold von (Counsellor of
Legation, then Ambassador in
Paris), 411
Hoetzsch, Otto (foreign policy
spokesman for DNVP), 488
Hofmannsthal, Hugo von (poet), 579
Homais (druggist in *Madame
Bovary*), 41
Homburg, Octave (French banker;
adviser to Poincaré), 461
homeowners, as interest group, 483,
494
Hoover, Herbert (Secretary of
Commerce, 1921–1928), 12, 287,
581
Horne, Robert (Chancellor of the
Exchequer), and reparations,
267, 283
Hotel Balkan, Trieste, burned by
Fascists, 309
Hotel Esplanade, Berlin, and German
tariff parleys, 525–526
Houghton, Alanson B. (U.S. Am-
bassador in Berlin), 287, 383, 488
Hue, Otto (leader of the Social
Democratic mine workers union),
140, 169, 218, 223, 366–367n
Hugenberg, Alfred (bitter DNVP
critic of Weimar; mass communi-
cations czar with industry connec-
tions), 59, 67, 257, 262–263, 485
Hughes, Charles Evans (Secretary
of State), 245
L'Humanité (SFIO, then Communist
daily), 158

Hungary, its revolution, 93; and
reaction, 136
Hythe Conference (April 1921), 240

Idea Nazionale (Nationalist daily),
181, 187, 307
ideology, in the 1920's, 593
I. H. Stein, Co. (Cologne bank), and
Rhineland bankscheme, 397
Ilva (Italian steel concern), 86, 187
Imbusch, Heinrich (Catholic trade
union leader), 67, 212, 221–223
income distribution, in Great Britain
and Europe, 44–45
income tax and surtax, in France
(*impôt général sur le revenu*),
466–469
Independent Socialists, German, or
Independents (USPD: left-wing
Socialist party, 1917–1922): and
elections, 171 (1920), 452 (1924);
and factory councils, 63, 139,
160–163; and issues under Wirth,
243, 270–271, 294–295; and socialization, 212, 223; and SPD, 164–
165, 172, 294–295, 301–302, 442;
splits, 294–295
Independents, French (Chamber
group of the far right), 274
index wages (tied to cost of living),
and the German inflation, 371–372
industry, and industrialists: and
election finances, 102–104; iron and
steel at mid-decade, 543; and labor
relations, 583–584; organization
of, 53–54; postwar aspirations, 154
British: and coal, 205; and
Foreign Office, 410n, 528n
French: alignments on coal and
reparations, 201–202; election
financing, 102–104; hostility to
planning, 76; Lorraine and Saar
holdings, 72, 533–536; protectionism, 280, 529; reparations, 388–389;
and Ruhr occupation, 411; and
trade negotiations, 520ff, 528–530
French and German compared:
attitude toward state, 84; in coal
and steel, 409; entrepreneurial
attitudes, 82–85; and inflation, 509;
interindustry exchanges, 388;
organization of, 70–71, 530; power
of, 70, 85, 530, 543; relations with
foreign ministries, 528n, 530, 543;
relations with Poincaré and Stresemann, 414; and reparations, 389;

and tariff compromises, 530–531;
and trade unions, 70

German: annexation plans, 71;
collaboration with regime, 481;
condemns parliament, 382; credit
action, 257–258; credit needs, 416,
448, 450; and Cuno, 371; and
currency reform, 377; divisions
within, 61–62, 66–67; and DNVP,
271, 485, 492; and DVP, 259–
260, 485; economic conditions of,
69–70, 538; and eight-hour day,
390, 448, 512; evades control, 225;
and Fehrenbach, 172–173; goes to
right, 444; and inflation, 68–69,
360; and Kapp Putsch, 168–169;
and MICUM negotiations, 391–393,
416–417; and National Liberalism,
374; pledges assets, 257–258, 369,
486n; and railroads, 264–265; and
reparations, 280, 388–389, 485;
resists stabilization, 301; and revaluation, 492; and Ruhr occupation,
390; and socialization, 218; Silesian
vis-à-vis Rhenish-Westphalian, 61–
62, 220; and Spa conference, 209;
social status of, 154; and Stinnes
negotiations (1924), 415; tariff
wishes, 66–67, 481, 524–525; trade-
agreement objectives, 520ff; and
trade unions and labor, 59; in war,
57–58; and Wirth, 248, 257–259,
272

Italian: and corporatism, 565;
and depreciation of lira, 573–576;
and fascism and Mussolini, 308,
322, 340, 552–553, 562, 572, 576–
578; and labor relations under
fascism, 561–562, 564–567; in Milan,
126; and Nationalist Party, 328;
and occupations of factories, 175–
176, 184–188; organization and
goals, 85–87; in recession, 191; and
Rossoni, 565–567; and the state,
570–571

See also Comité des Forges;
Confindustria; iron and steel indus-
try; Reichsverband der deutschen
Industrie

inflation: alternatives and social costs,
482–483; and bourgeoisie, 45; and
corporatism, 590–591; effects on
economic groups, 513; effects on
unions, 445; ending of, 482, 505;
and middle class, 387; and war, 43;
weakens parliaments and parties,
353, 515

French: and Briand, 274–275;
and Herriot, 497; and indirect taxes,
470; and iron and steel exports,
527, 531–532, 542; prefectural
reports of, 459, 473–474; and reparations, 470; and voter discontent,
473–474

French and German compared:
costs of, 45, 362; and party systems
and alignments, 503, 510–511;
and strength of respective industrial
groups, 508–509

German: causes of, 358; consequences of, 293, 359–363; and
industry, 361–362; and middle
classes, 359–362; and national income, 359; pace of, 247, 367, 376;
and passive resistance, 367;
political costs of, 385–386; price
and export policy, 68–69; and
wages and salaries, 360, 363

Italian: 49, 173

See also franc; lira; mark; prices
Interessenpolitik (interest-group
politics), 35
interest groups, 11, 21, 593–594; and
Luther, Stresemann, and Poincaré,
543; and ministries, 410; and
parliaments, 409; and stability, 482
Interior, Ministry of the, in Italy,
315; failure of, 321–322; removes
city councils, 319, 321. *See also*
prefects
international loan for reparations,
283, 286, 289
international steel agreement, *see*
Entente Internationale de l'Acier
international strike, July 1919
(*scioperissimo*), 94, 117–118
international trade, 479, 516, 587
Interparty Committee, in the Weimar
Republic, 512, 581
Intersyndical Committee, to weigh
Fascist labor demands (1929), 583
interventionists, in Italy, 49–50, 112n,
116; and 1919 elections, 123–128
intransigents, Fascist, 425, 546
IRMA (International Rail Manufacturers' Association), 524n, 533, 536,
542
iron and steel industry: conflicting
interests in France, 519, 528–530;
flow chart for, 518; and Franco-
German combination, 517; in
Germany, 61–62, 525ff; and government trade objectives, 520ff; in
Italy, 86, 185, 187, 191; in Lorraine,

iron and steel industry (*cont.*)
197–199, 209; organization of,
in France, Germany, Italy, Belgium,
516; overcapacity and overproduc-
tion, 519–520, 531; political
importance of, 543, 545; and
relations with coal producers, 409.
See also industry and industrialists;
Comité des Forges; Union of German
Iron and Steel Industrialists
(VdESI)
iron ore and coke exchanges, 198–
200, 388, 415–416, 522
Isaac, Auguste (rail executive; Bloc
National deputy and Minister of
Commerce), 157, 202, 465, 470,
475
Istituto per la Ricostruzione Industriale
(IRI: state holding company), 575
Italian-German Trade Treaty, 537
Italy: elites in, 14; and corporatism,
354; and councils, 139; failure of
liberalism, 305

Janus, Albert (German industrialist),
and MICUM negotiations, 393
Japy, Gaston (French industrialist),
and inter-industry ideas, 388
Jarres, Karl (Mayor of Duisburg;
on the right of the DVP), and
Rhenish policy, 376, 394, 399,
415; and parliamentary politics,
441, 456
Jarrow (Tyneside town with massive
unemployment), and rationalization,
544
Jaurès (leading French Socialist
spokesman before 1914), 94, 496,
505
Jenny, Frédéric (commentator on
finance), cited, 274 and 274n
Johannet, René (conservative com-
mentator), on bourgeoisie, 32
Jouhaux, Léon (CGT leader), urges
stabilization, 508
Journal des Débats (measured,
conservative paper), 93
Journée Industrielle (business daily),
cited, 78, 79, 94, 387, 407, 459, 470
Jouvenel, Henry de (middle-of-the-
road Senator, diplomat), on
Poincaré, 405
Jouvenel, Robert de, as author of
La république des camarades, 91
July Monarchy, 473
Junkers, 13, 35, 187, 377

Kahr, Gustav von (Bavarian Minister-
President, 1920–1921; emergency
executive, 1923), 170, 375, 383
Kaliski, Julius (corporative Socialist),
and economic planning, 143
Kanitz, Gerhard, Graf von (Minister
of Food and Agriculture), 441, 487
Kapp, Wolfgang (organizer of 1920
coup attempt), 167–169, 172
Kapp Putsch (rightwing seizure of
Berlin), 4, 160, 167–170, 203,
272, 580; and socialization thrust,
212–213, 215, 223
Kardorff, Siegfried von (mercurial
DNVP, then DVP member), 170,
374, 385
Kautsky, Karl (SPD theoretician), 140,
151, 224
Keil, Wilhelm (SPD champion of
mark revaluation), 490, 493–494,
510
Kempner, Franz (Ministerial Adviser
in Chancellery), 367
Kerensky, Alexander, 121
Kessler, Harry Graf (friend of
Rathenau; literary and political
dilettante), quoted, 293, 579
Keynes, John Maynard (economist):
and committee of economic experts
(1922), 297, 302–303; foresees
German default, 250, 253, 274;
and London schedule of payments,
242; and transfer problem, 251
Kilmarnock, Victor Alexander, Lord
(British delegate on Interallied
Rhineland High Commission), 398
Kirdorf, Emil (industrialist; director
of Gelsenkirchen firm), 210, 512
Klöckner, Peter (Ruhr industrialist),
303, 389–390, 393, 523, 532
Koch Weser, Erich (DDP leader),
161, 172, 246, 444, 456–457, 492
Kölnische Zeitung (pro-industry, DVP
oriented paper), 69
Köngeter, Eugen (Manager of Reichs-
kohlenrat, then Stumm executive),
219
Koeth, Colonel Joseph (head of
Demobilization Office), 62–63, 67,
140
Kolontai, Alexandra (leader of the
"workers' opposition," in Russia),
153
Korfanty Rebellion (pro-Polish uprising in Upper Silesia before final
partition), 245, 248

Social Democratic Party (*cont.*)
165, 442; and DVP, 166–167, 247,
260–261, 295, 511; economic
concerns, 69; and eight-hour day,
218, 246, 301, 383–384, 445; and
1924 elections, 440, 451, 454–455,
488; and factory councils, 65, 143–
144, 166, 449; and Great Coalition,
295, 301, 372–373, 382–385;
inflation policies, 365, 370–371;
out of power, 481; party congresses,
143, 260; and planning, 160; politics
under Wirth, 234, 243, 246, 249,
258–259, 261, 270, 272, 301–302;
in Prussia, 515; in the revolution,
54–55, 57; and "social power,"
514–515; and socialization, 139–
140, 144, 212, 215, 217, 221–225;
and the state, 356, 386–387; strikes
in East Prussia, 192; tariff stance,
487, 526; and tax compromise, 247,
249, 254–255, 257, 266, 269, 295;
and the USPD, 163–165, 256, 294–
295
social unrest: in Bologna, 177; and
fascism, 315, 317, 321–322
socialism and socialists or social
democrats: 6–8, 22–23, 136–137,
194, 581, 585
socialists, by country, *see* Social
Democratic Party, German; Socialist
Party, French; Socialist Party, Italian
Socialist Party, French (SFIO), and
Socialists: in 1914 elections, 31;
1919 elections, 97–98, 102, 105–
106; 1924 elections, 421, 458, 472,
474, 476, 478; formation and
organization, 29, 95; in parliament,
236, 240, 273–274, 290, 406, 496,
500, 505; presses railroad nationalization, 149, 155; tax and finance
policy, 465, 469, 494, 498–499,
506; and Third International, 151;
in war, 77, 92
Socialist Party, Italian (PSI), and
Socialists: Albertini on, 114, 188;
and Aventine, 549; in Bologna,
177; city council control attacked,
319–321; Congress of Livorno and
and schism, 187, 324, 334–335;
and constituent assembly movement,
50; and 1919 elections, 123–124,
126–131; 1920 elections, 189; 1921
elections, 326–327; 1924 elections,
436–437; and factory councils, 147;
and Fascists, 314–315, 322, 331,
343; and Fiat, 561; geographical

bases of support, 129–131; and
Giolitti, 183, 548; and "legality,"
328; and liberals, 325; loss of power,
183, 310, 312; Mussolini's cabinet
bid, 343; and pacification, 330; and
parliamentary participation, 133–
134, 325, 332–336; and Popolari
and Catholics, 179, 335; and proportional representation, 116, 123–
124; radicalization of, 27, 49, 112,
548; rally in war, 110; strikes, 113,
134, 176; and Third International,
151
socialization: in Germany, 63, 70,
140, 144, 158–159, 194, 212ff, 225;
Korsch's concepts of, 139–140. *See
also* nationalization
Socialization Commission: First
commission, 1918–1919, 140–141;
Second commission, 1920–1921,
215–216, 218, 221, 223, 251, 264
Socialization Subcommittee, *see* Subcommittee on the Socialization
Question Soleri, Marcello (Giolittian;
Minister of Agriculture), 311, 338,
431, 552
Sollmann, Wilhelm (SPD Interior
Minister under Stresemann), 382
Solmssen, Georg (manager of the
Diskonto-Gesellschaft bank), 397
Solons, 551, 564. *See also* Committee
of Eighteen
Sonnino, Sidney (conservative Italian
premier, then Foreign Minister,
1914–1919), 25–26, 28, 111, 115,
121, 123
Sorel, Georges (French syndicalist
theorist), 23, 563
Soresina (farming region near Cremona), and agrarian conflicts,
318–319
Sorge, Kurt (Krupp executive;
Chairman of the Reichsverband der
deutschen Industrie), 169n, 219,
263
South, Italian: electorale role, 124,
131, 133, 326–327, 432–434, 437–
438; elites in, 42, 424; and politics
321, 323, 440, 479, 548; and taxes,
427
Soviet Union, and Soviets, 150–151,
278. *See also* Russia
Sozialistische Monatshefte (publication
of the conservative SPD wing), 143
Spa Conference and Agreements, 203–
209, 224, 233; and coal issue in

644

LIBRARY OF CONGRESS CATALOGING IN PUBLICATION DATA

Maier, Charles S
  Recasting bourgeois Europe.

  Bibliography: p.
  Includes index.
  1. Europe—Politics—1918-1945.   2. Europe—Eco-
nomic conditions—1918-1945.   I. Title.
D727.M236   1975   320.9′4′051   73-2488
ISBN 0-691-05220-4
ISBN 0-691-10025-X